Julie A. Garrison
Editor

The Twelfth
Off-Campus Library Services
Conference Proceedings

The Twelfth Off-Campus Library Services Conference Proceedings has been co-published simultaneously as *Journal of Library Administration*, Volume 45, Numbers 1/2 and 3/4 2006.

Pre-publication
REVIEWS,
COMMENTARIES,
EVALUATIONS . . .

"If you could not attend the Off-Campus Library Services Conference, this is an excellent source of information on the presentations at the Conference. This publication covers all of the presentations and poster sessions with clarity. There are a number of sections providing good ideas and details about common practices in place for instructing distance education students about the library. This is a must have for all librarians providing assistance and service to a distance education community. Reading this publication is ALMOST AS GOOD AS BEING THERE."

Jodi Poe, MLIS
Distance Education Librarian/
Electronic Resources Manager
Houston Cole Library
Jacksonville State University

More pre-publication
REVIEWS, COMMENTARIES, EVALUATIONS . . .

"AN INVALUABLE TOOL TO BOTH THE PRACTITIONER AND THE SCHOLAR. . . . More than 70% of the proceedings include presentations on theoretical and research-based topics including copyright, teaching faculty use, career challenges for distance education librarians, and collaboration between institutions. For example, there is a very fascinating and useful paper on research comparing doctoral dissertations awarded by traditional versus non-traditional institutions using a citation analysis method. More importantly, there are several papers reporting applications of cutting edge, or near cutting edge technologies. To separate the hype that often accompanies new technologies from their actual usefulness, it is precisely these kinds of presentations that assist researchers and practitioners alike in advancing distance education. The proceedings include applications of e-books, use of PDAs in design of library services, weblogs for information literacy, email reference services, and integration of library services into Blackboard course pages. There are two other very useful sections of note. The proceedings include the record of three information rich workshops. One in particular, the use of firewalls, adblockers, and web accelerators, will aid most distance education designers. The inclusion of posters from the poster session was a welcome addition. POSTER SESSIONS, OFTEN IGNORED IN CONFERENCE PROCEEDINGS, OFFER A WEALTH OF INFORMATION AS WELL."

John B. Harer, PhD
*Library Science Program Coordinator
and Assistant Professor
East Carolina University*

The Haworth Information Press®
An Imprint of The Haworth Press, Inc.

The Twelfth
Off-Campus Library Services
Conference Proceedings

The Twelfth Off-Campus Library Services Conference Proceedings
has been co-published simultaneously as *Journal of Library
Administration*, Volume 45, Numbers 1/2 and 3/4 2006.

Monographs from the *Journal of Library Administration*®

For additional information on these and other Haworth Press titles, including descriptions, tables of contents, reviews, and prices, use the QuickSearch catalog at http://www.HaworthPress.com.

1. *Planning for Library Services: A Guide to Utilizing Planning Methods for Library Management,* edited by Charles R. McClure, PhD (Vol. 2, No. 3/4, 1982). *"Should be read by anyone who is involved in planning processes of libraries–certainly by every administrator of a library or system." (American Reference Books Annual)*

2. *Finance Planning for Libraries,* edited by Murray S. Martin (Vol. 3, No. 3/4, 1983). *Stresses the need for libraries to weed out expenditures which do not contribute to their basic role–the collection and organization of information–when planning where and when to spend money.*

3. *Marketing and the Library,* edited by Gary T. Ford (Vol. 4, No. 4, 1984). *Discover the latest methods for more effective information dissemination and learn to develop successful programs for specific target areas.*

4. *Excellence in Library Management,* edited by Charlotte Georgi, MLS, and Robert Bellanti, MLS, MBA (Vol. 6, No. 3, 1985). *"Most beneficial for library administrators . . . for anyone interested in either library/information science or management." (Special Libraries)*

5. *Archives and Library Administration: Divergent Traditions and Common Concerns,* edited by Lawrence J. McCrank, PhD, MLS (Vol. 7, No. 2/3, 1986). *"A forward-looking view of archives and libraries. . . . Recommend[ed] to students, teachers, and practitioners alike of archival and library science. It is readable, thought-provoking, and provides a summary of the major areas of divergence and convergence." (Association of Canadian Map Libraries and Archives)*

6. *Legal Issues for Library and Information Managers,* edited by William Z. Nasri, JD, PhD (Vol. 7, No. 4, 1986). *"Useful to any librarian looking for protection or wondering where responsibilities end and liabilities begin. Recommended." (Academic Library Book Review)*

7. *Pricing and Costs of Monographs and Serials: National and International Issues,* edited by Sul H. Lee (Supp. #l, 1987). *"Eminently readable. There is a good balance of chapters on serials and monographs and the perspective of suppliers, publishers, and library practitioners are presented. A book well worth reading." (Australasian College Libraries)*

8. *Management Issues in the Networking Environment,* edited by Edward R. Johnson, PhD (Vol. 8, No. 3/4, 1987). *"Particularly useful for librarians/information specialists contemplating establishing a local network." (Australian Library Review)*

9. *Library Management and Technical Services: The Changing Role of Technical Services in Library Organizations,* edited by Jennifer Cargill, MSLS, MSEd (Vol. 9, No. 1, 1988). *"As a practical and instructive guide to issues such as automation, personnel matters, education, management techniques and liaison with other services, senior library managers with a sincere interest in evaluating the role of their technical services should find this a timely publication." (Library Association Record)*

10. *Computing, Electronic Publishing, and Information Technology: Their Impact on Academic Libraries,* edited by Robin N. Downes (Vol. 9, No. 4, 1988). *"For a relatively short and easily digestible discussion of these issues, this book can be recommended, not only to those in academic libraries, but also to those in similar types of library or information unit, and to academics and educators in the field." (Journal of Documentation)*

11. *Acquisitions, Budgets, and Material Costs: Issues and Approaches,* edited by Sul H. Lee (Supp. #2, 1988). *"The advice of these library practitioners is sensible and their insights illuminating for librarians in academic libraries." (American Reference Books Annual)*

12. *The Impact of Rising Costs of Serials and Monographs on Library Services and Programs,* edited by Sul H. Lee (Vol. 10, No. 1, 1989). *". . . Sul Lee hit a winner here." (Serials Review)*

13. ***Creativity, Innovation, and Entrepreneurship in Libraries,*** edited by Donald E. Riggs, EdD, MLS (Vol. 10, No. 2/3, 1989). *"The volume is well worth reading as a whole. . . . There is very little repetition, and it should stimulate thought." (Australian Library Review)*

14. ***Human Resources Management in Libraries,*** edited by Gisela M. Webb, MLS, MPA (Vol. 10, No. 4, 1989). *"Thought provoking and enjoyable reading. . . . Provides valuable insights for the effective information manager." (Special Libraries)*

15. ***Managing Public Libraries in the 21st Century,*** edited by Pat Woodrum, MLS (Vol. 11, No. 1/2, 1989). *"A broad-based collection of topics that explores the management problems and possibilities public libraries will be facing in the 21st century." (Robert Swisher, PhD, Director, School of Library and Information Studies, University of Oklahoma)*

16. ***Library Education and Employer Expectations,*** edited by E. Dale Cluff, PhD, MLS (Vol. 11, No. 3/4, 1990). *"Useful to library-school students and faculty interested in employment problems and employer perspectives. Librarians concerned with recruitment practices will also be interested." (Information Technology and Libraries)*

17. ***Training Issues and Strategies in Libraries,*** edited by Paul M. Gherman, MALS, and Frances O. Painter, MLS, MBA (Vol. 12, No. 2, 1990). *"There are . . . useful chapters, all by different authors, each with a preliminary summary of the content–a device that saves much time in deciding whether to read the whole chapter or merely skim through it. Many of the chapters are essentially practical without too much emphasis on theory. This book is a good investment." (Library Association Record)*

18. ***Library Material Costs and Access to Information,*** edited by Sul H. Lee (Vol. 12, No. 3, 1990). *"A cohesive treatment of the issue. Although the book's contributors possess a research library perspective, the data and the ideas presented are of interest and benefit to the entire profession, especially academic librarians." (Library Resources and Technical Services)*

19. ***Library Development: A Future Imperative,*** edited by Dwight F. Burlingame, PhD (Vol. 12, No. 4, 1990). *"This volume provides an excellent overview of fundraising with special application to libraries. . . . A useful book that is highly recommended for all libraries." (Library Journal)*

20. ***Personnel Administration in an Automated Environment,*** edited by Philip E. Leinbach, MLS (Vol. 13, No. 1/2, 1990). *"An interesting and worthwhile volume, recommended to university library administrators and to others interested in thought-provoking discussion of the personnel implications of automation." (Canadian Library Journal)*

21. ***Strategic Planning in Higher Education: Implementing New Roles for the Academic Library,*** edited by James F. Williams, II, MLS (Vol. 13, No. 3/4, 1991). *"A welcome addition to the sparse literature on strategic planning in university libraries. Academic librarians considering strategic planning for their libraries will learn a great deal from this work." (Canadian Library Journal)*

22. ***Creative Planning for Library Administration: Leadership for the Future,*** edited by Kent Hendrickson, MALS (Vol. 14, No. 2, 1991). *"Provides some essential information on the planning process, and the mix of opinions and methodologies, as well as examples relevant to every library manager, resulting in a very readable foray into a topic too long avoided by many of us." (Canadian Library Journal)*

23. ***Budgets for Acquisitions: Strategies for Serials, Monographs, and Electronic Formats,*** edited by Sul H. Lee (Vol. 14, No. 3, 1991). *"Much more than a series of handy tips for the careful shopper. This [book] is a most useful one–well-informed, thought-provoking, and authoritative." (Australian Library Review)*

24. ***Managing Technical Services in the 90's,*** edited by Drew Racine (Vol. 15, No. 1/2, 1991). *"Presents an eclectic overview of the challenges currently facing all library technical services efforts. . . . Recommended to library administrators and interested practitioners." (Library Journal)*

25. ***Library Management in the Information Technology Environment: Issues, Policies, and Practice for Administrators,*** edited by Brice G. Hobrock, PhD, MLS (Vol. 15, No. 3/4, 1992).

"A road map to identify some of the alternative routes to the electronic library." (Stephen Rollins, Associate Dean for Library Services, General Library, University of New Mexico)

26. **The Management of Library and Information Studies Education,** edited by Herman L. Totten, PhD, MLS (Vol. 16, No. 1/2, 1992). *"Offers something of interest to everyone connected with LIS education–the undergraduate contemplating a master's degree, the doctoral student struggling with courses and career choices, the new faculty member aghast at conflicting responsibilities, the experienced but stressed LIS professor, and directors of LIS Schools." (Education Libraries)*

27. **Vendor Evaluation and Acquisition Budgets,** edited by Sul H. Lee (Vol. 16, No. 3, 1992). *"The title doesn't do justice to the true scope of this excellent collection of papers delivered at the sixth annual conference on library acquisitions sponsored by the University of Oklahoma Libraries." (Kent K. Hendrickson, BS, MALS, Dean of Libraries, University of Nebraska-Lincoln) Find insightful discussions on the impact of rising costs on library budgets and management in this groundbreaking book.*

28. **Developing Library Staff for the 21st Century,** edited by Maureen Sullivan (Vol. 17, No. 1, 1992). *"I found myself enthralled with this highly readable publication. It is one of those rare compilations that manages to successfully integrate current general management operational thinking in the context of academic library management." (Bimonthly Review of Law Books)*

29. **Collection Assessment and Acquisitions Budgets,** edited by Sul H. Lee (Vol. 17, No. 2, 1993). *Contains timely information about the assessment of academic library collections and the relationship of collection assessment to acquisition budgets.*

30. **Leadership in Academic Libraries: Proceedings of the W. Porter Kellam Conference, The University of Georgia, May 7, 1991,** edited by William Gray Potter (Vol. 17, No. 4, 1993). *"Will be of interest to those concerned with the history of American academic libraries." (Australian Library Review)*

31. **Integrating Total Quality Management in a Library Setting,** edited by Susan Jurow, MLS, and Susan B. Barnard, MLS (Vol. 18, No. 1/2, 1993). *"Especially valuable are the librarian experiences that directly relate to real concerns about TQM. Recommended for all professional reading collections." (Library Journal)*

32. **Catalysts for Change: Managing Libraries in the 1990s,** edited by Gisela M. von Dran, DPA, MLS, and Jennifer Cargill, MSLS, MSEd (Vol. 18, No. 3/4, 1993). *"A useful collection of articles which focuses on the need for librarians to employ enlightened management practices in order to adapt to and thrive in the rapidly changing information environment." (Australian Library Review)*

33. **The Role and Future of Special Collections in Research Libraries: British and American Perspectives,** edited by Sul H. Lee (Vol. 19, No. 1, 1993). *"A provocative but informative read for library users, academic administrators, and private sponsors." (International Journal of Information and Library Research)*

34. **Declining Acquisitions Budgets: Allocation, Collection Development and Impact Communication,** edited by Sul H. Lee (Vol. 19, No. 2, 1993). *"Expert and provocative. . . . Presents many ways of looking at library budget deterioration and responses to it . . . There is much food for thought here." (Library Resources & Technical Services)*

35. **Libraries as User-Centered Organizations: Imperatives for Organizational Change,** edited by Meredith A. Butler (Vol. 19, No. 3/4, 1993). *"Presents a very timely and well-organized discussion of major trends and influences causing organizational changes." (Science Books & Films)*

36. **Access, Ownership, and Resource Sharing,** edited by Sul H. Lee (Vol. 20, No. 1, 1994). *The contributing authors present a useful and informative look at the current status of information provision and some of the challenges the subject presents.*

37. **The Dynamic Library Organizations in a Changing Environment,** edited by Joan Giesecke, MLS, DPA (Vol. 20, No. 2, 1994). *"Provides a significant look at potential changes in the library world and presents its readers with possible ways to address the negative results of such*

changes. . . . Covers the key issues facing today's libraries . . . Two thumbs up!" (Marketing Library Resources)

38. **The Future of Information Services,** edited by Virginia Steel, MA, and C. Brigid Welch, MLS (Vol. 20, No. 3/4, 1995). *"The leadership discussions will be useful for library managers as will the discussions of how library structures and services might work in the next century." (Australian Special Libraries)*

39. **The Future of Resource Sharing,** edited by Shirley K. Baker and Mary E. Jackson, MLS (Vol. 21, No. 1/2, 1995). *"Recommended for library and information science schools because of its balanced presentation of the ILL/document delivery issues." (Library Acquisitions: Practice and Theory)*

40. **Libraries and Student Assistants: Critical Links,** edited by William K. Black, MLS (Vol. 21, No. 3/4, 1995). *"A handy reference work on many important aspects of managing student assistants. . . . Solid, useful information on basic management issues in this work and several chapters are useful for experienced managers." (The Journal of Academic Librarianship)*

41. **Managing Change in Academic Libraries,** edited by Joseph J. Branin (Vol. 22, No. 2/3, 1996). *"Touches on several aspects of academic library management, emphasizing the changes that are occurring at the present time. . . . Recommended this title for individuals or libraries interested in management aspects of academic libraries." (RQ American Library Association)*

42. **Access, Resource Sharing and Collection Development,** edited by Sul H. Lee (Vol. 22, No. 4, 1996). *Features continuing investigation and discussion of important library issues, specifically the role of libraries in acquiring, storing, and disseminating information in different formats.*

43. **Interlibrary Loan/Document Delivery and Customer Satisfaction: Strategies for Redesigning Services,** edited by Pat L. Weaver-Meyers, Wilbur A. Stolt, and Yem S. Fong (Vol. 23, No. 1/2, 1997). *"No interlibrary loan department supervisor at any mid-sized to large college or university library can afford not to read this book." (Gregg Sapp, MLS, MEd, Head of Access Services, University of Miami, Richter Library, Coral Gables, Florida)*

44. **Emerging Patterns of Collection Development in Expanding Resource Sharing, Electronic Information, and Network Environment,** edited by Sul H. Lee (Vol. 24, No. 1/2, 1997). *"The issues it deals with are common to us all. We all need to make our funds go further and our resources work harder, and there are ideas here which we can all develop." (The Library Association Record)*

45. **The Academic Library Director: Reflections on a Position in Transition,** edited by Frank D'Andraia, MLS (Vol. 24, No. 3, 1997). *"A useful collection to have whether you are seeking a position as director or conducting a search for one." (College & Research Libraries News)*

46. **Economics of Digital Information: Collection, Storage, and Delivery,** edited by Sul H. Lee (Vol. 24, No. 4, 1997). *Highlights key concepts and issues vital to a library's successful venture into the digital environment and helps you understand why the transition from the printed page to the digital packet has been problematic for both creators of proprietary materials and users of those materials.*

47. **Management of Library and Archival Security: From the Outside Looking In,** edited by Robert K. O'Neill, PhD (Vol. 25, No. 1, 1998). *"Provides useful advice and on-target insights for professionals caring for valuable documents and artifacts." (Menzi L. Behrnd-Klodt, JD, Attorney/Archivist, Klodt and Associates, Madison, WI)*

48. **OCLC 1967-1997: Thirty Years of Furthering Access to the World's Information,** edited by K. Wayne Smith (Vol. 25, No. 2/3/4, 1998). *"A rich–and poignantly personal, at times–historical account of what is surely one of this century's most important developments in librarianship." (Deanna B. Marcum, PhD, President, Council on Library and Information Resources, Washington, DC)*

49. **The Economics of Information in the Networked Environment,** edited by Meredith A. Butler, MLS, and Bruce R. Kingma, PhD (Vol. 26, No. 1/2, 1998). *"A book that should be read both by information professionals and by administrators, faculty and others who share a collective concern to provide the most information to the greatest number at the lowest cost in the*

networked environment." (Thomas J. Galvin, PhD, Professor of Information Science and Policy, University at Albany, State University of New York)

50. **Information Technology Planning,** edited by Lori A. Goetsch (Vol. 26, No. 3/4, 1999). *Offers innovative approaches and strategies useful in your library and provides some food for thought about information technology as we approach the millennium.*

51. **Managing Multicultural Diversity in the Library: Principles and Issues for Administrators,** edited by Mark Winston (Vol. 27, No. 1/2, 1999). *Defines diversity, clarifies why it is important to address issues of diversity, and identifies goals related to diversity and how to go about achieving those goals.*

52. **Scholarship, Research Libraries, and Global Publishing,** by Jutta Reed-Scott (Vol. 27, No. 3/4, 1999). *This book documents a research project in conjunction with the Association of Research Libraries (ARL) that explores the issue of foreign acquisition and how it affects collection in international studies, area studies, collection development, and practices of international research libraries.*

53. **Collection Development in a Digital Environment,** edited by Sul H. Lee (Vol. 28, No. 1, 1999). *Explores ethical and technological dilemmas of collection development and gives several suggestions on how a library can successfully deal with these challenges and provide patrons with the information they need.*

54. **Collection Management: Preparing Today's Bibliographers for Tomorrow's Libraries,** edited by Karen Rupp-Serrano, MLS, MPA (Vol. 28, No. 2, 1999). *For both beginners and professional,* Collection Development *addresses your vexing questions that librarians continually face to assist you in creating a cost-effective and resourceful library.*

55. **The Age Demographics of Academic Librarians: A Profession Apart,** edited by Stanley J. Wilder (Vol. 28, No. 3, 1999). *The average age of librarians has been increasing dramatically since 1990. This unique book will provide insights on how this demographic issue can impact a library and what can be done to make the effects positive.*

56. **Collection Development in the Electronic Environment: Shifting Priorities,** edited by Sul H. Lee (Vol. 28, No. 4, 1999). *Through case studies and firsthand experiences, this volume discusses meeting the needs of scholars at universities, budgeting issues, user education, staffing in the electronic age, collaborating libraries and resources, and how vendors meet the needs of different customers.*

57. **Library Training for Staff and Customers,** edited by Sara Ramser Beck, MLS, MBA (Vol. 29, No. 1, 1999). *This comprehensive book is designed to assist library professionals involved in presenting or planning training for library staff members and customers. You will explore ideas for effective general reference training, training on automated systems, training in specialized subjects such as African American history and biography, and training for areas such as patents and trademarks, and business subjects.* Library Training for Staff and Customers *answers numerous training questions and is an excellent guide for planning staff development.*

58. **Integration in the Library Organization,** edited by Christine E. Thompson, PhD (Vol. 29, No. 2, 1999). *Provides librarians with the necessary tools to help libraries balance and integrate public and technical services and to improve the capability of libraries to offer patrons quality services and large amounts of information.*

59. **Management for Research Libraries Cooperation,** edited by Sul H. Lee (Vol. 29, No. 3/4, 2000). *Delivers sound advice, models, and strategies for increasing sharing between institutions to maximize the amount of printed and electronic research material you can make available in your library while keeping costs under control.*

60. **Academic Research on the Internet: Options for Scholars & Libraries,** edited by Helen Laurence, MLS, EdD, and William Miller, PhD, MLS (Vol. 30, No. 1/2/3/4, 2000). *"Emphasizes quality over quantity. . . . Presents the reader with the best research-oriented Web sites in the field. A state-of-the-art review of academic use of the Internet as well as a guide to the best Internet sites and services. . . . A useful addition for any academic library."* (David A. Tyckoson, MLS, Head of Reference, California State University, Fresno)

61. **Research Collections and Digital Information**, edited by Sul H. Lee (Vol. 31, No. 2, 2000). *Offers new strategies for collecting, organizing, and accessing library materials in the digital age.*

62. **Off-Campus Library Services**, edited by Ann Marie Casey (Vol. 31, No. 3/4, 2001 and Vol. 32, No. 1/2, 2001). *This informative volume examines various aspects of off-campus, or distance learning. It explores training issues for library staff, Web site development, changing roles for librarians, the uses of conferencing software, library support for Web-based courses, library agreements and how to successfully negotiate them, and much more!*

63. **Leadership in the Library and Information Science Professions: Theory and Practice**, edited by Mark D. Winston, MLS, PhD (Vol. 32, No. 3/4, 2001). *Offers fresh ideas for developing and using leadership skills, including recruiting potential leaders, staff training and development, issues of gender and ethnic diversity, and budget strategies for success.*

64. **Diversity Now: People, Collections, and Services in Academic Libraries**, edited by Teresa Y. Neely, PhD, and Kuang-Hwei (Janet) Lee-Smeltzer, MS, MSLIS (Vol. 33, No. 1/2/3/4, 2001). *Examines multicultural trends in academic libraries' staff and users, types of collections, and services offered.*

65. **Libraries and Electronic Resources: New Partnerships, New Practices, New Perspectives**, edited by Pamela L. Higgins (Vol. 35, No. 1/2, 2001). *An essential guide to the Internet's impact on electronic resources management–past, present, and future.*

66. **Impact of Digital Technology on Library Collections and Resource Sharing**, edited by Sul H. Lee (Vol. 35, No. 3, 2001). *Shows how digital resources have changed the traditional academic library.*

67. **Evaluating the Twenty-First Century Library: The Association of Research Libraries New Measures Initiative, 1997-2001,** edited by Donald L. DeWitt, PhD (Vol. 35, No. 4, 2001). *This collection of articles (thirteen of which previously appeared in ARL's bimonthly newsletter/report on research issues and actions) examines the Association of Research Libraries' "new measures" initiative.*

68. **Information Literacy Programs: Successes and Challenges**, edited by Patricia Durisin, MLIS (Vol. 36, No. 1/2, 2002). *Examines Web-based collaboration, teamwork with academic and administrative colleagues, evidence-based librarianship, and active learning strategies in library instruction programs.*

69. **Electronic Resources and Collection Development**, edited by Sul H. Lee (Vol. 36, No. 3, 2002). *Shows how electronic resources have impacted traditional collection development policies and practices.*

70. **Distance Learning Library Services: The Tenth Off-Campus Library Services Conference,** edited by Patrick B. Mahoney (Vol. 37, No. 1/2/3/4, 2002). *Explores the pitfalls of providing information services to distance students and suggests ways to avoid them.*

71. **The Strategic Stewardship of Cultural Resources: To Preserve and Protect,** edited by Andrea T. Merrill, BA (Vol. 38, No. 1/2/3/4, 2003). *Leading library, museum, and archival professionals share their expertise on a wide variety of preservation and security issues.*

72. **The Twenty-First Century Art Librarian**, edited by Terrie L. Wilson, MLS (Vol. 39, No. 1, 2003). *"A must-read addition to every art, architecture, museum, and visual resources library bookshelf." (Betty Jo Irvine, PhD, Fine Arts Librarian, Indiana University)*

73. **Digital Images and Art Libraries in the Twenty-First Century**, edited by Susan Wyngaard, MLS (Vol. 39, No. 2/3, 2003). *Provides an in-depth look at the technology that art librarians must understand in order to work effectively in today's digital environment.*

74. **Improved Access to Information: Portals, Content Selection, and Digital Information,** edited by Sul H. Lee (Vol. 39, No. 4, 2003). *Examines how improved electronic resources can allow libraries to provide an increasing amount of digital information to an ever-expanding patron base.*

75. **The Changing Landscape for Electronic Resources: Content, Access, Delivery, and Legal Issues,** edited by Yem S. Fong, MLS, and Suzanne M. Ward, MA (Vol. 40, No. 1/2, 2004).

Focuses on various aspects of electronic resources for libraries, including statewide resource-sharing initiatives, licensing issues, open source software, standards, and scholarly publishing.

76. **Libraries Act on Their LibQUAL+™ Findings: From Data to Action,** edited by Fred M. Heath, EdD, Martha Kyrillidou, MEd, MLS, and Consuella A. Askew, MLS (Vol. 40, No. 3/4, 2004). *Focuses on the value of LibQUAL+™ data to help librarians provide better services for users.*

77. **The Eleventh Off-Campus Library Services Conference,** edited by Patrick B. Mahoney, MBA, MLS (Vol. 41, No. 1/2/3/4, 2004). *Examines–and offers solutions to–the problems faced by librarians servicing faculty and students who do not have access to a traditional library.*

78. **Collection Management and Strategic Access to Digital Resources: The New Challenges for Research Libraries,** edited by Sul H. Lee (Vol. 42, No. 2, 2005). *Examines how libraries can make the best use of digital materials, maintain a balance between print and electronic resources, and respond to electronic information.*

79. **Licensing in Libraries: Practical and Ethical Aspects,** edited by Karen Rupp-Serrano, MLS, MPA (Vol. 42, No. 3/4, 2005). *Presents state-of-the-art information on licensing issues, including contract management, end-user education, copyright, e-books, consortial licensing software, legalities, and much more.*

80. **Portals and Libraries,** edited by Sarah C. Michalak, MLS (Vol. 43, No. 1/2, 2005). *An examination of the organization of Web-based and other electronic information resources with a review of different types of portals, attached services, and how to make the best use of them.*

81. **Evolving Internet Reference Resources,** edited by William Miller, PhD, MLS, and Rita M. Pellen, MLS (Vol. 43, No. 3/4, 2005 and Vol. 44, No. 1/2, 2006). *This book surveys the availability of online information, both free and subscription-based, in a wide variety of subject areas, including law, psychology, health and medicine, engineering, Latin American studies, and more.*

82. **Library/Vendor Relationships,** edited by Sam Brooks, and David H. Carlson, MLS, MCS (Vol. 44, No. 3/4, 2006). Library/Vendor Relationships *examines the increasing cooperation in which libraries find they must participate in, and vice versa, with the vendors that provide system infrastructure and software. Expert contributors provide insights from all sides of this unique collaboration, offering cogent perspectives on the give and take process that every librarian, publisher, and database provider/producer can use.*

83. **The Twelfth Off-Campus Library Services Conference Proceedings,** edited by Julia A. Garrison, MLIS (Vol. 45, No. 1/2/3/4, 2006). The Twelfth Off-Campus Library Services Conference Proceedings *is a selection of the finest proceedings from the twelfth annual conference on library services held in Savannah, Georgia in April 2006. Topics include expert presentations on copyright issues, evaluating library services Web sites, best practices for distance learning instruction, Weblogs in instruction, collaborative efforts, and many other of the latest issues. The collection also contains workshop and poster abstracts, including full papers when provided by the author.*

The Twelfth
Off-Campus Library Services
Conference Proceedings

Julie A. Garrison
Editor

The Twelfth Off-Campus Library Services Conference Proceedings
has been co-published simultaneously as *Journal of Library
Administration*, Volume 45, Numbers 1/2 and 3/4 2006.

The Haworth Information Press®
An Imprint of The Haworth Press, Inc.

New York • London • Victoria (AU)
www.HaworthPress.com

Published by

The Haworth Information Press®, 10 Alice Street, Binghamton, NY 13904-1580 USA

The Haworth Information Press® is an imprint of The Haworth Press, Inc., 10 Alice Street, Binghamton, NY 13904-1580 USA.

The Twelfth Off-Campus Library Services Conference Proceedings has been co-published simultaneously as *Journal of Library Administration®*, Volume 45, Numbers 1/2 and 3/4 2006.

Library of Congress Cataloging-in-Publication Data

Off-Campus Library Services Conference (12th : 2006 : Savannah, Ga.) The Twelfth Off-Campus Library Services Conference proceedings / Julie A. Garrison, editor.
    p. cm.
    "Co-published simultaneously as Journal of library administration, volume 45, numbers 1/2/3/4."
    Proceedings of the conference held April 26-28, 2006, Savannah, Georgia.
    Includes bibliographical references and index.
    ISBN-13: 978-0-7890-3476-2 (alk. paper)
    ISBN-10: 0-7890-3476-X (alk. paper)
    ISBN-13: 978-0-7890-3477-9 (pbk. : alk. paper)
    ISBN-10: 0-7890-3477-8 (pbk. : alk. paper)
    1. Academic libraries–Off-campus services–Congresses. 2. Libraries and distance education–Congresses. 3. Academic libraries–Information technology–Congresses. 4. Distance education–Congresses. 5. Education, Higher–Effect of technological innovations on–Congresses. I. Garrison, Julie A. II. Journal of library administration. III. Title.

Z675.U5O36 2006
025.5–dc22

2006021456

Indexing, Abstracting & Website/Internet Coverage

This section provides you with a list of major indexing & abstracting services and other tools for bibliographic access. That is to say, each service began covering this periodical during the year noted in the right column. Most Websites which are listed below have indicated that they will either post, disseminate, compile, archive, cite or alert their own Website users with research-based content from this work. (This list is as current as the copyright date of this publication.)

Abstracting, Website/Indexing Coverage . . . . Year When Coverage Began

- *AATA Online: Abstracts of International Conservation Literature (formerly Art & Archeology Technical Abstracts) <http://aata.getty.edu>*. 2004

- *Academic Abstracts/CD-ROM (EBSCO)* 1993

- *Academic Search Complete (EBSCO)*. 1995

- *Academic Search Elite (EBSCO)* 1993

- *Academic Search Premier (EBSCO) <http://www.epnet.com/academic acasearchprem.asp>* 2006

- *Academic Source Premier (EBSCO)*. 2006

- *Advanced Polymers Abstracts (Cambridge Scientific Abstracts) <http://csa.com>* 2006

- *AGRICOLA Database (National Agricultural Library) (AGRICultural OnLine Access) A Bibliographic database of citations to the agricultural literature created by the National Agricultural Library and its cooperators <http://www.natl.usda.gov/ag98>* 1991

- *AGRIS/CARIS <http://www.fao.org/agris/>*. 1991

- *Aluminium Industry Abstracts (Cambridge Scientific Abstracts) <http://www.csa.com>* 2006

- *British Library Inside (The British Library) <http://www.bl.uk/services/current/inside.html>* 2006

- *Business & Company Profiles ASAP (Thomson Gale)* 1996

- *Business & Management Practices (Thomson Gale)* 2006

(continued)

(continued)

(continued)

(continued)

Special Bibliographic Notes related to special journal issues (separates) and indexing/abstracting:

- indexing/abstracting services in this list will also cover material in any "separate" that is co-published simultaneously with Haworth's special thematic journal issue or DocuSerial. Indexing/abstracting usually covers material at the article/chapter level.
- monographic co-editions are intended for either non-subscribers or libraries which intend to purchase a second copy for their circulating collections.
- monographic co-editions are reported to all jobbers/wholesalers/approval plans. The source journal is listed as the "series" to assist the prevention of duplicate purchasing in the same manner utilized for books-in-series.
- to facilitate user/access services all indexing/abstracting services are encouraged to utilize the co-indexing entry note indicated at the bottom of the first page of each article/chapter/contribution.
- this is intended to assist a library user of any reference tool (whether print, electronic, online, or CD-ROM) to locate the monographic version if the library has purchased this version but not a subscription to the source journal.
- individual articles/chapters in any Haworth publication are also available through the Haworth Document Delivery Service (HDDS).

The Twelfth
Off-Campus Library Services
Conference Proceedings

CONTENTS

CONTRIBUTED WORKSHOPS

CONTRIBUTED ELECTRONIC POSTERS

ABOUT THE EDITOR

Julie A. Garrison, MLIS, is currently the Director of Off-Campus Library Services at Central Michigan University where she works with off-campus faculty and adult learners fulfilling degree requirements in remote locations. Ms. Garrison is active in the library community, most recently with the Distance Learning Section of the Association of College and Research Libraries, and has served on several different library association committees. Prior to her appointment at Central, she held the position of Associate Director of Public Services at Duke University's Medical Center Library. Ms. Garrison has been a co-developer and instructor of a distance education Evidence-Based Medicine online course taught through the University of North Carolina at Chapel Hill's Graduate School of Information and Library Science and has researched and written articles on the design and effectiveness of online continuing education courses. She received her BA in English Literature from the University of Michigan in 1992 and her MLIS from the University of California at Los Angeles in 1995.

Preface

Welcome to the Twelfth Off-Campus Library Services Conference Proceedings. The Central Michigan University Libraries and the Central Michigan Off-Campus Programs have provided generous support of both this conference and these Proceedings.

This year, the Proceedings also contains workshop and poster abstracts, including full papers for these when provided by the author.

The papers, workshops, and posters included here were selected by the Program Advisory Board using a juried abstracts process. All of the contributed papers have been formatted to comply with the conference *Guidelines for Preparing Manuscripts* distributed to contributors. Typographical errors have been corrected and papers have been formatted for consistency, using the guidelines published in the *Publication Manual of the American Psychological Association* (5th ed.), *APA Publication Manual* Web site at http://www.apastyle.org/, and other reputable sources.

Julie A. Garrison
Editor

[Haworth co-indexing entry note]: "Preface." Garrison, Julie A. Co-published simultaneously in *Journal of Library Administration* (The Haworth Information Press, an imprint of The Haworth Press, Inc.) Vol. 45, No. 1/2, 2006, p. xxxi; and: *The Twelfth Off-Campus Library Services Conference Proceedings* (ed: Julie A. Garrison) The Haworth Information Press, an imprint of The Haworth Press, Inc., 2006, p. xxv. Single or multiple copies of this article are available for a fee from The Haworth Document Delivery Service [1-800-HAWORTH, 9:00 a.m. - 5:00 p.m. (EST). E-mail address: docdelivery@haworthpress.com].

Acknowledgments

The Twelfth Off-Campus Library Services Conference represents contributions of many working in this field. Thanks to all of the authors/presenters for their willingness to share their thoughts, experiences, and research on paper and for allowing Central Michigan University to publish their work for wider distribution.

Special thanks goes to Connie Hildebrand, Conference Coordinator, for all of the work she has done the past two years to plan, organize, and make this event and proceedings a reality. Recognition goes to the Program Advisory Board for lending their time and expertise to reviewing and selecting proposals for papers, workshops, and posters that are included in the following pages.

Special thanks also go to Linda Neely, Copyright Coordinator, and Tanya Fox for providing extra sets of eyes in reviewing papers and abstracts for formatting and grammatical consistency. Sherry Cole, in the CMU Libraries' Dean's Office also deserves recognition for lending her word processing expertise at a moment's notice when formatting difficulties surfaced.

In addition, recognition and thanks to our colleagues in CMU Off-Campus Library Services who have each contributed in their own personal way to the conference. These include: Laurie Bellinger, Mark Costa, Monica Craig, Dan Gall, Anita Gordon, Kristi Khan, Julie LaDell-Thomas, Jeanne Pilibosian, Sharon Southwick, TaLisa Wolosonowich, Cindy Worley, and student workers.

Program Advisory Board
and Executive Planning Committee*

Jackie AlSaffar
Reference Librarian/Centers Liaison
Buena Vista University

Rita Barsun
Walden Librarian
Indiana University

Michele D. Behr
Off Campus Services Librarian
Western Michigan University

David Bickford
Dean of University Learning
    Resources & University
    Librarian
University of Phoenix

Heather L. Brown
Distance Education/Outreach
    Librarian
University of Nebraska Medical
    Center

Consuela Cline
Coordinator of Reference Services
Mercer University

Mary Cassner
Subject Specialist Librarian
University of Nebraska-Lincoln

Mark Costa*
Off-Campus Librarian
Central Michigan University

Monica Craig*
Off-Campus Librarian
Central Michigan University

William Denny
Distance Learning/Government
    Documents Librarian
California University of Pennsylvania

Jack Fritts
Director of Library Services
Benedictine University

Daniel Gall*
Off-Campus Librarian
Central Michigan University

Julie Garrison*
Director, Off-Campus Library
    Services
Central Michigan University

Laura Heinz
Senior Director
Outreach/Extramural Services
Texas Tech University Health
    Sciences Center

Connie Hildebrand*
Conference Coordinator
    & Librarian
Central Michigan University

Julie LaDell-Thomas*
Off-Campus Librarian
Central Michigan University

Elaine Magusin
Reference Services Librarian
Athabasca University

Rob Morrison
Instructor, University Library
National-Louis University

Carol M. Moulden
Associate Professor,
    University Library
National-Louis University

Doris Munson
Systems/Reference Librarian
Eastern Washington University

Patrick Mahoney
Business Analyst
Ewing Marion Kauffman Foundation

Alexander (Sandy) Slade
Executive Director
Council of Prairie and Pacific
    University Libraries (COPPUL)

Terri Summey
Head of Distance and Access
    Services
Emporia State University

Beth Thomsett-Scott
Science Reference and Liaison
    Librarian
University of North Texas

Allyson Washburn
Distributed Learning Services
    Librarian
Brigham Young University

Justine Wheeler
EMBA/MBA Librarian
University of Calgary

CONTRIBUTED PAPERS

Copyright Concerns in Online Education: What Students Need to Know

Jackie AlSaffar

Buena Vista University

SUMMARY. As both users of and creators of copyrighted works, students must have a basic understanding of the principles regarding intellectual property. The chances of online students infringing copyright are greater simply because of the venue–nearly every activity has copyright considerations. Students need to take full advantage of the privileges copyright affords, yet realize the limitations of use. This article outlines the avenues of acceptable use of copyrighted works, defines key differences between copyright and plagiarism, and asserts the importance of librarians to provide guidance and education on these issues. doi:10.1300/J111v45n01_01

KEYWORDS. Copyright, intellectual property

WHY IS COPYRIGHT IMPORTANT?

Copyright has direct implications for online students. Not only are they users of copyrighted works, but as students, they are creators as

[Haworth co-indexing entry note]: "Copyright Concerns in Online Education: What Students Need to Know." AlSaffar, Jackie. Co-published simultaneously in *Journal of Library Administration* (The Haworth Information Press, an imprint of The Haworth Press, Inc.) Vol. 45, No. 1/2, 2006, pp. 1-16; and: *The Twelfth Off-Campus Library Services Conference Proceedings* (ed: Julie A. Garrison) The Haworth Information Press, an imprint of The Haworth Press, Inc., 2006, pp. 1-16.

Available online at http://jla.haworthpress.com
doi:10.1300/J111v45n01_01

1

well. Everyday activities such as forwarding an attachment to a fellow student, posting an entry to a discussion group, downloading a journal article from a database, inserting clip art into a PowerPoint™ presentation, or writing a paper for a course, all carry copyright considerations. The chances of infringing copyright in the online environment are greater *simply because of the venue.*

As both consumers and producers of copyrighted works, then, students must become savvy about what is and is not permissible, not only to avoid infringement of others' works, but to protect their contributions in this Information Age. If information is the currency of the Information Age, then students must be encouraged to build on prior knowledge, to forge linkages between knowledge and to create new knowledge. The new century needs workers that are reflective thinkers and creators of knowledge. Librarians have talked much and worked hard to promote the skills of information literacy. Why? Because students need skills to effectively locate, evaluate, and ultimately use information effectively to create new knowledge. That is the goal of information literacy, and it is a vital part of the mission of higher education.

DOES COPYRIGHT AFFECT STUDENTS IN A REAL WAY?

Let's face it: online course content can easily be scrutinized for possible violations of copyright. "In this environment of increasingly sophisticated tracking mechanisms and heightened sensitivity to copyright issues, it's just common sense for people who use outside materials . . . to be aware of potential copyright violations and to take the necessary steps toward compliance" (Zielinski, 1999, Conclusion section, para. 1). Corporate America, Hollywood studios and large record companies are becoming more aggressive in pursuing violators, often filing suit against individual students and universities. So from a practical standpoint, having knowledge of copyright law is imperative, since ignorance of the law is no excuse. Innocent infringement is infringement nonetheless.

Student projects and interaction in the online environment look different than in face-to-face classes, often taking the forms of online portfolios, small-group assignments, virtual collaboration, shared facilitation, synchronous or asynchronous chats, discussion boards and homework forums. That computers have a great capacity to connect users to information is both a good and a problematic thing. Already vast quantities of text, audio, video and images are available online that students may be incorporating into their assignments. As "the world's largest copying machine" (Committee on Intellectual Property Rights [CIPR], 2000, p. 23), the Web is in fact a publication medium for online students, allowing for easy reproduction and distribution of information–two of the "exclusive rights" reserved for copyright holders. Digital documents can be made accessible to an unlimited number of other users very easily. It is important to recognize that in this new media-rich, interactive, collaborative environment, the rules have not all been worked out. As online courses move further away from mimicking face-to-face courses, more issues will arise.

WHAT EXACTLY SHOULD STUDENTS KNOW ABOUT COPYRIGHT?

First and foremost, students should have an awareness and appreciation of the exclusive rights granted to authors as stated in 17 U.S.C. § 106. Copyright is in fact a bundle of rights, and includes the rights to:

(1) reproduce the work
(2) prepare derivative works
(3) distribute copies of the work to the public
(4) display or perform the work publicly

As important as knowing what those rights are, it is equally important that students be aware that the rights granted by copyright are *exclusive*, not *absolute*. This means that the rights of copyright are restricted by some very important exceptions and limitations. Copyright owners are not entitled to absolute dominion or a monopoly over the use of their work. Copyright is, at its heart, a balance between the conflicting interests of copyright owners with copyright users.

In order for students to exchange ideas, build on prior knowledge, and forge new links between knowledge, students need access to information. Fear of copyright infringement should not hinder students from taking full advantage of information, in all its various formats. That certainly would not serve to promote the advancement of science and the useful arts, as copyright is supposed to do.

Realistically, online students are at greater risk of violating copyright laws simply due to the delivery method of the course, and as we have witnessed from recent file-sharing rulings, students are not immune from lawsuits. In addition to being the venue through which online courses are conducted, the Web is in fact a publication medium for online students, allowing for easy reproduction, distribution and publication of information. We as educators and librarians know that engagement with the content of a course is what higher education is all about, is at the heart of an intellectual life, and is an objective of every course taught, whether face-to-face or online. Yet far from being an abstract concept in the online course, copyright is an integral part of the online operation. The common denominator is that whatever is captured in fixed form, whether words or sounds or images, is protected by copyright. And that accounts for nearly every activity that happens in an online course.

Copyright protects creators of original works–whether they are authors, musicians, artists, programmers, or simply college students. It is important for students to know they have protections when posting their work to a course site. While most are not worried that others will "scoop" their master plan for world peace, they nonetheless seek a reward for their efforts, even if it is only a good grade in the course. It is important to establish sensitivity toward copyright, so that students will ". . . be able to hold on to the value of what they create, to reap where they have sown" (Goldstein, 2003, p. 7). Much of what is posted to the Web seems transitory in nature–that hastily written e-mail or blog entry or forum posting. It may surprise students to learn, then, that such fleeting information, along with their doodles and scribbling and shopping lists, are afforded the same length of copyright protection as is their senior capstone project, or the great American novel–currently set at life of the author plus 70 years.

What should students know about copyright? They must have an awareness of both the rights and responsibilities they have when dealing with copyrighted works. In other words, we want students to take full advantage of the privileges copyright affords, yet realize the limitations of use. Just as important as knowing what might constitute infringement is knowing that there is a danger in being too risk-averse. It is worthwhile to consider these issues more fully, starting first with an exploration of the conditions and occasions under which use of copyrighted works is allowable.

LAWFUL USE OF COPYRIGHTED WORKS

Fair Use

Many uses of copyrighted information within higher education fall within the scope of fair use, so therefore do not constitute infringement.

The doctrine of fair use outlines a four-factor test by which to determine whether any particular use of a copyrighted work constitutes infringement. A fair use analysis using the four factors is done on a case-by-case basis; each factor will weigh in favor of or against a determination of fair use. The strength of an argument for or against a use will be made in light of all four factors: (1) the purpose and character of the use; (2) the nature of the copyrighted work; (3) the amount and substantiality of the portion used; (4) the effect on the potential market for or value of the work.

It should be noted that fair use is a defense to a claim of infringement. In the online environment, a fair use defense would be strengthened by restricting access to copyrighted works, by restricting the length of time of access, or by limiting the portion of the work used. The fair use doctrine affords us a degree of latitude in the educational setting, yet students must know that not every educational use will be fair. They must also realize that a use considered fair in education may not be lawful in the marketplace. Two scenarios below will serve to illustrate what issues would require a fair use assessment.

Scenario: An engineering student wants to present her research findings regarding the collapse of the Tacoma Narrows Bridge at a conference. She prepares a PowerPoint™ presentation that incorporates architectural drawings of the bridge, so as to illustrate the flaws in design. Can she print off and distribute handouts of the drawings without permission?

Scenario: A student has written a Readers Theatre script for *Five Little Monkeys Jumping on the Bed*. Her professor loves it and encourages her to add it to an online repository of scripts. Can she legally do this, considering that *Five Little Monkeys* is still under copyright protection?

Library Databases

Another avenue to lawful use of copyrighted materials is through license agreements. Libraries enter into contracts with database producers or vendors to make the content of databases available to their authorized users. We librarians know that access to periodical literature through these databases is most assuredly essential for online students. But do our students know that? How are online students made aware of these valuable resources? Do they know libraries spend a significant portion of their acquisitions budgets to license these resources? Do they know that these databases are not available to the general public–that they are subscription-based only? Whether or not online students have the benefit of a research library nearby, online databases have the advantages of being accessible, of making available a great number and a great array of journals, and of being available round the clock.

License agreements set forth specific terms and conditions of use. While terms vary from database to database, a license agreement typically addresses such issues as who is allowed access, what uses are authorized, who is liable for any misuse, and, of course, the fee for licensing the database. How is an online student to know what actions are permitted, and what actions prohibited, short of reading each license agreement? Licenses typically specify that use be restricted to persons affiliated with the institution (currently enrolled students, faculty, staff, and walk-in users). This means that sharing passwords with unauthorized users is prohibited. Additionally, forwarding or e-mailing information to unauthorized persons is not allowed. In regards to usage of a database, licenses generally allow users to print, download, and e-mail copies for their personal use, for the purposes of research, teaching and scholarship only. Any commercial use of a database is prohibited. Posting a persistent or stable link to an article is permissible (for those databases that incorporate that functionality). However, copying and posting licensed works to another Web site is not allowed. Systematic downloading of licensed works is also prohibited. A few examples of what situations may arise in regards to licensed databases follow.

Scenario: Mary graduates this semester. She is downloading articles from databases to retain for use later, so she can easily access them and distribute to co-workers during training sessions. Is this use permitted?

Scenario: A professor wants students to read an article from the *New York Times*. The article is available full text in Lexis-Nexis, but linking directly to the article is not possible. Can the professor scan the article and post online within the courseware, since the end result is the same?

Scenario: An online student is made aware of a supplemental issue of a magazine devoted to her chosen paper topic. The student wants to read the entire issue, and would, if she were reading the print version. However, she is accessing the issue online. Can she download every article contained in that issue or is that prohibited?

Scenario: An online student (Student A) is collaborating on a project with a student from another university (Student B). Student A locates an article in a database that Student B does not have access to at the other university. Can Student A send the article to Student B?

Permissions

Getting permission to use a work is the surest way to avoid infringement. Librarians and educators routinely seek permission to use copyrighted works. Students, on the other hand, do not see copyright as integral to their coursework, so it gets short shrift. From grade school on, students are warned not to copy others' works, yet they still have a hard time determining what actually constitutes plagiarism (Spanier & Sherman, 2005) They know even less about what constitutes copyright infringement! Even if a student knows a particular use goes beyond fair use, he may be disinclined to seek permission to use it. Perhaps he simply feels he is flying under the radar–a typical student in a typical class does not typically attract much attention, after all. Perhaps he feels it is worth a gamble–operating under the assumption that the chances of detection are minimal, and the penalties slight. Or maybe time is a critical factor. If the assignment is due tomorrow, that does not allow much time for corresponding back and forth with the copyright holder (if that person can even be identified). Or perhaps the student may fear the copyright owner may not grant permission, or may grant permission only if fees are levied–not what a student wants to hear.

Librarians and educators, we hope, take greater care when dealing with copyrighted works. Securing permissions for works posted on courseware can often be done quickly and easily through a clearinghouse such as the Copyright Clearance Center. A student may be unaware (and may not care) that permission has been secured for certain articles he accesses via courseware or coursepacks. He is more concerned that the article is readily available in a format that is easy to access and view.

Two scenarios below will illustrate when it would be prudent for students to seek permission to use a work.

Scenario: A student-teacher wonders if she can hang her students' art work up in the halls of the school. Technically, she should ask permission of each student before doing so.

Scenario: An online student is writing a report for class. He wishes to incorporate an idea and several quotes that a fellow student posted to a discussion forum. The student would be wise to obtain permission from the other student.

Public Domain

There are no copyright restrictions on works in the public domain. They can be used for any purpose without fear of infringement. "Wonderful," a student thinks, "then anything without a copyright notice on it is in the public domain." Therein lies one difficulty with public domain–the misconception that unless a work bears a copyright notice, it is in the public domain. Many students have the mistaken notion that information on the Web, unless it specifically includes a notice, is in the public domain just because it is publicly accessible. Another common misconception is that a work "out-of-print" equates to a work "out-of-copyright." The availability of a work has nothing to do with the underlying copyright. The copyright for a work remains intact whether or not the work is currently in print.

Works enter the public domain in a number of legalistic ways. One common way is through expiration of copyright. Determining when that happens for any particular work is difficult. Copyright laws have changed many times in the past century, on occasion extending the length of protection granted to works. United States' works created previous to 1923 are in the public domain; that is about the only thing one can assume. Lengths of protection vary, too, depending on whether a work is authored by an individual, anonymously, by a corporation, or is a "work made for hire." A chart prepared by Lolly Gasaway (2003), entitled *When U.S. Works Pass into the Public Domain*, can assist in determining if a work has entered the public domain through expiration of copyright.

Some works have fallen into the public domain due to a failure on the part of the copyright owner to register the work. This applies only to works published before 1978 that do not bear a copyright notice. Unlike now, registration of works was required for protection before that year.

If an author so desires, he can forego his copyright to a work and place it in the public domain. All that is required is a statement formally declaring his intent. A new avenue for authors interested in sharing their creative works without giving up ownership in them is Creative Commons (http://creativecommons.org/). This Internet-based service allows authors to place their works online using a flexible "some rights reserved" licensing structure. It offers a middle-ground between the "all rights reserved" protection of copyright and the "no rights reserved" free-for-all of public domain. As stated by Creative Commons, "Our licenses help you keep your copyright while inviting certain uses of your work–a 'some rights reserved' copyright" (Creative Commons, n.d., para. 1).

Federal government documents are in the public domain, if they are works created by government employees within the scope of their employment. Works produced by state and local governments, on the other hand, generally are copyrighted. Sounds straight-forward, but consider this: the maps produced by Lewis and Clark on their expedition are in the public domain. However, the private papers of William Clark, chronicling the voyage, were not part of the group's commission, so did not immediately fall into the realm of public domain, as did the maps (Samuels, 2000).

Lest you think that is the only complication in regards to government documents and public domain, think again. The federal government is not required to disseminate all governmental works (works regarding national security, for example), so naturally those documents are not in the public domain. Additionally, works created under a government contract or by government grant also do not fall into public domain. Certain works produced by the National Institute for Standards and Technology (NIST) and the United States Postal Service (stamps, for instance) are also not in the public domain. Information found on government Web sites, however, is in the public domain.

What advantages do works in the public domain offer to students? The fact that there are no restrictions on use gives students much freedom–no fair use guidelines to weigh, no permissions to seek, no charge attached to any use, nor any conditions to satisfy other than citing the source. What, then, are the disadvantages to the public domain? The major drawback is the difficulty in determining what falls into this category. Are ERIC documents in the public domain? How about the Mona Lisa? How about the Bible? How about a new translation of a work that has long since entered the public domain? There is no master database one can search to locate works in the public domain. Nor is it easy to determine whether the copyright has expired for a given work. A student may well be using a work that is in the public domain and never be aware of it. Another drawback to the public domain is the problem of orphan works. These are works still under copyright protection, but whose owners cannot be found. It is evident that public domain, like so many aspects of copyright law, is somewhat murky and complex.

Realistically, does a student care whether or not something falls into the public domain? Would such knowledge change the works he selects to use? Would it change the way he uses a work? It possibly could. Consider a student in a music composition course. A student who knows that Beethoven's *Fifth Symphony* is in the public domain might create (and maybe even sell!) a *Ragtime Fifth Symphony* based on Beethoven's work, with no fear of copyright infringement. He could not, however, create a Ragtime version of *Born in the U.S.A.* without first consulting Bruce Springsteen. It is not so far-fetched to imagine. Peter

Schickele, after all, has used the classics widely in his musical parodies. Knowing that Shakespeare's plays and Monet's water lilies and the *Gettysburg Address* and birth records are in the public domain could have important ramifications for student research.

TEACH Act

The TEACH (Technology, Education, and Copyright Harmonization Act) Act of 2002 impacts online educators more directly than online students. It brings into closer alignment uses of copyrighted materials that are permitted in a face-to-face class with similar uses in an online course. Essentially, it allows educators to perform or display certain copyrighted works in an online environment, if certain requirements are met, as part of "mediated instructional activities" in the course. Because of the TEACH Act, an online educator can incorporate film clips into a film studies course, or sound bytes into a music appreciation course. Institutions that have chosen to comply with the TEACH Act must, as a requirement of the Act, provide educational materials about copyright to their community and promote copyright compliance. Students in the course must be notified that the materials may be subject to copyright protection, that they cannot save materials to their computers, that they may not revise the materials in any way, and that they may not copy or distribute the materials.

PUSHING THE LIMITS OF COPYRIGHT

We live in interesting times! On the one hand, we have lobbyists in Washington working to ensure that the voices of the motion picture industry are heard. On the other hand, we have a major corporation (Google™) pushing the limits of copyright with its Google Book Search™ program. In another realm, we have students forming free culture groups on campuses who are promoting open-source software, hosting remixing contests, and speaking out against "extremist" copyright laws. At the same time, we see universities paying high copyright fees and erring on the side of caution when mounting works online rather than risk litigation.

What can recent case law and legislative activity tell us about where copyright is headed? It seems even the legislation is conflicting. In 1998 Congress passed the Sonny Bono Copyright Term Extension Act, which increased the term of protection from 50 years after an author's death to 70 years. That same year, the Digital Millennium Copyright Act (DMCA) was passed into law. It serves to partially shield institutions (and Internet service providers) from the infringing acts of students and faculty. Lipinski stated that "[r]ecent case law suggests an increased aggressiveness on the part of copyright owners to target nonprofit and individual copyright violators" (2003, p. 486). Hoffmann saw ". . . an attempt by powerful copyright owners to make a 'land grab' for all they can get, taking advantage of new technologies and copyright law's inability to address those technologies" (2005, p. 8).

Will the growing popularity of online education make it a target for increased scrutiny? Will the threat of lawsuits curb students' urges to download music, or simply lead to a disregard of copyright law? Will Creative Commons, open-source software, and other endeavors promoting sharing cause a fundamental change in the way we think about intellectual property? Globalization is sure to affect United States copyright law: "The recent introduction of copyright into the international trade bazaar, where intellectual property rights can be traded for subsidies to rice or rapeseed oil, promises to complicate both domestic and international copyright . . . " (Goldstein, 2003, p. 161).

How might these trends affect an online student who takes no interest in copyright? It is obvious to the online student that information commonly assumes a fixed form, and is therefore subject to copyright law. It should be obvious, too, that information in fixed forms will continue to play a central role in the Information Age. Students would be well served, then, to recognize the economic and political realities surrounding information.

COPYRIGHT CONUNDRUMS

Copyright vs. Plagiarism

Copyright and plagiarism are interrelated concepts, yet distinct. While similar in the respect that both involve the ethical use of intellectual property, and that violation can be done easily and even unknowingly, the similarity ends there.

A student who passes off the work of another as his own, or uses a source without giving credit is plagiarizing. In academia, this intellectual thievery is considered ethically wrong and is prohibited by university policy. While we usually associate plagiarism with education and copyright infringement with the marketplace, plagiarism is not confined to the hallowed halls, nor is copyright only the purview of the market-place. Not long ago, well-known historians Steven Ambrose and Doris Kearns Goodwin made headlines when both were accused of plagiarism. The punishment can be serious, as Goodwin learned.

> She is on leave from PBS's *The NewsHour with Jim Lehrer*, a number of universities and organizations have withdrawn their speaking invitations, and *The Harvard Crimson* has called for her resignation from Harvard's board of overseers. In addition, Goodwin resigned as a member of the Pulitzer Prize board, and the board has been asked to rescind her 1995 Pulitzer for *No Ordinary Time: Franklin and Eleanor Roosevelt: The Home Front in World War II.* (Ardito, 2002, p. 16)

Just as issues of plagiarism are not confined to academia, nor are issues of copyright infringement confined to the marketplace. As recent court cases have demonstrated, university students who helped themselves to an excessive number of MP3 music files have been found in violation of copyright, and have been fined up to $17,500 (Graham, 2004). Usually, a claim of copyright infringement surfaces when the fourth factor of fair use weighs in favor of the copyright owner, i.e., when the marketability of a work is lessened because of an act of intellectual thievery. Noted law professor Paul Goldstein succinctly stated that copyright is mostly about money (2003).

Not all instances of plagiarism constitute copyright infringement, nor do all violations of copyright constitute plagiarism (Manuel, n.d.). To illustrate the former, consider that even a clear-cut act of plagiarism, for the sole purpose of monetary gain, does not violate copyright law, if the work in question has passed into the public domain and is no longer under copyright protection, or is a government document that never was under copyright protection. Using such a work without giving proper attribution is clearly plagiarism, and while academically dishonest and an affront to our moral sensibilities, technically there is nothing illegal about it. On the flip side, consider how something may constitute copyright infringement, but not be considered plagiarism. A student who downloads a thousand music files from a file-sharing server will be in violation of copyright, yet he has not plagiarized anything.

Let us look at another difference between these two concepts. Facts cannot be copyrighted (a statement of someone's birth date, for example) for the reason that their creation does not stem from an act of authorship–it just "is." Yet a distinct arrangement or compilation of those facts into a fixed form becomes a copyrightable work (a published family genealogy, for instance). A re-statement of that work without proper attribution would constitute plagiarism.

Owning a Copy vs. Owning a Copyright

Owning a copy of a work is different than owning the copyright to that work. A student who purchases a book has the right to lend it to a neighbor, display it on the coffee table, re-sell it on Amazon.com™, or use it as a doorstop. But he does not have the right to scan a chapter from that book and load it onto a course Web site. While the book becomes his physical property, it does not become his intellectual property. Likewise, an e-mail or presentation that Student A forwards to Student B does not become the intellectual property of Student B, but remains that of Student A. An article retrieved from a database has its own copyright nuances. Technically speaking, libraries do not "own" the articles within subscription databases. They are simply paying for access to them, which is similar to "renting" them for a period of time.

The Free Web Is Not Free

"The Web is a particularly alluring temptress, beckoning with its wide selection of easily accessed content . . ." (Zielinski, 1999, "It's up there," para. 1). Contrary to what many students assume, information posted on publicly-accessible Web pages is, by default, copyrighted. A student operating under the assumption that publicly-accessible means copyright-free may liberally copy and paste portions of "found text" into a document. Plainly stated, registration with the Copyright Office is not necessary to secure copyright protection, nor is a statement of copyright notice necessary. Copyright is automatic once information assumes a fixed format. Information that is mounted on a publicly-accessible Web page makes it available for public viewing, but does not put it in the public domain. What this means for students is that without express consent of the copyright owner, downloading or copying files from the Internet is an act of infringement. However, the doctrine of fair use does apply to the Web, so affords students some latitude.

OUR ROLE AS LIBRARIANS

How can librarians best serve online students, most of whom we will never see face-to-face, or even personally interact? What is our role in the online environment? It is clear that there are copyright ramifications for nearly all of the services and resources the library provides to online students. It is clear, too, that there are copyright ramifications for nearly every activity that an online student does, due to the nature of the delivery method. In this Information Age, it is in a student's best interests to be knowledgeable about copyright. It is up to us to figure out ways to make this happen in the online environment. Following are some ideas of how we can "reach out and touch" online students in both direct and indirect ways, to improve their learning experience.

- Embedded librarian: Become an "embedded librarian" in an online course. Librarians can set up a discussion forum, assist students in locating resources, or post timely hints.
- Policy makers: Get involved with the development of copyright policies on campus. Get involved with other professionals to impact national policies.
- Policy promoters: Encourage students to become familiar with the institution's copyright policies, which may address such things as what to do if a claim of infringement is made. Be a model of ethical behavior by promoting lawful uses of copyrighted works.
- Educators: Capitalize on teachable moments! The student who wonders why he is not able to print off an entire chapter of an e-book is an ideal candidate.
- Partners: Team up with course developers and instructional designers. Faculty may know copyright from the standpoint of intellectual property rights for courses they design, yet be unaware of the restrictions of database licenses, the process for obtaining permissions, etc. Make sure instructional designers use persistent links to articles, instead of posting the full text. Team up with designers to create learning objects or tutorials relating to copyright.

The goal of educating students about copyright should be to raise awareness of what is at stake, to know where the gray areas lie, and to know when to question their actions. How this can be accomplished is another matter.

The fact that copyright education is mandated by law for institutions to be in compliance with the Digital Millennium Copyright Act (DMCA) and the TEACH Act gives us more leverage when making a case for its importance. Education must go beyond simply distributing copies of the institution's copyright policies to promoting responsible use of intellectual property. Key players in online education–including course developers, instructional designers, and adjunct professors–need to know when to play it safe and when to exercise fair use rights. Librarians need to be educated about copyright as well. Not only will we be asked to secure permissions for course materials, but we will need to negotiate license agreements with databases vendors. And like it or not, we will be consulted when sticky copyright questions arise.

To sum up, awareness of copyright is a necessity in a digital world.

A better understanding of the basic principles of copyright law would lead to greater respect for this law and greater willingness to abide by it, as well as produce a more informed public better able to engage in discussions about intellectual property and public policy. (CIPR, 2000, pp. 16-17)

REFERENCES

Ardito, S. C. (2002, July/August). Plagiarism, fabrication, and the lack of attribution. *Information Today, 19*, 16-17. Retrieved December 10, 2005, from Academic Search Premier database.

Committee on Intellectual Property Rights and the Emerging Information Infrastructure. (2000). *The digital dilemma: Intellectual property in the information age.* Washington, DC: National Academy Press.

Creative Commons. (n.d.). *Learn more about Creative Commons.* Retrieved December 12, 2005, from http://creativecommons.org/learnmore.

Gasaway, L. (2003). *When U.S. works pass into the public domain.* Retrieved December 1, 2005, from http://www.unc.edu/~unclng/public-d.htm.

Goldstein, P. (2003). *Copyright's highway: From Gutenberg to the celestial jukebox* (Rev. ed.). Stanford, CA: Stanford University Press.

Graham, J. (2004, March 24). College students sued over music downloads. *USA Today*, p. 5b. Retrieved December 10, 2005, from Academic Search Premier database.

Hoffmann, G. M. (2005). *Copyright in cyberspace 2: Questions and answers for librarians.* New York: Neal-Schuman.

Lipinski, T. A. (2003). Legal issues in the development and use of copyrighted material in Web-based distance education. In M.G. Moore & W.G. Anderson (Eds.), *Handbook of distance education* (pp. 481-505). Mahwah, NJ: Erlbaum.

Manuel, K. (n.d.). *Plagiarism and copyright.* Retrieved December 3, 2005, from http://lib.nmsu.edu/instruction/toolkit/Copyright.ppt.

Samuels, E. (2000). *The illustrated story of copyright.* New York: St. Martin's Press.
Spanier, G., & Sherman, C. H. (2005, December 2). Thou shalt not pirate thy neighbor's songs. *Chronicle of Higher Education, 52,* B24. Retrieved January 22, 2006, from Academic Search Premier database.
Zielinski, D. (1999). *Are you a copyright criminal?* Retrieved December 1, 2005, from http://www.3m.com/meetingnetwork/presentations/pmag_copyright_criminal.html.

doi:10.1300/J111v45n01_01

Helping Users Help Themselves: Evaluating the Off-Campus Library Services Web Site

Donna Bancroft
Susan Lowe

University College/University of Maine System

SUMMARY. Traditionally, distance students have completed their research in an electronic environment and off-campus librarians have strived to meet the needs of these students using a variety of methods. Today our students are familiar with the Web as a medium of interaction, and library usage has changed as a result of electronic services on the Internet. Given the dramatic increase in usage of our Off-Campus Library Services' Web site, a survey was conducted to determine whether the content of the site and the services offered were simple and useful to our users. This paper presents the results of the survey as well as a discussion of the changes to the site as a result of feedback from students. doi:10.1300/J111v45n01_02

KEYWORDS. Online resources, survey, Web pages, usage patterns, evaluation, assessment

UNIVERSITY COLLEGE/UNIVERSITY OF MAINE SYSTEM

University College is the organizational umbrella under which the University of Maine System's distance classes take place. The Univer-

[Haworth co-indexing entry note]: "Helping Users Help Themselves: Evaluating the Off-Campus Library Services Web Site." Bancroft, Donna, and Susan Lowe. Co-published simultaneously in *Journal of Library Administration* (The Haworth Information Press, an imprint of The Haworth Press, Inc.) Vol. 45, No. 1/2, 2006, pp. 17-35; and: *The Twelfth Off-Campus Library Services Conference Proceedings* (ed: Julie A. Garrison) The Haworth Information Press, an imprint of The Haworth Press, Inc., 2006, pp. 17-35.

Available online at http://jla.haworthpress.com
doi:10.1300/J111v45n01_02

17

sity College provides the University of Maine System community with a single point of service for current and emerging information technology and support for distributed learning. Approximately 6,000 students of every age and from every region of the state take classes at more than 75 off-campus sites and at 11 regional University Centers. Additionally, out-of-state and international students participate in the University of Maine System courses via the Web.

Interactive television is the primary medium of course delivery. Courses also are delivered via the Web, video conferencing, videotapes/DVDs, and other technology. Students can choose from 19 degree or 16 certificate programs at the associate, bachelor and master's levels and select from nearly 200 courses each semester (University College, 2005, Courses and Degree Section).

OFF-CAMPUS LIBRARY SERVICES

Since 1989, the Off-Campus Library Services (OCLS) office of the University College has been providing library services to distance learners. The office evolved from being part of a university campus library into being completely integrated as a system-wide service for the University of Maine System. The University of Maine System consists of seven universities each with its own distinct mission. The system serves nearly 35,000 students and each university campus offers distance education courses. Administratively OCLS reports to distance education which provides centralized services for each of the university campuses. This unique situation within the structure of the University of Maine System gives OCLS the opportunity to form both formal and informal bonds not only with the other libraries in the university system, but also with the front line distance education faculty and service providers for distance learners.

The Off-Campus Library Services office at University College/University of Maine System offers the following core services for faculty, staff and students. These are not accomplished in isolation, but rather in coordination with the system library directors and staff at the other campuses. The guiding principles for the program are based on the ACRL "Guidelines for Distance Learning Library Services" (2004).

The main goal of the OCLS office is to meet the unique needs of faculty, students, and staff using distance education technologies–wherever these individuals are located–by providing effective and appropriate services.

Current services include:

For Faculty:

- consultation with faculty regarding incorporation of information literacy into the curriculum
- library and information literacy instruction in the classroom (at centers), via ITV, and over the Web using Ask-a-Librarian
- faculty training regarding library technology and copyright and fair use issues in distance education
- use of electronic reserves for library reserves for students
- broadcast clearance for audiovisual materials used in Web-based, ITV, and compressed video courses
- copyright clearance for reserve material and faculty coursepacks
- assistance for faculty conducting research
- brochures providing faculty with information regarding library services

For Students:

- centralized interlibrary loan and circulation services (renewals, library cards, troubleshooting)
- toll-free and electronic reference and referral assistance
- Off-Campus Library Services Web site with interactivity for requesting library cards, interlibrary loan articles, links to information sources, reference services, course specific research guides, FAQs, etc.
- document delivery of journal articles to home addresses and electronically via e-mail and ILLiad
- development of point-of-use guides and brochures both in paper and online
- coordination of the library-use instruction component of the *Introduction to the College Experience* course (University of Maine at Augusta course)
- in-class library use instruction (as well as phone, e-mail, online live reference, and onsite instruction) in partnership of the campus-based librarians

For Distance Education Staff and Campus-Based Librarians:

- onsite training in library technologies for center/site staff
- staff manuals which include library policies, hours, forms, etc.

- cooperative agreement with a local public library
- clearinghouse for library-related problems
- training for campus bibliographic instruction librarians who use distance education technologies
- centralized listing of videos cleared for broadcast and video-streaming, vendor contacts, and payment of broadcast fees

System-Wide Administrative and Mariner Committees:

- Library Directors
- System Circulation Heads
- Database Subscription Task Force
- Information Literacy Subcommittee
- eReference Task Force
- System-Wide Heads of Reference Committee

Periodically over the years, the Off-Campus Library Services office has conducted, in accordance with the "Guidelines for Distance Learning Library Services," both formal and informal assessments of our user groups and evaluated the resources and services that OCLS provides. As part of our ongoing quality improvement process, OCLS staff monitor the Web pages for content and recommend new items or services to the site. For example, during our bibliographic instruction sessions we gave students a handout called "Mariner Basics" (Mariner is the name of the digital library of the University of Maine System). After a review of our Web pages, we added this handout as a PDF file for the students to freely print out as they needed. The immediate popularity of this one item, as shown by our Web server statistics, indicated the handout was viewed over 174 times in a three month period. This one addition encouraged us to make further changes to the site in anticipation of our users' needs.

As a result of our 2005 OCLS retreat, we revised the content of a number of pages, deleted some pages entirely, and added some new features. One new feature was the addition of our customized Web pages for specific classes. Each individual course page is directed toward the assignments for the class and makes the research process for the student more fluid. These pages are carefully constructed by combining several features already offered on our Web page. The rationale behind this project was to provide students with inclusive information intended for the subject of the class in one location. For example, the pages for the criminal justice class have database links to subject specific databases that the university system subscribes to in the criminal justice arena along with additional library and Internet resources.

Since 2002, OCLS has examined on a monthly basis our Web server statistics and usage patterns for our directory on the server. The report is generated by Analog which is a program that measures the usage and popularity of the pages (Analog, 2004). During the period from 2002 to 2005, we observed that usage of the OCLS site had risen dramatically. Overall hits on the site were 45,665 in the 2002-2003 academic year and they increased in 2003-2004 to 57,587 and continue at this level–an increase of nearly 12,000 hits. In the public sector during this same period there was a growing comfort level and familiarity with the Web as a medium of interaction. We deduced that the increased activity at our site mirrored that comfort level. Students were using the digital information we provided and increasingly interacting with our services via the Web. Coombs discussed this shift in user behavior toward the virtual library and her use of tracking software to track usage of their library's site (2005). We closely looked at our Web server logs to determine which pages of the Off-Campus Library Services' Web site generated the most traffic. These logs answered questions regarding popularity of some of the pages, but it did not answer all of the questions that we had. We wanted to take a closer look at our Web site to determine whether the content of the site and the services offered were straightforward and useful to our users.

INTRODUCTION

The "Guidelines for Distance Learning Library Services" provide a rationale for conducting an assessment. The first paragraph in the Management section of the Guidelines particularly addresses conducting a survey "to monitor and assess both the appropriateness of their [distance learning library users] use of services and resources and the degree to which needs are being met and skills acquired" (ACRL, 2004).

There have been several helpful articles published on conducting formal user surveys, focus group feedback, and other measurement options for obtaining information from users. After a careful review of the literature on assessment of library Web sites and services, we decided to conduct a user survey and measure user satisfaction in a systematic way. User surveys not only give feedback, but also inform users of features that they might be unaware of and do not use. Another function of the survey was to evaluate and assess our services. Are the support services meeting students' needs? What improvements could we make to assist them when they are conducting research and accessing our services? Are the support services offered by Off-Campus Library Services functional in a changing electronic environment? Plosker, in particular, provided practical advice on the survey process itself and grounded us with a clear mental picture of the goals of the survey (2002).

The main objective of the survey was to provide OCLS with a tool for measuring users' practices on the OCLS site as well as satisfaction with the online services that we provide. It would reveal any service issues that need fine-tuning and identify any unmet needs or future requirements. For purposes of this study, we were not evaluating the appearance, interface, and aesthetics of the page, but rather trying to ascertain if the *services and resources* we provide on the site meet users' needs.

When developing the survey, we examined all of the Off-Campus Library Services pages. The intent was to make sure that all of our resources and services were included. Figure 1 shows the home page for OCLS and provides a snapshot of our primary services.

After significant discussion, we decided what kind of information we needed from our patrons. Did we just want a "yes" or "no" answer or was some other type of feedback required in the assessment? Was the online library card application working for them? What degree of satisfaction do they have with the form? Have they used the "Ask-a-Librarian" service? Are they satisfied with this means of communication? We wanted the questions to be comprehensive and cover all of our services and resources.

METHODOLOGY

After deciding on the format of the questions, a twenty-question anonymous survey was developed by the Off-Campus Library Services office to evaluate the services we offer to students. Sixteen of the questions were multiple choice or multiple answer and four were open ended for comments. Three hundred and thirty-five (335) surveys were distributed by several different methods. Students were invited to fill out the survey in live classes at the outreach centers, Web-based classes, interactive television classes and via the phone. The Web-based surveys were filled out online via a designated Blackboard site set up specifically for this survey. The remainder of the paper-based surveys were

FIGURE 1. Off-Campus Library Services Home Page
(http://www.learn.maine.edu/ocls)

distributed and collected by other University College staff members and returned to Off-Campus Library Services. See Appendix for statistical breakdown of the survey results and responses to open-ended questions.

RESULTS

Three hundred and thirty-five surveys were distributed and sixty-seven were returned, for a 20% response rate. A high percentage of respondents (85%) were female, ranging in age from 26 to 65. These "non-traditional students" reflected enrollment statistics for distance learners taking classes through the University of Maine System. A high number (78%) indicated that they had used our services prior to taking the survey. Eighty-two percent (82%) told us they were required to use our library resources and services by the faculty teaching classes they were presently taking. Students indicated in high percentages (over

50%) that they became aware of our services in a number of ways–primarily from staff, faculty, and librarians.

As part of the survey, we wanted to obtain information in three major areas–the use and helpfulness of the links to library resources, the importance of the research guides and tools developed by the librarians, and the satisfaction level of the services OCLS offers. The basic tool that students need for remote access to the library's online resources for research is a university library card. Sixty-seven percent (67%) indicated that they used the online form to apply for the card and all indicated that they received the card in a timely fashion. Of the links available on our Web page, those most extensively used and beneficial to the students were our links for "Indexes and Databases" (69%) and the link to our online shared catalog URSUS (66%).

To respond to the students' requirements for research, OCLS has developed many tools to assist with this process. Our resource guides and tutorials are used on a regular basis. Forty-five percent (45%) had used the Mariner tutorials, thirty percent (30%) had used the Mariner Basics handout, and twenty-two percent (22%) had used the course specific Web guides. Students told us that the Mariner tutorials and the Mariner Basics handout were very useful (42% and 44% respectively).

Feedback on our services was also a priority of the survey. A popular service, as shown by the survey results, was our online interlibrary loan service. Forty-six percent (46%) had used the service to enhance their research and the same number indicated that they received their material in a timely manner. They also said that the online form was easy to complete (45%).

One of the many links we offer is an e-mail service. We asked students if they had used this service. Sixty-seven percent (67%) had never submitted an e-mail question, however, twenty-five percent (25%) indicated that the service was useful and prompt. The FAQs/Library Help area on the Web page was not utilized by many. Sixty percent (60%) had not used this option but, of those who had used it, thirty-eight percent (38%) had found it useful. See Appendix for statistical breakdown of the survey results and responses to open-ended questions.

DISCUSSION

The OCLS librarians have made a concerted effort to foster and develop relationships with the faculty and to integrate information literacy as a critical part of the curriculum. The results of our survey affirm the success of this professional relationship. Eighty-six percent (86%) of the respondents informed us that they are now required to use our services by their instructors.

How do students find out about our services? The majority of students are directed by faculty and OCLS librarians who are guest speakers in their classes. Faculty teaching online classes are encouraged by the librarians to put a direct link to our home page in their course software. As part of our mission, OCLS librarians travel extensively throughout the state to the outreach centers and sites where students take their classes, and we have established a comfortable presence with the students and staff at those locations. The survey shows that staff at the centers and sites are an important source of information about OCLS. According to the survey we have indeed become a known entity out in our distance learning community–forty-nine percent (49%) of the students had become aware of us through the staff at the sites and centers. An additional fact that came to our attention from the survey was that a significant number of students (19%) became aware of us via other students.

The OCLS Web site is designed specifically to assist students with the research process. The site offers tools for accessing material, links to digital library resources, online tutorials, handouts, course guides, and document delivery for material that are not available full-text online. The results of the survey showed that students were using all of these services consistently for their research.

Interestingly enough, despite the abundant amount of full-text material available online, the document delivery service is used extensively (46%). The article request form where students submit their interlibrary loan requests is a significant feature based on the number of request we process each year. Forty-five percent (45%) of the students indicated that they had used the form and of these thirty-one percent (31%) were satisfied with the delivery time. We offer a number of ways to deliver the material to our students–snail mail, fax, and electronically. Despite issues with electronic delivery to non-university e-mail accounts, the majority of students were very satisfied with this service.

The comments to the open-ended questions were positive. Based on the feedback, most of the students had a good understanding of what resources and services were available to them. Most felt comfortable using the links and services on our page. Several non-traditional students who had been away from formal study for a number of years were especially appreciative of the assistance we provided to them.

CONCLUSION

The survey validated the mission of Off-Campus Library Services and many of the underlying philosophies of the office. The outreach function for center and site personnel is a core value. Faculty partnerships are also central to our mission. Students clearly benefit from this relationship. A clear directive is given to the students of where to go to start their research and where to obtain the support services.

Based on the survey, we have several revisions planned for the OCLS Web site. We are going to develop more course-related pages and move them to a more prominent location on the Web page. We currently replaced our article request form with ILLiad which should facilitate a better mechanism of document delivery. We will produce online instructions for our site to support this new service. Presently, we are replacing our Web-creation software. By adding daily announcements, course resources, and updates, the software upgrade offers us new ways to enhance our services to students.

Overall, the survey gave us a better understanding of how students are using our Web-based services and their level of satisfaction with what we provide to them in the online environment.

REFERENCES

Analog: Introduction. (2004, December 19). Retrieved December 5, 2005, from http://www.analog.cx/intro.html.

Association of College and Research Libraries. (2004). Guidelines for distance learning library services. *College & Research Libraries News, 65*, 604-611.

Coombs, K. A. (2005). Using Web server logs to track users through the electronic forest. *Computers in Libraries, 25*, 16-21. Retrieved January 12, 2005, from Academic Search Premier database.

Plosker, G. (2002). Conducting user surveys: An ongoing information imperative [Electronic version]. *Online, 26*, 64-69. Retrieved January 13, 2005, from http://www.infotoday.com/online/sep02/Pl9osker.htm.

University College. (2005). Success starts here! Retrieved December 13, 2005, from http://www.learn.maine.edu/about.html.

doi:10.1300/J111v45n01_02

APPENDIX

University of Maine System Off-Campus Library Services
Survey Results

67 responses from 335 surveys, 20% returned

1. <u>What is your gender?</u>
   Male   15%
   Female   85%
   Not answered   0%

2. <u>What is your age?</u>
   16-25   31%
   26-35   28%
   36-45   30%
   46-55   4%
   56-65   6%
   Over 65   0%
   Not answered   1%

3. <u>Have you used our services before?</u>
   Yes   78%
   No   22%
   Not answered   0%

4. <u>Have you been required to use our services in your class?</u>
   Yes   82%
   No   16%
   Not answered   2%

5. <u>How did you find out about Off-Campus Library services? Select all that apply.</u>
   Center/Site Staff   49%
   Brochure/Poster   4%
   Librarian visited class   54%
   Faculty/Syllabus   42%
   Student   19%
   Librarian from another campus   0%
   Link from course Webpage   21%
   Other   9%
   Not answered   0%

APPENDIX (continued)

6. <u>What features of the Off-Campus Library Services Webpage have you used? Please check all that apply.</u>

Online Library Card Application	51%
Article Request Form	46%
E-mail Reference Service	10%
Live Chat "Ask a Librarian"	13%
Mariner Tutorials	45%
Online FAQ's Library Help	6%
Course-Specific Guides	22%
Link to Online Indexes and Databases	69%
Link to URSUS	66%
Out of State Student Information	0%
Search the Internet Link	13%
Book Renewal Link	15%
OCLS Toll-Free Numbers	4%
"Mariner Basics" Handout	30%
Not answered	0%

7. <u>What part(s) of our Webpage have been the most useful to you? You may select more than one.</u>

Online Library Card Application	42%
Article Request Form	37%
E-mail Reference Service	4%
Live Chat "Ask a Librarian"	7%
Mariner Tutorials	30%
Online FAQ's Library Help	4%
Course-Specific Guides	13%
Link to Online Indexes and Databases	52%
Link to URSUS	51%
Out of State Student Information	0%
Search the Internet Link	12%
Book Renewal Link	13%
OCLS Toll-Free Numbers	4%
"Mariner Basics" Handout	22%
Not answered	0%

8. <u>The library card application was easy to fill out.</u>

Yes	67%
No	1%
Have not used	28%
Not answered	4%

9. I received my library card in a timely manner by using the online library card application.

Yes   67%
No   3%
Have not used   30%
Not answered   0%

10. The Article Request Form was easy to fill out.

I agree   45%
I disagree   3%
Have not used the form   52%
Not answered   0%

11. After using the Article Request Form, I was _____ with the length of time it took to receive my article(s).

Very satisfied   13%
Satisfied   28%
Dissatisfied   3%
Not applicable   58%
Not answered   0%

12. After submitting my e-mail question(s), the response(s) was/were _____ prompt and complete.

Always   21%
Sometimes   4%
Never   1%
Not applicable   67%
Not answered   7%

13. I have used the Mariner Tutorials and found them _____ in learning how to use Mariner.

Very helpful   42%
Somewhat helpful   21%
Not helpful   0%
Not applicable   36%
Not answered   1%

14. The FAQ's / Library Help have been _____ in answering my questions.

Always helpful   22%
Sometimes helpful   16%
Never helpful   0%
Not applicable   60%
Not answered   2%

APPENDIX (continued)

15. <u>Please comment on the usability of the URSUS (book catalogue) link from the OCLS homepage.</u>
Excellent. Use quite often
Loved the service, it made college paper tolerable
I found it very easy to use
Not too hard to use
I think this is a very useful tool and have found it very easy to use
URSUS is quite usable once you become accustomed to the format. Initially I found it difficult to use, but after some practice it became much easier
I love using URSUS. It is so helpful when doing research for a report
There is always an array of information available
Fairly useful, need to know your way around
I found this very useful in doing research papers and had no trouble navigating thru the system
Never used
It worked fine
Very easy and helpful
Good
URSUS is very easy to use and helpful in finding information
Have not used yet
Very helpful to me
Fine
I think it fits its purpose
Good
Was easy and receive information I needed
I don't know if I used that I could not find what I was looking for if that is what I was on though
It was very easy to use and has a great amount of resources. My only problem was in trying to find the button to actually request the books that I wanted
It took me where I wanted to go, which made me happy
Easy
Have not used
I found it very useful. I successfully requested 5 books
Have not used
Very easy to use
I have used this program frequently. It is very helpful to have books sent to a close location
Very helpful
I have not used
Liked access to online journal articles

I have had a good time using URSUS

The URSUS was very useful when finding books and articles that went along with my research paper. Lets you look up and order books easily

User friendly

I have tried to use it several times and I just don't get it. It hasn't been easy for me

Very useful

It has been very easy to use and helpful

It makes it a lot easier to access

Worked well. Could have been more useful to me if I had a library card

Very easy and helpful

Useable

16. Please comment on the usability of the Indexes and Databases link from the OCLS homepage.

Excellent. Use all the time

Wonderful

Like this aspect, think that more attention should be paid to getting students to know how to use it

Very easy to use

Very easy to use

This again was extremely helpful in all research that I have been required to do for classes

Good

A little complicated until you realize what you are looking at in terms of the indexes! Then fairly easy to use

Again, easy to use and helpful as well

The indexes and databases link is easy to use

Very easy

Indexes and Databases link should not be black, can't tell it's a link

Haven't used them I don't think

Was very easy to navigate with a vast array of information

Loved it

I like it

I think it was slightly confusing to get to the link for the indexes

Easy

I found them easy to use

They are easily accessible and helpful

Good

Confusing at first

Like before if those were what I was on, I found titles with what I wanted but could not get into them

Very usable

I was able to find articles that were useful

Easy

APPENDIX (continued)

Very helpful and easy to understand
Very helpful
Have not used
I think it was very easy to find and it was easy to do searches in also
Very easy to use
I have really enjoyed having journals and other publications
Great to have so many accessible resources
I have found it easy to use and extremely helpful for research
Friendly
Easy to use
Did not use
Sometimes frustrating finding right wording for research
A bit confusing, but I usually find what I'm looking for
Very useful
Hard to get to online links but they are there
Good, seems to be easy to use
A lot of links were not available to the Augusta Campus, ex.- journal sites
Useable
Very good easy to follow

17. I have read or printed out the "Mariner Basics" hand out and found it _____ for doing my research.

Very useful	25%
Somewhat useful	19%
Not useful	0%
Not applicable	48%
Not answered	8%

18. How helpful were the Web pages which describe the library services for out-of-state students?

Very helpful	3%
Somewhat helpful	7%
Not helpful	1%
Does not apply–I am an out-of-state student but have not used these pages	4%
Does not apply–I am not an out-of-state student and have no need to use these pages	76%
Not answered	9%

19. What are the most important Off-Campus Library resources and services you use for completing coursework in your distance classes?
How to prepare a basic WORD document (for older adults–handouts)
Librarian in building
Mariner Tutorials
Links to online data bases and the ursus system
Mariner tutorials, ursus
Live chat is wonderful and very helpful. It makes doing research very easy and much more accessible
I use the sites for the specific classes, where the teacher has articles for you to read. I also like being able to find different articles that I know have credentials
I think the article request has been the most helpful for me
URSUS, links to databases
The most important ICL service is simply the availability of material that I, as a distance student, would have no access to if the OCLS did not exist. It would be impossible for me to continue with my course work
Academic Search Premier
URSUS
Do not use
Indexes and databases as well as MARINER
E-mail, grading
E-mail, coursework downloading, library
Looking up articles and the indexes and databases
Indexes and databases
Link to indexes and databases
Academic Search Premier
Guidance I received when I wasn't able to do it–from Donna
I don't know
The access to peer-reviewed journal articles, otherwise I don't know how I ever would have found the articles for my topic. Thank you for making that so much easier
The indexes and databases
Indexes and databases
Requesting books and articles; renewal of books
URSUS book catalogue Indexes and databases
I use the indexes and databases which makes a search for information easy and efficient
Indexes and databases for research and URSUS
Requesting texts and printing journals
Online full text indexes and databases
Download journal articles
URSUS

APPENDIX (continued)

Requesting books online and then picking them up at Augusta or a re-
mote site
Mariner
Having access to articles and journals, also finding books from my home
computer
Full text articles online
Journals, magazines
Online services for projects
Journal articles that are peer reviewed and in full text
Inter library loan
The "Ask-A-Librarian" feature was very helpful and fast
Journal articles
To get access to sites specified in our courses

20.   We welcome other comments you would like to make either about any
      of the above questions or about the services offered by the Off-Campus
      Library Services.
      All staff are very helpful for research–very patient with students
      College life is demanding for non traditional students with busy lives
      Library services make the work much easier
      The whole ITV program is a very helpful and appreciated way to return
      to school for those of us that are non-traditional students. I would not
      have been able to earn a degree without this program
      You're doing a fine job, keep up the informative work
      I am very thankful that the services exist, you are doing a great job
      Thank you
      Everyone I've spoken to in the library has been very helpful and nice
      Thank you
      Thank you
      The library works great. The cards that you take to the library and have
      entered take too long before you can get to the library resources
      Somewhat hard at first to figure out
      Very helpful
      First rate library system
      Going to try the tutor next and see what happens hopefully it will help
      me write your paper
      I just got my library card and hopefully it will help me with my resource
      shopping because I have been having a very hard time
      One of the peer review articles I requested never came

I am very impressed and appreciative of the Off-Campus Library Services. It saves time and is very nice to sit at home and research then in the library
Nice service
I enjoy being able to use it at home
Librarian was knowledgeable, enthusiastic, and helpful
Thanks to the staff for all your help

The Face of Regional Campus Libraries and Librarianship

John Brandt

California State University Stanislaus

Linda Frederiksen

Washington State University Vancouver

Tina Schneider

The Ohio State University at Lima

Darby Syrkin

Florida State University, Panama City Campus

SUMMARY. Based on differing missions and models, with unique populations and policies, regional campus libraries vary greatly in form and in function not only from those on a main campus but also among themselves. Demanding flexibility in personnel, administrative models, service philosophies, and collection development efforts while still meeting resource and service expectations to regional campuses presents increasing challenges to academic libraries. This paper discusses the findings of a survey distributed to regional campus librarians in the fall of 2005. doi:10.1300/J111v45n01_03

KEYWORDS. Digital libraries, electronic books, regional campus libraries, extended campus, branch campus

---

[Haworth co-indexing entry note]: "The Face of Regional Campus Libraries and Librarianship." Brandt, John et al. Co-published simultaneously in *Journal of Library Administration* (The Haworth Information Press, an imprint of The Haworth Press, Inc.) Vol. 45, No. 1/2, 2006, pp. 37-61; and: *The Twelfth Off-Campus Library Services Conference Proceedings* (ed: Julie A. Garrison) The Haworth Information Press, an imprint of The Haworth Press, Inc., 2006, pp. 37-61.

Available online at http://jla.haworthpress.com
doi:10.1300/J111v45n01_03

INTRODUCTION

Regional campus libraries go by many names. Are we a branch campus or are we off-campus? Extended campus or satellite campus? Each has a slightly different connotation, although they all approximate the same identity. But who are we exactly? And what do we know about each other?

One definition of a regional campus comes from the National Center for Education Statistics (NCES, 1992) which stated that it is "a campus or site of an educational institution that is not temporary, is located in a community beyond a reasonable commuting distance from its parent institution, and which offers organized programs of study, not just courses" (p. 156). Regional campus libraries, then, are the libraries located on those campuses. We have chosen to use the term "regional campus library" for this study because it seems the most complete. It is not a specialized branch library necessarily, nor is it orbiting a main campus as the term "satellite" might suggest. The students, faculty and staff who study and work at the regional campus do not consider themselves "off-campus." "Regional campus" appears to define its location and purpose in a permanent, current and comprehensive way.

This study presents an updated look at regional campus libraries and issues specific to them. What do they offer their campus and community that is different from a main campus library? How do staffing and funding differ from main campus? And most important, how do regional campus libraries relate to and communicate with their main campuses, both physically and in cyberspace? It has been eighteen years since these questions were asked last, and our educational system and library services have changed significantly since then. It is important that we reevaluate our place and our future.

LITERATURE REVIEW

Regional campus libraries, because they go by so many names and have no subject heading that is applied regularly, often disappear in the literature. Once the list of near-synonyms has been exhausted, though, it is clear that the literature is replete with case studies about individual regional campus libraries. Some of these studies address topics specific to regional campuses, others do not. However, it is equally clear that regional campus libraries have been only infrequently researched at the state or national level.

National or statewide surveys allow regional campus librarians to see how they fit into the larger picture. The surveys might point out areas that need attention in general at regional campus libraries, or they might make a library aware of what should be improved at their own campus specifically. Despite the paucity of surveys, they do offer a valuable baseline from which we can see ourselves today.

The earliest broad study of the services and structure of regional campus libraries in the United States was conducted by Fisher in 1978. Fisher attempted to contact the known regional campuses by using the directory of the National University Extension Association and ACRL, although admittedly this directory was not complete. In total, Fisher contacted and visited 57 different libraries. He examined the role of main libraries in providing services to extended campuses, and regional campus libraries themselves, in addition to the topic of using non-academic libraries for extension students. The summary found the libraries to be "inadequate" and that "a great deal remains to be done" (p. 69). Additionally, he found that "there is normally no member of staff in university libraries who has special responsibility for the services of extension students," and those regional campuses that actually have libraries were described as "minimal" (p. 70). As might be expected, Fisher found that "off-campus extension students receive an adequate service only when there is a separate extension library, adequately funded and staffed" (p. 70).

Power (1991) surveyed 124 extended campuses in the United States in 1988. Power examined in a systematic way the services and funding issues at regional campus libraries. Power asked a total of nineteen questions, many similar to the fifty-one questions posed in this study, including questions about degrees available at a regional campus, types of library services offered, interlibrary loan services, staffing, funding, and distance from main campus. Because Power's survey was conducted in the late 1980s, many questions are no longer easily comparable to the present survey, particularly those asking about CD-ROMS, charging for searches, and so forth. However, Power contributed a valuable line of comparison for today's libraries.

Fritts (1998) conducted a survey in which nineteen librarians discussed their involvement with extended campus library services. However, just three of the respondents were "strictly dedicated to extended campus library services" (p. 149). The other respondents were responsible for extended campus services, but in some cases these services constituted only five to fifteen percent of their workload. Fritts made some valuable points about the unique position of extended campus librarians, especially if they are located on a regional campus. The isolation of regional campus librarians can foster a "sense of alienation and separation" unless there are deliberate efforts to "maintain good, open communication channels" (p. 148).

It must be noted that a distant librarian is not always considered "distant." With a physical and permanent presence on a regional campus, regional campus librarians are not considered distant to their own campuses. It is only in relation to main campuses that this term comes into play and the tension of reporting channels revealed. Fritts' point is well taken that communication plays a valuable role in integrating services to remote sites, no matter where its librarian is actually located. However, the results of his survey reflect the responses of librarians for whom regional campuses are just a part of their responsibilities. The responses of just three regional campus librarians provide only a limited view from regional campus librarians themselves.

Schneider (2001) conducted a survey of regional campus libraries in Ohio, with a particular focus on outreach to the community. The survey focused on the different mission of regional campuses, with their common emphasis on presence in the local community, and how the libraries participated in that mission. Libraries on the whole were found to be active in their communities with partnerships of all kinds with local institutions, but they did not necessarily include such local activity as part of their formal mission.

METHODOLOGY

In early 2005, the authors each searched state and national education Web sites looking for institutions of higher learning that met the broad 1992 NCES definition of a regional campus. A state-by-state database directory of colleges and universities in this category was created and then matched against a listing of National Association of Branch Campus Administrators. Several specialized categories of regional campuses emerged during this phase of the project and decisions regarding inclusion in the directory and the survey were made based on the best available information. Off-campus centers with degree programs but no apparent library facility, for example, were removed, as were campuses that were affiliated with a larger university system but appeared to be independent of it. The final listing included 652 private and public, for-profit and non-profit, two-year and four-year institutions located in the United States.

During the same period, the authors developed an electronic cover letter and survey instrument which was approved by each of the authors' institutional research review boards. An informal invitation to pretest the questionnaire was sent to individuals belonging to the Regional Campus Libraries Discussion Group. Based on feedback from this pilot test, some modifications to the original set of questions were made. The final list of 51 questions concentrated primarily on library organization and administrative structure (see Appendix). Both the pre-test and final surveys were conducted electronically, using SurveyMonkey, an online, Web-based software product.

Invitations to participate in the Regional Campus Libraries survey were sent to 629 contacts with e-mail addresses in the directory database during the week of August 15, 2005, with a follow-up reminder sent three weeks later. A total of 169 responses, along with several e-mail messages sent outside the survey space, were received by the deadline date of September 15, 2005, at which time the data gathering phase of the project concluded. Using SurveyMonkey software, co-author John Brandt from California State University Stanislaus compiled and analyzed the descriptive data as received and the first phase of this exploratory study of regional campus libraries came to an end.

FINDINGS

The SurveyMonkey server recorded 172 different online sessions which submitted answers to the survey. Three of these were test sessions conducted by the authors, leaving 169 entries submitted by survey participants. The first question screened participants, asking if the respondent was responsible for library services at a regional campus, and 157 participants answered yes. However, only 140 proceeded further into the survey, submitting answers for the second and subsequent questions. One of the respondents reported their institution only had one campus, leaving 139 entries to be analyzed. Two respondents included detailed information on a total of three additional regional campuses supported by their institution, yielding a final total of 142 regional campuses reporting data.

Profile

The survey measured whether or not each regional campus met the definition of branch institution used by the NCES (1992). Almost all

(94%) respondents offered full-programs of study (e.g., degrees or certificates), not just individual courses. All but two (99%) indicated their regional campuses were permanent facilities. Most of the regional campuses (70%) reported to be within commuting distance of the parent institution. The regional campuses were located anywhere from 5 to 3000 miles from the parent institution, half (51%) within 50 miles, and nearly one quarter (22%) over 100 miles (see Table 1).

A large majority (82%) of the responses were from regional campuses of publicly funded institutions. The private campuses were mostly from non-profit institutions (14%), although a few (4%) represented for-profit organizations. Just under one third (32%) were regional campuses of community or other colleges which awarded only associate's degrees, almost half (47%) of the parent institutions awarded doctorates, and the rest were mostly from master's granting institutions (17%). A small but noteworthy number (18%) indicated their regional campus was co-located with another institution, most of these (13%) representing campuses shared by universities and community colleges.

While most of the regional campuses offered courses for undergraduates in their first and second years (77%), some only served upper-division undergraduates and graduate students (17%). Others served graduate students only (6%) (see Table 2). Nearly half (49%) reported having enrollments of under 1,000 students, over one third (37%) indicated enrollments of between 1000 and 3000, and the remainder (12%) recorded larger student bodies (3000 or more) (see Table 3).

Respondents

The invitation asked for the person responsible for library services at a regional campus to complete the survey. Most of the respondents were based on the regional campus (85%), but a number were based at the main campus (15%), including distance learning librarians and library administrators (see Table 4).

A large majority of those who answered the survey indicated the highest degree they had obtained was the MLS (86%). Five percent (5%) reported having a doctorate. Some had a bachelor's degree or lesser academic degree (9%). Respondents were asked to categorize their personal professional status. Almost half (45 %) reported having faculty status, while others were non-faculty professionals (34%), administrators (8%), paraprofessional/staff (10%), or had a librarian-specific status similar to tenure (3%).

TABLE 1. Distance from Regional Campus to Main Campus

Distance in miles	Campuses ($n = 139$)
5 to 25	25 (18%)
> 25 to 50	46 (33%)
> 50 to 100	33 (24%)
> 100 to 250	21 (15%)
> 250	10 (7%)
No Main Campus	2 (1%)

TABLE 2. Level of Coursework Offered at Regional Campuses

Level of coursework	Campuses ($n = 136$)
Undergraduate (all years) and graduate	46 (34%)
Undergraduate (all years) only (no graduate)	20 (15%)
Lower-division undergraduate only	39 (29%)
Upper-division undergraduate and graduate	23 (17%)
Graduate level coursework only	8 (6%)

TABLE 3. Number of Students Enrolled on Regional Campuses

Enrollment	Campuses ($n = 137$)
0-500	36 (26%)
500-1000	31 (23%)
1000-1,500	21 (15%)
1,500-3,000	30 (22%)
3,000-5,000	7 (5%)
5,000-10,000	8 (6%)
10,000-25,000	2 (1%)
Not Sure	2 (1%)

TABLE 4. Frequency of Commuting to the Regional Campus by Responsible Persons Based at the Main Campus

Frequency of commute to regional	Campuses ($n = 18$)
Do not commute on a regular basis	9 (7%)
2 times per month	3 (2%)
1 day/week	3 (2%)
2 days/week	2 (2%)
3 days/week	1 (1%)

Of those with faculty status, almost half had achieved tenure, and 7% were working for tenure; the rest had non-tenure track faculty status (17%). For the 37 librarians serving as tenured or tenure-track members of a faculty, three-quarters (76%) reported the main campus granted tenure, roughly one fifth (19%) indicated the regional campus served as the tenure granting institution, and the remainder (6%) reported other arrangements.

Differences in the Status of Librarians

While regional campus librarians reported having the same employment status as their counterparts at the parent institution, many institutions appear to assign a different status to librarians working at the regional site. Over half of the institutions provided faculty status to librarians on the main campus (62%), while a much smaller percentage reported some type of faculty status for regional campus librarians (39%). Eighteen libraries (14%) reported that no professional librarians serve at their regional campus (see Table 5).

Of the institutions that have tenure-track faculty on their main campuses, one third (33%) indicated that regional campus librarians had a different status. The largest group (22%) assigned non-faculty, professional status to their regional campus librarians.

Staffing

Respondents were asked to report the number of professional full-time and part-time librarians working at the regional campus, as well as the full-time equivalent (FTE) for librarians. Over half of the regional campuses reported being served by one or fewer full-time professional librarians with a Master of Library Science or equivalent degree. Just over one quarter (29%) indicated two or three full-time professional librarians worked in the regional library, and a smaller number (19%) were staffed by four or more. Roughly one third of regional campuses employed part-time librarians (35%). Most libraries (74%) also reported employing student workers (see Table 6).

As previously noted, eighteen libraries reported no professional librarians, full-time or part-time, working at the regional campus. Roughly one third (36%) indicated the full-time equivalent of 0.1 to 1.0 professional librarians at the regional library, almost one quarter (23%) from 1.1 to 2.0 FTE, and only 25% more than 2.0 FTE.

TABLE 5. Employment Status of Librarians on Main and Regional Campuses

Status	Status on main campus	Status on regional campus
	Campuses (*n* = 133)	
Faculty, tenure-track	59 (44%)	30 (23%)
Faculty, non-tenure track	21 (16%)	18 (14%)
Faculty, other	2 (2%)	2 (2%)
Non-faculty parallel to tenure	2 (2%)	1 (1%)
Academic Professional	30 (23%)	45 (34%)
Staff	8 (6%)	7 (5%)
Mixed	8 (6%)	10 (8%)
Other/don't know	3 (2%)	2 (2%)
No librarians on campus		18 (14%)

TABLE 6. Staffing Levels of Regional Campus Libraries

FTE	Professional librarians (*n* = 111)	Paraprofessional/staff (*n* = 113)	Student assistants (*n* = 109)
0	18 (16%)	24 (21%)	32 (29%)
0.1-1.0	40 (36%)	25 (22%)	23 (21%)
1.1-2.0	26 (23%)	24 (21%)	24 (22%)
2.1-3.0	7 (6%)	17 (15%)	13 (12%)
3.1-4.0	5 (5%)	4 (4%)	7 (6%)
More than 4	15 (14%)	19 (17%)	10 (9%)

Communication Between the Campuses

Librarians based at the regional campus reported a wide variety in the frequency of their travel to the main campus library. Reponses ranged from once a year or less (18%) to multiple times a month (21%). A majority reported visiting one to three times (31%) or four to twelve times (37%) each year (see Table 7).

Regional campus libraries hosted visits from main campus librarians far less often. Almost one third (35%) received visits less than once a year, just over half (59%) several times a year, and only a few (10%) were visited at least monthly (see Table 8).

Three quarters (75%) of the libraries reported travel was an important method of communication between the campuses. The most commonly reported communication media included e-mail (98%) and the telephone (94%). All other methods were mentioned by less than half of the

TABLE 7. Frequency of Visits to the Main Campus by Respondents Based at the Regional Campus

Frequency	Respondents (*n* = 113)
Never	4 (4%)
Once every few years	8 (7%)
Once a year	8 (7%)
2-3 times a year	27 (24%)
4-8 times a year	20 (18%)
Once a month	21 (19%)
2-3 times a month	12 (11%)
Every week	11 (10%)
As needed	2 (2%)

TABLE 8. Frequency of Visits to the Regional Campus by Librarians from the Main Campus

Frequency	Respondents (*n* = 128)
Never	10 (8%)
Once every few years	29 (27%)
Once a year	19 (15%)
2-3 times a year	36 (29%)
4-6 times a year	19 (15%)
Once a month	6 (5%)
2-3 times a month	4 (3%)
Every week	3 (2%)
Occasionally/When Asked	2 (2%)

respondents, including postal/interoffice mail (42%), video or Web conferencing (23%), faxes (2%) and other print media (2%).

Reporting and Funding

The data were split almost evenly on whether the regional campus library reports to the main campus library (31%), the regional campus administration (30%), or both of these organizations (29%). The remainder indicated they reported to university or system administrators (4%), or had other reporting structures (6%) (see Table 9).

Funding for regional campus library operations was less likely to be split between the main and regional campus. Sole funding from the

TABLE 9. Administrative Relationship of Main and Regional Campus Libraries

	Number of Regional Campus Libraries	
Administering body	Reporting to: ($n = 129$)	Receiving funding from: ($n = 130$)
Main Campus Library	40 (31%)	56 (43%)
Regional Campus Administration	39 (30%)	51 (39%)
Both	38 (29%)	14 (11%)
Other	12 (10%)	10 (8%)

main campus library (43%) or the regional campus administration (39%) accounted for the vast majority of respondents, and only a small number (11%) reported receiving funding for library operations from both. Several (3%) reported funding from other university or system sources, or contributions from other agencies (5%).

Services Available at the Regional Campus Library

All of the respondents (100%) reporting the duties performed by their regional campus library provided reference assistance. Almost all indicated the regional library was responsible for instruction (94%), collection development (94%), and collection maintenance (93%). Many also performed other duties independent of the main campus library, including interlibrary loan/document delivery (69%) and supporting distance education (54%). Other common responsibilities found at the regional campus library included providing technical support for faculty (63%), outreach (51%), and campus recruitment (18%).

A few of the regional libraries (12%) reported having a Friends of the Library organization at the regional campus, and one institution reported their regional group was affiliated with the Friends group at the main campus library. A number of respondents (14%) indicated their regional campus library supported a satellite library on another campus location. Over half of these (9% of all respondents) reported the "branch of a branch" library had its own staffing.

Collections

The vast majority of the regional campus libraries reported having their own print collection (91%), but over half (63%) also used the print collection of the main campus library. Several (7%) of the regional campus libraries also reported having their own print collections in off-campus storage. Funding for regional campus print collections came from the main campus library (54%), the regional campus administration (35%), or a mixture of both organizations (9%). Other sources supplementing the primary sources of funding include donations/endowment (3%), co-located institutions (3%), and other local sources (3%).

The reported size of the print collections housed at the regional campus libraries ranged from no collection (6%), under ten thousand volumes (36%), between ten and fifty thousand (34%), and larger (24%) (see Table 10). The number of current serial subscriptions also ranged widely, from zero (6%), 1 to 50 (27%), 51 through 250 (43%), and over 250 (24%) (see Table 11).

Funding for serials (print or electronic) in regional campus libraries was reported from a variety of sources, often from more than one source. Nearly two thirds (65%) received funding from the main campus library, but over one third (40%) received funding from the regional campus administration. Other funding sources for serials included membership in a consortium, either through the main library (20%) or independent membership for the regional campus library (7%).

Overall, half of the regional campuses (56%) reported all of the main campus library's subscriptions to electronic serials included access for the regional library. However, a number of regional campuses (15%) received their electronic serials through the main campus library subscriptions, but were excluded from some licenses due to vendor decisions. Over one-fifth (21%) of the libraries reported subscribing to some of their own electronic serial databases in addition to those provided by the main campus library. Only a small minority (7%) received no access to electronic serials from the main campus library.

TABLE 10. Number of Volumes in the Print Collection of Regional Campus Libraries

Volumes	Campuses ($n = 113$)
0	7 (6%)
1-1,499	11 (9%)
1,500-4,999	15 (13%)
5,000-9,999	16 (14%)
10,000-19,999	17 (14%)
20,000-49,999	24 (20%)
50,000-99,999	15 (13%)
100,000 and over	13 (11%)

TABLE 11. Number of Current Print Serial Subscriptions of Regional Campus Libraries

Subscriptions	Campuses (*n* = 113)
0	7 (6%)
1-25	16 (14%)
26-50	15 (13%)
51-100	17 (15%)
101-150	16 (14%)
151-250	16 (14%)
251-500	13 (12%)
501+	13 (12%)

Relationships with Library Consortia

About one third (32%) of respondents indicated their regional campus library was a member of a consortium independently of the main campus library. The most common types of these consortia include local, regional, or state consortia (21%), independent membership in OCLC (9%), and consortia for specialized subject libraries (5%).

The responses indicated a lack of familiarity with the parent institution's participation in library consortia. A number of respondents were not sure if the main campus library was a member of a multi-state (24%), state (15%), or local (31%) library consortium.

Respondents were also unsure if the parent's membership in multi-state (25%) consortia included the regional library, but some (10%) reported it did not. Greater percentages of libraries reported the parent's membership in state (15%) and local (24%) consortia did not include the regional (see Table 12). Some (9%) of the regional libraries reported having independent membership in local consortia due to the distance of the main library from the local area.

Relationships with Other Local Libraries

Sizable numbers of regional campus libraries reported having relationships with local academic (55%) and public (42%) libraries, and some also reported relationships with school (16%) and other types (17%) of local libraries. Almost half (46%) of the respondents reported having reciprocal borrowing agreements with other academic libraries, and smaller groups reported sharing facilities (11%) and programming

TABLE 12. Inclusion of Regional Campus Library in Main Campus Library's Consortia Membership

Main campus library's membership includes regional	Multi-state consortia (n = 111)	State consortia (n = 112)	Local consortia (n = 70)
Yes	72 (65%)	95 (85%)	53 (76%)
No	11 (10%)	17 (15%)	17 (24%)
Not Sure	28 (25%)	0 (0%)	0 (0%)

(6%) with other academics. A smaller portion of regional campus libraries (23%) reported reciprocal borrowing agreements and a few share programs (7%) and buildings (2%) with public libraries.

DISCUSSION

A national study of any kind is challenging and ambitious, but this study was particularly so. The most obvious challenge of this study was the absence of a pre-existing list and consistent definition for our subjects. The authors based their selection of subjects on the National Center for Education Statistics definition, but understood potential subjects may not define themselves as a regional campus library. Consequently, the authors purposefully decided to include and contact any institution that could even vaguely fit the NCES definition in the state-by-state directory and let the subjects define themselves. This relatively liberal selection of subjects created a directory of over 652 possible subjects. Still, because the survey addressed regional campuses and did not include all the variations of that designation, i.e., branch, satellite, etc., not all the contacts were certain they should complete the survey. Others completed the survey but did not fit the NCES criteria regarding "easily commutable distance." Others, as evidenced by the low return rate, did not complete the survey at all. Expanding and clarifying the NCES definition and including the possible variant names of a regional campus library might have helped increase the number of respondents.

Power (1991) did not seem to wrestle with this definition challenge and used a smaller mailing list of 149 names. Additionally, the Power survey was much shorter with only 19 questions. The current survey was available online and did not take long to complete, but its length of 51 questions could have contributed to the limited response rate.

The study illuminated the absence of a national regional campus directory, a conventional definition, and clear criteria for regional campuses and their libraries. Library literature indicates our profession often considers the regional campus as simply an extension of the main campus and regional campus libraries and their librarians as simply part of the main campus' off-campus or distant library. This is also evident in the previous studies. In 1991, Power relied on attendance lists of the Association of College and Research Libraries Extended Campus Libraries Discussion Group and the Off-Campus Library Services Conferences to create her survey mailing lists. Fritts (1998) surveyed librarians involved with "extended campus library services" (p. 147).

This current study should help clarify the nature of regional campus libraries and indicate changes in the regional campus library profile. Regional campuses today offer full-time programs, are permanent facilities, and often have their own funding. Regional campus libraries also have facilities, resources, and staff and often support distance education programs that are independent from the main campus. While some regional campus librarians report to the main campus library system, others report solely to the regional campus. The definition of regional campus librarians as distant librarians is erroneous and should be clarified in our field. The Association of College and Research Libraries (ACRL) Regional Campus Libraries Discussion Group should be a strong voice in the effort of redefining this unique area of academia and our profession.

It must be noted the absence of a clear definition for regional campuses may be partially due to the absence of a uniform regional campus identity. As mentioned, this is the first survey in eighteen years that explores the staffing, funding, and collection models of regional campus libraries and the relationships between regional and main campus libraries. The findings of this survey specify some of the variations among regional campus libraries and are discussed below.

Institution Profiles

A large majority of the respondents represented publicly-funded institutions, and most of the others were private, non-profit institutions. A small number of responses were from private, for-profit institutions. The survey responses indicate regional campus libraries may be anywhere from 5 to over 3000 miles from their main campus, with half within 50 miles and nearly one quarter over 100 miles. The number of students enrolled in regional campuses varies, but the majority of respondents reported relatively small populations of fewer than 3000 students. The regional campuses support lower division students (first- and second-year undergraduates only), upper division students (third- and fourth-year undergraduates only), lower and upper division students (four-year), upper division students and graduates, four-year students and graduates, and graduates only. Almost all respondents indicated they support full academic programs. While this survey did not ask about the delivery of class instruction, full academic programs on regional campuses generally suggests the campus has at least some resident faculty. This contrasts with the Power (1991) study in which the findings indicated professors mostly traveled to the campus to teach. The comparison between studies helps elucidate the transition from extended to regional campus.

In this study, several respondents reported their campus was co-located with another institution; most of the co-locations were between university and community colleges. A few respondents reported sharing buildings. Additionally, a number of regional campus libraries reported having satellite libraries of their own.

Staffing and Librarian Status

Only 21% of the respondents to the Power (1991) study indicated having onsite librarians at their campus. Both Power (1991) and Fritts (1998) indicated many extended campuses had no library services and/or resident library staff. According to the current survey, some regional campus libraries still do not have professional librarians and the majority of respondents reported having only one FTE professional librarian. More than half of the respondents indicated having less than 2.1 FTE in permanent staff or student workers. These numbers have strong implications for regional campus librarian position announcements, hiring, professional development, service expectations, and potential burnout. Regarding professional status, many of the regional campus librarians reported an "academic professional" status. This contrasts the larger number of "faculty, tenure-track" status librarians on main campuses.

Communication Between Regional and Main Campus

In this survey, communication methods between the regional and main campus libraries included travel, telephone, e-mail, postal mail, and Web or video conferencing. Fritts (1998) reported "a librarian at a remote site is not regularly included in library activities or meetings, which fosters a sense of alienation and separation" (p. 148). While this study did not address the possible marginalization felt by regional campus librarians, most regional campus librarians reported traveling to the main campus more often than they thought main campus librarians traveled to the regional campus. Considering the number of solo librarians on the regional campus, these reports of travel have implications for regional campus librarian staffing and possible future technological needs.

Reporting and Funding

A large majority of respondents indicated the person responsible for regional campus library services is based at the regional campus, but reports to both the regional and main campuses. This dual reporting has strong implications for both campus and library administrations, especially as funds get tighter every year. While the reporting is to both regional and main campuses, funding sources for the regional campus libraries generally comes from either the main or regional campus. Anecdotal evidence from the Regional Campus Libraries Discussion Group suggests this single-funding/dual-reporting structure can be confusing and problematic for some regional campus librarians.

Services and Collections

Power (1991) asked survey respondents to rate services from most to least often provided. "Document delivery" was listed first on the list by 61.1% of the respondents and "Designated librarian" was listed seventh on the list by 36.9% of the respondents (p. 202). The current study did not ask for a ranking of services but still indicated regional campus librarians provide traditional and thorough library services, such as reference, instruction and collection development. In addition, many regional campus libraries provide interlibrary loan and distance education services independently from the main campus.

Nearly 39% of the respondents in the Power (1991) study indicated their library signed a contract with other institutions to provide library services. While many regional campus libraries use and borrow resources from the main campus collection, the majority of the current survey respondents now reported owning their own print collection. This is important to note, especially when trying to dispel the traditional view of regional campus libraries. According to this study, the main campus often provides the funding for these collections. Funding for serials was reported to come from either the regional or main campus, and sometimes from both. Consortial and co-location agreements were also reported.

Many regional campus libraries reported belonging to consortia independently of the main campus library. However, when asked about the main campus consortia agreements, the responses indicated a limited awareness of the main campus library activities.

Community Relationships

The number of libraries (42%) in this study working with their local public libraries contrasts with a previous, smaller study on regional campus libraries and their involvement in the community. Schneider (2001) found only a small percentage (20%) of Ohio regional campus libraries worked with their local public libraries. Conversely, only a small percentage (16%) of respondents in this study reported having relationships with local schools, whereas Schneider found a much larger percentage of approximately 60% of regional campus libraries in Ohio who had a relationship with local school libraries: ten worked with local high schools, and two with local elementary schools. Another avenue for community involvement is the support from a Friends of the Library group. Findings suggest such support among regional campus libraries is limited, with only 12% of respondents reporting a Friends organization at the regional campus.

CONCLUSION

This study achieved its goal of revisiting the concept of regional campus libraries and librarianship. Still, ample room exists for much more research.

Location, Students, Programs, and Facilities

The institutional profile information gathered in the survey suggests the "easily commutable distance" of the NCES branch campus definition may need to be reexamined. In addition, future research could further explore the profiles of the libraries at different distances to determine the possible trends among the libraries closer or further away from the main campus. Correlations between distance and student levels, staffing, collections, services, and/or licensing agreements should also be studied.

The smaller populations, student levels, and possible variations in the kinds of academic programs supported by the regional and main campuses have implications for library staffing, funding, and collection development models and these correlations should be explored further.

While the topic of co-located libraries is increasing in library literature, future study in regional campus co-location trends and the direct impact on regional campus library administration, funding, and collection development policies is recommended. Co-location contractual agreements and funding allocations should be studied. Staff training programs and staffing models particular to regional campus co-locations should also be further explored. Finally, the expansion of regional campuses, with branches of their own, necessarily affects library budgets, collections, and staffing; the impact of these branches of branches, or "twigs," should be examined.

Staffing, Status, Duties, and Salaries

The trends in staffing regional campus libraries should be identified. Job announcements for regional campus librarians and staff could be studied to identify the qualifications expected by regional campuses. Studies of regional librarian professional backgrounds and progression goals are also encouraged. Correlations between staffing figures and student populations on the regional and main campuses and/or number of librarians and list of duties should be explored.

Anecdotal evidence from the ACRL Regional Campus Libraries Discussion Group indicates status, promotion, and tenure among regional campus librarians are very important issues and the apparent disparity of tenure track librarians on main and regional campuses must be explored further. Research specifically regarding the differences between main and regional campus promotion and tenure structures must be conducted. A regional campus salary study is also highly recommended.

A comparison between the number and types of services provided by regional and main campus librarians would also be interesting. In addition, future study in the correlations between number of staff and services provided in the regional campus library should be conducted. State-by-state comparisons on the number of regional libraries and their services could also be performed. Further, regional campus librarian involvement in campus-wide activities such as building developments, fundraising, and academic program development should be explored. Regional campus library marketing efforts and study of how those efforts relate to the main campus library would also be an interesting report.

Collections and Consortia

Library collection size, content, development, use, and maintenance on the regional campus are all potential areas of research. How regional campus library collection development policies may be influenced or controlled by the main campus and how decisions are made would be a particularly interesting study. Collection content and format comparisons between regional and main campus libraries could also be performed. In addition, the trends in the reliance on main campus library collections, interlibrary loan, and local library collections should be examined. The regional and main campus differences in academic programs, funding, licensing agreements and contracts and the availability of cataloging and processing staff should be explored. Future studies in the trends of consortial agreements of the regional and main campus libraries are necessary.

Administration, Communication, and Funding

Details and trends in dual-reporting management among regional and main campuses should be examined. Trends in and efficacy of various communication methods employed between regional and main campuses could also be identified. Main campus librarian perceptions and awareness of their regional campus counterparts should be studied. In addition, the requirement and/or desire of travel by the regional campus librarians to the main campus should be studied and correlations between travel performed by regional campus librarians to the main campus and campus distances could be considered. Finally, because funding sources and availability obviously affect staffing and collection development decisions, correlations between sources of funding, budgets, and collection size for regional campus libraries could be studied.

Community Relationships

Future study and state-by-state comparisons in the relationships between regional campus libraries with school, public, and academic libraries in the community are encouraged. A correlation study between funding and agreements with local libraries is also highly recommended. Examples of productive Friends of the Library groups for regional campus libraries should also be identified and studied.

This study lays out new groundwork for research on regional campus libraries. It not only provides another benchmark in the history of national studies of regional campus libraries, but also provides several avenues for further, more detailed research. The authors have provided online access to detailed statistics on each topic in this study to encourage and inform future discussion and research (Brandt, Frederiksen, Schneider, & Syrkin, 2005). Of continuing importance is establishing a sense of identity, and defining what makes regional campus libraries unique. Particularly important in future studies will be exploring the relationships with main campus libraries and their impact on administration, collection development, database licensing, and other regional campus library services. While case studies provide insight on individual libraries, at this point it seems broader studies would be more useful, so that regional campus libraries can have a better sense of national or statewide norms.

REFERENCES

Brandt, J., Frederiksen, L., Schneider, T., & Syrkin, D. (2005). *The face of regional campus libraries and librarianship: A national survey conducted August 15-September 15, 2005.* Retrieved December 13, 2005, from http://library.csustan.edu/jbrandt/regional/2005.html.

Fisher, R. K. (1978). Library services to university extension students in the U.S.A., a critical survey with comparative assessment of equivalent services in Great Britain. *British Library Research and Development Reports*, no. 5432.

Fritts, J. (1998). Administrative structures for extended campus library services: A survey of institutional operations. In P. S. Thomas & M. Jones (Comps.), *The Eighth Off-Campus Library Services Conference Proceedings* (pp. 147-154). Mt. Pleasant: Central Michigan University.

National Center for Education Statistics. (1992, July). *Postsecondary education facilities inventory and classification manual.* Retrieved October 24, 2005, from http://nces.ed.gov/pubs92/92165.pdf.

Power, C. (1991). A survey of extended campus library services and funding at American academic institutions. In C. J. Jacob (Comp.), *The Fifth Off-Campus Library Services Conference Proceedings* (pp. 199-208). Mt. Pleasant: Central Michigan University.

Schneider, T. (2001). The regional campus library and service to the public. *Journal of Academic Librarianship*, 27, 122-127.

doi:10.1300/J111v45n01_03

APPENDIX

Regional Campus Libraries Survey

1. Are you responsible for library services at a regional campus of a college or university (e.g., a campus with physical classrooms not on the main campus of your college or university)?
2. Does your regional campus offer full programs (e.g., degree or certificate programs), or just individual courses?
3. Is your regional campus within commuting distance of your parent institution/main campus?
4. Is your regional campus a "permanent campus" (e.g., classrooms owned/rented by your institution for the foreseeable future)?
5. Is your regional campus co-located with another college or university (e.g., is your regional campus located on the campus of another college or university)?
6. What is the name of your library?
7. What is the name of your regional campus?
8. What is the name of your parent institution?
9. Please estimate the distance (in miles) your campus is from the parent institution/main campus.
10. What level of students take classes at your regional campus? Lower-division undergraduates (freshman-sophomore); Upper-division undergraduates (junior-senior); Graduate students; Other (e.g., certificate programs).
11. What is the approximate number of students (in FTE) on your regional campus? (If your regional library is co-located with another institution, please indicate the total number of students served.)
12. What is your status? Tenured faculty; Tenure-track faculty (not yet tenured); Non-tenure track faculty; Non-faculty professional librarian (with MLS or equivalent degree); Library paraprofessional/support staff; Other (please specify).
13. What is the status of librarians on your main campus? Faculty, tenure track; Faculty, non-tenure track; Academic professional (non-faculty); Staff; Other (please specify).
14. What is the status of librarians on your regional campus? Faculty, tenure track; Faculty, non-tenure track; Academic professional (non-faculty): Staff: Other (please specify).
15. What academic degrees do you hold? (Please mark all that apply) Doctoral degree in Library Science; Doctoral degree in another discipline; Master's degree in Library Science (or equivalent): Master's degree in another discipline; Bachelor's degree in Library Science; Bachelor's degree in another discipline: Associate's degree in Library Science; Associate's degree in another discipline; None of the above; Other (please specify).

16. How many degreed librarians (having a Master's in Library Science or an equivalent degree) work in your regional campus library?
17. How many paraprofessionals and other permanent staff work in your regional campus library?
18. How many student assistants typically work in your regional campus library?
19. If you are tenure-track faculty (or have already received tenure), are you tenured: On your regional campus; Through the main campus library; Not in a tenure track position; Other (please specify).
20. The regional campus library reports primarily to: The parent institution/main campus library administration; The regional campus administration; Both the parent institution/main campus library administration and the regional campus administration; Other (please describe).
21. The duties performed and the service offered by your regional campus library include (please mark all that apply): Reference; Bibliographic/information literacy instruction; Collection development; Collection maintenance; Interlibrary loan/document delivery services independent of main campus ILL/document delivery department; Distance education support independent of main campus distance education programs; Technical support for faculty; Campus recruiting; Community outreach; Other (please describe).
22. Are you based at your regional campus or at the main campus (e.g., where do you consider your primary office to be)?
23. Do you regularly commute to your regional campus library (or libraries) from the main campus?
24. How often do you go to your main campus for library business?
25. How often does a main campus librarian or library committee come to your campus?
26. What are the usual methods of communication between regional and main campus librarians?
27. The funding for librarian and staff salaries and other administrative functions of your regional campus library originates from: The parent institution/main campus library administration; The regional campus administration; Both the parent institution library and the regional campus administration; Other (please specify).
28. Does your regional campus have its own "Friends of the Library" organization?
29. Is your regional campus "Friends of the Library" associated with a "Friends of the Library" organization from the main campus?
30. If yes, how is your regional campus "Friends of the Library" associated with the "Friends of the Library" found on the main campus?
31. Is your regional campus library a member of any consortium independent of your main campus library?

APPENDIX (continued)

32. Is your parent institution a member of a multi-state consortium of: Academic libraries; Multiple type libraries: Not a member of any multi-state library consortium; Not sure; Other (please specify).
33. If yes, does this membership include your regional campus library?
34. Is your parent institution a member of a state consortium of: Academic libraries; Multiple types of libraries; Not a member of any state library consortium; Not sure; Other (please specific).
35. If yes, does this membership include your regional campus library?
36. Is your parent institution a member of a local consortium of: Academic libraries; Multiple type libraries; Not a member of any local library consortium; Not sure; Other (please specify).
37. If yes, does this membership include your regional campus library?
38. Does your regional campus library have a satellite of its own at another campus location (i.e., a "branch of a branch")?
39. If yes, is the satellite library of your regional campus library staffed separately?
40. For print materials, does your regional campus library (mark all that apply): Have its own print collection on campus; Have its own print collection off campus; Uses the print collection of the main campus library; Other (please describe).
41. Funding for the print collection at your regional library comes from (please mark only one): the parent institution/main campus library administration; The regional campus administration; A combination of parent institution/main library and the regional campus; No print collection at the regional campus library; Other (please describe).
42. How many print monographs are in your regional campus library collection?
43. How many print serial titles are in your regional campus library collection?
44. How are serial subscriptions (in all formats) for your regional campus library funded? Parent institution/main campus library; Regional campus administration; Consortial agreement (dependent on parent institution); Consortial agreement (independent of parent institution); Other (please describe).
45. Are electronic databases licensed: By your main campus for all campuses, without exception; by your main campus, except for vendors that see each campus as a separate customer; By your regional campus in addition to your main campus; By your regional campus only (no support from the main campus); By state/regional consortia only (i.e., you have no independent subscriptions outside of what is provided by a consortium); Other (please describe).

46. Does your regional campus library have a relationship with a local academic library at another institution of higher education (e.g., a college or university other than your parent institution)?
47. Does your regional campus library have a relationship with a local public library?
48. Does your regional campus library have a relationship with a local school library?
49. Does your regional campus library have a relationship with any other kind of local library?
50. If you mentioned that your library has relations with a school library and has programs for their students, please describe the types of programs your library has for K-12 students.
51. If you would like to share any other comments about your regional campus library or about the survey, please include them here.

Collaboration for Distance Information Literacy Instruction: Do Current Trends Reflect Best Practices?

Stefanie Buck

Western Washington University

Ramona Islam

Fairfield University.

Darby Syrkin

Florida State University, Panama City Campus

SUMMARY. In 2005, the Distance Learning Section (DLS) Instruction Committee conducted a survey of Association of Research Libraries (ARL) members regarding collaboration in distance learning information literacy instruction. The results were published in an Association of Research Libraries/Association of College and Research Libraries (ARL/ACRL) SPEC Kit. This paper reexamines the data reported in the SPEC Kit and compares these data to a selection of current library literature about collaboration, distance education, and information literacy instruction. doi:10.1300/J111v45n01_04

KEYWORDS. Distance education, information literacy, library instruction, collaboration

---

[Haworth co-indexing entry note]: "Collaboration for Distance Information Literacy Instruction: Do Current Trends Reflect Best Practices?" Buck, Stephanie, Ramona Islam, and Darby Syrkin. Co-published simultaneously in *Journal of Library Administration* (The Haworth Information Press, an imprint of The Haworth Press, Inc.) Vol. 45, No. 1/2, 2006, pp. 63-79; and: *The Twelfth Off-Campus Library Services Conference Proceedings* (ed: Julie A. Garrison) The Haworth Information Press, an imprint of The Haworth Press, Inc., 2006, pp. 63-79.

Available online at http://jla.haworthpress.com
doi:10.1300/J111v45n01_04

INTRODUCTION

It could be argued that it takes an entire campus to teach information literacy. Collectively it requires the efforts of faculty, librarians and administrative support to implement a successful information literacy program. The expertise of librarians makes them essential partners with faculty who want to infuse information literacy concepts into their teaching. In the same way, members of the teaching faculty are essential partners for librarians who teach information literacy skills. Consultations between librarians and professors are necessary to ensure that information literacy learning objectives will be relevant to students and closely tied to whatever subject matter is studied. Support from administrators and information technology professionals further contributes to the likelihood that students will graduate as information literate adults.

If it takes a campus to realize effective information literacy education, then what is to be done in the absence of a physical site? How does the collaborative dynamic translate into the distance learning environment? The word "campus" as used above does not necessarily imply a physical location. Instead, it connotes a body of individuals working together under the umbrella of a particular institution. Collaboration is as essential to information literacy instruction when individuals are remote from one another as it is when individuals are in close proximity to one another.

This conundrum–the collaborative imperative paired with ostensible barriers to working collaboratively–inspired members of the Association of College and Research Libraries (ACRL) Distance Learning Section (DLS) Instruction Committee to investigate the state of collaboration for distance learning information literacy instruction at higher education institutions across the United States. In order to craft a survey that would measure meaningful data, DLS Instruction Committee members sifted through the literature on collaboration, distance learning, and information literacy instruction. This enabled the authors to compile a list of best practices in collaboration for distance information literacy instruction that informed the design of a questionnaire distributed to Association of Research Libraries (ARL) members in January, 2005. Results from this survey were published as the *ARL/ACRL SPEC Kit no.*

286: Collaboration for Distance Learning Information Literacy Instruction (SPEC Survey) in July, 2005.

While the need for collaboration in the distance learning environment is inescapable, it can be especially difficult to form collaborative relationships in the absence of a physical campus. In 2000, Caspers (Oregon State University) and Lenn (University of Oregon) predicted that,

> The changes in higher education, in particular, may drastically affect the idea and practice of collaboration with faculty. Pressures to economize are resulting in major cost-cutting initiatives on most campuses at the same time new technologies are changing the way people work and study. As faculty contend with an educational system in flux, these environmental pushes and pulls can help and hinder librarian-faculty collaboration. (p. 148)

The library community has clearly outlined the responsibilities of academic libraries to support the information needs of distance learners. Standards are also in place that identify information literacy skills that students are expected to master. Unfortunately, distance education faculty and students are often difficult to reach and subsequently not aware of available library services. As stated by one of the respondents to the SPEC Survey, the "invisibility of distance learning" is a particular challenge (ARL/ACRL, 2005, p. 45). "With so many of the faculty having never set foot on the campus," wrote D'Angelo and Maid in their discussion of integrating library services into a new program called Multimedia Writing and Technical Communication at Arizona State University, "they naturally possess little or no knowledge of campus services–including library services" (2005, p. 57).

Faculty and students who learn and work at a distance may view the library primarily as a physical space on the campus that is not within their reach. Consequently, distant faculty, particularly those developing online courses, may overlook services and resources they believe are too difficult to reproduce electronically (DeWald, Scholz-Crane, Booth, & Levine, 2000). Providing library support for these online courses is not easy. "Librarians charged with the support of students in online courses are often challenged to know what kind of assignments online students are required to complete, what resources they use, or even the name and the location of the instructor" (Reidel, 2002, p. 479), not to mention the difficulty of reproducing library instruction in an online environment (DeWald et al., 2000). Some comments from the SPEC Survey, such as

"I wonder if faculty see [information literacy] as a true need. . . ," "Faculty do not want to make room in the syllabus for [library instruction]," and "[I] see. . . just how unsound a lot of their pedagogical approaches are when developing online teaching resources" (ARL/ACRL, 2005, p. 45) clearly reflected some of these challenges.

Technology has also created instructional challenges for librarians and faculty. Teaching faculty may be inclined to view the presence of a librarian as less important since the students are computer literate and many more sources are available online (Caspers & Lenn, 2000). The "constant and rapid change in technology and information resources makes it very difficult for students, faculty, and librarians to stay current. It also makes it difficult to maintain the currency of training materials" (Cunningham & Lanning, 2002, p. 345). If librarians are viewed as less essential to the course because of the technology available, then the chances for team-teaching or other collaborative efforts diminish. While the presence of technology sometimes precludes librarians in the minds of faculty, the same technology can be overwhelming for librarians who work with distance learners. Sixteen (40%) out of 40 SPEC Survey respondents indicated the time spent dealing with technology issues was a challenge and included comments such as "Extremely time consuming developing online resources . . . ," "Spend a lot of time . . . working through technology issues . . . ," and "Time to learn technology and course content [is] of primary concern" (ARL/ACRL, 2005, p. 44).

Added to the challenges posed by distance learning technologies is the decentralized distance learning environment that is not always easy to navigate. Numerous SPEC Survey comments attested to this difficulty: "Highly decentralized," "There is no office for Distance Education in this campus; therefore, no coordination," "[The university] has yet to develop clear policies concerning distance education . . . ," "Distance programming at our university is not coordinated in any central way . . . ," "[The] university has a decentralized system . . . There is not a common support structure for distance learners" (ARL/ACRL, 2005, p. 45). While it is not clear from the survey responses, this decentralization of distance education programming probably contributed to the number of respondents citing administrative concerns (11 of 40, or 28%) and "institutional political issues" (9 of 40, or 23%) as challenges to effective collaboration for distance information literacy instruction (p. 44).

BEST PRACTICES FOR SUCCESSFUL DISTANCE LEARNING INFORMATION LITERACY COLLABORATION

Despite the challenges cited above and throughout this paper, many libraries have implemented creative solutions that nourish the development of collaborative relationships for the benefit of distance information literacy instruction. This paper reexamines the data reported in the SPEC Survey. Rather than repeating analyses of trends or correlations discussed in the SPEC Survey, a selection of best practices gleaned from the current library literature is presented against which data from survey respondents are compared. Examining how closely aligned the average ARL member library is with best practices reveals strategies that might be emulated to strengthen distance learning information literacy programs.

Create a Designated Library Contact

Not all universities are fortunate enough to have a librarian whose job is to provide library services to distance users. Nevertheless, that kind of contact can be beneficial. Kaufmann, for example, noted that when Seton Hall University was developing their distance learning program, having a librarian designated as a liaison to the distance education program proved to be very fruitful and resulted in a "commitment from [SetonWorldWide] to make the library information session a component of every program's orientation residency week" (2003, p. 57). This liaison attends staff meetings, providing the perfect opportunity to inform SetonWorldWide staff about information resources and other library services.

A majority (24 of 35, or 69%) of the SPEC Survey respondents reported having at least one professional in the library responsible for coordinating information literacy instruction for distance learners (ARL/ACRL, 2005, p. 24). Of that number, fifteen (63%) reported that the librarian bore a title specific to distance learning, and eight reported that the librarian was employed within a department dedicated to distance learning (pp. 25-26).

Know the Potential Collaborators

One study on the dynamics of collaborative teaching partnerships reported that, "Librarians and academics agreed that it is important for people to have established a good working relationship before attempting to develop a collaborative teaching partnership" (Ivey, 2003, p. 102). Levesque, from the University College of the Cariboo in British Columbia, Canada, suggested that one of the best strategies for fostering collaboration is to survey the faculty about their attitudes, expectations, and use of library resources and services (2002). While surveys are not always popular among faculty members and response rates tend to be low, it is an opportunity to discover what the faculty members truly know about the library and what their needs and concerns are. In addition, a survey may help identify who among the distance education faculty is interested in information literacy and could be a potential collaborator (Kotter as cited in Ivey, 2003; Markgraf, 2005).

Fourteen of 36 (40%) SPEC Survey respondents reported conducting needs assessments of teaching faculty members and other professionals serving distance learners (ARL/ACRL, 2005, p. 36). A majority of SPEC Survey respondents (32 of 34, or 94%) reported using personal contact and 65% (22 of 34) reported using local presentation to promote information literacy instruction for distance learners (p. 35).

Share Information

Most of the literature recommends keeping faculty informed through a variety of means, but D'Angelo, Maid and others acknowledged that doing so can be difficult (Caspers & Lenn, 2000; D'Angelo & Maid, 2005; Ivey, 2003; Markgraf, 2005). It requires not only outreach to a variety of faculty–adjunct, resident, local, and distant–but also continual refreshment to deliver the most current and accurate information.

> . . . . We must find ways to better educate our adjunct faculty, both local and distant, to the resources already available. The usual ways of making all faculty, including adjuncts, aware of services such as presentations by library staff at meetings, flyers, brochures, and the like are impossible. (D'Angelo & Maid, p. 62)

Making the initial contact is often one of the biggest hurdles. Adjunct faculty who teach in distance programs may have irregular schedules and do not usually spend a lot of time on campus (Caspers & Lenn, 2000), making it more difficult for librarians to build and maintain relationships over years and through regular interaction. Kaufmann suggested contacting new faculty members through an existing library liaison program can also be successful (2003). But, as one SPEC Survey respondent reported, "Many adjunct faculty are temp[orary] employees and are not entered into the university system until they receive their first paycheck halfway through the semester, i.e., there is no contact info[rmation] online for them" (ARL/ACRL, 2005, p. 35).

Once established, regular communication is also difficult to sustain. "Partnerships," Levesque reminded us, "like any relationships require involvement and ongoing communication" (2002, p. 7). The difficulties many librarians have noted in reaching members of the distance learning faculty, combined with the unresponsiveness of many of these individuals, can be frustrating.

Jeffries from Wayne State University, who surveyed on-campus faculty members and librarians regarding their collaborative needs and expectations, found that electronic communication was the preferred method of keeping in touch (2000). She also discovered that professors wanted librarians to promote library services and materials, and take the initiative to maintain ongoing communication. Promoting and sharing information about successful collaborations is one way to take the initiative. Caspers and Lenn noted that speaking at academic conferences attended primarily by scholars outside of the library and information science field has proved to be beneficial for librarians to make connections (2000).

The results of the SPEC Survey confirmed that frequent communication is a strategy that facilitates collaboration. The majority of the respondents reported promoting services through personal contact, Web-based information sharing, and/or e-mail communication techniques (ARL/ACRL, 2005, p. 35). In addition, the SPEC Survey findings suggested some electronic communication methods, such as informational alerts, blogs, or discussion lists, are used as additional services or "perks" offered to distance teaching faculty. Twenty-two of 34 (65%) SPEC Survey respondents reported giving local presentations and a few (6 of 34, or 18%) reported using promotional giveaways. Surprisingly, 18% (6 of 34) also reported not actively promoting information literacy instruction for distance learners (p. 35).

Participate Throughout Campus

One of the most useful strategies librarians can employ to build and maintain collaborative partnerships is to attend faculty meetings or other formal and informal gatherings that may lead to contact with faculty (Cunningham & Lanning, 2002). At Georgia State University, two librarians concluded that "since we attended faculty meetings with teaching faculty and participated in discussions about student learning, teaching techniques, successes, and problems, teaching faculty have come to recognize librarians as equal partners in the teaching mission of the university" (Edge, 2003, p. 137). A survey conducted by Jeffries also found that faculty members want librarians to be interested in faculty research and to be willing to attend faculty meetings (2000).

According to the SPEC Survey, "attending faculty meetings and meetings with distance education faculty" is a strategy that facilitates collaboration (ARL/ACRL, 2005, p. 41). SPEC Survey respondents also indicated building rapport with potential partners through less formal channels. Thirty-seven percent (13 of 35) reported meeting with colleagues over coffee or lunch (p. 36).

Librarians also understand the potential of campus-wide collaboration and seek collaborative opportunities with other programs, departments, or services on campus, such as technology and Blackboard user groups that support teaching and learning. The instructional technology department is another group with which to collaborate (Markgraf, 2005; Petrowski, Baird, Leach, & Noyes, 2000). "The good relationship spawned by work with instructional design teams," wrote Riedel, "has led to more work . . . I hope to work more with design teams to target and then develop the most likely courses to incorporate library instruction" (2002, pp. 485-486). At Austin Peay State University, librarians worked closely with the director of distance education and the Blackboard administrator to "make sure clear links to the library's Web site are visible within the online environment" (Buchanan, Luck, & Jones, 2002, p. 151). At the same institution, librarians working with technically savvy distance education staff and faculty established a multimedia development suite housed in the library where faculty could learn about instructional design in an online environment. The librarians hope that it will provide "additional opportunities for librarians to work with faculty to integrate appropriate information literacy concepts into the curriculum" (Buchanan et al., 2002, p. 164). Collaboration with faculty development centers or teaching and learning centers also helps to build a positive image of the library on campus (Cunningham & Lanning, 2002) and could improve course content. At Arizona State University East, a partnership between the library and Multimedia Writing and Technical Communications program led to the revision of courses, the creation of new courses, and the rewriting of program outcomes. Many librarians also serve on university committees and several examples in the literature reflect how this participation has led to successful collaboration (Argentati, 1999; Buchanan et al., 2002; Fletcher & Stewart,

2001). At Seton Hall University, a representative from the library serves on the university Academic Policy and Core Curriculum Committee. This committee involvement has led to a working relationship with Seton Hall's distance learning program and helped to establish the library's instructional component and first library Web page for students in the distance education program.

The SPEC Survey findings supported this trend: a majority of the respondents reported being involved in some non-library specific committee, with 66% (23 of 35) serving on information technology committees, 57% (20 of 35) on distance education support committees, 46% (16 of 35) on course management software committees, 46% (16 of 35) on committees of centers devoted to improved teaching, and 31% (11 of 35) on curriculum planning committees. Twenty-six out of 36 (71%) of the SPEC Survey respondents reported a strong relationship between the library and a center devoted to improving teaching, while 46% (16 of 35) reported direct participation of librarians in the activities of such a center (ARL/ACRL, 2005, p. 22). In addition, six out of 35 (17%) respondents reported library participation in instructional design committees (p. 23). Several respondents commented that they planned to have "more librarians presenting at faculty sessions," "participating in university-wide formal distance education support groups," and "working with . . . staff from the Campus Media Center" in the future (p. 43).

Expand Online Presence

Creating a Web site for distance learners and faculty is one of the most basic ways to improve contact with the distance education faculty (Kaufmann, 2003; Markgraf, 2005). Cassner and Adams reported that the majority (36 of 51, or 71%) of the libraries they surveyed in 2004 had a Web site dedicated to distance learners (2005). Contacting a department and offering to make Web pages is another way to strike what Riedel called a "preemptive blow," alerting the faculty to services provided by the library (2002, p. 480). A Web site for distance students can be more than just a description of library services and links to databases; it can also initiate collaborative opportunities. Kaufmann wrote that the initial work on a Web site project led to more customized Web pages among various academic departments (2003).

Launching a distance education Web site is not a substitute for other collaborative learning strategies.

> The most effective way for librarians to reach distance learners is not through publications distributed to students or pages linked from the library's home page promoting library services for distance learners; rather, it is through cooperation (at least) and collaboration (at best) with teaching faculty. (Caspers & Lenn, 2000, p. 150)

Yet, a Web presence is a good starting point. This and other Web-related activities, such as creating distance education resources and services Web pages and advocating links to library Web sites within online courses, or providing Web-based guides and handouts, should not be overlooked (Buchanan et al., 2002; D'Angelo & Maid, 2005).

Many distance courses are offered via a course management system that often includes some kind of synchronous or asynchronous communication module, such as a blog, a chat, a listserv, or other communications tool. Taking advantage of these tools is an opportunity for librarians to become closer to distance learners and faculty, even if a collaborative relationship has not yet formed. Markgraf described the experience of the "lurking librarian" who, while not a fully integrated instructor in the program, was still able to participate in the course management system and provide a positive library presence throughout the semester (Markgraf, 2005). Giles' participation in an online course also proved to be a positive experience. During the course, Giles noticed students having difficulty with basic research concepts and suggested a refresher in basic library skills to the instructor, who then made time for such an instruction session. Giles noted that both the professor and the students "welcomed my presence and contributions on Blackboard and felt much more comfortable in asking for research help in this course and others" (2004, p. 263).

Both Giles and Markgraf agreed that the privilege of participating in an online course needs to be handled carefully. It is imperative that the librarian will be able to fulfill expectations, because the reputation of the entire library may be at stake. In addition, it is important that the students understand the role of the librarian and that the librarian does not try to overshadow the main instructor (Giles, 2004; Markgraf, 2005). These "foot-in-the-door" opportunities have the potential of leading to more collaboration in the future.

Ninety-four percent (94%, or 35 of 36) of SPEC Survey respondents indicated that their libraries have a presence on their institutions' home page (ARL/ACRL, 2005, p. 22). Several respondents submitted examples of Web pages designed specifically for their distance education students and faculty (pp. 52-107). The strategy of "creating a web site for a specific [distance education] class" was also mentioned in the SPEC Survey as useful for facilitating collaboration (p. 42).

SPEC Survey respondents realized the necessity of being involved with online course management systems and communication software and indicated improvement plans such as "encouraging instructors to allow librarians [sic] participation in their course discussion boards," "information literacy modules for web courses," and "more integration into course management system of subject-related literacy/library resources" (ARL/ACRL, 2005, p. 43).

Establish Roles, Responsibilities, and Objectives

One of the issues that arises in the literature regarding collaborative teaching is the question of whose responsibility it is to teach information literacy skills. How much of a role can and should the librarian play in the actual course? This may be one of the biggest roadblocks to a successful collaborative teaching partnership. Collaborative teaching partners should embrace a shared definition of information literacy and decide who is responsible for teaching which skills (Ivey, 2003). In the past, teaching information literacy was often viewed as a separate field of study, discipline independent, as exemplified in the prevailing "one-shot" instruction sessions. Teaching students to find, evaluate, and use information is still often viewed by faculty and librarians as the role of the librarian alone. Such perceptions are changing slowly due to the increased role of technology and a deepening focus on teaching and learning at many colleges and universities (Cunningham & Lanning, 2002).

As Buchanan et al. noted, collaboration is the most successful approach to integrating information literacy skills into the classroom (2002) and a successful collaborative partnership is based on both partners being involved in the process from start to finish; from the early stages of development to establishing the goals and outcomes through to the assessment and evaluation of the project (Laverty et al., 2003; Levesque, 2002). Defining information literacy teaching roles and responsibilities early is likely to prevent conflict in the future. All of the faculty surveyed by Ivey agreed that there is a "need for information literacy policies to be developed so that information literacy programs can be adequately resourced in terms of time and staffing," although there were definite variations in the amount and type of collaboration that faculty and librarians thought was appropriate (2003, p. 110). Collaboration also helps librarians and professors to envision mutual goals and objectives, in particular when it comes to information literacy. "As a result of all these activities [the revision of a humanities 101 course], both the librarians and the communications professor possess a greater understanding of information literacy learning outcomes, as well as having the experience of working together" (Buchanan et al., 2002, p. 151). Riedel wrote that one of the immediate results "of library integration in online courses is that more faculty members are interested in learning about our databases" and that "faculty aware of the multiple choices of library integration in course design will doubtlessly raise the bar for their students as well as for librarians" (2002, p. 486).

Collaborative teaching librarian roles reported in the SPEC Survey included one-shot guest lecturer (88%, or 30 of 34) and ad hoc resource person (65%, or 22 of 34). Seven out of thirty-four (21%) respondents indicated they were either the primary instructor or a team teacher (ARL/ACRL, 2005, p. 37). Collaborative teaching requires the librarian to be a part of course development from the beginning and, as indicated by the SPEC Survey findings, time is an issue. Sixty-five percent (65%, or 26 of 40) of respondents indicated "time/workload issues" as one of the biggest challenges librarians encounter when attempting to work collaboratively to deliver distance information literacy instruction to distance learners. As one respondent noted, "The amount of time it takes to develop many online resources cuts into the amount [sic] of faculty we can assist . . . " (p. 43).

Capitalize on Expertise

In a successful collaboration, different members of the group will bring different expertise and experiences to the table (Buchanan et al., 2002; Raspa & Ward, 2000). As Kaufmann stated, "By capitalizing on the collective expertise of librarians, faculty, administrators, and the information technology staff across the campus, existing services and resources were enhanced and new services were created for SetonWorldWide's learning community with little additional expense" (2003, p. 52). Many authors who have had a successful collaboration agree that the sharing of information and expertise between librarians and faculty leads to more collaboration (Buchanan et al., 2002; Ivey, 2003; Markgraf, 2005). It also helps librarians gain insight into students' research behavior, develop classroom management skills, and learn about curriculum development, while improving the image and credibility of the library (Buchanan et al., 2002; Shank & DeWald, 2003).

Librarians need to take a more proactive approach to market their unique expertise. Such marketing might begin "through liaison librarians" (ARL/ACRL, 2005, p. 43) and continue by capitalizing on previous successful collaborations (Buchanan et al., 2002; Ivey, 2003). One respondent to the SPEC Survey noted that "departmental workshops to faculty demonstrating existing examples [of collaboration] . . . gives faculty an idea of what type of collaboration is possible and the value" (p. 41).

Conduct and Take Part in Training

As the amount of information available escalates, knowledge of how information is organized and published, and the capacity to teach the skills needed to gain efficient access to it, will continue to be highly valued and will mark the role of the contemporary librarian in the era of collaborative enterprise. (Caspers & Lenn, 2000, p. 153)

The literature suggests that taking advantage of training opportunities is a key element to a successful collaborative relationship (Ivey, 2003; Markgraf, 2005). To be accepted by faculty as partners in the classroom, librarians, who generally are not hired for their teaching abilities, but rather for their research expertise, may need to demonstrate their teaching abilities before true collaboration occurs.

Librarians who have teaching qualifications and experience are in great demand (Buchanan et al., 2002; Ivey, 2003). Understanding educational theories and principles can make a difference in the level of collaboration achieved. The "key to establishing a good collaborative effort is to deliver a proposal that is not only pedagogically sound but also addresses or assists the faculty members as they deal with the pressures of economy" (Caspers & Lenn, 2000, p. 149). Librarians need to constantly educate themselves and teach faculty about information literacy concepts, standards, learning outcomes and objectives.

Eighty-one percent (29 of 36) of SPEC Survey respondents reported having teacher training available to the librarians (ARL/ACRL, 2005, p. 23). The survey findings also indicated strong connections with and reliance on instructional designers and committees (pp. 23,42).

Attending training workshops with faculty can also lead to some exciting opportunities. Giles is an example of a librarian who successfully applied this strategy. After attending a Blackboard workshop, she met a new faculty member. This led to Giles' participation in an online history course (2004). Another option is to become a student again. Cunningham & Lanning described a case where a librarian took art courses. Such endeavors, though sometimes beyond the call of duty, help librarians to develop positive relationships with faculty members (Cunningham & Lanning, 2002, p. 346). At the Rochester Institute of Technology, faculty members were offered quarterly workshops on how and where to integrate library services into their online courses. This workshop was developed by the distance learning librarian, who reported a "good turnout with enthusiastic attendees" (Buehler, 2004, p. 78).

Perform Assessments

Assessment and documentation are critical to the success of any library initiative. For relatively new and challenging programs, such as distance learning information literacy instruction, keeping records and collecting feedback is crucial to document successes, inform promotion decisions, facilitate future collaborative endeavors, and plan improvements (Cunningham & Lanning, 2002; Levesque, 2002). "... If a case is to be made for collaborative partnerships between librarians and academics and the development of information literacy programs," then, Ivey noted, "evidence of how these partnerships and programs can increase student's information literacy is crucial" (2003, p. 108).

The responses from the Survey indicated that there is support for this practice with 50% (three of six) reporting solicitation of student feedback from surveys, focus groups, and other means, and 83% (five of six) reporting receipt of feedback from faculty about the quality of student work after instruction (ARL/ACRL, 2005). Only five survey respondents indicated whether the latest assessment they used revealed anything about the distance learning students' information literacy skills. Only one of the five (20%) reported that students' information literacy skills improved. Two out of the five (40%) reported having no comparison data from previous years and another two (40%) indicated the library had yet to compile or analyze the results of the assessments (ARL/ACRL).

CONCLUSION

The distance learning environment poses unique and sometimes extreme challenges to working collaboratively toward the development and promotion of information literacy among students. It is clear from the SPEC Survey findings that, in spite of these challenges, distance learning librarians are actively pursuing collaborative opportunities with some success. Trends revealed by the SPEC Survey indicate many libraries serving distance learners have established a Web or online presence and many librarians are availing themselves of training opportunities and are participating in campus-wide activities.

Findings also indicate that libraries serving distance education programs may be struggling with assessment of information literacy instruction programs and the incorporation of information literacy skills into the curriculum. Because the data collected do not reveal how collaborations between librarians and faculty or others on- and off-campus affect these continued challenges, further research in these areas is necessary. In addition, because information literacy assessment and information literacy infusion across curricula are challenging issues for distance and on-campus librarians alike, another potential area of research might examine collaborations between distance librarians and their own on-campus colleagues, and compare distance learning information literacy programs with similar programs targeted to on-campus students.

Further study of collaborative efforts at both ARL and non-ARL members libraries is also strongly recommended. More focused research on specific topics such as time, workload, compensation, and staffing among distance learning instruction librarians could be performed. Research that explores how collaborative relationships are initiated and by whom could help future librarians and teaching faculty. Additionally, correlation studies between size of distance learner populations and library staff dedicated to distance learners would be interesting. Finally, future researchers could repeat this survey after specific intervals to determine collaboration trends in distance learning information literacy instruction and related issues.

By increasing the library presence on campus and online, participating in university-wide committees, communicating and promoting services effectively, and initiating progressive and sound information literacy instruction, librarians can enjoy the ultimate success of helping create information literate distance learners.

REFERENCES

Argentati, C. (1999). Library-university partnerships in distance learning. In IFLA Council and General Conference. *Conference Program and Proceedings* (65th Bangkok, Thailand, August 20-28, 1999). (ERIC Document Reproduction Service No. ED441 406).

Association of Research Libraries/Association of College and Research Libraries (ARL/ACRL). (July, 2005). *Collaboration for Distance Learning Information Literacy Instruction. SPEC Kit no. 286.* Washington, DC: Association of Research Libraries & Association of College and Research Libraries.

Buchanan, L., Luck, D. L., & Jones, T. C. (2002). Integrating information literacy into the virtual university: A course model. *Library Trends, 51*(2), 144-166.

Buehler, M. A. (2004). Where is the library in course management software? *Journal of Library Administration, 41*(1/2), 75-84.

Caspers, J., & Lenn, K. (2000). The future of collaborations between librarians and teaching faculty. In D. Raspa & D. Ward (Eds.). *The collaborative imperative: Librarians and faculty working together in the information universe* (pp.148-154). Chicago: Association of College and Research Libraries.

Cassner, M., & Adams, K. E. (2005). A survey of distance librarian-administrators in ARL libraries: An overview of library resources and services. In P. B. Mahoney (Ed.), *The Eleventh Off-Campus Library Services Conference proceedings* (pp. 85-96). Binghamton, NY: Haworth Information Press.

Cunningham, T. H., & Lanning, S. (2002). New frontier trail guides: Faculty-librarian collaboration on information literacy. *Reference Services Review, 30*(4), 343-348.

D'Angelo, B. J., & Maid, B. M. (2005). Beyond instruction: Integrating library service in support of information literacy. *Internet Reference Services Quarterly, 9*(1/2), 55-63.

DeWald, N., Scholz-Crane, A., Booth, A., & Levine, C. (2000). Information literacy at a distance: Instructional design issues. *Journal of Academic Librarianship, 26*(1), 33-44.

Edge, S. (2003). Faculty-Librarian collaboration in online course development. In S. Reisman, J. G. Flores, & D. Edge (Eds.). *Electronic learning communities: Issues and practices* (pp. 136-185). Greenwich, CT: Information Age Pub.

Fletcher, J., & Stewart, D. (2001). The library: An active partner in online learning and technology. *Australian Academic and Research Libraries, 32*(3), 213-221.

Giles, K. L. (2004, May). Reflections on a privilege: Becoming part of the course through a collaboration on Blackboard. *C&RL News, 65*(5). Retrieved May 27, 2004, from http://www.ala.org/ala/acrl/acrlpubs/crlnews/backissues2004/may04/may04.htm.

Ivey, R. (2003). Information literacy: How do libraries and academics work in partnerships to deliver effective learning programs? *Australian Academic and Research Libraries, 34*(2), 100-113.

Jeffries, S. (2000). The librarian as networker: Setting the standard for higher education. In D. Raspa & D. Ward (Eds.). *The collaborative imperative: Librarians and faculty working together in the information universe* (pp. 114-129). Chicago: Association of College and Research Libraries.

Kaufmann, F. (2003). Collaborating to create customized library services for distance education users. *Technical Services Quarterly, 21*(2), 51-62.

Laverty, C., Leger, A., Stockley, D. McCollam, M., Sinclair, S., Hamilton, D., & Knapper, C. (2003, November 3). Enhancing the classroom experience with learning technology teams. *Educause Quarterly*, 19-25.

Levesque, N. (2002). Partners in education: The role of the academic library. In *The Idea of Education Conference, Mansfield College, Oxford, England*. Retrieved September 12, 2005, from http://www.inter-disciplinary.net/levesque.pdf.

Markgraf, J. (2005). Librarian participation in the online classroom. *Internet Reference Service Quarterly, 9*(1/2), 5-19.

Petrowski, M. J., Baird, D., Leach, K., & Noyes, J. (2000, December). Building a successful collaboration. *College and Research Library News, 61*(11), 1003-1005.

Raspa, D., & Ward, D. (2000). Listening for collaboration: Faculty and librarians working together. In D. Raspa & D. Ward (Eds.). *The collaborative imperative: Working together in the information universe* (pp. 1-18). Chicago: Association of College and Research Libraries.

Riedel, T. (2002). Added value, multiple choices: Librarian/faculty collaboration in online course development. *Journal of Library Administration, 37*(3/4), 477-487.

Shank, J. D. & DeWald, N. H. (2003). Establishing our presence in courseware: Adding library services to the virtual library. *Information Technology and Libraries, 22*(1), 38-43.

doi:10.1300/J111v45n01_04

Assessing
the Professional Development Needs
of Distance Librarians
in Academic Libraries

Mary Cassner
Kate E. Adams

University of Nebraska-Lincoln

SUMMARY. Professional development is essential for academic librarians to keep current with skills, knowledge, and competencies in rapidly changing times. The authors surveyed distance librarians in academic libraries to determine their professional development needs. Respondents were asked to indicate which professional development activities they are currently participating in and those they are likely to engage in within the next five years. Findings from the survey will inform library administrators, distance librarians, and professional associations of the professional development needs of distance librarians. doi:10.1300/J111v45n01_05

KEYWORDS. Professional development, career development, distance librarians, academic librarians

INTRODUCTION

The *ACRL Statement on Professional Development* (2000) affirmed that professional development is essential for academic librarians to keep

[Haworth co-indexing entry note]: "Assessing the Professional Development Needs of Distance Librarians in Academic Libraries" Cassner, Mary, and Kate E. Adams. Co-published simultaneously in *Journal of Library Administration* (The Haworth Information Press, an imprint of The Haworth Press, Inc.) Vol. 45, No. 1/2, 2006, pp. 81-99; and: *The Twelfth Off-Campus Library Services Conference Proceedings* (ed: Julie A. Garrison) The Haworth Information Press, an imprint of The Haworth Press, Inc., 2006, pp. 81-99.

current with skills, knowledge, and competencies in rapidly changing times. That effort is a shared responsibility among individual librarians, library institutions, and professional associations (ACRL, 2000). When the Association of College & Research Libraries (ACRL) surveyed its members in 2000, responses revealed that librarians consider professional development to be very important, and that ACRL members also seek professional development opportunities from other library organizations (Cast & Cary, 2001). When ACRL began its strategic planning process in 2003, the organization again sought input from division members. Input obtained from focus groups, surveys, phone interviews, and leadership council sessions indicated that professional development was the service that ACRL members value the most (Petrowski, 2004).

The ACRL Statement on Professional Development sets a context for change: "Technology is reshaping the world of learning and of scholarly communication, and the effects on academic and research librarians are profound" (ACRL, 2000, p. 933). To address these multiple changes, academic librarians face learning new skills and knowledge to perform their jobs.

Distance librarian Burich observed, "As new technologies are introduced, often it is the distance learning community that first incorporates them into its instructional delivery options" (2004, p. 32). The *Guidelines for Distance Learning Library Services* briefly mention the concept of professional development in the Personnel section, by stating that the higher education institution should provide "opportunities for continuing growth and development . . . including continuing education, professional education, and participation in professional and staff organizations" (ACRL, 2004, Personnel section, para. 2). The authors of this study wanted to know, what are the professional needs of distance librarians? This question formed the basis of the authors' investigation. Findings from the study will inform library administrators, distance librarians, and professional associations of the professional development needs of distance librarians at the present time and anticipated needs within the next five years.

LITERATURE REVIEW

While the library literature includes numerous articles on professional development for librarians, many of the articles provide an overview of the topic, offer suggestions to practicing librarians, or focus on the needs of tenure-track librarians. Although many articles are research based, an empirically based study of distance librarians' professional development needs, to the authors' knowledge, has not been addressed.

Stone (1969), in a seminal study on professional development of librarians, looked at factors that motivate librarians to pursue professional development after receiving their graduate degree. Stone examined factors that are both most important and those that are deterrents to professional development activities. She surveyed library school graduates from the classes of 1956 and 1961, with final data based on returns from 138 librarians. The Stone study addressed respondents' activities to upgrade their "knowledge, abilities, competencies and understanding in [their] field of work or specialization" (p. 21), particularly from the aspect of an individual's motivation to develop professionally.

Havener and Stolt (1994) examined the topic from the perspective of whether formal institutional support made a difference in the extent to which professional development was sought. The authors studied data from a 1991 survey of academic librarians in Oklahoma. White (2001) discussed how professional development activities benefit reference librarians, particularly those in tenure-leading positions. The article by Flatley and Weber (2004) enumerated a variety of professional development opportunities that new academic librarians might consider. An article by Jones (2002) offered advice to novice distance librarians, based on the results from queries Jones posted on two distance education-related listservs. Practicing distance librarians suggested a number of professional development opportunities.

METHODOLOGY

For the purposes of this research study, the authors used the following definition of professional development:

> [the] further study undertaken during employment by a person trained and educated in a profession, sometimes at the initiative of the employer but also through voluntary attendance at conferences, workshops, seminars, or enrollment in postgraduate courses, particularly important in professions that have a rapidly changing knowledge base. (Reitz, 2004, P section, para. professional development)

The authors' research is based on a survey of distance librarian practitioners currently employed in academic libraries. The research questions included: What professional development opportunities do distance librarians seek? What unmet professional development needs do distance librarians have? What challenges do distance librarians face in obtaining professional development? What knowledge or skill sets will distance librarians need in the next five years?

The authors identified activities that fall broadly under the concept of professional development. The survey instrument consisted of 11 questions, some with multiple parts. Six questions were partially close-ended, offering the opportunity to mark suggested responses. Five questions were completely open-ended. All but two of the questions provided an option for respondents to expand their answer or add comments.

The survey was submitted to the University's Institutional Review Board for required approval. Following approval, survey questions were formatted using Flashlight Online software to create the test instrument. The authors pre-tested the survey and cover letter with five librarians from three different units within the libraries. The librarians had different academic backgrounds and a range of years of experience in libraries.

An e-mail message was sent to OFFCAMP, an electronic discussion listserv for distance librarians, on November 14, 2005. As of that date there were 657 registrants on OFFCAMP. While the majority of OFFCAMP registrants are from North America, particularly the United States, a number of other countries are also represented. The e-mail message consisted of a cover letter outlining the research and inviting distance librarians in academic libraries to participate in the study. The message provided a deadline date for completing the survey, which could be accessed via a Web link from the e-mail message. A reminder e-mail was sent prior to the deadline. A final message was sent to the listserv stating that the deadline date had been extended. The survey was closed as of December 1, 2005.

The survey was anonymous as it did not ask questions that could identify individuals, institutions, or e-mail addresses. When each Web survey was submitted, the data were sent to a secure server operated by Flashlight Online. Both raw and compiled data were collected and made available to the researchers. The researchers later analyzed the raw data.

RESULTS

In response to the e-mail message seeking participation in the survey, 103 surveys were submitted through the Flashlight Online Web link.

Below are the questions asked in the survey and answer results. Many respondents used the comments box to expand on their responses. A synopsis of these comments is included, with the occasional quote.

Q1. What percentage of your current job duties relates to distance library services?

The portion of job duties relating to distance library services ranges widely among the respondents. The most frequent responses in descending order were 25% (15), 50% (13), 100% (12), 60% (9), 90% (8), and 20% (8).

At the low end, two respondents indicated 5%, two indicated 10%, and six indicated 15% of their job is distance library services. The range of answers ran from 0% (one response) to 100% (12 responses), with 54% as the average.

Q2. Job Duties–Mark all that apply to your current distance librarian job duties.

34	Circulation functions
64	Collection development
47	Document delivery
64	Electronic resources
82	Instructional design (such as tutorials or course modules)
92	Library instruction
98	Reference
81	Web page design/updating

The most frequently noted job duties are reference and library instruction. Nearly all of the respondents (95%) indicated that reference activities are included as part of their distance librarian duties. Five individuals mention participating in virtual reference or coordinating reference services. Eighty-nine percent noted duties related to library instruction. Two reported that they sometimes travel to off-campus sites for library instruction. Several teach college classes. One librarian teaches three subject-specific classes for undergraduate and graduate students, while another has served as instructor for an asynchronous credit course in information literacy.

Distance librarians' work often involves electronic resources, instructional design, or Web page design/updating. Eighty percent of respondents reported job duties related to instructional design, while 79% perform Web page design or updating for distance learners. Sixty-two percent reported duties associated with electronic resources. One librarian has a number of job responsibilities–EZ Proxy support and maintenance, federated search set up and rollout, and End Note distribution, instruction, and support.

Collection development in support of distance learners is an activity reported by 62% of respondents. Nine librarians indicated that they serve as liaisons or subject specialists. Several are subject specialists for business, education, and forensic sciences. Not surprisingly, some stated that they are liaisons to their campus unit involving continuing education or services for distance students. One individual is liaison for the courseware systems management groups on campus.

Some respondents indicated that their job duties for distance learners included document delivery or circulation functions. Slightly fewer than half indicated their position included document delivery for distant learners, and one-third noted circulation activities.

Eighteen respondents replied that their job duties included marketing or outreach functions. Librarians reported mail and e-mail communication to students and in-person contact with students at off-campus sites. Other job duties can include outreach activities with distance faculty, administrative staff, and the community. One person reported communication with students, faculty, the campus distance learning unit, IT staff, Web designers, and other academic librarians around the state. Others indicated membership on campus committees, attendance at relevant meetings, and advocacy promotion activities related to distance education.

There were 59 optional comments. Survey respondents reported other job duties beyond typical distance librarians. Some duties are managerial in nature, such as department chair, head of a branch library, and supervisor of other distance librarians. One respondent also serves as library director. Several librarians mentioned administrative duties such as strategic planning, accreditation and licensure issues, budgetary responsibilities, and policy development for extended library services. The occasional specialized duty includes faculty professional development and copyright specialist for the library.

Q3. For how many years have your job duties involved library services to distance learners?

Answers to this question ranged from a low of three months to a high of 30 years. Respondents average six years of job duties that include library services to distance learners, while the mean equals five years. The most frequent responses were 1, 2, 4, and 5 years. One respondent had been on the job for three months, another for four months.

Years followed by numbers of responses:

1 (9)	1.5 (1)	2 (12)	3 (7)	4 (12)	4.5 (1)
5 (15)	5.5 (4)	6 (7)	7 (3)	8 (7)	9 (2)
10 (6)	11 (3)	12 (1)	12.5 (1)	13 (1)	14 --
15 (2)	16 (1)	17 (2)	18 --	19 (1)	20 (1)
30 (1)					

Q4. Type of institution in which you are currently employed.

45	Research university
39	Four-year college or university
8	Community college
3	Medical or special library
8	Other

Most distance librarians are currently employed at research universities (44%) or four-year colleges or universities (38%). In addition, eight respondents (7%) indicated they work at community colleges, while three respondents are employed at medical or special libraries. Only eight individuals stated they work in other types of institutions.

There were 27 open-ended comments. Some of the comments specified private college, religious affiliation, small state university, Canadian university, and large, private Mexican university. One individual reported working for a university system and not for a specific library. Another is employed by a community college district that provides distance learning space to six major state universities offering undergraduate and graduate degrees. One librarian serves students from three institutions–research university, four-year college, and community college.

Q5. How important have the following been in addressing your professional development needs as a distance librarian?

Professional journal articles

| 42 Essential | 45 Important | 15 Somewhat Important | 1 Not Important |

Professional monographs

| 10 Essential | 43 Important | 37 Somewhat Important | 11 Not Important |

Listserv targeting distance librarians (such as OFFCAMP)

| 51 Essential | 42 Important | 9 Somewhat Important | 0 Not Important |

Distance Learning conferences (such as the Off-Campus Library Services Conference)

| 45 Essential | 36 Important | 17 Somewhat Important | 4 Not Important |

Workshops or staff development programs offered by your library

| 9 Essential | 23 Important | 36 Somewhat Important | 33 Not Important |

Workshops offered by your college or university

| 6 Essential | 30 Important | 40 Somewhat Important | 26 Not Important |

Library/Information Science classes taken before completing your Master's degree program

| 3 Essential | 21 Important | 30 Somewhat Important | 47 Not Important |

Library/Information Science classes taken after completing your Master's degree program
[If not applicable, leave blank]

| 5 Essential | 14 Important | 10 Somewhat Important | 28 Not Important |

College or university classes

| 3 Essential | 11 Important | 25 Somewhat Important | 50 Not Important |

One half of all respondents considered listservs targeting distance librarians to be essential in addressing their professional development needs. Overall, listservs received the highest ratings with 91% of respondents stating that they are either essential or important to them. Nine percent rated listservs as somewhat important. No respondents considered listservs as unimportant for professional development. The ratings are likely influenced by the fact that the survey was solicited via listserv.

Eighty-five percent of distance librarians who responded to the survey reported that professional journal articles are essential or important for their professional development. One librarian reported reading business literature, especially management journals, and articles and monographs on leadership.

Forty-three percent of respondents rated monographs as important, 37% as somewhat important, and only 10% as essential. One librarian reported reading not only books but also dissertations and education documents found in ERIC. It appears that monographs may not be as important as journal articles to distance librarians.

Seventy-nine percent of respondents viewed distance learning conferences as being essential (44%) or important (35%) in addressing their professional development needs. One librarian said, "Unfortunately, I have not been able to travel to any of the off campus library services conferences due to poor travel funding. However, I hope to go to the one in 2006. I think conferences would be extremely helpful!" Others reported attendance at regional conferences or conferences and workshops offered by state library associations. One librarian noted that the Association of Christian Librarians' annual conference often has workshops pertinent to distance library services. Another respondent reported finding the programs and discussions at ALA conferences useful. One individual stated that reading conference papers is a way to keep current.

Survey respondents did not find workshops as useful in meeting professional development needs in comparison to listservs, professional literature, and distance learning conferences. Workshops, whether offered by the library or the university, were rated essential or important by only one third of the librarians. One fourth indicated that workshops offered by their university are not important in addressing their professional development needs, while one third stated that those offered by their library are not important in meeting their needs. A respondent said, "My library rarely offers workshops or staff development programs, but does support travel to off-site locations for professional development." Others reported attendance at workshops offered by professional association and vendors demonstrating new software. Another individual attends consortial meetings specific to distance services.

In general, classes ranked lowest in meeting professional development needs. Approximately 50% of respondents rated library/information sciences classes and university classes taken after completion of the master's degree as not important in addressing professional development needs. However, one respondent commented, "I obtained my MLS in 1978, so the concept of distance learning was hardly discussed. This year I earned an advanced certificate in management of libraries using a combination of videoconferencing and online classes." Another respondent reported current enrollment in a PhD education program.

Respondents provided 35 comments related to meeting professional development needs. Three respondents indicated that blogs are very useful. One individual stated:

> Blogs, especially those of other distance librarians, have been extremely important to me, possibly more so than any other source. A blog has the currency of good journals or news sources, the analysis of a journal article, and the response possibilities of a listserv.

Many respondents noted the value of informal networking with peers or mentors. Others mentioned cross training in other areas of the library, on the job experience, and training related to technology, communication, ITV, and Blackboard. Two librarians answered from the perspective of personal experience as distance learners. One stated, "I learned a lot by being a distance learner, and being poorly served."

Q6. Consider possible core activities that you believe will benefit you as a distance librarian in the next five years. How important is it for you to increase your knowledge in the following areas?

Budget/finances
25 Very Important   43 Somewhat Important   25 Not Important   8 Have already achieved

Human resources personnel
24 Very Important   37 Somewhat Important   33 Not Important   6 Have already achieved

Management training
20 Very Important   52 Somewhat Important   23 Not Important   7 Have already achieved

Marketing/public relations
65 Very Important   30 Somewhat Important   6 Not Important   2 Have already achieved

Supervisory skills
16 Very Important   46 Somewhat Important   29 Not Important   10 Have already achieved

Instructional design
80 Very Important   20 Somewhat Important   2 Not Important   1 Have already achieved

Web page design
58 Very Important   35 Somewhat Important   6 Not Important   4 Have already achieved

Nearly all distance librarians believe it is important to increase their knowledge of technology in the next five years. Seventy-eight percent of respondents feel it is very important to expand their instructional design skills. More than half, 56%, believe that it is very important to increase their skills in Web page design.

Many of the 18 comments centered on the need to keep current with technology. One respondent stated that it is essential to understand new technologies that can be used in online instruction, such as RoboDemo, Impatica, and Soft Chalk. These tools can be used in creating tutorials, research guides, and reusable learning objects. Another distance librarian supported learning XML, Cold Fusion, RoboDemo or View Lets to aid in managing complex tutorials, design online questionnaires, and online testing. Another respondent valued skills in compressed video, chat, and voice-over IP.

Nearly two-thirds of the respondents believe it is very important to increase their knowledge of marketing or public relations. A respondent stated, "Marketing is a current passion and I'm active in several aspects of it."

In terms of core activities, ratings for budget/finances, human resources personnel, management training, and supervisory skills were evenly divided between very important, somewhat important, or not important.

Several respondents commented that leadership, assessment and evaluation skills, data analysis, and strategic planning would be useful for the future. One individual stated that training in these areas is not as important as it is unlikely that her institution will have the financial resources to fund additional distance librarians. Another respondent remarked that some of these skills were covered in the advanced certificate program.

Respondents were asked to mark "have already achieved" for the listed core activities. Fewer than 10% of the respondents indicated they had already gained knowledge or competency in any of these areas. One reason for this might be that half of the survey respondents have distance librarian experience for six or fewer years.

Q7. What knowledge or skills do you think will be important for distance librarians to possess in the next five years?

Many thoughtful comments were offered in response to this question. Technology knowledge and skills, particularly those related to instructional and Web page design, were mentioned most often. Distance learning pedagogy is another frequently mentioned theme, as is marketing and outreach. Other comments centered on administrative or management skills. Communication and interpersonal skills were deemed important by some respondents. Such comments reflected findings from Jones (2002) who reported from her study that respondents recommended developing instructional technology skills and learning the course management software adopted by the local campus.

Technology knowledge or skills facilitating the teaching of students via distance media is thought to be essential for librarians, currently and in the future. One librarian stated that technology and instructional design knowledge and skills are needed to improve services to meet students' wants and needs. That librarian commented, "Currently, I don't think libraries do this very well when faced with what our competition is doing."

Many respondents stated that knowledge of instructional or Web page design will continue to be important in the future. Several respondents believe that distance librarians need a basic knowledge of Web design and application skills. This will be a job requirement, rather than an option, in coming years, one librarian averred. Online tutorial development is also noted as a necessary skill for distance librarians. Another commented that distance librarians should be knowledgeable about software to create online instructional materials in a variety of multimedia formats. One respondent stated that distance librarians will need a mastery of rich media instruction production, such as short videos and screen casts or pod casts. Distance librarians will need a basic understanding of course management software and its integration with the library's electronic platform and resources.

One respondent stated that all technology skills possible will be needed, as well as creativity in applying new technologies to distance education. Distance librarians should have a basic understanding of games and gaming and know how these can be used for information literacy instruction. Also required will be knowledge of instant messaging, blogging, RSS feeds, wireless technologies, and the use of cell phones as a learning technology.

A familiarity with integrating access to electronic sources including e-journals, e-books, databases, and Internet sites will continue to be needed. An understanding of how to use technology to improve access and services will be essential.

Some indicated that administrative or management training and knowledge will continue to be necessary in the future. Forecasting, strategic planning, budgeting skills, and contract or license negotiation skills will be useful. Assessment and data analysis skills are also considered essential for distance librarians.

Not surprisingly, communication and collaboration skills also ranked as important. Distance librarians require the ability to team with other professionals inside and outside the library to deliver services and resources. Communication will necessitate a variety of delivery methods including in-person, phone, e-mail, chat, videoconferencing, and technologies yet to make it to the mainstream markets. Advocacy skills to work with vendors to improve electronic interfaces will be required of distance librarians.

Significant knowledge of marketing and outreach skills were also viewed as important by many respondents. Librarians should take advantage of opportunities to partner and collaborate with faculty teaching distance courses as well as other campus staff who work with distance students. It was noted that distance librarians need an understanding of marketing, which means product development, not just publicity. Public relations skills are necessary to increase awareness of the services offered.

When asked what knowledge or skills each thought important for distance librarians to possess in the next five years, one respondent stated "everything." Another individual commented, "Nothing new, but distance librarians have to be very adaptable and quick to spot the best ways to serve their clientele." Two respondents indicated that diverse language skills would be useful. One answered that "the idea of distance librarianship as a separate service must be on the way out." A somewhat similar statement was made by a respondent who said that the "ability to 'integrate' services for distance students with those for on-campus students to benefit both populations" was necessary.

Q8. What challenges do you face in obtaining professional development for distance learning? Mark as many as apply.

89	Time constraints at work
37	Obligations outside the job
55	Insufficient funding to attend conferences/workshops
40	Insufficient funding to take online workshops/seminars
32	Insufficient funding to take "for credit" classes
44	Limited choice of distance learning offerings that relate to my job

Respondents were asked to mark as many of the responses that applied to them. There were 21 optional comments. Eighty-six percent of distance librarians experience time constraints at work. Three individuals commented that they have other job duties unrelated to distance learning services. One respondent stated, "Working at a small institution with so many responsibilities means having trouble finding time for any professional development, let alone for distance learning." One respondent indicated that other library staff do not completely understand the needs of a satellite campus and the time it takes.

Half of the options that respondents could mark pertained to funding considerations. Fifty-five individuals reported insufficient funding to attend conferences or workshops. Forty perceive funding to attend online workshops or seminars to be a challenge. Thirty-two respondents believe there is insufficient funding to take for-credit classes. One respondent reported, "While our university doesn't fund all conferences, I am willing to use personal funds. However, I can't possibly attend all the conferences I'd like to. I make frequent use of free online seminars."

Forty-four respondents believe that limited choice of distance learning offerings that relate to their jobs is a challenge. One individual from a small university reported that it is difficult to find relevant training since often training is focused on the needs of larger institutions. Another librarian noted it is difficult to determine which training will be of most benefit to the particular position. Sometimes, training opportunities provide a "rehash what those of us who have been doing this for a while already know." One respondent desired additional offerings on management specific to distance services.

Three respondents commented there are limited professional development opportunities in their geographic area. One believed that since there are relatively few distance librarians, professional development only takes place at national conferences and online. This respondent would prefer such activity be done on a regional level.

Thirty-seven respondents noted that obligations outside the job are challenges to acquiring professional development. However, none of the optional comments address what these obligations might be. Perhaps these might relate to inadequate funding, the travel that would be required, or perceived limited time outside the job.

Several librarians reported that there is limited administrative support for professional development. One respondent believed there is a lack of recognition of the importance of continuing education for librarians at her institution. Similarly, one respondent believed there is limited awareness, prioritization, and administrative support of distance learning. A third reported unwillingness at the institutional level to fund development that is perceived as unnecessary, and commented, "I think I need the development, they don't. I have to fund it myself, although they allow me to do it within the workday."

One individual was allowed ample time and funding for professional development. However, this comment stands out because this is the only remark of such a nature.

Q9. What would be of most benefit to you personally when trying to meet your professional development needs?

When responding to this question, one respondent stated,

> A cadre of computer/digital savvy, professional librarians (law, science, med, generalists), instructional designers, online educators from small and large institutions, K-12 educators and librarians, finishing library school students and profs, and tech geeks coming together at an online conference (via web casts, i.e., learning times) addressing topics coming from this survey!

Many of the 72 responses pertained to funding, time, and instruction. Others related to networking and professional development opportunities. One individual was uncertain what would benefit her most.

A perceived lack of time is a common theme. One librarian indicated a need for "a 48-hour day." Some would like to spend additional time on distance learning duties but also have other job responsibilities. Others would use extra time for professional reading, getting away to concentrate on learning, networking with colleagues, or working on the research prior to publishing. One librarian would use extra time to participate in online sessions without interruptions. Another would use extra time to work with colleagues on skill-building and practice projects. Two others raised the possibility of telecommuting as a means to save time.

Funding concerns are an issue for many librarians. Comments indicated an interest in free or low-cost professional development opportunities or an increased level of institutional funding. Some librarians would use additional monies for professional travel and costs associated with research, conferences, workshops, and classes or training.

A few respondents reported that increased administrative support would be useful to them. Three respondents said it would be helpful to have increased staffing in their offices. Another said it would be of benefit to have reliable computing equipment and infrastructure.

A significant number of comments related to instructional needs. Many individuals indicated a preference for online conferences, workshops, and classes. Several were proponents of anytime, anywhere learning. One individual stated,

Put all classes/courses/workshops/seminars, etc., online. Some of us live in the middle of nowhere with small budgets and do not have the time or money to physically go anywhere. We are in the business of supporting distance education so we should be able to get all of our professional development needs met via distance education technology.

Respondents reported a wide range of needs. Two respondents would like to take self-paced classes or training. Others prefer to leave the worksite for training or education, which they want at local, in-state, or perhaps regional locations. One respondent preferred programs and articles that focus on specific issues rather than general topics. Another appreciated the Madison distance education conference and MERLOT (Multimedia Educational Resource for Learning and Online Teaching). Two individuals indicated they would benefit from additional professional reading. One respondent suggested a database containing professional development opportunities and a calendar of workshops and conferences.

Ten librarians indicated that networking with distance colleagues would be beneficial. One said, "I'd just like to hear more success stories about how other librarians have provided different kinds of services to distance learners and how others can replicate their successes." A respondent noted that these discussions could take place in a variety of venues including OFFCAMP, conferences, newsletters, and Web sites.

Q10. How likely are you to take advantage of the following opportunities or activities during the next five years?

Live Web casts

60 Very Likely	26 Likely	14 Somewhat Likely	3 Not Likely

Interactive Web courses/seminars

57 Very Likely	26 Likely	17 Somewhat Likely	3 Not Likely

Virtual attendance at conferences

36 Very Likely	21 Likely	31 Somewhat Likely	14 Not Likely

RSS (Really Simple Syndication)

36 Very Likely	19 Likely	25 Somewhat Likely	16 Not Likely

Journal alert services

40 Very Likely	32 Likely	25 Somewhat Likely	5 Not Likely

Reading professional journals

70 Very Likely 26 Likely 7 Somewhat Likely 0 Not Likely

Reading monographs

38 Very Likely 33 Likely 24 Somewhat Likely 8 Not Likely

Listservs

83 Very Likely 14 Likely 5 Somewhat Likely 1 Not Likely

Blogs

32 Very Likely 29 Likely 37 Somewhat Likely 4 Not Likely

Networking with colleagues

73 Very Likely 24 Likely 5 Somewhat Likely 1 Not Likely

Programs at the American Library Association annual conferences

33 Very Likely 22 Likely 25 Somewhat Likely 23 Not Likely

Association of College and Research Libraries conferences

34 Very Likely 24 Likely 30 Somewhat Likely 15 Not Likely

Off-Campus Library Services conferences

48 Very Likely 31 Likely 15 Somewhat Likely 8 Not Likely

Regional or state library conferences

45 Very Likely 34 Likely 16 Somewhat Likely 7 Not Likely

Preconferences for library conferences

18 Very Likely 23 Likely 42 Somewhat Likely 18 Not Likely

Q11. Do you have additional comments related to the survey?

There were 19 comments. Comments related to lack of funding to attend conferences or online workshops, finding time to develop instructional materials, networking, and balancing different job roles or duties. Lack of administrative support and lack of office space is problematic for one respondent. One individual stated that "distance librarians need to be leaders to do their jobs really well, so leadership training should be part of any offerings for them."

Three individuals asked that survey results be shared. One respondent asked for wide dissemination of results to share with administrators. One comment reported that the survey was very "American centered."

CONCLUSION

Professional development is essential for academic librarians to keep current with skills, knowledge, and competencies in rapidly changing times. The results from this study can inform library administrators, distance librarians, and associations of the professional development needs of distance librarians. The findings from the authors' survey reveal practitioners' assessment of anticipated knowledge and skills in the next five years. Specific activities support obtaining knowledge and skills are rated by preference. The authors also provide a brief profile of academic distance librarians.

Profile of a Distance Librarian Working in an Academic Library

- Over 80% of respondents are employed by research universities or four-year colleges or universities.
- On average, the distance librarian has six years of experience in the position.
- Distance learning job responsibilities typically represent half of the respondent's assignments.

The most common job responsibilities are reference and library instruction. Document delivery or circulation functions are less frequently reported, while instructional design and Web page responsibilities are apparently becoming more common.

Preferences of Distance Librarians

- Listservs targeting distance librarians, distance learning conferences, and professional journal articles are the most important in meeting professional development needs.
- Professional monographs are less important than journal articles.
- Distance librarians will likely continue to use listservs, read professional journals, and network with colleagues in the next five years.
- Blogs, which provide currency, analysis, and quick communication, are increasing in importance.
- Core activities that will be most important in the next five years are instructional design, Web page design, and marketing/public relations.

• Knowledge or skills that will be important in the next five years are instructional technology and Web page design.

A big challenge that distance librarians face in obtaining professional development for distance learning is time constraints. Sufficient funding is also a concern. One librarian commented that when institutions do not provide funds for courses or travel to conferences, resources such as listservs and online access to professional journals are important. Access to relevant professional development opportunities is essential in meeting the needs of distance librarians.

REFERENCES

Association of College & Research Libraries. (2000). ACRL statement on professional development. *College & Research Libraries News, 61*, 933-936.

Association of College & Research Libraries. (June 2004). *Guidelines for distance learning library services.* Retrieved July 28, 2005, from http://www.ala.org/acrl/resjune02.html.

Burich, N. (2004). Providing leadership for change in distance learning. *Journal of Library & Information Services in Distance Learning, 1*(2), 31-41.

Cast, M., & Cary, S. (2001). Members assess ACRL: Results of the 2000 membership survey. *College & Research Libraries News, 62*, 623-628.

Flatley, R. K., & Weber, M. A. (2004). Professional development opportunities for new academic librarians. *Journal of Academic Librarianship, 30*, 488-492.

Havener, W. M., & Stolt, W. A. (1994). The professional development activities of academic librarians: Does institutional support make a difference? *College & Research Libraries, 55*, 25-36.

Jones, M. F. (2002). Help! I'm the new distance librarian–Where do I begin? *Journal of Library Administration, 37*, 397-410.

Petrowski, M. J. (2004). ACRL offers development opportunities. *American Libraries, 35*(2), 9.

Reitz, J. M. (2004). *ODLIS: Online dictionary for library and information science.* Retrieved December 22, 2005, from www.lu.com/odli.

Stone, E. W. (1969). *Factors related to the professional development of librarians.* Metuchen, NJ: Scarecrow Press.

White, G. W. (2001). The professional development of reference librarians: Implications of research, publication, and service. *Reference Librarian, 73*, 337-350.

doi:10.1300/J111v45n01_05

Blogging It into Them:
Weblogs in Information Literacy Instruction

Priscilla Coulter
Lani Draper

Stephen F. Austin State University

SUMMARY. Online learning, while broadening opportunities for many, has the unfortunate effect of isolating or even alienating students who crave interaction and/or are uncomfortable with information technology. Weblogs (blogs) are an easy-to-use, informal means of online interaction that have become widely popular in recent years; their potential value as community-building and learning tools in higher education has only just begun to be explored. We report on our use of blogs as a supplement to face-to-face information literacy instruction and as a sole means of library outreach to graduate distance learners. We also explore the current uses of blogs in libraries nationwide. doi:10.1300/J111v45n01_06

KEYWORDS. Weblogs, blogs, information literacy, library instruction, libraries, education

INTRODUCTION

Weblogs (blogs) are, simply put, unedited Web sites of varying complexity wherein individuals or groups can freely publish information. In

[Haworth co-indexing entry note]: "Blogging It into Them: Weblogs in Information Literacy Instruction." Coulter, Priscilla, and Lani Draper. Co-published simultaneously in *Journal of Library Administration* (The Haworth Information Press, an imprint of The Haworth Press, Inc.) Vol. 45, No. 1/2, 2006, pp. 101-115; and: *The Twelfth Off-Campus Library Services Conference Proceedings* (ed: Julie A. Garrison) The Haworth Information Press, an imprint of The Haworth Press, Inc., 2006, pp. 101-115.

January of 2005, the Pew Internet & American Life Project proclaimed blogs "a key part of online culture" (2005, para. 1), citing a three-fold increase in blog participation since 2003. By their count, 27% of 120 million Internet users in the United States read blogs, while 12% and 7% post to and create them, respectively. A number of free blogging sites have made Internet publication as simple as e-mail and, while they are gaining popularity amongst organizations (e.g., the Association of College and Research Libraries: http://www.acrlblog.org/), blogs are best known (and both criticized and celebrated) as the voice of the individual on the Internet (see Downes, 2004). The uses of blogs are naturally widely variable (personal journal, fan site, political/social commentary, news, professional discourse), but the result of their sudden popularity is that blogs have become worldwide icons of self-expression and freedom of speech.

Blogs in Libraries

Not surprisingly, librarians are interested in blogs, which represent a relatively inexpensive, quick means of collecting and sharing information (Carver, 2003). A simple search in Google for *library AND blog* brings around 53.5 million hits (in December, 2005); at a glance, librarianship and library news and services are common themes, though difficult to quantify. A search of the profession's literature delves deeper: blogs focused on professional discourse, library news, reference, marketing, outreach, book clubs, and internal communication are reported (e.g., Cohen, 2005; Fichter, 2003; Harder & Reichardt, 2003; Kenney & Stephens, 2005; Vogel & Goans, 2005), though seldom in detail (see Vogel & Goans for an exception). There is, in fact, a blog devoted to the use of blogs and similar technologies in libraries: http://www. blogwithoutalibrary.net. However, there is scant mention of blogs as tools in information literacy (IL) instruction. Some call for librarians to explore blogs as educational tools (Clyde, 2005; Ross Embrey, 2002), but there are no reports of their successful implementation in library classrooms.

Blogs in Education

IL skills are, at face value, dry learning material. Librarians, themselves all too aware of the inherent worth of research skills, often teach them for their own sake, forgetting that most students have little context in which to appreciate those skills beyond, perhaps, a class assignment. It is up to librarians, then, to create a learning context that highlights the relevancy of IL to students' lives, future careers, interests and/or experiences. Interactive pedagogy can do much to engage and motivate students, even where the subject matter at hand is dry (Honkimäki, Tynjälä, & Valkonen, 2004). Providing opportunities for reflective learning in higher education is vital to creating lifelong learners (Masui & De Corte, 2005). Further, applying a constructive approach (essentially: allowing room for creativity, reflection, social interaction and authentic, or problem-based, learning activities) to IL instruction results in meaningful acquisition, transference and retention of "abstract" IL concepts (Cooperstein & Kocevar-Weidinger, 2004). While implementation of such techniques in the classroom are challenging for many librarians, who are often time-constrained, blogs have been used to prompt student reflection, critical thinking and collaboration with considerable success in a variety of educational settings (Aylward, 2004; Downes, 2004; Huffaker, 2004; Kessler & Lund, 2004; Oravec, 2002; Poling, 2005).

In addition, blogs can be valuable community-building tools for students who are physically isolated from their classmates and instructors. Dickey (2004) encouraged distance education students to use blogs to share their frustrations and successes, in addition to posting course-related reflections. In so doing, students naturally formed a more cohesive and supportive social unit, dispelling perceptions of solitude in the online environment. There is evidence, as well, that these communal blogs sparked reflective learning and satisfaction in learning as students coached one another through difficulties, shared ideas and considered the sources of their successes and failures.

At Stephen F. Austin State University (SFA), librarians teach one-shot IL sessions to individual classes, typically scheduled by faculty near the assignment of a research project. As IL sessions are time-constrained, it is difficult for librarians to effectively demonstrate every aspect of the research process, much less the application of critical thinking to that process. Students are therefore encouraged to visit subject librarians as they begin their projects (and many take advantage of this invitation), but they are not typically required to do so. Librarians have no efficient, reliable means, then, of communicating with these students after that initial 50- to 75-minute IL session. Librarians are also hard pressed to uniformly reach distance education students. Given the growing popularity of blogs and their potential to encourage student reflection and interaction, we chose to investigate the efficacy of blogs as teaching and learning tools in IL instruction. Our goals were (1) to more consistently communicate with, and continue to teach IL skills to, both traditional and distance education students and (2) to engage students in an open dialogue of research-related questions, encouraging reflective, collaborative learning. In this paper, we report on our use of blogs as IL teaching tools; we also attempt to gauge the attitudes of both librarians and students toward blogs as learning aids.

METHOD

Blogs in IL Instruction

During the spring and fall semesters of 2005, Coulter used Google's Blogger (http://www.blogger.com/) to create a blog for each of ten courses for which she provided face-to-face IL instruction. She also created a blog for an online graduate degree program in one of her liaison departments. Each blog was configured to allow any reader to comment (generating an automatic e-mail notification to Coulter) and to e-mail posts. The blog created for distance education students can be viewed at http://sfasumsri.blogspot.com/.

To avoid the impression that other means of contacting Coulter for research help (e.g., e-mail, phone, office) were discouraged, the blogs were not promoted intensively. In the spring semester, students were introduced to their blogs during face-to-face IL sessions. The blogs' URLs were provided on any printed handouts, alongside more traditional contact information. Distance education students and faculty were alerted to their blog via e-mail. All blogs were also linked to appropriate subject guides on the library's Web site; these online subject guides are heavily featured by all librarians during IL sessions and reference interviews. During the fall semester, in response to students' survey responses, an attempt was made to better market the blogs: fliers, consisting of printouts of the blogs' first pages (all stating the blogs' purpose and location, instructions for commenting and Coulter's contact information), were handed out during face-to-face IL sessions. Distance education students were again contacted by e-mail, and associated faculty members were asked to promote the blog to their students. A link inside WebCT courses was suggested; such a link was put into place on a course home page by one of the distance education faculty, albeit later in the semester.

An open-source hit counter, TDStats (http://www.tdstats.com/), was placed on most of the blogs in an attempt to record the number of visits to each. However, the counters were not configured to distinguish between hits by visitors and hits by Coulter as she updated the blogs. As the reported traffic on all blogs was overwhelmingly low, and our interest was primarily in student participation (rather than simple observation), these figures were ultimately ignored.

Information was posted to the blog periodically throughout the semester. Research tips (e.g., Boolean logic, wildcards, Web site evaluation) and databases not covered during IL sessions, new products or services available to students and information specific to remote searching and access were among the topics.

At the end of each semester, a brief survey (see Appendix) was created using SurveyMonkey (http://www.surveymonkey.com/). The survey's URL was posted to each blog, and faculty members were asked to encourage students to take it. Descriptive analyses of the resultant data was performed by SurveyMonkey.

Blogs in Libraries Nationwide

A pilot survey was designed and distributed by Draper in May of 2005 via the Information Literacy Instruction (ILI-L) online community provided by the Association of College & Research Libraries' Instruction Section. The survey was created using Zope software and results were exported to Microsoft Excel for analysis.

In June of 2005, a second online survey was created using SurveyMonkey and distributed by Coulter and Draper via several library-related e-mail listservs. This survey was also promoted in an article in the School Library Journal (Oatman, 2005), as well as numerous library-related blogs and RSS feeds. It remained available through November 2005. Descriptive analyses of the survey data was provided by SurveyMonkey. Questions and responses of both surveys are available online (see Results).

RESULTS

Student Surveys

Twenty-six, or 15.1%, of 172 targeted students responded to the spring 2005 survey. Of these, 15.4% indicated that they had a blog, or read those of others. 73.1% reported that they never checked their class research blog, and none of the remaining 26.9% used the blog's comments feature. The blog was judged "not helpful" by 46.2%, though, in response to the same question, 61.5% commented that they never used it, didn't know about it, or didn't know what a blog was. Several indicated that they looked at the blog when they visited it to access the survey, and that it looked as though it would have been useful to them. Interestingly, students seemed to like much about the blog, particularly the "information/answers given by librarian" and that it was available online. Seven indicated that they liked nothing about the blog; seven also left comments explaining that they had not used it, or did not know about it. When asked for suggestions about the research blog, 40.9% of those who commented voiced the need for increased marketing. Complete results of the spring survey can be seen in the Appendix.

Only one student (of 101 targeted students) responded to the fall 2005 survey. This student, part of the distance education program, was 38 years old and not a recreational blogger. S/he reported checking the blog once without posting a comment, but rated it not helpful, commenting that, "I was mostly past my lit[erature] research phase. It would have been more useful last year. It will be great for upcoming students." Like the spring respondents, this student liked the information that Coulter posted to the blog, as well as its online availability and informal qualities, but also pointed out that "I don't check [the] blog for new postings unless I'm directed to do so."

Librarian Surveys

The pilot survey found 82 respondents. The majority (78%) were from four-year academic institutions; 19.5% reported from community colleges or two-year academic institutions. The remaining respondents were from corporate and public libraries. All reported having some familiarity with blogs, while 26.8% have posted to at least one blog. Of those who responded, 12.2% reported owning a blog; 12.2% also use blogs to communicate with students. Of these blogs, 50% are deemed regularly used. Blog topics include: course-specific information, discussion and literature research, information for off-campus or nontraditional students, Internet culture, current events. When prompted for potential improvements to their blogs, four of eight respondents felt that better marketing and/or visibility were called for. One each mentioned educating users about blogs and making the blog's content "more interesting" and/or interactive. One felt that faculty support (i.e., requiring students to use the blog) was necessary, while another, apparently a course instructor, was entirely satisfied with his/her blog. The final question of the pilot survey asked respondents for general comments about the use of blogs in IL instruction. Of the 37 who complied, 14 were unequivocally positive (four expressing plans to create educational blogs in the near future), while five were more or less negative about the use of blogs as tools in IL instruction. Five pointed out that blogs provide a function much like the discussion/bulletin board features of most courseware products and are therefore likely to be perceived as redundant. Three felt that "faculty buy-in," or some other means of motivating students to use blogs (e.g., assignments and grades), was necessary. One was concerned with students' ability to critically analyze the information found on blogs, and thus was apparently hesitant to encourage their use for academic research. Another expressed enthusiasm for learning and using new technology. Complete results of the pilot survey are available at http://www.faculty.sfasu.edu/pcoulter/OCLS/pilot.pdf.

Two hundred and fifty four individuals responded to the second survey. While most (61.8%) hailed from four-year colleges and universities, librarians from K-12 schools (4.3%), public libraries (10.6%), community colleges (10.2%), special libraries (9.1%) and library schools (0.8%) responded as well. The vast majority (96.1%) reported having at least some experience with blogs, whether as readers or contributors; 31.5% are currently using blogs to communicate with their users. Library news is the most common topic in these blogs (75.3%), though reference (44.3%), information literacy (36.1%) and readers' advisories (19.6%) are represented as well. Other topics include: world news, discipline-specific news and information sources, popular culture, article/tables of contents alerts, government reports, intellectual freedom, course-specific information and discussion and remote access to library resources. Though we are primarily concerned with librarians' use of blogs to communicate with library patrons, 12.5% reported using blogs to communicate with colleagues.

Of librarian bloggers, 67.9% judge that their blogs are used regularly and 71.8% feel that blogs are an effective means of communicating with, or teaching, library users. Fifty-two percent cited a blog's subject matter as key to its success or failure; marketing and user interest in and/or knowledge about blogs also ranked high (49.3% and 46.7%, respectively). Respondents also suggested that the blog's ease of use, visibility on the library's Web site and frequency of updates and posts play a large role in a blog's success. When asked what they would or could do to improve their blogs' effectiveness, 63.2 % of respondents indicated that they would increase marketing, promotion and/or online visibility of their blog. Some felt that their blog's content could be improved (10.5%) or updated more frequently (10.5%), while 7% stated a need for user education. Seven percent expressed a lack of adequate software and/or technical support, while 5.3% wish for more time to maintain and update library blogs.

Ninety six respondents shared a number of insightful (and humorous) thoughts and ideas on the use of blogs in libraries. Of these, 29 were unequivocally positive toward blogs as tools for communicating with or instructing library users; nine were largely or entirely negative. Thirteen indicated that they plan to begin blogging in the near future; five of these envision educational blogs. One respondent expressed a concern with the hierarchical organization of posts on most blogs (early posts are lost beneath a "sea" of more recent additions), while another pointed out that blogs are often searchable. The long-term viability of blogs as a communication tool was questioned by some, while others seemed inclined to favor their adoption as part of a tradition of embracing new information technologies. Concern with commercial blogging software placing library blogs next to less-than-authoritative blogs was raised; others touted the time- and money-saving qualities of free, push-button publishing. Several stressed the value of the potential interactivity of blogs when used to communicate with students. Complete responses to the second survey can be accessed at http://www.faculty.sfasu.edu/pcoulter/OCLS/survey2summary.html.

DISCUSSION

Our attempt at blogging as a means of IL instruction was, at best, a neutral effort. Our goal of prompting students to engage and collaborate in learning research skills certainly was not met: not a single student posted a comment to a research blog. Their survey responses, however, indicate that they rarely, if ever, checked their blogs; once students looked at them, they realized that the blogs might have been helpful. This experience confirms what some of our librarian survey respondents asserted: faculty collaboration is key to the success of an IL blog. Indeed, the sole fall student respondent, a distance education student, admitted that s/he only checked the blog when directed to do so (presumably by his/her professor). Like most instructional librarians in the United States (Coulter, Clarke, Draper, & Scamman., 2005), SFA librarians teach IL in one-shot sessions. We do not assign grades or award extra credit; we lack the ability to motivate students, aside from what we can conjure via masterful presentation and force of personality. Without faculty support, therefore, it will always be difficult for us to persuade students to return to, much less participate in, a blog (or any similar tool) focused on literature research. This general lack of motivational power, alongside concerns about blogs expressed by librarians in our survey, may well explain the absence of IL-focused blogs from the library literature.

It seems obvious, per student survey comments, that improved marketing and/or visibility has the potential to improve these blogs' use; again, students indicated that, had they known about or remembered the blogs' existence, they would have used them. Many librarian bloggers, as evidenced by our survey, have evidently reached the same conclusion (see Bell, 2005). Interestingly, increased marketing (fliers) and visibility (link to course home page) in the fall 2005 semester had no apparent impact on our blogs' usage. In fact, one female undergraduate student, tattered blog flier in hand, came to Coulter's office for help weeks after her face-to-face IL session. Her question was one that Coulter had addressed on the blog, yet she had never visited it.

Courseware may present significant competition to educational blogs, particularly in distance education. Most courseware programs feature a discussion forum or bulletin board, designed to foster student interaction and reflection. Participation in these discussions is often encouraged or required by distance learning faculty to facilitate community building. As pointed out by several respondents to our pilot survey, blogs function similarly, and so may be resisted by students and dismissed by faculty. Indeed, Coulter found that, while students occasionally shared their research strategies and problems in the WebCT discussion forum and chat room (even posting e-mail correspondence with Coulter), they were silent on the blog, despite its prominent location on their course Web page. Of course, where the luxury of access to online courses is not granted, blogs still offer a way for librarians to efficiently communicate with remote students.

In the end, it may be that the average college student is not a part of the blog culture. The Pew Internet and American Life Project's January 2005 report found that, despite the impressive recent increase in blogging, 62% of American Internet users do not know what a blog is. Too, they supply further characteristics of the typical blog creator that seem to exclude the average college student: young (under 30 years of age) but "veteran" Internet users (6 or more years' experience) who are likely to hold a college or graduate degree and to live in relatively wealthy households. The typical United States undergraduate is certainly young, but may be too much so (under 24, see U.S. Department of Education, 2005) to have obtained sufficient Internet experience, postsecondary education and/or wealth. It seems likely, then, that the students in most of Coulter's face-to-face IL sessions, and possibly much of SFA's student population, will not be serious bloggers. Students' survey responses confirm this suggestion: nearly 85% indicated that they did not blog, and several commented that they did not know what blogs were. Similarly, interviews with faculty in the targeted distance education program revealed that these students are typically older than 30, having returned to graduate school after some years in the workforce, and are often challenged by distance learning technology, which indicates relative inexperience with the Internet. This, too, was confirmed in part by our single fall student survey respondent, who was 38 years old.

Still, blogs are an inexpensive, easy-to-use and, quite frankly, fun means of communication. While their popularity continues to grow (and they themselves to evolve), there is little to be lost in attempting to use them to teach IL skills. After all, traditional library instruction (i.e., one-shot sessions) often falls short of its goals, primarily because it is time-constrained and leaves no time for student reflection. Blogs offer one-shot instructional librarians a means of maintaining contact with students throughout a semester, providing continued instruction and opportunities for collaborative and reflective learning. Librarians teaching semester-long courses, of course, have the ability to fully exploit blogs, whether as required reflective student journals or community-building tools. Our survey respondents reported that other types of library blogs are effective; we believe that, with increased marketing and collaboration with teaching faculty (translating into increased motivational power), librarians can emulate their teaching colleagues' success with educational blogs.

REFERENCES

Aylward, M. L. (2004). Web logs as an independent study tool. *Journal of Interactive Instruction Development, 16*, 22-26.

Bell, S. (2005, October 15). Where the readers are. *Library Journal*. Retrieved on December 6, 2005, from http://www.libraryjournal.com/article/CA6269278.html.

Carver, B. (2003, January 15). Is it time to get blogging? *Library Journal*. Retrieved on December 6, 2005, from http://www.libraryjournal.com/article/CA266428.html.

Clyde, L. A. (2005). Educational blogging. *Teacher Librarian, 32*, 43-45.

Cohen, S. M. (2005). Weblogs and public libraries. *ePublications*. Retrieved on December 6, 2005, from http://www.ala.org/ala/pla/plapubs/epublications/weblogs.htm.

Cooperstein, S. E., & Kocevar-Weidinger, E. (2004). Beyond active learning: A constructivist approach to learning. *Reference Services Review, 32*, 141-148.

Coulter, P., Clarke, S., Draper, L., & Scamman, C. (2005). [Survey of current information literacy practice in academic libraries]. Unpublished raw data.

Dickey, M. D. (2004). The impact of Web-logs (blogs) on student perceptions of isolation and alienation in a Web-based distance-learning environment. *Open Learning, 19*, 279-291.

Downes, S. (2004). Educational blogging. *Educause Review, 39*, 14-26. Retrieved on December 6, 2005, from http://www.educause.edu/ir/library/pdf/erm0450.pdf.

Fichter, D. (2003). Why and how to use blogs to promote your library's services. *Information Today*, 17. Retrieved December 6, 2005, from http://www.infotoday.com/mls/nov03/fichter.shtml.

Harder, G., & Reichardt, R. (2003). Throw another blog on the wire: Libraries and the Weblogging phenomena. *Feliciter, 49*, 85-88.

Honkimäki, S., Tynjälä, P., & Valkonen, S. (2004). University students' study orientations, learning experiences and study success in innovative courses. *Studies in Higher Education, 29*, 431-449.

Huffaker, D. (2004). The educated blogger: Using Weblogs to promote literacy in the classroom. *First Monday*, 9. Retrieved December 6, 2005, from http://www.firstmonday.org/issues/issue9_6/huffaker/.

Kenney, B., & Stephens, M. (2005). Talkin' blogs. *Library Journal, 16*, 38-41.

Kessler, P. D., & Lund, C. H. (2004). Reflective journaling: Developing an online journal for distance education. *Nurse Educator, 29*, 20-24.

Masui, C., & De Corte, E. (2005). Learning to reflect and to attribute constructively as basic components of self-regulated learning. *British Journal of Educational Psychology, 75*, 531-372.

Oatman, E. (2005). Blogomania! *School Library Journal, 51*, 36-39.

Oravec, J. A. (2002). Bookmarking the world: Weblog applications in education. *Journal of Adolescent & Adult Literacy, 45*, 616-621.

Pew Internet & American Life Project (2005, January). *The state of blogging*. Retrieved December 6, 2005, from http://www.pewinternet.org/pdfs/PIP_blogging_data.pdf.

Poling, C. (2005). Blog on: Building communication and collaboration among staff and students. *Learning and Leading with Technology, 32*, 12-15.

Ross Embrey, T. (2002). You blog, we blog: A guide to how teacher-librarians can use Weblogs to build communication and research skills. *Teacher Librarian, 30*, 7-9.

U.S. Department of Education, National Center for Education Statistics, Higher Education General Information Survey (HEGIS). (2005). *Table 173: Total fall enrollment in degree-granting institutions, by attendance status, age, and sex: selected years, 1970 to 2014*. Retrieved on December 6, 2005, from http://nces.ed.gov/programs/digest/d04/tables/dt04_173.asp.

Vogel, T. M., & Goans, D. (2005). Delivering the news with blogs: The Georgia State University Library experience. *Internet Reference Services Quarterly, 10*, 5-27.

doi:10.1300/J111v45n01_06

APPENDIX

Questions and responses of the surveys administered to students for whom blogs were created in the spring and fall of 2005. Complete responses are supplied for the spring semester; fall responses are summarized in the results section. Comments are copied verbatim.

1. What class were you in?*

2. Do you blog (have your own blog, or read those of others)?

response	
yes	15.4% (4)
no	84.6% (22)

3. Which best describes how often you checked your class' research blog?

response	
never	73.1% (19)
once	15.4% (4)
a few times	3.8% (1)
several times	7.7% (2)
a lot	0% (0)

4. How many questions/comments did you post to the research blog?

response	
none	100% (26)
one	0% (0)
a few	0% (0)
several	0% (0)
a lot	0% (0)

5. On a scale of 1 to 10, how useful was the research blog to you this semester? Choose only one number, but feel free to leave comments.

response	
1 (not helpful)	46.2% (12)
2	3.8% (1)
3	3.8% (1)
4	0% (0)
5 (somewhat helpful)	7.7% (2)
6	3.8% (1)
7	3.8% (1)
8	3.8% (1)
9	0% (0)
10 (very helpful)	7.7% (2)

Comments: 61.5% (16)
1. didnt ever use it so i can really say
2. i didnt know about it!
3. I did not find out about it until late in the semester.
4. it helped me gain knowledge of certain topics
5. honestly, I have no idea what a blog is! I'm sure it would be helpful, but I just don't have a clue.
6. I don't know I never used it.
7. This is a good idea. It would work best for large classes that meet infrequently, which does not describe us (and great for online classes). However, I think this is a great idea and I plan to use it more in the future
8. No experience to rate
9. It was helpful but I only used it for one thing . . . but for that one thing it was very helpful
10. Blogs are useful I forgot to use it though
11. i never used the blog, but as i looked over it for this survey it looked like it would be very helpful
12. I am not sure what a blog is.
13. I feel I can not comment on this question because I have never used a blog and really don't even understand what it is.
14. I do not feel that should grade the blog since I never participated in the use of them.
15. But, I never used it and I am sure that it is very helpful if you do use it.
16. I'm sure it would have been helpful if I'd remembered it was there and checked it!

APPENDIX (continued)

6. What did you like about the research blog? Check all that apply.

response	
information/answers given by librarian	34.6% (9)
questions/answers/comments given by classmates	23.1% (6)
online	34.6% (9)
informal	23.1% (6)
ability to post anonymously	23.1% (6)
nothing	26.9% (7)

Other/Comments: 26.9% (7)

1. i didnt know about it!
2. I generally go straight to the research indexes.
3. What is this blog thing? I don't guess I heard about it.
4. I like this option in spite of having not used it.
5. didn't use the blog
6. I still feel I can not comment.
7. Never used them

7. What DIDN'T you like about the research blog? Check all that apply.

response	
information/answers given by librarian	3.8% (1)
questions/answers/comments given by classmates	3.8% (1)
online	0% (0)
informal	0% (0)
ability to post anonymously	0% (0)
nothing	76.9% (20)

Other/Comments: 19.2% (5)

1. Don't know too much about blogging.
2. not sure because I didn't use it enough
3. Unknown
4. didn't use the blog
5. Once again, I did not use them.

8. Any comments about blogs (this one, or blogs in general)? Any suggestions? (Anything goes!)

Comments: 84.6% (22)
1. nope. i never used it so i cant say
2. Somehow publicize this blog more. If I had remembered it existed I might have used it.
3. i had no idea it was here, if i knew about it i would have been able to use it!
4. More advertisement would probably be more helpful.
5. Not really they just dont help that much to me
6. I would need to use the blogs more to be able to answer this question.
7. I think you should spread the word more!
8. Again. . . I don't know what a blog is. Sorry!
9. I do not know what a blog is and have not heard of the one that you are speaking of
10. The blog is a good idea that needs to catch on better.
11. I guess I missed the whole blog thing. I don't have a clue what it is. I do know that I had a hard time finding research articles on calli.
12. Again, great idea and I plan to use it more in the future
13. i did not know much about it, but i thought it was cool.
14. Students should be more informed of this tool and its funtionality. It should be course related information.
15. I was very helpful.
16. No comments
17. Thanks for the help at the beginning of the semester! I learned a lot
18. just emphasize more in the intro held in the library how helpful this site could be :)
19. All I know about blogs is what I have heard on the news that they are online type journals that people keep. I guess I was unaware that one was available to us, or maybe I just forgot.
20. It's all good.
21. Sorry I was unable to use this blog. I'm sure it would have been helpful in some way.
22. none
23. No comments
24. No comments
25. I haven't begun to use the Blog system yet.
26: I think blogs can be nifty tools if used appropriately.

*In the Fall of 2005, an additional question was added to the beginning of the survey: How old are you? See results and discussion.

E-mail Reference
in a Distributed Learning Environment:
Best Practices, User Satisfaction,
and the Reference Services Continuum

Rosie Croft
Naomi Eichenlaub

Royal Roads University

SUMMARY. Royal Roads University (RRU) Library uses e-mail reference as its primary point of contact for reference services. Learners working off-site are encouraged to request reference help at a central e-mail address which routes questions to librarians. Questions are monitored cooperatively and answered via an informal protocol. RRU prides itself on excellent client service and the librarians endeavor to be responsive and helpful. Recent staff turnover and a need to orient new librarians led to the development of a set of best practices for e-mail reference. This paper examines the role of e-mail reference in the continuum of digital reference services and discusses best practices together with staff training and development issues that are particular to the conduct of e-mail reference in a distributed learning environment. To measure the success of this model, learners were surveyed for their satisfaction with responses to questions and for their preferred mode of contact. doi:10.1300/J111v45n01_07

[Haworth co-indexing entry note]: "E-mail Reference in a Distributed Learning Environment: Best Practices, User Satisfaction, and the Reference Services Continuum." Croft, Rosie, and Naomi Eichenlaub. Co-published simultaneously in *Journal of Library Administration* (The Haworth Information Press, an imprint of The Haworth Press, Inc.) Vol. 45, No. 1/2, 2006, pp. 117-147; and: *The Twelfth Off-Campus Library Services Conference Proceedings* (ed: Julie A. Garrison) The Haworth Information Press, an imprint of The Haworth Press, Inc., 2006, pp. 117-147.

Available online at http://jla.haworthpress.com
doi:10.1300/J111v45n01_07

KEYWORDS. E-mail reference, reference services, digital reference, best practices, distance librarianship, user satisfaction

INTRODUCTION

Royal Roads University (RRU) Library has been developing collections and services for distance learners since shortly after the university's inception in 1995. A small university with a learner base of approximately 2000 full-time students, RRU has a mandate to provide applied professional online degree programs. Most programs offered currently are at the graduate level and are delivered using a distributed learning model which combines on-campus residencies of two to four weeks with online distance courses. As a consequence, the development of a suite of online collections and services has been central to the mission of the library.

The library's e-mail reference service is integral to the support of RRU distributed learners. Moreover, many learners use the e-mail reference service as their first point of contact with the library. Over time, librarians have developed a set of best practices in order to ensure that e-mail reference services maintain a consistently high level of quality. Anecdotal feedback from learners in the form of thank-you responses suggests that they are satisfied with the help they receive via the library's e-mail reference service. However, in order to validate this informal feedback and to ensure that the library is meeting learners' research needs, the authors developed a survey to measure satisfaction with the library's e-mail reference service. The survey also investigated learner satisfaction with e-mail versus other modes of contact for assistance with their research.

LITERATURE REVIEW

E-mail reference has become a standard service offering within the academic library setting, and as Moyo wrote, "emphasis in a typical modern academic library is increasingly shifting to electronic access to resources and services in support of e-learning" (2004, p. 222). Even as early as 1998, the vast majority (91%) of universities with a distance library contact used e-mail in reference services (Casey, 2004), and RRU was no exception. Though many articles cite some decline in reference transactions in libraries generally (for example, Fritch & Mandernack,

2001; Jackson, 2002; Ury & Johnson, 2003), statistics on reference questions in academic libraries seem to have remained stable (Jackson). Some academic libraries, like RRU, have had an increase in the number of e-mail reference inquiries (Lee, 2004). Furthermore, learners' need for reference help is not diminished by new technologies, but rather is enhanced by it:

> Electronic resources have generated an even greater reference and instruction need. First, to help library users understand the individual information resources available to them, and help them select the appropriate database to search based on the subject content and scope of the database. Second, to help users learn and apply the techniques of searching that will yield the best results. (Moyo, p. 224)

The types of questions asked via e-mail reference are very similar to those asked via other contact methods, regardless of whether the service was intended to serve the full gamut of question types or not (Diamond & Pease, 2001; Garnsey & Powell, 2000). Indeed, as resources migrate increasingly to online formats, questions about access are becoming as important as guiding learners to the appropriate resources:

> The ramifications of this technology is that today's energetic librarian not only needs to know how to go about finding and supplying answers, how to explain the use of a full-text journal database, and how to translate the sometimes intricate processes of electronic reserves, she must also know something about trouble-shooting various technical aspects of access. (Backhus & Summey, 2003, p. 197)

E-mail has certain advantages over other contact methods for both the user and the librarian. It "provides a way for shy people, and those inhibited by the library setting, to be a part of the reference process" and also allows the librarian more time to reflect on the question and find sources without the pressure of waiting users (Straw, 2000, p. 377). E-mail also allows questions to be routed easily to librarians with subject expertise (Garnsey & Powell, 2000). The e-mail response also serves as a tailored pathfinder to which a learner can refer back at a later date. Links to tutorials and help guides can be included in e-mail reference responses, thereby enriching the content and increasing the instructional value of the transactions. There is also the consideration of non-native speakers who may be more fluent in writing than speaking and therefore may be more comfortable with e-mail reference (Moeller, 2003). Furthermore, e-mail alleviates some of the telephone tag that plagues phone reference (Philip, 1997; Spinks, Wells, & Meche, 1999). E-mail also allows learners to ask questions as they arise rather than wait for a time when a librarian is available (Garnsey & Powell; Stacey-Bates, 2003).

How a patron should be encouraged to ask a question is a matter of debate. There is much mention in the literature for the need for a reference form, some even consider it critical (Abels, 1996; Kratzert, Richey, & Wassman, 2001; McClennen & Memmott, 2001). A reference form can gather contact and demographic information that may be helpful in answering the question. However, while a form may prompt learners to ask their questions "succinctly" (Casey, 2004), it also creates "a barrier for users who must answer a series of questions in order to even ask their own question" (Diamond & Pease, 2001, p. 216). In general, in an age when the Internet is most often the first stop for researchers, reference questions may be more sophisticated (because "users only come to the reference librarian after first trying Internet sites and coming up short" (Jackson, 2002, p. 309). The study of question types in academic libraries by Diamond and Pease also indicates this increased sophistication.

Whether e-mail is an appropriate or even adequate communication method for complex reference questions has been debated in the literature. Many articles point to the lack of "non-verbal cues" that some deem essential indicators of the progress of a reference interview (Abels, 1996; Fritch & Mandernack, 2001; Garnsey & Powell, 2000; Ladenson, 2003; Straw, 2000), as well as the inherently time-consuming back and forth that has also been touted as an inevitable component of an e-mail reference interview (Abels; Backhus & Summey, 2003; Coffman, 2001; Moyo, 2004; Straw). However, there is controversy in the literature as to whether or not the reference interview is essential even in person (Bidwell, 2003; Lee, 2004), and certainly there is no certainty that librarians better serve patrons in person than they do online (Bidwell).

Responses to e-mail reference questions may skip the reference interview process by and large. Abels (1996) was the first to characterize approaches to e-mail reference, which she listed as the following: piecemeal, feedback, bombardment, assumption, and systematic. Her study found that the "systematic" approach of sending back numbered questions as an online interview technique was the most successful. It may be useful to consider that Abels' study was done in an era when the librarian frequently was doing searches on behalf of the learner and sending results, rather than pointing learners toward resources that they also might access. Other authors have endorsed a combination of the "assumption" and "feedback" approaches, where librarians respond to e-mail reference questions by making assumptions about what users need, providing information based on those assumptions, and inviting them to ask further questions if those assumptions are incorrect, thus not forcing users into time-consuming e-mail interviews (Diamond & Pease, 2001). Lederer (2001) also preferred to "reply with some kind of answer."

A certain amount of intuition is required to interpret e-mail reference queries, and on this subject, the Rosenfeld Library specified that "the research strategy is often an interpretation of what is requested in light of available information–the librarian's best judgment" (Gomez Borah, 2000, para. 6). The reference interview is described by Lee (2004) as "both crucial and unnecessary. Not at the same time, but with different students who have different needs and different questions" (para. 48). The need for a back and forth interview via e-mail has been discounted in another recent study, where the number of e-mail questions that led to further questions to clarify any part of the initial question was 4% (Moeller, 2003). The Rosenfeld Library stated in their best practices document that "re-emails for clarification are almost never necessary; responses to our answers are usually 'thank-you's' or new questions, spurred by the successful handling of the first inquiry" (Gomez Borah, para. 6).

A complicating factor for e-mail reference service at some universities is the nature of the clientele. Many university libraries serve members of the public via e-mail reference–whether it is their policy to do so or not–as well as their own university community (Stacey-Bates, 2003). Not knowing who or where the user is can complicate answering e-mail reference questions in an academic library (Moeller, 2003). Lederer (2001) noted that care must be taken when handling non-affiliate questions if it is not a library's policy to serve them: the unaffiliated person who asks a question has the potential to be affiliated in the future or may pay for the tuition of someone who is an affiliate. Some services have created a separate role of "filterer" which assures that the questions that are answered are from those who are eligible for the service. This function is often separate from the role of answering because it "often involves subtle questions of policy" and is better left to more experienced staff members (McClennen & Memmott, 2001, p. 146).

Studies of user satisfaction with e-mail reference in academic environments suggest that users prefer e-mail over other contact methods (Moeller, 2003; Lee, 2004). E-mail reference has been a standard service in academic libraries for some years. Chat reference, by comparison, is a relatively new service that is getting much attention and has eclipsed the intense investigation given to e-mail reference in the late 1990s and early part of this century. Chat is seen as advantageous because it promises "instant gratification" to the user, and this is seen to put it on par with similar services in the commercial sector (Moyo, 2004). To further meet a perceived immediacy in the needs of users, chat reference services that offer 24/7 coverage are also considered to be a goal to work toward by some librarians. Others question the validity of that need and the cost of trying to meet it (Moyo, 2004; Jackson, 2002; Lederer, 2001). Furthermore, there is some question as to whether or not chat really saves the time of the user over e-mail (Taher, 2002; Lee, 2004). Lee's direct comparison of e-mail versus chat reference service at two Australian university libraries revealed that:

> If the content of these communications (as measured by number of words) is an indication then it probably involves more of the student's time using chat than e-mail. The amount of text alone in a student's e-mail is half that of a chat message. This does not even take into account the time spent waiting for a reply to (on average) 19 turns. (para. 63)

Lee added that in a rather large number of chat sessions the user just "disappears," but went on to note that the screen-sharing option that is often part of chat services can be "worth a thousand words."

So where does e-mail fit within the continuum of reference services? E-mail reference is not mutually exclusive from other methods of reference contact: e-mails can turn into phone calls, or in-person interviews or phone reference can turn into e-mail, etc. Indeed, these are not the only interdependencies that define the success of e-mail reference or reference services generally:

> Inadequacies in, or lack of, any of its components threaten this intricate mutual dependence. The most exalted reference skills cannot make up for seriously inadequate collections. Lack of sympathy toward the library user can make even the most knowledgeable reference librarian ineffective, even when the collections are adequate. Knowing the reference collections well is important to good refer-

ence work, but so is an intimate knowledge of wider collections. If we can use technology and electronic collections to enhance this complex structure, so much the better. (Gorman, 2001, p. 171)

Good reference service is critical for the overall success of the library and in so far as e-mail reference is an element of this critical service "the issue of approachability is just as important in the electronic environment as it is at the traditional reference desk. The perception of accessibility sets the tone of the user's entire encounter with the library" (Straw, 2000, p. 377).

A service standard is critical to reference service (Bidwell, 2003). A number of documents defining best practices for digital reference services have emerged over the last few years providing guidelines specific to e-mail reference services (Gomez Borah, 2000; IFLA, 2005; IPL, 2005b; Roesner, 2005; VRD, 2005a). The Internet Public Library's (IPL) "Ask A Question" service offers free e-mail reference to anyone around the globe. "[A]n educational initiative designed to provide students and professionals in the library and information science (LIS) profession a place to explore and learn about the practice of librarianship in the digital age" (2005a, para. 1), the IPL aims to provide "a consistently high quality in answers to reference questions" (2005b, p. 1).

Regarding the components of an e-mail reference reply, the IPL prescribes six elements as mandatory for inclusion in an IPL e-mail reference reply: salutation, acknowledgement of the question, answer, citations for sources provided, path(s) to show how the resources or answers were located, and some type of closing statement (2005b). The IFLA digital reference guidelines recommend similar e-mail components, including a heading (which should contain a greeting and a "notice of thanks for using the service"), body, and signature (2005, sect. 2.2). The VRD, a network of "internet-based question-and-answer services" (2005b, para. 2) outlines basic best practices for the e-mail reference transaction, including greeting the questioner, suggesting a variety of resources, providing a path to these resources, and ensuring clarity by including generous amounts of white space in e-mail responses (2005a).

IFLA guidelines also specify that digital reference services should "promote information literacy by providing patrons with information on how [the librarian] found an answer to their question" (2005, sect. 2.2). The UCLA Rosenfeld Library includes a similar emphasis on the opportunities for information literacy afforded by e-mail reference in their best practices document, indicating that they provide "search command syntax with every database recommendation" (Gomez Borah, 2000, para. 8). This document also highlights the importance of pre-testing database and catalog searches before prescribing them to patrons (Gomez Borah). Many academic libraries that serve primarily distance learners must also "keep cultural nuances in mind when sending e-mail abroad or to persons in this country who may be from another cultural background" (Spinks et al., 1999, p. 150), and these too should be noted in best practices.

Quality control for e-mail reference services is highlighted by The Alberta Library (TAL), which operates a consortial Web-based e-mail reference service for participating members. Regarding quality control and evaluation of e-mail reference services, TAL states that "the quality of [their Ask A Question] service is essential to ensure its success" and that "monitoring of responses is essential to maintain the high quality of the service" (Roesner, 2005, p. 3). Responses are monitored by coordinators and the TAL checklist document includes an evaluation form that serves as "a tool for coordinators and staff to use as a guideline for quality control" (Roesner, p. 9). Eight points on the form, each with a ranking of 1 to 5, evaluate the response in terms of quality, accuracy, audience, focus, depth, courtesy, clarity, and objectivity. The checklist document includes nine points to review before sending an answer to a patron, including reviewing for spelling and grammatical errors, URL formatting, using clear, jargon-free language, verifying the visual appeal of the answer, ensuring the tone is receptive and cordial, focusing the answer to the question, providing a sufficient level of detail that matches the question, and ensuring that presentation, style, and language are appropriate to the request (Roesner). When taken together, these elements of excellence can help to mold the individual e-mail reference transaction into what all reference transactions can ideally be: "[A] reference query can be seen either as a closed loop (a question asked, a question answered, and no more) or as a knock on a door. Opening the door may lead to a lifetime of learning" (Gorman, 2001, p. 178).

E-MAIL REFERENCE AT ROYAL ROADS UNIVERSITY

From an initial staff of one librarian, RRU now has grown to include five full-time and three part-time librarians. By the time the librarian staff had increased to a complement of two, RRU Library had established a general e-mail address–reflib@royalroads.ca–to divert incoming e-mail to the inboxes of all librarians. This paralleled a similar general e-mail address for computer support offered by the university. RRU librarians strongly encourage patrons to send e-mail reference questions to the "reflib" address (in instruction, on handouts and business cards, on the Web site), and reinforce this message by sending responses from this address.

Client service has high priority at RRU Library, and reference is currently available for almost all library open hours, with a mandated question turnaround time of 24 hours or less. RRU librarians do not take set shifts for reference coverage; while some librarians are designated to answer the bulk of the reference questions that are received in any format, all librarians help with reference based on their availability, volume of questions, and to some degree subject matter of questions. The reflib@royalroads.ca address is also copied on all replies so that all librarians may view and add to reference responses as appropriate. While this approach can present workload challenges, it encourages a continuous and collegial learning environment among librarians, as well as continuity for patrons in extended interactions and the enhanced quality of responses. Furthermore, the emphasis on e-mail reference has led not only to the development of a set of best practices, but also to the inclusion of a mock e-mail reference question in the interview process for librarian hires. While this innovation has met with limited success to date, the hiring committee continues to refine this element, hoping to accurately elicit the related competencies of applicants.

The bulk of reference transactions at RRU are conducted by e-mail. The percentages of reference questions that have been received in the past three years via e-mail can be broken down according to the data in Table 1.

Based on data collected over the past three years, reference librarians respond to an average of 139 questions per month, including e-mail, telephone, and in-person queries, where in-person measures include both walk-in questions and scheduled appointments. While e-mail is therefore the primary point of contact for reference services, it is frequently used in tandem with a phone call to walk a learner through a process, or as a follow-up to an in-person query.

RRU librarians are fortunate to have the opportunity to conduct formal classroom instructional sessions with almost all learners at least once during the course of their programs. This provides learners with an introduction to the resources, and offers librarians the opportunity to

TABLE 1. Percentage of Reference Inquiries by Method of Contact

	2002	2003	2004
E-mail	68.6%	58%	72.8%
Telephone	13.2%	18.2%	12.5%
In person	18.2%	23.8%	14.7%

meet the learners and convey a personable, knowledgeable, and approachable image of librarians for learners to take into their distance learning environment. Learners are encouraged to ask ready reference or indepth questions.

The RRU campus is situated in an outlying suburb of a major Canadian city, and even within that suburb it is in an isolated spot. There is a public library branch close by that is more accessible than the RRU Library. This results in low use of the RRU library by the public, and given that RRU Library's highest priority is its university community, the few e-mail reference questions from the public are generally deflected politely to the local public library and to free online services. RRU Library is also very fortunate to have technological infrastructure; a simple e-mail directory lookup, that almost always allows librarians to discern not only whether incoming e-mail is from a member of the university community, but also with what program that person is affiliated. Consequently, questions that may need special handling by a senior librarian may be filtered with relative ease, and librarians may concentrate on their primary customer base. RRU therefore does not require that an online form be filled out for the purpose of gathering demographic information about the user.

Furthermore, though e-mail reference request forms are often used elsewhere to encourage users to refine their questions, this has not been necessary at RRU. It rarely happens that a learner sends a question which leaves the librarian with no choice but to return a set of questions. In most cases the e-mail query has been well thought out and developed, regardless of whether it is a search for a known item or a request on how to get started researching a topic. Generally, librarians are able to provide learners with a level of response to get them started in their research, inviting them to contact the library again if they require further information, greater level of detail, clarification, etc. The majority of responses received include positive feedback and to a lesser extent, new questions.

E-MAIL REFERENCE BEST PRACTICES

Best practices for e-mail reference transactions at RRU Library (see Appendix A) were identified and documented during the summer of 2004 in response to a need to orient new reference librarians. Previously, reference inquiries were fielded by a team of two to three librarians. As such, it was fairly easy to ensure that responses were consistent in terms of quality, courtesy, clarity, and resources suggested. When the number of librarians employed at RRU doubled within 1.5 years, accompanied by some staff turnover, a reference lead was appointed to coordinate the reference function and to provide training and coaching to new reference librarians. The reference lead developed a set of best practices to ensure consistency in the responses to questions answered through "reflib." Quality and consistency in reference responses is especially important in a distributed environment where the library in general, and librarians in particular, are characterized by the quality of responses sent from the reference librarian e-mail address.

The RRU e-mail reference best practices document was originally modeled on a version of the Virtual Reference Desk training manual for VRD network information specialists. The VRD document was designed and developed to train volunteers answering reference questions for K-12 students via the Virtual Reference Desk Network (now the Digital Reference Education Initiative (DREI)). The RRU e-mail reference best practices document was tailored to a predominantly graduate-level post-secondary environment and enriched with home grown best practices, lessons learned, challenges specific to providing reference in the RRU environment, and existing service strengths.

The best practices document is useful not only for teaching new reference librarians but also as a consultative tool for practicing reference librarians. In the collaborative and shared reference environment of RRU Library where reference librarians see all incoming reference queries as well as all outgoing replies, the best practices document reinforces excellence in e-mail reference services and reminds librarians of the importance of modeling quality responses. This collaborative reference environment also fosters ongoing professional development, promoting a continuous learning environment where librarians learn from each other's replies, for example, learning about resources that one librarian might have suggested or overlooked. Finally, completed transactions are filed and saved for future reference, providing a searchable archive of past questions and a resource for future research questions on similar topics. This archive can also be very useful for reference training purposes as well as development of best practices.

SURVEY METHODOLOGY

The authors developed a survey (see Appendix B) to send out to the RRU learner base in order to measure satisfaction with the e-mail format for sending research inquiries and receiving responses. The survey consisted of sixteen short questions which asked learners to indicate their levels of satisfaction with the answer(s) to their question(s), the general helpfulness of the reply, and the speed of the reply. The survey also polled learners on the hours that they would be most likely to request research assistance, their first and second choices of methods for requesting assistance, and the amount of time that they consider reasonable to receive a reply. In order to determine the suitability of e-mail reference to promote information literacy, learners were also asked if they felt more confident in their ability to use the library's resources as a result of the e-mail reply they received. Finally, learners were given the opportunity to comment on how the e-mail response they received to their question and library services in general could be improved.

Learners were sent a separate, follow-up form e-mail (see Appendix C) with a link to the survey in response to each e-mail inquiry to the reflib@royalroads.ca e-mail address during the three month period of September 1 to November 30, 2005. The survey link was sent at the end of each question transaction, where a transaction was defined as any number of e-mail exchanges required to answer a particular question. One transaction could therefore include a series of questions on a similar topic. For the most part, the survey was sent out at the end of the transaction, though sometimes it was difficult to predict if a learner would reply with additional questions, and whether this would become a new transaction. As the research was meant to focus on learners who contacted the library for research help via the reference librarian e-mail address, learners who sent inquiries via phone, in person, or via a Web form available on the library Web site did not receive a survey, nor did university staff, alumni, and members of the public who asked questions during this period. Repeat patrons who contacted the library multiple times during the three month period received the form e-mail invitation to complete the survey following each transaction. E-mail inquiries that were directional in nature, for example, referrals to other library services such as circulation, were also excluded from receiving the survey, as were learners who received e-mails sent by librarians to follow up on phone calls or in-person questions.

SURVEY RESULTS

In total, 178 surveys were sent out with 67 responses received for a response rate of 37.6%. The vast majority of the respondents–88%– were graduate degree learners. The representation of graduate learners by program was proportionally consistent with the relative size of each of the programs. The other 12% of respondents were an even mix of undergraduate learners and learners in graduate certificate or diploma programs. Although RRU has fewer undergraduate than graduate learners, the number of survey respondents was even lower than would reflect the actual relative proportions. On examination of the e-mail reference inquiries to which surveys were sent, it became apparent that there were simply few undergraduates contacting reflib@royalroads.ca by e-mail.

While the librarians hoped for a good level of learner satisfaction with reference services, the results exceeded those hopes. In rating their satisfaction with the answers to their questions, 81% were "very satisfied" and 19% were satisfied. No respondents were dissatisfied or very dissatisfied. Similarly, when rating the level of helpfulness of the reply, 91% chose "excellent" and 9% chose "good." None responded "fair" or "poor." High satisfaction levels also extended to the speed of reply to the reference question, with 94% "very satisfied" and 6% "satisfied," with no respondents "dissatisfied" or "very dissatisfied." Of perhaps greatest reward to RRU librarians were learner responses to "Do you feel more confident in your ability to use our library's resources as a result of our e-mail reply to you?" with 92% saying yes, and 8% saying no. Moreover, satisfaction did not appear to be influenced by whether the question was a first time use of reflib@royalroads.ca or not: 48% had not used the service before, 51% were repeat customers, and 1% could not remember.

In addition to the satisfaction expressed with the content and speed of the replies, learners also indicated satisfaction with the method of communication: 75% of learners were "very satisfied" with e-mail as a contact method and 25% were satisfied, with no "dissatisfied" or "very dissatisfied" users. The results when asked to rate preferred methods of contact from a list of five choices are shown in Figures 1 and 2.

Some demographic information from the respondents was collected. To an extent reflective of RRU graduate learners overall, 68% of re-

FIGURE 1. Method of Contact, First Choice

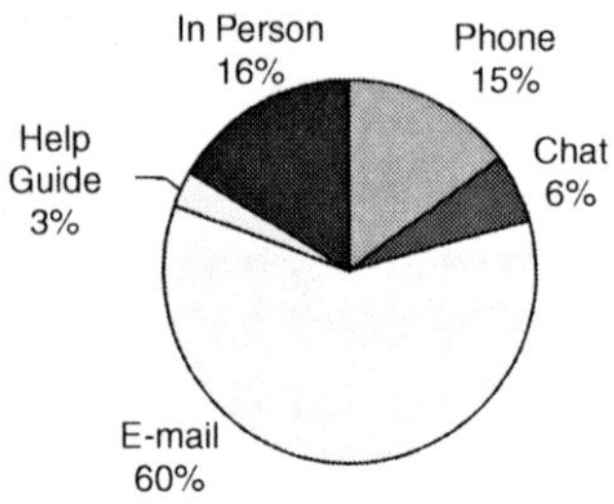

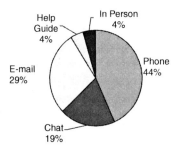

FIGURE 2. Method of Contact, Second Choice

spondents were women and 32% of respondents were men. Given the predominantly mid-career demographic of graduate learners at RRU and the low level of response from the undergraduate population, the respondent age groups were cross-tabulated against the contact method of first choice to see if there were correlations with certain contact methods and age. Figures 3-5 show the most preferred method of contact by age.

Learners were asked to comment on contact method options. While most comments preferred e-mail reference, four respondents noted that free phone contact would be helpful (RRU does not currently have such a service, though librarians will call learners back or initiate a call based upon an e-mail request so that the university covers the cost of the call). Three learners also commented in support of chat, and two thought an FAQ page might be helpful (RRU Library has a link to such a page already).

RRU Library also asked questions regarding hours of access and response time. Most learners were likely to require assistance be-

FIGURE 3. Method of Contact, First Choice, Age Group 18-35

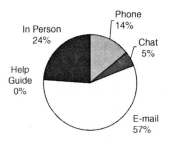

FIGURE 4. Method of Contact, First Choice, Age Group 36-49

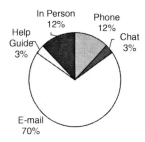

FIGURE 5. Method of Contact, First Choice, Age Group 50+

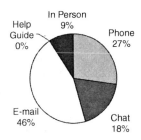

tween 6 p.m.-10 p.m. PT (54%), followed by 8 a.m.-6 p.m. PT (31%), and only 15% noted either 10 p.m.-5 a.m. PT or 5 a.m. to 8 a.m. PT as a likely time to need help. Reference service is officially available seven days a week for at least eight hours a day. Coverage is sometimes more or less available than this given the availability of staff. The library tries to ensure that e-mail reference questions are answered within 24 hours. When asked about expectations regarding question turnaround time, 7% of learners responded that less than one hour was a reasonable response time, followed by 29% with an upper limit of 12 hours or less, 48% for 24 hours or less, 11% for 48 hours or less, and 5% for 72 hours or less. Again, however, the satisfaction level with speed of the reply for the questions that respondents had most recently asked was 94%.

DISCUSSION

The results of the survey indicated a high degree of satisfaction with e-mail reference service at RRU in all major categories of measure, which would indicate that the best practices and oversight mechanisms that have been developed for the service are working well. The survey results also showed that a majority of RRU learners who are using e-mail prefer it as their first choice for contacting the library. While learners were not asked to explain their reasons for their preferences and did not divulge reasons in commentary, it can be surmised that some or all of the advantages that e-mail has to offer learners in general are true for learners at RRU. It is noteworthy that an online chat service did not figure prominently in the wishes of RRU learners. And, interestingly, preferences for chat did not follow a predictable pattern among age groups. Rather, other synchronous forms of communication–phone calls and visits in person were preferred. As a few learners commented, RRU Library should more clearly outline its reference service parameters on the library Web site so that learners can more easily select from among the service options. It is difficult to assess the preferences for all contact methods given that chat reference is not available for users to evaluate. However, clients are clearly not frustrated with e-mail as a primary option.

Why has the library retained e-mail as the preferred form of online reference assistance over newer technologies such as virtual reference software packages and chat? In 2001, RRU Library began investigating reference tools that could enrich existing reference services provided in-person, over the telephone, and via e-mail. Librarians considered virtual reference software as a means of providing synchronous support for the individual distance learner at the point of need in her/his research process. While there were appealing features offered by such software, including the ability to co-browse with and push Web pages to learners, the advantages offered by e-mail and telephone appeared to outweigh those of the virtual reference software packages that were examined. Furthermore, maintaining chat service hours with a small reference librarian staff and a distributed user population in various time zones remains a challenge that requires more resources than the return on investment of virtual reference software packages would warrant (McFarland & Eichenlaub, in press).

The library has only anecdotal evidence regarding satisfaction with e-mail reference services previous to the implementation of best practices and as such no correlation can be drawn between the implementation of best practices and user satisfaction. However, the level of satisfaction of learners with the answers to their questions (100% very satisfied or satisfied), the helpfulness of the reply received (100% excellent or good), and their increased confidence in using library resources as a result of the reply received (92% yes) could indicate that best practices are contributing to excellence in e-mail reference services at RRU Library.

CONCLUSION

The survey of e-mail reference satisfaction indicated that not only were learners very satisfied with the speed of the reply they received, but they were satisfied with receiving this help via e-mail, and with the quality of the response. Perhaps most important was the finding that a significant majority of learners felt empowered to use the library resources as a result of the reply that they received. While RRU may eventually offer chat reference, perhaps in partnership with other libraries, as part of a complement of reference services, there is currently little apparent demand to assume the cost and staffing requirements that such a service entails. E-mail reference, in the context of rapid response time and effective quality control measures, is an effective tool for providing reference services in a graduate-level distributed learning environment.

REFERENCES

Abels, E. G. (1996). The e-mail reference interview. *RQ, 35*(3), 345-358.

Backhus, S. H., & Summey, T. P. (2003). Collaboration: The key to unlocking the dilemma of distance reference services. *Reference Librarian, 40*(83/84), 193-202.

Bidwell, P. (2003, October). Wrestling with an octopus: Reference quality issues. Paper presented at the LIANZA annual conference: *Oceans of opportunity: Whakawhitihia te moana,* Napier, New Zealand.

Casey, A. M. (2004). A historical overview of Internet reference services for distance learners. *Internet Reference Services Quarterly, 9*(3/4), 5-17.

Coffman, S. (2001). Distance education and virtual reference: Where are we headed? *Computers in Libraries, 21*(4). Retrieved December 10, 2005, from http://www.infotoday.com/cilmag/apr01/coffman.htm.

Diamond, W., & Pease, B. (2001). Digital reference: A case study of question types in an academic library. *Reference Services Review, 29*(3), 210-218.

Fritch, J. W., & Mandernack, S. B. (2001). The emerging reference paradigm: A vision of reference services in a complex information environment. *Library Trends, 50*(2), 286-305.

Garnsey, B. A., & Powell, R. R. (2000). Electronic mail reference services in the public library. *Reference & User Services Quarterly, 39*(3), 245-54.

Gomez Borah, E. (2000). *E-mail reference at UCLA Rosenfeld Library. UC best practices in instruction & reference for digital resources workshop*, Los Angeles: CA, June 23, 2000. Retrieved December 4, 2005, from http://personal.anderson.ucla.edu/virtual.library/EmailRef.htm.

Gorman, M. (2001). Values for human-to-human reference. *Library Trends, 50*(2), 168-182.

International Federation of Library Assocations. (2005). *IFLA digital reference guidelines*. Retrieved November 9, 2005, from http://www.ifla.org/VII/s36/pubs/drg03.htm.

Internet Public Library. (2005a). *IPL educational initiative*. Retrieved December 4, 2005, from http://www.ipl.org/div/about/edinit.html.

Internet Public Library. (2005b). *Policy: Answering IPL reference questions*. Retrieved December 10, 2005, from http://drei.syr.edu/pdf/AnsweringIPLRefQuestions.pdf.

Jackson, M. G. (2002). A rush to serve: Digital reference services and the commitment to 24/7. *Advances in Librarianship, 2*, 299-317.

Kratzert, M., Richey, D., & Wassmann, C. (2001). Tips and snags of academic cyberreference. *College & Undergraduate Libraries, 8*(2), 73-82.

Ladenson, S. (2003). E-mail reference: Improving service by working cooperatively. *Reference Librarian, 40*(83/84), 183-191.

Lederer, N. (2001). E-mail reference: Who, when, where, and what is asked. *Reference Librarian,* (74), 55-73.

Lee, I. J. (2004). Do virtual reference librarians dream of digital reference questions? A qualitative and quantitative analysis of e-mail and chat reference. *Australian Academic and Research Libraries, 35*(2), 95-110.

McClennen, M., & Memmott, P. (2001). Roles in digital reference. *Information Technology and Libraries, 20*(3), 143-148.

McFarland, D., & Eichenlaub, N. (in press). Using virtual classroom software for library instruction. In S. Clayton (Ed.), *Going the distance: Library instruction for distance education students*. New York: Neal-Schuman.

Moeller, S. E. (2003). Ask-A-librarian: An analysis of an e-mail reference service at a large academic library. *Internet Reference Services Quarterly, 8*(3), 47-61.

Moyo, L. M. (2004). Electronic libraries and the emergence of new service paradigms. *Electronic Library, 22*(3), 220-230.

Philip, B. (1997). *"mayihelpyou@theelectronicreferencedesk? An examination of the past, present and future of electronic mail reference service."* Retrieved November 25, 2005, from http://hollyhock.slis.ualberta.ca/598/brenda/emailref.htm.

Roesner, M. (2005). *The Alberta Library virtual reference training materials & checklist.* Retrieved December 4, 2005, from http://drei.syr.edu/pdf/roesner.pdf.

Spinks, N., Wells, B., & Meche, M. (1999). Netiquette: A behavioral guide to electronic business communication. *Corporate Communications: An International Journal, 4*(3), 145-156.

Stacey-Bates, K. (2003). E-mail reference responses from academic ARL libraries: An unobtrusive study. *Reference & User Services Quarterly, 43*(1), 59-70.

Straw, J. E. (2000). A virtual understanding. *Reference & User Services Quarterly, 39*(4), 376-379.

Taher, M. (2002). The reference interview through asynchronous e-mail and synchronous interactive reference: Does it save the time of the interviewee? *Internet Reference Services Quarterly, 7*(3), 23-34.

Ury, C., & Johnson, C. (2003). Reference beyond the walls of the library: Interacting with faculty and students in the 21st century. *Reference Librarian, 40*(83/84), 203-218.

Virtual Reference Desk. (2005a).*VRD volunteer training module for MLS students: DREI training manual 2005.* Retrieved December 4, 2005, from http://eduref.org/~nsdl/QABuilder/Manual2005.pdf.

Virtual Reference Desk. (2005b). *About VRD.* Retrieved December 14, 2005, from http://vrd.org/about.shtml.

doi:10.1300/J111v45n01_07

APPENDIX A

E-mail Reference Best Practices

Royal Roads University Library

Steps to creating a quality e-mail reference response:

1. Greet and sign off
2. Analyze the question
3. Suggest a variety of resources
4. Provide paths to resources
5. Language and tone
    5.1 Questions from international learners
    5.1.1 Questions from Iran MBAs
6. Style and structure
7. Role of instruction
8. How much is enough?
9. Role of canned responses
10. Check for typos!
11. Send from reflib and Cc reflib
12. Reply promptly!
13. Referrals
14. Following up
15. A note regarding citation questions

1. Greet and sign off

Greet learners by name and offer a tone of supportiveness towards their learning and their decision to contact the library for research assistance. Thank them for their e-mail, question, comment, feedback, etc., and make sure to personalize the e-mail response.

Hi Rebecca,

Thanks for your question! It sounds like you are off to a great start.

When it comes time to close the e-mail, always encourage learners to contact the library again if they have any further questions. It is good practice to also always include your signature. It looks professional and it gives people important contact information as well as a 'face' to their e-mail interaction. It is also best practice to end with a formal salutation (Kind regards, etc.). It adds an additional degree of politeness and professionalism to e-mails.

I hope this helps, Rebecca. Please let us know if you have any further questions.

Best regards,

Naomi

Naomi Eichenlaub, MLIS
Librarian
Royal Roads University Library
2005 Sooke Road, Victoria BC, V9B 5Y2
Tel: (250) 391-2600 ext. 4241
naomi.eichenlaub@royalroads.ca
http://library.royalroads.ca

2. Analyze the question

Study the question in order to determine what the learner is looking for. Why did s/he e-mail us? Sometimes it can be a bit difficult to discern what a learner is actually looking for. Be careful not to overwhelm the learner with too many questions though. Try to provide some kind of answer to get him/her started, if only a limited one based on your understanding of the question, and if you need further clarification, follow up with just a few questions at the end. This will both build the learner's confidence in you to be helpful, and give him/her something to get going if s/he is working on a very short timeline.

A great answer considers not only the question asked by the learner, but also the depth of answer that will best serve the learner. Does s/he want a detailed pathfinder for a particular research question or just want a couple of book titles?

Also, if a learner contacted you via e-mail, s/he is probably looking for a response via e-mail. Sometimes it can be prudent to offer to follow up via phone, but remember, this may not work for all patrons. Doing a little of each might be a good compromise. Similarly, a phone call would be expected if that was the initial form of contact, but further follow-up via e-mail may also be warranted. If a phone call is really the only thing that makes sense for an e-mail question, ask to have his/her phone number so the charge is against the university and not the learner.

3. Suggest a variety of resources

Provide recommendations for a balance of sources in a variety of formats. Sure, online articles are a great source of information, but do not forget to suggest other useful resources beyond our online database collections:

APPENDIX A (continued)

Books–still wonderful and useful–let the learners know a couple of useful titles and remind them about our free Doc Del service that includes return postage!

e-books–we have nearly 25,000!

RRU Theses–there could be a past major project perfect for someone's topic. Plus, RRU theses are available online in full text via our Current Research @ Royal Roads database and are also searchable via our library catalogue.

Web Resources–there are some great treasures out there–random full text of journal articles, government reports, etc.

Also, just as we add new electronic collections to our database listings on a regular basis, there are also sources that we use much less frequently than resources such as Ebscohost and Current Research. Take some time to regularly review the great sources we have that we might not use as often as we could.

4. Provide paths to resources

Always provide the path you took to find any resources that you recommend so that learners can replicate both your strategy and your results.

When referring people to the library home page, always provide the URL (http://library.royalroads.ca). If you refer a learner to one of our help guides, provide a direct link to that as well as direction. If you suggest a Web resource, let the learner know what search engine you used and how you found the Web site or document and include the URL.

I would suggest you take a look in Ebscohost. To access our databases, go to the library home page (http://library.royalroads.ca), click on Search for Articles, log in, and scroll down to select the database you wish to search.

5. Language and tone

Many learners approach the library for the first time via e-mail. Be as friendly and encouraging as possible. Make sure to use clear, concise, and coherent language with a professional tone. It is also best to avoid colloquial language and expressions that one would use in conversation but not in writing, such as "stuff," "you know what I mean," etc. It is also a good idea to avoid using library jargon, such as OPAC, "collection gaps," etc.

It is also important to always have a positive tone to your message. We have great resources, both print and electronic, and great service delivery. If someone stumbles across an issue or title that we do not have in full text, for whatever reason, or a book that we do not have in our collection, avoid taking an apologetic tone. Instead, highlight the positive: There is always a useful resource that we can point a learner towards. Similarly, while it might be tempting to sympathize with a learner who is expressing some frustration with their research, we need to frame our support in the most positive light possible:

Our full text access to this journal via ScienceDirect is for the most recent 5 years only. Since your article is a bit older than that, we do not have full text access to it. However, we can get it for you via Interlibrary loan (ILL) for $7.50 / item. Please forward the citation to rruill@royalroads.ca if that option appeals to you. You could also check another library near you to see if they subscribe to this journal in print.

We are also happy to suggest other resources that may be helpful–what is your topic? *Be careful also to try not to appear defensive about costs/fees, for example with ILLs, though that can be difficult at times.*

5.1 Questions from international learners

5.1.1 Questions from Iran MBAs

Special note: With regards to Iran MBA learners and points of cultural formalities, please note the following as being very desirable points to include in our responses:

- Always greet the learner with "Dear. . . ." and if gender is difficult to determine, put in their name as they have sent it. Try not to use "Hi" or even "Hello." Try to use formal letter writing etiquette.
- Your first line should either be "How are you?" and/or "I hope you are well."
- Try very hard not to speak in metaphor or jargon. Remember they are all ESL speakers.
- Always finish with the offer of more help.
- Always finish with "Regards" or "Best regards."

Please feel free to follow up with the International Office for more advice. As much as we can, we would like these learners to feel welcome and comfortable in asking us for our assistance.

6. Style and structure

Your e-mail reply could be full of relevant resources and helpful information, but if it is not clear, all of this helpful information could be lost on the learner.

APPENDIX A (continued)

With e-mail reference it is crucial that information be both written and presented in as clear a manner as possible. Be especially clear and concise when doing e-mail reference as it is easy to be overwhelmed by too much text. Are different ideas represented in separate paragraphs? Put yourself in the learner's shoes. Could you follow the structure, logic and instructions that you provide?

Here are a few more tips:

- Be liberal in the use of white space
- Keep each paragraph to one idea (very short paragraphs)
- Font: use colour and type to highlight, not to show that you copied and pasted something from another e-mail.

7. Role of instruction

As much as possible, the general tone of our e-mail replies should be one of enabling the learner to find information on their own ("teach them how to fish"). Providing step by step instructions for accessing resources, as well as always explaining how you located the information that you did is the best way to accomplish this (see also 4. Provide paths to resources).

Also, during our first reference retreat, we reaffirmed the importance of including links to relevant database help guides and tutorials in replies that we send out. This will also serve to cut down on lengthy instructions as well as to highlight our help guides.

8. How much is enough?

One of the more difficult aspects of e-mail reference can be interpreting how much information someone is seeking. It is best to be as concise as possible. Try to provide enough information to be helpful and informative, without burdening the learner with irrelevant information that clutters up the response. There is a fine balance between providing just enough information and bombarding someone. This is part of the intuitive nature of reference, and especially e-mail reference, which lacks the face-to-face cues of more formal reference interactions. You need to intuit how much information a learner needs to get them started, or to help them out of a hole, and then encourage them to be in contact again when they get to the next stage of their research process.

This should help get you started. We can help you find full text when you get to that stage. Remember too that your suggestions should never be random, always pre-test your recommended keywords and search strategies in the databases you recommend. In some instances, it may be most prudent to provide the learner with search strings to copy and paste into the databases. In other cases, actually attaching documents found might be the best course of action. Again, try to be sensitive to the learner's needs. Ideally, e-mail reference is the same learning opportunity on information discovery that an in person reference interview might be, but this may not always best serve the learner.

9. Role of canned response

Try to avoid the use of canned responses as much as possible. While there are certainly elements of responses that can be recycled, such as instructions for accessing article databases, etc., most questions are unique in nature and deserve a unique response. With regards to standard sets of instructions, for example, how to access the database listings, inasmuch as we start from a similar set of instructions, it's a good idea to modify the reply to suit each unique question and scenario. A word of caution: Be very careful when using past replies to make sure that you have the correct name, journal info, etc.

10. Check for typos!

While mistakes are unavoidable, typos do look sloppy and should be avoided. Using the spellcheck function in Outlook can help. Be especially watchful for errors that will prevent someone from obtaining critical information, such as a typo in an e-mail address (reflib@royalroads.ca) or in the library home page address (http://library.royalroads.ca).

11. Send From reflib and Cc reflib

Our process for handling e-mail reference is to encourage learners to contact us at our central e-mail address (reflib@royalroads.ca). When replying to an e-mail, enter this address into the From field so that you are sending from Reference Librarian. In order to let other librarians know that you have responded to a question, Cc the reflib address as well. This also helps to promote an environment of learning whereby we can all learn from each other's responses.

If someone e-mails you a question directly, please reply from Reflib and let the learner know that in future they should send inquiries to this central address in case one of us is away from a computer and does not see their question.

12. Reply promptly!

Please remember to make replying to e-mails sent to reflib a priority. While we have informally stated that we like to have all e-mails responded to within 24 hours, the reality is that we try and answer questions ASAP. If someone has sent a question on a particular day, they should hear back from us that same day.

APPENDIX A (continued)

If a question comes in late in the day and you do not get a chance to reply, or if the question requires more digging than you anticipated, send an e-mail to the learner acknowledging receipt of the question and let him/her know that we are working on it and will be back in touch. In the case of a complex question, you can also include a few preliminary suggestions to get him/her going and let him/her know that you will be back in touch with more details.

13. Referrals

When someone e-mails with a request that should be referred along to either ILL, Circulation staff, Thesis Office, etc., please reply directly to the learner, from reflib, and Cc the appropriate other party. Avoid forwarding the e-mail directly along without providing the learner with any response from reflib. The learners have gone to the trouble of contacting us so we should acknowledge this and reply back to let them know that we received their e-mail and are forwarding their request along.

- ILL
  Specific to ILL referrals, remember to let the learner know that you are forwarding the request to ILL, and let him/her know in advance that there is a fee of $7.50 / item for this service. If someone is looking for a thesis or dissertation from another university, you might want to let him/her know that the fee will be in excess of our usual $7.50.
- Computer Help Desk
  When a learner e-mails with an access problem, e.g., a login and password that are not working, it is best to do a bit more troubleshooting before forwarding the request on to the Computer Help Desk. For example, we need to first identify whether it is a simple matter of forgetting a password or something else that is our responsibility to fix such as a broken ezproxy link, a database that is down for maintenance or exceeded its user limit, a learner who is trying to access Ebsco from www.ebsco.com instead of going through our Search for Articles, etc.

14. Following up

Sending an e-mail to follow up on inquiries that come in by phone or in person can serve to remind the learner about the information that was mentioned, as well as to provide an opening for further questions and/or future contact.

15. A note regarding citation questions

Fortunately, our job is not to interpret any style manual for our learners. When learners e-mail with questions asking for referencing help, please do not provide detailed citation help beyond letting them know that there is a complete APA manual available to view or borrow in our library and can be purchased at most book stores.

You can also let learners know that "Our role is to guide you to resources that will help you with your citation questions."

For specific questions or help interpreting style, refer the learner back to his/her instructor. Do not, under any circumstances, read the APA manual yourself! Many learners also inquire about citing second and third hand sources (cited somewhere else). We should remind these learners that it is proper research practice not to cite something you have not seen, but to go to the original source and cite that directly.

It can be hard not to answer learner's specific citation questions, but it is best that we not set a precedent in this area.

APPENDIX B

E-mail Reference Services @ Royal Roads University Library Learner Survey

To help improve reference services provided by Royal Roads University Library, we need your help! In particular, please fill out the following survey on the e-mail reference services we offer via reflib@royalroads.ca.

This is a short survey that should only take between 5 and 10 minutes to complete. Your response to this survey will be anonymous. While service improvement is the primary goal of this survey, summary data may be used in a research project.

Thank you very much for helping to improve RRU Library reference services!

---

1. What type of program are you enrolled in?

Graduate certificate
Graduate diploma
Graduate degree
Undergraduate certificate
Undergraduate degree

APPENDIX B (continued)

2. If you are in a **degree** program, please specify which one you are affiliated with.

BCom
BSc
BJus
BAAC
HSP
KM
MAC
MAEEC
MAIIC
MACAM
MADL
MALT
MBA
MEM

3. Was your most recent e-mail the first time that you have used reflib@ royalroads.ca to contact RRU Library for help?

Yes
No
Can't remember

Please answer the following 4 questions based on the reply to your most recent request sent to reflib@royalroads.ca

4. How would you rate your satisfaction with the **answer to your question**(s)?

Very satisfied
Satisfied
Dissatisfied
Very dissatisfied

5. How would you rate the **general helpfulness** of the reply to your question(s)?

Excellent
Good
Fair
Poor

6. How would you rate your satisfaction with the **speed of the reply** that you received?

Very satisfied
Satisfied
Dissatisfied
Very dissatisfied

7. Do you feel more confident in your abililty to use our library's resources as a result of our e-mail reply to you?

Yes
No

8. What hours are you most likely to require research assistance from library staff when you are working away from campus? **Please note these times are Pacific Time. Please check all that apply.**

8AM-6PM
6PM-10PM
10PM-5AM
5AM-8AM
Never

9. How satisfied are you with using e-mail as a contact method for your research assistance inquiries?

Very satisfied
Satisfied
Somewhat satisfied
Dissatisfied
Very dissatisfied

10 a. Of the following methods of contact that you could use, which one would be your first choice for research assistance while off campus?

Talking to a person on the phone
Talking to a person via online chat
Asking your question via e-mail
Using a print or online guide

APPENDIX B (continued)

10 b. Of the following methods of contact that you could use, which one would be your second choice for research assistance while off campus?

Talking to a person on the phone
Talking to a person via online chat
Asking your question via e-mail
Using a print or online guide

11. Are there other methods of contact that you think we should explore? If so, please specify:

12. If you need help finding information and have chosen to ask via e-mail, what do you regard as a reasonable response time for a reply? **Please specify what unit of time you are using (hours, days, etc.)**

13. Do you have any suggestions or comments on how our e-mail response to your question may have been better for you?

14. Do you have any other comments about RRU Library services?

15. This question is optional. Please indicate the age range into which you fall.

16. This question is optional. Please indicate your gender.

Thank you very much!

_____

APPENDIX C

E-mail Reference Services @ Royal Roads University Library
Survey E-mail

Dear XXXXX,

Thank you for your recent research question sent to reflib@royalroads.ca.

We are inviting you to participate in a short anonymous survey on our e-mail reference services here at RRU Library. Please take a few minutes to let us know what you think!

http://www.tinyurl.com/cvefu

If you have already completed our survey, we thank you for your participation and invite you to provide us with feedback by completing this short survey each time you send a question to reflib@royalroads.ca. We will be collecting data via this survey through November.

Thanks very much,

RRU Reference Librarian Team

If you have any questions about this survey, please e-mail rosie.croft@royalroads.ca. Thanks!

Getting Beyond Institutional Cultures:
When Rivals Collaborate

Frances A. Devlin
Nancy J. Burich

University of Kansas

Marcia G. Stockham

Kansas State University

Terri Pedersen Summey

Emporia State University

Elizabeth C. Turtle

Kansas State University

SUMMARY. As library service providers for distance learners, we are constantly searching for ways to improve communication, share our knowledge, and make distance learners aware of our resources. Virtual (real-time chat) reference is yet another tool to utilize in reaching these students. While virtual reference has been around for several years, and is offered by many libraries, the four institutions comprising this service have taken a variety of paths to reach the current stage–a collaboration among academic state university libraries of varying size. This paper discusses collaboration aspects such as differences in institutional cultures,

[Haworth co-indexing entry note]: "Getting Beyond Institutional Cultures: When Rivals Collaborate." Devlin, Frances A. et al. Co-published simultaneously in *Journal of Library Administration* (The Haworth Information Press, an imprint of The Haworth Press, Inc.) Vol. 45, No. 1/2, 2006, pp. 149-168; and: *The Twelfth Off-Campus Library Services Conference Proceedings* (ed: Julie A. Garrison) The Haworth Information Press, an imprint of The Haworth Press, Inc., 2006, pp. 149-168.

Available online at http://jla.haworthpress.com
doi:10.1300/J111v45n01_08

negotiations, planning and implementation, developing policies and best practices, staff training, technology issues, and lessons learned that can be applied to any collaborative project. doi:10.1300/J111v45n01_08

KEYWORDS. Academic libraries, institutional culture, collaboration, virtual reference

INTRODUCTION

The *Oxford English Dictionary* (OED Online) gives the origin of collaborate as "co + labor + ate," and provides the primary definition as "working in conjunction with others, to co-operate." The secondary definition is "cooperating traitorously with the enemy." The original meaning of rival was "a small stream" and it became "one living on the opposite bank of a stream from another." Now the most common meaning is "one who strives to equal or outdo another in any respect."

Collaboration within an institution can be challenging, even when all individuals share a common vision and goal. Imagine how hard it is to collaborate with other institutions whose priorities and goals may be very different. Each grouping of individuals shares a culture, "the shared beliefs, ideologies and ideas which serve as a normative guide for behavior within the group or the organization" (Harmon, 2002, p. 97). In the Kansas Academic Cooperative Chat Service, collaboration goes beyond cooperation and includes agreement on policies, processes, and philosophies to institute a shared service. The cooperative consists of the University of Kansas (KU), Kansas State University (K-State), Emporia State University (ESU), and Wichita State University (WSU). WSU issues are not discussed in detail in this paper since they began offering the service at their institution at the beginning of the fall semester 2005.

Today, budgets are stretched thin and staff size is static or shrinking while the demand for new resources and services increases. Fenner and Fenner (2004) predicted that as the cost of storage for materials increases and storage space diminishes, librarians will show renewed interest in working together. Technology enables librarians to work together in new and creative ways (Murray & Tschernitz, 2004). Fritch and Mandernack (2001) admonished librarians to recognize the value of community and the social context of information in providing reference services. A sense of community needs to be developed and fostered for the success of any collaborative venture. As a result, interesting groups of institutions are working together, even those competing for students, budgets, and athletic victories. The common goal is to maximize the use of institutional resources.

One of the early issues collaborative partners face is building a trusting relationship. In this context, Niehoff and Paul (2001) discussed the "psychological contract." Most of these contracts apply to relations between employees and management in a business context, but it is relevant here to understanding how partnerships work. Because there can be a perceived breach or violation to the contract when either party fails to fulfill their obligations, those expectations must be clearly understood from the beginning. That means that new partners must be introduced to the culture of the partnership or, in this case, of the service. The norms of acceptable behavior as well as the standards and expectations need to be negotiated at the outset.

It is collaboration that is the topic of this paper, focusing on a united operation with common policies and procedures. Each partner institution developed its own ways of providing the cooperative chat service within its own culture to function effectively within the collaborative environment.

LITERATURE REVIEW

The literature that discusses inter-institutional or intra-institutional partnerships in academic libraries is very sparse. Examples of two academic collaborative chat reference services are provided in articles written by Truelson (2004) and Wilson and Keys (2004). Two articles describe using strategic planning or project management techniques to build cooperation between academic libraries and computing centers (Creth, 1993; Favini, 1997). Other articles discuss administrative support and planning for inter-institutional collaboration for electronic collection development (Simpson, 1997), for a statewide newspaper preservation database project (Hayman, 1997), for information literacy (Hope & Peterson, 2002), and for live Web reference training among several libraries (Anonymous, 2004). Stockham, Turtle, and Hansen (2002/2003) and Smith, Race and Ault (2001) discussed issues in developing a statewide system for collaborative reference.

An article by Davidson, Schofield and Stocks (2001) described collaboration between different professional cultures. His article illustrated how different institutional routines and values can generate different agendas, assumptions, and expectations about outcomes that can lead to a variety of issues and dynamics. Simpson (1997) discussed the challenges and consequences of inter-institutional collaboration for collection development.

Relevant literature in business and higher education includes Harmon's article (2002) that described the consequences of merging academic institutions and highlights the importance of the human factor to make new collaborative efforts successful. Kezar and Eckel (2002) provided a discussion of the impact of culture on organizational behavior and the importance of understanding Bergquist's (1992) cultural archetypes that exist within the academy: collegial, managerial, developmental, and negotiating.

COLLABORATION AND DISTANCE LEARNING

Librarians serving distant learners have a long tradition of collaboration. The proceedings of every Off-Campus Library Services Conference highlight instances of institutions working together by sharing information to provide solutions to common problems. These conferences also bring together professionals searching for research partners. In today's world, distance education opportunities are steadily increasing and that is true also in Kansas. Each of the institutions collaborating to provide the chat reference services described here has a strong distance learning program and is committed to providing reference services to these students. K-State, as the land grant institution in the state, has a long tradition of providing courses across the state; ESU has an established library and information management program in several states and is expanding distance learning offerings in several disciplines; and KU offers a growing number of Web-based and Web-enhanced courses.

One of the main reasons that many institutions are interested in providing a virtual reference service is to be able to serve those faculty members, staff members and students at a distance from the institution. The Guidelines for Distance Learning Library Services (ALA, 2004) state that institutions offering distance education courses should have equivalent services for all those affiliated with that institution regardless of location, including reference services that should be offered from the originating institution. Virtual reference using chat technology allows the user and the librarian to interact in the electronic realm, regardless of location.

COLLABORATIVE CHAT IN KANSAS

Academic librarians in Kansas began to think about offering virtual reference services in 2001. Librarians wanted a service beyond e-mail that would serve students remote from the traditional campus setting. K-State piloted their own project to examine the viability of offering chat reference services. As this was one of the largest institutions in the state, the colleges and universities that were the same size or smaller monitored the K-State pilot project with interest to see whether their results might have implications for implementation of chat reference services at other institutions. One of the most important findings was that the service was not sustainable because of the lack of available staff to offer sufficient hours to make it attractive to users (Stockham & Turtle, 2002).

KANAnswer

In 2002, the Kansas Library Network board authorized funding for a statewide virtual reference pilot project. An executive director was named and an eighteen-member task force was convened. The task force was charged with designing and implementing the service that was given the name KANAnswer (http://skyways.lib.ks.us/KSL/KLNB/ KANAnswerWeb/). The intent of the project was to determine whether this type of service could work on a statewide basis using librarians from multiple types of libraries.

The KANAnswer service was launched in January of 2003 and continues today. Throughout the history of the service there have been approximately twenty-five libraries involved in the project and over ninety operators. Usage statistics rose in the first couple of years of the service and then leveled off during the last year. The service has been well received by users as both "quantitative and qualitative data point to a relatively high degree of satisfaction with the service" (Hansen, 2004, Project Goals subsection, item 2). The librarians staffing the service are dedicated and work hard to ensure quality service is provided. Many of the questions received by operators were about legal issues, high school assignments, or fall into the realm of "public library" questions. However, in general, college and university students were not using the KANAnswer service even though several academic institutions participated in staffing the service.

Consequently, academic librarians decided that a service needed to be offered that was geared strictly to students and faculty at academic institutions. If a group could pool funds and staff to provide a common service for its users, limited resources could be used most efficiently. The collaboration between the four academic institutions that resulted has helped to extend service hours for a chat service, in addition to sharing subscription costs for software.

HawkHelp LIVE

As it became clear that KU students were not using the KANAnswer service, the question of how to address their needs was examined. Because of political implications, KU decided to continue to provide operators for the statewide service. However, during the spring semester of 2003, the KU Libraries implemented its own chat reference service to offer online research assistance to students and faculty. The service was limited to KU students, staff and faculty. Although the chat service gradually gained popularity over the first year, its usage was low due to restricted hours of availability. The service was staffed sixteen hours per week during the first semester it was offered. KU continued to further expand its schedule and tried different hours of availability, believing that the success of the service depended on making it accessible and convenient for its users. A year later, the schedule had been increased to thirty-two hours per week. But there were still significant staffing challenges. Library staff already had full work schedules and participation in chat was voluntary. This added responsibility was viewed as one more thing to add to already full plates. So, KU looked for other ways to increase the hours of the chat reference service by finding additional operators. Library staff members from other units (such as branch libraries, access services, and cataloging) were solicited. A group of highly trained peer reference student assistants were also added as operators on a trial basis. The students staffed the service during the early morning, late evening and weekend hours. Initially, this was successful and the use of peer students increased the service hours significantly. However, it was difficult to maintain this staffing pool, as constant specialized training was required and turnover was high. Many students found it difficult to refer specialized questions to more experienced staff members and this was problematic in ensuring high quality service. During this period, discussions were also initiated with K-State librarians to investigate the possibility of setting up a trial cooperative chat service.

KANSAS ACADEMIC COOPERATIVE CHAT SERVICE

Initial talks between KU and K-State started in the fall of 2003, followed by a more formal meeting that included representatives of other interested schools in early 2004. The exploratory talks resulted in an agreement by KU and K-State to conduct a limited pilot project with the provision that other partners could be included at a later date. The purpose of the pilot project was to test the viability of a collaborative academic chat service.

A Memorandum of Understanding (MOU) was drafted to aid in negotiation and also to serve as a model for other Kansas Regents institutions that might be interested in joining the collaboration at a later date. There was a consensus that it was important to have a written document outlining the parameters of the partnership. A sample MOU was identified with a Web search and customized to address the issues of software and technology, staffing/training, budget, project duration and assessment. The final MOU was forwarded to the deans of each institution for signature. Both deans were extremely supportive of the collaborative project and did not hesitate to sign the MOU (see Appendix).

An informal assessment prepared by the K-State coordinators for their administration in December 2004 highlighted the fact that one of the largest benefits from the project was the opportunity to work with librarians at another institution. It gave all the librarian/operators a chance to experience and appreciate the differences and similarities of the two libraries. There were some rough spots along the way (low usage, increased communication problems when working with a large group of operators, problems with the software) but overall the arrangement worked well. Based on the success of that trial collaboration, invitations were extended to other state academic institutions in Kansas.

With this broader interest, a second draft MOU was prepared and circulated to the deans and directors at the five potential partner schools. Institutional cultures resulted in different expectations and comfort levels with the concept of the MOU. Some questioned the language of the document, treating it as a contractual agreement rather than a memorandum of understanding. A few directors could not sign the document without review by legal counsel at their respective institutions and felt that the language and expectations of the document needed to be more precise with more formal structure. Negotiations on the MOU were conducted by e-mail, but it was eventually decided to proceed without the document because it threatened to delay the service with our new partners. ESU and WSU libraries joined the collaborative, known as the

Kansas Academic Cooperative Chat Service in 2005. The service continues today without an MOU, but an informal agreement is understood between schools and works because a level of trust has been established.

Implementation

During the planning stage for the pilot project between KU and K-State, a timeline was developed for implementation that outlined specific steps and target dates for each institution. Guidelines were written for the combined staff to provide parameters for the service. These policies were prepared, keeping in mind the standards for collaborative digital reference services already developed by the Reference and User Services Association (RUSA) of the American Library Association (ALA) and the International Federation of Library Associations and Institutions (IFLA). Other service documentation included strategies for serving each other's students, ways to deal with authentication issues, how to provide assistance using the common databases, and when to make referrals to each institution's subject specialists. As the cooperative service expanded, these guidelines were adapted to include the new partner institutions.

Even though it was decided to use databases common to all institutions to answer questions, the curriculum of each institution resulted in librarians being more comfortable with some databases than others. Consequently, brief guides were prepared for each of the common databases to aid operators in their use. The guides included tips on search strategies, the use of wildcards, the presence of a thesaurus, and other useful features that were not shared by all the databases.

A collaborative Web page was developed to gather service and institutional documentation into a tool to assist operators when chatting with users from other schools (http://www.lib.ku.edu/~public/ReferenceChat/). From this URL, operators could locate institutional Web pages containing local policies, procedures, and links to various collections. An e-mail listserv was also created to facilitate communication between the group of combined operators from all institutions regarding technical or software issues, scheduling, and information updates.

Administrative Responsibilities

KU acts as the lead administrator for the cooperative service and is primary liaison with QuestionPoint 24/7 (http://www.questionpoint.

org/) for training, software and cost-sharing arrangements. Other responsibilities include statistical reporting, scheduling, maintaining the listserv and Web page, and reviewing transcripts. Meetings with the site coordinators from the four institutions are scheduled twice a year in conjunction with Kansas Library Association's professional conferences.

It became evident early on that each site would need a responsible party to facilitate local issues, training, questions, monitoring QuestionPoint for new information that needed to be shared with operators, participating in scheduled meetings, and staff scheduling. Partner institutions chose librarians with experience in providing virtual reference to administer the service. This left more time for the KU site coordinator to administer the broader issues of the collaborative service such as group administration, vendor communication, and assessment activities.

Training

The issue of training was one of the priorities when planning the joint service. While each institution conducted training in the best and most appropriate way for their group of operators, all parties adhered to certain agreed-upon standards. General guidelines assumed that all operators should be familiar with the technology used (e.g., online training guides provided by Convey and later QuestionPoint 24/7), all would have hands-on practice time, and all would keep up their skills and be advised of any software or policy changes. The initial collaboration between only two institutions included a one-day training session where the coordinators from KU spent a day at K-State. This was a formal training session with an agenda that included a virtual reference overview, tips and techniques, demonstrations and tutorials of the software, and hands-on training with predetermined exercises. The hands-on session was used as a starting point for the site coordinators to develop further training and practice sessions within the institution.

Training again became an issue when the decision was made to change the software to OCLC's QuestionPoint 24/7 and include more partners in the service in early 2005. KU had been leasing chat software from Convey Systems for its own service and continued to use it for the pilot with K-State. At this point, the experience and comfort level with different software packages was quite varied. Some operators had past experience with three different products, others one or two, with training programs ranging from telephone consultation to Web-based demonstrations to formal onsite vendor visits. Original discussions included the possibility of having an onsite visit from the QuestionPoint vendor, but not everyone felt it necessary. The final decision was to receive Webcast/telephone training sessions at each institution to train a core group of operators. These operators would then be able to work with new operators as they joined the service. Several sessions were held at each institution. The same basic guidelines for training mentioned above applied to the new software and partners, but individual institutions developed their own scheduling and methods of training. Besides the hands-on training, practice sessions between operators at the same institution were scheduled and encouraged before going live.

Several help guides and handouts facilitated the training process. A brief "cheat sheet" outlining login procedures, how to pick up calls, co-browsing procedures, and other important highlights was very well received by the operators. Guidelines explaining what the service is, who can use it, and a legal disclaimer were also helpful. The most useful tool is the collaborative Web page that lists important information for each institution with a link to each site. This Web page allows operators to look up such things as library hours, technical help, contacts, and policies that are needed when helping students from a different school. As each institution joined the service, the site coordinator was responsible for supplying information to be added to the page. These institutional facts helped alleviate some of the anxiety operators had about answering each other's reference questions. Another helpful piece was a PowerPoint presentation that two operators developed to be used as a "refresher" after the first semester of service.

Staffing and Scheduling

As mentioned earlier, one of the main benefits of the collaboration was to increase the number of staff to extend the hours of the service. By combining resources for the pilot between KU and K-State, staff was more than doubled. When ESU and WSU joined later in 2005, our operator numbers increased even more. Having additional operators to staff the service provided greater flexibility in scheduling. Staff providing the service are composed of professional librarians, generalists, and paraprofessionals from each partner institution. Once the collaborative service expanded beyond the KU/K-State pilot, KU discontinued using the peer reference students.

It was decided that the service would be offered only when classes are in session at the four institutions. For the fall semester 2005, the cooperative chat service was available forty-six hours per week (11 a.m.-9 p.m.,

Monday to Thursday and 11 a.m.-5 p.m. Friday). E-mail reference services at each institution provide backup during downtime. The schedule is distributed equitably (even though the staff number varies at each library), with each partner responsible for staffing one day each week. Friday hours are split among three institutions, with the service closed on weekends. Discussions are continuing to evaluate the possibility of increasing the service hours in the evenings after 9 p.m.

An issue that has surfaced with a collaborative service is that students may be working with a librarian from another university. Those staffing the service need to be mindful of that and provide the best service possible to the person requesting assistance, regardless of their institutional affiliation. In order to do that, operators need to be familiar with the databases, online catalogs, and the Web sites of both the respective libraries and the universities.

Publicity and Marketing

Because KU already had a presence at their institution with the name HawkHelp *LIVE*, each school decided to use separate icons and names for the service. Names used at the other schools include Cat Answers, Hornet Help and Wu Knows! Therefore, no unified marketing slogan or plan was developed, and each school was responsible for its own marketing. This aspect of the service was stronger in some schools than others, and coordinators believe that this should be developed further and become a priority at all schools.

KU has marketed HawkHelp *LIVE* in a variety of ways. A logo was developed using the Jayhawk mascot typing at a computer. Links to the service were placed prominently on the library Web pages and a series of posters and flyers were distributed on campus. The service is also featured prominently in presentations and library instruction sessions to our undergraduate level courses each fall semester. In the last few years, the library has distributed promotional items such as travel mugs, business card and CD holders and t-shirts with the service logo during campus events in the fall. One year, a film modeled after "The Matrix" was made to promote the use of the library to incoming freshmen and online chat was mentioned as a way to get research assistance at the library. The service has been featured in the campus newspaper, *The Kansan.*

At K-State, the *Manhattan Mercury*, the *Collegian*, and the *Library Link* published articles describing the service. Librarians were encouraged to promote the service in instruction classes. The PR team created and distributed flyers announcing the service. After the first semester, icons and messages were placed in more visible locations on the library Web site, resulting in increased usage by K-State students.

At ESU, a formal marketing strategy has not yet been used. Initially, the academic virtual reference service was publicized through word of mouth in library instruction sessions and through links on the library's Web page. With a redesign of the Web page, the link was changed to Ask-A-Librarian and moved to a more prominent place on the Web site. This move has resulted in increased usage from ESU students.

ESU would like to reach distance education students and faculty with chat reference. A new brochure was created to distribute to not only distance education students but also to faculty across campus and at remote locations. Studies have indicated that keeping faculty informed about distance services offered by the library is important (Kelley & Orr, 2003). Faculty can assist the library by alerting students to services provided by the library. The next step for ESU is to develop a marketing plan and promotional materials for virtual reference to reach all segments of the university. Staff members are also working to redesign the distance services page to provide information for those remote from the campus.

Software/Technical Issues

KU used software from Convey Systems Inc. for the first two years of service. There were often problems associated with the "co-browse" or "application sharing" feature. Use of the service also required that the patron download a plug-in on their computer and this was viewed as a deterrent. Some partners had problems when trying to coordinate the download for remote students using EZProxy (http://www.ezproxy. com/support/). A combination of communication problems, the perception of low priority, and different expectations between the IT department and the library contributed to a very frustrating time while trying to get the issues resolved.

In early 2004, KU was a member of a working group formed by a consortial group called the Greater Western Library Alliance (GWLA) to investigate potential chat collaborations among member libraries. Although KU decided not to join a GWLA pilot cooperative at that time, the use of the Convey software was re-evaluated. A decision was made to move to OCLC's QuestionPoint 24/7 in January 2005. OCLC's acquisition of 24/7 in August 2004 allowed the continued use of the co-browse feature, in addition to standard chat and Web page-pushing. QuestionPoint also had a strong e-mail reference component and allowed the development of a knowledge base, both of which were of interest to KU for future development.

The decision by KU to change vendors was met with relief at K-State, although QuestionPoint would probably not have been the first choice. Because K-State and KU started using the software at a time when QuestionPoint was transitioning to 24/7 software, there was confusion concerning when to use each product's interface.

Since operators at ESU had been staffing the KANAnswer service prior to beginning the academic collaborative service, getting used to the software was not a problem. However, when ESU operators started with the collaborative service, an issue emerged with operators not seeing the patron's pages when using the co-browse feature. The ESU computers were networked using Novell, which includes ZENworks (http://www.novell.com/coolsolutions/zenworks/) to help manage platforms and assist in providing security to the computers connected to the network. It was discovered that the ZENworks applications were interfering with the operator's ability to use QuestionPoint features and needed to be disabled.

Assessment

No formal assessment has been done, but ongoing analysis of the statistical reports indicates that usage of the cooperative chat service has been steadily increasing each semester since its inception in 2003. The mix of students using the service has also been changing. During the pilot with K-State, usage by KU students was higher. But this was probably due to the fact that KU had been offering the service for a year and had already begun to build a user base. As the cooperative service matures and is offered longer by each partner, we are finding that usage is gradually increasing by students from all four institutions.

Survey results show a high degree of satisfaction with the quality of the service provided, although some users have expressed surprise that their questions are being answered by librarians from another institution.

CONCLUSIONS AND LESSONS LEARNED

Three themes emerge from this description of our Kansas collaborative chat service: the benefits of collaboration; the recognition that each institution has its own culture; and the value of the psychological contract. "The success of any collaborative venture lies mainly with communication" (Fletcher, Hair, & McKay, 2004, p. 6). Because of open communication about these themes, four institutions have created a trusting relationship to get beyond institutional culture and to develop a successful collaborative partnership.

Many public institutions value collaboration as a politically advantageous goal, including these four institutions governed by the Kansas Board of Regents. Similarities in our institutional cultures have made it easier to collaborate. We have similar library resources and curricular guidelines from the Board of Regents. We share common electronic databases purchased by the Kansas State Library and a common consortium that serve as a basis for providing service to each other's users without violating contracts with vendors. This use of electronic resources is especially important in distance learning because staff and users may not have access to print resources. The group can achieve more than any of the participants can accomplish individually. We share a common motivation to collaborate, and the leadership at each school has supported our venture. From our common needs, each of us took what we learned from our KANAnswer experience and modified it to fit our users' needs.

Institutional culture can thwart or facilitate change. An institution's values can generate differing goals, agendas, assumptions, and expectations. Each institution wants to maintain its own culture and identity, and each wants to take advantage of the benefits of working together. When our four institutions decided to collaborate, we developed strategies to examine one another's values to avoid misunderstandings. Each institution determines its own staffing and scheduling needs, training requirements, and its technical configurations. The parts of the service come together under the collaborative umbrella represented by the service name and the common Web page.

The idea of a psychological contract was unspoken when the collaborative service began, but it has represented a powerful tool in creating the trusting relationship we share. This mutual trust and respect provide the context for staff acceptance of working with colleagues from other institutions. If the members of any group do not buy into the idea of being part of the new venture, it can hinder the project's success. The experiment of using peer students as chat operators provides an example of a failed contract. Though students were very comfortable with the technology of chat and instant messaging, supervisors' assumptions that students would embrace this new responsibility were wrong. Students did not expect this new and complex duty, and they resented the time that was needed for training to improve their reference skills.

If a MOU had been negotiated in the example above, the outcome might have been more positive. The MOU takes interpretation out of the mix by putting obligations in writing. It acts as a translator to bridge the gap between cultures and articulates a clear philosophy of service. For our current collaboration, even though no MOU was implemented, the psychological contract provides the framework for delivering quality service to each other's students and outlines how we will work with a new, combined audience in creative ways.

Sharing questions from our combined student populations has provided challenges, but ultimately, the benefits of collaboration have outweighed the negatives. Operators have been able to provide support, share experiences and exchange knowledge with colleagues from partner institutions to develop best practices. The Kansas Academic Chat Service continues to evolve and grow. Future plans include extending the service hours, utilizing more operators expressing an interest in participation, and developing a formal assessment plan. It is hoped that this successful collaboration will continue to benefit each institution and serve as a model for other collaborative ventures with the state universities.

REFERENCES

American Library Association. (2004). *Guidelines for distance learning library services.* Retrieved November 27, 2005, from http://www.ala.org/ala/acrl/acrlstandards/guidelinesdistancelearning.htm.

American Library Association. (2004). *Guidelines for implementing and maintaining virtual reference services.* Retrieved December 13, 2005, from http://www.ala.org/ala/rusa/rusaprotools/referenceguide/virtrefguidelines.htm.

Anonymous. (2004). Project management done here. *Library Journal, 129*(5), 44.

Bergquist, W. (1992). The four cultures of the academy. San Francisco: Jossey Bass.

Coffman, S. (2002). What's wrong with collaborative digital reference? *American Libraries, 33*(11), 56-58.

Creth, S. D. (1993). Creating a virtual information organization: Collaborative relationships between libraries and computing centers. *Journal of Library Administration, 19*(3/4), 111-132.

Davidson, A. L., Schofield, J., & Stocks, J. (2001). Professional cultures and collaborative efforts: A case study for technologists and educators working for change. *Information Society, 17*, 21-32.

Favini, R. (1997). The library and academic computing center: Cultural perspectives and recommendations for improved interaction. *ACRL 8th National Conference*

Papers. Retrieved October 11, 2005, from http://www.ala.org/ala/acrlbucket/ nashville1997pap/favini.htm.

Fenner, J., & Fenner, A. (2004). The future in context: How librarians can think like futurists. *Library philosophy and practice (7.1).* Retrieved August 11, 2005, from Gale Expanded Academic ASAP.

Fletcher, J., Hair, P., & McKay, J. (2004). Online-librarian–real time/real talk: An innovative collaboration between two university libraries. *Breaking boundaries: Integration & interoperability.* Retrieved November 21, 2005, from http://www.vala. org.au/vala2004/2004pprs/prgm2004.htm.

Fritch, J. W., & Mandernack, S. B. (2001). The emerging reference paradigm: A vision of reference services in a complex information environment. *Library Trends, 50*(2), 286-305.

Hansen, E. (2004). *KANAnswer pilot project assessment.* Retrieved November 23, 2005, from http://skyways.lib.ks.us/KSL/KLNB/KANAnswerWeb/ KANAnswerProjectAssessmentWeb.htm.

Harmon, K. (2002, July). Merging divergent campus cultures into coherent educational communities: Challenges for higher education leaders. *Higher Education, 44*(1), 91-114.

Hayman, L. M. (1997, July). Database design for preservation project management. *Library Resources & Technical Services, 41*(3), 236-49.

Hope, C. B., & Peterson, C. A. (2002). The sum is greater than the parts: Cross-institutional collaboration for information literacy in academic libraries. *Journal of Library Administration, 36*(1/2), 21-38.

International Federation of Library Associations and Institutions. (2002). Digital reference guidelines. Retrieved December 13, 2005, from http://www.ifla.org/VII/s36/ pubs/drg03.htm.

Jacob, C. J. (1991). *The Fifth Off-Campus Library Services Conference Proceedings: Albuquerque, New Mexico, October 30-November 1, 1991.* Mt. Pleasant, MI: Central Michigan University Press.

Jacob, C. J. (Ed.). (1993). *The Sixth Off-Campus Library Services Conference Proceedings: Kansas City, Missouri, October 6-8, 1993.* Mt. Pleasant, MI: Central Michigan University Press.

Jacob, C. J. (Ed.). (1995). *The Seventh Off-Campus Library Services Conference Proceedings: San Diego, California, October 25 -27, 1995.* Mt. Pleasant, MI: Central Michigan University Press.

Kelley, K. B., & Orr, G. J. (2003). Trends in distant student use of electronic resources: A survey. *College & Research Libraries, 64*(3), 176-191.

Kezar, A., & Eckel, P. D. (2002, July-August). The effect of institutional culture on change strategies in higher education: Universal principles or culturally responsive concepts? *Journal of Higher Education, 73*(4), 435-461.

Lessin, B. M. (Ed.). (1983). *The Off-Campus Library Services Conference Proceedings: St. Louis, Missouri, October 14-15, 1982.* Mt. Pleasant, MI: Central Michigan University Press.

Lessin, B. M. (Ed.). (1986). *The Off-Campus Library Services Conference Proceedings: Knoxville, Tennessee, April 18-19, 1985.* Mt. Pleasant, MI: Central Michigan University Press.

Lessin, B. M. (Ed.). (1987). *The Off-Campus Library Services Conference Proceedings: Reno, Nevada, October 23-24, 1986.* Mt. Pleasant, MI: Central Michigan University Press.

Lessin, B. M. (Ed.). (1988). *The Off-Campus Library Services Conference Proceedings: Charleston, South Carolina, October 20-21, 1988.* Mt. Pleasant, MI: Central Michigan University Press.

Mahoney, P. B. (Ed.). (2002). *The Tenth Off-Campus Library Services Conference Proceedings: Cincinnati, Ohio, April 17-19, 2002.* Mt. Pleasant, MI: Central Michigan University Press.

Mahoney, P. B. (Ed.). (2004). *The Eleventh Off-Campus Library Services Conference Proceedings: Scottsdale, Arizona, May 5-7, 2004.* Mt. Pleasant, MI: Central Michigan University Press.

Murray, J., & Tschernitz, C. (2004, June). The Internet myth: Emerging trends in reference enquiries. *Australasian Public Libraries and Information Services, 17*(2), 80-89.

Niehoff, B. P., & Paul, R. J. (2001, Spring). The just workplace: Developing and maintaining effective psychological contracts. *Review of Business, 22*(1), 5-8.

Oxford English Dictionary. (2005). Retrieved November 5, 2005, from OED Online.

Simpson, D. B. (1997). Solving the challenges presented by electronic resources: Creating opportunities through inter-institutional collaboration. *Journal of Library Administration, 24*(4), 49-60.

Smith, R. M., Race, S. F., & Ault, M. (2001). Virtual desk: Real reference. *Journal of Library Administration, 32*(1), 371-382.

Stockham, M., & Turtle, E. (2002). Exploring the challenges of virtual reference in an academic library. In C. Ury & V. Wainscott (Eds.), *Brick and click libraries: Changes and challenges. Proceedings of a regional academic library symposium.* (pp. 69-75). Maryville, MO: Northwest Missouri State University.

Stockham, M., Turtle, E., & Hansen, E. (2002/2003). KANAnswer: A collaborative statewide virtual reference pilot project. *Reference Librarian, No. 79/80,* 257-266.

Thomas, P. S. (Ed.). (2000). *The Ninth Off-Campus Library Services Conference Proceedings: Portland, Oregon, April 26-28, 2000.* Mt. Pleasant, MI: Central Michigan University Press.

Thomas, P. S., & Jones, M. (Eds.). (1998). *The Eighth Off-Campus Library Services Conference Proceedings: Providence, Rhode Island, April 22-24, 1998.* Mt. Pleasant, MI: Central Michigan University Press.

Truelson, J. (2004, December). Partnering on virtual reference using QuestionPoint: Guidelines for collaboration between academic libraries in Australia/New Zealand and the U.S. *Australian Academic & Research Libraries, 35*(4), 301-309.

Wilson, F., & Keys, J. (2004, June). AskNow! Evaluating an Australian collaborative chat reference service: A project manager's perspective. *Australian Academic & Research Libraries, 35*(2), 81-95.

doi:10.1300/J111v45n01_08

APPENDIX

Memorandum of Understanding
University of Kansas and Kansas State University

Introduction

Involvement with the state-wide virtual reference service (KANAnswer) for the past year has given us the experience to look at other options that will directly serve our students. While KANAnswer is a worthwhile service project that serves Kansas citizens, the shared interests and expertise of academic librarians seems a better partnership than the current model of mixed library groupings. In these times of budget uncertainties, starting a virtual reference project where collaboration and shared resources are emphasized is a reasonable strategic move. Since K-State and KU use the Voyager OPAC, and share many of the same databases, it will be relatively easy for librarians to help students from the other institution. In addition, both universities have a large distance education component that would be helped through this venture.

Project Description

A collaborative arrangement between the University of Kansas (KU) and Kansas State University (K-State) libraries to offer a virtual reference (live chat) service to the students, faculty, and staff of those institutions.

Technical/Software Issues

KU will:

- Maintain the current contract with Convey Systems (www.conveysystems. com). (lease arrangement, technical support provided).
- Resolve start-up issues with authentication.
- Bring in K-State as a "group" within the current contract.

K-State will:

- Pay for one seat (operator license).
- Work closely with K-State and KU technical staff to implement authentication with EZProxy, facilitate download of Convey plug-in, and customize the group account with administrative rights.
- Determine a name and logo for the K-State group account.

Budget

KU will:

- Negotiate with Convey to add additional seats as needed under the current contract.
- Maintain at least two current seats.
- Determine methods and costs of publicity for their institution.

K-State will;

- Provide one seat/month at a cost of $300/month.
- Determine methods and costs of publicity for their institution.

Staffing

Total hours provided will be negotiated between K-State and KU based on the need for services and usage statistics.

KU will:

- Provide approximately 27 staff hours per week.
- Be responsible for assigning staff schedules at their institution.

K-State will:

- Provide 12-15 staff hours per week until operators become comfortable with the training, schedule, and new mode of delivering service.
- Expect to increase hours by the beginning of the 2004 fall semester.
- Be responsible for assigning staff schedules at their institution.

Training

It is anticipated that on-going training will be needed (type to be determined) and will be the responsibility of each institution. Excellent communication will be needed between the two institutions regarding training issues, new features, software updates, etc.

KU will:

- Provide initial training to selected K-State operators based on materials already developed. Issues to be covered include but are not limited to: policies, unique databases, software mechanics, and referrals.

APPENDIX (continued)

K-State will:

- Train the remaining operators and provide ongoing communication.

Project Duration

- December 2003-January 2004. Preliminary discussions.
- February-March 2004. Sign Memorandum of Understanding, finalize issues in training and implementation.
- March-April 2004. K-State begins staffing of service.
- March-Fall semester 2004. Ongoing assessment of the service and library collaboration.
- December 2004. Decision concerning continued participation.
- The project can be reevaluated at any time and terminated with the consent of both parties.

University of Kansas Libraries _____ Date _____

Kansas State University Libraries _____ Date _____

Fostering a Community
of Doctoral Learners

Rosemary Green

Shenandoah University

SUMMARY. This paper describes a newly designed graduate course developed and taught by a librarian. Basic information literacy attributes are emphasized in the course, enabling students to develop more specialized capabilities of locating, evaluating, and synthesizing research literature. Students in the course participate as members of a graduate cohort, so there is opportunity for them to evolve as a cohesive learning community. The theoretical framework of communities of practice is used to inform the instructional design of this course. Observations of early teaching and learning experiences as well as reflections upon this approach to course development are offered. doi:10.1300/J111v45n01_09

KEYWORDS. Communities of practice, information literacy, literature review, doctoral pedagogy, graduate education, distance education

INTRODUCTION

With an increasing emphasis upon student-centered learning, discussions have turned toward aspects of community and students learning

[Haworth co-indexing entry note]: "Fostering a Community of Doctoral Learners." Green, Rosemary. Co-published simultaneously in *Journal of Library Administration* (The Haworth Information Press, an imprint of The Haworth Press, Inc.) Vol. 45, No. 1/2, 2006, pp. 169-183; and: *The Twelfth Off-Campus Library Services Conference Proceedings* (ed: Julie A. Garrison) The Haworth Information Press, an imprint of The Haworth Press, Inc., 2006, pp. 169-183.

Available online at http://jla.haworthpress.com
doi:10.1300/J111v45n01_09

from each other as community peers. The environment of distance education draws even greater attention to learners' sense of community. Given the flexible nature of distance education, a community of teachers and learners need not come together in exclusively face-to-face exchanges. Course management software and other means of instructional delivery allow students and instructors to share information, skills-building, and knowledge through several communication venues. Regardless of location, learner interaction may be generated by course tasks as well as by socially-generated factors. Learning communities may be established formally among distance learners enrolled in the same program and informally as those same learners share common backgrounds, interests, and motivations for learning.

Drawing on the theoretical framework of communities of practice (Lave & Wenger, 1991; Wenger, 1998), this paper focuses on an instructional environment of graduate learners and aspects of community that these learners display, viewed through the lens of participating members of an online information literacy course. Elements adopted to facilitate community participation were used when designing the instructional components of a first-term graduate information literacy course taught entirely using Blackboard course management software. Early experiences and reflections upon the process are offered from the perspective of the librarian-instructor, with illustrative comments from student participants. Relevance of the communities of practice framework to graduate learning communities and information literacy instruction is also considered.

COMMUNITIES OF PRACTICE FRAMEWORK

Lave and Wenger's contributions to the theories of learning in practice, legitimate peripheral participation and communities of practice, are brought forward in *Situated Learning: Legitimate Peripheral Participation* (1991) and further developed in *Communities of Practice: Learning, Meaning, and Identity* (Wenger, 1998). In a community of practice, participants engage to varying degrees in community aspects that are defined as common purpose, mutual engagement, and shared repertoire of resources and practices. Drawing from their anthropological studies of apprentice learning and enculturation, Lave and Wenger pose the notion of legitimate peripheral participation to explain how novices develop expertise in the communities where they are positioned. A foundational assumption of this model is that learning is accomplished through participation whereby novices and experienced members share their own particular expertise with each other. Legitimate peripheral participation accounts for this process as one by which neophyte members are engaged with a given community of practice, becoming more proficient in community enterprises.

Typically, the shared activity of learning characterizes a community of practice. As a function of the community, learning is "an integral and inseparable aspect of social practice within the classroom community" (Lave & Wenger, 1991, p. 31). In a setting where meaning and knowledge are jointly constructed among co-participants, learning becomes a social practice (Bird, 2001). Learning, "the engine of practice" (Wenger 1998, p. 96), is focal to a community of practice, taking place through the sharing of purposeful, patterned activity as individuals turn community resources to their advantage. Learner, activity, and community mutually constitute each other. "Situated learning also extends the importance of the social nature of learning, where learning takes place through the communication and participation of members within a community" (Stacey, Smith & Barty, 2004, p. 108). Knowledge is constructed in the informal and formal social contexts that become established in learners' cohorts, courses, programs, and curriculum.

As novices and transitional researchers, graduate students may interact with others in the academic community from a beginning position of peripherality, drawing upon community resources. Within a community of practice, "legitimate peripheral participation provides a way to speak about the relations between newcomers and old-timers, and about activities, identities, artifacts and communities of knowledge and practice" (Lave & Wenger, 1991, p. 29). Student participants are positioned differently within the community, depending upon factors such as their range of skills and experience, length of candidature, and opportunities for enculturation. The trajectory of legitimate peripheral participation offers students the opportunity to be drawn into an academic community of practice. In the presence of dialogue, collaboration, feedback, and new tasks, mentored students become better acclimated to academic expectations, achieving performance that comes closer to that of the experts (Belcher, 1994). The exchange of artifacts, such as topical bibliographies and personal narratives, affords community discourse and knowledge creation. Practice is opened to newcomers to the community through legitimate peripheral participation, where "participation consists of the shared experiences and negotiations that result from social interaction among members within a purposive community" (Pallas, 2001, p. 7). Community members may be neophytes, competent others, and experts. Wenger (1998) centralized the concept of practice, referring to activities that community members negotiate and mutually perform, drawing on community resources with the purpose of furthering shared goals. The elders of the community, referred to as mentors, master-practitioners, masters, old-timers, and experts (Belcher, 1994; Hager, 2003; Lave & Wenger; Merriam, Courtenay & Baumgartner, 2003; Wenger, 1998), provide this access. All members then gain from the community by practicing and acquiring more complex abilities and knowledge.

In a collective of novices and experts, students, librarians, faculty and others share varying levels of participation and engagement. As newcomers to the academic community, doctoral students actively engage with other members, many with tenure and expertise, to learn the norms, habits, and discourse of the community. Participation with a learning community in this way fosters students' socialization into academic disciplines. In learning more about community enterprise and practices, novices begin the transition from the periphery to a position of proficiency, eventually approaching centrality and more competent participation. The notion of legitimate peripheral participation serves as a metaphor for the progress that doctoral candidates make during candidature, engaged in varying degrees with academic community members and resources. "In an academic community of practice, students, academics, professionals and indeed anyone else who shares this site of practice, are responsible for the maintenance of the community of practice, for inducting newcomers into it" (Brew, 2003, p. 12). Students engage in generational encounters (Wenger, 1998) with academics, librarians, and other educators who, in part, constitute the learning resources of the community. Given the opportunity to co-participate with an "attuned expert" (Freedman & Adam, 1996, p. 403) and performing increasingly challenging tasks, students learn requisite and discipline-specific levels of academic activity through practice.

When professional doctorate students, viewed first as participants in their own professional communities, re-enter higher education, they find that they must move among multiple communities. In particular, practitioners returning to the environment of higher education find that their roles, status, and peer groups undergo noticeable change. For some, "engaging with a research community focused on, and usually based in, a university is logistically difficult" (Wikeley & Muschamp, 2004, p. 132). Frequently profiled as practitioners and part-time students, doctoral education students continue to share multiple positions as they interact with professional, academic, and other discrete groups in a constellation of communities (Pallas, 2001; Wenger, 1998). Within the wider university community, learning environments are dispersed, and multiple communities of practice co-exist (Boud & Lee, 2004; Lea, 2004; Lee & Roth, 2003). Depending on their levels of experience, learners identify with multiple groups and communities of fixed, individual courses, academic programs, and schools. They may also be joined in cohorts that are formed to complete an educational program together, and sometimes these learners find that they share professional as well as academic commonalities (Stacey et al., 2004; Wilson, 2001). Students in education and the social sciences are likely to find that "peer cultures of research students" (Deem & Brehony, 2000, p. 152) are highly influential in their research training.

Competing roles and requirements of multiple communities, part-time enrollment, and enrollment in distance-based rather than on-campus courses all contribute to doctoral students' sense of separation, even isolation. Attentiveness to community dynamics in online course design and teaching can sustain an otherwise disengaged group of learners. "Traditions, curriculum (in the widest sense) and values, established through a specialised vocabulary" (Wikeley & Muschamp, 2004, p. 130) contextualize practices of a distance learning community and reify such practices. Regardless of the medium of instructional delivery, the enterprises of "jointly constructed meaning and knowledge" (Bird, 2001, p. 95) can bring together students through practice. Members of the group need not be physically present with each other to engage as learners. Instructional practices such as knowledge sharing, peer collaboration, and discussion-based learning foster a sense of learning within a group rather than a sense of being detached from the peer community (Boud & Lee, 2004; Cousin & Deepwell, 2005). Where students regularly engage with each other, academic community members, and institutional resources, the issue of community participation may not be pressing. But the doctoral journey is often viewed as one taken in isolation, and doctoral students are known to experience separation from the learning community (Boud & Lee, 2004). However, when the community of practice model is applied, the journey of the doctoral student may become a shared and supported one.

CONTEXT OF THE COURSE COMMUNITY

Following a curriculum revision in the doctorate of educational leadership at Shenandoah University, a core of three courses was established to prepare students for the literature review process that would eventually support their doctoral research proposals. Each of the three courses is paired with a co-requisite content course and taught in separate academic semesters. The first course in the sequence emphasizes basic information literacy attributes, with the overall goal of introducing students to the process of conducting productive, targeted, and critical literature searches. To that end, students are required to demonstrate the ability to identify useful tools, apply pertinent search strategies, and screen and interpret results effectively. At first, information literacy is approached from an informational perspective, as students are oriented to the process of identifying their information needs, then screening and acquiring supporting materials. Thereafter, information literacy takes on an educational perspective (Smith & Oliver, 2005) closely associated with the content and learning processes of a co-requisite course and embedded in the curriculum. The subsequent two courses that follow in later academic terms build on basic information literacy skills, enabling students to deploy more specialized aspects of locating, evaluating, and synthesizing research literature. Students enrolled in the new curriculum are mentored in the development of their information skills throughout their program (Lloyd, 2005). Courses in the sequence have been developed by a faculty librarian, incorporating instructional design and strategies to support the communities of practice model. Courses are taught online by librarians, using Blackboard course management software. The teaching and learning environment of the first course is the focus of this paper.

These doctoral students are early postgraduates and all share membership in co-requisite courses, one which meets entirely online and the other which meets both online and occasionally face-to-face; both courses emphasize a tutorial dimension of individualized instruction. Students enrolled in these courses also participate as members of individual postgraduate cohorts, the design being that they enter and proceed through the program as an intact group. The cohort model has been found to enhance supportive peer relationships as well as engender a sense of community, particularly among postgraduates who blend professional and academic lives (Winston & Fields, 2003). Because the three online courses are co-requisite with three content courses that meet in the traditional classroom environment, students engage both in person and online; consequently, personal and virtual interactions are encouraged throughout the academic sequence. Students are given opportunities to join together as a group and potentially to coalesce as a doctoral learning community.

COURSE DESIGN AND INSTRUCTIONAL METHODS

The course, *Locating and Examining Research Literature*, was essentially designed to accommodate two curricular contexts. First, it is taught in tandem with a content course, *Introduction to Research Methods*, in which new students in the doctorate of educational leadership are introduced to the literature of educational philosophy and methodology and are prepared to investigate preliminary research topics from a broad, theoretical perspective. The activities and assignments required in *Locating and Examining Research Literature (LERL)* support the acquisition and refinement of information literacy skills by familiarizing students with the university library's research sources, providing tools that students use to practice locating, evaluating, and organizing research literature, and enabling them to undertake investigation of individual research topics. In its emphasis on teaching and learning information literacy in an environment of guided participation, *LERL* is patterned after *Locating and Interpreting Research Literature*, an online seminar offered to commencing doctoral students in education at Deakin University in Australia.

LERL is the first of three courses that scaffold learning the literature review process, so the foundation laid in the first course supports later tasks of critiquing and synthesizing the literature, and eventually producing a literature review. The required sequence of research core courses provides students opportunities to develop information literacy skills along with disciplinary knowledge (Smith & Oliver, 2005). All courses in the sequence are Blackboard-based to accommodate scheduling requirements of the students and to allow them to access instructional materials at the time best suited to the content course. In an incremental approach, information literacy and other elements of the literature review process are mentored throughout the course sequence, taught in the context of the curriculum (Lloyd, 2005).

The interdependence of *LERL* with a co-requisite content course and with other courses in the doctoral education curriculum, the online environment where the course is offered, and the unique dynamics of the learning group all affect course structure and pedagogy. Students and instructor are assumed to be members of this learning community, to whom practice, resources, and opportunities for engagement are open (Wenger, 1998). The course is characterized by a clearly defined infrastructure that provides flexibility in topic development, opportunities for individual participation and cooperation, complementary activities that support learning in *LERL* and a co-requisite course, and modeling and coaching from instructors of both courses. As Wilson, Ludwig-Hardman, Thornam, and Dunlap (2004) recommended, the course features a supportive environment, shared goals, collaboration among all members, respectful inclusion of different perspectives, progressive discourse toward knowledge building, and distribution of learning through participation.

Together, *LERL* and the research methods course blend skills-based and process-oriented approaches. New learners are expected to arrive at the "pedagogic setting with congealed practices from another kind of setting, often a more didactic one" (Cousin & Deepwell, 2005, p. 61), so methods of instructing information literacy attribute skills are at first didactic and direct. However, a checklist approach to learning information literacy skills (Smith & Oliver, 2005; Webber & Johnston, 2000) is avoided; information literacy is presented as an initial and fundamental phase in the recursive cycle of gathering, evaluating, and synthesizing research literature. Instructional support for information literacy is embedded in the disciplinary context (Smith & Oliver, 2005) of the graduate education curriculum, presented as an integral part of reviewing literature. A basic instructional framework is established through a course syllabus, course materials, and explicit directions that guide students to larger university community resources, including library tools and collections. Clear deadlines for submission of learning activities are established. Fresh content is added periodically, depending on learners' needs and progress. The final course project is an annotated bibliography wherein each student presents a nascent body of literature to support an evolving research project. Within this infrastructure, students are encouraged to explore process and product, and members of the cohort demonstrate a willingness to engage in both.

Undertaking information literacy as an early phase of reviewing research literature and writing about that process are essential to the *LERL* course. The process commences with students developing the skills to locate and acquire research materials that support their identified information needs, based upon potential research interests. Development of research topics occurs in a dynamic cycle of identifying an area of focus, searching for supporting literature, reading and analyzing the literature, sharing procedural and reflective writings, receiving feedback from the group, and revising the focus. Central to the cycle is each student's articulation of individual, progressive experiences of identifying and locating topical literature. In a recursive approach to information literacy, several students make a point of returning to earlier discussions as they discover that a recent activity has contributed further insights into earlier learning. Course postings constitute individual diaries, outlining both group interactions and progress toward establishing mature research topics. Online course discussions provide a forum for proposing, exploring, testing, and shaping research areas related to their professional experiences and circumstances. Learning occurs through improvisation (Lave & Wenger, 1991) as students experiment with online searching methods, starting with basic information seeking strategies that soon evolve into more complex methods.

Reflecting the ubiquitous nature of writing activities in the doctoral curriculum, both conversational and academic writing are required in *LERL*. Students engage with each other through informal and formal writing activities as practice for eventual discursive exchanges with the larger academic community. Practitioners tend to favor narratives for communication (Riehl, Larson, Short & Reitzug, 2000), so an initial personal introduction from each opens the first discussion. Online communication, both relative and tangential to course content, continues among the students as they become more familiar with each others' backgrounds and interests, and as they offer feedback and encouragement to each other. As educational practitioners, all group members easily adopt techniques of shared dialogue, cooperation, and interest in others' progress. Peer learning is commonly found in the professional context of these practitioner students (Boud & Lee, 2004), and they bring that mode of collaborative and communicative learning with them to the course. Often, students deliberately request that the group share reactions to their postings. Learning occurs in an intellectual collectivity (Mentis, Ryba & Annan, 2001) of participation, reflected by students mutually engaging in the discovery and sharing of literature-searching tools, resources, and methods. Over time and through practice, students demonstrate greater fluency in the informational and methodological tools of their discipline (Hager, 2003).

While course structure and materials are intended to facilitate distributed relationships, a clear teaching presence is maintained in the course. In a guided practice approach, the instructor makes a point of posing questions, offering suggestions, and providing feedback on a regular basis. The virtual classroom potentially allows immediate responses, so feedback following each required assignment can be timely and pertinent. Coaching and mentoring are integral to interactions between novices and experts (Brown, Collins & Duguid, 1989); instructors in both *LERL* and the research methods course deliberately check and balance ongoing interactions with the students. The two courses are intended to complement, and both instructors are able to engage with students simultaneously; the Blackboard environment easily facilitates concurrent interactions. Topic development within the broad framework of educational theory and methodology in one is supported by information literacy learning in the other. Learning is facilitated and guided, generally through a combination of hints, suggestions, and direct feedback from instructors. When appropriate, instructor responses to individuals' writing activities are expressed broadly so that all can benefit. For example, when students concentrate on mastering a bibliographic and citation management program, they are encouraged to use an online tutorial, brainstorm, and ask questions of each other and the instructors. Commenting candidly, one student wrote, "I have also enjoyed and hated RefWorks. It is a great feature in collecting wanted information yet incorrect data input can put you in a bind . . . time wasted." Students are given suggestions on how the software might be helpful to them in the long run, but they are not required to commit to its use.

STUDENT PERSPECTIVES

Several critical events relative to topic selection, information seeking, and learning bibliographic format take place during the first weeks of the course. Members of the learning group negotiate and adjust, first as individuals, and then collectively as they share personal and collegial reflections after the events (Farmer, 2004). Most of the students enter the course with what appears to them to be an explicit, defined research question that will be sustainable for the next few years of the program. Because the overarching philosophy of the Shenandoah University's doctoral education program centers on inquiry and process, students must learn to redefine research questions into much broader, preliminary areas of inquiry. At the same time, they discover that investigating broadly stated research topics in research databases is an ineffective approach. As they conceptualize their topics more generally and generously, simultaneously they learn to investigate more explicit search strategies. One student reflected, "For me, one of the biggest benefits of this process has been broadening my topic while simultaneously narrowing my topic. Reading through the abstracts and finding different descriptors, which would then propel me into another direction." Both approaches allowed new ways of seeing research areas and knowing the practices for using published literature to investigate those areas.

All share the experience of viewing the research process in a new light, and they take advantage of the supportive learning environment to modify their topics. Another student recommended, "When you have time, wander around any of the databases that have something to do with business, psychology, sociology, any of the social sciences. I've been amazed by how many 'education' type articles show up." *LERL* requires that students meet the challenges of learning new online research tools and library databases; as professional educators, they openly share their own learning paths and insights with each other. In a further critical event that stimulates many postings, participants share that the nuances of American Psychological Association bibliographic formatting requires another set of skills that must be learned quickly, sometimes contradicting earlier experience with other formats. Drawing on formal course-acquired knowledge and professional experience from each member, the group filters each of these experiences through peer-sharing, advice, and feedback.

The literature on doctoral pedagogy reveals that often students are presumed to bear skills and knowledge commensurate with doctoral research and research writing (Deem & Brehony, 2000; Riehl et al., 2000; Wikeley & Muschamp, 2004). However, no assumptions that *LERL* students possess prior knowledge concerning information seeking or familiarity with scholarly literature and current research methodology are made. As one student reminded us, many learners return to graduate education remembering earlier experiences with print-dominated and early-phase computerized resources. "While I used ERIC searches with my MA degree in the late 80s, the librarian would type the descriptors into the computer and return the 'hit' list to me. . . . What a difference a decade and a half make!"

Scaffolded activities guide the learners in developing new information literacy skills in an environment of supported communication. Early learning activities, such as searching online local and union library catalogs, are used as practical pedagogy (Boud & Lee, 2004) to provide clear structure in the first weeks, and gradually students assume responsibility over subsequent learning tasks as they master necessary skills. Learning, not teaching, is at the center of the course. In the process, learning occurs through structured tasks, observation, and by reflective practice, all essential to participation (Benzie, Mavers, Somekh & Cisneros-Cohernour, 2005; Merriam et al., 2003). The students employ trial and error, a popular technique that supports confidence gaining through experimentation. As this comment from one of the group members illustrated, "I have hit some of the same problem areas in searching as you have, and I just kept going at it until I got around it." Even as novices, students are encouraged to construct, share, and practice their own relative research frameworks, based on their professional and personal experiences (Lloyd, 2005). Students entering doctoral programs in educational leadership typically bring with them "a strong orientation to practice" (Riehl et al., 2000, p. 411), and this point of reference typically guides and sustains topic development. As the semester advances, peer learners in *LERL* construct a community where learning about research tools and methods is supported. "For me, it's been about improving and simplifying old processes. I keep getting clearer about what 'Information Generation' really means . . . I've enjoyed it and our communal struggle." As online discourse and interactions are practiced, learning assumes both social and academic functions (Benzie et al., 2005).

REFLECTIONS AND IMPLICATIONS

A community of practice provides the opportunity to "take part in meaningful activities and interactions, in the production of sharable artifacts, in community-building conversations, and in the negotiation of new situations" (Wenger, 1998, p. 184). Students in *LERL* participate collectively in the processes of building information literacy attributes, reflecting on the challenges and successes of learning new methods of literature searching, sharing bibliographic findings, and negotiating critical events. The course structuring of *LERL* encourages students to apply prior inquiry skills and knowledge to designating potential research topics, to which they add a complementary set of information literacy skills. Adopting and adapting explicit approaches suggested by the instructor, students explore their own research interests and interact with peer investigators. Even online, the environment becomes one of mutual improvisation, experimentation, questioning, and modification in an intellectual collective of novices and experts. Eventually, the novices grow into competent participants, learning with and from each other. At times the boundaries blur, and all participants act interchangeably as learners and teachers. In this way, learning is not held with any one person but is distributed among all participants. After reflecting that "two heads are better than one," one student concluded, "It has been quite an adventure and thanks for all your feedback. You have made the journey even more exciting and I look forward to our continued work together."

In the end, a community of practice may possibly evolve or not, depending on group dynamics, timing, individuals' profiles and experiences, and other factors. The uniqueness of any group depends on its members, and the learning group presented in this paper is distinguished by early collective engagement and open interactions with one another. A continual "flow of information between members" (Wenger, 1998, p. 125) begins in the earliest days of the cohort's association. While this learning community has not been formed spontaneously, members readily find common ground in their goals and reasons for engagement with one another. Considering the exchanges of encouragement, collaborative problem-solving, and the frequent sharing of search strategies and reading recommendations, members of the cohort exemplify an overall sense of "having something to offer" (Stacey et al., 2004, p. 113) each other in the information literacy process.

The literature continues to associate information literacy with the information seeking and synthesizing needs of graduate and distance learners. At the same time, empirical and propositional discussions increasingly situate information literacy in the academic curriculum. In the context described here, the paired *LERL* and research methods course provide building blocks in the doctoral education curriculum, integrating practices for acquiring information literacy attributes into the process of project development. As distance education pedagogies continue to emerge, information literacy becomes established not only as a set of identifiable attributes but also as a process that is valued in a community of online teachers and learners. Lloyd (2005) encouraged us to consider information literacy "as a cultural practice and social process which is situated and contextual" (p. 234). Many students now arrive at higher education acclimated to learning collaboratively and in groups; teachers and learners are well positioned to take advantage of this predisposition. Taking the view of information literacy as not only a process but also as a means of enculturation accommodates further understanding of the participative learning that occurs in both physical and virtual communities. The contextualization of information literacy within the communities of practice framework is a relatively new perspective, and, from that perspective, this paper is presented to inform the online information literacy courses designed for graduate learners and to offer new points for discussion.

AUTHOR NOTE

Appreciation is extended to Dr. Peter Macauley and Dr. John Goss for their critiques and helpful recommendations.

REFERENCES

Belcher, D. (1994). The apprenticeship approach to advanced academic literacy: Graduate students and their mentors. *English for Specific Purposes, 13*, 23-34.

Benzie, D., Mavers, D., Somekh, B., & Cisneros-Cohernour, E. J. (2005). Communities of practice. In B. Somekh & C. Lewin (Eds.), *Research methods in the social sciences* (pp. 180-187). Thousand Oaks, CA: Sage.

Bird, L. (2001). Virtual learning in the workplace: The power of communities of practice. In G. Kennedy, M. Keppell, C. McNaught & T. Petrovic (Eds.), *Meeting at the crossroads: Proceedings of the 19th Annual Conference of the Australasia Society for Computers in Learning in Tertiary Education* (pp. 93-100). Melbourne, Victoria: University of Melbourne.

Boud, D., & Lee, A. (2004). Peer learning as pedagogic discourse for research education. In M. Kiley & G. Mullins (Eds.), *Quality in postgraduate research: Re-imagining research education. Proceedings of the 2004 Quality in Postgraduate Research Conference*, Adelaide, South Australia.

Brew, A. (2003). Teaching and research: New relationships and their implications for inquiry-based teaching and learning in higher education. *Higher Education Research & Development, 22*, 3-18.

Brown, J., Collins, A., & Duguid, P. (1989). Situated cognition and the culture of learning. *Educational Researcher, 18* (1), 32-42.

Cousin, G., & Deepwell, F. (2005). Design for network learning: A communities of practice perspective. *Studies in Higher Education, 30*, 57-66.

Deem, R., & Brehony, K. J. (2000). Doctoral students' access to research cultures–Are some more unequal than others? *Studies in Higher Education, 25*, 149-165.

Farmer, L. S. J. (2004). Narrative inquiry as assessment tool: A course case study. *Journal of Education for Library and Information Science, 45*, 340-351.

Freedman, A., & Adam, C. (1996). Learning to write professionally: Situated learning and the transition from university to professional discourse. *Journal of Business and Technical Communication, 10*, 395-427.

Hager, M. J. (2003). *Mentoring relationships in doctoral education: Doctoral students' socialization into communities of practice.* Unpublished doctoral dissertation, University of Michigan, Ann Arbor.

Lave, J., & Wenger, E. (1991). *Situated learning: Legitimate peripheral participation.* New York: Cambridge University Press.

Lea, M. R. (2004). Academic literacies: A pedagogy for course design. *Studies in Higher Education, 29*, 739-756.

Lee, S., & Roth, M. W. (2003). Becoming and belonging: Learning qualitative research through legitimate peripheral participation. *Forum: Qualitative Social Research, 4* (2), 64 paras.

Lloyd, A. (2005). No man (or woman) is an island: Information literacy, affordances and communities of practice. *Australian Library Journal, 54*, 230-237.

Mentis, M., Ryba, K., & Annan, J. (2001, December). *Creating authentic on-line communities of professional practice.* Paper presented at Australian Association for Research in Education Conference, Fremantle, Western Australia. Retrieved October 15, 2005, from http://www.usqu.edu.au/electpub-jst/docs/html2002/pdf.mentis.pdf.

Merriam, S. B., Courtenay, B., & Baumgartner, L. (2003). On becoming a witch: Learning in a marginalized community of practice. *Adult Education Quarterly, 53,* 170-188.

Pallas, A. M. (2001). Preparing education doctoral students for epistemological diversity. *Educational Researcher, 30* (5), 6-11.

Riehl, C., Larson, C. L., Short, P. M., & Reitzug, U.C. (2000). Reconceptualizing research and scholarship in educational administration: Learning to know, knowing to do, doing to learn. *Educational Administration Quarterly, 46,* 391-427.

Smith, J., & Oliver, M. (2005). Exploring behaviour in the online environment: Student perceptions of information literacy. *ALT-J, Research in Learning Technology, 13* (1), 49-65.

Stacey, E., Smith, P., & Barty, K. (2004). Adult learners in the workplace: Online learning and communities of practice. *Distance Education, 25,* 107-123.

Webber, S., & Johnston, B. (2000). Conceptions of information literacy: New perspectives and implications. *Journal of Information Science, 26,* 381-397.

Wenger, E. (1998). *Communities of practice: Learning, meaning, and identity.* Cambridge: Cambridge University Press.

Wikeley, F., & Muschamp, Y. (2004). Pedagogical implications of working with doctoral students at a distance. *Distance Education, 25,* 125-142.

Wilson, B. G. (2001, July). *Sense of community as valued outcome for electronic courses, cohorts, and programs.* Paper presented at VisionQuest PT3 Conference, Denver. Retrieved October 25, 2005, from http://carbon.cudenver.edu/~bwilson/SenseOfCommunity.html.

Wilson, B. G., Ludwig-Hardman, S., Thornam, C. L., & Dunlap, J. C. (2004, April). *Bounded community: Designing and facilitating learning communities in formal courses.* Paper presented at the meeting of the American Educational Research Association, San Diego CA. Retrieved October 25, 2005, from http://carbon.cudenver.edu/~bwilson/BLCs.html.

Winston, B. E., & Fields, D. L. (2003). Developing dissertation skills of doctoral students in an Internet-based education curriculum: A case study. *American Journal of Distance Education, 17,* 161-172.

doi:10.1300/J111v45n01_09

Observations from the Field:
Sharing a Literature Review Rubric

Rosemary Green
Mary Bowser
Shenandoah University

SUMMARY. This paper reports an ongoing research project aimed at developing an analytic rubric used with graduate literature reviews, focusing on the process of adapting and testing it as an instructional and assessment instrument. Early data are presented with explanations of instrument adaptation and our reflections on training and implementation. Emphasis is given to our techniques for transferring the project from one off-campus graduate program to a similar one, while continuing the faculty-librarian model of collaboration. We offer recommendations for modifications to the process and highlight strengths of the rubric. doi:10.1300/J111v45n01_10

KEYWORDS. Scoring rubric, faculty-librarian collaboration, information literacy, literature review, graduate education, academic writing

INTRODUCTION

Preparing a thesis may be the first large-scale writing task that many graduate students undertake, and often students are exposed to the scholarly writing process for the first time in their master's program. From the student's point of view, writing a thesis and reviewing the

[Haworth co-indexing entry note]: "Observations from the Field: Sharing a Literature Review Rubric." Green, Rosemary, and Mary Bowser. Co-published simultaneously in *Journal of Library Administration* (The Haworth Information Press, an imprint of The Haworth Press, Inc.) Vol. 45, No. 1/2, 2006, pp. 185-202; and: *The Twelfth Off-Campus Library Services Conference Proceedings* (ed: Julie A. Garrison) The Haworth Information Press, an imprint of The Haworth Press, Inc., 2006, pp. 185-202.

Available online at http://jla.haworthpress.com
doi:10.1300/J111v45n01_10

literature present opportunities for considerable anxiety,. but direct guidance in graduate research writing may not be available (Bruce, 1994a; Green & Bowser, 2002). Graduate students are not necessarily equipped with the requisite skills to execute large research writing projects, including mastery of the literature, nor can it be presumed that they will be taught these skills during their program. Students' writing skills and knowledge about those conventions are assumed, yet they are expected to perform competently and to write a thesis relatively unassisted. Even such basic skills as citing and attributing proper reference to others' work may be taken for granted (Hendricks & Quinn, 2000). In actuality, the graduate student will find very little guidance for combining linguistic attributes with structure in order to complete a literature review (Swales & Lindemann, 2002).

In response to the difficulties observed when our graduate education students at Shenandoah University began constructing their literature reviews, we developed a rubric to guide students in constructing this section of the thesis. This paper reports an ongoing research project aimed at developing an instrument used with graduate literature reviews. In a faculty-librarian partnership, we created an instructional and assessment rubric with formative, summative, and evaluative applications. Students use the rubric as a writing guide, instructors use it to assess individual literature reviews, and evaluators use it to compare literature reviews across class groups. In an initial pilot phase, the rubric was used with off-campus graduate education students in team-taught thesis courses, and data were collected. On the basis of the adaptive construction of the rubric, a project at a second university was undertaken to test the rubric for transferability to a similar instructional context.

The process of adapting and testing the rubric at a second institution is the focus of this report. We present early data from "Best Practices University" (BPU) with explanations of instrument adaptation and our reflections on training and implementation. Emphasis is given to our techniques for transferring the project from one off-campus graduate program to a similar one, while continuing the faculty-librarian model of collaboration. We offer recommendations for modification to the process as we experienced it and highlight the strengths of the rubric.

UNDERTAKING THE LITERATURE REVIEW

As it is expected of graduate students, the literature review process requires accumulating, reading, comprehending, evaluating, organising, and synthesizing relevant literature. Knowledge of the empirical, theoretical, and methodological foundations of one's research is demonstrated in the literature review, a central feature in both the research proposal and completed thesis. The literature review contextualizes current issues, describing art and science, theory and practice. Undertaking the literature review eventually leads to determination of existing scholarship, support for problem formulation, and location of one's research within existing bodies of knowledge. The review of literature contributes insights or applications otherwise not identifiable in existing literature (Rumrill & Fitzgerald, 2001), grounding the new research and establishing its individuality. Furthermore, the literature review offers epistemological context, revealing the knowledge of previous researchers and knowledge of the review writer (Lea & Street, 1998). As students learn to speak from the text, relying less on received wisdom and personal opinion, they become critical readers of research (Riehl, Larson, Short, & Reitzug, 2000), able to situate an argument by evaluating and incorporating relevant literature.

Developing and composing the literature review takes place over a period of time, following a nonlinear path from emergence to completion. In a cycle punctuated by gathering, analysing, organising, drafting, and reflecting, the literature review process is characterized by intertwining functions. While the literature review is ubiquitous throughout most postgraduate research, literature about the literature review is negligent in addressing the complexity of the process and end product. Academic interest in the literature review as a topic for research is rather limited and seldom turns toward identifying, evaluating, and integrating past research (Bruce 1994b; Cooper, 1988).

Descriptive or instructional reports address application of the literature review in scholarship and research (e.g., Miller & Crabtree, 2004; Rumrill & Fitzgerald, 2001); advice on construction of a review of the literature (e.g., Afolabi, 1992; Swales & Lindemann, 2002); and information literacy events such as acquiring, evaluating, and organising the literature as elements of the literature review process (e.g., Morner, 1993; Nimon, 2002). A second and smaller group of empirical studies focuses on the review of literature as a phenomenon that frames a research study or serves as an object of inquiry. Qian (2003) and Krishnan and Kathpalia (2002) reported small-scale studies in which literature review writing was used as a vehicle for understanding students' strategies for learning academic writing. As the focus of inquiry, investigations of the literature review and practices in teaching and learning the process appear in a comparably small cohort. Bruce's phenomenographic analysis of doctoral students' experiences of the literature (1994a) and subsequent reflection model (1994b, 1996) spoke to the consolidation of the gathering, evaluating, and synthesizing stages of the literature review process. Two studies reported by faculty-librarian teams employed criterion-reference rubrics that assess the quality of literature reviews written by doctoral or master's students (Boote & Beile, 2005; Green & Bowser, 2003). Both articulated criteria for the graduate literature review and pointed to clearer standards and instructional strategies for achieving well-constructed literature reviews. In a single doctoral dissertation devoted to the influence and role of the doctoral literature review, Zaporozhetz (1987) reported on doctoral advisors' instructional practices and attitudes toward the review of literature, concluding that the literature review is given the least instructional consideration among dissertation chapters.

Literature from the past two decades offers very few discussions of teaching and learning the literature review process, with the assumption made that students bear sufficient skills and knowledge specific to researching, interpreting, and writing about scholarly literature (Dreifuss, 1981; Libutti & Kopala, 1995; Williams, 2000; Zaporozhetz, 1987). Authors of academic research belong to a scholarly club (Macauley 2001a), writing for members of that club. Much of the research that is read by graduate students presumes an ability to use earlier research literature, yet novice researchers may experience difficulty deciphering research literature, perceiving it to be privileged discourse (Bruce, 1994b; Riehl et al., 2000). Hart (1998) noted that the quality of literature reviews produced by students varies considerably, and annotated bibliographies rather than critiques of research are all too common. The literature describes a constellation of assumptions regarding student preparedness for graduate research and writing. Added to the presumption that postgraduates are well equipped for the literature review task are further assumptions that they are able to negotiate the information environment and, overall, that they are sufficiently prepared to conduct graduate level research (Hernandez, 1985; Kiley & Liljegren, 1999). As integral to the research process as the literature review should be, students have been known to produce a problem statement, hypothesis, and research design in advance of reviewing relevant literature. The hypothesis or research problem should emerge naturally from the literature review, yet when the quality of graduate research is assessed, rarely is a qualifying literature review that supports a testable hypothesis articulated as a competency (Winston & Fields, 2003).

While most introductory research textbooks in education and the social and behavioral sciences contain a section on reviewing prior research (e.g., Creswell, 2005: Gall, Gall, & Borg 2003), they concentrate to a greater degree on methods of data collection and analysis. In a review of research writing texts and handbooks, Paltridge (2002) found that less attention is afforded thesis or dissertation writing itself than other elements such as methods and analysis; the same can be said for the treatment of the literature review in these texts. Where the literature review is outlined, texts primarily emphasize procedures for literature gathering and interpreting. Recent texts in information science research (e.g., Gorman & Clayton, 2005; Powell & Connaway, 2004) outlined a similar approach to accumulating literature, and students are left to wonder how to treat that material once gathered. Mauch and Birch (1998) segregated the steps in literature searching from the written review of the literature; the benefits of reviewing the literature are outlined, but no clear strategies for organizing and writing are given. The preference in many texts is for literature searching and reviewing sources rather than constructing a written synthesis; perhaps the authors assume that, once the student has resources in hand, writing a literature review follows readily. Generally, criteria and prescriptions for researching and writing a scholarly literature review remain vague and diverse (Boote & Beile, 2005; Bruce, 1994c).

Three notable exceptions to these segregating approaches are Hart's (1998), Pan's (2003), and Galvan's (2005) guides, devoted entirely to writing the literature review from first draft to completed review. Throughout *Doing a Literature Review*, Hart offered formulae, checklists, and criteria intended to help students establish a supportable argument and develop attributes in academic writing. Galvan's *Writing Literature Reviews* and Pan's *Preparing Literature Reviews* presented complementary workbook approaches, recommending exercises in reading empirical research and writing evaluative essays. Galvan assured students that they will learn how to write a review of the literature, but he, too, distinguished literature seeking from writing about research and failed to define the literature review clearly. Much advice on literature reviewing is given, with little evidence that such advice is taken and, if so, to what effect.

INFORMATION LITERACY:
GENERATING THE LITERATURE REVIEW

The literature consistently shows that the practice of reviewing the literature may have two meanings–accumulating relevant literature and writing about such literature. Cooper (1985) encapsulated these two meanings in his definition of a literature review:

> First, a literature review uses as its database reports of primary or original scholarship, and does not report new primary scholarship itself . . . Second, a literature review seeks to describe, summarize, evaluate, clarify, and/or integrate the content of the primary reports. (p. 7)

To any student commencing the process, reviewing the literature means that topic and relevant sources must first be located, acquired, interpreted, and analysed.

A decade ago, Ackerson (1996) and Libutti and Kopala (1995) attested that little in the literature of the day addressed the uniqueness of graduate student literature seeking and literature review needs. At one time, information literacy initiatives in higher education concentrated largely on undergraduate education (Dewey, 2001; Grassian & Kaplowitz, 2001). Postgraduates' instructional needs have been overlooked, perhaps because of the assumption that commencing graduate students have already reached required levels of information skills, either by osmosis or through their undergraduate studies (Macauley, 2001a). Historically, efforts toward training and supporting research students have been extensions of undergraduate programs rather than separate programs based on specific needs of research postgraduates. That imbalance is being adjusted, and more initiatives with pedagogically appropriate foundations are now directed toward the master's and doctoral student (Genoni & Partridge, 2000). Effective information literacy instruction targeted toward the graduate learner incorporates methods such as peer collaboration, direct instruction, and a discipline-specific emphasis (Green & Bowser, 2002; Nimon, 2002; Smith & Oliver, 2005; Squires, 1998). Student-centered methods of delivering information literacy instruction include academic coursework (Bruce, 1990; Green, 2006; Kingston & Reid, 1987; Rader, 1990) that incorporates active learning, action research, or problem-based components (Bruce, 2001; Nimon, 2002).

Postgraduate researchers have highly specialized information needs that require skills sets that differ from those needed by undergraduates (Ackerson, 1996; Macauley, 2001b; Morner, 1993; Williams, 2000). Advanced information skills of identification, advanced browsing, critical evaluation, and presentation are particularly required of graduate researchers (Barry, 1997). Foreshadowing later research, Zaporozhetz (1987) and Alire (1984) spoke with groups of graduate students and found that the majority admitted a need for proper instruction in acquiring and using bibliographic sources. Macauley (2001a, 2001b) and Nimon (2002) documented interviews in which students acknowledge the need for information literacy skills in order to complete their dissertations successfully.

With information literacy integrating into the mission of higher education institutions, those in the community who share the same educational goals are brought together in more coordinated efforts. Expanding venues for information retrieval offer new opportunities for faculty-librarian cooperation. The literature documents an increase in information literacy partnerships established across academic units (Dewey, 2001; Doskatsch, 2003; Green & Bowser, 2002; Isbell & Broadus, 1995; Macauley & Cavanagh, 2001). Zaporozhetz (1987) concluded that "the process of writing the dissertation provides a unique interaction among advisors, doctoral candidates, and librarians" (p. 129). Bailey (1985), Bruce (2001), and Macauley and Cavanagh (2001) echoed this observation, describing partnerships shared by postgraduates, librarians, and academics. The impetus for many of these initiatives comes from librarians, especially regarding the stages at which students need and acquire information literacy skills. Nevertheless, academics and librarians agree upon the importance of information literacy to student learning (Bruce, 2001; Macauley, 2001b). Regardless of the pedagogical approach, information literacy training for research students must deal with effective information management in the domain of the students' discipline if the initial stages of identifying the research question and pursuing relevant literature are to proceed.

METHODS

This paper presents and updates ongoing research. With the intention of developing a rubric that could be used for both instructional and evaluation purposes, we first identified our focus as the quality of literature reviews written by students in our master's of education program at

Shenandoah University and devised a scoring instrument to apply and scrutinize criteria relevant to thesis literature reviews. The rubric reflected our perspectives on the ways that students accumulate, evaluate, and use research sources in the process of reviewing literature. The first analytic rubric had twelve criteria measured in a range of three scores; we modified the rubric to include ten criteria and a five-score scale, reasoning that smaller differences between samples can be difficult to read in a shorter scale (Perlman, 2002). In a recent study (Green & Bowser, 2003), we used a ten-item, three-category, five-score rubric to rate literature reviews written for theses by master's of education students at our university. Five criteria articulated elements of content, three addressed presentation, and two described writing/format features. Scores ranged from a low of one to a high of five across deficient, undeveloped, emerging, developed, and exemplary scoring ranges; a total score of 50 was possible. All points on the scale and all criteria were clearly labeled and described. We continue to take the rubric through an applied cycle of data collection, interpretation, and revision.

An essential feature of the rubric continues to be the instructional framework in which it is implemented. The rubric is introduced to commencing master's students during the information literacy stages of literature review development, when students are initially gathering and evaluating research literature and preparing to draft their first syntheses of the literature. In later stages of the graduate program, a librarian-instructor collaborates with graduate education faculty to co-teach a thesis course that concentrates on the final stages of completing and writing up research projects. The rubric is used for teaching purposes to communicate clear guidelines for expectations of well-constructed literature reviews, and students use it consistently through literature seeking and writing phases until their theses are completed. Instructors score and match the rubric with each student's series of drafts, and students are able to see progress in their conceptualizing and writing. Additionally, students are aware of and attempt to meet the articulated assessment criteria of the rubric (Moskal & Leydens, 2002).

Introducing and Analyzing the Rubric at a Second Site

In 2003 we were invited to share the rubric and our instructional model with another, comparably sized institution. Initially, we recognized the feasibility of a joint venture because the structures of graduate education programs at Best Practices University (BPU) and Shenandoah University (SU) are similar. Graduate education programs in both institutions are targeted toward teacher practitioners, constructed around cohort models, share similar instructional methods, and use a combination of face-to-face methods and course management software to deliver instruction to off-campus graduate students. At both institutions, librarians collaborate with faculty to teach graduate education courses centered on information literacy and methods in gathering, evaluating, and synthesizing research literature. We welcomed this opportunity to test the rubric and our instructional model for transferability to a similar context and to examine the dependability of our research procedures. By examining the rubric in the new setting, we hoped also to study the rubric for flexibility as well as utility for formative, summative, and evaluative purposes.

As the joint project began to take shape, one critical difference between the two institutions became apparent. Graduate education students at SU organize their research projects around topics of personal interest and professional expertise, so each project is relatively unique. In contrast, all graduate education students at BPU are required to encompass educational best practices into their scholarly projects. BPU students are grouped as they enter the program, students write initial literature reviews of single topics within best practices literature, and the capstone research projects and literature reviews are written by the student groups. Therefore, in the first months of this phase we concentrated on modifying and adapting our rubric. With a faculty-librarian team at BPU, we designed a best practices rubric to match expectations that their beginning students would incorporate the literature of best practices in K-12 teaching into initial project literature reviews. As we operationalized the criteria to fit the best practices context, six criteria from our original rubric were revised; of those, two content criteria and one composition criterion underwent substantive changes to accommodate the emphasis on current best practices literature. During the fall 2004 term, the BPU librarian-instructor taught new graduate education students in an introductory research course, using the best practices rubric to provide guidelines for constructing early literature reviews and to provide feedback on students' drafts.

Using the foundation of our original rubric, the three categories for criteria–content, presentation, and writing/format–were retained in the best practices rubric, as was the five-point scoring scheme. In the best practices rubric, content criteria address (1) inclusion of historical, theoretical and seminal literature; (2) inclusion of best practices literature; (3) quality of literature; (4) relevance of literature to current topic; and (5) relevance of studies to each other. Presentation criteria describe (6) organization; (7) transitions; and (8) justification for further research. Finally, the writing/format criteria articulate (9) clarity of writing and interpretation of literature; and (10) bibliographic (APA) format.

Following implementation of the adapted rubric at BPU, we sought to test the efficacy of the instrument, instructional model, and our research methods. We engaged BPU raters to apply the rubric as an evaluative instrument, comparing samples of literature reviews written by BPU students using the rubric with samples written before the rubric was introduced into their graduate education program. We were conscious of the potential for imposing our biases and preferred to use independent raters rather than read the trial samples ourselves, so we continued to use that approach here. We prepared two BPU trainers, the graduate librarian-instructor and a member of the education faculty, who then trained their own faculty readers to read and rate samples of literature reviews using the best practices rubric. In the process of preparing the two BPU trainers to use the rubric, we checked for criterion-related reliability by matching their scores with our ratings of the same samples. Inter-rater reliability was also checked by determining that the two trainers reached consensus independently when rating literature review exemplars drawn from BPU students' work. The trainers proceeded to act as our agents and continued the project at their institution for one academic term. They randomly selected 16 samples, equally distributed between literature reviews written with and without the use of the rubric. Then they selected, trained, and paired eight raters from among their institution's graduate education faculty to read and score the samples. Each sample was read and scored twice. As our research agents, the graduate librarian and faculty member coded and distributed samples to their raters, then returned the scored rubrics to us for analysis.

Because the data were inconclusive, we decided to take these samples through another reading and analysis. We trained a second group of four raters, this time faculty and librarian readers from Shenandoah University. Again, criterion-related rater reliability and inter-rater reliability were confirmed by reaching consensus between experts and raters and between raters. In this reading, raters were not paired; instead, each of the 16 samples read by the first raters was read again by one new rater.

FINDINGS AND DISCUSSION

Sixteen literature reviews emphasizing best practices research and written by commencing master's of education students at BPU were scored twice by paired raters from their home institution. Several months later, the same samples were read a third time by raters selected from our university. The literature reviews were scored on a five-point scale according to criteria to include use of best practices literature and to accommodate early-stage literature reviews. A two-sample *t* test assuming unequal variances was conducted on the total score means, but no significant differences were found between scores of samples written without rubrics and scores of samples written with rubrics. When mean scores by criteria were examined, a range from a low of 2.8 (*SD* 1.3) for criterion 1, historical, theoretical, seminal literature, to a high of 3.8 (*SD* 1.1) for criterion 10, APA format, emerged first in samples of literature reviews written without the rubric. Among the samples of literature reviews written with the rubric, mean scores ranged from a low of 2.4 (*SD* 1.3), again criterion 1, to a high of 4.2 (*SD* 0.9), again criterion 10. Samples written with the use of the rubric showed slight gains in criterion 4, relevance of published studies to current topic, from 3.5 (*SD* 0.7) to 3.7 (*SD* 0.8), in criterion 8, justification for further research, from 2.6 (*SD* 1.3) to 3.2 (*SD* 1.2), and again in criterion 10, APA format, from 3.8 (*SD* 1.1) to 4.2 (*SD* 0.9). Table 1 describes these findings, derived from three readings of each group of sample literature reviews.

Raters at Best Practices University consistently scored their students' literature reviews higher than did the Shenandoah University raters. While total scoring from BPU raters improved slightly in the samples written with the rubric, data from SU raters indicate that total scores decreased in the samples written with the rubric. High standard deviations in all scores are noted. Those findings are described in Table 2.

By sharing and adapting the rubric to a second setting, we introduced new variables into our project. For example, we learned that our original rubric was designed for students concluding their literature reviews and theses, not necessarily for students who were just beginning the literature review process as were those at Best Practices University. For this reason, further revisions to the rubric for both instructional and evaluative functions are needed. At BPU, adjunct education faculty as well as the librarian and faculty we trained taught the literature review process using the rubric; whereas, at SU, the same librarian-instructor and education faculty have consistently team-taught the thesis course, including for-

TABLE 1. Comparison of Samples Written Without and With Rubric, by Criterion

Rubric Criterion	Without Rubric Mean (SD)	With Rubric Mean (SD)
1. Historical & theoretical background; seminal literature	2.8 (1.3)	2.4 (1.3)
2. Best practices literature	3.0 (1.4)	3.0 (1.4)
3. Quality of literature	3.1 (1.3)	3.1 (1.4)
4. Relevance of published studies to current topic	3.5 (0.7)	3.7 (0.8)
5. Relevance of published studies to each other	3.3 (1.1)	3.1 (1.3)
6. Organization	3.7 (1.2)	3.3 (1.1)
7. Transitions	3.7 (1.1)	3.4 (1.1)
8. Justification for further research	2.6 (1.3)	3.2 (1.2)
9. Clarity of writing and interpretation of literature	3.6 (1.0)	3.4 (0.8)
10. Bibliographic (APA) format	3.8 (1.1)	4.2 (0.9)

Note: Values are rounded to tenths.

TABLE 2. Comparison of Total Scores of Samples Written Without and With Rubric, by Raters

	Best Practices University Raters	Shenandoah University Raters
Without Rubric, Total Scores *Mean (SD)*	34.3 (9.3)	29.9 (7.4)
With Rubric, Total Scores *Mean (SD)*	34.9 (7.2)	28 (6.8)

Note: A total score of 50 points was possible.

mative and summative uses of the rubric. Faculty, librarians, and our trained raters at SU typically examine literature reviews in their final drafts rather than in the beginning stages, and that background possibly resulted in their assigning lower scores to the BPU first-stage literature reviews. Nevertheless, when taken together, the total scores suggest the students are able to demonstrate emergent capability in reviewing literature.

Our conclusions should be tempered with an appreciation for the preliminary nature of the revised rubric and its use in the second setting. Most significant, perhaps, is that BPU trainers, faculty, and students were new to the process of using formative and summative rubrics, and our literature review rubric was one of the first introduced into their graduate programs; consequently, a period of adjustment was to be expected. As an analytical tool, the rubric was newly introduced to the

BPU environment, possibly accounting for the relatively broad range of scores given to individual criteria.

We have reached encouraging conclusions regarding the abilities of novice graduate students to appropriate practices for reviewing the literature. They seem to be able to apply bibliographic formatting accurately and consistently, regardless of instructional model. In the introductory research class, students begin to use the literature to articulate the relationship between published research and the newly defined research topics and to justify their research studies. We would expect that other criteria for quality and relevance of studies and for presentation to improve over time as students gain more experience with the literature. At the lowest points of standard deviation, mid-level, undeveloped to emerging scores are maintained for criteria 4, relevance of published studies to current topic, and 10, bibliographic format, and for criteria 6, organization, 7, transitions, and 9, clarity of writing and interpretation. These scores encourage us to conclude that these learners are able to demonstrate relevance of the literature using conventions required in early stages of academic writing, even though they may be entering the cycle of gathering, analyzing, and synthesizing research literature for the first time.

The process of sharing, adapting, and revising the original rubric to the second setting showed interesting and informative results, and we learned that circumstances affecting rater training and instrument use required significantly different approaches at each site. We were able to establish criterion-related and inter-rater reliability with two BPU trainers and with SU raters by seeking consensus at the time that training exemplars were read. However, inter-rater reliability at the training was not statistically determined with correlation coefficients. The variability of scores among raters and between groups of raters indicated that we should continue to examine training procedures throughout the reading process. Rater checking, begun during the training phase, should also continue throughout data collection.

We observed, too, that matters of course outcomes and program design affected the manner in which we modified and recommended using the rubric. Translations from classroom practice to examination of practice are not necessarily seamless. If the rubric is to serve dual functions as an instructional and evaluative instrument, it requires further modification and exploration. We found evidence of differences in perceptual frameworks of trainers, raters, instructors, and student writers, emphasizing the need to operationalize criteria for literature reviews and for master's research projects as a whole. All participants in the rubric implementation process should be able to differentiate well developed and comprehensible criteria, yet when the new rubric was put into practice, we observed that criteria were not necessarily understood consistently across participating groups, including students, instructors, and readers.

We question now whether a five-score rubric functions best as an assessment tool; returning to Perlman (2002), we recognize that long scales present difficulties in differentiating adequately between scale points and challenge raters to reach agreement on scores. The next phase of instrument development will examine whether the rubric as it is currently written functions equally well for both instruction and evaluation or whether two instruments are now required. As an unexpected outcome from the process of adapting our original rubric, we have been able to reorganize the first instrument's criteria and refine criteria descriptions. We realize, too, that the best practices rubric and our original rubric represent two instructional tools that may potentially serve as bookends in the process of literature review construction, one at the first draft phase and one at the final phase of completion.

CONCLUSION

Teaching and learning the literature review process in graduate education deserves exploration, discussion, and innovation. We have concluded that the body of research relevant to teaching, learning, and evaluating literature reviews is quite small. Despite this apparent lack of conversation, the importance of giving pedagogical support to improving the conceptualization and structure of literature reviews cannot be overstated. Sources included in the review are chosen largely based on research needs perceived by the graduate writer, following criteria that may or may not meet standards of objectivity. Depending on the skills and inclinations of the writer, justification for inclusion of literature in the review may be quite subjective, in part because graduate students may not be sufficiently guided in the process of reviewing the literature. Ideally, tools such as rubrics can be used as part of the instructional scheme of modeling good literature reviews, scaffolding methods for learning the process, and coaching students in the gradual, recursive process of writing and revising. Our study contributes to this discussion by proposing an instructional model, describing an analytical instrument for the process, and sharing the procedures by which both instruction and evaluation can be refined and distributed among colleagues.

REFERENCES

Ackerson, L. G. (1996). Basing reference service on scientific communication: Toward a more effective model for science graduate students. *RQ: Reference Quarterly, 2*, 248-60.

Afolabi, M. (1992). The review of related literature in research. *International Journal of Information and Library Research, 4* (1), 59-66.

Alire, C. A. (1984). *A nationwide survey of education doctoral students' attitudes regarding the importance of the library and the need for bibliographic instruction.* Unpublished doctoral dissertation, University of Northern Colorado, Greeley.

Bailey, B. (1985). Thesis practicum and the librarian's role. *Journal of Academic Librarianship, 11*, 79-81.

Barry, C. (1997). Information skills for an electronic world: Training doctoral research students. *Journal of Information Science, 23*, 225-238.

Boote, D., & Beile, P. (2005). Scholars before researchers: On the centrality of the dissertation literature review in dissertation preparation. *Educational Researcher, 34* (6), 3-15.

Bruce, C. (1990). Information skills coursework for postgraduate students: Investigation and response at the Queensland University of Technology. *Australian Academic & Research Libraries, 21*, 224-232.

Bruce, C. (1994a). Research students' early experiences of the dissertation literature review. *Studies in Higher Education, 19*, 217-119.

Bruce, C. (1994b). Supervising literature reviews. In O. Zuber-Skerritt & Y. Ryan (Eds.), *Quality in postgraduate education* (pp. 143-155). London: Kogan Page.

Bruce, C. (1994c). When enough is enough: Or how should research students delimit the scope of their literature review? In G. Ryan, P. Little & I. Dunn (Eds.), *Challenging the conventional wisdom in higher education* (pp. 435-439). Sydney: University of New South Wales.

Bruce, C. (1996). From neophyte to expert: Counting on reflection to facilitate complex conceptions of the literature review. In O. Zuber-Skerritt (Ed.), *Frameworks for postgraduate education* (pp. 239-253). Lismore, New South Wales: Southern Cross University.

Bruce, C. (2001). Faculty-librarian partnerships in Australian higher education: Critical dimensions. *Reference Services Review, 29*, 106-115.

Cooper, H. (1985). *A taxonomy of literature reviews.* Washington, DC: National Institute of Education.

Cooper, H. (1988). Organizing knowledge syntheses: A taxonomy of literature reviews. *Knowledge in Society, 1*, 104-126.

Creswell, J. W. (2005). *Educational research: Planning, conducting, and evaluating quantitative and qualitative research* (2d ed.). Upper Saddle River, NJ: Pearson.

Dewey, B. I. (2001). *Library user education: Powerful learning, powerful partnerships.* Lanham, MD: Scarecrow Press.

Doskatsch, I. (2003). Perceptions and perplexities of the faculty-librarian perspective: An Australian perspective. *Reference Services Review, 31*, 111-121.

Dreifuss, R. A. (1981). Library instruction and graduate students: More work for George. *RQ: Reference Quarterly, 21*, 121-123.

Gall, M. D., Gall, J. P., & Borg, W. R. (2003). *Educational research: An introduction* (7th ed.). Boston: Allyn and Bacon.

Galvan, J. L. (2005). *Writing literature reviews: A guide for students of the social and behavioral sciences* (3rd ed.). Glendale CA: Pyrczak Press.

Genoni, P., & Partridge, J. (2000). Personal research information management: Information literacy and the research student. In C. Bruce & P. Candy (Eds.), *Information literacy around the world: Advances in programs and research* (pp. 223-235). Wagga Wagga, New South Wales: Centre for Information Studies, Charles Sturt University.

Gorman, G. E., & Clayton, P. (2005). *Qualitative research for the information professional; A practical handbook* (2d ed.). London: Facet.

Grassian, E. S., & Kaplowitz, J. R. (2001). *Information literacy instruction: Theory and practice.* New York: Neal-Schuman.

Green, R. (2006). *Fostering a community of doctoral learners.* Paper presented at the Eleventh Off-Campus Library Services Conference, Savannah, GA.

Green, R., & Bowser, M. (2002). Managing thesis anxiety: A faculty-librarian partnership to guide off-campus students through the thesis process. *Journal of Library Administration, 37,* 341-354.

Green, R., & Bowser, M. (2003, April). *Evolution of the thesis literature review: A faculty-librarian partnership to guide off-campus research and writing.* Paper presented at the Eleventh Annual Conference of the Association of College and Research Libraries, Charlotte, NC.

Hart, C. (1998). *Doing a literature review: Releasing the social science research imagination.* Thousand Oaks, CA: Sage.

Hendricks, M., & Quinn, L. (2000). Teaching referencing as an introduction to epistemological empowerment. *Teaching in Higher Education, 5,* 447-457.

Hernandez, N. (1985). *The fourth, composite 'R' for graduate students: Research.* University of Wyoming, Laramie (ERIC Document Reproduction Service No. ED267671).

Isbell, D., & Broadus, D. (1995). Teaching writing and research as inseparable: A faculty-librarian teaching team. *Reference Services Review, 23* (4), 51-62.

Kiley, M., & Liljegren, D. (1999). Discipline-related models for a structured program at the commencement of a PhD. *Teaching in Higher Education, 4,* 61-75.

Kingston, P., & Reid, B. (1987). Instruction in information retrieval within a doctoral research program: A pertinent contribution? *British Journal of Academic Librarianship, 2,* 91-104.

Krishnan, L. & Kathpalia, S. S. (2002). Literature reviews in student project reports. *IEEE Transactions of Professional Communication, 45,* 187-197.

Lea, M. R., & Street, B. (1998). Student writing in higher education: An academic literacies approach. *Studies in Higher Education, 23,* 157-172.

Libutti, P., & Kopala, M. (1995). The doctoral student, the dissertation, and the library: A review of the literature. *Social Science Reference Services, 48,* 5-25.

Macauley, P. (2001a). *Doctoral research and scholarly communication: Candidates, supervisors and information literacy.* Unpublished doctoral thesis, Deakin University, Geelong, Victoria.

Macauley, P. (2001b). Menace, missionary zeal or welcome partner? Librarian involvement in the information literacy of doctoral researchers. *New Review of Libraries and Lifelong Learning, 2,* 47-66.

Macauley, P., & Cavanagh, A. K. (2001). Doctoral dissertations at a distance: A novel approach from down under. *Journal of Library Administration, 32,* 331-46.

Mauch, J. E., & Birch, J. W. (1998). *Guide to the successful thesis and dissertation: Conception to publication. A handbook for students and faculty.* New York: Marcel Dekker.

Miller, W. L., & Crabtree, B. F. (2004). Depth interviewing. In S. N. Hesse-Biber & P. Leavy (Eds.), *Approaches to qualitative research* (pp. 185-202). New York: Oxford University Press.

Morner, C. J. (1993). *A test of library research skills for education doctoral students.* Unpublished doctoral dissertation, Boston College, Boston.

Moskal, B. M., & Leydens, J. A. (2002). Scoring rubric development: Validity and reliability. In C. Boston (Ed.), *Understanding scoring rubrics: A guide for teachers* (pp. 25-33). College Park, MD: ERIC Clearinghouse on Assessment and Evaluation. (ERIC Document Reproduction Service No. ED471518).

Nimon, M. (2002). Preparing to teach "the literature review": Staff and student views of the value of a compulsory course in research education. *Australian Academic & Research Libraries, 33,* 168-179.

Paltridge, B. (2002). Thesis and dissertation writing: An examination of published advice and actual practice. *English for Specific Purposes, 21,* 125-143.

Pan, M. L. (2003). *Preparing literature reviews: Qualitative and quantitative approaches* (2d ed.). Glendale, CA: Pyrczak Press.

Perlman, C. (2002). An introduction to performance assessment scoring rubrics. In C. Boston (Ed.), *Understanding scoring rubrics: A guide for teachers* (pp. 5-13). College Park, MD: ERIC Clearinghouse on Assessment and Evaluation (ERIC Document Reproduction Service No. ED471518).

Powell, R. R., & Connaway, L. S. (2004). *Basic research methods for librarians* (4th ed.). Westport, CT: Libraries Unlimited.

Qian, J. (2003). *Chinese graduate students' experiences with writing a literature review.* Unpublished master's thesis, Queen's University at Kingston, Ontario.

Rader, H. B. (1990). Bringing information literacy into the academic curriculum. *College & Research Libraries News, 51,* 879-880.

Riehl, C., Larson, C. L., Short, P. M., & Reitzug, U. C. (2000). Reconceptualizing research and scholarship in educational administration: Learning to know, knowing to do, doing to learn. *Educational Administration Quarterly, 46,* 391-427.

Rumrill, P. D., & Fitzgerald, S. M. (2001). Using narrative literature reviews to build a scientific knowledge base. *Work, 16,* 165-170.

Smith, J., & Oliver, M. (2005). Exploring behaviour in the online environment: Student perceptions of information literacy. *ALT-J, Research in Learning Technology, 13* (1), 49-65.

Squires, D. (1998). The impact of new developments in information technology on postgraduate research and supervision. In J. A. Malone, B. Atweh & J. R. Northfield (Eds.), *Research and supervision in mathematics and science education* (pp. 299-322). Mahwah, NJ: Lawrence Erlbaum Associates.

Swales, J. M., & Lindemann, S. (2002). Teaching the literature review to international graduate students. In A. M. Johns (Ed.), *Genre in the classroom: Multiple perspectives.* Mahwah, NJ: Lawrence Erlbaum Associates.

Williams, H. C. (2000). User education for graduate students: Never a given, and not always received. In T.E. Jacobson & H.C. Williams (Eds.), *Teaching the new library to today's users* (pp. 145-172). New York: Neal-Schulman.

Winston, B. E., & Fields, D. L. (2003). Developing dissertation skills of doctoral students in an Internet-based education curriculum: A case study. *American Journal of Distance Education, 17*, 161-172.

Zaporozhetz, L. (1987). *The dissertation literature review: How faculty advisors prepare their doctoral candidates.* Unpublished doctoral dissertation, University of Oregon, Eugene OR.

doi:10.1300/J111v45n01_10

Indiana's Statewide Distance Education Library Services Task Force: Past, Present, and Future

Anne Haynes

Indiana University, Bloomington

Susan Mannan

Ivy Tech Community College-Central Indiana

SUMMARY. The authors present a case study in statewide cooperation in the delivery of library services to distance students throughout Indiana. This paper is the first to tie together all efforts of Indiana academic librarians, since 1994, to create an academic library services consortium focused on services to distance learners. Indiana has a history of interest in libraries serving distance students, but organizing activity in that area was not sustainable until recently when an organization was formed, under the Academic Libraries of Indiana, that shows promise of supporting distance education library services throughout the state. doi:10.1300/J111v45n01_11

KEYWORDS. Library consortia, partnerships, Indiana

A REVIEW OF CONSORTIA EFFORTS IN DISTANCE LIBRARY SERVICES

The authors present a case study in statewide delivery of library services to distance students throughout Indiana. This paper is the first to

[Haworth co-indexing entry note]: "Indiana's Statewide Distance Education Library Services Task Force: Past, Present, and Future." Haynes, Anne, and Susan Mannan. Co-published simultaneously in *Journal of Library Administration* (The Haworth Information Press, an imprint of The Haworth Press, Inc.) Vol. 45, No. 1/2, 2006, pp. 203-213; and: *The Twelfth Off-Campus Library Services Conference Proceedings* (ed: Julie A. Garrison) The Haworth Information Press, an imprint of The Haworth Press, Inc., 2006, pp. 203-213.

Available online at http://jla.haworthpress.com
doi:10.1300/J111v45n01_11

tie together all of the efforts of Indiana academic librarians to date at creating an academic library services consortium focused on services to distance learners. The idea for this paper came from the authors' desire to share the Indiana experience of working through several incarnations of a consortium and finally arriving at the current configuration, a group that is sponsored by a statewide library organization, the Academic Libraries of Indiana (ALI) (http://ali.earlham.edu/). The authors will show that although the first two generations of the Library Services Task Force, sponsored by Indiana's Higher Education Telecommunication System (IHETS), recommended initiatives that for the most part did not result in formal adoption of changes, they laid the foundation for further work. As of this writing, the third iteration of the task force showed promise of fulfilling some of the goals of the previous two task forces and considering new initiatives.

A search was done of the library and information science literature on the subject of statewide consortia for academic library distance education services in the United States and for articles on distance library services in Indiana. No articles were found that documented the complete history of Indiana's consortium, but several articles and reports discussed parts or aspects of Indiana's history of cooperative distance library services. Fry, Lucas, and Miller (1999) wrote about the history of the Private Academic Library Network of Indiana (PALNI), but that organization excludes public institutions. Scott (2002) discussed the successes of Indiana's virtual university consortium, the Indiana College Network (ICN), and the Indiana Partnership for Statewide Education (IPSE) in meeting the distance and online learning needs of the state. Two reports documented the work and recommendations of the IHETS Library Committee and the IHETS/IPSE Library Services Task Force (IPSE/IHETS, 1995; IPSE/IHETS, 2004).

Few articles appear in the literature about similar efforts in other states. The search produced articles on two other states' efforts to join academic libraries' distance or electronic services in a network of cooperation and mutual support: The Utah Academic Library Consortium (UALC) and the Louisiana Academic Library Information Network Consortium (LALINC) and its Resource Sharing Committee (Brunvand et al., 2001; Wittkopf, Orgeron, & Del Nero, 2001). There were other examples of consortia covered in the literature, but most were regional rather than statewide consortia. The scarcity of close comparisons to the Indiana model is not surprising when one considers that each state has its own approach to funding and organizing higher education and related library services.

INDIANA'S DISTANCE EDUCATION ORGANIZATION

Indiana colleges and universities have been offering distance education courses for many years. As long ago as the early 1900s, Indiana University was offering independent study courses, and Purdue University was broadcasting courses via radio starting in the 1930s. These two universities began to deliver courses between their campuses in 1961. As a result of this inter-campus activity, IHETS was created in 1967 to help coordinate the distance education activities among the various Indiana higher education institutions (Scott, 2002). In the early years, courses were delivered to campuses around the state through a closed-circuit one-way video/two-way audio television system, managed by IHETS. A student in southern Indiana could, for example, take a course from Purdue University by going to a regional university campus or a local two-year college site.

When the Internet offered the possibility of online courses, the college and university IHETS members took steps to coordinate and promote the growing number of courses to an even faster growing market of students. In 1992 the IHETS' Board of Directors formed the Indiana Partnership for Statewide Education (IPSE). This "consortium within a consortium" was to develop collaborative ways of bringing a broad range of educational opportunities to Indiana citizens through a variety of technologies that would allow them to pursue their education at a distance, at work or at home (Scott, 2002, Indiana's Virtual University section, para. 2). To accomplish this, IPSE created the Indiana College Network (ICN), one of the earlier virtual universities in the country and the first such consortium (Scott).

Institutions participating in the ICN both then and now include the seven state-supported schools (Ball State, Ivy Tech Community College, Indiana State University, Indiana University, Purdue University, University of Southern Indiana, and Vincennes University) plus many of Indiana's independent/private colleges, including Indiana Wesleyan, the University of Indianapolis, and the University of Saint Frances. Together these institutions have increased the distance offerings in spring of 2005 to 3,005 classes in 194 programs, ranging from certificate programs to master's degree programs and even one Ph.D. program. As in other areas of the country, growth in online course enrollments was the greatest. By the spring of 2005, there were 89,478 online course enrollments. Including all forms of delivery (including live television, video tape, DVD, and CD), enrollments totaled 103,853 for 2003-04 (Indiana Higher Education Telecommunication System. 2005). IPSE/IHETS has taken several steps to support students in their pursuit of distance education. They have established 59 learning centers in 49 counties where students may view courses, get online access, and receive other help, especially assistance with registration issues.

IHETS LIBRARY COMMITTEE–ROUND 1

In addition to the above efforts, a number of committees were formed to coordinate activities and encourage best practices. One of these was the IHETS Library Committee, formed in the 1994/95 school year. The 19 members of the committee represented the academic libraries of the IHETS member institutions, plus representatives of high school and public libraries, IHETS, the Indiana State Library, and the Indiana Cooperative Library Services Authority. This group, chaired by Pat Steele from Indiana University, was charged with recommending infrastructure, criteria, policies, and procedures that would ensure effective library support to ICN students. The committee met several times during the year and produced a report with several recommendations, including a mission statement for IPSE library services, and a set of assumptions and proposed model for library services.

That report of the IPSE/IHETS Library Committee (1995) stated, "The mission of the libraries involved in the Partnership for Statewide Education is to provide library resources and library services through a seamless and equitable support system for distance learners who are enrolled in the Indiana College Network" (p. 4). Recognizing the complex variety of colleges and universities in the partnership, the committee's stated assumptions included the idea that each originating institution had overall responsibility for providing library services to its own students in its own courses. It was never intended that any cooperative effort or organization replace that responsibility. Cooperative efforts were intended to facilitate and enhance what individual institutions would do. It was seen as a multi-layered, networked approach.

The proposed model included four features: (1) originating institutions providing the base support for their own courses and students through a designated "coordinating librarian," (2) ICN affiliate libraries and librarians, which would be local public and perhaps school libraries and librarians agreeing to give some assistance and connect students to the libraries of their "home" institutions (those originating the courses), (3) the ICN learning centers, which would provide Internet access, low level library service, and a connection to the home library as needed, and (4) an ongoing IPSE/IHETS library committee to implement, assess, and continue to develop a library service model for the ICN.

It was recommended that each originating institution appoint a "coordinating librarian" to work with the students, the faculty teaching the courses, others in the home institution as needed, the learning centers, and local libraries throughout the state. This librarian would proactively contact faculty, students, and learning centers to assist and train in the use of library resources. The committee went so far as to recommend issuing IPSE identification cards to ICN students to help establish visibility for the programs and to ensure effective service.

It was also assumed that students would need convenient access to libraries that could help them with searches and other library needs. The committee intended to work with local libraries to encourage them to grant library privileges to ICN students. They envisioned creating a list of possible places students could get library help, to include local libraries that had agreed to become "affiliate libraries" (designated providers of library service to ICN students). The list would also include the libraries on all campuses in the state. Students would be required to choose a "home library" from this list of participating libraries. That "home library" would serve as the students' main point of library contact and could be one close to them or could be at the institution originating their course. Selecting a home library would facilitate communication among the student, the home library, the learning center, and the coordinating librarian at the originating institution. This network was also envisioned to provide training activities for students and librarians.

Finally, as IPSE instituted a peer review process to evaluate the new online courses from each institution, it was assumed that the coordinating librarians would also be involved in that process as consultants. A library impact form was developed and recommended as part of every course proposal. The report closed with an appeal to the two statewide academic library networks, the State University Library Automation Network (SULAN) and the Private Academic Library Network of Indiana (PALNI) to examine the possibility of negotiating with online database vendors to open remote database access to ICN students regardless of the particular university from which their courses originated.

The report was submitted to the IHETS Management Committee in June of 1995. The committee did not formally reconvene after submission. Learning centers developed along a different model, as did interinstitutional faculty peer review, and the library committee's work was never formally implemented within the IPSE/IHETS/ICN framework. Nonetheless, the librarians had explored the issues together, developed a network, and gained an understanding of what was needed for good library service. Some member institutions implemented some of the report's recommendations, and librarians continued to work together informally, supporting their own courses and reaching out when needed.

IHETS LIBRARY COMMITTEE–ROUND 2

In 2003 a second library services task force sponsored by IPSE was convened by Susan Scott of IHETS. The environment had changed in the ensuing eight years. Online courses were in full swing, supported by robust course management systems. The distinction between distance students and those on campus also taking online courses had become blurred. Libraries in Indiana were offering a wide array of online resources, including journals and newspapers, citation indexes, books, reference works, online dissertations and abstracts, digital libraries, sound, video, and online tutorials for information literacy. A cooperative state-funded project called INSPIRE (http://www.inspire.net/) was making core databases and online journal articles available to all Indiana K-12 schools; public, academic, and special libraries; and the State Library. It was possible to request document delivery and interlibrary loan services online, and e-mail and chat reference services and online course reserves were offered by at least some libraries. Search engines such as Google made it possible for students and faculty to access so much information that the librarian's role had become more vital in interpreting the flow from the proverbial "fire hose" of online information.

In the second task force, ten of the twelve members were the "distance education librarians" from various colleges and universities actively engaged in distance and online education. The remaining two members represented IHETS and the Indiana State Library. Judy Tribble from Indiana State University served as chair. The task force's charges were: (1) to review the report of the previous committee, (2) "to consider the current context and recommend optimal ways to provide enhanced library services for e-learning," and (3) to "assess the potential for collaboration in developing information-literacy courses and/or training for faculty and students in use of e-library resources" (IPSE/IHETS, 2004, p. 1).

A survey of Indiana public librarians was conducted, asking about the public libraries' experience with distance students using their libraries. Sixty-one librarians responded. The results of this survey demonstrated in general the willingness of public librarians to support their users who were distance students, and also showed that more and better communication was needed between the public libraries and the students' originating institution libraries.

The task force met jointly with the IPSE Faculty Services Team (http://www.ihets.org/about/comm/faculty/) in an effort to increase communication with faculty about the availability of library services offered to distance learners. They also updated information for the ICN's Web site for library support (http://www.icn.org/services_and_resources/library_support.html), which has links to the library Web sites of all participating schools in the state. The result of this task force was a 2004 report, which called for the formation of an IPSE Library Services Team as a continuing committee. This IPSE/IHETS report updated the mission statement of the libraries involved in IPSE and recommended a "framework for supporting students learning at a distance" in Indiana (2004, p. 6). Public libraries were recognized as having a potentially important role in supporting distance students. The report emphasized one of the most basic premises of the ACRL Guidelines for Distance Learning Library Services (ACRL, 2004), which is that the primary responsibility for providing library services rests with the originating institution. The "originating institution" is defined in the ACRL Guidelines as "the entity . . . responsible for the offering or marketing and supporting of distance learning courses and programs: the credit-granting body" (ACRL, 2004, p. 2). In addition, the report encouraged the Academic Libraries of Indiana (ALI) "to examine the possibility of negotiating with online resource vendors to open remote access to distant students" (IPSE/IHETS, p. 6).

A NEW ORGANIZATION BECOMES INVOLVED

Following the submission of the 2004 IHETS report, committee members kept in touch and waited for IHETS to give the group an ongoing charge. Discussion of the report surfaced some confusion about overlapping roles of IHETS and a newly formed organization, the Academic Libraries of Indiana (ALI). By 2005, it was apparent that this confusion and other priorities and budgetary constraints at IHETS had curtailed the ability of IHETS to pursue creation of such an ongoing group. This time committee members felt the need to move forward with or without IHETS sponsorship, and they sought out a new home with the Academic Libraries of Indiana (ALI). ALI, formed in 2003, was made up of all the academic libraries in Indiana, represented by their directors. One of the directors, Susan Mannan from Ivy Tech Community College, had been a member of both of the IHETS library committees and was now on the board of ALI. Mannan proposed to the ALI board that it was a logical home for a group interested in furthering library services to distance learning students. The directors were just the people whose attention and support were needed to promote services to distance learning students. The board accepted the idea and appointed the director who had brought them the issue as the chair of the newly formed task force.

The task force is composed of volunteers and appointees from several member institutions. Backgrounds of the volunteer task force members included experience as distance education and off-campus library services librarians, librarians who had taken, developed and or taught distance (mostly online) courses, a former distance education coordinator, an "embedded librarian" in a distance course, and a librarian doing outreach efforts. Four members had served on the earlier IHETS/IPSE Library Committee. Six members are library directors who have been involved with distance education. The board gave the task force the following initial charge/mission:

- Explore issues and opportunities related to distance education and off-campus library use.
- Identify distance education/off-campus library-related needs for ALI consideration.
- Explore possible cooperative or coordinated projects and services related to distance education or off-campus library use among ALI members.
- Identify other organizations and institutions with which ALI could cooperate and explore potential joint programs or projects that might improve library services to distance education or off-campus users.

The task force will be challenged to find issues and projects that can be cooperatively pursued at the statewide level in an environment that has a diverse range of large and small public and private libraries ranging from two-year community colleges to graduate research universities. These diverse institutions vary greatly in their involvement in distance education. Some deliver hundreds of courses to many thousands of students. Others have few or no courses via distance. Further, defining and identifying distance students is surfacing as an issue. The definition of a distance learner is problematic in relation to library services, especially in institutions whose main activity is through face-to-face, on-campus courses. Many students who take distance courses are also taking courses on campus. Should the library treat these students as distance students or on-campus students? Further complicating the picture is the emergence of hybrid courses, which meet face-to-face on campus, but for fewer than the usual number of hours, making up that lost time with online activities and communications. Are these students distance learners? How does the library identify distance learners so that they can receive "distance learner" services, if those services are different?

The first efforts of the task force are concentrating on an environmental scan. A survey in the spring of 2006 will seek input on the practices of the academic libraries in the state with regard to their distance learning services. The group is also gathering statistics on distance learning enrollments at the various institutions, reviewing information on and links to the libraries on the ICN Web sites, reaching out to public and school library partners who might be serving the distance learning students, and reaching out to the coordinators of ICN distance learning centers around the state. In the spring of 2006 the task force will host a session at the Indiana Library Federation annual state conference designed to inform public librarians about services available to distance learners and how they can help students access those services. Task force members also hope to visit with the ICN learning center coordinators on the same topic. The task force plans to look for ways to highlight best practices in the state in serving distance learners and will seek to encourage more dialogue among the distance learning librarians and between them and distance learning faculty. They may also consider ways to highlight online library tutorials that could be shared.

From these activities, the task force and ALI board hope to discover ways to improve services to distance learners and off-campus students. The first result should be a new level of awareness of the issues and a broader and deeper understanding on the part of the task force members, ALI library directors, ICN learning center coordinators, and public librarians. In the future, the task force may consider contact with institutional campus distance education and off-campus services coordinators. Future work will likely focus on continued awareness activities, sharing and promoting of best practices, and promoting the ACRL Guidelines for Distance Learning Library Services. Future projects might also involve exploring the need/possibility for more joint licensing of academic databases that would offer statewide access for distance learning students. More awareness of distance learner database needs may also lead to a strengthening of the statewide state-funded INSPIRE suite of databases that could be used by a student at any institution. There is also interest in researching how librarians are currently involved with distance education faculty, how the use of library resources is now incorporated into distance education courses as compared to on-campus courses, and how the involvement of librarians with faculty during the development of distance courses can be promoted. In general, the focus will be on activities that can be pursued at a statewide cooperative level because of the nature of ALI as a statewide organization of academic libraries. ALI had already implemented statewide reciprocal borrowing and no-charge interlibrary loan agreements and is exploring cooperative database purchases. The work of the Distance Education/Off Campus Library Services Task Force may uncover new ways to cooperate, although it is too soon to be more specific.

CONCLUSION

Finding concrete projects on which to cooperate may not be easy. There are varying levels of involvement in distance education on the part of the seventy-plus academic institutions in the state, all the way from having 35,000 students enrolled in several hundred courses to minimal or no involvement. Indiana has a history of interest in libraries serving distance students, but that activity formerly was not sustainable. There is hope now that, under the auspices of library directors through the ALI organization, activity and interest can be sustained.

AUTHOR NOTE

The authors would like to acknowledge Rita Barsun and Susan Scott for their critical reading of the manuscript.

REFERENCES

Association of College and Research Libraries. (2004, June 29). *Guidelines for distance learning library services.* Retrieved October 5, 2005, from http://www.ala. org/ala/acrl/acrlstandards/guidelinesdistancelearning.htm.

Brunvand, A., Lee, D. R., McClosky, K. M., Hansen, C., Kochan, C. A., & Morrison, R. (2001). Consortium solutions to distance education problems: Utah academic libraries answer the challenges. *Journal of Library Administration, 31*(3/4), 75-92. Retrieved November 13, 2005, from The Haworth Press, Inc. database.

Frye, L., Lucas, V., & Miller, L. (1999). Technology partnerships: The PALNI success story. *Indiana Libraries, 18* (suppl), 39-43. Retrieved November 13, 2005, from Wilson Library Literature and Information Science database.

Indiana Higher Education Telecommunication System. (2005). *IHETS by the numbers.* Retrieved September 1, 2005, from http://www.ihets.org/about/bkg/stats/index. html.

Indiana Partnership for Statewide Education/Indiana Higher Education Telecommunications System. Library Committee. (1995, June 8). *Report.* (Available from Indiana Higher Education Telecommunications System, 714 North Senate Avenue, Indianapolis, IN 46202.)

Indiana Partnership for Statewide Education/Indiana Higher Education Telecommunications System. Library Services Task Force. Library Services for Students in Distance Learning. *Report.* (2004, May 21). (Available from Indiana Higher Education Telecommunications System, 714 North Senate Avenue, Indianapolis, IN 46202.)

Scott, S. B. (2002). Coping with success: Distance learning in Indiana higher education. *Indiana Libraries, 21* (1), 2-5. Retrieved March 15, 2005, from Wilson Library Literature and Information Science database.

Wittkopf, B., Orgeron, E., & Del Nero, T. (2001). Louisiana academic libraries: Partnering to enhance distance education services. *Journal of Library Administration, 32*(1/2), 439-447. Retrieved November 13, 2005, from The Haworth Press, Inc. database.

doi:10.1300/J111v45n01_11

What Do Distance Education Faculty Want from the Library?

Samantha Schmehl Hines

University of Montana-Missoula

SUMMARY. Much has been written on the importance of working with instructors teaching at a distance to provide library services to distant students and instructors. However, what distant instructors want and expect from the library has not been explored as directly, and definitely not on a large scale. Examining the small-scale studies that have been performed at various institutions, we can (1) identify what distance education faculty generally want from their library to supplement their instruction; (2) look at what services faculty would commonly like to see the library offer to their students; and (3) discover what further steps need to be taken to better understand the faculty we seek to serve. doi:10.1300/J111v45n01_12

KEYWORDS. Distance education, faculty, library services, attitudes

INTRODUCTION

I initially presented the results from my assessment of distant faculty at my institution at ALA Annual 2005, with a poster titled, "What do distance education faculty want from the library?" This caught several conference attendees' eyes. A number of people stopped by to ask what,

[Haworth co-indexing entry note]: "What Do Distance Education Faculty Want from the Library?" Hines, Samantha Schmehl. Co-published simultaneously in *Journal of Library Administration* (The Haworth Information Press, an imprint of The Haworth Press, Inc.) Vol. 45, No. 1/2, 2006, pp. 215-227; and: *The Twelfth Off-Campus Library Services Conference Proceedings* (ed: Julie A. Garrison) The Haworth Information Press, an imprint of The Haworth Press, Inc., 2006, pp. 215-227.

Available online at http://jla.haworthpress.com
doi:10.1300/J111v45n01_12

indeed, did the faculty want, and if there were any conclusions they could take back to their own libraries.

My evaluation of distance education faculty services via an assessment of their needs, opinions and desires started out as a way for this new librarian to get to know her constituency, and it is certainly not unique. While preparing for the poster session, I learned of a number of similar studies at other institutions. These studies ranged from informal information gathering via telephone interviews and face-to-face meetings, to elaborate questionnaires with prepaid return mailing envelopes. This led me to wonder if there were any commonalities between what I found at my institution and what others found at theirs. Were there certain things that faculty everywhere wanted, that could be used as a baseline for providing services or starting discussions?

STUDIES EXAMINED

This paper examines thirteen other studies or surveys, besides my own, of distant faculty dating from 1986 to 2004. These studies came primarily from public universities from across the United States.

These studies varied in how they were carried out. Generally, they consisted of formally gathered survey data, with surveys ranging in length from eight to sixteen questions. Six studies used surveys conducted wholly on paper, which were sent to respondents either via campus mail or the postal service. Three were conducted entirely online, and one sent out the surveys on paper but allowed for either paper or e-mail responses. Interestingly, this last survey's e-mail responses beat out paper responses nearly two-to-one (Adams & Cassner, 2001). Otherwise, the reported response rates varied from 24% to 50%.

The non-survey studies included focus groups (*Distance Learning*, 1998), in-person collaboration on projects (Feldheim, King & Sherman, 2004), and analyses of services and statistics (Markgraf, 2002). One study that had a formal survey also used focus groups (Shaffer, Finkelstein, Woelfl & Lyden, 2004) and another used telephone interviews in addition to a survey (Steffen, 1986).

In order to better analyze the conclusions, this paper breaks down the survey items and analyses from the studies into two foci: services provided to faculty directly, and services for students. There were no universal themes across all studies but some points were mentioned repeatedly.

Commonalities with Faculty Services

Something that came up in a number of studies was the difficulty in finding out who is teaching at a distance, and how to contact them. Four studies (Cook & Cook, 1987; Hufford, 2004; Markgraf, 2002; Shaffer et al., 2004) mentioned this as a specific problem and all four attributed it to a decentralized system of distance education management at their institution.

One interesting finding is that faculty seemed to not have an understanding of what bibliographic/information literacy instruction entailed or how it could be performed at a distance without taking up valuable class time (Steffen, 1986). There was a definite lack of interest in librarian-facilitated instruction in many of the studies on the part of faculty (Adams & Cassner, 2001; Lebowitz, 1993; Shaffer et al., 2004). Anecdotally, this seems to also be a problem with face-to-face instruction. Some studies showed that faculty feel that it is their role, primarily, to instruct their students on using the library (Steffen, 1986; Hufford, 2004; O'Neal, 1995).

A service that was suggested or supported by some faculty is some sort of library integration into the courseware used, such as Blackboard or WebCT (*Distance Learning*, 1998; Feldheim et al., 2004; Markgraf, 2002). Integration into the courseware could include components such as discussion forums monitored by librarians, modules on library research techniques and resources, subject guides, online lectures, and so forth. This approach depends on the faculty understanding what information literacy instruction involves, good communication and collaboration between librarian and instructor, and whether instructors can spare the time or "space" necessary in the course framework.

This ties in with another key issue that emerged. Faculty are very concerned with a perceived lack of time in the distant classroom (*Distance Learning*, 1998; Markgraf, 2002; Steffen, 1986). Even though time is not measured in the traditional sense of the hour-long class meeting, the amount of information the instructor needs to pass on in a semester can seem daunting. Devoting resources to library instruction may seem like wasted time.

Another concern was copyright issues. Faculty were worried about what they could and could not use in their distance courses and wanted librarians to provide guidance (*Distance Learning*, 1998; Shaffer et al., 2004). Copyright in general poses a challenge in the classroom, but with online courses and a constantly changing technological landscape instructors often do not know clearly what is allowed under copyright laws.

Also of concern was technical support. Many faculty felt the library should assist them with troubleshooting resources at a distance (Markgraf, 2002). Problems with proxy access were mentioned in more than one study (Adams & Cassner, 2001; Shaffer et al., 2004). Libraries deal with access and troubleshooting materials in differing ways–for this issue, it is a matter of communicating with faculty to make sure they know whom to contact with problems, especially so they can pass this information on to students having problems.

Faculty asked to be kept better notified about available services and materials (Adams & Cassner, 2001; *Distance Learning*, 1998; Lebowitz, 1993; Shaffer et al., 2004; Stockham & Turtle, 2004). A reoccurring theme was that faculty rarely use the library services for themselves but wanted to be able to help guide students to library services and resources. Periodic communication by e-mail was mentioned as a good way to facilitate this type of notification by a number of studies (*Distance Learning*, 1998; Markgraf, 2002; Stockham & Turtle, 2004).

A point of interest and enthusiasm to librarians is that faculty are generally requiring the use of library resources in their assignments (Adams & Cassner, 2001; Hufford, 2004; Lebowitz, 1993; Stockham & Turtle, 2004). For the most part there were few concerns about the availability of resources and assignments were not being redesigned because of a lack of resources.

Another interesting and encouraging element that emerged is faculty place a high value on library services (Cook & Cook, 1987; Fender, 2001; O'Neal, 1995; Steffen, 1986). Our services are recognized as important and are seen in at least one study as lending legitimacy to distance education ventures (*Distance Learning*, 1998).

Commonalities with Student Services

Handouts were desired for students (*Distance Learning*, 1998; Lebowitz, 1993; Stockham & Turtle, 2004). Faculty mentioned course-specific handouts but also brought up a desire for more general guides that students can print and take away for later use (*Distance Learning*; Lebowitz). Online tutorials, research guides, and orientations were suggested for students as well (*Distance Learning*; Hufford, 2004; Markgraf, 2002; Stockham & Turtle, 2004). Some faculty felt this would be beneficial to their own learning about the library and its resources, as well.

In some studies, faculty assumed that students already knew how to use library resources and services, and didn't need instruction. (Lebowitz, 1993; Shaffer et al., 2004). Faculty may forget about their students' learning curves when researching or dealing with unfamiliar resources, because they think that students already have done similar research.

Minimizing differences between students' on campus access and distant access to resources was of concern to faculty (Adams & Cassner, 2001; *Distance Learning*, 1998). They praised libraries' purchases of full text online resources, and asked for more of these databases (Adams & Cassner; Hufford, 2004; Lebowitz, 1993). There was some expressed concern about the speediness of delivery of library materials, mostly in older studies (Adams & Cassner; O'Neal, 1995).

Marketing and student awareness of what the library had to offer also came up in the surveys (Hufford, 2004; Stockham & Turtle, 2004). Although faculty themselves feel aware of what the library has to offer, they really are not sure whether their students know what resources and services are available.

UNIVERSITY OF MONTANA'S FACULTY EVALUATION OF SERVICES

Methodology

During November 2004, a ten-question online survey of brief multiple choice questions (Appendix A) was created to assess the awareness and usefulness of library services available to distance education faculty at the University of Montana-Missoula and to learn more about potential services of interest to faculty. At the end of the assessment, instructors were offered the chance to contact the author via e-mail or phone with questions and/or feedback.

When designing the questions, chief concerns were to find out if instructors knew about library's resources, if they expected their students to use these resources, and what special efforts to educate distant students about library resources they would most appreciate. In the studies discussed above, services like discussion boards, online lectures and tutorials, or special subject guides were used by other institutions, and there was interest to see if a demand for similar services among our faculty existed. The survey needed to be brief so a question about subject areas taught was not included. In order to encourage honest responses, no identifying characteristics of the professors responding were gathered.

On December 1, 2004, a link to the assessment Web site was e-mailed to 35 of the instructors of distance education classes at the University of Montana-Missoula that semester (Appendix B). Compiling this list was made easier by the University's attempt to centralize information about online and distant courses. The instructors' names were gathered via the UMOnline Web site, which contains information about courses taught at a distance at the University of Montana. Blackboard is the primary delivery system for distance education at our institution. Some faculty have Blackboard components for their face-to-face courses, but those courses are not listed on the UMOnline site. Some faculty who teach correspondence courses or closed circuit television courses are also not listed on the UMOnline site, but those courses are not common at the University of Montana. The names of eight instructors teaching technical courses such as Algebra or Surgical Techniques were removed from the list, as it was unlikely that these courses had any research component or required the use of library resources. As of December 8, one week later, sixteen responses had been received, which represented a response rate of approximately 46% of the professors teaching courses with potential research components that semester.

The assessment was housed on the Web site SurveyMonkey.com. This Web site will collect and tally surveys with 10 or fewer questions and 100 or fewer respondents for free. The results of the free surveys are presented in a bar graph and tally for each question and are not downloadable. No identifying information is collected unless specifically requested in the survey. SurveyMonkey also offers a professional subscription for $19.95 a month, which allows the user more questions, respondents and other options. It is a remarkably easy site to use and it comes highly recommended for short surveys of this nature.

As the assessment was conducted entirely online, and notification and solicitations were sent out via e-mail to instructors, this study cost nothing to carry out materially. There were no mailing or printing costs. Additionally, the study could be run quickly since there were no printing or mailing time delays.

Length of Time Teaching at a Distance

The majority of those responding had been teaching courses through UMOnline for three or more years. Fourteen (87.5%) respondents had been teaching online or at a distance for two years or more. The remaining respondents had only just begun teaching at a distance this past semester. It is interesting to note that, based on these results, distant instructors at the University of Montana are either relatively experienced at teaching at a distance or are complete novices.

Use and Awareness of Mansfield Library Resources

Twelve (75%) of those responding required some sort of research for their class. Fourteen (87.5%) respondents knew that the Mansfield Library at the University of Montana offered online academic library resources. However, results were evenly divided (7 to 7, with two not sure) when asked if they felt their students were aware of these resources. Seven of the respondents, comprising 43.8%, did not provide their students with a link to the Mansfield Library Web site from their Blackboard course shells. An additional two respondents indicated they would link to the library's site but didn't know how.

Useful Services for UMOnline Instructors

We were interested in what sort of specific library services would be beneficial to instructors, and designed a series of appropriate questions. The majority, at eight respondents, would find it useful to have a resource guide prepared by a librarian available for their course subject matter. This is a service that is currently available to distant instructors via their subject librarian or the outreach coordinator–perhaps instructors are not aware of how to request this service.

Seven respondents would find it useful to have a course unit on library skills for integration into their Blackboard course shells. This is something that the Library has been working on and hopes to have ready by spring 2006.

Interestingly, a clear majority of 62.5% (10) would not find a library research discussion thread in their Blackboard area, monitored by a librarian, to be useful. This is an idea that has proven popular at other institutions using Blackboard. It is unclear whether the instructors feared it would take time and attention away from their course, or if they just felt it would be an ineffective resource for students.

Instructors Would Recommend a Stand-Alone Research Skills Class

The Mansfield Library was, at the time of the assessment, attempting to implement a one-credit class, via Blackboard, dealing with library and research skills. Distant instructors were receptive to this idea, with eleven respondents (73.3%) saying they would encourage their distance students to take such a class. Ten respondents also indicated that they would also encourage their students in face-to-face classes to take such a course. However, the only e-mail feedback received on the assessment was from a participant who disagreed strongly with this point. This professor, who teaches in the School Library Media Endorsement Program, felt that library instruction is only effective when tied to another discipline or assignment outside the library.

Conclusions

Through this assessment we learned:

- UMOnline instructors have generally been teaching courses at a distance for two or more years.
- They are giving assignments that require the use of library resources.
- They feel informed about the services the library offers, but are not sure their students are aware of what is available.

When discussing concrete options for informing students about library services, it seems that the instructors who responded to our survey prefer stand-alone options such as research guides and independent library research courses, although they do have some interest in a library skills unit that could be incorporated into their courses.

DISCUSSION

The impetus to compare results from our study and the others examined earlier came from the hope that there would be some consistent desires or views across institutions that could be assembled, but nothing universal emerged. However, some interesting commonalities did surface in this analysis, as outlined above. Some of the common concerns or needs provide librarians with valuable insights regarding library services at a distance. None of this information can be generalized on a statistical level, but taken as a whole, these studies offer some interesting trends, tips and techniques we as librarians can employ when serving faculty at a distance.

Librarians need to better publicize to our distant population what we do with instruction and how we do it. This is true for both the faculty and the student population. Our services will not be used if our users do not know they exist. The studies examined demonstrated that faculty do want to hear from us, and also informed us that e-mail is an effective way to communicate with them. One study showed that faculty who have existing contacts with librarians use library services more frequently (Markgraf, 2002).

Librarians could use faculty concerns to help market services. Regarding the lack of time available in classes, demonstrate that consulting with a librarian in some way can result in better assignments, better-prepared students, and less time spent on mechanics in the classroom environment. Showing faculty we can save them time will get their attention and open up avenues of communication.

Addressing issues of copyright can also be a way to attract faculty into consulting with a librarian. Becoming knowledgeable on what resources can be used in the distant classroom, and how they can be used, will provide a valuable service that is not always offered to those teaching at a distance. Providing this information will again create opportunities to promote other library services to faculty and, through them, to their students.

The creation of handouts, subject guides, or online tutorials develops further prospects for librarians to reach out to both students and faculty. Along with increasing awareness and use of library resources, these guides provide another great opportunity for outreach to both our constituent distant audiences. Collaborating with faculty on a handout or resource is an excellent way to connect and promote library services (Feldheim et al., 2004).

As for further steps that can be taken, it would be useful to complete a wide, statistically valid study of distance education faculty across several campuses assessing library services. Based on my small experience with my institution's service evaluation and the research for this presentation, there is definitely interest among librarians in finding out how to best provide service to this population. However, the question remains as to whether we can generalize across campuses to discover universal library needs.

Another potential research project would be the design and testing of a survey instrument to assess faculty satisfaction with and recommendations for library services, which could be used at individual campuses as a tool to determine what they do well and where they could improve. Many librarians with whom I spoke about this paper and my study wanted to compare survey questions. We all desire to use well-tested questions to get the best information possible.

My research did not lead to a generalizable baseline of library services for distant faculty, as I had hoped, but it did open discussion on what is generally wanted by faculty. A universal set of services may not be discovered, but perhaps further research will lead us to find a set of appreciated core services to offer, or an evaluation instrument to demonstrate where we excel institutionally and what we can improve.

REFERENCES

Adams, K., & Cassner, M. (2001). Marketing library resources and services to distance faculty. *Journal of Library Administration, 31*(3/4), 5-22.

Cook, J., & Cook, M. L. W. (1987). Faculty perspectives regarding educational supports in off-campus courses. In B. Lessin (Ed.) (1991), *Off-campus library services: Selected readings from Central Michigan University's Off-Campus Library Services Conference* (pp. 105-115). Metuchen, NJ: Scarecrow Press.

Distance learning: What faculty say about distance learning and library support. (1998). Retrieved March 8, 2005, from University of Minnesota Libraries Web site: http://www.lib.umn.edu/dist/testing/dlfocus.phtml.

Feldheim, M. A., King, A. O., & Sherman, S. (2004). Faculty-librarian collaboration: Meeting the information technology challenges of distance education. *Journal of Public Affairs Education, 10*(3), 233-246.

Fender, D. (2001, April). *Student and faculty issues in distance education.* Paper presented at the Mid South Instructional Technology Conference.

Guidelines for Distance Learning Library Services. (2004). Retrieved October 12, 2005, from American Library Association Web site: http://www.ala.org/acrl/resjune02.html.

Hufford, J. (2004). Library support for distance learners: What faculty think. *Journal of Library & Information Services in Distance Learning, 1*(3), 3-28.

Lebowitz, G. (1993). Faculty perceptions of off-campus student library needs. In C. Jacob (Comp.), *The Sixth Off-Campus Library Services Conference proceedings* (pp. 143-154). Mt. Pleasant, MI: Central Michigan University.

Markgraf, J. (2002). Collaboration between distance education faculty and the library: One size does not fit all. *Journal of Library Administration, 37*(3/4), 451-464.

O'Neal, W. (1995). Faculty and liaison for the Off-Campus Library Services Conference. In C. Jacob (Comp.), *The Seventh Off Campus Library Services Conference proceedings* (pp. 269-276). Mt. Pleasant, MI: Central Michigan University.

Shaffer, J., Finkelstein, K., Woelfl, N., & Lyden, E. (2004). A systematic approach to assessing the needs of distance faculty. *Journal of Library Administration, 41*, 413-428.

Steffen, S.S. (1986). Working with part-time faculty: Challenges and rewards. In B. Lessin (Comp.), *The Off-campus Library Services Conference Proceedings.* Reno, NV.

Stockham, M., & Turtle, E. (2004). Providing off-campus library services by team: An assessment. *Journal of Library Administration, 41*, 443-457.

doi:10.1300/J111v45n01_12

APPENDIX A

Survey Questions

1. How long have you taught courses online/at a distance?
   A. This is my first semester
   B. One year
   C. Two years
   D. Three or more years

2. Did your course(s) in Fall 2004 require your students to do any sort of research (for papers, presentations, assignments, etc.)?
   A. Yes
   B. No

3. Did you know that there are online academic library resources available for distance education students and faculty?
   A. Yes
   B. No

4. Would you have found it useful to have a librarian prepare a resource guide for your students on your course's subject matter?
   A. Yes
   B. No
   C. Not sure/not applicable

5. Would you have found it useful to have a brief unit on library resources and services, prepared by a librarian, as part of your Blackboard class?
   A. Yes
   B. No
   C. Not sure/not applicable

6. Would it be useful to your course to have a discussion thread area for research-related questions that a librarian could monitor and join in on?
   A. Yes
   B. No
   C. Not sure/not applicable

7. Do you feel your students are aware of the library resources and services available to them through the Mansfield Library at the University of Montana?
   A. Yes
   B. No
   C. Not sure/not applicable

APPENDIX A (continued)

8. Would you encourage your distance students to take a class via UMOnline covering research skills?
   A. Yes
   B. No

9. Would you encourage students in your face-to-face classes to take a class via UMOnline covering research skills?
   A. Yes
   B. No
   C. I do not teach face-to-face classes

10. Do you provide a link to the library Website via your Blackboard course home page?
    A. Yes
    B. No
    C. I would but I don't know how
    D. My class does not use Blackboard

APPENDIX B

E-mail Solicitation Text

Dear [UMOnline Instructor],

As the Outreach Coordinator at the Mansfield Library, University of Montana-Missoula, I work specifically with distance education students and instructors to provide them with library services.

As part of our mission to offer the best possible services to faculty and students, I would like to ask you a few questions about your course and online teaching experiences. The survey should take only 2-3 minutes of your time. It is available online at http://www.surveymonkey.com/s.asp?u=34409750039.

Please don't hesitate to contact me if I can assist with your classes for next semester or if you have any questions or concerns about library services for distance education students or faculty.

Sincerely,
Samantha Hines

–

Samantha G. S. Hines
Outreach Coordinator/Reference Librarian
Assistant Professor
Mansfield Library
University of Montana
Missoula, MT 59812-9936
Toll-free Reference Assistance 1.800.240.4939
samantha.hines@umontana.edu

Creating an Informational CD for Distance Clinical Laboratory Science Students

Cotina Jones
Julie Dornberger

Winston-Salem State University

SUMMARY. Traditionally the distance clinical laboratory science students visit Winston-Salem State University three or four times during the course of the semester. These visits are usually for orientation and testing purposes. While the students are aware that there is a library on campus, they are not familiar with all of the library's electronic resources that they have access to from their home computers. The distance and health science librarians decided to collaborate to design an informational CD-ROM specifically for these students. doi:10.1300/J111v45n01_13

KEYWORDS. Distance library services, collaboration, informational CD-ROM

INTRODUCTION

Enrollment in the distance education program at Winston-Salem State University (WSSU) is steadily increasing. Between 2000 and 2004 the number of distance students rose by fifty. While the number of

[Haworth co-indexing entry note]: "Creating an Informational CD for Distance Clinical Laboratory Science Students." Jones, Cotina, and Julie Dornberger. Co-published simultaneously in *Journal of Library Administration* (The Haworth Information Press, an imprint of The Haworth Press, Inc.) Vol. 45, No. 1/2, 2006, pp. 229-243; and: *The Twelfth Off-Campus Library Services Conference Proceedings* (ed: Julie A. Garrison) The Haworth Information Press, an imprint of The Haworth Press, Inc., 2006, pp. 229-243.

Available online at http://jla.haworthpress.com
doi:10.1300/J111v45n01_13

distance education students is increasing, coming to the O'Kelly library and using the library's resources and services is not. During the past three school years, the number of student contacts has continually decreased–from 118 in 2002-2003 to 38 in 2004-2005.

According to the Association of College and Research Libraries (ACRL) Guidelines for Distance Learning Library Services, "Members of the distance learning community are entitled to library services and resources equivalent to those provided for students and faculty in traditional campus settings" (ACRL, 2004, para. 11). It is equally important for distance learners to gain lifelong learning skills through general bibliographic and information literacy instruction that has typically been provided for traditional students. Traditional methods of library instruction and research assistance, however, will not meet the needs of the distance learners at Winston-Salem State University. Considering the above precepts, it was important to design a library instruction package to assist the distance learner at WSSU.

In the fall of 2004, the Associate Dean of Allied Health and the Chairperson of the Graduate Nursing program were asked about the library's use by the health science students including the distance learners. During this session, it was learned that the distance learners were assigned research topics, but they did not use the library to conduct their research. Instead, they used the Internet, textbooks, and other assigned readings to complete their research. Various methods of library instruction were discussed during this meeting, including face-to-face and online instruction. Through this discussion, it was realized that the most effective method of reaching the distance learning student was via a CD-ROM.

At the conclusion of this initial meeting, the distance librarian and the health science librarian met and discussed creating a CD-ROM that would target the distance clinical laboratory science students for a pilot study. These students were selected due to their class size (approximately twenty) and the fact that they were required to come on campus four times per semester. The distance clinical laboratory science program is Internet-based and specifically designed for students who are experienced medical laboratory technicians in need of a clinical laboratory science degree.

Distance learners visit the campus four times per semester for orientation and to take exams. In the distance clinical laboratory science program, students typically visit the campus at the beginning of the semester for an overview of the class. During the semester, the students have an opportunity for face-to-face contact with the instructors to complete any tests and address any concerns. This provides an opportunity for the library staff to meet face-to-face with students to distribute and explain the purpose of the CD-ROM. An evaluation is also given at this time to gather general information about each student. A post-evaluation is given at the end of the semester to find out if the CD-ROM was an effective tool for informing students in how to use remote library services.

OVERVIEW OF THE DISTANCE PROGRAM

Distance learning has been a part of Winston-Salem State University since 1938, with summer sessions offered at locations throughout the remote regions of North Carolina. The program is now geared towards those students whose workday or distance prevents them from participating in on-campus courses (Winston-Salem State University, 2005).

The university's distance education program currently includes a face-to-face component mainly for nursing and education students in the rural counties surrounding the university. These courses are taught primarily by adjunct faculty.

Distance learning incorporating the use of technology has been available to students since 1996. The online offerings include Bachelor's degrees in Clinical Laboratory Science and Interdisciplinary Studies. Certificates are also offered in Social Work, Physical Education, Clinical Chemistry and Clinical Microbiology. A graduate program in Rehabilitation Studies offers several online courses. A majority of the online courses are taught by on-campus faculty.

LIBRARY RESOURCES
FOR THE ONLINE VIRTUAL CAMPUS

Virtual campus students are able to remotely access any of the library's electronic resources, including the online catalog and over ninety electronic databases. Students also have access to a comprehensive electronic book collection.

Reference assistance is available to the distance learners in a variety of formats. "NC Knows," a 24-hour reference service available to North Carolina students, offers access to librarians for answering reference questions. Students are required to use their campus login to receive this service. A toll-free telephone number has also been established for students to call directly to the reference desk for assistance. Students also have the opportunity to e-mail their questions to the reference desk staff, who answer them during the library's operating hours. A Web blog has been created which addresses general questions that students may have.

A distance services librarian was added to the O'Kelly Library staff in 2000 to provide reference and research assistance to distance learners. The librarian was also responsible for providing instruction to distance learners as requested.

A distance services Web site has also been created that provides distance learners with access to the library's online catalog and electronic resources, without having to access them through the library's Web site. Students are also provided with links to the library's tutorials, as well as useful tutorials from other university libraries.

RATIONALE

The literature does not provide much discussion on library instruction offered for distance learners via CD-ROM. However, it has been acknowledged as a tool for providing supplemental information to learners, both distance and traditional. According to Swenson and Evans (2003), CD-ROMs can reach adults who have different types of learning styles. The Clinical Laboratory Science CD-ROM has information in formats geared to the auditory and visual learner. The introduction contains narration as well as visual cues. The PowerPoint which explains PubMed in detail is narrated to help the user fully understand the various search strategies.

According to Swenson and Evans (2003), another noted advantage of CD-ROMs is the ability of the user to move between the CD-ROM and the Internet. Therefore, the Clinical Laboratory Science CD-ROM was specifically designed to open each link in a new window. Doing this enabled the user to view new information and refer back to the original page. The goal of this project was two-fold: assist the students in becoming more successful learners while exposing them to the library's electronic resources. This goal is accomplished by keeping the students' technology requirements at a minimum thus allowing them to spend more time on learning and less on technology (Swenson & Evans, p. 39).

Upon further examination of the literature we found that WSSU distance clinical laboratory science students are similar to other off-campus students in that they "have problems finding enough references for their assignments" (Porter, 2003, p. 57). We believe this is due in part to a lack of awareness of the available resources and how to search them. Many of our distance learners have fallen into what Burgstahler referred to as the "second digital divide"(Burgstahler, 2002, p. 421). This simply means that students are not using all of the tools available to them over the Internet–in our case the library's electronic resources. Instead they rely heavily on various search engines to find information. None of our distance learners have had an opportunity to receive library instruction. As such, they have not developed their research skills or learned how to access the library's resources. Therefore a component of each PowerPoint or Camtasia program included on the Clinical Laboratory Science CD-ROM is information on how to search the different health science databases. In essence each PowerPoint or Camtasia program is a small library instruction session.

METHODOLOGY

After speaking with the Associate Dean of Allied Health about possible instruction methods, we decided to create an informational CD-ROM. Upon this decision the distance librarian, health sciences librarian, and Webmaster met several times to determine the information to be included and the format. The Webmaster was consulted to find out what software was needed and the timeline necessary to complete the project.

It was during these meetings that we decided to include information that was specific to clinical laboratory science as well as other information that was useful to the health sciences in general. Since the students had not received any library instruction, general library information was also included.

PowerPoint presentations were included to teach students how to search PubMed, CINAHL, Science Direct, and the ProQuest databases. PubMed was included on the CD-ROM because it is available through the National Library of Medicine (NLM) without having to login to the library's electronic databases. It provides access to indexing and abstracts and some full-text articles related to biomedical literature. The user was also given access to links to the NLM's molecular biology resources. A PowerPoint presentation on CINAHL was included because it is a database which provides indexing and abstracts to nursing and allied health literature. It is also one on the most heavily used health science databases. Science Direct was selected for inclusion on the CD-ROM because it contains full-text information on a variety of subjects including biology and allied health.

Students were taught how to use the online catalog by viewing a step-by-step guide in the Camtasia program. Along with showing students how to use the various electronic resources, access to the sites was included in the CD-ROM. Information about the library's Web site and distance services Web page were included to provide students with additional assistance.

In creating the CD-ROM it was extremely important to follow the university's current Web site guidelines. This gave the CD-ROM the same look as the library's Web site. This helped to make the CD-ROM more user-friendly.

After a demo version of the CD-ROM was completed, select students and library staff who were not familiar with searching these particular databases were asked to critique it. Once this crucial step was completed and corrections were made, the final copy of the CD-ROM was produced. The Associate Dean of Allied Health and the Clinical Laboratory Science Chairperson were given the opportunity to review it and make suggestions as well. When the review was completed class visits were scheduled to survey the students and distribute the informational package.

After the Clinical Laboratory Science Chairperson reviewed the instructional package, students were given the CD-ROM and encouraged to use it. They were also shown parts of the CD-ROM to hopefully influence student use. A survey was given to students on the first visit to gather information on their demographics and computer use. The students were also made aware of a scheduled return visit, during which time they would be asked for their opinion of the informational package.

DESCRIPTION OF CD-ROM

The CD-ROM is organized into four tiers and designed with Macromedia Dreamweaver to simulate Web pages. The first tier provides an opening screen or portal to the content. The second includes instructional content with links to PowerPoint presentations and Camtasia movies. The third tier provides informational content with links to descriptions of library services. The fourth offers outside links to the library's Web site and a guided tour.

There is a brief recorded introduction that plays automatically when the CD-ROM is launched giving contact information and an overview of what is included on the CD-ROM. The opening screen displays the major links as the audio plays.

In the second tier, there are nine PowerPoint presentations including *Accessing CINAHL and PubMed, PubMed Demystified* (narrated), *Clinical Laboratory Science Links, Navigating the Library Website, Introducing the Distance Library Services Website,* and *Journal Finder.* Two of the presentations have been converted into Windows Media movies as there is no need for interactive links for students within the presentations. There are three more PowerPoint presentations that have been converted into movies using the Camtasia software including *An Overview of Library Services, Electronic Resources: An Introduction,* and *the Online Catalog: An Introduction.*

Also in the second tier are Camtasia "movies" that demonstrate searching of the online catalog and an online database. These screen recordings show both keyword and subject searches. The step-by-step process is shown along with annotations.

The third tier screen offers two main categories with links for "How to Use" and "Where to Find." Included under the former category are links for the National Library of Medicine and O'Kelly Library's electronic resources, online catalog, and journal finder. "Where to Find" includes links to distance library services, clinical laboratory and health sciences informational links, and contact information.

The links chosen from the library Web site to include in the fourth tier provide direct access to the homepage, online catalog, electronic resources, research guides, online tutorials, a guided library tour, and the university homepage.

FINDINGS

Twenty-one students completed an introductory survey (see Appendix for evaluation results). This evaluation gathered information on ease of computer access, electronic resource and Internet use, and knowledge of who to contact for research assistance. Ready access to computers was important for students to be able to use the CD-ROM and view the various links included. Ninety-five percent of those students surveyed had access to a computer either at home or at work.

Students were also asked about the types of resources most often used. Approximately 62% of the students surveyed admitted to using the Internet instead of the library's electronic resources. This figure is closely related to a Pew Internet & American Life Project study reporting that 73% of college students said they used the Internet more than the library (Jones, 2002). The distance learning students were asked this question to determine what format would best serve our distance learning students in the future and if they were using the library's electronic databases.

Knowledge of who to contact for research assistance was another question on the survey. This question was to test student awareness of available library resources and services. It was also to learn if students were knowledgeable about the distance services librarian that was available to them.

Eight students completed the post-evaluation. This evaluation was designed to determine if the students used the CD-ROM and if it was useful. A majority of the questions that were on the first evaluation were on the second, just in a different format. Comparing the pre- and post-evaluations, we were able to determine that the CD-ROM was beneficial to a majority of the students. Since the CD-ROMs were distributed to the students the number of questions to the distance services librarian has increased. New partnerships have developed between the health sciences librarian and the health sciences faculty and staff, since they have been made aware of the CD-ROM that was created for the distance clinical laboratory science students.

ADVANTAGES

Overall this project has allowed the library the opportunity to provide distance students with guidance and instruction in using the library remotely. One advantage of using the CD-ROM is that it provides students with one-on-one instruction that can be accessed at their convenience. In addition, it does not need to be used sequentially. A student can use it as a reference tool to look up "how to" information as necessary. It not only provides general information on library services but also in-depth content focusing on a specific discipline, clinical laboratory science. Step-by-step visual demonstrations of how to search online databases gives students relevant tools to complete research assignments. The project has also been a marketing tool for showcasing library services and staff as an integral part of the academic community, for students and faculty. As word spread that the clinical laboratory science distance students had received a CD-ROM, faculty from the School of Nursing also became interested in working with the library to design one for their students. Although costly in staff time, the project is not a technically difficult or expensive endeavor. The CD-ROM can be replicated for various disciplines using PowerPoint, Camtasia and Dreamweaver, all well-known software.

DISADVANTAGES

There are two disadvantages that can be pointed out. Planning and executing the content for the CD-ROM was time intensive for the two librarians involved. Additionally, the librarians must constantly update information as the library Web site and database interfaces change. Students currently in possession of the CD-ROM already have out-of-date information. In the case of O'Kelly Library, the technical expertise to turn the content provided by librarians into a CD-ROM product was available. Other libraries may need to provide special training or additional staff to handle the technical aspects.

OBSTACLES

Although the Clinical Laboratory Science program enrolled a small number of online students and required them to come to campus for orientation and exams, it was still difficult to meet with all the students at one time. The initial expectation was for 40 students to be present at the first orientation but there were only 21. The next meeting with the group of students was to assess their use of the CD-ROM. Testing was occurring in various rooms and each student had to be individually asked to fill out the form. At that time, the faculty member teaching the immunology class had also begun giving her students the exams online. This eliminated the students' need to visit the School of Health Sciences during the semester. Allowing the students to take their exams online was beneficial to them; however, it was a barrier in terms of gathering information to make the informational package more useful to future students. To assist us in surveying those students who completed the exams online, the professor was able to provide a list of students and their e-mail addresses. To thank students for responding to the online survey we sent them gifts of appreciation.

In addition, there are considerable general problems faced in serving distance learners at Winston-Salem State University. Although a distance learning librarian is provided to support learners with equitable access to library resources and services, there is not a centrally administered distance program. Each discipline that provides distance courses employs a coordinator but is inconsistent in providing timely information concerning courses offered and contact information for faculty and students. Therefore, it is difficult for the librarian to identify or serve the distance community. Attempts to contact faculty through e-mail, newsletters, and Blackboard have been unsuccessful. In some cases, as with clinical laboratory science, the faculty who teach online courses also teach face-to-face courses on campus and are easier to identify and locate.

CONCLUSIONS

In the future updated CD-ROMs will be provided to those students in the clinical laboratory science program. Plans are in progress for a CD-ROM for the distance nursing students. This project will be less time intensive to create since much of the information from the clinical laboratory science CD-ROM can be updated and used. They will be evaluated using a form of online evaluation, whether through a link included in the CD-ROM or distributed to students via e-mail. A Web site will eventually be established that contains the information presently included on the CD-ROM.

The Winston-Salem State University distance learning program is comparatively small (approximately 400 students), with clinical laboratory science comprising only about 40 students per semester. The CD-ROM project was a solution to the long standing problem of providing these students with library services, especially access to electronic resources. Initiating contact with clinical laboratory science faculty also opened the door to potential partnerships in the future. Since the completion of this project nursing faculty members have requested a similar project for their students.

The collaborative efforts of the distance learning librarian and health science librarian was beneficial in updating health sciences instructional content and providing library visibility in the School of Health Sciences. It will most likely be a factor in the continuance of the project for years to come.

AUTHOR NOTE

Special thanks to Beverly Murphy, Assistant Director of Marketing and Publications at Duke University for critiquing this article.

REFERENCES

Association of College and Research Libraries. (2004, June 29). *Guidelines for Distance Learning Library Services.* Retrieved July 13, 2005, from http://www.ala.org/ala/acrl/acrlstandards/guidelinesdistancelearning.htm.

Burgstahler, S. (2002). Distance learning: The library's role in ensuring access to everyone. *Library Hi Tech, 4* (2), 420-432.

Jones, S. (2002). *The Internet goes to college: How students are living in the future with today's technology.* Retrieved October 25, 2005, from Pew Internet & American Life Project Web Site: http://www.pewtrusts.com/pdf/vf_pew_internet_college.pdf.

Porter, S. (2003). Chat: From the desk of a subject librarian. *Reference Services Review, 31* (1), 57-67.

Swenson, P.W., & Evans, M. (2003). Hybrid courses as learning communities. In S. Reisman, J. G. Flores, & D. Edge (Eds.), *Electronic Learning Communities: Issues and Practices* (pp. 27-71). Greenwich, CT: Information Age.

Winston-Salem State University. (2005). *Distance learning.* Retrieved October 26, 2005, from http://www.wssu.edu/WSSU/LifelongLearning/Distance+Learning/.

doi:10.1300/J111v45n01_13

APPENDIX

Evaluation Results

Evaluation One Results

1. Do you have access to a computer?

Yes
20 (95%)
No
1 (5%)
Total: 21

2. Have you ever used O'Kelly Library's electronic resource?

Yes
4 (19%)
No
17 (81%)
Total: 21

3. If yes, were you able to find the information needed?

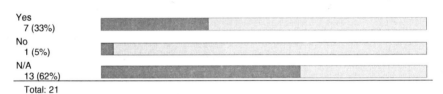

Yes
7 (33%)
No
1 (5%)
N/A
13 (62%)
Total: 21

If no, what resources did you use? Select all that apply:

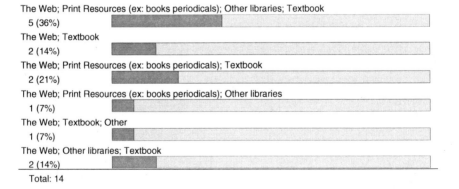

The Web; Print Resources (ex: books periodicals); Other libraries; Textbook
5 (36%)
The Web; Textbook
2 (14%)
The Web; Print Resources (ex: books periodicals); Textbook
2 (21%)
The Web; Print Resources (ex: books periodicals); Other libraries
1 (7%)
The Web; Textbook; Other
1 (7%)
The Web; Other libraries; Textbook
2 (14%)
Total: 14

4. Which health science electronic resources have you used? Select all that apply:

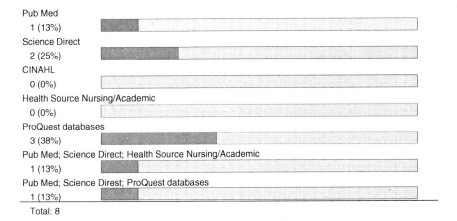

Pub Med
  1 (13%)
Science Direct
  2 (25%)
CINAHL
  0 (0%)
Health Source Nursing/Academic
  0 (0%)
ProQuest databases
  3 (38%)
Pub Med; Science Direct; Health Source Nursing/Academic
  1 (13%)
Pub Med; Science Direst; ProQuest databases
  1 (13%)

Total: 8

5. Do you know how and who to contact at O'Kelly Library for assistance?

Yes
  7 (33%)
No
  14 (67%)

Total: 21

Evaluation Two Results

1. The CD provided me with helpful and sufficient information.

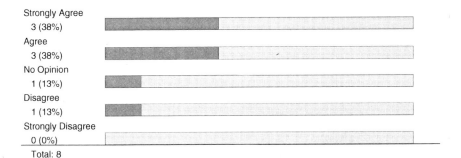

Strongly Agree
  3 (38%)
Agree
  3 (38%)
No Opinion
  1 (13%)
Disagree
  1 (13%)
Strongly Disagree
  0 (0%)

Total: 8

APPENDIX (continued)

2. My knowledge about searching PubMed has increased.

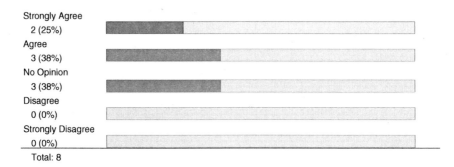

Strongly Agree
2 (25%)
Agree
3 (38%)
No Opinion
3 (38%)
Disagree
0 (0%)
Strongly Disagree
0 (0%)
Total: 8

3. My knowledge about searching Science Direct has increased.

Strongly Agree
1 (13%)
Agree
3 (38%)
No Opinion
4 (50%)
Disagree
0 (0%)
Strongly Disagree
0 (0%)
Total: 8

4. I know how and who to contact at O'Kelly Library for research assistance.

Strongly Agree
1 (13%)
Agree
3 (38%)
No Opinion
3 (38%)
Disagree
1 (13%)
Strongly Disagree
0 (0%)
Total: 8

5. The CD-ROM was a useful format to accessing information.

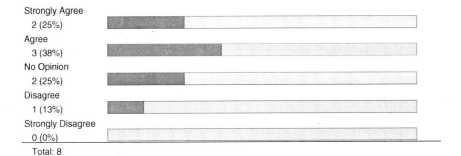

Strongly Agree
  2 (25%)
Agree
  3 (38%)
No Opinion
  2 (25%)
Disagree
  1 (13%)
Strongly Disagree
  0 (0%)
    Total: 8

6. If not, which format would be most useful?

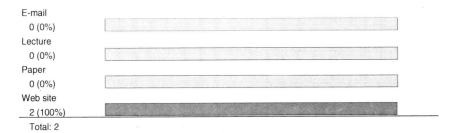

E-mail
  0 (0%)
Lecture
  0 (0%)
Paper
  0 (0%)
Web site
  2 (100%)
    Total: 2

Blackboard on a Shoestring: Tying Courses to Sources

Dan H. Lawrence

Rocky Mountain Center for Health Promotion and Education
Prevention Information Center

SUMMARY. Blackboard Learning System™ enhancements can provide high levels of sophistication and make it relatively simple to provide a seamless connection between online courses and library services. But not all institutions are willing or able to make the investment for these additional features. Yet providing direct links to library resources from Blackboard courses may still be the best way to facilitate a connection between the two Web environments. This paper is intended to introduce the key points for consideration as an institution begins a project to insert a library presence into online and courseware-enhanced classes taught on Blackboard. A general "primer" on the potential functionality of Blackboard is included as well as instructions for the various means of creating links from course menus to a library Web page. doi:10.1300/J111v45n01_14

KEYWORDS. Blackboard, academic libraries, distance education, integration, linking, course management systems

INTRODUCTION

It is widely accepted that online access and exposure to information technology from an early age has created expectations for ease of access

---

[Haworth co-indexing entry note]: "Blackboard on a Shoestring: Tying Courses to Sources." Lawrence, Dan H. Co-published simultaneously in *Journal of Library Administration* (The Haworth Information Press, an imprint of The Haworth Press, Inc.) Vol. 45, No. 1/2, 2006, pp. 245-265; and: *The Twelfth Off-Campus Library Services Conference Proceedings* (ed: Julie A. Garrison) The Haworth Information Press, an imprint of The Haworth Press, Inc., 2006, pp. 245-265.

Available online at http://jla.haworthpress.com
doi:10.1300/J111v45n01_14

and use. Libraries have been forced to reconsider traditional services and develop new or evolved services models (Lawrence & Lowell, 2005). This is particularly true among the "Net Generation": learners born in the 1980s or after who have grown up with ready access to technology (Oblinger & Oblinger, 2005). Increased exposure to applications that allow for customization and personalization only exacerbates students' expectations that technology should adapt to their needs rather than the other way around (Gibbons, 2005a).

Students and faculty who have difficulties locating information will often move on to easier and more familiar information resources. In research, as in other tasks, people tend toward the path of least resistance. Ease and convenience are often cited as reasons why many students prefer commercial search engines, such as Google and Yahoo! (Jackson, 2002). In online classes, there may be very little incentive for students to find their way to the academic library when entering a short URL such as "Google.com" may make information seem much more convenient.

One way to help ensure students and faculty will use library resources is to provide just-in-time access to information within the context of their academic work, that is, from their classes. In an ideal scenario, time and resources would be available to develop fully customized library assistance for every class. However, there is rarely funding to implement such time-intensive collaboration for all online courses.

For those institutions that use the Blackboard Learning System™ as the course management system (CMS) for their online classes, expensive enhancements can provide high levels of sophistication and make providing a seamless connection between online courses and online library services through the use of tabs or a predefined space for a library presence relatively simple. Though not all institutions are willing or able to make the investment for these additional features, providing direct links to library resources from Blackboard courses may still be the best way to facilitate a connection between the two Web environments.

Blackboard has the potential to be a very complex system. However, the first step toward integrating library resources into the CMS does not need to be overly burdensome. Rather than establishing a desired level of deep course integration with only one or two courses, it can be argued that a generic, global link to the library will better serve *all* students by increasing the ease of access to library resources.

This paper will provide guidance in inserting the library into the Blackboard CMS by addressing the following:

- Why a library would choose to establish a library presence on a CMS.
- Explaining what the different versions of Blackboard are and what they do.
- Discussing where a library can start to establish a presence on a CMS.

WHY ESTABLISH A LIBRARY PRESENCE ON A CMS?

As far as the library is concerned, reasons for providing direct access to library resources in course management systems have been fairly well documented in the literature. Several authors cite the CMS as an opportunity to offer library instruction, to help faculty develop better research assignments, or to provide higher quality class readings (Buehler, 2004; Getty, Burd, Burns, & Piele, 2000; Shank & Dewald, 2003). Others are concerned with securing a place in the CMS in order to avoid marginalization by Google (Gibbons, 2005a) or other "competitors" that provide digital library collections (Cohen, 2002; *Course management software*, 2001). Still more authors argue that librarians need to get involved with the CMS or campus teaching centers in order to ensure they secure a seat at the table in campus-wide discussions about online learning and digital resource provision (Baker & Starratt, 2005; Hisle, 2005; Jacobson, 2001; Lovett, 2004; Murray, 2004).

The online classroom is the locus for learning. The CMS is the place for instruction, online discussions, group projects, as well as the holding area for research assignments and recommended readings. If the library can push relevant content into this domain, the resources gain importance to the students simply by their presence within the course (Gibbons, 2005c).

However, there is research that indicates that faculty are not always aware that distance and on-campus students have the same access rights to library resources and some are not aware of how library resources can apply to their classes (Rieger, Horne, & Revels, 2004). More disappointing are Markland's findings that faculty are most likely to use Web searches to identify suitable online resources for their students (2003).

But this does not mean that faculty cannot recognize benefits from librarians stepping forward and taking a role in the CMS. Better resources for students, the time savings accompanying course-specific research guides, and the removal of the burden of securing copyright clearance for electronic reserves are just a few of the easily articulable benefits (Gibbons, 2005c).

Libraries must also insert themselves into the CMS to preserve and/or reinvent their symbolic place in the institution. The monumental architecture and placement of many academic libraries has historically served as a visual cue to the significance of the library's role in the academic enterprise (Freeman, 2005). Distance students, however, may not experience a campus at all, let alone a campus with boundaries enclosing classrooms, professors' offices, and student services, such as a library. For online students, there is not necessarily a perception of the library as a monumental building sitting prominently in their image of the "university." Their primary contact with the university may be through the framework of their classes taught on a CMS. In the online environment, "it is not the space that demands our attention now so much as our representation of space, and our ability to mould and manage ideas within boundaries that are fundamentally intangible" (Garrett, 2004, pp. 56-7).

If the academic library does not have a visible presence in this domain, students will, and do, function without the academic library—and this is, arguably, to the detriment of their learning. So it falls to the librarian "to design an imaginative, easily identifiable space in cyberspace as the centrality of the library as a physical phenomenon slowly fades. . . [librarians must] construct the image of libraries to mirror the image of the service they wish to promote" (Martell, 2000, p.104). That is to say, librarians must be responsible for creating a mental picture of the library for students that is central and relevant to their academic experiences.

THE DIFFERENT "VERSIONS" OF BLACKBOARD
AND WHAT THEY DO

With the $180 million acquisition and merger of WebCT by Blackboard to finalize (at the time of writing) in early 2006–pending a second round of U.S. Department of Justice antitrust review questions–there is no doubt that Blackboard will continue to have a major presence in the academic course management system market (O'Hara, 2005). Blackboard will have, according to some analysts' reports, a combined 80-90% of the higher education CMS market (*Blackboard, WebCT to merge*, 2005). Keeping track of current, and future product offerings and functionality will be more important than ever for library planning.

Blackboard is not a one-size-fits-all software solution. Blackboard sells two product suites. The Blackboard Commerce Suite™ manages campus commerce and financial transactions. It integrates disparate campus financial networks and allows a universal personal account to pay for services such as tuition, room and board, books, and fines. The other product suite–Blackboard's primary product for higher education–is the Blackboard Academic Suite™.

Blackboard has versions that are known as "releases." At the time of writing, most institutions use the Blackboard Academic Suite Release 6; however Blackboard announced Release 7.0 in October 2005. There are also several "application packs" (three in Release 6: 6.1, 6.2, and 6.3) which are distributed as part of a company strategy to release patches and upgrades in well-tested small bundles (*Blackboard launches new*, 2004). Release 7.0 adds multiple language support and the ability to manage Blackboard Backpacks™, a new for-fee personal information manager that students can use to organize notes and assignments and that allows offline and mobile device access to course content.

The Blackboard CMS Product

The Blackboard Academic Suite is made up of three separate yet integrated products. The Blackboard Learning System™ is the CMS, which provides an online learning platform that incorporates course management and content creation tools, e-mail, chat, discussion boards, assignment functions, assessment tools, a grade book, and course statistics. Blackboard also offers an entry-level CMS product, the Blackboard Learning System-Basic Edition™, which compared to the fully functioning "Enterprise" Learning System, lacks the security features and ability to add extensions and building blocks (discussed below).

The other two products–the Blackboard Community System™ and the Blackboard Content System™–supplement and add functionality to the Learning System.

The Blackboard "Portal" Product

The Blackboard Community System™ (formerly known as the Portal System or Community Portal System) is a module that allows for the creation of customizable content through tabs, modules, channels, tools, courses and organizations. Different content can be pushed to different individuals based on their roles in the organization (*Blackboard community*, n.d.).

Every user that logs in to the Blackboard Learning System enters into a "main menu" by default. This main menu contains tabs leading to "common areas." The Blackboard Learning System and Blackboard Learning System-Basic Edition include tabs to four common areas:

- My Institution: acts as the gateway to the CMS and is populated with default modules of content. There are two views for displaying courses the user is enrolled in, announcements, a calendar, and task list.
- Courses: provides a list of courses in which a user is enrolled or is teaching.
- Academic Web Resources: provides a link to a Web resources list created by Blackboard. This tab is disabled by default (this content can conflict with libraries' efforts to provide local access to particular resources).
- System Admin: is only accessible to those with Blackboard administrator privileges.

There is very little that can be customized in these common areas, that is, unless the institution purchases the Blackboard Community System™. This additional enhancement provides an institution with extra common area tabs, including community, services, and Web. Community tabs can include campus organizations. The services tab can include modules for various campus services (including the library). The Web tab can be used to point to a URL that will open within Blackboard (for instance, the library home page). Blackboard Community System™ comes with over 100 modules and allows for the creation of new modules and customized tabs.

With the Community System, modules can be created using "channels." Channels use RSS feeds to bring in content from outside of the Blackboard system. This can be useful to a library, for instance, if the OPAC can generate RSS feeds of preset searches; it would be possible to create a channel on a library tab for specialized resources such as discipline-specific reference materials. If a library maintains a blog of new and interesting happenings or resources the RSS feed from this blog could potentially be captured and displayed inside a Blackboard module. Users could then opt to switch any modules on or off, depending on their preferences.

The Blackboard Content Product

As the name implies, the Blackboard Content System™ (now on Release 2.0) allows for the managing and sharing of content and files. Files can be shared by individuals as well as by classes, departments, and the library. This system includes a searchable, hierarchical, taxonomic cataloguing system for learning objects and would be well suited as the foundation for an institutional repository project. It also has an e-reserve component that allows for the creation of individual e-reserve folders for each class.

The Content System can be extremely useful to libraries in that it provides virtual storage areas for each class where library staff can potentially add customized content without having to gain access to the course itself. The instructor can then later choose whether to implement this content into the course. This has potential for not only electronic reserves, but also for instructional materials, course guides, and other discipline specific library resources.

Blackboard Building Blocks

It is also possible to add enhancements to Blackboard using "Building Blocks." The Blackboard Building Blocks Software Development Kit (SDK) is available for free as a download. Institutions can use the JAVA-based SDK to create local Building Blocks which will enable additional functionality or create bridges between Blackboard and external systems or applications.

There is a tremendous amount of potential for the use of Building Blocks for local library applications. One example is from Baylor University, which developed a Building Block to provide an automatic link to e-reserves hosted on the Innovative Millennium Media Management module from within individual Blackboard courses on the Blackboard Learning System (Build 6.0) with the Blackboard Community System "upgrade" (Bennet & Steely, 2004). The link to e-reserves is automatically embedded in the Tools menu, without faculty, librarian, or Blackboard administrator intervention. However, they were not able to solve the problem of requiring re-authentication while accessing the reserves. The code for this building block has been made freely available for use by institutions with similar software configurations.

There is also momentum toward inter-vendor relationships. Several library vendors have joined the Blackboard Developers Network in order to partner with Blackboard for the development of Building Blocks which work to facilitate integration of their products with the CMS (Ritter, 2003). However, despite the potential and all of the partnerships, there are few library-related building blocks that have been made available thus far.

There is a catalog of building blocks at http://www.blackboard.com/extend/b2/. Many are free and others are available for purchase from the developer. A few of the more interesting open source and freeware building blocks for libraries are:

- Copyright Permissions Building Block–provided by Copyright Clearance Center to allow instructors to register for clearance of items from their courses.
- LinkMaker Building Block–a project of the Washington Research Library Consortium that allows links to electronic reserves, journal articles, and databases without re-authentication by rewriting the URL to pass through an authentication server. A list of databases that the building block works with and handouts illustrating how faculty would use it is provided by American University at http://american.edu/cte/faculty/teachingbb.html.
- RefWorks Bridge–jointly developed by RefWorks and Northwestern University, this building block allows linking to Refworks databases and individual accounts from within the Blackboard course tools page.

Hosting and Administration

The Blackboard system can be hosted by the university or by Blackboard, on their servers via ASP. If the system is hosted locally, several departments may be involved in providing maintenance and support. If the system is hosted off-site, there are likely to be additional support issues that will arise with respect to IP recognition and authentication for access to library databases.

Since Blackboard is a software application with versions and optional add-ons, libraries will be subjected to the limits of their local system configurations. Furthermore, local knowledge and motivation can greatly impact whether all optional functionality is utilized. Librarians who wish to embark on a project to establish a presence in Blackboard for their library need to be keenly aware of more than just what is possible on their local system. They will also need to know about the people and departments that can help or hinder the process.

Whether the system is hosted locally or off-site, a person or persons will be assigned to be the Blackboard administrator. Knowing who is responsible for the various functions, and having a good relationship with them, is vital. Blackboard administrators are responsible for:

- Courses: creating courses and having users enrolled, either manually or by automated loads from registrar data. Courses can also be reused, copied, and archived. A course catalog specific to Blackboard is available.
- Users: updating, creating, and removing users and observers (observer status allows a parent or administrators to view course content without being able to interact).
- Portal Areas: managing tabs, modules, channels, the tool panel, and system settings which set the look, feel and functionality of the site.
- System Options: installing and managing system extensions.
- Creating system wide announcements.
- Setting up and modifying security settings.
- Providing access to support materials.

Additionally, Blackboard administrators are the people who can grant librarians access (either through institutional mandate or with faculty permission) to individual Blackboard courses. Blackboard has six user "roles" that allow varying levels of access to course maintenance and content (*Blackboard Learning System Administrator Manual: Release 6*, 2003). These roles are:

- Instructor: able to control all aspects of the course. Some Blackboard administrators allow instructors to add other instructors and teaching assistants.
- Teaching Assistant: same as the instructor but cannot add instructors or teaching assistants.
- Course Builder: can add course content but is not able to administer tests, assign grades, or put students in groups.
- Grader: has access to the assessment area and the grade book.
- Student: has access to visible course content and is added to the grade book.

- Guest: has access to all parts of a course that are not locked by the instructor.

Librarians working with Blackboard should identify which version of Blackboard their institution uses. Gaining access to the Blackboard Administrator Manual for the version of Blackboard used at their institution will quickly remove any mystery about what is possible on the local system. The Blackboard administrator may be willing to provide library staff with a copy of the Administrator Manual for the version of the system that is loaded. If not, the Administrator manual for Release 6 (*Blackboard Learning System Administrator Manual: Release 6*, 2003) is available at: http://company.blackboard.com/docs/cp/learning_system/release6/administrator/.

An effort should also be made to be aware of other local players who might take an interest in any project to establish a presence for the library on Blackboard. Those librarians at mid-size or larger campuses should acquire a thorough understanding of their campus' departmental structures and responsibilities for providing IT support and user training. It is recommended that a representative of the library call or pay a visit to the Blackboard administrator and others who may be impacted by any projects that will be undertaken. If persons resist talking to the library, or seem overly guarded about sharing their responsibilities, they can probably be ruled out as potential collaborative partners.

ESTABLISHING A LIBRARY PRESENCE ON BLACKBOARD

Shank and Dewald (2003) provided a useful framework for discussing how to establish a library presence in an institution's CMS. The authors pointed to two primary methods by which libraries can become more visible in online courses. One method is a micro-level approach that involves individual librarians teaming with teaching faculty in order to create customized components in individual courses. The second method is a macro-level approach, which involves inserting a generic presence into the software that is available across all courses.

For the purposes of this discussion it is important to differentiate between "levels" for integration in the Blackboard system. The "course level" is content that is only available to users who can gain access to a class. The "common area level" is made up of the content accessible by the tabs at the top of the Blackboard interface. All users have access to these tabs, though in some system configurations, users may be given the choice of whether or not to display the tab.

Micro-Level Approaches

Shank and Dewald (2003) defined a micro-level approach as "individual librarians working with individual faculty members to provide more customized library research assistance within courseware" (p. 40). While they provided a useful framework for discussing CMS integration, they wrote from the perspective of traditional on-campus librarians and offered few strategies for CMS integration that will meet the needs of distance students. They insisted that course-level integration of resources is best viewed as a supplement to in-class library instruction by using the CMS as a platform to deliver supplementary materials such as library instruction outlines, bibliographies, recommended databases, librarian contact information, post-class surveys and librarian contact information. In essence, their vision of the library's use of the CMS was primarily as a means of ensuring that students cannot throw away the handouts that librarians have worked so hard to prepare. They did suggest that it is possible to mount Web-based tutorials but discouraged their use except as a supplement before or after an in-class training session.

Gibbons (2005b) provided a more recent and thorough overview of how libraries are working toward using the full potential of CMS's to provide a seamless connection between course content and research materials. She provided a discussion and examples of how libraries are importing course-specific resources, electronic reserves, library-created subject course guides, and means of communication with libraries. She highlighted the obstacles involved in linking to customized resources, including problems with lacking persistent URLs and multiple authentications. Gibbons suggested that gaining access to individual courses is the first step to any micro-level approach. This is a step that will require good relationships with faculty.

Collaboration with faculty has emerged as a research priority for those providing services to distance students (Islam et al., 2005; Slade, 2004). Cox (2002) provided a general overview to how library instructors can utilize Blackboard to do one-shot instruction. He emphasized course-by-course collaboration with faculty. Lenholt, Costello, and Stryker (2003)–and again in Costello, Lenholt, and Stryker (2004)–discussed a collaborative project with business faculty to use Blackboard to supplement traditional instruction sessions by assisting faculty to upload Microsoft Word format library guide handouts into their courses.

Roberts (2003) discussed a project to mount TILT (Texas Information Literacy Tutorial) on Blackboard in order to take advantage of the assessment function. Cubbage (2003) discussed the issues Northwestern University faced as it decided to use Blackboard as a delivery vehicle for electronic reserves. Giles (2004) discussed a collaborative project that included the librarian as a participant in a Blackboard course, able to answer library research-related questions directly through the discussion list. She did however provide a warning concerning the time commitment involved in a semester long project like this.

In fact, the time and effort required to establish relationships with individual faculty, and then the work involved in maintaining support for individual classes, is the primary drawback to micro-level approaches to CMS integration (Gibbons, 2005b; Shank & Dewald, 2003). There is no way to reach every student by focusing on individual classes. According to Gibbons, "a low librarian-to-course ratio can create unachievable expectations" (2005b, p. 32).

The Blackboard Community System™ and the Blackboard Content System™ provide valuable enhancements to the CMS for pushing customized content to students and faculty. With these enhancements, and the in-house technical skills to adapt or create building blocks, course level integration can be reasonably automated. But lacking the time, skills, and resources, course level integration of customized resources may be too costly to achieve on a global level.

If there really is, as the ACRL *Guidelines for Distance Learning Library Services* (2004) suggest, "an increased concern and demand for equitable services for all students in higher education, no matter where the 'classroom' may be" (Introduction section, para. 3), then focusing on a few classes while ignoring the rest should be considered an equity issue–even if the neglect is due to limited staff and budgets.

While it is certainly preferable to provide fully customized class resources, the drain on library staff resources and energy may outweigh the advantages of increased contact with students and faculty that a micro-level approach can offer. This paper advocates for the use of a generic, global, macro-level insertion into Blackboard as a first step toward full integration–before turning attention to more staff intensive projects.

Macro-Level Approaches

A macro-level approach, according to Shank and Dewald (2003), involves providing information or services uniformly so that all courseware enhanced classes have direct access to them. A macro-level strategy allows a library to have the highest level of visibility, in the least amount of time, for the lowest expenditure of staff effort. Macro-level approaches make the provision of library services a scalable endeavor while working to increase the ease of access for students and faculty (Shank & Dewald, 2003).

Providing a global, uniform library presence into Blackboard will breed familiarity and trust as students come to expect and rely on the same link or resource, regardless of the class they are viewing (Gibbons, 2005b). This type of integration can take several forms. Uniform access to a resource can be achieved either through insertion at the common area level, or by creating access to a resource in all classes at the course level.

Macro Integration at the Common Area Level

As was noted earlier in the *Blackboard "Portal" Product* section, every Blackboard Learning System has common areas where a Blackboard administrator can create announcements or link to help resources. Any place where the library can appear in one of these tabs will certainly help toward integration of online courses and research materials. Links to virtual reference desk services, the OPAC and databases, global pathfinders and handouts, or document delivery services are all possible destinations for links from common area modules, and require very little work when an institution has access to the Blackboard Community System™ (Shank & Dewald, 2003). If the system allows the creation and customization of tabs, modules, and channels, it would be possible to:

- Add a library tab that would create a library common area that could include a wide variety of customizable content for personalization. If this content duplicates content on the library Web site, it would have to be maintained.
- Create a Web link tab that would open a page from the library's Web site in Blackboard. This would eliminate the need to duplicate content, but would not direct integration with Blackboard tools and modules.
- Create library modules that could be added to any of the common areas, such as a "campus services" tab.

Unfortunately, without the Blackboard Community System™ none of the common area level customization is possible. This leaves course level integration as the only option for libraries to create a macro-level presence.

Macro Integration at the Course Level

Even without the Community System module, it is possible, and quite simple, to create a default link to library resources that opens within the "shell" of every Blackboard class. Students can "visit the library" and access resources without navigating away from their class. While it may be preferred by some to offer fully customized links for each class or discipline, providing a link to the library that opens "within" a course helps to create a seamless connection between the two Web environments. Such a connection may facilitate a student's ability to find relationships between the class assignments and the concepts and ideas of the research materials (Koohang, 2004).

A direct link to a library Web page from within a class enhances discovery-based learning by enabling students to use the library and resources to gather and make connections between different knowledge domains (Weigel, 2005). Furthermore, access to the library from an online course takes advantage of the technology in a way that encourages active learning that allows students to discover and articulate connections between the course content, research materials, and their own work (Dewald, Scholz-Crane, Booth, & Levine, 2000).

Shank and Dewald (2003) pointed to several drawbacks of a macro-level approach. Their primary concern was the lack of human contact with librarians. They worried that students would become virtual library users only and would not be able to fully develop their online searching skills. Another major concern is the lack of personalization and customization that online users have come to expect (Gibbons, 2005b).

If the library experience is designed to be easy to navigate, welcoming, and self-instructing, the user can be guided through the research process as they are performing (Lowell, 2005). In his discussion of how performance-centered design principles can be applied to library instruction, Lawrence (2005) asserted:

> It should not be the goal of those developing and maintaining a library's web presence to force a person to concentrate on learning to "search" the library. Rather, a better goal is to only provide a library user with the information they need to successfully complete

their activity when they need help, and without making them stop what they are doing to go look for it. (p. 1)

Creating a Link to the Library from the Course Menu

This section describes the various methods for adding a link to the library in the course menu of classes taught on the Blackboard system. This type of link opens a Web page within the frame of the course. When the instructor or a student clicks on the link, the library will appear to be part of the course. Students are able to seamlessly move between the content of the class and the research environment without "leaving class." Rather than just inserting a piece of the library into a course, the library becomes part of the course.

In every Blackboard course, there is a course menu on the left side of the screen listing all of the course areas for that particular class. Course areas are the various parts of the course that hold content, tools, and links. A link to the library built into the course menu ensures that no matter where a student is in a course, the library will be a visible part of the class.

Adding a Default Link from the Course Menu of All New Courses

The Blackboard administrator can create new content areas, tool areas and external links that can be added to the course menu. They can also decide which course areas will be visible, by default, for every new course that is generated in the system. It is a very simple process for the Blackboard administrator to create a course area as an external link that can go to any URL. This link can be set to open in a new window or to open within the frame of the Blackboard course.

Defaults will apply to every new course shell generated on the system. As with any course areas on the course menu, instructors have the option of removing the link from their course menu.

Most instructors, if they teach the same class over multiple semesters, have the option of reusing content. Depending on the permissions that instructors are allowed, either the instructor or Blackboard administrator can implement any of the methods for reusing the content. There are three ways that content can be reused:

- Copy: creates a new course from an existing course. The user interactions, grades, and course statistics do not transfer.

- Exporting/importing: export saves a copy of a course, excluding the user information, to be stored as a zip file. It is then possible to import the course structure and content at a later date.
- Archiving/restoring: archive creates a copy of the course in its entirety, including all user interactions, grades, and statistics. Restore is a means of picking up where the course left off. All users and data will be included.

It is common for instructors that teach the same class over consecutive semesters to copy the course. The Blackboard administrator can do batch copies of many courses simultaneously. Unfortunately, Blackboard's default functionality does not provide an automated means of inserting a new course area into the course menu during copying, importing, or restoring. If an older course does not contain the library link in the course menu, the copy, import, or restored version of the class will not have it either. This also means that once an instructor removes the link from the course menu, as long as he or she continues to copy the content, there is no automated means of restoring the link. Inserting links into the course menus of the courses that are reused from previous semesters will have to be done manually.

Deciding Where the Link Should Go

Knowing it is possible to create a link is one thing. Deciding where the link should go, and what the destination page will "do" for the user is the next step. The page that the generic link leads to will be the point of entry page to the "library" and will therefore play a significant role in the mental model of the library and its services that each user will develop. A library home page may not provide the type of first impression that will encourage further use.

It should also be remembered that this link is likely to be the same for students in both online-only and Blackboard supplemented courses. Even at institutions where structural changes to a library home page are unlikely due to staff resources or political resistance, it may be possible to use the Blackboard link as an opportunity to approach online services from a new perspective. At the very least, this entry page may provide an opportunity for those who advocate for distance support to provide an additional "library hub" that will better serve all users.

Moore asserted that while there needs to be some level of customization to make library resources seem relevant, there is a generic set of skills common to all disciplines and that the "use of customized examples and customized opportunities for practice will increase engagement and ownership" (as cited in Gibbons, 2005b, p. 32). When customization of library resources is discussed, librarians tend to categorize along disciplinary or subject lines. There are humanities resources, business resources, nursing resources, etc. Since the library shelves are arranged this way, and librarians are trained to think this way, there is a general expectation among those in the library field that users will, or should, follow similar lines of logic. But the interdisciplinary nature of many majors, coupled with the breadth of classes a student takes to meet general education requirements, makes it unlikely that students will be comfortable approaching all research tasks from a disciplinary perspective. Customization is not the overriding issue in Moore's argument. Rather, the question of making the library resources seem relevant so that users will want to use them is most pressing.

A TASK-BASED ENTRY POINT TO THE LIBRARY

Any point of entry into the library should make links to common tasks readily visible. When patrons reaches this page, they should intuitively know where to go next in order to accomplish the task they have set out to complete. If they cannot figure out what to do, there needs to be brief, easy to follow directions for the next step. By anticipating the most common tasks as well as the questions related to these tasks, it is possible to compile a "short list" of the most necessary components to include in the entry page. For example:

- How can I find and get books?
- How can I find and get articles?
- How can I find materials related to the class I am currently taking?
- What services are available for distance students?
- What services are available for faculty?
- How can I get help from a person if I need it?
- What do I do if I have questions that are not answered here?

It is easy to imagine how a page organized to answer such questions could guide users toward existing resources in the library Web site, such as the OPAC, databases, subject guides, distance student handbooks, faculty handbooks, virtual reference services, instructional resources, and more. The entry page, whatever it is, should provide visible, yet unobtrusive help functions that will allow novice researchers to get the help they need to perform more like expert researchers. The entry page should not, however, force an expert user to click through several layers to reach the most common tools that they will use.

CONCLUSION

Given the changing nature of the way students seek information for assignments in the online course environment, the library home page is becoming one of the Web's best-kept secrets. Students believe in the acronym WYSIWYG–What You See is What You Get, but they are also coming to believe in WYDSDE (pronounced wids-dee)–What You Don't See Doesn't Exist (Garrett, 2004). It is absolutely necessary that libraries "integrate and expose" library services within the learning activities taking place in CMS courses (OCLC E-learning Task Force, 2003).

This strategy is based on one simple principle: start small and work bigger. The excitement of "new" technologies should not be allowed to push librarians into projects that require large investments of time, with very little return. Starting with a small project that has high visibility is better than getting bogged down in a personally rewarding, yet low impact, project that reaches just a few students. Once a generic link is in place, it is then possible to move on to other projects that may yield deeper learning.

Dempsey wrote of library portals as a "library hub" (2003). If the library Web site is to be a portal, it cannot stand on its own, isolated from the rest of the university learning experience. The single entry point becomes more akin to the constricted opening between the two sides of an hourglass. There is one way in and one way out. The library services grouped together within a Web site must be broken apart and projected throughout the entire research and learning experience as unbundled, specific resources delivered at the time and place of need.

It is better to take a task-focused rather than a discipline-based perspective when determining the entry point to the library from a generic link in Blackboard. Students and faculty should be able to accomplish their intended tasks as quickly and easily as possible without having to break the flow of their work. If they have to stop what they are doing to seek out help or dig for resources that are buried deep in a site, they are likely to lose interest in what they are doing and go elsewhere to meet their information needs (Lawrence, 2005).

Staying informed about what Blackboard is capable of will help to generate ideas about what may be possible at any given institution. It does not take a great deal of time or library staff knowledge to get started. As library staff skills develop over time, libraries can begin to incrementally work toward the realization of a more fully integrated online learning environment.

REFERENCES

Association of College and Research Libraries. (2004). *Guidelines for distance learning library services*. Retrieved December 12, 2005, from http://www.ala.org/ala/acrl/acrlstandards/guidelinesdistancelearning.htm.

Baker, B. F., & Starratt, J. (2005). *The Library and the academic enterprise: Trends in Illinois*. Paper presented at the ACRL Twelfth National Conference. Minneapolis: ACRL.

Bennet, S., & Steely, J. (2004). *Blackboard and electronic reserves: Access, service, and copyright compliance*. Paper presented at the Innovative Users' Group 2004 Conference. Boston.

Blackboard community system brochure. (n.d.). Retrieved December 12, 2005, from http://www.blackboard.com/docs/AS/Bb_Community_System_Brochure.pdf.

Blackboard launches new software release strategy for education industry. (2004, May 26). Retrieved December 12, 2005, from http://forbes.ccbn.com/releasetext.asp?ticker=bbbb&coid=177018&client=forbes&release=582647.

Blackboard learning system administrator manual: Release 6. (2003). Retrieved December 12, 2005, from http://company.blackboard.com/docs/cp/learning_system/release6/administrator/.

Blackboard, WebCT to merge. (2005, October 13). *Inside Higher Ed News*. Retrieved October 14, 2005, from http://www.insidehighered.com/news/2005/10/13/merger.

Buehler, M. (2004). Where is the library in course management software? *Journal of Library Administration, 41*(1), 75-84.

Cohen, D. (2002). Course-management software: Where's the library? *EDUCAUSE Review, 37*(3), 12-13.

Costello, B., Lenholt, R., & Stryker, J. (2004). Using Blackboard in library instruction: Addressing the learning styles of generations X and Y. *Journal of Academic Librarianship, 30*(6), 452-460.

Course management software: Where is the library? (2001). *Online Libraries & Microcomputers, 19*(10), 1-2.

Cox, C. (2002). Becoming part of the course: Using Blackboard to extend one-shot library instruction. *College & Research Libraries News, 63*(1), 11-14.

Cubbage, C. (2003). Electronic reserves and Blackboard's course management system. *Journal of Interlibrary Loan, Document Delivery & Information Supply, 13*(4), 21-32.

Dempsey, L. (2003). The recombinant library: Portals and people. *Journal of Library Administration, 39*(4), 103-136.

Dewald, N., Scholz-Crane, A., Booth, A., & Levine, C. (2000). Information literacy at a distance: Instructional design issues. *Journal of Academic Librarianship, 26*(1), 33-44.

Freeman, G. T. (2005). The library as place: Changes in learning patterns, collections, technology, and use. In *Library as place: Rethinking roles, rethinking space.* Washington, DC: Council on Library and Information Resources.

Garrett, J. (2004). The legacy of the Baroque in virtual representations of library space. *Library Quarterly, 74*(1), 42-62.

Getty, N. K., Burd, B., Burns, S. K., & Piele, L. (2000). Using courseware to deliver library instruction via the Web: Four examples. *Reference Services Review, 28*(4), 349-359.

Gibbons, S. (2005a). Defining the challenge. *Library Technology Reports, 41*(3), 4-6.

Gibbons, S. (2005b). Strategies for the library: CMS integration barriers. *Library Technology Reports, 41*(3), 24-32.

Gibbons, S. (2005c). Who should care and why. *Library Technology Reports, 41*(3), 21-23.

Giles, K. L. (2004). Reflections on a privilege: Becoming part of the course through a collaboration on Blackboard. *College & Research Libraries News, 65*(5), 261-264.

Hisle, W. L. (2005). *The changing role of the library in the academic enterprise.* Paper presented at the ACRL Twelfth National Conference. Minneapolis: ACRL.

Islam, R., Barsun, R., Behr, M. D., Buck, S., Buehler, M., Chakraborty, M. et al. (2005). *SPEC Kit 286: Collaboration for Distance Information Literacy Instruction.* Washington, DC: Association of Research Libraries.

Jackson, M. E. (2002). The advent of portals. *Library Journal, 127*(15), 36-39.

Jacobson, T. E. (2001). Partnerships between library instruction units and campus teaching centers. *Journal of Academic Librarianship, 27*(4), 311-316.

Koohang, A. (2004). Students' perceptions toward the use of the digital library in weekly Web-based distance learning assignments portion of a hybrid programme. *British Journal of Educational Technology, 35*(5), 617-625.

Lawrence, D. H. (2005). *EPSS and library instruction.* Retrieved December 5, 2005, from http://danhlawrence.com/et500/documents/500_615_final_paper_EPSS.pdf.

Lawrence, D. H., & Lowell, K. E. (2005). Distance services: Sharing services, collections and users. *Colorado Libraries, 31*(3), 3-4.

Lenholt, R., Costello, B., & Stryker, J. (2003). Utilizing Blackboard to provide library instruction: Uploading MS Word handouts with links to course specific resources. *Reference Services Review, 31*(3), 211-218.

Lovett, D. G. (2004). Library involvement in the implementation of a course management system. *Medical Reference Services Quarterly, 23*(1), 1-11.

Lowell, K. E. (2005). Information architecture: Distance services from the back room. *Colorado Libraries, 31*(3), 23-24.

Markland, M. (2003). Embedding online information resources in Virtual Learning Environments: Some implications for lecturers and librarians of the move towards delivering teaching in the online environment. *Information Research.* Retrieved June 12, 2005, from http://informationr.net/ir/8-4/paper158.html.

Martell, C. (2000). The disembodied librarian in the digital age, part II. *College and Research Libraries, 61*(2), 99-114.

Moore, K. (2004). Embedding information skills in the subject-based curriculum. In P. Brophy, S. Fisher & J. Craven (Eds.), *Libraries without walls 5* (pp. 79-86). London: Facet.

Murray, P. (2004, Fall). A new convergence. *netConnect, 129*, 40.

Oblinger, D., & Oblinger, J. (2005). Is it age or IT: First steps toward understanding the net generation. In D. G. Oblinger & J. L. Oblinger (Eds.), *Educating the net generation*. Boulder, CO: EDUCAUSE.

OCLC E-Learning Task Force. (2003, October). *Libraries and the enhancement of e-learning*. Retrieved December 12, 2005, from http://www.oclc.org/index/elearning/default.htm.

O'Hara, T. (2005, November 26). Blackboard's WebCT deal spurs antitrust questioning. *Washington Post*, p. D01. Retrieved December 12, 2005, from LexisNexis database.

Rieger, O. Y., Horne, A. K., & Revels, I. (2004). Linking course Web sites to library collections and services. *Journal of Academic Librarianship, 30*(3), 205-211.

Ritter, G. (2003). *Blackboard, building blocks and libraries: A position paper on the untapped potential of library integration with Blackboard's e-Education Systems*. Retrieved August 29, 2005, from http://www.blackboard.com/docs/BuildingBlocks/Bb_datasheet_Building_Blocks_Libraries.pdf.

Roberts, G. (2003). The yin and yang of integrating TILT with Blackboard. *Computers in Libraries, 23*(8), 10-13.

Shank, J. D., & Dewald, N. H. (2003). Establishing our presence in courseware: Adding library services to the virtual classroom. *Information Technology and Libraries, 22*(1), 38-43.

Slade, A. L. (2004). Research on library services for distance learning: An international perspective. *Journal of Library and Information Services in Distance Learning, 1*(1), 5-43.

Weigel, V. (2005). From course management to curricular capabilities: A capabilities approach for the next-generation CMS. *EDUCAUSE Review, 40*(3), 54-67.

doi:10.1300/J111v45n01_14

Marketing Research Relationships to Promote Online Student Success

Linda L. Lillard

Emporia State University

SUMMARY. Many creative and unique plans for serving the distance learning population are being designed to stay in compliance with the ACRL Guidelines for Distance Learning Library Services (2004). These guidelines promote providing services for the distance learning community that are equivalent to those provided for students and faculty located in a traditional campus setting. The guidelines also acknowledge that designing services for this population may result in a more personalized approach than the campus community might expect. This paper will examine the application of relationship marketing, defined as mutual interest between companies and customers that emphasizes customer retention and long term relationships, to the design of library services for distance learners. doi:10.1300/J111v45n01_15

KEYWORDS. Research relationships, libraries, online courses, relationship marketing

INTRODUCTION

In an era when 73% of college students say they use the Internet more than the library (Jones, 2002), academic librarians are trying to find new

[Haworth co-indexing entry note]: "Marketing Research Relationships to Promote Online Student Success." Lillard, Linda L. Co-published simultaneously in *Journal of Library Administration* (The Haworth Information Press, an imprint of The Haworth Press, Inc.) Vol. 45, No. 1/2, 2006, pp. 267-277; and: *The Twelfth Off-Campus Library Services Conference Proceedings* (ed: Julie A. Garrison) The Haworth Information Press, an imprint of The Haworth Press, Inc., 2006, pp. 267-277.

Available online at http://jla.haworthpress.com
doi:10.1300/J111v45n01_15

ways to reach their patrons who prefer to access resources online. Many creative and unique plans for serving this population are being designed to stay in compliance with the ACRL Guidelines for Distance Learning Library Services (2004) that promote providing equivalent services for the distance learning community to those provided for students and faculty located in a traditional campus setting. Furthermore, the ACRL guidelines acknowledge that designing services for the distance learning population may result in a more personalized approach than the campus community might expect. Suggestions that alliances be formed between librarians and teaching faculty are frequently found in the library literature (Markland, 2003) and McColl (2001) asserted that "librarians should seek to ensure that they remain part of the process as virtual learning takes hold. They must explain their role in the information management chain clearly to their academic colleagues . . ." (p. 238).

EMBEDDING LIBRARIES AND LIBRARIANS INTO ONLINE COURSES

According to the 2001 National Survey of Information Technology in U.S. Higher Education, more than 80% of the public four year colleges and almost 70% of the private universities that participated in the survey reported the purchase of instructional software (Green, 2001). This proliferation of Web-based course software has allowed librarians to design creative ways of reaching students in online courses that definitely have the possibility of being more personalized as the ACRL Guidelines (2004) suggest. For example, Burns integrated library instruction into courses delivered via Web-based course software, Getty integrated tutorials into Web-based course software at University of California Riverside and Piele did the same at University of Wisconsin Parkside. Burd used the software to provide a pass/fail information literacy course at Regent University and actually considered providing synchronous lessons (Getty, Burd, Burns, & Piele, 2000). At Rochester Institute of Technology, subject specialist librarians were expected to use Web-based course software to provide services such as demonstrating the resources and providing annotated links to materials (Buehler, Dopp & Hughes, 2001).

Shank and Dewald (2003) asserted that librarians and libraries are being left out of the design and implementation of Web-based course software and offered several models they believed librarians could use to integrate themselves into online courses. One model (called Macro-Level

Library Courseware Involvement) consists of "working with the developers and programmers of courseware to integrate a generic, global library presence into the software" (p. 28). Shank and Dewald suggested that virtual reference desk services could be integrated into the Web-based course software so that students could ask reference questions when they were logged into their online course. Direct links to the OPAC and online databases could be made from the online course software and global pathfinders, help sheets and document delivery services could be made available. Their second model (called Micro-Level Library Courseware Involvement) promotes collaboration of individual librarians with faculty to develop "customized library instruction and resource components for the courseware-enhanced courses" (p. 38). The micro-level model incorporates some of the suggestions from the macro-level model but is more in-depth and customized. Shank and Dewald recommended e-mail links to the librarian, real-time chat reference service, specific recommended databases for assignments, tutorials, and quizzes in this model. They believed strategic positioning of the library resources and services was the major advantage of this model.

These methods and models mesh well with the ACRL statement regarding the development of more personalized approaches to the provision of library services for distance learners. They also support McColl's (2001) assertion that librarians remain part of the virtual learning process and Wynne, Edwards and Jackson's (2001) insistence that the key to the future of higher education is the collaboration between teachers, learners, information specialists, Web designers, and technical and educational development staff. It is necessary, then, for librarians to make the most of any collaborative opportunity and push hard to become totally involved in the teaching of online courses. Markland (2003) discussed embedding online information resources in virtual learning environments and what those implications might be for lecturers and librarians. But why not embed the actual librarian in the online courses and promote the development of a "research relationship" with students?

LIBRARIAN IN THE ONLINE CLASSROOM: A RESEARCH RELATIONSHIP PROJECT

In the fall semester of 1999, the library liaison to the nursing department at Central Missouri State University was asked by the faculty member to participate in an online course, Nursing 4010, Nursing Research. The librarian readily agreed and was given the opportunity to act as a co-instructor of this online course through the Blackboard Web-based course software. This invitation provided an opportunity for the librarian to participate in course instruction to a greater extent than was ever possible through traditional instruction sessions where the instructor brought a class to the library (Dinwiddie & Lillard, 2002).

Teaming with the distance learning librarian, the nursing librarian began by compiling an arsenal of useful information resources related to nursing and medical information and making that available on a Web page. The distance learning librarian prepared a special Web page for distance learning students that brought together information necessary for their success such as how to access library catalogs and general Web resources, how to access the online databases from off campus, how to use the cooperative borrower card at partner libraries throughout the state, and how to initiate interlibrary loan. The nursing librarian learned how to use the Web-based course software and began communicating with students in the class. While the communication consisted mainly of offers to provide research assistance from a distance and to assist in the completion of assignments, the ultimate outcome hoped for was to develop research relationships so that the librarian could work with students one-on-one throughout the entire class. Disappointingly, students displayed some reluctance to contact the librarian and also exhibited confusion about what was appropriate to ask. One student made the comment: "I appreciate the service. But that isn't to say that it isn't difficult sometimes to overcome my feeling that utilizing this service is 'cheating!'" Another student responded to some offers from the librarian by actually coming to campus:

> I did meet with the librarian for a tour of the library, resources available and using my computer to find those resources. Due to rain and my phone lines, I did have some technical difficulties retaining my connections. I would have benefited if I had utilized her assistance more. It is through my own stubbornness that I refuse help and insist that my work is ALL MINE!

Even though a relationship in the ideal sense did not appear to develop as evidenced from these comments, a relationship did develop nevertheless as the second student came to the library and met with the librarian (Dinwiddie & Lillard, 2002).

This project continued for five years and was eventually expanded to include students in the criminal justice program as the nursing liaison was also the liaison to that department. Responses to the administered Likert scale survey showed that overall, students seemed to get some benefit from the librarian in the online classroom. For example:

Question: The announcements provided by the library liaison were timely and useful in helping me conduct my research.

Response	Criminal justice N = 87	Nursing N = 28	Overall N = 115
Strongly Agree	20.7%	35.7%	24.3%
Agree Somewhat	42.5%	46.4%	43.5%
Disagree Somewhat	11.5%	3.6%	9.6%
Strongly Disagree	9.2%	7.1%	8.7%
No Opinion	16.1%	7.1%	13.9%
Total	100.0%	100.0%	100.0%

Question: Having a librarian available to assist in my research via e-mail or telephone is a service I would like to have for other classes.

Response	Criminal justice N = 87	Nursing N = 28	Overall N = 115
Strongly Agree	61.0%	67.9%	62.6%
Agree Somewhat	29.9%	21.4%	27.8%
Disagree Somewhat	2.3%	0	1.7%
Strongly Disagree	1.1%	0	.9%
No Opinion	5.7%	10.7%	7.0%
Total	100.0%	100.0%	100.0%

Question: I felt comfortable asking for assistance from the librarian working with this course.

Response	Criminal justice N = 87	Nursing N = 28	Overall N = 115
Strongly Agree	35.6%	53.6%	40.0%
Agree Somewhat	31.0%	21.4%	28.7%
Disagree Somewhat	4.6%	0	3.5%
Strongly Disagree	8.0%	0	6.1%
No Opinion	20.7%	25.0%	21.7%
Total	100.0%	100.0%	100.0%

Question: Because of her involvement with this course, I will ask for assistance from the Blackboard librarian for future research needs while I am continuing my degree program at Central.

Response	Criminal justice N = 87	Nursing N = 28	Overall N = 115
Strongly Agree	40.2%	64.3%	46.0%
Agree Somewhat	37.9%	25.0%	34.8%
Disagree Somewhat	3.4%	0	2.6%
Strongly Disagree	3.4%	0	2.6%
No Opinion	14.9%	10.7%	13.9%
Total	99.8%	100.0%	99.9%

(Tables and questions adapted from Dinwiddie & Lillard, 2002). Used with permission from Central Michigan University.

The response to the survey questions revealed that in theory students wanted the services of the librarian in the online classroom; however, these services were not utilized to the extent hoped for at the onset of the project. This could be due to the fact that they were not marketed properly. An examination of the literature on relationship marketing could inform this project.

Having the librarian actually present in the online course has many advantages. One of the major advantages of this model is that as a member of the instructional team, the librarian can become more familiar with the course content and assignments, thus enhancing his/her ability to interact with students in a personalized way by customizing services and resources toward class and individual student needs. This is an opportunity that rarely arises in the face-to-face world of the librarian/instructor collaboration. Many times instructors simply send students to the library to do research with specific requirements, take students to the library for a one time instruction session or have the librarian come to their classes for a one time instruction session. Shank and Dewald (2003) asserted that because the librarian has the opportunity to discuss the assignment details with teaching faculty, library assistance for students will improve as well as the assignments and that faculty members may begin to view the librarians as consultants. Furthermore, access to the librarian within the online class allows students point-of-need assistance. If links to resources, tutorials and contact information are available within the online course software, students are afforded more of a one-stop shopping atmosphere that alleviates the time-consuming need to leave the online class environment and search for assistance. The availability of this two-way contact on an ongoing basis can assist in the development of a research relationship. Once a student has had an initial consultation with the librarian in the online classroom, that librarian can point out resources that might help the student as the class progresses. This is just not possible in the face-to-face world without a major expenditure of effort. The Web-based course software enhances seamless involvement and collaboration.

MARKETING THE SERVICE

Now the question becomes, if academic libraries offer this type of personalized and customized service, will students use it? Longitudinal studies of library users in academic, public, and school libraries conducted by Kuhlthau (1993) revealed ". . . a limited, insignificant role for librarians . . ." and "a perception of the librarian as a 'last resort' source locator." White (1997) defined marketing as "a destabilizing process of creating in the client an awareness for a need of which the client may be totally ignorant" (p. 116), and in many cases, as Kuhlthau discovered, library patrons simply do not see the need for a librarian. So, White advocated that librarians must awaken a hunger for their services. Why do patrons not see the need for a librarian? How can librarians market library services to the student who makes the comment: "I believe this could be good and useful, but I would guess that most people will not use the librarian's help unless they have to" (Dinwiddie & Lillard, 2002)? Several survey questions were asked for which the results showed the preference for a personalized solution was questionable. For example:

Question: I would like to have an online tutorial available that explains use of the electronic library resources in detail.

Response	Criminal justice N = 87	Nursing N = 28	Overall N = 115
Strongly Agree	47.1%	50.0%	47.8%
Agree Somewhat	36.8%	21.4%	33.0%
Disagree Somewhat	6.9%	17.9%	9.6%
Strongly Disagree	2.3%	0	1.7%
No Opinion	6.9%	10.7%	7.8%
Total	100.0%	100.0%	99.9%

Question: I would benefit from an interactive "real time" tutoring session presented by the librarian working with this course.

Response	Criminal justice N = 87	Nursing N = 28	Overall N = 115
Strongly Agree	21.8%	42.9%	27.0%
Agree Somewhat	50.6%	21.4%	43.5%
Disagree Somewhat	11.5%	28.6%	15.7%
Strongly Disagree	5.7%	0	4.3%
No Opinion	10.3%	7.1%	9.6%
Total	100.0%	100.0%	100.1%

(Tables and questions adapted from Dinwiddie & Lillard, 2002).

While a greater percentage of the students seemed to prefer the tutorial over the real time tutoring session by the strongly agree and agree somewhat response (80.8%), 70.5% of the students did reply with the strongly agree and agree somewhat response to the real time tutorial.

Upon examination of the survey responses, it is obvious that the services need to be marketed properly. According to White (1997), marketing can be used to awaken a desire for products and services, and libraries could make use of the process if they tell the public how great libraries can be. He went on to say ". . . it should be fairly clear that librarians do not market and that they never have marketed" (p. 116). McKenna (1991) asserted that marketing is not just a function in an organization but actually a way of doing business that must be pervasive and built into the job description of every member of that organization. An entity does not need to be a business to market itself, and McKenna made the point that the purpose of marketing is not to mislead a customer nor falsify the organizational image but "to integrate the customer into the design of the product and to design a systematic process for interaction that will create substance in the relationship" (p. 5).

Parasuraman, Berry, and Zeithaml (1991) found that customers want relationships. In addition, many of the customers interviewed in their research indicated that they wanted to be known and cared about, preferring "ongoing personalized relationships with the same representatives" of the firms they deal with who could be considered as partners (p. 43). Consequently, we could look to the concept of relationship marketing, which Cram defined as utilizing timely knowledge of individual customers to design products and services, which when communicated interactively promotes a mutually beneficial long term relationship

(1994). Furthermore, "libraries need relationship marketing" according to Besant and Sharp (2000). "Can there be a more straightforward way to create a vigorous library of value to users than by understanding and cultivating relationships with users?" (Besant & Sharp, p. 22).

Keating and Hafner (2002) examined one-to-one patron relationship management in the college or university campus library environment asserting that the academic library home page "represents a new portal for the promotion, delivery, and utilization of academic library services" (p. 428). They promoted incorporating knowledge based software programs that record patron's interests automatically. "By tracking usage by major or professional discipline, the database can be analyzed to provide real-time feedback to patrons of what services have been recently used by their peer group, or a subset of their peer group" (p. 429). This is similar to the method used by online bookseller Amazon.com when suggestions are made to purchasers regarding other items in which they might be interested based on items ordered by customers with like preferences (Keating & Hafner, 2002). While this is definitely a more personalized method of service, it could be termed more as a pseudo-relationship described by Gutek and Welsh (2000) as when a large company claims that it has a relationship with customers that is nothing more than just a matter of collecting data about the buying habits of its customers. Gutek (1995) asserted that relationship transactions take place when customers have repeated contact with the same provider. They get to know each other as individuals and as occupants of their particular roles and with an expectation for future interactions. There is an opportunity for a shared history to develop in each interaction that increases efficiency in subsequent interactions. The shared history developed in each interaction allows subsequent transactions to be more efficient. In the case of the librarian in the online classroom, there is the opportunity for a relationship to be developed between students and the librarian and faculty and the librarian.

Singh (2003) stated that "today's information customer is a very different person than the patron of just a few years ago" (p. 36). Expectations are raised because of technology not just in the area of delivery but also in quality. Value-added services such as encapsulating information and supplying it on a continuous basis are becoming important because, as St. Clair (1997) asserted, the information and services we provide can be obtained somewhere else. The customer service paradigm has shifted and this must be incorporated into the library management approach. Consequently, while marketing a research relationship by customizing library services is an outstanding service for online students, building this network of service through resources, facilities, services, and service providers must be accomplished by the library and information professions, or other professions and disciplines will become the information providers and leave today's information providers behind (Singh, 2003).

REFERENCES

Association of College and Research Libraries. (2004). *Guidelines for distance learning library services.* Retrieved December 1, 2005, from http://www.ala.org/ala/acrl/acrlstandards/guidelinesdistancelearning.htm.

Besant, L. X., & Sharp, D. (2000, March). Upsize this! Libraries need relationship marketing. *Information Outlook,* 17-22.

Buehler, M., Dopp, E., & Hughes, K. A. (2001). It takes a library to support distance learners [at Rochester Institute of Technology]. *Internet Reference Services Quarterly, 5*(3), 5-24.

Cram, T. (1994). *The power of relationship marketing: How to keep customers for life.* London: Pitman Publishing.

Dinwiddie, M., & Lillard, L. L. (2002). At the crossroads: Library and classroom. In P.B. Mahoney (Ed.), *The Tenth Off-Campus Library Services Conference Proceedings* (pp. 199-212). Mt. Pleasant, MI: Central Michigan University.

Getty, N. K., Burd, B., Burns, S. K., & Piele, L. (2000). Using courseware to deliver library instruction via the Web: Four examples. *Reference Services Review, 28*(4), 349-359.

Green, K. (2001). *The 2001 national survey of information technology in U.S. higher education.* Retrieved December 1, 2005, from http://www.campuscomputing.net/.

Gutek, B. A. (1995). *The dynamics of service: Reflections on the changing nature of provider/customer interactions.* San Francisco: Jossey-Bass.

Gutek, B. A., & Welsh, T. M. (2000). *The brave new service strategy: Aligning customer relationships, market strategies and business structures.* New York: AMACOM.

Jones, S. (2002, September 15). *The Internet goes to college: How students are living in the future with today's technology.* Retrieved April 30, 2003, from http://www.pewinternet.org/reports/pdfs/PIP_College_Report.pdf.

Keating, J. J., III, & Hafner, A. W. (2002). Perspectives on supporting individual library patrons with information technologies: Emerging one-to-one library services on the college or university campus. *The Journal of Academic Librarianship, 28*(6), 426-429.

Kuhlthau, C. C. (1993). *Seeking meaning: A process approach to library and information services.* New Jersey: Ablex.

Markland, M. (2003). Embedding online information resources in Virtual Learning Environments: Some implications for lecturers and librarians of the move towards delivering teaching in the online environment. *Information Research, 8*(4). Retrieved February 24, 2006, from http://informationr.net/ir/8-4/paper158.html.

McColl, J. (2001). Virtuous learning environments: The library and the VLE. *Program*, *35*(3), 227-239.

McKenna, R. (1991). *Relationship marketing: Successful strategies for the age of the customer*. Cambridge, MA: Perseus Books.

Parasuraman, A., Berry, L. L., & Zeithaml, V. A. (1991). Understanding customer expectations of service. *Sloan Management Review*, *32*(3), 39-48.

Shank, J. D., & Dewald, N. H. (2003, March). Establishing our presence in courseware: Adding library services to the virtual classroom. *Information Technology and Libraries*, *22*(1), 38.

Singh, R. (2003). Developing relationship marketing with customers: A Scandinavian perspective. *Library Management*, *24*(1/2), 34-43.

St. Clair, C. (1997). *Quality management in information services*. London: Bowker-Saur.

White, H. (1997, February 15). Marketing as a tool for destabilization. *Library Journal*, *122*(3), 116.

Wynne, P., Edwards, C., & Jackson, M. (2001). Hylife: Ten steps to success. *Ariadne*, *27*. Retrieved December 1, 2005, from http://www.ariadne.ac.uk/issue27/hylife/intro.html.

doi:10.1300/J111v45n01_15

The Faculty-Library Connection: An Online Workshop

Erin McCaffrey
Tina J. Parscal
Tom Riedel

Regis University

SUMMARY. With the proliferation of distance education programs, it is essential to consider methods to reach faculty who are often at a distance themselves. This paper discusses how the Libraries and School for Professional Studies Distance Learning department at Regis University collaborated to develop an online workshop in WebCT designed to raise faculty awareness of library resources and services and to train them to integrate library activities into the courses they teach. doi:10.1300/J111v45n01_16

KEYWORDS. Librarian faculty collaboration, instructional design, distance education

INTRODUCTION

The Regis University School for Professional Studies (SPS) has offered courses at the undergraduate and graduate levels at extended campuses for over 20 years. In the past ten years, an increasing number of

[Haworth co-indexing entry note]: "The Faculty-Library Connection: An Online Workshop." McCaffrey, Erin, Tina J. Parscal, and Tom Riedel. Co-published simultaneously in *Journal of Library Administration* (The Haworth Information Press, an imprint of The Haworth Press, Inc.) Vol. 45, No. 1/2, 2006, pp. 279-300; and: *The Twelfth Off-Campus Library Services Conference Proceedings* (ed: Julie A. Garrison) The Haworth Information Press, an imprint of The Haworth Press, Inc., 2006, pp. 279-300.

Available online at http://jla.haworthpress.com
doi:10.1300/J111v45n01_16

279

courses have been delivered online. Currently, over 40% of SPS enrollments are in online classes; fifteen degrees and numerous certificate programs are available entirely online. With this increase in the number of online classes has come an increase in affiliate faculty, many of whom are as geographically dispersed as the distance students.

The SPS distance learning department, charged with developing and maintaining online courses, has a good, collegial relationship with Regis distance learning librarians. The two groups have worked together over the past several years to ensure that the library is integrated into online courses. An informal meeting in the summer of 2004 led to collaboration on an online faculty development project that would focus on raising faculty awareness of library resources and services as well as to train faculty to integrate library activities into the courses they facilitate.

A REVIEW OF THE LITERATURE

Academic librarians consistently wrestle with new and innovative ways to reach out to faculty, and there is much in the literature of the fields of library and information science and education addressing library orientations for faculty as well as general faculty development. Traditionally, libraries have offered single session workshops for faculty ranging from the "one-shot" orientation to more tailored topic or subject-specific workshops (Hall, 1999; Mosely, 1998; Werrell & Wesley, 1990). The library might also be one component of a larger orientation for administrators, faculty or support staff (Hurst, 2003).

While somewhat dated, Lacey (1980) presented considerations relevant to contemporary faculty development and recommended that programs focus on helping faculty identify improvements for the teaching-learning process. "The librarian who can help a faculty member learn to use the tool-box more effectively can make an enormously important contribution to every aspect of faculty development" (p. 23). The modern toolbox has expanded from print-based resources and now includes navigating the enormous wealth of electronic resources. Stamps (1984) wrote of reaching out to "invisible" faculty who are often unaware of library facilities and technological changes. As a result, their unfamiliarity impacts their students' awareness. Stamps' objective in offering faculty orientations was to make the faculty feel "as comfortable and competent in the library as possible" (p. 90). Haynes (1992) emphasized the role of faculty as both teachers and learners. Brancato (2003) recommended that those planning faculty development efforts recognize faculty as adult learners and encourage lifelong learning activities.

Active collaboration between librarians and faculty or other university departments is one method for creating effective tools for faculty development. Cook (2000) proffered a useful review of the literature emphasizing the connections between librarians and faculty, noting that librarians have become more proactive in creating connections within their institutional communities. Cook addressed collaboration and types of collaborative or cooperative endeavors, and stated that "members of a collaborative effort work in a team-like setting toward a common goal" (p. 33). Palloff and Pratt (2005) presented the cyclical relationship between community and collaboration, where "collaboration supports community and community supports the ability to collaborate" (p. 4). For example, Florida International University librarians collaborated with the university's Academy for the Art of Teaching to develop a series of faculty workshops addressing such topics as information literacy and intellectual development, power assignments, and teaching for transfer (Iannuzzi, 1998). The University of Maryland University College's Graduate School of Management and Technology (GSMT) produced a faculty development program that includes library workshops. Originally presented as classroom-based workshops, offerings were expanded online as their distance education program grew. The Web-based workshops include using online library resources, using the Internet, and developing library assignments for students in the online environment (SchWeber, Kelley & Orr, 1998). With the proliferation of distance education programs, it is essential to consider methods to reach faculty that are often themselves at a distance.

INSTRUCTIONAL DESIGN OF THE WORKSHOP

In July 2004, the two Regis University distance learning librarians met with the assistant director of distance learning, who is responsible for online faculty development within the School for Professional Studies, to constitute the core team charged with an interdisciplinary course development. The resulting design and development of the workshop over the fall of 2004 loosely followed the Morrison, Ross, and Kemp (2004) instructional design model.

The Team

The distance learning librarians served as subject matter experts and facilitators of the workshop while the assistant director of distance learning served as the instructional designer and project manager. Other contributors were brought in at various junctures of the project. These included other librarians and a faculty member who contributed expert tips via vignettes, two multimedia specialists who contributed interactive learning objects, a Web developer and usability expert who designed the course layout, an accessibility expert, and an e-learning technologist who loaded the demonstration media files on the streaming server.

Instructional Problems

The team discussed current practices for training faculty on library resources, existing tools and resources and how they are utilized, and needs for faculty and their students related to using the library, its services, and resources. The team also brainstormed topics and potential instructional formats during these early meetings.

Learner Analysis

A learner analysis performed in the first meeting determined that the workshop would primarily target faculty from the School for Professional Studies, but would still be open to faculty from all three schools within the university. The team ascertained that the audience had the following characteristics: (a) busy faculty with multiple demands for their time and attention, (b) from a broad range of disciplines, (c) from all three schools, (d) highly educated adult learners, (e) geographically dispersed, (f) diverse range of experience with online learning, (g) broad range of prior knowledge about the library and the services offered, (h) computer and Internet skills ranging from basic to advanced, and (i) desire skills and information that they can apply immediately.

Task Analysis

A formal task analysis was not completed. However, the team did discuss what knowledge, skills, and abilities were required by faculty to integrate library resources into their courses in all formats. After the first meeting the team decided to reflect on their decisions and come to the next meeting to propose goals for the workshop. Five goals were identified:

1. Introduce concepts of information literacy.
2. Update online research skills, applying basic search concepts.
3. Provide criteria for critically evaluating online information.
4. Address issues of copyright.
5. Provide ideas and opportunity to draft a library research assignment.

Learning Objectives

These discussions led to the generation of five learning objectives for the workshop. Learning objectives are what a learner should be able to demonstrate as a result of the workshop. After completing the Faculty-Library Connection, the learner should be able to do the following five things:

1. Discuss information literacy.
2. Effectively search relevant databases for a subject area.
3. Critically evaluate information.
4. Define copyright.
5. Design an effective library assignment.

Based on these identified learning objectives, the content was sequenced using a mix of content expertise sequencing of conceptual elaboration and task expertise sequencing (Morrison et al., 2004). Early in the workshop the theoretical concepts of information literacy would be introduced and discussed. Participants would then be introduced to the resources and tools for searching relevant databases. Search techniques would be demonstrated and participants would be given an opportunity to practice searching databases within their disciplines. The search activities would be followed by a section on evaluating information and copyright. The final "capstone" activity would involve designing an effective library assignment.

Performance Outcomes

The team decided that the course would be organized into sections related to the five learning objectives. Performance outcomes were identified for each learning objective.

1. Discuss information literacy.
   a. Examine several definitions of information literacy.
   b. Retrieve an electronic reserve article addressing information literacy.

2. Effectively search relevant databases for a subject area.
   a. Identify at least one database within a subject area.
   b. Conduct basic and advanced searches using a database.
   c. Apply common search concepts and techniques and utilize limit features to focus a search.

3. Critically evaluate information.
   a. Contrast materials found on the Internet with an article retrieved from a database.
   b. Apply evaluation criteria to both items.

4. Define copyright.
   a. Review general copyright guidelines.
   b. Locate reserve policy and procedure information.
   c. Retrieve materials on electronic reserve.

5. Design an effective library assignment.
   a. Locate information on library instruction.
   b. Create effective library assignments.
   c. Identify contact information for library liaisons.
   d. Generate an instructional activity utilizing the Regis library resources.

Instructional Strategies and Content Development

The distance learning librarians divided up the content sections and began writing content, identifying resources and readings, and developing activities and discussion questions for each section. The team determined that it was realistic to cover all five areas in two weeks of asynchronous online learning in which participants invest five to seven hours per week on the workshop. It was decided that participants should be given an authentic experience of interacting with the library resources remotely. Therefore, such elements as electronic reserves, searching databases, and locating discipline-specific resources on the library Web site were included. Several sections were enhanced with interactivity to help motivate and engage learners. One of the distance learning librarians recorded a demonstration for searching *Academic Search Premier* using Camtasia software. Multimedia specialists were consulted to develop two games for self-assessment, an interactive crossword puzzle which provided practice for generating synonyms for keywords and a concentration game on copyright.

Another goal of the workshop was to reinforce the fact that libraries are also about people. As many faculty interface with the university library from branch campuses or online, it is also important to put a human face on library services. To that end, several of the librarians and one SPS faculty member were asked to provide a photo and a piece of expert advice related to a section of the workshop. This approach also models expert strategies for research and integrating library resources into teaching.

The team intended for the workshop to provide participants with the opportunity to collaborate in the online discussion forum. One or two discussion questions were crafted for each section. Because of the highly interactive nature of the workshop an introductory icebreaker question was developed. In addition to posting an introduction, participants were asked about how they currently use the library for research or teaching as well as if they physically visit or remotely connect to the library. This activity also provided the facilitators with additional information about the participants' level of entry knowledge about library resources and provided the participants with a safe opportunity to practice posting messages to the discussion forum.

Writing the content and producing the demonstration took several months. Once the content was written and the interactive pieces identified, the course content was passed to production. The production team developed color scheme and look and feel for the course. While the production was happening, the distance learning librarians embarked on the assessment and training process for online faculty.

Preparing the Facilitators

While there are many similarities between facilitating a face-to-face classroom and facilitating an online class, SPS recognizes that the online environment can still present special challenges to new facilitators. Therefore, they are required to complete a 10-day Teaching Online Preparation (TOP) course. Before the launch of the Faculty-Library Connection workshop, the librarians were invited to participate in the preparatory course. The course is structured to mirror the layout and types of activities a facilitator would find in a typical Regis online course. The TOP course builds on the theoretical study of the traits of adult learners, examination of national guidelines for best practices in distance learning, principles of ethical teaching, and Bloom's Taxonomy of Educational Objectives (ADEC, 2003; Chickering & Ehrmann, 1987; WCET, 2000). Activities range from the theoretical to the practical, from discussing the ethical principles of teaching and working in groups to composing discussion questions for two different levels on Bloom's Taxonomy, to creating introduction and expectation documents, and initiating, managing and closing a forum discussion thread. An equally important aspect of the course for all of the participants was observing how the facilitation process was modeled. The TOP facilitator (also the instructional designer for the Faculty-Library Connection) encouraged discussions to run their course with minimal intervention, then summarized individual topics and moved the participants on to the next module.

Preparing the Participants/Learner Support

Research underscores the importance of setting clear expectations for online learners as well as providing ongoing support. Therefore, the invitation and introduction letters were carefully crafted to include the learning objective, time investment and pacing of the workshop, technical requirements, and a personal contact to whom to direct questions or concerns. Participants were also provided with a link to Regis' online interactive *Guide to Distance Learning* which demonstrates how to navigate the learning management system, as well as a link to the forum tour which provides instructions for using the discussion forum tools. Technical support was also made available through the university's Information Technology Services Help Center.

The Workshop Pilot and Formative Evaluation

The team beta-tested the workshop with a group of faculty developers from graduate and undergraduate programs and distance learning and library staff. This "learning community" quickly became interactive and congenial, although, unlike most communities formed during an online class, the participants already were well acquainted with each other from previous work together. Several issues arose from the standpoint of facilitation that were transferable to the subsequent live launch–the challenge of keeping an asynchronous group discussion on schedule, keeping everyone involved in the discussion, and ultimately, attrition.

Once the pilot concluded, the team held a formative evaluation meeting. First, participants were asked to share their general impressions. Targeted questions were then asked related to the workshop description, goals, learning objectives, and performance outcomes; learner perceptions; workshop activities and interactions; technical components; and overall learning experience.

The feedback from the pilot group was mainly positive. The accessibility specialist provided critical information on ways in which the online materials could be made more accessible. Specifically, the alternative text for the Camtasia demonstration needed to be rewritten for non-sighted individuals using a screen reader to interact with the remote database. Also, *Academic Search Premier* articles linked to from the workshop were not in accessible PDF format, so they needed to be tagged and re-saved on electronic reserve. It was suggested that the activity for integrating the library resources be introduced earlier in the workshop, developed in stages, and that participants be asked to pre-select a lesson (not a course) that could be enhanced by a library activity. Members of the formative evaluation group reported that the section on copyright was worthy of its own course or tutorial. Because of this, the section was removed along with the concentration game.

Once the workshop underwent final edits, it was advertised via targeted e-mail to faculty (Appendix A). Initial response from faculty was good, with over 40 expressing interest in participating, so the group was divided into two sections, each with its own facilitator. However, the team learned from this first offering that registration numbers did not necessarily indicate the number of faculty who would actually complete the course. It also became clear that some faculty were challenged by the role of being students in an online environment. Although some of the participants were seasoned online instructors, others may never have taken or facilitated an online class. More than one tried to participate in the forum without consulting the course content; in fact, one even admitted he had no idea there *was* content, and asked where it was. Private e-mails and phone calls from the facilitators helped to iron out some of these special challenges. Generally, forum discussions participation was good and faculty enjoyed the interaction and "best practices" sharing they were able to do in the online environment.

COURSE FEATURES

The course map (Appendix B) outlines the workshop sections and the activities performed by the facilitator and participant in each section.

Within the course, there are some notable features including forum discussions, advice from the experts, opportunities for exploratory learning, opportunities for application, and engaging interactivity.

Forum Discussions

Participation involved not only interacting with online workshop content, but also with colleagues in a facilitated asynchronous discussion forum (see Figure 1). The forum discussions were facilitated by the distance learning librarians and provided for thoughtful reflection on the workshop content. Although the activity questions are included within the course text, the facilitator posts the discussion questions at the appropriate point in the forum so that discussions can be conducted in that environment. The distance learning librarians had some initial experience participating in forum discussions as "visiting experts" or "guest lecturers" in online classes. While those visits were normally brief and focused on answering direct questions or making research suggestions based on students' stated research topics, we still learned a great deal from monitoring how course instructors facilitated their courses.

This facilitative method of teaching positions the facilitator as a participant as well as a guide to learning. This model popularly refers to a facilitator as a "guide on the side" in contrast with a lecturer, or "sage on the stage," who would be more likely to impart information than to facilitate learning in an interactive way. A facilitator acknowledges that:

> the knowledge and experience that each student brings to the classroom is just as important as the knowledge the facilitator brings. So each student learns from fellow students as well as from the instructor as a result of the facilitated learning discussions. (Addesso, 2000, p. 112)

Advice from the Experts

Vignettes of advice or expert testimonials were seeded throughout the workshop online content. These vignettes not only provided information related to specific skills and concepts, they also served to introduce some of the key library personnel (see Figure 2).

Exploratory Learning

The instructional strategy of exploratory learning was used throughout the workshop. This strategy provided participants with the authentic

FIGURE 1. Sample Forum Discussion Topic

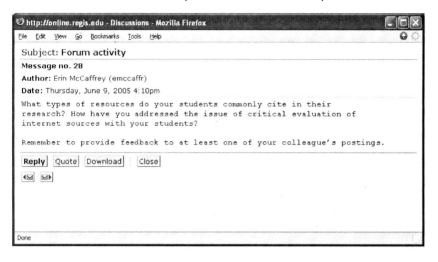

FIGURE 2. Sample of Advice from Experts

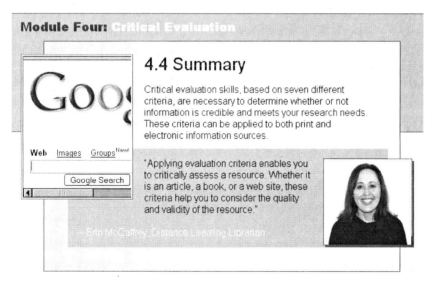

experience of searching for, locating, and evaluating library, Web, and database resources (see Figure 3).

Opportunities for Application

To make the workshop relevant and readily applicable, participants were asked to complete a "capstone" activity in which they revise a lesson from a current course to include a library activity (see Figure 4). Participants were asked to share their assignment in the forum for peer review and reflection.

Engaging Interactivity

Interactive activities like multimedia demonstrations and games were included in the workshop to make the content more engaging and motivating (see Figure 5).

FIGURE 3. Sample of Exploratory Learning Activity

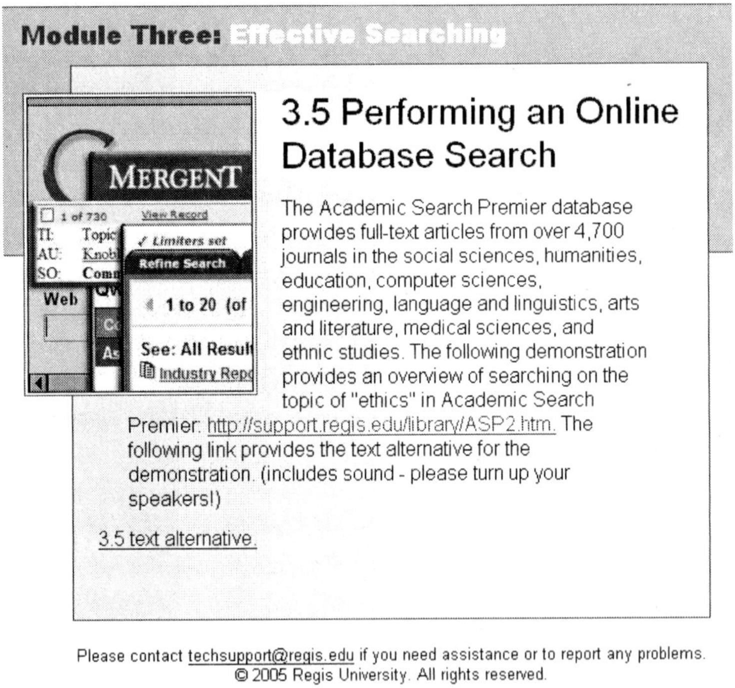
Module Three: Effective Searching
MERGENT
Limiters set
Refine Search
1 to 20 (of
See: All Resul
3.5 Performing an Online Database Search
The Academic Search Premier database provides full-text articles from over 4,700 journals in the social sciences, humanities, education, computer sciences, engineering, language and linguistics, arts and literature, medical sciences, and ethnic studies. The following demonstration provides an overview of searching on the topic of "ethics" in Academic Search Premier: http://support.regis.edu/library/ASP2.htm. The following link provides the text alternative for the demonstration. (includes sound - please turn up your speakers!)
3.5 text alternative.
Please contact techsupport@regis.edu if you need assistance or to report any problems.
© 2005 Regis University. All rights reserved.

Used with permission.

FIGURE 4. Sample Application/Integration Activity

Module Five: Design an Effective Library Learning Activity

5.2 Integrating Library Resources and Research

There are many ways to integrate library resources and research into courses, but some are more effective than others. Like any good learning activity, good library activities are well integrated with the overall objectives and content of the course and have clearly worded instructions. A library activity should be designed to improve skills and build confidence rather than invoke anxiety. Feel free to collaborate with a librarian in developing library activities—your anxiety level shouldn't be raised, either!

"I use the vast resources of the Regis Libraries to aid my teaching and research in ways that constantly evolve, as does the library itself, but these ways always seem to revolve around the wealth of material available and the superb staff who help me and my students to access this material. Indeed, the libraries' vast databases and related access services not only facilitate my own scholarly and personal research, they have hugely impacted a great many students of mine, both in immediate ways (help with projects due soon) and in larger, world-view expanding, ways (help with understandings of the breadth of knowledge and perspective available to the seeker). Still, I have found that what energizes the value of this information and of the access services associated with it is the expertise and demeanor of the library staff: they openly and actively invite student inquiry, and then they come through, generously, with the help requested—an outstanding combination!"

—Mike Zizzi, SPS Communication Faculty

Used with permission.

Remote Access to Electronic Reserves and Databases

Participants were provided with an electronic demonstration for searching remote databases (see Figure 6). The workshop also utilized electronic reserve articles that were available directly from the online course area.

ATTRITION

One of the key issues that surfaced in the delivery of the workshop involved attrition. While the anticipated level of work is clearly expressed

FIGURE 5. Crossword Puzzle Used for Generating Keywords

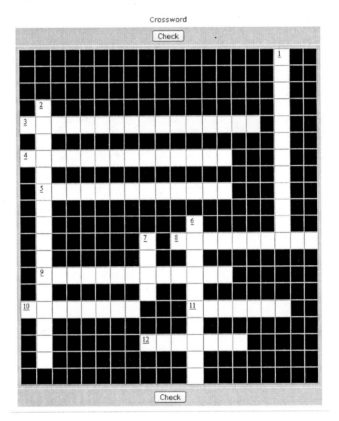

in the workshop expectations (Appendix C), the workshop experienced about 30% attrition. In response to this issue, we sent a Web-based survey to query all individuals who registered for the workshop about their experience and impressions. Nineteen registrants responded to the survey.

Workshop Completion

Ten respondents stated that they did not start or complete the workshop. Seven reported that they did not start or complete due to work and time constraints, one respondent reported technical problems, two re-

FIGURE 6. Screen Capture of Database Search Demonstration

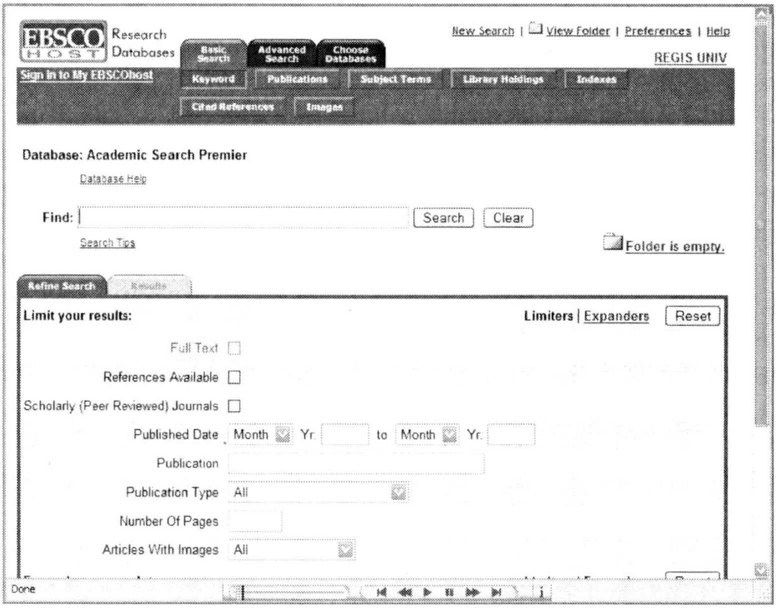

ported family medical issues, and one stated the reason for not participating was that "no one followed up." Other comments were also included in the response to this question. One respondent thought the workshop was only one week, rather than two, and could not commit to two weeks. Another reported being hesitant about online learning with a dial-up modem. Although the individual completed the workshop, someone reported feeling "left behind" when the facilitators kept to the posted schedule and summarized a discussion thread before the individual had a chance to post his/her activity. Finally, two reported that they completed but by lurking and observing rather than participating. One respondent claimed dropping the workshop but returning later to read all of the discussion and to download the activities.

Workshop Expectations

Ten respondents reported that the workshop met or exceeded their expectations. Comments included the following statements:

- I was able to design a unit that I can use with my students in EN203.
- I wanted to know about locating scholarly articles through the Regis Web site.
- I learned some tricks to better navigate the numerous resources online and how to find 'credible' resources.
- I found value reading the comments of the participants and learned from that. There was good discussion by the group.

One reported a mixed response, "Yes, to the extent that I was able to see the work done by other workshop participants. No, due to an inability to keep up with the pace and add my own work to the discussions." One respondent replied, "So-So, I've already used library resources, so it was a bit repetitive." None of the individuals who started the workshop reported that it did not meet their expectations.

Additional Aspects of Library or Library Use They Would Have Liked to Learn

Responses to this question varied and included:

- Build in more activities that step students through increasing levels of skill and critical analysis of online sources.
- Identifying specific resources for the various courses in my discipline areas.
- Examples of research librarians helping students and faculty find information they needed.
- Copyright.
- Procedures for checking currency of library holdings.
- How to access the library at a distance, what is available through full-text, and what can be requested.
- Require practicing more databases.
- Additional examples of moderately complex library-based assignments for online students.

Evaluation of Usefulness of What Was Learned

All of the respondents who answered this question stated that the material in the workshop was useful. Several reported that they have already incorporated new strategies and techniques into their teaching.

Positive Feedback

Positive feedback focused on the organization and content of the workshop as well as the quality and expertise of the facilitators.

Negative Feedback

Respondents reported that the negative aspects of the workshop involved the accelerated pace of the workshop and the lack of active participation by some of the participants. One individual asked that the facilitators share more of their expertise through the discussion forum.

Suggestions for Other Library Workshops

No suggestions were offered.

Technical Difficulties

Only one respondent reported some slowness with the library site but not with the course site.

CONCLUSIONS

Both librarians and faculty benefit from the Faculty-Library Connection workshop. While only the distance learning librarians have facilitated the workshop so far, we hope our reference librarians will be trained to serve as co-facilitators, giving them the opportunity to expand their knowledge of the online course experience. The workshop allows the library to reach a large population of dispersed faculty with whom we might otherwise not interact with because of their physical location. It affords faculty the opportunity to receive instruction in available library resources and the WebCT format provides faculty interested in teaching with technology the opportunity to experience a technology-mediated environment. The workshop also raises the visibility of librarians as facilitators; as a result of this workshop, one of the early participants contacted her departmental library liaison to participate in a chat session for her online course.

The biggest challenge has been course facilitation. Facilitation can be an extremely time-intensive process. The larger the group of participants, the more time spent communicating with individuals and summarizing discussion forum postings. As a result, we recommend the workshop be offered at those times of the term when it will not conflict with our bibliographic instruction schedules.

Collaborating with other university departments has served as a tremendous learning opportunity and both the library and the SPS distance learning department benefit from this collaboration. Greater collaboration with the distance learning instructional designers will hopefully lead to the development of other online workshops. The instructional designers have also asked librarians to participate on online course development teams. Since the workshop can target specific populations of faculty by subject specialty or location, we are working to offer the workshop to a select group of faculty at the Regis Las Vegas campuses.

REFERENCES

Addesso, P. (2000). Online facilitation: Individual and group possibilities. In K.W. White & B. H. Weight (Eds.), *The online teaching guide* (pp. 112-123). Boston: Allyn and Bacon.

American Distance Education Consortium. (2003). *Guiding principles for distance teaching and learning.* Retrieved December 13, 2005, from American Distance Education Consortium Web site, http://www.adec.edu/admin/papers/distance-teaching_principles.html.

Brancato, V. C. (2003). Professional development in higher education. *New Directions for Adult and Continuing Education, no. 98,* 59-65.

Chickering, A., & S.C. Ehrmann. (1987). Implementing the seven principles: Technology as lever. Retrieved December 13, 2005, from TLT Group Web site: http://www.tltgroup.org/programs/seven.html.

Cook, D. (2000). Creating connections: A review of the literature. In D. Raspa & D. Ward (Eds.), *The collaborative imperative: Librarians and faculty working together in the information universe* (pp. 19-38). Chicago: Association of College and Research Libraries.

Hall, L. (1999). Faculty information competence. *Computers in Libraries, 19*(8), 29-34.

Haynes, E. (1992). The role of the academic library in providing support for faculty development. In J. L. Pence & E. Haynes (Eds.), *Academic libraries in the service of faculty development: A collection of essays commissioned by the Colorado academic library committee* (pp. 47-84). Colorado: Colorado Academic Library Committee (ERIC Document Reproduction Service No. ED355942).

Hurst, L. (2003). The special library on campus: A model for library orientations aimed at academic administration, faculty, and support staff. *Journal of Academic Librarianship, 29*(4), 231-236.

Iannuzzi, P. (1998). Faculty development and information literacy: Establishing campus partnerships. *Reference Services Review, 26*(3-4), 98-102+.

Lacey, P. A. (1980). The role of the librarian in faculty development: A professor's point of view. In N. Z. Williams & J. T. Tsukamoto (Eds.), *Library instruction and faculty development: Growth opportunities in the academic community* (pp. 17-28). Ann Arbor, MI: Pierian Press.

Morrison, G. R., Ross, S. M., & Kemp, J. E. (2004). *Designing effective instruction.* Hoboken, NJ: J. Wiley & Sons.

Mosely, P. A. (1998). Creating a library assignment workshop for university faculty. *Journal of Academic Librarianship, 24*(1), 33-41.

Palloff, R. M., & Pratt, K. (2005). *Collaborating online: Learning together in community.* San Francisco: Jossey-Bass.

SchWeber, C., Kelley, K. B., & Orr, G. J. (1998). Training, and retraining, faculty for online courses: Challenges and strategies. In *Distance Learning '98. Proceedings of the Annual Conference on Distance Teaching & Learning* (pp. 347-352). Madison: University of Wisconsin System (ERIC Document Reproduction Service No. ED422874).

Stamps, D. (1984). Out of the woodwork: Orienting the "invisible" faculty. *Georgia Librarian, 21,* 90-92.

Werrell, E. L., & Wesley, T. L. (1990). Promoting information literacy through a faculty workshop. *Research Strategies, 8*(4), 172-180.

Western Cooperative for Educational Telecommunications. (2000). *Principles of good practice for electronically offered degree and certificate programs.* Retrieved December 13, 2005, from Western Cooperative for Educational Telecommunications Web site, http://www.wcet.info/projects/balancing/principles.asp.

doi:10.1300/J111v45n01_16

APPENDIX A

Professional Development Opportunity–The Faculty-Library Connection Workshop

Workshop Description

This two-week workshop is designed to allow you as faculty to update your research skills and increase your familiarity with library resources so that you can better integrate library activities into your courses. This workshop also addresses some of the challenges of online research from the perspective of your own research as well as that of your students–you might encounter many of the same frustrations that your students experience. Finally, you will have the opportunity to explore the concept of information literacy, and the application of information evaluation. Finding, retrieving and critically thinking about information are essential to life-long learning!

Workshop Outcomes

The participants will accomplish five things:

- Discuss information literacy.
- Retrieve electronic reserve article addressing information literacy.
- Apply common search concepts and techniques to conduct basic and advanced searches using a database.
- Contrast materials found on the Internet with an article retrieved from a database and apply evaluation criteria to both items.
- Generate an instructional activity utilizing the Regis library resources.

Dates

4/11/05-4/22/05 online in WebCT

Facilitators

Tom Riedel
Erin McCaffrey

Commitment

Participants will be asked to invest 5-7 hours per week during the workshop.

System Requirements

Please check this link to ensure that your computer meets the technical requirements for online courses.

http://www.regis.edu/regis.asp?sctn=onl&p1=ol&p2=tech

To sign up, please send a message to facsup@regis.edu. You will receive a confirmation message with instructions for logging onto the workshop.

APPENDIX B

Faculty-Library Connection Workshop Course Map

Module	Content Elements	Facilitators Role	Participant Role
Workshop Overview	Welcome, setting the stage and getting acquainted.	Facilitators post introductions and expectations documents. Facilitate discussion and provide feedback, clarification, and guidance.	Participants introduce themselves in the discussion forum and discuss how they currently use the library, both physically and virtually.
Information Literacy	Define information literacy and eReserves reading on information literacy, and expert advice.	Facilitators facilitate discussion and provide feedback, clarification, and guidance.	Participants discuss how do they use the libraries for research; what they want students to know about doing research; their level of satisfaction of the quality of students' research; reflect on the reading; and share strategies for library activities that they have used in the past.
Effective Searching	Introduce electronic databases; how to select the correct database; multimedia media demonstration of searching strategies using Academic Search Premier; different approaches to searching; interactive keyword activity using a crossword puzzle game; and expert advice.	Facilitators facilitate discussion and provide feedback, clarification, and guidance.	View the demonstration; complete the interactive crossword activity; and perform a database search for topic related to discipline or research interest, describe strategies used, report finding, and discuss experience.
Critical Evaluation	Present strategies and resources for critically evaluating information; contract library database and information found on the Web; apply evaluation criteria to both types of searches; and expert advice.	Facilitators facilitate discussion and provide feedback, clarification, and guidance.	Perform Google search; discuss the types of sources students often cite; and generate strategies for communicating expectations for appropriate resources within respective disciplines.
Design an Effective Library Learning Activity	Tips for integrating library activities; the importance of aligning outcomes, instructional strategy, and assessments; examples of library activities; and one faculty member's strategies are presented.	Facilitators facilitate discussion and provide feedback, clarification, and guidance.	Participants craft a library learning activity, share with other participants and solicit feedback; and provide feedback to each other.
Final Reflection	Learning Objectives are reviewed and participants are asked to reflect on their experience.	Facilitators facilitate discussion; provide feedback, clarification, and guidance; and summarize the workshop.	Participants share their reflections in the discussion forum.

APPENDIX C

Workshop Expectations

If you have questions or concerns related to this workshop, please feel free to discuss them with me by contacting me via e-mail.

Name, **Facilitator**

Contact Information

E-mail:
Phone:
Fax:

The best way to contact me is by e-mail. I check my e-mail several times daily, so you should expect a reply from me within 24 hours or less. My office hours are Monday through Friday from 8:00 a.m. to 5:00 p.m., although these might vary slightly depending upon other commitments.

Purpose

The purpose of this workshop, the Faculty Library Connection, is to enable faculty to update their research skills and familiarize themselves with library resources so that they can better integrate library activities into their courses. Critically thinking about information is essential to independent life-long learning.

Forum Postings

To ensure manageable discussion, please post a REPLY to a discussion question. If your comments warrant a new discussion, use COMPOSE MESSAGE to start a new thread. I will facilitate the discussion to keep us moving through the workshop content. Please be respectful of others in your postings.

Level of Work

You should plan to spend one to two hours a day in this workshop. Each module builds on the work of the previous section. I expect you to be an active participant, reflecting on the course material and posting to the Forum. If you are unable to meet a submission deadline, please contact me.

Privacy

Students using online formats for study at Regis University do so in a protected environment. However, these learning environments may at times be viewed by faculty (both current and those learning to become online facilitators), Distance Learning staff and other experts who are working with us to maintain the highest quality online courses.

Feedback

During the workshop, you will be expected to respond to fellow participants who will also be responding to your work. Please be respectful and constructive in your feedback.

Designing Library Services for the PDA

Dana McFarland
Jessica Mussell

Royal Roads University

SUMMARY. Handheld electronic devices are becoming popular and are playing an increasingly important role in the distributed learning environment. Enabling library users to maximize their access to library resources through these devices involves challenges that include determining the level of interest among users, identifying relevant resources, and establishing technical and compatibility standards. Affordability of devices for consumers, and availability of resources and support for handheld computing initiatives within libraries must also be considered. This study examines issues and challenges surrounding the design and delivery of library services and resources for personal digital assistants (PDAs) at Royal Roads University Library, finding that there are beneficial research applications for handheld devices that can be implemented even while related technologies continue to evolve. doi:10.1300/J111v45n01_17

KEYWORDS. Personal digital assistants, library services, distributed learning

INTRODUCTION

Personal digital assistants (PDAs) of various sorts are increasingly owned by members of the Royal Roads University community, with

[Haworth co-indexing entry note]: "Designing Library Services for the PDA." McFarland, Dana, and Jessica Mussell. Co-published simultaneously in *Journal of Library Administration* (The Haworth Information Press, an imprint of The Haworth Press, Inc.) Vol. 45, No. 1/2, 2006, pp. 301-314; and: *The Twelfth Off-Campus Library Services Conference Proceedings* (ed: Julie A. Garrison) The Haworth Information Press, an imprint of The Haworth Press, Inc., 2006, pp. 301-314.

Available online at http://jla.haworthpress.com
doi:10.1300/J111v45n01_17

33% of participants in a learner survey reporting ownership in 2004. Access to information resources such as e-books, news, and journal articles figured prominently among the services most desired by survey respondents (Hawksworth, 2005). Further, a pilot project in 2005 in the use of Blackberry devices by university staff and faculty indicated that a more fully featured PDA, such as Pocket PC or Palm, would better satisfy some requirements, such as browsing the Internet and reading e-books (Grundy, 2005). In light of the findings of these two earlier studies, the Royal Roads University Library decided to identify faculty and staff who use PDAs, other than Blackberries, and to assess their level of interest in PDA-friendly services to complement existing desktop-based access to online library resources. A secondary objective was to explore which PDA applications our clients perceive to be of most use.

To date, programs at Royal Roads University have been delivered primarily online to distance learners across Canada and beyond. To support the university's commitment to e-learning and its interest in mobile learning (m-learning) environments, the library focuses on providing resources in electronic formats over print. This mandate to provide access to resources in electronic format wherever possible and practical makes it appealing to explore PDAs as another mode of access for online resources. With the growing popular adoption and increasing evolution of smaller devices, it seems natural to anticipate a demand for PDA-accessible library services. As Michael Seadle noted in his introductory article to the PDA issue of *Library Hi Tech*, we need to "[consider] how our patrons will use PDAs, just as in the past we had to plan for their use of computers, laptops, and Internet access" (Seadle, 2003, p. 391).

LITERATURE REVIEW

The decision to embark on this study coincided with the implementation of a wireless network across the university. An earlier study (Carney, Koufogiannakis, & Ryan, 2004) suggested wireless as a necessary precondition to support a growing academic PDA user community. In another study where a wireless network was being implemented, the authors expected patrons with PDAs to become their main wireless users (Seadle, 2003). With so many libraries and academic institutions implementing wireless networks, librarians are well positioned to consider the experiences of early adopters in determining what services might be relevant for this new constituency within their own user groups.

Initially, health libraries took the lead in providing PDA services and instruction to medical students and clinical staff, with the Arizona Health Sciences Library in Tucson leading the way (Garrison, Anderson, MacDonald, Schardt, & Thibodeau, 2003; Peters, Dorsch, Bell, & Burnette, 2003; Shipman & Morton, 2001; Stoddard, 2001). More recently other academic libraries and some school systems have begun to explore the potential of this service area (Carney et al., 2004; Dahl, Koufogiannakis, & Ryan, 2005). Their experiences demonstrate the benefits and limitations of the PDA as a medium for instruction and for providing access to library resources.

PDAs allow for learning on the go. The phrase "anytime, anywhere" becomes much more meaningful in the context of a device that can both fit in a pocket and exploit the power and resources of an institution's wireless network. Postsecondary institutions increasingly find themselves operating within this context: users may regard PDAs as an economical and more portable alternative to laptops, whereas institutions may find provision of a wireless network more attractive than maintaining costly and space-consuming labs full of desktop computers in constant need of renewal (Carlson, 2000). Besides saving space, Peters et al. (2003) pointed out that wireless access to online resources may actually facilitate increased use, reflected in usage statistics, with access no longer limited to the available conventional computers.

As part of the ongoing development of PDA services, some ILS vendors have begun offering PDA modules. In 2004, Innovative Interfaces, Inc. launched airPac, a wireless OPAC interface that works with Internet-ready PDAs and cellphones (Innovative Interfaces, 2004). Some progressive Web sites are being designed to enable viewing and use through PDA browsers. In their article on a PDA deployment at the University of Minnesota Duluth, Allert and Deneen noted that:

> viewing normal Web pages from the iPAQ [pocketpc] may require considerable scrolling, both horizontally and vertically . . . faculty needed to set aside time to reformat all crucial course Web pages to fit the iPAQ . . . The need to reformat Web pages, however, places additional requirements on the provider of this content. Ideally, Web sites should be formatted to reconfigure themselves to suit the device that is accessing them, but this also requires additional programming. (Deneen & Allert, 2003, p. 423)

If automatic configuration is not possible due to restrictive templates or the nature of the content, Web designers may still enhance PDA usability by paying attention to how content appears in browsers on the tiny screen.

The potential offered by the technology, together with growing ubiquity and apparent cost savings afforded by PDAs and wireless connectivity, are compelling reasons to experiment and to begin to develop services. Of course libraries will learn through experience which applications are viable and well-received, but initial efforts can be guided by research related to the pedagogy of online learning and interface design. The University of Minnesota Duluth project, focusing on PDA applications for computer science students, advised that:

> with productivity tools holding only marginal importance, the investigation centered on the capabilities of other iPAQ software, the role of the Internet and the wireless network, and the possibility of creating instructional software. Instructors needed to consider the curriculum and to identify key interaction points in which mobile computers could be effective. (Deneen & Allert, 2003, p. 420)

A user study by the University of Alberta Libraries found that "the services proving most popular with users . . . were: the ability to download database search results to a PDA, the PDA training sessions, maintaining a Web site with listings of PDA resources, providing consultations, and loaning of PDA books" (Carney et al., 2004, p. 397). These approaches and findings are consistent with online design principles that favor minimal screen scrolling.

Of the resources that are available for a fee through subscription, medical resources are most prevalent due to the profession's early adoption of handheld devices for point-of-care reference. These resources include MD Consult's Pocket Consult, PEPID (Portable Emergency and Primary Care Information Database), Ovid@Hand, Harrison's On Hand, and Medline on Tap, to name a few. The scarcity of available content is a current limitation for non-medical libraries that are considering the incorporation of PDA resources into the collection.

Value-added features for PDAs are not yet common in existing online information products, but there are examples. Libraries that hold netLibrary e-book titles have been able to purchase an additional "gateway" license that allows for download of selected titles to a PDA, although it is unclear at the time of writing whether this will be the case in future. Other information providers are developing features that can be used to enhance the research potential of the PDA. Highwire Press offers RSS feeds and table of contents alerts that integrate well with PDAs. A new area with exciting potential is for audio or video file downloads, known as podcasting. McGraw-Hill's Access Medicine already offers weekly downloadable podcasts on a variety of medical topics. Good quality non-medical podcast sources are also emerging, including Earthwatch Radio, Out of the Past (Film Noir), public radio documentaries, and others.

METHOD

The library convened a focus group to assess the level of interest in PDA-friendly library services among university faculty members and staff. Potential participants were identified from among respondents to a questionnaire about PDA ownership and use (see Appendix for questionnaire).

The questionnaire was delivered online using a Web-based survey tool because many staff and faculty work off-campus To reach the greatest number of potential respondents, the link to the questionnaire was distributed as part of an online staff newsletter that is delivered weekly to each staff e-mail address. The link was advertised twice.

Respondents were asked to identify themselves and to indicate their willingness to be contacted for further participation. The responses received from the questionnaire were used to solicit potential focus group participants who were accustomed to using wireless enabled PDAs (other than Blackberries) to identify applications that were currently in use or of interest, and to gauge initial interest in having the library develop PDA-accessible services. Based on the responses, researchers contacted individuals to form a focus group to experiment with and discuss a pilot collection of resources compiled by the library. Investigators also anticipated learning about new resources and applications for PDAs, particularly since most participants in the focus group had strong backgrounds in information technology or related fields. In the focus group one librarian-researcher acted as facilitator and demonstrated a selection of PDA resources and applications while the other recorded the events and discussion.

The pilot collection of PDA resources was identified through a review of the recent professional literature and listserv discussions, together with an analysis of existing online collections. This entailed testing the usability of the library's current online resources, and looking for features in them that were specifically tailored to PDA use. For inclusion in the list, resources had to be:

a. relevant to the academic programs offered at Royal Roads University;
b. easy to view or navigate on a small-screen;
c. supported by both Pocket PC and Palm Pilot operating systems (unless freely available on the Internet); and
d. accessible preferably via browser with additional software requirements limited to stable and free or affordable applications.

The list of free and subscription resources was compiled and added to the library Web site.[1] The entries included e-journal and e-book collections, article databases, and an Internet search engine. Links to enabling applications, such as Acrobat Reader for PDA, RSS readers for PDA and e-book readers for PDA were included to support the various file formats used to encode content.

The focus group met in a seminar room in the library. The demonstration of resources for PDAs was facilitated by displaying the PDA output on a laptop computer using the Microsoft Remote Display Control application. The laptop display was then projected to the screen using a data projector. Speakers were used to provide sound for RSS feed items with audio enclosures. Participants were encouraged to follow using their own devices, and to comment freely throughout the session.

RESULTS

The questionnaire to solicit focus group participation was made available to approximately 300 staff and faculty. Fifteen staff and faculty responded to the questionnaire. Because only eleven respondents actually owned a PDA, only eleven were able to complete the questionnaire. Of the eleven full respondents, ten (91%) used their PDA on a daily basis. Pocket PC (6) was the most popular type of device, followed by Palm (3) and BlackBerry (1).[2]

Respondents to the questionnaire expressed preferences for various applications for the PDA. Only six of the eleven respondents (55%) had wireless-capable PDAs. Figure 1 illustrates respondents' current uses for the PDA, while Figure 2 illustrates how they reported they would like to use the PDA.

Ten respondents (67%) reported using the PDA on a daily basis at work primarily for the purposes of managing their schedules, contacts, and e-mail. Eight respondents (73%) felt that the ability to conduct research using the PDA would be beneficial to their work. Specifically, there was interest in having access to e-book collections, databases, online journals, PDA or small-screen friendly Web sites, and RSS feeds (Figure 2). Of the respondents who expressed interest in using the PDA to conduct research, three took part in our focus group.

FIGURE 1. What do you use your PDA for?

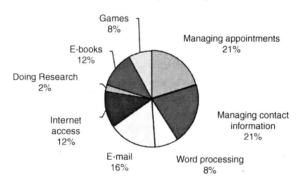

FIGURE 2. What types of research resources would you like to be able to access via PDA?

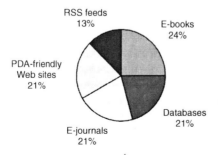

DISCUSSION

The questionnaire was intended to recruit a focus group, so although the questionnaire responses are of interest they are not statistically significant.

Respondents to our questionnaire were from units across the university. However, two of the three participants in the focus group were from information technology or related departments. This suggests that although PDA ownership is increasing, uptake of wireless-enabled PDAs to support academic research remains with the early adopters.

The focus group began with a librarian-researcher introducing the purpose and plan for the meeting, and inviting participants to follow along with the demonstration and to make comments or ask questions in the moment. A number of themes emerged.

Enabling Applications

The session began with a demonstration of online journal access for the PDA via the library Web page for PDA resources. PDA display was projected for the benefit of focus group participants by means of a laptop computer using the Microsoft Remote Display Control (MSRDC) application, which was then displayed using a data projector. One participant remarked that he had used MSRDC, but only to enlarge the PDA display for viewing on a desktop computer, and not for the purpose of projection. Other discussion followed that related to enabling software, including the suggestion that a browser other than Internet Explorer for the PDA might offer more functionality for research purposes. Access NetFront was mentioned as an example of a browser that allows for viewing of multiple pages, minimizing pages, etc.

In viewing the library catalog via a PDA, one participant noted a marked difference in the appearance of the same pages on his own device. The group proceeded to explore browser settings to optimize the appearance of content on the page and thus improve navigability of the library catalog for that device. Discussion as to whether it might be possible to configure a browser to view Web pages in landscape orientation on PDA was inconclusive.

Wireless Infrastructure

Participants remarked that load on the wireless network may compromise speed, with perceptible consequences for Internet browsing, downloading files, etc. The stability of the wireless network and its limited availability, in only select buildings on campus, were also noted as factors that might compromise reliability of access.

Availability of Content

In questionnaire responses each focus group participant expressed interest in reading e-books on PDA. Unfortunately, at the time of the focus group meeting the library had no e-book product that supported download to a PDA for offline reading. Furthermore, testing confirmed that the library's existing e-book products (netLibrary, ebrary, EnviroNetbase) did not support online viewing by PDA browser versions. Consequently the demonstration of e-books for PDAs relied on viewing and discussing freely available e-books, particularly those from the Electronic Text Center of the University of Virginia Library. Librarians were concerned that these free e-book collections would not catch the interest of the participants, who might have been expected to prefer more recent and more technical content. However, participants clarified that their interest in e-books to date was principally recreational. In fact, one participant had previously visited the Electronic Text Center and commented favorably on the content available for download there. For viewing e-books on PDA, participants preferred the MSReader format.

All focus group participants had experimented with downloads of MP3 files for music, but none had used the PDA for spoken word podcasting. There was general agreement that producing podcasts for local curriculum requirements could be done relatively simply, but there was also debate about the pedagogical value of podcasting "lectures" and some apprehension that the technology might not be accessible enough for users. There was greater enthusiasm in anticipating applications in education for video podcasting.

Discussion Summary

The majority of our questionnaire respondents and focus group participants currently use the PDA primarily for time management tasks such as scheduling and e-mail. It is perhaps surprising that focus group participants had not taken more initiative to explore the resources and services that they reported to be of interest in their questionnaire responses.

Usability was identified as a fundamental barrier to more diverse employment of the PDA. While Web sites can be created with formatting and templates that facilitate viewing content on a PDA, most are not developed that way at present. In the absence of a critical mass of accessible content that demonstrably enriches the PDA environment, there was speculation in the focus group that the "killer app" for PDA has yet to emerge. Enhancing discussion group applications for e-learning to permit offline reading and processing of posts was suggested as an area with potential for the PDA.

Until usability improves and the added value of the PDA becomes obvious, focus group participants felt that economic factors will constrain uptake of this tool for research to early adopters. Older PDA models are not wireless capable and owners have to consider replacing or upgrading to enable wireless. Committing to a device that uses one or another of the available operating systems also has the effect of restricting access to content. These limitations notwithstanding, participants concurred that the university and the library should monitor developments in the PDA environment so as to anticipate demand and enrich and integrate applications where possible. The question was posed as to whether this is the device with evolutionary impetus: perhaps convergence between laptop and PDA devices will address problems of portability versus ergonomics, resulting in a more functional device to support research activities.

CONCLUSION

Examination of the literature and the outcomes of this study suggest both strengths and challenges to using a PDA for library research. The handheld device is not a technology that applies equally well to every aspect of retrieving and managing information. There are significant variations in functionality among available devices, challenging the notion that a library might present a uniform suite of services and resources for this format. Use of PDAs for library research is also limited by the availability of resources. Currently, most online resources are not designed for viewing on handheld screens. Scrolling and the distortion of graphical images are disincentives to using the PDA for some applications. As well, many resources and applications that have been developed for PDAs are not compatible with diverse operating systems, but rather are most frequently made available for either Palm OS or Windows CE operating systems. It is difficult to gauge which of the competing standards may prevail.[3]

Although the PDA is one of the least expensive and most portable options for access to online collections, it is best employed as a supplementary tool. The devices presently do not have access to a critical mass of content that is easily viewed and navigated. Furthermore, to best serve PDA users until there is convergence of the technology to a set of standards, libraries may have to select and support resources for multiple operating systems. Nevertheless, within these constraints there are exciting niche applications, particularly in downloading video or audio files for mobile use. Much can be done using existing tools in ingenious ways.

To make research via a PDA more appealing, Web designers and online content providers should consider designing interfaces to be viewable on both desktop and small screen devices. Failing this, a solution that may be within the purview of the library would be to explore mediation by a PDA-compatible federated search interface to retrieve, compile, and present search results from across various online repositories within a PDA-compatible view. Beyond these solutions, the future may offer devices that allow for greater flexibility of application to research without compromising portability and convenience (Thurrott, 2002).

NOTES

1. The list of PDA resources is found at <http://library.royalroads.ca/info/pda.htm>.

2. One respondent did not know what type of PDA he/she owned.

3. Recently Palm Inc. has announced the production of a version of the Palm Treo that will run on the Windows operating system, suggesting that Microsoft may be winning the battle (Avery, 2005).

REFERENCES

Avery, S. (2005, September 24). New Palm to embrace Microsoft. *Globe and Mail*, p. B5.

Carlson, S. (2000). Universities find wireless systems bring them convenience and savings. *Chronicle of Higher Education, 47*(7), p. A64.

Carney, S., Koufogiannakis, D., & Ryan, P. (2004). Library services for users of personal digital assistants: A needs assessment and program evaluation. *Portal: Libraries and the Academy, 4*(3), 393-406.

Dahl, S., Koufogiannakis, D., & Ryan, P. (2005). Just another format integrating resources for users of personal digital assistants. *Acquisitions Librarian, 16*(33/34), 133-135.

Deneen, L., & Allert, J. (2003). Hand-held computers in the classroom and the library: Teaching and learning resource issues resulting from widespread deployment at the University of Minnesota Duluth. *Library Hi Tech, 21*(4), 419-425.

Garrison, J. A., Anderson, T. L., MacDonald, M. H., Schardt, C. M., & Thibodeau, P. L. (2003). Supporting PDAs: The experiences of a health sciences library. *Library Hi Tech, 21*(4), 412.

Grundy, S. (2005). [BlackBerry Pilot Project]. Unpublished raw data.

Hawksworth, J. (2005). *The formulation of a feasibility study and business case for mobile learning (m-learning) with PDAs at RRU: A consulting report for Royal Roads University.* Unpublished master's thesis, Royal Roads University, Victoria, British Columbia, Canada.

Innovative Interfaces. (2004). *Innovative celebrates its first twenty-five years!* Retrieved September 27, 2005, from http://www.iii.com/about/25.shtml.

Peters, T., Dorsch, J., Bell, L., & Burnette, P. (2003). PDAs and health sciences libraries. *Library Hi Tech, 21*(4), 400-411.

Seadle, M. (2003). Mental models for personal digital assistants (PDAs). *Library Hi Tech, 21*(4), 390-392.

Shipman, J. P., & Morton, A. C. (2001). The new black bag: PDAs, health care and library services. *Reference Services Review, 29*(3), 229-237.

Stoddard, M. J. (2001). Handhelds in the health sciences library. *Medical Reference Services Quarterly, 20*(3), 75-82.

Thurrott, P. (2002). *Microsoft brings out celebrities, new hardware for tablet PC launch.* Retrieved November 7, 2005, from http://www.windowsitpro.com/Article/ArticleID/27185/27185.html.

doi:10.1300/J111v45n01_17

APPENDIX

**Personal Digital Assistant (PDA) Use at Royal Roads University:
Survey**

Disclaimer:

The purpose of this survey is to investigate the use of personal digital assistants (PDA) by faculty and staff at Royal Roads University in order to determine whether or not there is an interest in the library providing PDA-friendly services to complement our current collection of online and print resources. From this survey, we hope to identify a group of individuals who would be willing to participate in a focus group where we will provide library instruction via PDA for PDAs. If you have more than one PDA, we ask that you fill out one survey for each device. All responses will be kept confidential.

1. Name: _____

2. Position: _____

3. Program/Department _____

4. a) Do you own a personal digital assistant (PDA)?
   ☐ Yes
   ☐ No

   b) If yes, is it:
   ☐ Owned personally
   ☐ Owned by Royal Roads University
   ☐ Other (please specify) _____

5. What brand is your PDA?
   ☐ Pocket PC
   ☐ Palm
   ☐ BlackBerry
   ☐ Don't know
   ☐ Other (please specify) _____

6. What operating system does your PDA use? (choose one)
   ☐ Palm OS
   ☐ Windows
   ☐ Don't know
   ☐ Other (please specify) _____

7. Is your PDA wireless capable?
   ☐ Yes
   ☐ No
   ☐ It can be made wireless capable by adding a card or accessory
   ☐ Don't know

8. How often do you use your PDA?
   ☐ Daily
   ☐ Weekly
   ☐ Less than weekly

APPENDIX (continued)

9. What do you use your PDA for? (check all that apply)
   - ☐ Managing appointments
   - ☐ Managing contact information
   - ☐ Word processing
   - ☐ E-mail
   - ☐ Web/Internet access
   - ☐ Research
   - ☐ Reading e-books
   - ☐ Games
   - ☐ Other (please specify) _____

10. Do you use a PDA at work?
    - ☐ Yes
    - ☐ No (if no, skip to question 12)

11. How do you incorporate PDA use into work?

    _____
    _____
    _____

12. Would the ability to conduct research using your PDA be beneficial to work?
    - ☐ Yes
    - ☐ No (if no, skip to question 14)

13. What types of research resources would you like to be able to access via PDA?
    - ☐ e-books
    - ☐ Databases
    - ☐ e-Journals
    - ☐ PDA-friendly Websites
    - ☐ RSS feeds
    - ☐ Other (please specify) _____

14. May we contact you for further information?
    - ☐ Yes (if yes, please provide contact details below)
    - ☐ No

Contact details:
Phone: _____ E-mail: _____

Thank-you for participating in our survey.

Providing Library Instruction to Distance Learning Students in the 21st Century: Meeting the Current and Changing Needs of a Diverse Community

Evadne McLean

Mona Campus
University of the West Indies

Stephen H. Dew

University of Iowa

SUMMARY. This study examines the variety of instructional practices employed in distance learning librarianship from the end of the 20th Century through the early beginnings of the 21st Century. The authors provide a thorough review of the literature on distance learning library instruction, and the study highlights the instructional services provided at two academic institutions with distinctly different clienteles and missions–one a large American university and the other a large Caribbean university. doi:10.1300/J111v45n03_01

KEYWORDS. Instruction, video conferencing, online classes, tutorials, information literacy

---

[Haworth co-indexing entry note]: "Providing Library Instruction to Distance Learning Students in the 21st Century: Meeting the Current and Changing Needs of a Diverse Community." McLean, Evadne, and Stephen H. Dew. Co-published simultaneously in *Journal of Library Administration* (The Haworth Information Press, an imprint of The Haworth Press, Inc.) Vol. 45, No. 3/4, 2006, pp. 315-337; and: *The Twelfth Off-Campus Library Services Conference Proceedings* (ed: Julie A. Garrison) The Haworth Information Press, an imprint of The Haworth Press, Inc., 2006, pp. 315-337.

Available online at http://jla.haworthpress.com
doi:10.1300/J111v45n03_01

INTRODUCTION

According to the Association of College and Research Libraries' (ACRL's) *Guidelines for Distance Learning Library Services*, it is "essential" that each institution provide distance learning students with instructional services "equivalent" to those provided on-campus students, including the provision of a "program of library user instruction designed to instill independent and effective information literacy skills" (2004, p. 611). How academic institutions provide instructional services vary widely depending on the personnel, facilities, and resources employed by the individual institution. In some cases, librarians travel to classrooms located at various sites, where they meet face-to-face with classes, lecture on library resources and services, and interact with students–the traditional method of library instruction prevalent throughout the last half of the 20th Century. In an ever-increasing number of situations, however, librarians are using the interactive capabilities of new technologies, especially the Web, television, and videoconferencing, to communicate simultaneously with students who can be located at many different sites. In addition, through online tutorials, course management systems, and other software, a great deal of library instruction is being conducted asynchronously. With resources and clientele varying greatly among academic institutions, pedagogical practices for distance learning librarians also vary greatly. Frequently large institutions' practices may vary depending upon the nature of the particular program or course being supported.

For librarians looking for pedagogical practices for providing bibliographic instruction to distance education students, there are several resources that are immensely valuable. *Library Literature and Information Science Full Text* (a commercial *WilsonWeb* database) and *Library, Information Science & Technology Abstracts* (a free *EBSCOhost* database) are two of the best resources available. Fortunately, both were available at the University of Iowa and utilized for this study. Possibly the best free resource, however, is *Library Services for Distance Learning: The Fourth Bibliography*, a Web-based resource originally edited by Alexander Slade (the editorial responsibility for the Web site was transferred in 2005 to the Distance Learning Section of ACRL). Other resources that should prove informative and useful for distance education librarians interested in instructional issues would be the LOEX (Library Orientation Exchange) Web site, a self-supporting, non-profit educational clearinghouse for library instruction and information literacy information, and the Web sites and listservs for the two most relevant sections of ACRL–Distance Learning and Instruction.

INFORMATION LITERACY AND ACTIVE LEARNING

According to ACRL, information literacy is the "set of skills needed to find, retrieve, analyze, and use information" (ACRL, 2006), and in order to guide instruction librarians interested in promoting information literacy skills, ACRL published the "Information Literacy Competency Standards for Higher Education" (ACRL, 2000). Building upon this, ACRL's Distance Learning Section developed a SPEC Kit for the Association of Research Libraries entitled *Collaboration for Distance Learning Information Literacy Instruction* (ACRL/DLS, Instruction Section, 2005), and in its study, the committee observed,

> The ability to utilize a variety of tools and technologies, from face-to-face instruction to synchronous and asynchronous online assistance, appears to be a trend for libraries that are taking the lead in distance information literacy instruction. . . . Many of those libraries that are engaged in the distance information literacy instruction appear to be approaching the unique challenges of the distance learning environment dynamically and creatively. (p. 18)

Orr and Wallin also recognized the need for creativity, that the "individualistic" information literacy needs and learning styles of off-campus students require a realignment of traditional services and flexible delivery of instruction (2001). During the last four years, the Off-Campus Library Services Conference and a number of journals have produced a good deal of scholarship concerning the creative development of information literacy programs for distance education students (Buchanan, Luck, & Jones, 2002; D'Angelo & Maid, 2004; Dewald, Scholz-Crane, & Booth, 2000; Heller-Ross & Kiple, 2000; Holmes, 2002; Kearley & Phillips, 2002; Kelley, Orr, & Houck, 2001; Lockerby, Lynch, Sherman, & Nelson, 2004; Manuel, 2001; McFarland & Chandler, 2002; Mulherrin, Kelley, & Fishman; 2004; Reynolds, 2001; Walsh, 2002).

LEARNING STYLES

In order to connect with as many students as possible, distance education librarians must be aware of the wide variety of student learning styles, especially when their instruction involves new technology. For example, Du noted that, for online courses, students with "concrete" learning styles are naturally more satisfied with the learning experience, so instructors may increase overall student satisfaction by including more active/reflective dimensions for "abstract" learners (2004, pp. 60-61). Brown-Syed, Adkins, and Tsai discovered that, although "visual and intuitive learners may gravitate to the Web with ease," sequential and aural learners may have problems. To help alleviate such problems, they concluded, "Just as with classroom presentations, distance education programming demands the employment of a variety of teaching methods to accommodate a variety of learning styles" (2005, p. 22). Holmes also emphasized the need to better understand the variety of learning styles among distance education students, concluding "When we offer a diversity of learning approaches, we enable all students to choose the best environment (possibly multiple environments) for their learning" (2002, p. 292).

THE UNIVERSITY OF THE WEST INDIES AT MONA INFORMATION LITERACY: GETTING UWI MONA DISTANCE LEARNERS ON BOARD!

The University of the West Indies (UWI) consists of three campuses–Cave Hill in Barbados, St. Augustine in Trinidad, and Mona in Jamaica. In addition there are UWI Distance Education Centres (UWIDECs) in the non-campus countries, which give the university a presence in those islands, as well–Anguilla, Antigua and Barbuda, the British Virgin Islands, Dominica, Grenada, Montserrat, St. Kitts/Nevis, St. Lucia and St. Vincent, the Grenadines, Belize, the Bahamas, the Cayman Islands, and the Turks and Caicos Islands.

UWI's programs are delivered face-to-face on-campus, through tertiary level institutions (TLIs), and by distance education methodologies. Formal distance education at UWI began in 1983 with audio-graphic teleconferencing. However, in 1996 print became the primary medium of dissemination of instruction, while teleconferences and face-to-face tutorials became supportive strategies.

In recent years, the drive has been to improve the quality of UWI distance education offerings, so beginning with the academic year 2005, blended learning was introduced. The components of this new approach are a self-study print-based instructional package (course material, compilation of readings and course guide); *Moodle*, a Web-based learning management system (LMS); E-Tutor to monitor activities; and CD-ROM to provide students with *PowerPoint* presentations (with audio narration) of some aspect of the course content.

Mona has a relatively small distance-student population, the majority of whom work in education, the financial sector, or the civil service. Students pursue undergraduate degrees in accounting, economics, management studies, education, educational administration, agribusiness, and the diploma in gender and development studies. In addition, there is a postgraduate diploma in construction management, and master's degrees in agricultural and rural development, counseling, family medicine, and education.

Distance students attend classes at UWIDEC sites, and each of the three UWI campuses is responsible for a number of these sites. Mona Campus, for example, is responsible for ten off-campus sites across Jamaica and four in the northern Caribbean–in the Bahamas, Belize, Cayman and the Turks and Caicos Islands. It is the responsibility of each campus library to provide support to underpin the academic programs.

LIBRARY INSTRUCTION AND INFORMATION LITERACY AT UWI MONA

As one of its offerings to on-campus undergraduates, the Mona Library delivered face-to-face bibliographic instruction from 1985 to 2000. Instruction was compulsory for students taking an English usage and writing class sponsored by the Department of Language, Linguistics and Philosophy. The sessions involved a lecture by a reference librarian and a two-hour tutorial, which were complemented by optional sessions on the use of the Internet and information about database searching.

Unfortunately, these sessions were never offered to the distance learning community, although their informational needs were not different from their on-campus counterparts. But there was a reason for this. For many years, the library was not involved with the campus's distance education programs. However, in 1996 when UWIDEC was established, its staff invited librarians from the three campuses to join them and other UWI personnel in Barbados for a five-day workshop conducted by personnel from the International Extension College of the Open University. The workshop addressed support for distance learners and sensitized the librarians to this segment of the student population and to their information needs. As a consequence, the Mona Campus librarian identified someone to coordinate services to the distance learners. This resulted in the introduction of some basic library services, such as on-site core collections, mediated database searching, and reference service.

The university administration declared that UWI students upon graduation should possess certain attributes which clearly highlight the need for information literacy instruction. For example, the current principal stated, "The Mona Campus remains committed to the delivery of a quality education to our students and to the producing of graduates who are independent critical thinkers . . . " (UWI Calendar, 1999, p. 119). And the following was found in the *Mona Development Plan 1990-2000*: "The campus will emphasize sound undergraduate education . . . to produce good graduates capable of thinking, researching material, analysis, integrating knowledge and coherent expression of ideas" (UWI Mona, 2001, p. 6). Against this backdrop, in her report for the academic year 1999-2000, the university/campus librarian remarked:

> It is hoped that the Library will soon be able to establish a bibliographic instruction unit to spearhead the thrust towards an Information Literacy program which will equip students with the competencies to gain maximum benefits from their university education. (UWI Mona, 2000, p. 6)

Mona's Information Literacy Unit (MILU) was established in the 2000-2001 academic year. Training sessions were offered to all librarians and paraprofessionals, and this resulted in the development of a cadre of librarians who were able to offer a variety of training courses to clients. According to the departmental report for 2001-2002, over 1500 students were given information literacy training via library modules in foundation courses. Along with the customary introductory courses on using the online public access catalog (OPAC), postgraduates and undergraduates could access the following: "Introduction to the WWW," "Internet Strategies," "Web Databases," and "Citing and Evaluating Information Resources." In addition, the unit provided group-specific training courses at the request of lecturers.

By 2001, the distance library services coordinator, in keeping with ACRL's *Guidelines for Distance Learning Library Services*, surveyed a sample of the distance-learner population to ascertain their satisfaction with the existing library services and to determine new service requirements (McLean & Dew, 2004). Unfortunately, when asked how useful information literacy (the meaning of information literacy was explained) would be to their course of study, the majority gave it a "moderately useful" score. This may have indicated a lack of understanding of information literacy skills to their studies and for life-long learning. Convinced that the time for information literacy instruction had arrived, the distance library services coordinator commenced training at the sites. The idea was to offer training similar to that offered to the on-campus students, bearing in mind the necessity to give distance learners services and resources comparable to those offered to the on-campus students. As a result the module developed by MILU was slightly modified for the purpose of off-site training.

THE MODULE

The module is entitled "Locating, Evaluating and Using Information from a Variety of Sources," and it covers the following search strategies:

- Analyzing and brainstorming the topic.
- Determining the information needed–background, statistical, current, historical.
- Identifying resource options–reference books, text books, newspaper articles, scholarly journal articles.
- Using appropriate tools to locate the resources–the library catalogs, databases, the Internet, printed indexes and abstracts.
- Evaluating sources (some criteria–Does the information answer the question? Is it current? Is it complete? Is the article signed? Is the writer an expert in his field?).
- Citing information sources.

The tutorials are conducted in the computer labs of the UWIDDEC sites and aim to introduce students to the library services and resources, search strategies, and print and online resources available from the library, and to teach them how to evaluate sources and use information responsibly. During the two-hour-long session, the distance library services coordinator uses the distance learners' Web page as the center-piece to introduce the scope of the library services and resources available to the students. Then, using a *PowerPoint* presentation, the librarian takes students through the steps in the research process, stopping at intervals to engage in the following activities: brainstorming and analyzing a given topic; using the Web version of the library catalog to locate resources on the topic; and searching databases, using search engines, accessing the subject portals and other resources from the distance learners' home page. An important bit of information for the students is the fact that they can access the databases from the UWIDC sites only, as authentication is by IP address, but they can access past exam papers and reference sources anytime anywhere. Finally, students are taken through the criteria for evaluating information resources and reminded of the need to note information sources carefully and to cite them accurately.

CHALLENGES

Both on-campus and off-campus students are required to take the English usage and writing course through which the module is delivered. However, as part of their course requirement, the on-campus students must attend the lecture in the library (most times their lecturers accompany them and mark the register). However, there is no such requirement for those in the distance program, and herein lies one reason for poor attendance at training sessions scheduled at the sites. Another reason for this is the fact that the distance library services coordinator has to depend on the willingness of the site administrators to schedule the sessions and encourage attendance, and more often than not, this is not easily achieved. In other cases it is the unwillingness of students to attend. One can only speculate that some have yet to grasp the importance of the tutorial and others cannot find the time to attend because of their packed schedules. Another contributory factor to the poor attendance might be the time of the academic year that the classes are scheduled. The English usage and writing course is delivered in the first semester, but more often than not, information literacy training is not delivered at the sites until the second semester.

Another issue is that of follow-up. While the face-to-face students have their lecturers to reinforce aspects of the training through class activity, there is no such experience for the off-campus students. They have one class only, sometimes for less than the scheduled two hours, and that is the sum total of their exposure. However, their on-campus counterparts have the option of attending additional sessions offered by MILU. Finally, undergraduate distance students, in the northern Caribbean and those in postgraduate programs by distance are not given information literacy training. This is so because the distance library services coordinator does not visit sites out of Jamaica nor have classes with those in the postgraduate programs.

THE WAY FORWARD

The provision of the information literacy instruction for UWI Mona distance students is still in its infancy and is not reaching the majority of distance students. However, those who have attended the sessions have given positive feedback and lamented that they had not been exposed to the information earlier in the academic year. This is one good reason to improve the offering and delivery of instruction. Another is that distance learning is one of the nine strategic objectives of the UWI *Strategic Plan 11, 2002-2007* (2002, p. 24). Additionally, there is the library's own commitment to improve library services for distance learners.

The first step in this direction involves lobbying the Department of Language, Linguistics and Philosophy, which is responsible for the English usage and writing course, to integrate the information literacy module into the course for all undergraduate distance students, as it is for the on-campus students. The librarians also need to encourage the course coordinators of the distance master's programs to integrate an information literacy module in their program, as well.

Over the longer term all Mona distance students should be required to take an information literacy course for academic credit. Since there are a number of students to be reached, the methodology by which the course will be disseminated is a factor for careful consideration. However, contemporary trends in course delivery, dictate that a Web-based solution is the way forward. According to Dennis and Broughton (2000), "a clear and distinct advantage of using a Web-based tutorial is that it can be offered to anyone in the world at any time of the day or night, to the benefit of independent learners and those at a distance" (p. 32). If this delivery method is adopted, it will allow students to complete the course independently, without having to attend classes. However, they would be encouraged to seek the help of the distance library services coordinator by telephone, fax or e-mail, if they need help to complete their course work. A best practice that could be benchmarked for this module is that done by Texas Tech University, in which students are required to go to the nearest public library to use printed resources in order to complete two practicum exercises (Hufford, 2004). An appropriate evaluation instrument should also be developed to measure the effectiveness of the module and to make adjustments where necessary. Finally, a variety of methods including e-mail, brochures, and the learning management system, *Moodle*, should be used to publicize information literacy instruction, including its benefits and means of access.

LIBRARY INSTRUCTION AND INFORMATION LITERACY AT THE UNIVERSITY OF IOWA

The University of Iowa (UI) sponsors about fifteen different degree-granting programs (Dew, 2002). Approximately 2,000 students are enrolled in graduate or professional degree-granting programs, and another 4,000 are enrolled each year in bachelor-level, liberal-arts-and-sciences courses. Although most of UI's distance learners are located in the state, a significant number are located throughout the United States and in many foreign countries. To meet a growing demand for distance education, the University of Iowa has increased its course and degree offerings by utilizing a wide variety of teaching methods, formats, and technologies. Although some distance-education classes continue to conform to the traditional correspondence-course format, others are conducted entirely over the Internet or by videotape. Most distance-education classes, however, involve some level of live interaction between faculty and students. For some courses, faculty members travel to classrooms located at various sites throughout the state, where they lecture, hold class, and interact with students. In an ever-increasing number of situations, faculty members use the interactive capabilities of television, especially the Iowa Communications Network (ICN), and they conduct their classes while communicating simultaneously with students who are located at several different sites around the state.

The University of Iowa Libraries support the informational, research, and instructional needs of UI students and faculty participating in distance-education programs regardless of course format or location. Prior to the beginning of each semester, the distance education coordinator sends an e-mail to each faculty member involved in distance education, offering formal face-to-face instruction when appropriate, as well as other instructional services, including reference assistance (by e-mail and toll-free telephone) and course-specific chat communications through the university's course management system–ICON (Iowa Courses On-line, a Desire2Learn system) (see Appendix). For the coordinator, the preferred method of instruction remains the face-to-face alternative, especially when each student has access to a computer with an Internet connection. In such face-to-face instruction, the coordinator can take advantage of the hands-on experience, taking each student through the research process of using library resources and services, while highlighting information literacy components. In most cases, the coordinator travels to the off-campus site where the class meets, but for some programs, the distance education students visit the campus for a general orientation to their program, and while on campus, they visit the library for face-to-face instruction.

For joint videoconferencing with on-campus and off-campus courses, the University of Iowa has the great fortune to have access to the Iowa Communications Network (ICN), a statewide fiber optic network providing connections to over eight hundred classrooms located in libraries, schools, colleges, hospitals, and a wide variety of government offices throughout the state. With comfortable seating and individual microphones for students located in each classroom, instructors can communicate directly with off-campus students and promote discussions between a number of sites simultaneously during a class session. A significant number of UI distance education classes utilize the ICN, and the coordinator of library services for distance education usually meets with several of the classes each semester. Since individual student computers are not available in the ICN classrooms, however, the coordinator must rely on a general presentation and demonstration to the students, instead of taking advantage of a hands-on experience. In spite of the lack of the hands-on option, the coordinator attempts to enliven the presentation with discussion, questions, and feedback from the students at the off-campus classrooms.

As McCarthy at the University of Rhode Island observed, a positive attitude about learning through the medium of videoconferencing can be increased by interactivity and the active participation of distant students, and as she concluded, "the benefits of interactive video far outweigh the barriers" (2004, p. 25). At Nova Southeastern University, Chakraborty and Victor were involved in an innovative delivery method for library instruction to graduate students using compressed video, and in a study presented at the Eleventh Off-Campus Library Services Conference, they highlighted the many challenges confronting instructors using videoconferencing (2004). Chakraborty and Victor emphasized the need to incorporate active learning techniques whenever possible, and they concluded that each remote site needs to be set up to be "conducive to a positive learning process," with access to computers for hands-on experience at the sites being the ideal (p. 111). In addition, several other studies have emphasized the positive aspects of reaching distance education students through the use of videoconferencing technology (Bean, 1998; Dunlap, 2002; Ronayne & Rogenmoser, 2002; Ruttenberg & Housewright, 2002).

UI ONLINE COURSES, COURSE MANAGEMENT SYSTEMS, AND TUTORIALS

For several years, the University of Iowa supported two different course management systems–*Blackboard* and *WebCT*–and although most faculty and students were generally satisfied with the systems, technical support was quite demanding, and the dual support sometimes led to confusion. After a university-wide assessment indicated that the university should adopt a single, centrally-supported course management system with full enterprise integration, a faculty review led to the adoption of Desire2Learn. The implementation allowed for a common institutional-wide strategy, encouraged local adaptation and innovation, and gave colleges and departments local control over "look and feel" aspects, as well as the flexibility to develop their own best practices. In 2005, the university began a one-year transition to the Desire2Learn courseware, which the university named ICON, standing for "Iowa Courses Online." For the coordinator of distance education library services, working with faculty using the course management systems has involved the creation of special resource pages, the provision of electronic reserves, and occasionally, chat reference. In order to take greater advantage of the university's courseware, in 2005, the libraries created a course management system integration task force (with the coordinator for distance education library services as a member). The task force interviewed librarians and teaching faculty in order to determine current and potential uses of the courseware. The investigation will continue into 2006, with the goal of promoting librarian and faculty collaboration in order to utilize the full potential of the courseware for instructing and assisting students.

In 2005, the UI Libraries offered only one online class focused on instructing students in the use of library resources and services; it was a course designed for undergraduate business students entitled "Competitive Intelligence Resources." The librarians involved in the course have begun preliminary discussions on how the course might be adapted and offered to off-campus students involved in the university's distance education MBA program. In addition, the coordinator began preliminary discussions on developing an online course on the use of library resources and services that would be offered to off-campus undergraduate liberal arts students. The UI Libraries will continue to investigate ways to use online courses and course management systems to provide instruction, resources, and services to distance education students.

Other institutions have taken different advantages of online courses and course management systems. For instance, librarians at Central Missouri State University used *Blackboard* to create a "pseudo course" that was designed to provide library instruction, research assistance, and communication to all of the institution's nursing students (Dinwiddie & Winters, 2004). Librarians at the University of Kentucky have developed faculty/librarian co-instructor teams for online courses, allowing "students to work with the course librarian throughout the entire life of a research project or a course, thus providing greater continuity in their projects and alleviating the need for constant re-explanation" (Lillard, 2003, pp. 209-210; Lillard, Wilson & Baird, 2004). Several institutions have used courseware to develop for-credit courses in information literacy and library instruction, including the Open University (Needham, 2004; Parker, 2003), Royal Roads University (McFarland & Chandler, 2002), Austin Peay State University (Buchanan et al., 2002), Louisiana State University (Wittkopf, 2003), Purdue University (Reynolds, 2001), Texas Tech University (Hufford, 2004), Washington State University (Lindsay, 2004), Rollins College (Zhang, 2002); Regent University (Lee & Yaegle, 2005), California State University, Chico (Blakeslee & Johnson, 2002); California State University, Hayward (Manuel, 2001), University of Texas at Austin (Ardis, 2003), and University of Maryland, University College (Kelley et al., 2001; Mulherrin et al., 2004). Librarians at the Houston Community College System have expanded upon the concept of the online course by having embedded librarians in the online classes. They have creatively used a blog, available through links in all of the online classes, to serve as an instructional and communication tool with large numbers of students (Drumm & Havens, 2004).

During the last decade, as the Internet has continued to expand as an enormously powerful tool for providing services and resources to distance education students, significant numbers of libraries have turned to Web-based tutorials to provide instruction and promote information literacy skills. Although some institutions still utilize CDs as an option for reaching a certain segment of distance learners, there is an overwhelming trend to transition from CD to Web access (Arnold, Sias, & Zhang, 2002; Jones, 2004). Web-based tutorials, many of which are in-house creations, can work effectively, especially for introductory information, but they do vary greatly in quality, and those lacking active learning components appear to be the least effective (Viggiano, 2004). According to Hrycaj, almost 60% of libraries in the Association of Research Libraries (ARL) have created their own tutorials, and in addition, approximately 60% have active learning components–a learning process involving the gathering of information, critical thinking, and problem solving (2005). The *TILT* (Texas Information Literacy Tutorial), developed by the University of Texas, is probably the best known of the Web-based tutorials, and many institutions have developed tutorials around that model (Fowler & Dupuis, 2000; Orme, 2004). A significant number of institutions have developed effective, interactive tutorials for distance education students and other remote users, including Western Michigan University (Behr, 2004), Deakin University (Churkovich & Oughtred, 2002), Shippensburg State University (Cook, 2002), University of Illinois at Chicago (Koenig & Brennan, 2003), University of Wyoming (Kearley & Phillips, 2002), and the Resource Discovery Network in the United Kingdom (Place & Dawson, 2002). A trend seems to be shifting toward the use of mini-tutorials or short-tutorials, focusing on particular subjects or research techniques, so that students do not have to go through long tutorials containing information superfluous to their particular needs. In addition to the use of Web-based tutorials, the University of Calgary has utilized Web-based worksheets for instruction, so that students can follow along interactively during hands-on instruction, or they can use the worksheet later asynchronously after the session (MacMillian, 2004). For the last ten years, the UI Libraries supported an introductory tutorial, *Library Explorer*; however, since the tutorial lacked interactive components, the libraries terminated support for the tutorial in 2005, turning to more active models, such as a *PsycINFO* tutorial co-developed with Kirkwood Community College.

CONCLUSION

The particular delivery method used for library instruction is usually mirrored by (or determined by) the nature of the particular program or course being supported. When institutions offer courses in a variety of formats utilizing a variety of technologies, instructional methods are necessarily offered in a variety of modalities, and they should include a full array of instructional services, from high-tech to low-tech. Librarians must be flexible; they must understand the variety of learning styles; and they should provide instruction to distance education students through a variety of learning environments. According to Heller-Ross and Kiple, "Instruction formats are usually closely connected to the technology and format of the other academic course offerings" (2000, p. 196). Heller-Ross and Kiple also noted that:

> every possible format is currently in use somewhere. . . . (but no particular one) is any better than the others. They have developed from the practical experiences and philosophical ideas of the librarians who shaped them and represent different institutional profiles in terms of size and types of degrees offered. (pp. 196-197)

Tuñón (2002) reinforced the conclusions of Heller-Ross and Kiple when she observed that no particular instructional technique or format is a "silver bullet," offering the perfect solution for library instruction. Offering flexibility and variety in the instructional process are the keys to success, but Tuñón also noted a political campus reality: "Decisions about whether to offer library training online or in a face-to-face format often are made by academic programs, and are based on the administrative and political constraints of those academic programs and curricula rather than fundamental pedagogical considerations" (2002, pp. 525-526).

The University of the West Indies and the University of Iowa have very different off-campus and distance education programs, but the librarians at both institutions are using many of the same teaching techniques and technologies to provide library instruction and information literacy training to their distance learners. All colleges and universities with distance learning programs must support the informational, research, and instructional needs of all of their off-campus students and faculty, regardless of course format or location. Face-to-face instruction continues to be a very important and very effective method of teaching, but increasingly, new technologies are providing important and useful alternatives for reaching many distance learners who would otherwise not receive instruction. The challenge to each distance learning librarian is how to use staff time and resources to provide a particular variety of instructional options that best fits an institution's course offerings and student needs.

REFERENCES

Ardis, S. B. (2003). A tale of two classes: Teaching science and technology reference sources both traditionally and through distance education. Issues in Science & Technology Librarianship, 37, 1092-1206.

Arnold, J., Sias, J., & Zhang, J. (2002). Bringing the library to the students: Using technology to deliver instruction and resources for research. In P. B Mahoney (Ed.), The Tenth Off-Campus Library Services Conference Proceedings (pp. 19-25). Mt. Pleasant, MI: Central Michigan University.

Association of College and Research Libraries. (2000). Information literacy competency standards for higher education [Electronic Version] College & Research Libraries News, 61, 207-215.

Association of College and Research Libraries. (2004). Guidelines for distance learning library services [Electronic version]. College & Research Libraries News, 65, 604-611.

Association of College and Research Libraries. (2006). Introduction to information literacy. Retrieved February 21, 2006, from http://www.ala.org/ala/acrl/acrlissues/acrlinfolit/introtoinfolit/introinfolit.htm.

Association of College and Research Libraries, Distance Learning Section. (2005a). Home page. Retrieved September 22, 2005, from http://caspian.switchinc.org/~distlearn.

Association of College and Research Libraries, Distance Learning Section. (2005b). OFFCAMP Listserv. Retrieved September 22, 2005, from http://caspian.switchinc.org/~distlearn/news/14_1.pdf.

Association of College and Research Libraries, Distance Learning Section, Instruction Committee. (2005). Collaboration for distance learning information literacy instruction: SPEC kit 286. Washington, DC: Association of Research Libraries, Office of Leadership and Management Services.

Association of College and Research Libraries, Instruction Section. (2005a). Home page. Retrieved September 22, 2005, from http://www.ala.org/ala/acrlbucket/is/welcome/welcome.htm.

Association of College and Research Libraries, Instruction Section. (2005b). ILI-L (Information Literacy Instruction Listserv). Retrieved September 22, 2005, from http://www.ala.org/ala/acrlbucket/is/ilil.htm.

Austen, G., Schmidt, J., & Calvert, P. (2002). Australian university libraries and the new educational environment. Journal of Academic Librarianship, 28, 63-67.

Bean, R. J. (1998). Lights–camera–instruction: Library instruction via interactive television. In P. Thomas & M. Jones (Eds.), The Eighth Off-Campus Library Services Conference Proceedings (pp. 29-34). Mt. Pleasant, Mi: Central Michigan University.

Behr, M. D. (2004). On ramp to research: Creation of a multimedia library instruction presentation for off-campus students. Journal of Library Administration, 41, 19-30.

Behrens, S. J. (1998). Developing a curriculum for an information literacy course for off-campus students: A case study at the University of South Africa. In P. Thomas & M. Jones, (Eds.), The Eighth Off-Campus Library Services Conference Proceedings (pp. 35-45). Mt. Pleasant, MI: Central Michigan University.

Blakeslee, S., & Johnson, K. (2002). Using HorizonLive to deliver library instruction to distance and online students. Reference Services Review, 30, 324-329.

Brown-Syed, C., Adkins, D., & Tsai, H. (2005). LIS student learning styles and Web-based instruction methods. Journal of Library and Information Services in Distance Learning, 2, 5-25.

Brunvand, A. (2004). Integrating library reference services in an online information literacy course: The Internet Navigator as a model. Internet Reference Services Quarterly, 9, 159-177.

Buchanan, L., Luck, D., & Jones, T. (2002). Integrating information literacy into the virtual university: A course model. Library Trends, 51, 144-166.

Chakraborty, M., & Victor, S. (2004). Do's and don'ts of simultaneous instruction to on-campus and distance students via videoconferencing. Journal of Library Administration, 41, 97-112.

Churkovich, M., & Oughtred, C. (2002). Can an online tutorial pass the test for library instruction? An evaluation and comparison of library skills instruction methods for first year students at Deakin University. Australian Academic & Research Libraries, 33, 25-38.

Clayton, S. (2004). Your class meets where? Library instruction for business and education graduate students at off-campus centers. Reference Services Review, 32, 388-193.

Cook, D. L. (2002). Ship to shore: An online information literacy tutorial using BlackBoard distance education software. Journal of Library Administration, 37, 177-187.

D'Angelo, B., & Maid, B. (2004). Beyond instruction: Integrating library service in support of information literacy. Internet Reference Services Quarterly, 9, 55-63.

Dennis, S., & Broughton, K. M. (2000). FALCON: An interactive library instruction tutorial. Reference Services Review, 28: 31-38.

Dew, S. H. (2002). Documenting priorities, progress, and potential: Planning library services for distance education. In P. B. Mahoney (Ed.), The Tenth Off-Campus Library Services Conference Proceedings (pp. 217-242). Mt. Pleasant, MI: Central Michigan University.

Dewald, N., Scholz-Crane, A., & Booth, A. (2000). Information literacy at a distance: Instructional design issues. Journal of Academic Librarianship, 26, 33-44.

Dinwiddie, M., & Winters, J. (2004). Two-stepping with technology: An instructor/librarian collaboration in health promotion for baccalaureate nursing students. Journal of Library and Information Services in Distance Learning, 1, 33-45.

Drumm, M., & Havens, B. (2004). A foot in the door: Experiments with integrating library services into the online classroom. Journal of Library and Information Services in Distance Learning, 2, 25-32.

Du, Y. (2004). Exploring the difference of "concrete" and "abstract": Learning styles in LIS distance education. Journal of Library and Information Services in Distance Learning, 1, 51-64.

Dunlap, S. (2002). Watch for the little red light: Delivery of bibliographic instruction by unconventional means. In P. B. Mahoney (Ed.), The Tenth Off-Campus Library Services Conference Proceedings (pp. 221-225). Mt Pleasant, MI: Central Michigan University.

Erasmus, S. (2001). Information literacy and distance education: The challenge of addressing the lack of (basic) information skills in a lifelong learning environment. Mousaion, 19, 15-22.

Espinal, J., & Geiger, S. (1995). Information literacy: Boole to the Internet and beyond. In C. J. Jacob (Ed.), The Seventh Off-campus Library Services Conference Proceedings (pp. 75-100). Mt. Pleasant, MI: Central Michigan University.

Ferguson, K., & Ferguson, A. (2005). The remote library and point-of-need user education: An Australian academic library perspective. Journal of Interlibrary Loan, Document Delivery & Information Supply, 15, 43-60.

Fourie, I. (2001). The use of CAI for distance teaching in the formulation of search strategies at the University of South Africa. Library Trends, 50, 110-129.

Fowler, C. S., & Dupuis, E. A. (2000). What have we done? TILT's impact on our instruction program. Reference Services Review, 28, 343-348.

George, R., McCausland, H., & Wache, D. (2001). Information literacy: An institution-wide strategy. Australian Academic & Research Libraries, 32, 278-293.

Gibson, C., & Scales, B. (2000). Going the distance (and back again): A distance education course comes home. Reference Librarian, 69/70, 233-244.

Grobler, L. M. (1998). Towards the virtual library: Meeting remote business students' library and information needs. In P. Thomas & M. Jones (Eds.), The Eighth Off-Campus Library Services Conference Proceedings (pp. 165-173). Mt. Pleasant, MI: Central Michigan University.

Guillot, L., & Stahr, B. (2004). A tale of two campuses: Providing virtual reference to distance nursing students. In P. B. Mahoney (Ed.), The Eleventh Off-Campus Library Services Conference Proceedings (pp. 105-114). Mt. Pleasant, MI: Central Michigan University.

Hansen, C. (2001). The Internet Navigator: An online Internet course for distance learners. Library Trends, 50, 58-72.

Heller-Ross, H., & Kiple, J. (2000). Information literacy for interactive distance learners. In T. Jacobson & H. Williams (Eds.), Teaching the new library to today's users (pp. 191-219). New York: Neal-Schuman.

Henner, T. A. (2002). Bridging the distance: Bibliographic instruction for remote library users, Medical Reference Services Quarterly, 21, 79-85.

Holmes, K. E. (2002). A kaleidoscope of learning styles: Instructional supports that meet the diverse needs of distant learners. In B. Mahoney (Ed.), The Tenth Off-Campus Library Services Conference Proceedings (pp. 287-294). Mt. Pleasant, MI: Central Michigan University.

Holmes, K., Stahley, M., & Whyle, S. (1998). Library instruction at a distance: The high tech/high touch mix; three case studies. In P. Thomas & M. Jones (Eds.), The Eighth Off-Campus Library Services Conference Proceedings (pp. 183-195). Mt. Pleasant, MI: Central Michigan University.

Hosein, S. (2001). Developing information literacy programs for distance learners: Accepting the challenge at the University of the West Indies, St. Augustine. In Distance education in small states conference proceedings (pp. 193-198). Bridgetown, Barbados: University of the West Indies Distance Education Centre.

Hrycaj, P. L. (2005). Elements of active learning in the online tutorials of ARL members. Reference Services Review, 33, 210-218.

Hufford, J. R. (2004). User instruction for distance students: Texas Tech University System's main campus library reaches out to students at satellite campuses. Journal of Library Administration, 41, 153-165.

Iowa Communications Network. (2005). Retrieved September 22, 2005, from http://www.icn.state.ia.us/index.html.

Ivanitskaya, L., Laus, R., & Casey, A. (2004). Research readiness self-assessment: Assessing students' research skills and attitudes. In P. B. Mahoney (Ed.), The Eleventh Off-Campus Library Services Conference Proceedings (pp. 125-136). Mt. Pleasant, MI: Central Michigan University.

Jayne, E., Arnold, J., & Vander Meer, P. (1998). Casting a broad net: The use of Web-based tutorials for library instruction. In P. Thomas & M. Jones (Eds.), The Eighth Off-Campus Library Services Conference Proceedings (pp. 197-205). Mt. Pleasant, MI: Central Michigan University.

Jones, M. F. (2004). Creating a library CD for off-campus students. In P. B. Mahoney (Ed.), The Eleventh Off-Campus Library Services Conference Proceedings (pp. 137-149). Mt. Pleasant, MI: Central Michigan University.

Kearley, J., & Phillips, L. (2002). Distilling the information literacy standards: Less is more. In P. B. Mahoney (Ed.), The Tenth Off-Campus Library Services Conference Proceedings (pp. 137-149). Mt. Pleasant, MI: Central Michigan University.

Kearley, J. P. (1998). The evolution of the virtual library and its impact on bibliographic instruction for distance learners. In P. Thomas & M. Jones (Eds.), The Eighth Off-Campus Library Services Conference Proceedings (pp. 207-212). Mt. Pleasant, MI: Central Michigan University.

Kelley, K., Orr, G., & Houck, J. (2001). Library instruction for the next millennium: Two Web-based courses to teach distant students information literacy. Journal of Library Administration, 32, 281-294.

Kinder, R. (2002). Instructional services for distance education. Reference Librarian, 77, 63-70.

Koenig, M., & Brennan, M. (2003). All aboard the etrain: Developing and designing online library instruction modules. In P. B. Mahoney (Ed.), The Tenth Off-Campus Library Services Conference Proceedings (pp. 331-339). Mt. Pleasant, MI: Central Michigan University.

Lee, M., & Yaegle, S. (2005). Information literacy at an academic library: Development of a library course in an online environment. Journal of Library and Information Services in Distance Learning, 2, 33-44.

Library services for distance learning: The fourth bibliography. (2005). Retrieved September 22, 2005, from http://uviclib.uvic.ca/dls/bibliography4.html.

Lillard, L. L. (2003). Personalized instruction and assistance services for distance learners: Cultivating a research relationship. Research Strategies, 19, 204-212.

Lillard, L., & Dinwiddie, M. (2004). If you build it, they will come, but then what: A look at issues related to using online course software to provide specialized reference services. Internet Reference Services Quarterly, 9, 135-145.

Lillard, L., Wilson, P., & Baird, C. (2004). Progressive partnering: Expanding student and faculty access to information services. In P. B. Mahoney (Ed.), The Eleventh Off-Campus Library Services Conference Proceedings (pp. 169-180). Mt. Pleasant, MI: Central Michigan University.

Lindsay, E. B. (2004). Distance teaching: Comparing two online information literacy courses. Journal of Academic Librarianship, 30, 482-487.

Lockerby, R., Lynch, D., Sherman, J., & Nelson, E. (2004). Collaboration and information literacy: Challenges of meeting standards when working with remote faculty. In P. B. Mahoney (Ed.), The Eleventh Off-Campus Library Services Conference Proceedings (pp. 181-187). Mt. Pleasant, MI: Central Michigan University.

LOEX (Library Orientation Exchange). (2005). Retrieved September 22, 2005, from http://www.emich.edu/public/loex/index.html.

MacMillian, D. (2004). Web-based worksheets in the classroom. Journal of Library and Information Services in Distance Learning, 1, 43-51.

Manuel, K. (2001). Teaching an online information literacy course. Reference Services Review, 29, 219-228.

May, F. A. (2003). Library services and instruction for online distance learners. In J. Nims, R. Baier, R. Bullard, & E. Owen (Eds.), Integrating information literacy into the college experience: Papers Presented at the 30th National LOEX Library Instruction Conference (pp. 165-168). Ann Arbor, MI: Pierian Press.

McCarthy, C. A. (2004). Interactive video technology for distance learning: An assessment of interactive video technology as a tool. Journal of Library and Information Services in Distance Learning, 1, 5-27.

McFarland, D., & Chandler, S. (2002). "Plug and play" in context: Reflections on a distance information literacy unit. Journal of Business & Finance Librarianship, 7, 115-129.

McGill, L. (2001). Any which way you can: Providing information literacy to distance learners. New Review of Libraries and Lifelong Learning, 2, 95-113.

McLean, E., & Dew, S. (2004). Assessing the library needs and preferences of off-campus students: Surveying distance-education students, from the Midwest to the West Indies. In P. B. Mahoney (Ed.), The Eleventh Off-Campus Library Services Conference Proceedings (pp. 197-226). Mt. Pleasant, MI: Central Michigan University.

Mulherrin, E., Kelley, K., & Fishman, D. (2004). Information literacy and the distant student: One university's experience developing, delivering, and maintaining an online, required information literacy course. Internet Reference Services Quarterly, 9, 21-36.

Muth, M., & Taylor, S. (2002). Comparing online tutorials with face-to-face instruction: A study at Ball State University. In J. K. Nims & A. Andrew (Eds.), First impressions, lasting impact: Introducing the first-year student to the academic library (pp. 113-119). New York: Pierian Press.

Needham, G. (2004). Information literacy–Who needs it? In P. Brophy, S. Fisher, & J. Craven (Eds.), Libraries without walls 5: The distributed delivery of library and information services (pp. 109-119). London: Facet Publishing.

Nichols, J., Shaffer, B., & Shockey, K. (2003). Changing the face of instruction: Is online or in-class more effective? College & Research Libraries, 64, 378-388.

O'Hanlon, N. (2001). Development, delivery, and outcomes of a distance course for new college students. Library Trends, 50, 8-27.

Orme, W. A. (2004). A study of the residual impact of the Texas Information Literacy Tutorial on the information-seeking ability of first year college students. College & Research Libraries, 65, 205-215.

Orr, D., & Wallin, M. (2001). Information literacy and flexible delivery: Are we meeting student needs? Australian Academic & Research Libraries, 32, 192-203.

Parise, P. (1998). Information power goes online: Teaching information literacy to distance learners. Reference Services Review, 26, 51-52.

Parker, J. (2003). Putting the pieces together: Information literacy at The Open University. Library Management, 24, 223-228.

Pival, P., & Tuñón, J. (2001). Innovative methods for providing instruction to distance students using technology. Journal of Library Administration, 32, 347-360.

Pival, P., & Johnson, K. (2004). Tri-institutional library support: A lesson in forced collaboration. Journal of Library Administration, 41, 345-354.

Place, E., & Dawson, H. (2002). Building the RDN virtual training suite to teach Internet information skills via the Web. In P. Brophy, S. Fisher, & Z. Clarks (Eds.), Libraries without walls 4: The delivery of library services to distant users (pp. 161-172). London: Facet Publishing.

Reynolds, L. J. (2001). Model for a Web-based information literacy course: Design, conversion and experiences. Science & Technology Libraries, 19, 165-178.

Ronayne, B., & Rogenmoser, D. (2002). Library research instruction for distance learners: An interactive, multimedia approach. In P. Brophy, S. Fisher, & Z. Clarks (Eds.), Libraries without walls 4: The delivery of library services to distant users (pp. 187-196). London: Facet Publishing.

Ruttenberg, J., & Housewright, E. (2002). Assessing library instruction for distance learners: A case study of nursing students. In J. Nims, & E. Owen (Eds.), Managing Library Instruction Programs in Academic Libraries: Selected papers presented at the 29th National LOEX Library Instruction Conference (pp. 137-148). Ann Arbor, MI: Pierian Press.

Sedam, R., & Marshall, J. (1998). Course-specific World Wide Web pages: Evolution of an extended campus library instruction service. In P. Thomas, & M. Jones (Eds.), The Eighth Off-Campus Library Services Conference Proceedings (pp. 251-258). Mt. Pleasant, MI: Central Michigan University.

Smyth, J. B. (2001). Using a Web-based MOO for library instruction in distance education. Journal of Library Administration, 32, 383-392.

Sochrin, S. (2004). Learning to teach in a new medium: Adapting library instruction to a videoconferencing environment. Journal of Library Administration, 41, 429-442.

Ten Krooden, E. (2004). Teaching information literacy courses in southern Africa: Lessons learned in training on constructing personal bibliographic databases. Journal of Education for Library and Information Science, 45, 221-228.

Toth, M. (2005). Research and writing and theses–Oh my! The journey of a collaboratively taught graduate research and writing course. Reference Librarian, 89/90, 81-92.

Tuñón, J. (2002). Creating a research literacy course for education doctoral students: Design issues and political realities of developing online and face-to-face instruction. Journal of Library Administration, 37, 515-527.

University of Iowa Libraries. (2005a). Distance education library services. Retrieved September 22, 2005, from http://www.lib.uiowa.edu/disted/.

University of Iowa Libraries. (2005b). ICON: Iowa Courses Online. Retrieved September 22, 2005, from http://icon.uiowa.edu/index.shtml.

University of Iowa Libraries. (2005c) Information literacy. Retrieved September 22, 2005, from http://www.lib.uiowa.edu/instruction/infolit.html.

University of Iowa Libraries. (2005d). Library Explorer on the World Wide Web. Retrieved September 22, 2005, from http://explorer.lib.uiowa.edu/.

University of Iowa Libraries, & Kirkwood Community College Library. (2005). PsycINFO Tutorial. Retrieved September 22, 2005, from http://www.lib.uiowa.edu/psych/PsycINFO/PsycINFO/Pages_01Frame.htm.

University of the West Indies, Mona. (1999). Calendar, Vol.1.

University of the West Indies, Mona. (2000). Departmental report, 1999-2000.

University of the West Indies, Mona. (2002). Strategic plan 11, 2002-2007.

University of the West Indies, Mona, Library. (2005a). Home page. Retrieved September 22, 2005, from http://mona.uwi.edu/library/.

University of the West Indies, Mona, Library. (2005b). Library services for distance learners. Retrieved September 22, 2005, from http://mona.uwi/library/distance_learners.html.

University of the West Indies, Mona, Office of Planning and Institutional Research. (2001). Mona Development Plan 1990-2000.

Viggiano, R.G. (2004). Online tutorials as instruction for distance students. Internet Reference Services Quarterly, 9, 37-54.

Walsh, R. (2002). Information literacy at Ulster County Community College: Going the distance. Reference Librarian, 77, 89-105.

Wittkopf, B. (2003). Recreating the credit course in an online environment: Issues and concerns. Reference and User Services Quarterly, 43, 18-25.

Zhang, W. (2002). Developing Web-enhanced learning for information literacy. Reference & User Services Quarterly, 41, 356-363.

doi:10.1300/J111v45n03_01

APPENDIX

E-mail Sent to University of Iowa Distance Education Faculty Prior to the Start of Each Semester

Dear Professor X:

As the coordinator of library services for distance education, I am writing to inform you about the library resources and services that are available to you and your students enrolled in 021:120, "Design of Automated Systems." If you think that your students will find it useful, I will be glad to work with you on adding a library component to your ICON course site, and I also will be glad to give a presentation to your class on research strategies and how students can best use library resources and services. In addition, if you would like, I can set up an electronic reserve module for your class reading list.

I have attached a handout that summarizes library services for distance education students. Your students should have received a copy of this handout in their course registration packets from the Center for Credit Programs. The handout emphasizes the "Library Services for Distance Education Web Site" located at the following URL:

http://www.lib.uiowa.edu/disted

Through the Web site, students have access to the following:

- **Shortcuts to Electronic Resources:** Each shortcut links to a list of resources relevant to a particular subject, and I believe that many of your students will find the shortcut to "Library Science" useful.
- **Document-Delivery Service:** For a small fee, students can request that articles be faxed to them, mailed, or sent by desk-top delivery. Students also can request that books be sent to them by UPS.
- **Reference Service, by E-mail and Toll-Free Telephone:** Students can ask for help developing basic research strategies, finding information, and using library resources and services.

If I can assist you or your students in any research or library matter, please feel free to contact me at any time.

Sincerely,

Stephen H. Dew, Ph.D., Coordinator
Library Services for Distance Education
100 Main Library
University of Iowa
Iowa City, IA 52242-1420
E-mail: stephen-dew@uiowa.edu

Library Use in the E-learning Environment: A Profile of Penn State's World Campus Faculty and Students

Lesley Mutinta Moyo
Ellysa Stern Cahoy

Penn State University Libraries

SUMMARY. Are the library needs and expectations of students and faculty at a distance different than those of on-campus students and faculty? This article details and synthesizes the results of two studies conducted to assess Penn State University's World Campus students and faculty perceptions, expectations and use of Web-based library resources and services. The results provide insight into challenges and issues surrounding service to a virtual academic community. This article will highlight which library resources and services were rated as being the most valuable and important to World Campus users, and how the combined results of the two studies illuminate a widely applicable path for further development of library services to patrons at a distance. doi:10.1300/J111v45n03_02

KEYWORDS. Distance education, e-learning, Penn State University World Campus, distance learners–library services, distance education faculty–library services

---

[Haworth co-indexing entry note]: "Library Use in the E-learning Environment: A Profile of Penn State's World Campus Faculty and Students." Moyo, Lesley Mutinta, and Ellysa Stern Cahoy. Co-published simultaneously in *Journal of Library Administration* (The Haworth Information Press, an imprint of The Haworth Press, Inc.) Vol. 45, No. 3/4, 2006, pp. 339-359; and: *The Twelfth Off-Campus Library Services Conference Proceedings* (ed: Julie A. Garrison) The Haworth Information Press, an imprint of The Haworth Press, Inc., 2006, pp. 339-359.

Available online at http://jla.haworthpress.com
doi:10.1300/J111v45n03_02

339

INTRODUCTION

Online distance education has become part of the mainstream of higher education. According to *Growing by Degrees: Online Education in the United States, 2005*, nearly two-thirds of colleges and universities offering traditional face-to-face courses now offer courses online (Allen & Seaman, 2005). With over 2.3 million students in the United States taking at least one Web-based course, online distance education has become a sizable field to be served by academic libraries.

The growth of online distance education and the corresponding surge of students participating in online distance education programs have provided both opportunities and challenges for academic libraries. Libraries are now empowered to become dynamic participants in the emerging virtual academic environment while they are also challenged to provide equitable services to patrons in both the physical and the virtual environments. A key success factor in meeting the needs of the virtual academic community is getting to know online distance users and their needs. In order for libraries to fully meet the needs of e-learning programs, they must engage the e-learning community in much the same way as they do on-campus communities, effectively and proactively developing collections and services that meet their needs. Many libraries are using the ACRL *Guidelines for Distance Learning Library Services* (2004) to develop strategies that enable them to meet the needs of both categories of patrons.

In 2002 and 2004, studies of Penn State World Campus students and faculty were conducted. The World Campus is Penn State's online distance education initiative. The studies sought to determine World Campus student and faculty perceptions, expectations and use of Penn State University Libraries' resources and support services, highlighting the extent to which World Campus students' information needs were met (or unmet). The two studies were also designed to reveal the information seeking behavior patterns of World Campus students and World Campus faculty's perception of the importance of libraries in online distance education. The combined results of the two studies point to the need for academic libraries to be proactive in engaging and serving the e-learning community, including active promotion and marketing of services. Furthermore, the results of the two studies provide an opportunity for much discussion of and further research on the quality, adequacy and effectiveness of current library support for online programs, and strategies that academic libraries can employ to facilitate increased library integration in e-learning and more focused information-seeking behavior among e-learners.

Penn State's World Campus–Overview

Penn State's World Campus, the University's 25th campus and the online arm of the continuing and distance education program, was founded in 1998, initially offering three programs and serving forty-one students (Hons, 2002). By 2005, the World Campus had grown to offer fifty degree and certificate programs with over 5,600 enrolled students (Penn State University Faculty Senate, 2005). Most World Campus students are working, non-traditional students. Emphasizing academic programs over individual courses, the World Campus features four different types of courses, three of which are online: Web-based multi-media courses featuring interaction with instructors and fellow students; 'paced' courses featuring e-mail-based interaction with instructors and Web-based instructional materials; rolling enrollment courses (which students must complete within six months) featuring e-mail interaction with the instructor, Web-based course materials and print-based independent learning courses (Penn State University Faculty Senate, 2005). Full-time Penn State faculty members will teach 51% of undergraduate and 83% of graduate World Campus courses in 2005-06. The program prides itself on connecting students with the same faculty members who might teach them in an on-campus course offering. Throughout the World Campus, the focus is on providing courses that promote active learning and function as online learning communities (Hons, 2002).

Each World Campus course is created by a team that includes the course instructor, an instructional designer, a graphic designer, a technical typist, and a production specialist. The team helps make certain that World Campus courses are innovative yet streamlined and cost-effective. According to Penn State's President, Graham Spanier, "There's a rare faculty member who may be able to do it all himself or herself, but the instructional designer brings it all together" (Carnevale, 2000, p. A37). Each course-focused team also revisits and revises each course periodically, ensuring that previous students' feedback and new resources and emerging technologies are incorporated into the course as appropriate (Carnevale).

Penn State University Libraries' e-Learning Support

Boasting over 4.6 million print volumes, 56,000 serial subscriptions, and over 350 online databases, the Penn State University Libraries provide a wealth of resources and services to e-learners. As a partner with the World Campus in serving online users at a distance, the Penn State Libraries ensure that all students, on- or off-campus, are afforded the same access to all materials and services. Dean of the University Libraries, Nancy Eaton, has served on the World Campus' Steering Committee since the initiative's inception, and an Associate Dean of Libraries provides programmatic leadership for the libraries' online distance education initiatives.

The libraries worked cooperatively with the World Campus to design a gateway to library resources and services, bringing together a portfolio of amenities available to World Campus library users, including at-home delivery of library materials, full-text databases, and instructional tutorials (Penn State University Libraries, 2005). Penn State librarians have also worked collaboratively with World Campus administration and instructional designers to promote and integrate library resources within World Campus courses. By 2004, over 4000 distance education/World Campus users were registered with the Penn State Libraries, placing over 1600 journal article requests each year (Coopey, 2004).

LITERATURE REVIEW

Looking broadly at distance education literature, the role of the library is not often explored (except in library and information science-focused publications), yet access to information resources is a key factor in online program quality and success. For online distance education to be successful, there is need for library support at various levels. The *ACRL Guidelines for Distance Learning Library Services* (2004) have been adopted by most academic libraries as a benchmarking document for providing equitable library services to off-campus library patrons. Regular revision of the guidelines ensures incorporation of new issues brought about by technological changes which have in turn increased the diversity of learning environments.

With the proliferation of online distance learning programs, teacher student interactions are changing. There is a need for online distance education faculty to adapt their teaching styles and instructional methods to suit this online environment. One of the key findings of a study of distance education faculty at the University of Wisconsin was that faculty felt that their role in the distance learning environment had changed from that of authority figure to that of facilitator, and that this role required more effective communication with students. Furthermore, relationships with students in the online environment, although lacking face-to-face contact, were reported as strong, comfortable and enduring (Ryan, Carlton, & Ali, 2004). Merisotis and Phipps (1999) highlighted some shortcomings of the research literature addressing the differences between distance and traditional classroom-based teaching. One of the gaps they identified in the literature is the fact that the research does not adequately address the effectiveness of digital libraries. They questioned whether digital libraries provide adequate services for the online programs they are established to support, and suggest that there is anecdotal evidence that curricular objectives of some distance-learning courses have been altered because of a limited variety of resources available online.

Lorenzo (2003) put the library at the center of online learning, highlighting the role of the library in teaching and learning as a provider of vital services to its patrons. Lorenzo discussed how the new technology environment in higher education impacts campus libraries and creates a need for online information literacy programs and collections of full-text electronic resources to meet the needs of learners at a distance. Lebowitz (1997) presented several models used by libraries in administering and serving distance learners. In addition to emphasizing the need for institutional commitment to supporting distance education, she noted an important issue: that although the library may be generally perceived as central to the academic programs in the university, it is often not integrated into the courses prepared for distance delivery. The literature indicates that to a large extent, faculty determine the level of library integration, if any, in their distance learning courses. Hufford (2004) highlighted how a clear understanding of the needs and expectations of distance education faculty is fundamental to meeting those needs. He stated that:

> what the teaching faculty thinks about library support for their off-campus courses is not clearly understood among librarians . . . An accurate understanding of the needs and expectations of teaching faculty will enable librarians to provide more effective library support for their institutions' off-campus courses. (pp. 4-5)

Jobe and Grealy (2000) provided a comprehensive overview of library support for distance learning courses. Reviewing a significant amount of literature, they discussed library support for both the traditional modes of distance learning, and the new, technology-based modes, emphasizing that technology coupled with appropriate support is the key to providing library services to students at a distance.

Collaboration between distance education faculty, librarians and other academic support units is identified by the literature as a key factor in integration of the library in distance education and provision of effective support for online programs. Kaufmann (2003) demonstrated how faculty, librarians, administrators and technology staff collaborated to provide enhanced distance education services at Seton Hall University. Faculty perspectives on the role of the library in distance education will ultimately determine whether the library is integrated into distance education, and the degree of this integration. Professional literature indicates that when faculty members place value and emphasis on the library, so will their students (Ruddy, 1993). In a study presenting librarians' perspectives on serving distance education students, Jurkowski (2003) cited lack of contact and collaboration with faculty as one of the issues hampering library support to online students. Markgraf (2003) suggested that tailoring the nature of library support to match program requirements is important because of the different nature and needs of distance education programs. In another study, Markgraf (2004) provided a case study in which librarians participate in the online classroom using the 'lurking' method. Although this level of collaboration and participation is time-consuming, it has advantages of increasing librarian accessibility to students. Frisby and Jones (2000) presented an ideal situation of the library's involvement as an integral partner in the design and creation of a distance learning program and planning of the library services to support the program at Thomas Jefferson University.

Overall, many academic libraries have adopted various models of supporting distance education. ACRL's Academic Library Trends and Statistics is an annual survey that captures data from all institutions of higher learning in the United States and Canada. Each year the survey focuses on a different theme, with the focus in 2000 on distance learning. The overall findings of the survey indicated that for over 90% of the 1678 responding libraries, distance learning library services are mainstream services and are not administered separately. Furthermore, 90-95% of all responding libraries indicated they did not have a separate budget for library services to distance learners. In many institutions, services to distance learners are still in the developmental phase, with the focus on introducing new services, such as virtual reference for learners at a distance (Thompson, 2002). As part of the planning to support distance learners, it is also necessary to consider library services offered by other institutions as part of the resources available to e-learners. Libraries can work out reciprocal agreements with other institutions to ensure that distance education students have access to a local library. However, this may not be easy where student populations are dispersed (Caspers, 1999). Barsun (2002) highlighted the need and use of local libraries by distance learners, stating that:

> when distance library services and resources are available, students may still use local libraries for various reasons: they are more comfortable there, they are unaware of what their home library offers, or they experience difficulty using the internet for communication and library research. (p. 72)

Another key factor to providing effective support to e-learners is communication and marketing the services and resources available to them. Nicholas and Tomeo (2005) stated that even though many academic libraries are providing a variety of resources and services such as online databases, virtual reference services, online tutorials, e-reserves, etc., to their distance students, the students are often not fully aware of what is available to them. Moreover, the authors explored use of the Web as a marketing tool, suggesting creating distance learning gateways to serve as pathfinders to online information.

Finally, a literature review by Gandhi (2003) presented an overview of library services to distance learners and highlighted new issues and areas of emphases in serving distance learners and the evolving nature of librarians' roles in this dynamic environment.

METHODOLOGY

Conducted two years apart, the methodology used was very similar in the studies of World Campus faculty and students. A Web-based survey instrument was selected as the most effective and efficient way of reaching e-learners and was employed in both studies. Creating the surveys involved designing a Web-based questionnaire for each study using HTML and an accompanying Microsoft Access database for direct data capture. ColdFusion tagging of the Web-based questionnaire facilitated transfer of captured data into a database for analysis. Deliberate effort was made to keep the questionnaires short to encourage participation. The student survey included twelve questions while the faculty survey featured fifteen. Multiple-choice as well as open-ended questions were used in both studies. Random samples of 200 World Campus students and 250 World Campus faculty were selected for the studies. Sample participants were e-mailed a message inviting them to participate in the survey of their user population. In each of the studies, the invitation e-mail included a link to the Web-based questionnaire. As participants responded, data were captured directly into the MS-Access database created for the study and were later exported to SPSS for analysis. The studies also capitalized on the opportunity to promote library resources to e-learners by including links in the questionnaires to all the resources referred to in the respective studies. The response rates were relatively modest for both studies. The student survey yielded a 37.5% (75 total students) response rate while the faculty survey yielded a 22.3% (57 total faculty) response rate. See Appendix A and B for the text of each survey.

STUDENT SURVEY FINDINGS

Conducted in 2002, the survey of World Campus students marked the Penn State Libraries' first effort to formally assess how well users at a distance were served. The results of the student study were formally disseminated in an article published in *Library Management* (Moyo & Cahoy, 2003). Overall, students expressed general satisfaction with the library. Using a four-point Likert scale, a combined 69.3% of students responded that it was *very* easy (12%) or *easy* (59.3%) to *find* the library materials that they needed for their World Campus coursework. Conversely, 20.3% of students reported that it was *difficult* to find the materials that they needed. None of the respondents reported that it was *very difficult* to find what they needed, and 10.7% of students did not provide a response to the question. Students were also asked how easy it was for them to *get* the library resources that they needed. A combined 66.6% reported that it was *very easy* (9.3%) or *easy* (57.3%). A combined 22.6% of students indicated that it was *difficult* (21.3%) or *very difficult* (1.3%) to get the library resources that they needed. Eight students (10.7%) provided no response to the question.

Students' General Satisfaction with Library Resources and Services

Approximately 65% of the World Campus students felt that the library provided adequate support and assistance to library users at a distance. However, 21.3% felt that the support offered by the library to remote students was inadequate, and 13.3% did not respond to this question. Of those students who felt that support for World Campus users was inadequate, 14.7% suggested that there should be more instructional tutorials, 13.3% felt that there should be more reference help, and 12% of responding students suggested improved home document delivery of library materials.

Students' Use of Library Resources and Services

The most frequently used Web-based resources were the library catalog (76%) and full-text databases (68%). There was low usage of Web-based instructional resources and support services, such as tutorials (16%), interlibrary loan (26.7%) and virtual reference service (in 2002, e-mail reference) (10.7%). The libraries' electronic gateway to resources for World Campus students was only used by slightly more than one-third of responding students (34%). Throughout the survey, students articulated a very strong preference for full-text databases and other Web-based resources.

Student Use of Libraries–Penn State and Beyond

A majority of students (62.7%) indicated that they used local libraries in their communities. Of those who did so, 42.7% indicated that they visited a local Penn State campus library. This high percentage is not surprising, as Penn State operates 24 physical campuses located throughout Pennsylvania, and 47% of World Campus students are in-state (Penn State University Faculty Senate, 2005). Nearly one-third of students using local libraries were served by a public library in their community; 13.3% used a non-Penn State local college/university library, and an additional 13% utilized the services and/or resources of a local special library or information center. Students who reported receiving inadequate help via the Penn State Libraries Web-based resources and services were much more likely to report using a local library in their community (81.3%).

WORLD CAMPUS FACULTY SURVEY FINDINGS

Conducted in 2004, the survey of World Campus faculty was also the Penn State Libraries' first effort to discern online instructor's perceptions of the library and its resources. The pool of respondents (57 of 250) was predominantly comprised of experienced distance educators; a majority (53%) indicated that they had served as distance education faculty for four or more years. This high percentage is likely owed in part to Penn State's lengthy history of providing courses to students at a distance. Faculty were also asked how they most frequently corresponded with their online students. E-mail was overwhelmingly the most popular mode of communication (over 93%).

Faculty Perceptions on the Role of the Library in e-Learning

Faculty shared their perceptions of the library's major role in online distance education. Of those responding, 77% of faculty felt that the library's major role was in providing access to library resources. Half of the faculty surveyed felt that the role of the library in the online environment was *more significant* than in the on-campus environment. Approximately 29% of faculty felt that the library played a role in helping e-learners learn how to navigate the library research process, and 19% of faculty felt that it was the library's responsibility to teach students how to evaluate the quality and relevance of library resources.

Use of Library Resources in Online Instruction

A major finding of the survey was that a majority of World Campus faculty do not actively encourage students to use the library. Over 62% of faculty responded that they do not require students to use the library as part of their course(s). Instead, 60% of World Campus faculty indicated that they supply and package all of the research information for students in their course(s). As one faculty member stated:

> I provide my students with a comprehensive study guide and textbook, for my entry level course. As such, I do not require my students to use any library facilities (although I believe the university libraries are critical to support research in my area).

Over half of faculty (51%) indicated that they themselves have used or they have referred their students to at least one or more of the resources listed on the survey. When asked how the library might better support distance education courses, the most frequent response was a request for additional full-text online resources.

Faculty Perceptions of Students' Library Research Skills

Fully 55% of faculty felt that their students did not have difficulty finding and accessing library resources. Of those who did acknowledge their students' struggles, nearly one-quarter of faculty identified a general lack of awareness as the primary factor in students' difficulty using the library. Only 10% of faculty reported actively directing their students to use Web-based library resources, and 22% of faculty indicated that they consider finding research information to be the sole responsibility of the student. However, 62% of faculty indicated that they actively assessed the credibility/quality of research sources that their students used for course-related assignments.

Faculty Awareness of Existing e-Learning Library Services and Resources

World Campus faculty rated their own personal awareness of specific Penn State Libraries electronic resources and services. Nearly one-third of responding faculty (32%) were aware of the libraries' full-text databases and instructional tutorials. Fewer faculty members noted an awareness of the libraries' electronic gateway for World Campus/distance education users (24%), the libraries' delivery service for distance learners (22%), the virtual reference service (Web-based chat reference) (15.5%), online library research guides (17%), and instructional tutorials (17%). Of the resources and services included on the survey, 51% of faculty had either used one or more of the resource(s) themselves or referred their students to them for use. Faculty most frequently used full-text databases (39.7%). The least-used resource was the libraries distance learning delivery service (home delivery of library materials) (8.6%). In the survey's comments section, the libraries' virtual reference service was identified as one of the resources most helpful to students using the library from a distance.

DISCUSSION

During the initial study of World Campus students in 2002, it quickly became apparent to the authors that there was a need to survey World

Campus faculty as well because of their role in influencing and shaping their students' use or non-use of the library, and because of the authors' assumptions that:

- If faculty perceives that the library has a significant role in supporting online distance education, they would integrate it in their courses through appropriate assignments requiring library use.
- If the library is valued and emphasized by the faculty, their influence would lead their students to place similar value and emphasis on the library.
- Faculty members who use the library themselves are also likely to expect their students to use it.

The studies were conducted in sequence; the first survey focused on determining the students' information seeking behavior, while the faculty study sought to determine whether those student behaviors could be attributed to faculty's perceptions/use of the library and their pedagogical approach. The questions included in the questionnaires for the two studies did not match closely enough to yield one-on-one correlations of the results of the two studies. Nevertheless, there were a significant number of questions in both studies pertaining to common issues such as levels of awareness of resources/services, use, satisfaction, preferences, etc., to provide clear links between the two studies. The studies did confirm that online distance education faculty's own use of the library and course integration of library resources impact e-learners' library usage. More of the faculty (46.6%) who stated that they required use of the library as part of their courses, also reported that they had themselves used at least one or more of the library resources listed in the study, compared to only 20% of faculty who stated that they did not require use of the library as part of their courses and had used the listed resources themselves. Furthermore, 75% of the faculty who said they supplied all of their course information also said they did not require use of the library and 69% of the faculty who said research information for their courses was primarily the responsibility of students to find on their own also said they did not require use of the library.

In terms of adequacy of current services and resources offered to e-learners, 65% of the students surveyed felt that their needs were adequately met. This number seemed rather high given that many of the students were not even aware of the full scope of services and resources available to them. This perceived adequacy of services and resources by the students may be due in part to the fact that 60% of their faculty supplied all of the research information required for their courses, thereby diminishing the students' needs and expectations of the library. Furthermore, the fact that a majority of faculty (62%) do not require use of the library may have also contributed to reduced expectations of the library by the students.

The studies showed a difference between the students' perceptions of their library research skills, and the faculty's perceptions of their students' research skills. More students were confident about their research skills whereas fewer faculty were confident about their students' skills. A significant majority (69%) of the students reported that they found it very easy/easy to conduct online research remotely, while only a slight majority (55%) of their faculty felt that their students had no difficulty. The reasons for the difficulty also differed. Students who reported difficulty with online research felt that their skills could be improved through instructive tutorials and one-on-one assistance such as that provided via chat reference. Faculty who responded that their students had difficulty conducting online research remotely cited lack of awareness of resources as the main impediment.

Actual usage of services and resources by both students and faculty was minimal to moderate as reflected by both studies. This may be in part a result of the significant lack of awareness reflected in both groups. The resources known by the students and faculty, respectively, indicated that most of the respondents checked less than a third of the available resources/services listed on each survey. Responses to questions on awareness and usage of the resources by both groups showed that the most known and used resources were the online catalog and the databases, with a high preference for full-text databases by both groups. Moreover, both groups showed that electronic resources such as e-journals and full-text databases were more known and used than Web-based support services such as interlibrary loan, virtual reference and online tutorials.

Students and faculty who reflected knowledge of more resources and higher usage levels were also more likely to include positive comments acknowledging the supportive role that the library played in their academic work.

Some contradictions also emerged in each of the studies. Although 50% of the faculty responded that they perceive the role of the library in the online environment as being more significant than in the face-to-face environment, this perception did not translate into a corresponding number of faculty requiring library use. Instead, only 38% required library use, while 60% supplied all the research information required for their courses. Similarly, the students' study reflected a high level of satisfaction with the library, and yet only a low level of usage.

When the data from the two studies are compared, the combined results shed light on how online distance faculty influence library use among e-learners, and how some of the students' information seeking behaviors may be attributed to faculty's perceptions and pedagogical approach. To shed even further light on this scenario, it is necessary to conduct a study of librarians providing services to the e-learning community and ascertain additional issues that may be impediments to library use in the virtual environment.

RECOMMENDATIONS AND CONCLUSION

The surveys of World Campus faculty and students provide a thought-provoking depiction of the needs and use patterns of online users at a distance. Within both of these audiences, a prevailing theme is one of unawareness–World Campus faculty and students are still relatively uninformed of the wealth of library resources and services afforded them. As Lebowitz (1997) stated:

> One goal of an effective program of library services should be to ensure that students are aware that, albeit at a distance from their parent institution, they have a full array of services available, provided by a staff which is concerned with fulfilling their needs. (p. 307)

Penn State faces a challenge echoed in many academic libraries: effectively promoting and marketing library resources and services to users at a distance. While the Penn State Libraries have developed an electronic gateway and an accompanying portfolio of services for this audience, much of the library's support services for e-learners and online instructors still go unused. To remedy this, an overall marketing plan must be created, making certain that further development and promotion of library services to e-learners is prominently included in it. Wallace and Barber (2002) also suggested treating electronically-based services and resources as a 'branch library,' making provisions for funding the development and marketing of e-learning collections and services in the same manner that one would a physical library.

Assessing user needs is also primary in academic libraries' continued successful development of electronic resources and services for e-learners. As the ranks of learners at a distance continue to grow, academic libraries must gain formal feedback from these users to ensure that future online library resources and services are based on actual needs and not just assumptions or perceived needs. Additionally, academic libraries must regularly assess how their institution is meeting the *Guidelines for Distance Learning Library Services.*

Lebowitz (1997) noted that students who are not able to access adequate library resources are placed at an academic disadvantage. Her observation speaks to the importance of conducting longitudinal studies, both nationwide and locally, on the impact of library use on remote learners' academic performance and information literacy skills. Armed with conclusive data that confirm the importance of library research skills as an integral part of e-learners' academic experience, librarians will be able to build further collaborative partnerships with campus distance education faculty and administration. The importance of online distance learning in higher education will only continue to grow–academic libraries must embrace it as a mainstream audience and develop future collections and services accordingly.

REFERENCES

Allen, I. E., & Seaman, J. (2005, November). *Growing by degrees: Online education in the United States, 2005.* Retrieved December 6, 2005, from http://www.sloan-c.org/resources/growing_by_degrees.pdf.

Association of College and Research Libraries. (2004). *Guidelines for distance learning library services.* Retrieved November 11, 2005, from http://www.ala.org/ala/acrl/acrlstandards/guidelinesdistancelearning.htm.

Barsun, R. (2002). It's my library too, isn't it? *Journal of Library Administration, 37*(1/2), 59-82.

Carnevale, D. (2000). Turning traditional courses into distance education. *Chronicle of Higher Education, 46*(48), A37.

Caspers, J. S. (1999). Outreach to distance learners: When the distance education instructor sends students to the library, where do they go? *Reference Librarian, 67/68,* 299-311.

Coopey, B. (2004). *Libraries' distance learning delivery services: 2003-2004.* Penn State University Libraries.

Frisby, A. J., & Jones, S. S. (2000). The initiation of distance learning at Thomas Jefferson University: The library as integral partner. *Medical Reference Services Quarterly, 19,* 19-37.

Gandhi, S. (2003). Academic librarians and distance education: Challenges and opportunities. *Reference & User Services Quarterly, 43*(2), 138-154.

Hons, C. (2002). Big ten school in cyberspace. *T.H.E. Journal, 29*(6), 27.

Hufford, J. R. (2004). Library support for distance learners: What faculty think. *Journal of Library and Information Services in Distance Learning, 1*(3), 3-28.

Jobe, M. M., & Grealy, D. S. (2000). The role of libraries in providing curricular support and curricular integration for distance learning courses. *Advances in Librarianship, 23,* 239-267.

Jurkowski, O. (2003). Reaching out to online students: Librarian perspectives on serving students in distance education. *New Review of Libraries and Lifelong Learning, 4*(1), 77-89.

Kaufmann, F. G. (2003). Collaborating to create customized services for distance education students. *Technical Services Quarterly, 21*(2), 51-62.

Lebowitz, G. (1997). Library services to distant students: An equity issue. *Journal of Academic Librarianship, 23*(4), 302-308.

Lorenzo, G. (2003). At the online library. *Educational Pathways.* Retrieved November 22, 2005, from http://www.edpath.com/ollib.htm.

Markgraf, J. J. S. (2003). Collaboration between distance education faculty and the library: One size does not fit all. *Journal of Library Administration, 37*(3/4), 451-464.

Markgraf, J. S. (2004). Librarian participation in the online classroom. *Internet Reference Services Quarterly, 9*(1/2), 5-19.

Merisotis, J. P., & Phipps, R. A. (1999). What's the difference? Outcomes of distance vs. traditional classroom-based learning. *Change, 31*(3), 12.

Moyo, L. M., & Cahoy, E. S. (2003). Meeting the needs of remote library users. *Library Management, 24*(6/7), 281-290.

Nicholas, M., & Tomeo, M. (2005). Can you hear me now? Communicating library services to distance education students and faculty. *Online Journal of Distance Learning Administration, 8.* Retrieved Summer 2005, from http://www.westga.edu/%7Edistance/ojdla/summer82/nicholas82.htm.

Penn State University Faculty Senate Commitee on Outreach. (2005, October 25). Penn State World Campus update. Retrieved December 6, 2005, from http://www.psu.edu/ufs/agenda/2005-2006/oct25-05agn/appl.pdf.

Penn State University Libraries. (2005). Library resources and services for World Campus and distance education. Retrieved December 12, 2005, from http://www.libraries.psu.edu/instruction/world/.

Ruddy, M. (1993). *Off-campus faculty and students perceptions of the library: Are they the same?* In C. J. Jacob (Ed.), The The Sixth Off-Campus Library Services Conference (pp. 227-240). Mt. Pleasant, MI: Central Michigan University.

Ryan, M., Carlton, K. H., & Ali, N. S. (2004). Reflections on the role of faculty in distance learning and changing pedagogies. *Nursing Education Perspectives, 25*(2), 73-80.

Thompson, H. A. (2002). The library's role in distance education: Survey results from ACRL's 2000 academic library trends and statistics. *College & Research Libraries News, 63*(5), 338-340.

Wallace, L., & Barber, P. (2002). *On marketing virtual reference services.* Retrieved December 5, 2005, from http://ssdesign.com/librarypr/download/odds_and_ends/marketing_vps.pdf.

doi:10.1300/J111v45n03_02

APPENDIX A

Survey Instrument–World Campus Faculty

Faculty Perspectives on Remote Learners' Library Research Needs

1. Please tell us your College/Department:

2. How long have you been teaching distance education (DE) courses? [check one]
   0-3 Years
   4-6 Years
   7 + Years

3. Currently, what is your primary means of communication with your DE students?
   Telephone
   Fax
   E-mail
   Chat
   Regular mail (snail mail)

4. What role do you perceive the library plays in Distance Education? [check all that apply]
   Providing access to library resources
   Educating students on how to use the library
   Teaching students how to evaluate the quality/relevance of library resources
   None of these
   Other, please specify:

5. You perceive the role of the library in the online environment as?
   The same as in the physical environment
   More diminished in the online environment as compared to the physical environment
   More significant in the online environment, especially in facilitating access to and navigation of electronic resources

6. Research Information for your courses is primarily:
   Supplied by yourself as part of the course package
   Available online via the Libraries' Web site and students are referred to it
   The responsibility of students to find on their own
   Other, please specify in the text box below

APPENDIX A (continued)

7. Do you require your DE students to use the library as part of your course(s)?
Yes
No

8. Do you feel that your students have difficulty in finding and accessing the proper library resources necessary for their course work?
Yes
No

9. If YES to the above question, what problems do you find your DE students facing with regard to finding and accessing information for their course work? [check as many as apply]
They do not know how to search for and access library resources
They rely primarily on general Web sites as research sources
They do not know how to evaluate the credibility/quality of a resource
They are not aware of the existence of many useful resources/services available to them

10. Do you assess the credibility/quality of research resources (i.e., books, articles, etc.) that your DE students use for their assignments?
Yes
No

11. Are you aware of the following existing Penn State Libraries' resources that are supportive of DE? [Check all that apply]
Gateway to library resources created for distance education students
ASK! Virtual Reference Service (real-time, electronic reference assistance)
Remotely accessible databases (many with full-text resources)
Library Distance Learning Delivery (books and other print resources delivered door to door)
Research Guides by Subject
Online tutorials on how to use the libraries' resources

12. Have you used any of the resources noted above or referred your DE students to them?
Yes
No

If Yes, which resources have you used?

> Gateway to library resources created for distance education students
> ASK! Virtual Reference Service (real-time, electronic reference assistance)
> Remotely accessible databases (many with full-text resources)
> Library Distance Learning Delivery (books and other print resources delivered door to door)
> Research Guides by Subject
> Online tutorials on how to use the libraries' resources

13. What University Libraries resources do you find particularly useful in teaching DE courses?

14. What other resources and services would you like the University Libraries to offer in support of DE?

15. Please comment on/make suggestions for Penn State Libraries' support for DE students:

APPENDIX B

Survey Instrument–World Campus Students

Meeting the Needs of Remote Library Users

1. Which PSU library resources have you used? (check as many as apply)
    a.   The CAT (PSU online catalog)
    b.   Fast Track (menu of electronic databases)
    c.   Online Reference Shelf
    d.   PSU Subject Libraries home pages
    e.   None of the above

2. Have you ever visited the PSU Libraries' home page for World Campus students?
    a.   Yes
    b.   No

3. Have you ever used any of the PSU Libraries' **full-text** databases? (A full-text database provides access to entire articles online. An example of a full-text database is ProQuest.)
    a.   Yes
    b.   No

4. Have you ever requested to have a book or journal article sent to you through the **Library Distance Learning Delivery Service** (interlibrary loan)?
    a.   Yes
    b.   No

5. Have you ever e-mailed the **Electronic Reference Desk** for help with a research question?
    a.   Yes
    b.   No

6. Have you ever used one of the PSU Libraries' online research tutorials, such as "Information Literacy & You"?
    a.   Yes
    b.   No

7. How easy is it for you to **find** the library resources that you need?
    a.   Very easy
    b.   Easy
    c.   Difficult
    d.   Very difficult

8. How easy is it for you to **get** the library resources that you need?
   a. Very easy
   b. Easy
   c. Difficult
   d. Very difficult

9. As a distance learner, does the library provide enough help for you to find and get the resources that you need?
   a. Yes
   b. No

10. If 'No' to above, what can we do to help you find and get the library resources you need more easily? (check as many as apply)
    a. Provide more Web-based tutorials on how to do library research
    b. Make available electronic, one-on-one research help
    c. Home delivery of books, journal articles and other materials

11. Do you visit a local library in person to do your research or coursework?
    a. Yes
    b. No

12. If 'Yes' to above, which type of local library do you visit?
    a. PSU Library (main library or branch campus)
    b. Public library in your area
    c. Other college or university library (non-PSU)
    d. Other type of library

13. Do you have any additional comments on the quality of library services to World Campus and other remote students? Please feel free to make suggestions!

Comparison
of Summit Union Catalog Borrowing
and Interlibrary Loan Returnables
at Eastern Washington University

Doris M. Munson

Eastern Washington University

SUMMARY. In 2000, Eastern Washington University became part of the Cascade Consortium and participated in consortial borrowing through the Cascade Union Catalog. In 2003, the Orbis and Cascade consortia merged into the Orbis Cascade Alliance, which manages the Summit Union Catalog. In fall 2004, the Pickup Anywhere option of Innovative Interfaces' INN-Reach module was implemented, allowing patrons to pick up consortial materials at many of the member libraries, not just their own institution's library. Since 2000, Cascade or Summit consortial borrowing has increased while other interlibrary loans of borrowed returnables has decreased. It is too early to tell if Pickup Anywhere will have an effect on Eastern Washington University's Interlibrary Loan department. The problems library staff reported regarding Pickup Anywhere are also examined. doi:10.1300/J111v45n03_03

KEYWORDS. Interlibrary loan, Pickup Anywhere, INN-Reach, union catalogs

---

[Haworth co-indexing entry note]: "Comparison of Summit Union Catalog Borrowing and Interlibrary Loan Returnables at Eastern Washington University." Munson, Doris M. Co-published simultaneously in *Journal of Library Administration* (The Haworth Information Press, an imprint of The Haworth Press, Inc.) Vol. 45, No. 3/4, 2006, pp. 361-376; and: *The Twelfth Off-Campus Library Services Conference Proceedings* (ed: Julie A. Garrison) The Haworth Information Press, an imprint of The Haworth Press, Inc., 2006, pp. 361-376.

Available online at http://jla.haworthpress.com
doi:10.1300/J111v45n03_03

INTRODUCTION

Eastern Washington University (Eastern) joined the Cascade Consortium when it was formed in 2000 by legislative mandate to increase resource sharing among the six public baccalaureate-granting institutions in Washington State. The Cascade Consortium had a union catalog that allowed students, faculty, and staff to place patron-initiated holds on materials owned by member libraries.

In June 2003, the Cascade Consortium merged with the Orbis Consortium, an Oregon consortium, to form the Orbis Cascade Alliance (the Alliance). The Alliance maintains the Summit Union Catalog (Summit) that allows students, faculty, and staff to place patron-initiated holds on loanable materials in member libraries. Eastern patrons went from having six library collections in just Washington State at their disposal to having twenty-eight library collections in Washington State and Oregon from which they could request materials. By October 2005, the Summit Union Catalog contained over eight million bibliographic records and over twenty-six million items from its thirty-three member libraries (Orbis Cascade Alliance Statistics, n.d.).

Eastern hoped that joining the Cascade Consortium, and then the Orbis Cascade Alliance, would help relieve the increasing pressure on the interlibrary loan department by shifting some of the borrowing and lending activity of returnables to the circulation department. Also, Eastern hoped the Orbis Cascade merger would help provide better library service to distance education students. In addition to patron-initiated borrowing in the Summit Union Catalog, there is a reciprocal borrowing agreement among Orbis Cascade Alliance libraries that allows patrons from any member library to borrow returnables from all other member libraries on-site. However, until recently, Eastern distance education students could not request that materials from another Summit library be delivered to a non-Eastern library. Instead, they had to request the materials from Eastern's Interlibrary Loan (ILL) department, which would be mailed to them at their home address, and would then have to be returned by mail to Eastern. This changed in April 2004, when the Pickup Anywhere service was introduced. Eastern's distance education students can now request that an item in Summit be sent to any Pickup Anywhere library and may also return the item to any member library.

Pickup Anywhere does not replace interlibrary loan. Patrons must still request non-returnables, such as journal articles and material not available from Summit, through the interlibrary loan department. Also, libraries are not required to participate in Pickup Anywhere nor does a library's participation in Pickup Anywhere mean that all of the library's branch locations will be Pickup Anywhere sites. The library determines which of its locations may be used for this purpose. Eastern became a Pickup Anywhere library in October 2004. However, Eastern patrons began using the service to have books sent to other libraries almost as soon as the service became available six months earlier, indicating the existence of a need for remote delivery.

All Alliance libraries use Innovative Interfaces' Millennium Integrated Library System. Each library maintains its own system, contributing records and holdings to the Summit Union Catalog using the INN-Reach module. One of the major benefits of INN-Reach is that holdings and circulation information are updated in real time, which allows a patron to know immediately if an item is available for loan. Patron-initiated borrowing is also more cost effective than interlibrary loan because it requires less staff time and can take advantage of courier services. A recent Association of Research Libraries study of twenty-nine INN-Reach libraries found that the cost of an item borrowed using INN-Reach cost $2.89 versus $17.50 for a mediated interlibrary loan. Of these costs, the staff portion was $2.14 for INN-Reach and $10.39 for mediated interlibrary loan (Jackson, 2004a).

The INN-Reach system allows libraries to shift many of the mediated interlibrary loan requests for returnables to patron-initiated requesting in the union catalog. When a patron requests an item from another library, the system automatically decides which owning library will receive the request. A load balancing feature evenly distributes requests among members so that a few libraries do not bear the brunt of filling most of the requests. Each request is for a known item with a known status, so staff does not have to verify citations. The INN-Reach system tracks the status of the item from the placing of the hold to the final return of the item to the owning library. Items are shipped between libraries using a courier service and are at the pickup site usually within two to three days after the hold slip is generated at the owning library. Borrowing of material held by other member libraries becomes less labor intensive because patron-initiated borrowing does not need the staff intervention required for mediated interlibrary loan.

At Eastern, and many other libraries, INN-Reach loans are handled through the circulation department instead of the interlibrary loan department. The circulation department generates hold slips, pulls and processes materials requested by patrons at other libraries, processes materials received and sent by courier, and checks INN-Reach materials in and out. Shifting much of the workload for returnables to the circulation staff leaves the interlibrary loan staff more time to deal with more difficult and labor-intensive interlibrary loan requests.

Although Eastern has participated in patron-initiated borrowing since 2000, no formal study has been done to determine the effect of patron-initiated borrowing on interlibrary loan. This paper examines whether participation in the Cascade Union Catalog and then the Summit Union Catalog has resulted in a decrease in returnables borrowed through interlibrary loan. It also looks at Pickup Anywhere statistics of Eastern students to see what effect, if any, Pickup Anywhere has had on interlibrary loan and examines the problems library staff has reported with Pickup Anywhere.

LITERATURE REVIEW

One of the reasons INN-Reach libraries are trying to shift loans of returnables from mediated interlibrary loans to patron-initiated borrowing is that patron-initiated loans require less staff time, are therefore less costly, and are delivered more quickly (Jackson, 2004a).

The OhioLINK network was the first service to offer patron-initiated borrowing in 1994 and has been the subject of a number of research papers, including several on its effect on interlibrary loan. Ohio State University saw an initial drop-off in its borrowed returnable interlibrary loans when it implemented patron-initiated requesting in 1995. After the initial drop-off, interlibrary loan borrowing of returnables remained steady over the next five years, although borrowing shifted from English-language books to "materials such as dissertations/theses, microfilm and non-English books" (Kuehn, 2001, p. 2).

The University of Toledo saw an increase in the number of photocopy transactions and a decrease in returnable transactions after the implementation of OhioLINK. Overall, there was no significant decrease in its interlibrary loan activity (Breno, 1998). Another OhioLINK member, Miami University, also saw a drop in returnable transactions and an increase in the number of photocopy transactions. Miami University's Interlibrary Loan department now specializes in photocopy requests that are unobtainable from full-text services and returnables that cannot be obtained through OhioLINK (Van Dam, Block, & Pettitt, 1997).

Eimer and Loomis (2000) investigated the impact of the VIVA, GALILEO, and OhioLINK consortia on interlibrary loan departments. They found that "membership in the consortia did not bring about substantial staffing changes, or staggering increased budgetary costs" (p. 54). There was one major change in interlibrary loan in the majority of OhioLINK libraries: Book loan transactions were shifted from the interlibrary loan department to the circulation department. GALILEO, on the other hand, kept the transactions with the interlibrary loan department and "hired additional students to handle the extra materials being processed" (p. 54).

HKALL (the Hong Kong Academic Library Link) tested using INN-Reach for patron-initiated borrowing. The project concluded that INN-Reach cannot replace interlibrary loan because there "will always be needed items that can only be provided by libraries outside the INN-Reach sphere" (Chan, Ferguson, & Chan, 2004, p. 15). Also, the patron sometimes has incomplete bibliographic information and it takes trained interlibrary loan staff to determine what is really wanted. INN-Reach and interlibrary loan are complementary (Chan et al.).

Chmelir (2005) has done the only study to date on the effect of patron-initiated borrowing on interlibrary loan in the Cascade system before it merged with the Orbis consortium in 2003. She found that for each of three years, interlibrary loans for returnables decreased while consortial borrowing increased. The demand for interlibrary loan copies remained fairly constant. She pointed out that "Cascade transactions required considerably less staff mediation than traditional interlibrary loans and anecdotal evidence indicates that turn-around time was fast and patron satisfaction high."

The only published study of the Orbis consortium's impact on interlibrary loan compares interlibrary loan statistics for consortium members as a whole for the three months prior to patron-initiated borrowing and for the three months after patron-initiated borrowing was implemented. Member libraries saw a "10% decrease in borrowing and almost 18% decrease in lending" (Halgren, 1993, p. 16).

There is some disagreement in the literature as to whether patron-initiated borrowing is interlibrary loan or circulation. Preece and Logue (1996) characterized patron-initiated borrowing in the ILLINET Online union catalog as interlibrary loans. The phrase "self-serve interlibrary loan" was used by Preece and Kilpatrick (1998). A recent study comparing mediated interlibrary loan with patron-initiated borrowing also classified patron-initiated borrowing as interlibrary loan (Jackson, 2004a).

Kohl (1998) maintained that patron-initiated borrowing in OhioLINK is a circulation system.

Jackson (2004b) summed up the ambiguity when she stated that the libraries have not yet reached a consensus on what "user-initiated ILL" means.

> The latest ARL study defines user-initiated ILL as the process by which users search a catalog, identify items, and initiate requests for those materials without the assistance or mediation of library staff. . . . Many characterize user-initiated ILL as remote circulation or direct consortial borrowing as this service shares more in common with circulation than with traditional, mediated ILL. (p. 89)

Innovative Interface's Pickup Anywhere module is fairly new. It was first implemented by OhioLINK in July 2003. A search of the literature found no articles on Innovative Interface's Pickup Anywhere module or a similar product by another vendor.

METHODOLOGY

Interlibrary loan statistics were obtained from Eastern Washington University's Interlibrary Loan department for the year before the formation of the Cascade Consortium, the three years of membership in the Cascade Consortium, and the first two years of membership in the Orbis Cascade Alliance.

Cascade Consortium borrowing statistics were obtained from Gary Jeffries, Eastern's Circulation Unit Manager, in conversation on November 3, 2005 . Eastern shared a catalog with Washington State University until June 2003; and because the shared system could not break down Cascade borrowing and lending between the two universities, Jeffries kept manual records on Eastern's consortial borrowing and lending. Eastern implemented its own integrated library system about the same time Cascade merged with Orbis. Summit borrowing statistics were obtained from the Alliance's Web site for the two years after the merger (Orbis Cascade Alliance Statistics, n.d.).

Pickup Anywhere statistics were obtained by downloading them from Eastern's Millennium Pickup Anywhere module. The statistics were uploaded into Excel and sorted a variety of ways to determine if there was any pattern. The "shipped" status was used to calculate the number of Pickup Anywhere requests because it is the status that begins the Pickup Anywhere transaction and is the status least likely to be missed. Pickup Anywhere statistics for Eastern patrons were compared to statistics for all Summit patrons. Jeffries was also interviewed for insights on INN-Reach and Pickup Anywhere. To examine the extent of Pickup Anywhere problems as reported anecdotally by circulation staff, transactions for both Eastern and all of Summit were reviewed to determine what percentage of transactions were missing one or more statuses.

Annual statistics are calculated on a July through June basis to coincide with Eastern's fiscal year.

DISCUSSION

The number of returnables borrowed through the union catalog increased dramatically after the Orbis Cascade merger. As hoped, the number of returnables requested through interlibrary loan has dropped. Table 1 compares consortial borrowing with interlibrary loan borrowing.

In 2002/3, the year before the Orbis Cascade merger, interlibrary loans increased over the previous two years. This could possibly be attributed to the fact that Eastern split its system from Washington State University in early June 2003, the same time the Cascade Consortium was merging with the Orbis Consortium. Eastern patrons had no access to a union catalog or Washington State University's collection from early June to late August. They had to rely on the interlibrary loan department to supply materials they might otherwise have obtained through the union catalog or from Washington State University. However, interlibrary loans of returnable materials in 2003/4 were less

TABLE 1. Returnables Borrowed by Eastern Washington University by Year

	1999/2000	2000/1	2001/2	2002/3	2003/4	2004/5
Interlibrary loans	2,073	1,665	1,545	1,706	1,252	1,056
Cascade/Summit	n/a	4,602*	4,132*	4,710*	5,478	8,180
Pickup Anywhere	n/a	n/a	n/a	n/a	n/a	171
Total borrowed	2,073	6,267	5,677	6,416	6,730	9,407

*EWU/WSU shared system

than in any of the preceding years. They were down 27% when compared with 2002/3 ILLs and down 19% when compared with 2001/2 ILLs. At the end of the second year after the merger, 2004/5, interlibrary loans of returnables were only 51% of what they had been in 1999/2000, the year before Eastern began patron-initiated borrowing.

In the first year after the Orbis Cascade merger, 2003/4, there was a 16% increase in consortial borrowing. This is partly due to the fact that Eastern no longer shared a catalog with Washington State University. Materials that were once obtained from Washington State University via the shared catalog were now obtained through the Summit Union Catalog. However, consortial borrowing increased dramatically in 2004/5, up 49% over the previous year. This increase is well above the overall 20% increase in Summit borrowing for the same period (Orbis Cascade Alliance Statistics, 2005). The increase in consortial borrowing and decrease in interlibrary borrowing is illustrated in Figure 1.

Another reason patron-initiated borrowing has increased while interlibrary loans of returnables have decreased is that Eastern's Interlibrary Loan department will not borrow an item for a patron when it is available through Summit. Eastern's policy is that this is a patron education issue and that the patron should learn how to use Summit. The request is returned to the patron with a letter explaining that the material can be borrowed through Summit. Eastern's reference librarians are available to help patrons learn how to use Summit and place the request. Some patrons have complained that they would prefer to use interlibrary loan because they are familiar with it even though they obtain the material faster through Summit than by using interlibrary loan.

FIGURE 1. Decrease in EWU Interlibrary Loan Returnables Borrowed and Increase in Consortial Borrowing

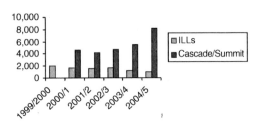

Table 2 compares all interlibrary loan statistics for the years 2000 through 2005. Although total interlibrary loans showed a slight drop in the first year of the Cascade Consortium, the overall number of interlibrary loans has remained relatively constant since then. Requests for returnables have decreased, while non-returnable (i.e., article copy) requests have steadily increased. Figures 2 and 3 offer a graphical view of Table 2.

Initiated in April 2004, Pickup Anywhere is the newest service to be offered to patrons of Alliance member libraries. The Alliance initiated the service in April 2004. Eastern became a Pickup Anywhere site in October 2004. Eastern Washington University is located in a small town twenty miles from the nearest large city in eastern Washington and sees much less Pickup Anywhere activity than Pickup Anywhere libraries in western Washington and western Oregon, where the majority of the population lives.

The Pickup Anywhere statistics thus far are interesting, although it will take a few more years to determine just what impact the service has on interlibrary loan. Table 3 compares monthly Eastern ILL borrowed returnables for the years 2003/4, 2004/5, and Pickup Anywhere statistics for Eastern patrons and all of Summit in the first year of service. The number of Pickup Anywhere transactions by Eastern patrons in 2004/5 is almost equal to the decline in interlibrary loan returnables.

Eastern patrons used Pickup Anywhere most during spring quarter, with forty percent of transactions occurring April through June. Overall use of Pickup Anywhere more than doubled in the second half of Eastern's fiscal year. There were 1334 transactions in the July to December period versus 2841 transactions in the January to June period.

TABLE 2. Eastern Washington University Filled Interlibrary Loans

	Return. borrowed	Nonreturn. borrowed	Total borrowed	Returnables loaned	Nonreturn. loaned	Total loaned	Total filled
1999/2000	2,073	4,288	6,361	3,758	2,841	6,599	12,960
2000/1*	1,665	4,481	6,146	2,766	2,198	4,964	11,110
2001/2*	1,545	5,007	6,552	2,683	2,749	5,432	11,984
2002/3*	1,706	5,248	6,954	2,530	2,487	5,017	11,971
2003/4	1,252	5,441	6,693	2,390	2,177	4,567	11,260
2004/5	1,056	5,154	6,210	2,178	3,324	5,502	11,712

*Cascade Consortium

FIGURE 2. EWU Interlibrary Loan Borrowing of Returnables and Nonreturnables

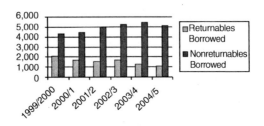

FIGURE 3. EWU Interlibrary Loan Lending of Returnables and Nonreturnables

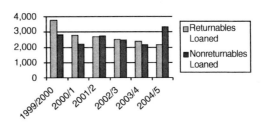

TABLE 3. Eastern Washington University ILL Borrowed Returnables and Pickup Anywhere Compared

	ILL 2003/4	ILL 2004/5	EWU patron PUA 2004/5	Summit PUA 2004/5
July	216	78	3	183
August	155	72	1	132
September	111	68	5	183
October	119	102	19	325
November	105	95	13	321
December	72	59	0	190
January	74	124	30	586
February	108	95	29	428
March	77	70	4	441
April	77	133	25	463
May	53	99	12	501
June	85	61	30	422
Total	1,252	1,056	171	4,175

While it is difficult to determine the impact on interlibrary loan at this time, several general observations can be made. The majority of Eastern patrons using Pickup Anywhere are graduate students (Tables 4 and 5). Most of the requested material is sent to libraries in the Seattle, Washington area. This correlates with two facts: Most of Eastern's distance education programs are at the graduate level and the majority of Eastern's distance education students live in the Seattle metropolitan area.

In 2004/5, Pickup Anywhere accounted for 1.3% of the total Summit borrowing. Graduate students were the primary users of Pickup Anywhere while undergraduate students accounted for the majority of regular Summit borrowing. The distribution of regular requests among type of patron in Summit is similar to that reported by Prabha and O'Neill (2001) for OhioLINK. Summit use is 49% undergraduates, 27% graduates, 19% faculty, and 5% staff compared to OhioLINK's "42% undergraduates, 37% graduates, 14% faculty, 5% staff, and 1% each, courtesy permits and affiliated faculty and staff" (p. 332).

Although Pickup Anywhere shows great potential, anecdotal evidence indicates there are a number of problems with the Pickup Anywhere module. When one examines how Pickup Anywhere works, it is not too difficult to anticipate problems if staff is not familiar with the module.

TABLE 4. Type of Patron Using Pickup Anywhere and Summit for 2004/5

	EWU patron PUA	Summit PUA	Summit INN-Reach borrowing
Undergrad	10	1,094	159,999
Graduate	140	2,431	87,061
Faculty	13	602	60,576
Staff	8	36	15,886
Total	171	4,163	323,522

TABLE 5. Type of Patron Using Pickup Anywhere and Summit as a % for 2004/5

	EWU patron PUA	Summit PUA	Summit INN-Reach borrowing
Undergrad	6%	26%	49%
Graduate	82%	58%	27%
Faculty	8%	15%	19%
Staff	4%	1%	5%
Total	100%	100%	100%

With INN-Reach, the item is actually checked out twice. The owning library checks out the item to the patron's library. The patron's library then checks out the item to the patron. When the patron returns the item, the patron's library checks the item in and then returns it to the owning library. The transaction is not completed until the owning library also checks in the item. Fortunately, almost all INN-Reach activity can occur in the regular Millennium Circulation module.

With Pickup Anywhere, a different procedure is followed. Each Pickup Anywhere loan transaction has five steps that update the status of an item. Some of the steps must be done in the Pickup Anywhere module, a sub-module of Millennium Circulation. The owning library starts the transaction when it checks the item out to the pickup site using the "check out to remote site" function in the INN-Reach module of Millennium Circulation. This step gives the item a status of "shipped." The pickup library "receives" the item using Pickup Anywhere. The item is then "checked-out" to the patron, also using Pickup Anywhere. If the item is returned to the pickup library or a library that is not the patron's library or the owning library, the library must use Pickup Anywhere to update the item's status to "returned" and then sends the item back to the owning library. If the item is returned to the patron's library or the owning library, the item can be checked in using the regular Millennium Circulation check-in mode. For the final step, the owning library uses the INN-Reach module to set the transaction to "completed."

The status of an item is important because it is used to track the item throughout the Pickup Anywhere process. The "shipped" status indicates the item is in possession of the courier until the status is updated by the pickup site. The "shipped" status helps hold the courier accountable for items that were placed in transit and never received by the pickup site. The "returned" status also holds the courier accountable for items placed in transit to the owning library. The "checked out" status indicates that the item is still in possession of the patron. Libraries and patrons can track the request.

To help staff identify Pickup Anywhere materials, a special sticker is affixed on the exterior book band used for INN-Reach materials. The sticker is attached at the time of initial checkout to alert the receiving library that it is a Pickup Anywhere item. It is not uncommon for the owning library to forget to affix the Pickup Anywhere sticker to the book band. It is also easy for pickup library staff to ignore or miss the sticker and use the regular circulation module to check material in and out to the patron.

The regular circulation module will not recognize Pickup Anywhere transactions. Library staff must use the Pickup Anywhere mode at certain points in the process to correctly process the materials. Unfortunately, the process is not intuitive and not parallel with the rest of the system. This is where many of the problems with Pickup Anywhere occur.

Anecdotal evidence indicates that steps to update the status of an item are often missed. Pickup Anywhere statistics (Table 6), support the anecdotes. Of the 171 transactions involving Eastern patrons, 78, or 46%, had all five statuses while 93 were missing one or more statuses. This mirrors the percentage of all Summit Pickup Anywhere transactions with all five statuses. Fortunately, staff is more likely to do all the Pickup Anywhere steps to update an item's status as he/she becomes used to the routine. Summit Pickup Anywhere transactions with all five statuses rose from 40% in November 2004 to 55% in May 2005.

Looking at overall statistics for the five statuses for both Eastern patrons and all Pickup Anywhere transactions (Table 7), the least likely statuses to be updated were "checked-out" and "returned." The "returned" discrepancy may partly be accounted for by the way items are checked in, which depends on where they are returned. If an item is returned to the owning library or the patron's library, the Millennium Circulation module is used to check in the item. If an item is returned to the pickup location or any other pickup location, the Pickup Anywhere module is used to check in the item. However, the most likely explanation is that circulation staff are inadvertently using the Circulation module rather than the Pickup Anywhere module to perform these tasks because regular INN-Reach transactions use the Circulation module. Pickup Anywhere transactions are the only circulation transactions that happen outside the normal circulation course of business. Also, many academic libraries employ work-study students and part-time workers at the circulation desk who may not be familiar with Pickup Anywhere

TABLE 6. Pickup Anywhere Transactions with All Steps and Missing Steps

	EWU patrons 2004/5		Summit 2004/5		Summit Nov. 2004		Summit May 2005	
All 5 statuses	78	46%	1,931	46%	129	40%	278	55%
< 5 statuses	93	54%	2,244	54%	192	60%	223	45%
Total	171	100%	4,175	100%	321	100%	501	100%

TABLE 7. Pickup Anywhere Transaction Steps Completed

Pickup Anywhere Status	Eastern Patrons	All Pickup Anywhere
Shipped	171	4,175
Received	136	3,576
Checked-out	134	3,111
Returned	119	2,834
Completed	170	4,129
Cancelled by Owning Library	0	6

and create "on-the-fly" records when an item shows up as not being in the database.

Comparing all Pickup Anywhere "Shipped" and "Completed" statuses in Table 7, it appears that 46 Pickup Anywhere transactions were not completed after being shipped. There are two possible explanations. The first is that the owning library forgot to update the status of the item when it was returned. The second is that the borrowed items were not returned by the patrons. Examination of the transactions indicates that 21 of the transactions were canceled or returned, leaving 25 items that may not have been returned by the patron. The loss rate for Pickup Anywhere items is less than 1%. Patrons have an incentive to return Summit items. Any Alliance patron who fails to return an item borrowed through Summit is charged a $75 replacement charge and $15 processing fee per item.

CONCLUSIONS

Participation in the Cascade Union Catalog and the Summit Union Catalog decreased the demand for mediated interlibrary loan returnables. Furthermore, patron-initiated borrowing decreased the amount of interlibrary loan department staff time spent on borrowing materials from other libraries and, at Eastern, shifted much of the workload to the circulation department. This left the interlibrary loan department more time to deal with the increasing demand for nonreturnables. Also, patrons often receive requested materials within two to three days, versus one to three weeks for mediated interlibrary loans.

Distance education graduate students are the most likely to use the Pickup Anywhere service. It is too soon to tell if Pickup Anywhere will have an effect on mediated interlibrary loan returnables. Data are needed for another two or more years to determine if use of the Pickup Anywhere service is increasing among Eastern patrons and if it affects the use of mediated interlibrary loans.

The number of statuses not being updated in Pickup Anywhere transactions is a concern. Although staff is more likely to update the status as s/he becomes more used to the module, the error rate is still fairly high. To help alleviate the problem, the Alliance held a Pickup Anywhere training session in July 2005. Also, a future project will compare statistics for 2004/2005 to 2005/2006 to see if additional training helps libraries do a better job of performing all the steps in a Pickup Anywhere transaction. Many Alliance libraries hope that Innovative Interfaces' future plans for Pickup Anywhere include a redesign so that transactions can be conducted in the regular circulation module.

REFERENCES

Breno, P. M. (1998). *Impact of OhioLINK resource sharing options on the workload of the Interlibrary Loan Department at the University of Toledo, Carlson Library.* Unpublished master's thesis, Kent State University, Kent, Ohio.

Chan, G., Ferguson, A., & Chan, L. (2004). HKALL and ILLIAD: The search for improved interlibrary loan. *ASAIHL Conference on Regional Cooperation in Higher Education.* Retrieved September 12, 2005, from http://www.ln.edu.hk/asaihl/pdf/papers/2_4_25.pdf.

Chmelir, L. (2005). Patron-initiated borrowing and traditional ILL: The Cascade experience. *Interlending & Document Supply, 33*(1), 35-41. Retrieved May 18, 2005, from Emerald.

Eimer, M. B., & Loomis, K. L. (2000). The future of sharing: The effect of statewide consortia on select interlibrary loan departments. *Journal of Interlibrary Loan, Document Delivery & Information Supply, 10*(3), 43-62.

Halgren, J. V. (1998). Resource sharing, interlibrary loan and Orbis: How did we get here and where are we going? *Journal of Interlibrary Loan, Document Delivery & Information Supply, 8*(4), 5-18.

Jackson, M. E. (2004a). *Assessing ILL/DD services: New cost-effective alternatives.* Washington, DC: Association of Research Libraries.

Jackson, M. E. (2004b). The future of interlending. *Interlending & Document Supply, 32*(2), 88-93.

Kohl, D. F. (1998). How the virtual library transforms interlibrary loans–the OhioLINK experience. *Interlending and Document Supply, 26*(2), 65-69.

Kuehn, J. (2001). We're still here: Traditional ILL after OhioLINK patron-initiated requesting and ejournals. *IFLA Council and General Conference, 67.* Retrieved September 12, 2005, from http://www.ifla.org/IV/ifla67/papers/063-108e.pdf.

Orbis Cascade Alliance Statistics. (n.d.). Retrieved October 26, 2005, from http://www.orbiscascade.org/staffhome/sharing-stats.html.

Prabha, C. G., & O'Neill, E. T. (2001). Interlibrary borrowing initiated by patrons: Some characteristics of books requested via OhioLINK. *Journal of Library Administration, 34,* 329-338.

Preece, B. G., & Kilpatrick, T. L. (1998). Cutting out the middleman: Patron-initiated interlibrary loans. *Library Trends, 47,* 144-157.

Preece, B. G., & Logue, S. (1996). Empowering the patron: Redesigning interlibrary loan services. *Journal of Library Administration, 23,* 155-166.

Van Dam, S., Block, J., & Pettitt, R. N. (1997). The impact of the OhioLINK Network on traditional interlibrary loan. *Journal of Interlibrary Loan, Document Delivery & Information Supply, 8* (1), 1-19.

doi:10.1300/J111v45n03_03

Keeping Your Eye on the Prize: Remaining Focused on the End User When Everything Around You Appears Chaotic

Edward W. Murphy

Embry-Riddle Aeronautical University

SUMMARY. Digital library services have become integral components of 21st century educational institutions. Librarians have been quick to adopt new technologies to serve their new remotely located patrons. This eagerness to adopt new technology, along with a willingness to adapt to new working environments and a continuing emphasis on the end users of our services have enabled success with regards to serving the distance education patron. This paper will review and discuss the evolution of Embry Riddle Aeronautical University's (ERAU) Extended Campus Library Services (ECLS), and how a conscious effort to focus on the end users of Embry-Riddle's ECLS has helped Embry-Riddle manage and respond to the explosive growth of its distance learning population over the last 30 years. doi:10.1300/J111v45n03_04

KEYWORDS. Distance education, managing growth, technology trends, student centered services

---

[Haworth co-indexing entry note]: "Keeping Your Eye on the Prize: Remaining Focused on the End User When Everything Around You Appears Chaotic." Murphy, Edward W. Co-published simultaneously in *Journal of Library Administration* (The Haworth Information Press, an imprint of The Haworth Press, Inc.) Vol. 45, No. 3/4, 2006, pp. 377-385; and: *The Twelfth Off-Campus Library Services Conference Proceedings* (ed: Julie A. Garrison) The Haworth Information Press, an imprint of The Haworth Press, Inc., 2006, pp. 377-385.

Available online at http://jla.haworthpress.com
doi:10.1300/J111v45n03_04

INTRODUCTION

There is a growing body of literature that discusses the changes and fluidity of librarianship as a profession, especially the segment supporting remotely located patrons. Technology, delivery methods, changes in both library personnel and in the distance education students themselves are forcing us to step back and examine where the profession is headed and how to best manage our way there. By embracing new technologies, adapting to the forces of change within the workplace, and by not forgetting who, ultimately, we are trying to serve, libraries will give themselves the best chance to succeed in an era that may seem chaotic, as well as difficult to plan for and effectively manage.

While Embry-Riddle Aeronautical University has established a fine reputation of providing a quality engineering and aviation/aerospace education, in actuality the main residential campus and the Hunt Library that supports it and the distance learning programs are not unusual. Embry-Riddle is a medium-sized academic institution serving a population of approximately 5000 students in Daytona Beach, Florida, with an additional 25,000 distance learning students scattered throughout the world.

Embry Riddle began its extended campus operations in 1970; the earliest classes were offered at army bases in Georgia, Alabama, Texas, and Virginia. Enrollment in 1970 was only a modest 175 students. The United States Army, Air Force, and eventually the Navy soon realized that Embry-Riddle's niche within the field of aviation and aerospace education was a perfect fit for many of their own educational goals and they were eager to establish partnerships with the newly formed extension services. The early growth of Embry-Riddle's distance learning programs was remarkable, with new centers opening every few months throughout the seventies. By 1980, Embry-Riddle had offered its first graduate degree programs through the extended campus and would soon have satellite operations across much of the United States and Western Europe.

The 1980s would see further expansion to include the opening of Embry-Riddle's 100th extended campus center. However, since it was still closely allied with the military, the distance education student population would rise and fall with the military buildups and draw downs of the United States government, and enrollments would fluctuate from anywhere between 1000 and 13,000 students. The 1990s would see the extended campus remain relatively stable with further expansion to 135 centers worldwide and ultimately to 25,000 students in FY 2004-2005.

Within 25 years, Embry-Riddle's distance learning population had exploded from 175 students to an astounding 25,000 students. Embry Riddle's College of Continuing Education (as it was now called) had quietly grown to be one of the largest off campus, regionally accredited (by the Southern Association of Colleges and Schools) colleges in the United States.

Ten years ago my predecessor submitted a paper to the 7th Off-Campus Library Services Conference relating the experiences of Embry Riddle's extension services as they began to develop a plan for providing resources to a new type of distance education student, one now equipped with a personal computer and online access. Although Embry-Riddle had been in the business of providing distance education courses and supporting materials for 25 years prior to 1995, many new and exciting developments were just coming online that would eventually transform the extended campus into something totally unrecognizable to my earlier colleague.

Young (1995) sounded almost weary as he wrapped up his presentation regarding the successful, and the not so successful, trials of delivering library services to a student population of roughly 1500 graduate and undergraduate students, at that time distributed across 37 states and 22 different countries.

> As explained above, it is a daily challenge for ECLS to prepare for and anticipate the needs of such a geographically diverse user population. One solution to these problems is to provide the students with access to the appropriate resources, which would allow them to identify, evaluate, and procure the information they need for their graduate research.

> The universities extended campus library services (ECLS) looks forward to the day when all independent study students can conduct research from home. This will allow the reference librarians to educate students and help them find information "on their own." Until then, ECLS must meet the challenges of working with existing technologies and access issues in order to provide quality reference service. (p. 401)

LITERATURE REVIEW

It is soon apparent to anyone surveying the current state of the electronic library and/or the delivery of library services to a remotely located distance learning population that the working environment is in a continuous state of change. What is also evident is that the basic needs of our end users have remained uncannily the same regardless of the era; "we need it, and we need it now" is the message that has reverberated from the earliest attempts to support our distance learning patrons up until the most recent requests for assistance.

The digital or electronic library has had such a dramatic impact on traditional library services that much of the literature is full of absolutes and calls to immediate action before it is too late to react. Ferguson and Bunge (1997) began by calling for the complete "metamorphosis of the user services particularly reference and instruction." Tenopir and Ennis (2002, p. 265) reiterated, stating "there is no doubt that digital information sources have had profound effects on university reference departments over the last decade and have changed libraries forever." Studies identifying and calling for "paradigm shifts" and "organizational restructuring" within the library as a place as well as librarianship as a profession routinely appear in library literature as we struggle to come to terms with phenomenal changes in our physical and technological environments.

Radical changes of the workplace must also have an effect on those in the workplace, and again there is ample evidence in the literature calling for training, understanding, and adoption of new workplace models before we can expect the success of our technological achievements to translate into the success for our students. Voulalas and Sharpe (2005) felt that the "characteristics of 'good' schools or learning institutions are those that participate in a lifelong learning culture, a commitment to professional development" (p. 191). This will foster a spirit of "vitality and empowerment" among those immediately concerned with the delivery and utilization of new methods of instruction and support, and would eventually transfer to improved student outcomes. Smith (2005b) saw libraries a little more challenging than other types of workplaces, but stated however "by developing the capability to make radical changes (the library) has the opportunity to position and solidify the libraries role in a new information age" (p. 153). Lamont (1999) underscored the above sentiments by identifying the "human issues as more likely to determine the success of a project," and "without the support and understanding by staff members, a project may well be doomed" (p. 390). Article after article reiterates the importance of continued training and support of librarians as they cope with rapid organizational changes, and article after article concludes that without additional training and support from library administration many librarians might be left struggling with the pace of technological change (Farley, 1998; Moore, 2003; Pankl, 2004; Smith, 2005a).

Today's students come equipped with a wide array of technology. It would not be unreasonable to expect to find a cellular phone, a personal digital assistant (PDA), a laptop computer, a digital camera, perhaps even a global positioning system (GPS) inside a student's book bag. These devices can now be coupled together and can communicate with other users with an equally impressive array of networking and communication technologies. Wireless (WAP) protocols, Bluetooth, and the World Wide Web can now all be used to communicate between each of the individual's devices as well as communicating with other individuals. This is not to say that a significant number of students may have never learned to program their VCRs, let alone their digital video recorders, or their Tivos. Garfinkel (2003) in his article "The Myth of Generation N," did not feel that there is enough evidence yet to argue that today's students are any more computer literate than those of a few years ago, although he does admit that there are plenty of statistics supporting the growing number of personal computers and the growing percentage of homes with Internet access throughout the United States.

Now that we have identified the library has undergone radical change, and that the librarians themselves have had to react in order to keep pace with the fluid nature of delivering library services to distance learners, what about the end users themselves? Are there any generalizations that can be made about today's distance learning students? Kazmer's (2002) year-long survey of distance education library students intimated comfortableness with both current technology and with methods of delivery and support services available; however, these were students enrolled in library school and likely had a fairly good grasp on what to expect from a distance education program. Prensky (2001, 2005) wrote numerous articles warning us not to underestimate or "dumb down" technology or resources for today's students. He believes that the generation of students in our schools now could very well teach us a few things about technology and about adapting and adopting new technology with regards to completing coursework, in communicating electronically, and with locating information online.

DISCUSSION

Many of Embry-Riddle's remotely located students attend classes at physical satellite locations (extended campus centers): about a third of them are completing a good deal of their coursework without seeing the inside of an ERAU classroom. The remaining are an interesting breed of "hybrid" students–those who have combined (either by choice, or by circumstance) the experience of attending classes at one of our residential campuses along with classes at one of our extended campus centers or with one of our entirely Web-based courses. These hybrid students have become increasingly more comfortable with the experience of attending a university and completing coursework over the Internet (Prensky, 2001; Long, 2005) or through any number of alternative outreach methods, and many of them are now reporting that they actually prefer this method of instruction (Prensky, 2005) as the generation of students who have grown up with the desktop computer takes its place at the university.

Embry-Riddle's extended campus students are now probably somewhere between Prensky's and Garfinkel's examples. For many years the extended campus did not have many of what would be considered "traditional" age undergraduates. The Embry-Riddle distance learning students of just ten years ago could have easily been characterized as "non-traditional" as they were predominantly serving members of the military enrolled in the Professional Aeronautics program. However, the university's latest institutional research reports indicate that the majority (63%) of our distance education students are now from the civilian sector, and the remaining (37%) are currently serving members of the armed forces. This is a complete turnaround from just ten years ago. The number of undergraduate courses now being offered through Embry-Riddle's extended campus has also increased significantly, which may also indicate a shift towards a more "traditional" age student.

In the late 1990s Embry-Riddle began to re-examine and consolidate its support to the extended campus and to the distance learning community. Before that the Extended Campus Library Support (ECLS) staff had been a separate entity from the Hunt Library, for many years existing in buildings a few blocks from the main campus. ECLS eventually moved onto the main campus and was fully incorporated into the Hunt Library under the Associate Director for Reference and Extended Campus Services. There are now 13 professional positions that deal directly with the extended campus community assisted by four paraprofessionals along with a cadre of student workers.

In the ten years since my predecessor presented his paper to the 1995 Off Campus Library Services Conference, the changes in technology and in the support services now available to a distance education student are astounding. Online services were just being explored by Embry-Riddle's extended campus in 1995; CompuServe and text-based browsers were just beginning to complement the print resources, co-operative agreements, video, toll-free telephone numbers and regular mail services used by the Hunt Library at that time as a means of student support.

Since then numerous e-mail programs, graphical browsers, intranets, the World Wide Web, VHS videotapes, CD-ROMs, DVDs, chat services, instant messaging, electronic document delivery, online databases and periodical indexes, full-text digital documents–including e-books, and streaming media content have all been used to support distance education students.

Is it surprising that students have reported that the simpler the design of the support operations to distance learners, the easier it is for them to navigate and to utilize the services? "Having a single contact point for all transactions was preferable since they didn't have to explain themselves each time they contacted the home campus" (Kazmer, 2002, pp. 396-397). Zheng and Smaldino (2003) and McGuigan (2002) also reported that by surveying end users, responding to their particular needs, and by making contact with the main campus as uncomplicated and unencumbered as possible reduces frustration levels and goes a long way to ensuring successful transactions.

Embry-Riddle and the Hunt Library in particular have made a concerted effort to reduce what the students have ruefully called the "Riddle runaround." ECLS utilizes tracking mechanisms and reference transaction transcripts to avoid precisely the concerns stated above. Regardless of which librarian handles a particular contact, they can quickly scan previous reference transactions and avoid potential redundant and frustrating contacts. The Hunt Library has also consolidated all of its contact information and services into a "one-stop-shopping" model; now any and all contact with the library and with library personnel can be made through one e-mail address. This single e-mail access point is "post mastered" by a librarian who ensures that the messages get to the correct department or to the correct contact person. In Embry-Riddle Aeronautical University's 2003 online distance learning student satisfaction survey, students overwhelmingly reported favorable responses to contact with the Hunt Library with regard to ease of use and with the overall effectiveness of their transactions.

The Hunt Library's ECLS has also been vigorously surveying and soliciting their end users in an attempt to be proactive in meeting their needs. Many of the successful initiatives and collaborative partnerships have come directly from in-house user surveys and end of semester course feedback. One of the latest initiatives has been to give the virtual/electronic library more of a sense of place. There had been an overwhelming response indicated on training feedback forms and from in-house surveys requesting tours and instruction in the physical library whenever members of the distance learning community were in Daytona Beach. It was a simple enough request to accommodate and now tours, meet and greets, and training are routinely conducted at the Hunt Library whenever possible.

CONCLUSIONS

Embry-Riddle has been in the business of providing quality distance education programs for over thirty years. The Hunt Library has been supporting the distance learning community since the inception of the extended campus and the College of Continuing Education in 1970. There have been so many dramatic changes in the types of support services that we have offered to our distance education patrons that my predecessor from only ten years ago would not recognize today's library support operation.

Technologies have come and gone, our student populations have literally exploded, and physical satellite locations have opened in the most remote of locations imaginable. Any attempt to predict how and where Embry-Riddle will be operating any significant length of time from now is definitely a challenge. From past experience it would appear first and foremost that the easier we make it for students, staff and faculty members to simply communicate with us the more successful we will be.

Technology has proved to be tenuous and fleeting; the constants have always been the information providers and the end users. By continuing to focus on these end users, responding to their feedback, and supporting and training those who deal with the extended campus community at the immediate service points we will give ourselves the greatest chance for continued success, and our students the greatest chances for their success.

REFERENCES

Farley, T. B. (1998). Academic libraries, people and change: A case study of the 1990's. *OCLC System and Services, 14*(4), 151-164.

Ferguson, C. D., & Bunge, C. (1997). The shape of services to come: Values-based reference service for the largely digital library. *College & Research Libraries, 58*(3), 252-265.

Garfinkel, S. (2003). The myth of generation N. [Electronic Version] *Technology Review*. Retrieved February 24, 2006, from http://www.mit-technologyreview.com/ InfoTech/wtr_13263,294,p1.html.

Kazmer, M. M. (2002). Distance education students speak to the library: Here's how you can help even more. *Electronic Library, 20*(5), 395-400.

Lamont, M. (1999). Critical human factors in emerging library technology centers. *Library Hi-Tech, 17*(4), 390-395.

Long, S. A. (2005). Digital natives: If you aren't one, get to know one. *New Library World, 106*(1210/1211), 187-189.

McGuigan, G. S. (2002). The common sense of customer service: Employing advice from the trade and popular literature of business to interactions with irate patrons in libraries. *Reference Librarian, 75/76*, 197-204.

Moore, M. G. (2003). From Chautauqua to the virtual university: A century of distance education in the United States. (Report No. 393). Columbus, OH: ERIC Clearinghouse on Adult, Career and Vocational Education.

Pankl, R. (2004). Baby boom generation librarians. *Library Management, 25*(4/5), 215-222.

Prensky, M. (2001). Digital natives, Digital immigrants. *On the Horizon, 9*(5), 1-5.

Prensky, M. (2005). Listen to the natives. *Educational Leadership, 63*(4), 8-13.

Smith, I. (2005a). Achieving readiness for organizational change. *Library Management, 26*(6/7), 408-412.

Smith, I. (2005b). Continuing professional development and workplace learning. *Library Management, 26*(3), 152-155.

Tenopir, C., & Ennis, L. (2002). A decade of digital reference: 1991-2001. *Reference & User Services Quarterly, 41*(1), 264-273.

Voulalas, Z. D., & Sharpe, F. G. (2005). Creating schools as learning communities: Obstacles and processes. *Journal of Educational Administration, 43*(2), 187-208.

Young, J. B. (1995). Providing reference service to graduate independent study students worldwide. In C. Jacob (Ed.), *The Seventh Off-Campus Library Services Conference Proceedings San Diego* (pp. 399-402). Mt. Pleasant, MI: Central Michigan University.

Zheng, L., & Smaldino, S. (2003). Key instructional design elements for distance education. *Quarterly Review of Distance Education, 4*(2), 153-166.

doi:10.1300/J111v45n03_04

Monthly Check-Up:
Using a Monthly Survey
to Monitor and Assess
Library and Information Services
for Distance Learners

James T. Nichols

State University of New York at Oswego

SUMMARY. As part of implementing a continuous improvement approach to quality service for distance learners, we identified a need for a measurement that could feasibly be repeated monthly, and could include both quantitative and qualitative components. We mounted the instrument on our Web-based survey system and plan to invite 30-50 students a month to complete the survey. The quantitative ratings will be tracked using run charts and control limits using the methods of W. Edwards Deming. The qualitative open-ended responses will be read and analyzed in regard to pre-established and emerging categories, with an interest in understanding successful information literacy experiences but especially with an eye to how we can remove barriers that our learners report. doi:10.1300/J111v45n03_05

KEYWORDS. Quality service, user feedback, surveys

[Haworth co-indexing entry note]: "Monthly Check-Up: Using a Monthly Survey to Monitor and Assess Library and Information Services for Distance Learners." Nichols, James T. Co-published simultaneously in *Journal of Library Administration* (The Haworth Information Press, an imprint of The Haworth Press, Inc.) Vol. 45, No. 3/4, 2006, pp. 387-395; and: *The Twelfth Off-Campus Library Services Conference Proceedings* (ed: Julie A. Garrison) The Haworth Information Press, an imprint of The Haworth Press, Inc., 2006, pp. 387-395.

Available online at http://jla.haworthpress.com
doi:10.1300/J111v45n03_05

INTRODUCTION

Wouldn't it be nice to have a convenient and regular report on how well your services meet the needs of your students? And better yet, if it would be easy to generate and to understand the results? Libraries commonly rely on informal feedback for information about users' needs and satisfaction, or on periodic surveys. The informal communication is important, but remains anecdotal and dependent on the listening skills and the perspectives of librarians. Surveys are systematic and can elicit the perspectives of users, but they have their problems which will be explored later in this article. Few libraries have been able to follow the urgings of the service quality and continuous improvement movements to truly stay close to the experiences of users. The procedures laid out in this article will allow for the kind of measurement of user satisfaction that will support development and improvement of quality services.

SURVEYS

The typical survey of library users is not conducted any more often than annually and leaves librarians with numbers that are difficult and time-consuming to interpret. Often a survey is done in anticipation of an accreditation visit. Although an effort may be made to conduct the survey on a scientific basis, the formulation of questions is often left to a committee with no real research framework in hand. And issues about the scientific standing of a one shot survey are ignored. The numbers have no meaning without a theoretical framework and a plan for comparing the current set of numbers to previous or future surveys or to similar surveys at other libraries.

The best developed and probably most used survey at this time is LibQUAL+. State University of New York at Oswego Library took part in this in 2003 and found it helpful, but we find that we cannot make use of LibQUAL+ more than every three to five years. The survey instrument and the means to analyze and understand the results have been developed to very high scientific standards. The theoretical framework focuses on establishing library user expectations and documenting the user's perceptions of how those expectations have been met. The items have been tested for reliability and validity. The dimensions, such as library as place and personal control, are the result of extensive factor analysis and been shown to represent the major areas of concern for library users (LibQUAL+ , 2006).

The questionnaires are lengthy, consisting of 22 statements for which each respondent is to indicate three ratings: acceptable level, perceived level, and desired level; and several other questions to address demographic and overall satisfaction data. Users need about 30 minutes to complete the form. The results are delivered as an institutional results notebook, as raw data in a form that can be loaded into applications for further analysis, and as tables of national norms. Once one is oriented to reading the charts, it is fairly easy to understand the results notebook. In our case, the results were generally moderate, and we needed to conduct additional analysis to identify areas that required attention. It took several months to complete the analysis, although on a number of issues we were able to take early results and act on them.

MEASURES FOR CONTINUOUS IMPROVEMENT

Developing and maintaining high quality service requires service providers to understand user needs and user experiences with the service from the users' points-of-view. Professional experience is no guarantee of understanding–generally, the longer one has delivered a service the less one really knows about the users' experiences without taking special steps. It requires great and continued effort to really listen to users. A formal program of feedback from users can be invaluable.

Ideally one could measure the quality of service from the perspective of the user very frequently, even daily, or in industrial settings hourly (Deming, 1982). In academic libraries we have to settle for something much less frequent. It is tempting to settle for once a semester, but that gives one little time to respond to the results and initiate improvements. Monthly seems to suit our current situation in distance learning at SUNY Oswego, but if we had a larger volume of activity, we would want to have measures on a weekly basis.

The advantage to frequency is that it provides a chance to track performance over time. By charting the monthly numerical results as a series, we can quickly and easily see changes and trends in satisfaction. This way we can document that improvements have had an impact, and also identify potential problems that need to be addressed. Data analysis needs to be speedy so that library responses can happen in time to make a difference. A good way to analyze changes and trends is to lay out the data in process behavior charts (Deming, 1982; Laughlin, Shockley, & Wilson, 2003).

PROCESS BEHAVIOR CHARTS

Process behavior charts (or control charts in Deming) are based on graphing measurements in sequence over time and calculating and graphing an Upper Control Limit (UCL) and a Lower Control Limit (LCL). The control limits are three standard deviations above and below the average of the measures. These limits can also be established through a moving range method that can be done in minutes with paper and pencil (Deming, 1982; Laughlin et al., 2003).

The chart below is based on a run of monthly statistics. The run plots the total for each month. The average, upper limit and lower limit have been calculated and entered on the chart. Successive years can be charted out in this manner, and the changes over time can be analyzed. In subsequent periods, one will hopefully see changes in the average in the desired direction: upward for something like the number of requests, but downward for something like the number of cancelled requests. Also, improvements in quality and in processes should lead to decreasing the span of the upper and lower limits.

Two main concepts are important in reading a process behavior chart. The first is that variations within the limits are most likely due to the design of the system and processes, staff effort and staff expertise. This is called common variation, and responsibility for reducing this variation is shared by management and staff, with the understanding that staff effort is one of the smaller factors and should never be focused on in isolation. Variations outside the limits, called special variations, are usually due to environmental or historical factors, such as snowstorms and network outages, but might be the result of poor planning. Management has the responsibility to identify the causes of special variations and make arrangements to insulate the system from them if possible (Deming, 1982).

The process improvement chart below (Figure 1) records the number of document delivery requests submitted to Penfield Library monthly for the 2003-2004 academic year. The average number of requests submitted had increased from eight a month in the previous year to 14 a month, but the span of the limits had also increased dramatically.

The requests for March were a case of special variation. Investigation showed that many of those requests were from a single student who had mistakenly submitted delivery requests for several items that should have been submitted to interlibrary loan. The requests had been cancelled for delivery and the student was referred to the correct service. In part because of stories like this, we have consolidated requests for document delivery into our ILLiad system, and basically direct the requests for the

FIGURE 1. Process Behavior Chart for Document Delivery Requests

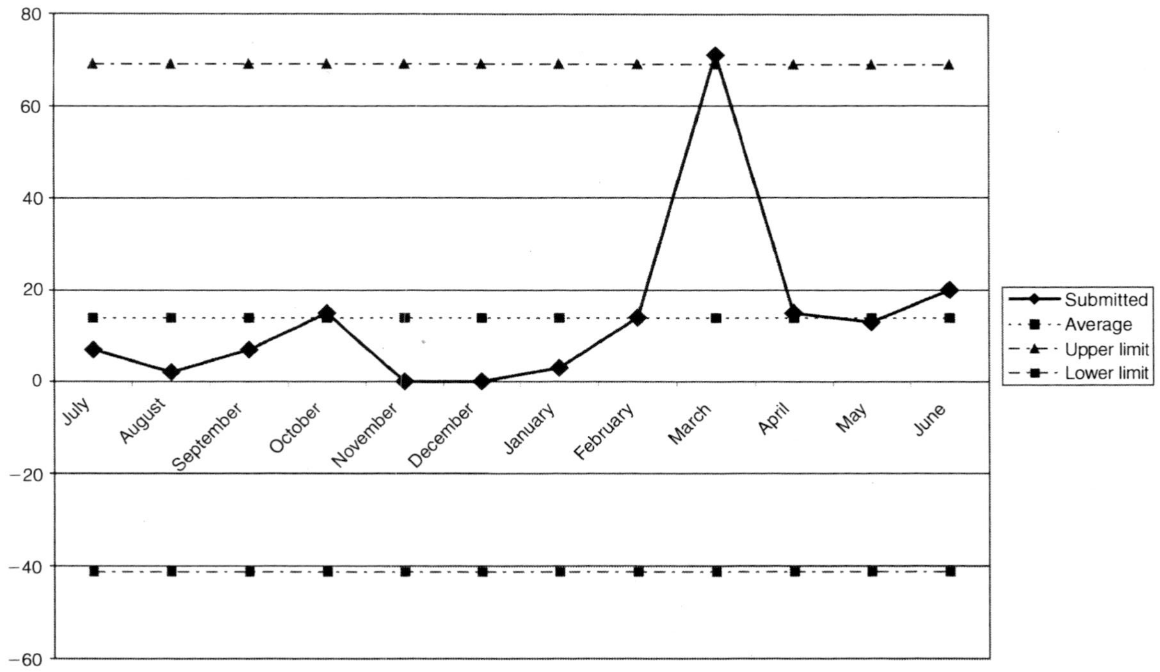

Legend:
- Submitted
- Average
- Upper limit
- Lower limit

users based on whether we own the material and whether the student qualifies for document delivery. We have eliminated the possibility of patron errors and eliminated one cause for special variation.

PLANS FOR A MONTHLY SURVEY AT SUNY OSWEGO

As part of implementing a continuous improvement approach to quality service for distance learners, we identified a need for a feasible measurement that could be repeated monthly, and could include both quantitative and qualitative components. We needed a qualitative, open-ended item that could help us understand the experiences of our distance learners from their points of view. We needed one to three items with numerical rating responses that could allow us to track our learners' needs and satisfaction over time. Above all, we needed something that could be sustained over time.

Initial needs assessment for distance learners was based on largely demographic observations and assumptions, and on input from faculty and administrators. We have attempted to meet the needs identified in this initial assessment, but do not as yet have information on the impact of our improvements, and do not have ready access to new or emerging needs. The evaluation questions for this survey included:

- To what extent do distance learners need library and information resources and services?
- How do distance learners rate the services of Penfield Library, and how do those ratings change over time?
- What do distance learners have to say about their experiences with library and information resources and services? What themes seem to be prominent, what needs remain unmet, and what improvements seem to be suggested in what they have to say?

SURVEY INSTRUMENT

In order to encourage wide participation in a monthly survey we saw a need for the questionnaire to be brief and easy to complete. We also saw a need to generate a combination of quantitative and qualitative data. The quantitative data will produce a process behavior chart to easily analyze changes over time. The qualitative data will be used to identify needs, to explore possible improvements, to explain the quantitative data responses more fully, and to identify need for additional items for future surveys. The questionnaire is appended.

The items for the questionnaire are being tested as a part of the end-of-semester course evaluation surveys. The results of this test will be available on the conference Web site.

The first part will provide data on the categories of information sources students view they are required to use as part of a course. The categories are arranged progressively by the complexity of independent searching and learning processes that may be involved. Initially, analysis of these data will be descriptive. With experience we should be able to develop a weighting scheme and an index number that will indicate the relative difficulty or complexity of the information use challenges that students face. Variation and change over time in this index will tell us about changes in the needs of students for library and information resources.

The second part will provide satisfaction scale responses from 1 to 6, plus a categorical marker for "did not use." The frequencies, averages, and variances of the responses should give us general ideas about distance learners' satisfaction with Penfield Library services. Laid out over time, these data will indicate trends and the impacts of improvements.

The third part is designed to invite open-ended statements about specific experiences with library and information systems.

DATA COLLECTION

A Web-based form will be set up with the responses automatically formatted for import into database systems. Two or three selected courses of distance learners will be invited to complete the form each month. These invitations will be extended through the course instructors, but no data will be collected that identify the course, instructor, or student. We will also invite users of the document delivery service to complete the form, and give a link to the form from the distance learners' library Web site.

ANALYSIS

On a monthly basis the quantitative data will be compiled. The average frequencies, or eventually the index, of the first part, and the averages of the second part responses will be entered into run charts so that changes over time will be evident. The use of averages will serve to normalize the varied numbers of responses. Statistical control limits will be calculated and entered on the charts as well. These limits will help indicate the likely sources for rises and falls in the responses, and will indicate progress if the span of the limits is reduced and the averages increase.

At the same time, the qualitative data will be analyzed to identify and track themes in the stories, to identify ideas for improvements, and to generate questions for additional research. The open-ended responses will be read and analyzed in regard to pre-established and emerging categories, with an interest in successful information literacy experiences but especially with an eye to how we can remove barriers that our learners report.

The results of the analysis will be included in annual reports on library services for distance learners. The process control charts will be made available to library staff, and possibly to distance faculty and students.

DISCUSSION

The conference presentation will report results to date. In addition, it will report how the results are used to document successes and failures, and most importantly, to identify ways to improve services. The presentation will also consider how this approach to assessment may be used in other distance learning settings, or in mixed onsite/distance learning services.

REFERENCES

Association of Research Libraries. (2006). *LibQual+: Charting library service quality*. Retrieved February 28, 2006, from http://www.libqual.org.
Deming, W. E. (1982). *Out of the crisis*. Cambridge, MA: Massachusetts Institute of Technology.
Laughlin, S., Shockley, D. S., & Wilson, R. (2003). *The library's continuous improvement fieldbook: 29 ready-to-use tools*. Chicago: American Library Association.

doi:10.1300/J111v45n03_05

APPENDIX

Survey Questionnaire for Distance Learners

Your need for library and information resources: Mark all statements that describe information use **required** by your online course.

To complete work for my course, I need to:

Look information up on the Web or in books	_Yes _No _I don't know
Read one or more articles posted or linked in the course or on electronic reserve	_Yes _No _I don't know
Select at least one article or book from a list or on my own and review or critique it in some way	_Yes _No _I don't know
Locate and read several sources on a topic of my choosing and write a paper or other presentation on what I learned	_Yes _No _I don't know

Other information need–Please specify

Your rating of library and information resources: Mark one response for each statement.

Penfield Library Web site and online resources are helpful and convenient to use.

Strongly Disagree	Disagree	Slightly Disagree	Slightly Agree	Agree	Strongly Agree	Never Used It

Telephone and e-mail reference assistance are helpful and convenient to use.

Strongly Disagree	Disagree	Slightly Disagree	Slightly Agree	Agree	Strongly Agree	Never Used It

Book Delivery and Article Delivery services are helpful and convenient to use.

Strongly Disagree	Disagree	Slightly Disagree	Slightly Agree	Agree	Strongly Agree	Never Used It

Your story or comments about using library and information resources for your course: How have libraries or online information systems helped you in completing your coursework or made your work more difficult?

Follow up: Provide your phone number or e-mail address if you desire an answer to a question or problem concerning library and information resources:

Distance Learning Librarianship Research Over Time: Changes and the Core Literature

Beth A. Reiten

Oklahoma State University

Jack Fritts

Benedictine University

SUMMARY. Central Michigan University has hosted 11 Off-Campus Library Services Conferences since 1982. This paper studies the proceedings of the 11 conferences to identify patterns of research. The authors were interested in determining how the field of distance learning library services has changed over that 22 year period as evidenced by the topics presented and the types of papers included in the proceedings. The authors analyzed the contributed papers and assigned those papers to specific subject tracks. The authors also considered the sources used by the presenters in order to identify works that may be considered seminal in this field. Distance learning librarianship is a field that has grown and matured, but there has been little research to date into the core literature of the field. This paper attempts to identify some of those core works through an analysis of the citations used in these sets of proceedings. doi:10.1300/J111v45n03_06

KEYWORDS. Core literature, research, Off-Campus Library Services Conference, distance learning librarianship scholarship

---

[Haworth co-indexing entry note]: "Distance Learning Librarianship Research Over Time: Changes and the Core Literature." Reiten, Beth A., and Jack Fritts. Co-published simultaneously in *Journal of Library Administration* (The Haworth Information Press, an imprint of The Haworth Press, Inc.) Vol. 45, No. 3/4, 2006, pp. 397-410; and: *The Twelfth Off-Campus Library Services Conference Proceedings* (ed: Julie A. Garrison) The Haworth Information Press, an imprint of The Haworth Press, Inc., 2006, pp. 397-410.

Available online at http://jla.haworthpress.com
doi:10.1300/J111v45n03_06

INTRODUCTION

Since the first Off-Campus Library Services (OCLS) Conference in 1982, librarians involved in providing service to distant students have shared their successes and issues through this venue. In that time over 500 librarians have presented papers and shared stories about their work. The authors of this paper wanted to identify any changes in the literature of distance learning librarianship over that time period. The authors took a two-part approach to this project. The table of contents of each set of proceedings was analyzed and the submitted papers were classified into specific categories. At the same time, the citation lists for each paper were entered into a database for analysis. The intent of this approach was to identify those works cited multiple times by conference presenters, with the intent of identifying the basic underpinning literature of distance learning librarianship.

Libraries have been providing service to distant patrons much longer than there have been Off-Campus Library Services Conferences. The librarians involved in providing distant support have frequently been required to offer such support as an adjunct to other full-time responsibilities. In the past twenty-five years the growth in institutional offerings to remote students has driven an upsurge in library support for those programs. The conferences sponsored by Central Michigan University have offered practitioners an opportunity and an outlet to share their work, their concerns, and their expectations. These conferences began in 1982 and have continued to be a regular feature on the distance learning landscape ever since. As of 2004, participants have gathered 11 times to share research, but more importantly, to share conversation.

The expectation of the researchers at the beginning of this project was that the study would reveal that the underlying content of submitted presentations would not show any major change over the 22 year span, but that there would be evident change in the technology used. In general, distance learning librarians are strongly driven to serve their populations to the best of their abilities. In some ways this is no different than the service orientation of any librarian, but it seems to be more visibly expressed by distance learning librarians. In some ways, this may reflect the different environment many distance learning librarians inhabit. Until recently, distance learning was frequently separate from the mainstream of library service. Many distance learning librarians worked almost as solo librarians, divorced from their colleagues, even within an institution. In some instances, the distance learning component was not a part of the institution's library structure, but was instead attached to an extension or an adult/continuing education operation. The authors believe that this isolation, whether real or perceived, has led to the emergence of distance learning librarianship as a distinct area of librarianship.

In more recent times, there has been a fundamental shift in focus as more institutions begin moving toward nontraditional, distant, and even electronic delivery of programs. Distance learning librarians are now finding themselves more part of the mainstream than ever before, and they are leading the rest of the library into their territory. However, that same service orientation still shows through, and distance learning librarians continue to serve their populations with the same intensity, regardless of delivery method.

SUBJECT TRACKS

The first OCLS Conference in 1982 identified six program tracks. The tenth conference used a different set of 10 track designations. The authors used an amalgam of the two to arrive at a consistent set of designations for classifying the papers presented at the 11 OCLS conferences. The track descriptors used at the first conference were:

- Administration and Planning
- Bibliographic Instruction
- Document Delivery
- Model Programs
- Program Evaluation
- Uses of Technology

The Tenth Conference used a more granular list of tracks:

- Administration–Cooperative Efforts
- Administration–Program Development
- Administration–Standards
- Needs Assessment–Program, Students, Librarian
- On-line Systems and Services
- Program Support Services–Electronic Reserves
- Program Support Services–Document Delivery
- Program Support Services–Interlibrary Loan

- Reference Services
- Student Instruction

The authors decided to revise some of the category designations to better reflect the shift in paper topics over time. One additional category, *Distance Librarianship Education*, was added to recognize a small number of papers presented over the course of the 11 conferences that did not fit into the primary seven categories. In general these papers represented research or studies of educational programs in library science offered to remote students or programs relating to distance learning librarianship offered by library schools. For the purposes of this paper, the track designations are:

- Administration and Planning
- Bibliographic Instruction
- Distance Librarianship Education
- Model Programs
- Program Evaluation
- Program Support Services
- Reference Services
- Uses of Technology

SUBJECT TRACK ANALYSIS

At the first conference, 25 titles were listed in the table of contents, one of which was a keynote address (Lessin, 1986). The keynote was not included in the program tracks listing and was not counted as part of this paper's material. The 24 paper presentations were divided among the six original tracks. These have been mapped to the revised list as follows:

Track	# of Papers	% of Presentations
Administration and Planning	4	16.67%
Bibliographic Instruction	3	12.50%
Distance Librarianship Education	0	0.00%
Model Programs	7	29.17%
Program Evaluation	4	16.67%
Program Support Services	2	8.33%
Reference Services	0	0.00%
Uses of Technology	4	16.67%

The second conference showcased 23 presentations (Lessin, 1986). The two most popular topics at this conference were *Model Programs* and *Program Evaluation*, with seven papers each.

Track	# of Papers	% of Presentations
Administration and Planning	3	13.04%
Bibliographic Instruction	0	0.00%
Distance Librarianship Education	1	4.35%
Model Programs	7	30.43%
Program Evaluation	7	30.43%
Program Support Services	2	8.70%
Reference Services	0	0.00%
Uses of Technology	3	13.04%

There were 30 presentations at the third conference (Lessin, 1987). The largest number of papers fell into the *Model Programs* category.

Track	# of Papers	% of Presentations
Administration and Planning	5	16.67%
Bibliographic Instruction	0	0.00%
Distance Librarianship Education	0	0.00%
Model Programs	11	36.67%
Program Evaluation	3	10.00%
Program Support Services	6	20.00%
Reference Services	0	0.00%
Uses of Technology	5	16.67%

The fourth conference reflected the growing influence of distance learning library services. At this conference there were 32 presentations (Lessin, 1988). As with the third conference, *Model Programs* was again the largest category.

Track	# of Papers	% of Presentations
Administration and Planning	9	28.13%
Bibliographic Instruction	3	9.38%
Distance Librarianship Education	0	0.00%
Model Programs	12	37.50%
Program Evaluation	1	3.13%
Program Support Services	3	9.38%
Reference Services	0	0.00%
Uses of Technology	4	12.50%

The fifth conference was the second largest of the 11 in terms of papers presented. In total, 41 papers were presented at this conference (Jacob, 1991). The largest category of presentations at this conference was *Administration and Planning*.

Track	# of Papers	% of Presentations
Administration and Planning	14	34.15%
Bibliographic Instruction	3	7.32%
Distance Librarianship Education	2	4.88%
Model Programs	6	14.63%
Program Evaluation	8	19.51%
Program Support Services	1	2.44%
Reference Services	0	0.00%
Uses of Technology	7	17.07%

The 30 papers presented at the sixth conference fell mainly into four areas, with *Administration and Planning* holding the largest number, followed by *Uses of Technology* (Jacob, 1993).

Track	# of Papers	% of Presentations
Administration and Planning	11	36.67%
Bibliographic Instruction	1	3.33%
Distance Librarianship Education	0	0.00%
Model Programs	5	16.67%
Program Evaluation	5	16.67%
Program Support Services	0	0.00%
Reference Services	0	0.00%
Uses of Technology	8	26.67%

The papers presented seemed to be most evenly spread across the categories at the seventh conference. A total of 37 papers were offered (Jacob, 1995).

Track	# of Papers	% of Presentations
Administration and Planning	8	21.62%
Bibliographic Instruction	6	16.22%
Distance Librarianship Education	0	0.00%
Model Programs	9	24.32%
Program Evaluation	5	13.51%
Program Support Services	2	5.41%
Reference Services	2	5.41%
Uses of Technology	5	13.51%

The number of accepted papers dropped in the eighth conference. Nearly half of the 27 papers presented dealt with *Uses of Technology* (Thomas & Jones, 1998).

Track	# of Papers	% of Presentations
Administration and Planning	5	18.52%
Bibliographic Instruction	0	0.00%
Distance Librarianship Education	0	0.00%
Model Programs	7	25.93%
Program Evaluation	3	11.11%
Program Support Services	0	0.00%
Reference Services	0	0.00%
Uses of Technology	12	44.44%

The ninth conference's 34 papers continued the trend for *Administration and Planning* and *Uses of Technology* to be the most active categories (Thomas, 2000).

Track	# of Papers	% of Presentations
Administration and Planning	9	26.47%
Bibliographic Instruction	0	0.00%
Distance Librarianship Education	1	2.94%
Model Programs	3	8.82%
Program Evaluation	3	8.82%
Program Support Services	3	8.82%
Reference Services	1	2.94%
Uses of Technology	14	41.18%

With 44 presented papers, the tenth conference was the largest of the 11. The *Administration and Planning* and *Uses of Technology* tracks represented 35 of the papers (Mahoney, 2002).

Track	# of Papers	% of Presentations
Administration and Planning	18	40.91%
Bibliographic Instruction	4	9.09%
Distance Librarianship Education	0	0.00%
Model Programs	1	2.27%
Program Evaluation	1	2.27%
Program Support Services	3	6.82%
Reference Services	0	0.00%
Uses of Technology	17	38.64%

There were 36 papers presented at the eleventh conference, and again the majority fell into the *Administration and Planning* and *Uses of Technology* categories (Mahoney, 2004).

Track	# of Papers	% of Presentations
Administration and Planning	13	36.11%
Bibliographic Instruction	1	2.78%
Distance Librarianship Education	1	2.78%
Model Programs	2	5.56%
Program Evaluation	2	5.56%
Program Support Services	4	11.11%
Reference Services	0	0.00%
Uses of Technology	13	36.11%

The 11 conferences offered a total of 358 papers. The most represented category over the 22 year span was *Administration and Planning*. *Uses of Technology* was a close second, with *Model Programs* showing the third largest total.

Track	# of Papers	% of Presentations
Administration and Planning	99	27.65%
Bibliographic Instruction	21	5.87%
Distance Librarianship Education	5	1.40%
Model Programs	70	19.55%
Program Evaluation	42	11.73%
Program Support Services	26	7.26%
Reference Services	3	0.84%
Uses of Technology	92	25.70%

With the exception of *Distance Librarianship Education*, which the authors added when the initial analysis showed the need for another category, the smallest category was *Reference Services*. The authors feel that this category had so few papers listed because most of the papers dealing with providing reference support to distant students were more focused on the delivery (technology) aspect than on the actual reference practices themselves. To a lesser degree, this also applies to the *Bibliographic Instruction* category, since many papers about bibliographic instruction dealt with the engine rather than the content to be delivered.

Administration and Planning accounted for 27.65% of the presentations offered. Within this category presenters covered a range of topics from the most basic 'starting a program on a shoestring' through papers on accreditation and licensure. Along the way, these presenters offered guidance and ideas that have been reviewed, discussed, dissected, adopted, and adapted by other practitioners. *Uses of Technology* was the second largest category. This logically follows the notion that distance learning librarians will be alert for new ways to utilize technologies to better enable the delivery of their content to their student populations.

Two additional questions the authors hoped to address had to do with the technological base for distance learning librarianship. As mentioned earlier, the apparent driving force behind distance learning librarianship is an intense service orientation. Distance learning librarians have been perceived as being leaders in technology because of their willingness to adopt new tools as they become available and to adapt those tools to their specific needs. This early adopter role is driven by the desire to provide the highest possible level of service and support to remote students. As the available technological tools have evolved, so have the delivery methods used in distance learning services. The base content does not seem to have changed tremendously over time, although there are new slants on content, such as the current focus on information literacy. Most of the papers included in these proceedings speak to the need to provide a high level of support by using the best available technological tools to deliver that support. In some ways, distance learning librarians are still mainly focused on how to teach their students the basics of research and online scholarship, even if they are doing so with state of the art media tools rather than the postal service or e-mail delivery. Whether a paper addresses delivering content via radio or streaming video, the content continues to take precedence over the method.

CORE LITERATURE

In addition to reviewing the papers from the 11 OCLS conferences to identify the patterns of research over the past 22 years, the authors reviewed the sources cited in these papers. While distance learning librarianship has been around for many years, research within the field has really grown and matured within the past two decades. In this time, there do not appear to have been any systematic attempts to identify a distance learning librarianship core literature. By analyzing the 2,914 individual citations from the 358 OCLS conference papers, the authors attempt to address this lack.

The initial step in this analysis was to identify items cited multiple times. There were 2,330 unique items, with 286 items being cited multiple times (13.99%) and 2,044 items being cited once. The multiple citations were then grouped by number of times cited and marked with the numbers of the conference in which they were cited. Unsurprisingly, over half of these items were cited twice with the number of items dropping as the number of cites increased. The authors were surprised to discover some items were cited as many as 26 times.

Times Cited	Number of Items
2	154
3	60
4	33
5	22
6	6
8	4
9	1
12	2
19	1
20	1
25	1
26	1

A preliminary scan through the multiple citations seemed to indicate the need for a revision to the authors' initial idea of creating a single core literature. Instead, three groupings suggested themselves:

- a **core literature** where the items included have spanned a substantial time period up through the near-present;
- a **historical core** where the items included were clearly seminal during the early conferences but have not been cited in the near-present;
- and a **potential core** where the items are too new to be included in the core with confidence, although they may become part of the core literature over time.

With these three groupings in mind, each set of citations was then evaluated individually for inclusion or exclusion. The authors utilized slightly different criteria for each set as required with a small handful of overarching criteria. Current news sources (i.e., *The Chronicle of Higher Education*) were not included, as they are reporting rather than research. General library topics (i.e., university-level library budgets) and non-library related topics (i.e., survey creation) were also excluded to provide a more focused distance learning librarianship literature.

To be included in the core literature, items cited twice must have been cited in two different conferences with the most recent citation being in the ninth through the eleventh conferences (2000-2004). To be included in the potential core, both citations must appear in the ninth through the eleventh conferences, with two citations in the same conference being acceptable. No items with two citations appear in the historical core as the authors did not feel that two citations were significant enough for inclusion.

Items with three citations were included in the core literature if they were cited in any three conferences with the latest appearance being in the seventh through eleventh conferences (1995-2004) or if they were cited twice in one conference with the latest citation occurring in the ninth through the eleventh conferences (2000-2004). If all three citations came within the ninth through eleventh conferences, the item was placed in the potential core. To appear in the historical core, the citations must be in any three conferences with the latest being no more recent than the sixth conference (1993).

If the items cited four times were cited three times in the same conference and the most recent citation was in the eighth conference (1998) or before, they were not included in the core literature. If all four citations occurred in the ninth through eleventh conferences (2000-2004), the item was placed in the potential core. Items cited in a minimum of two conferences where the most recent citation was no more recent than the sixth conference (1993) were included in the historical core.

Items cited five times where four of those citations occurred in the same conference and the most recent citation was in the eighth conference (1998) or before were not included in the core literature. The item was placed in the potential core if all five citations appeared in the ninth through eleventh conferences (2000-2004). If none of the citations were any more recent than the sixth conference (1993), the item was placed in the historical core.

With six citations, items were included in the core literature unless they were cited five times in the same conference with the most recent citation being in the eighth conference (1998) or before. If all six citations occurred in the ninth through eleventh conferences (2000-2004), the item was placed in the potential core. They were placed in the historical core if the most recent citation was from the sixth conference (1993) or prior.

If an item was cited eight or more times, it was automatically included in the core literature, unless all citations were from the ninth through eleventh conferences (2000-2004), in which case it was placed into the potential core, or if the most recent citation was from the sixth conference (1993) or prior. If this was the case, it was placed in the historical core.

By applying these criteria, the authors were able to create the listings of the core literature (78 references), the historical core (23 references), and the potential core (62 references). These bibliographies may be found at http://e-archive.library.okstate.edu/ocls. The analysis of the 2,914 citations pointed to the importance of two groups of items that appear in various places within the three bibliographies: the Off-Campus Library Services Conference Proceedings and various countries' guidelines for distance learning library support. While individual items within these groups were cited in vastly differing numbers, their importance as a whole was notable. Because of this, the authors have created two additional bibliographies, one for each of these two vital groups of references. These may also be found at the above URL.

The 358 papers from the 11 OCLS conference proceedings were presented by a total of 525 persons. Ninety-four persons in this group have presented at multiple conferences. Of those who presented at multiple conferences, eight offered two papers at a single conference. Two of this group of eight have presented two papers at each of two conferences. In addition to the 94 multiple conference presenters, four individuals offered two papers at the single conference where they presented.

Eleven individuals have presented at four or more conferences since the inception of the OCLS conference, while an additional two have presented four or more papers, one over two conferences and the other over three conferences.

The first table shows those individuals who have presented at four or more conferences:

Presenter	Presented Conferences
Adams, Kate F.	5, 8, 9, 10, 11
Barsun, Rita	8, 9, 10, 11
Bean, Rick	5, 6, 7, 8
Cassner, Mary	8, 9, 10, 11
Fritts, Jack	5, 6, 7, 8, 9, 11
Gilmer, Lois	4, 7, 8, 9
Morrison, Rob	5, 7, 9, 11
Moulden, Carol M.	4, 5, 6, 7
Ruddy, Sr. Margaret	3, 4, 6, 7, 8
Slade, Alexander	2, 3, 4, 5, 6, 8
Witucke, Virginia	4, 5, 6, 7

The second table shows those individuals who have presented four or more papers:

Presenter	Papers by Conference
Adams, Kate F.	5, 8, 9, 10, 11
Barsun, Rita	8, 9, 10, 11
Bean, Rick	5, 6, 7, 8
Cassner, Mary	8, 9, 10, 11
Fritts, Jack	5, 6, 7, 8, 9, 11
Gilmer, Lois	4, 7, 8, 9
Morrison, Rob	5, 7, 9, 11
Moulden, Carol M.	4, 5, 6, 7
Pival, Paul R.	10 (2x), 11 (2x)
Ruddy, Sr. Margaret	3, 4, 6, 7, 8
Slade, Alexander	2, 3 (2x), 4, 5, 6, 8
Tuñón, Johanna	9 (2x), 10 (2x), 11
Witucke, Virginia	4, 5, 6, 7

In addition to being frequent presenters, 10 of these individuals have also contributed 19 papers to one or more of the three core literature lists. They have contributed eight papers to the core literature, nine to the potential core, and two to the historical core. It is interesting to note how many of these sources were presented at an OCLS conference: three from the core literature, seven from the potential core, and one from the historical core.

The authors are aware that by limiting their analysis to the papers presented at the 11 OCLS conferences, they have selected only a subset of the distance learning library scholarship that is available. While this may have introduced some bias in the results, the authors felt that the 22-year span of the conference and the international scope of the presenters provided a sample representative of the scholarship in the field of distance learning librarianship as a whole.

These lists are not intended to be static; the authors welcome feedback from other practitioners in the field regarding inclusion and exclusion of references. In addition, the authors intend to revisit these analyses after each Off-Campus Library Services Conference to update the data and to continue to report on growth and changes in the literature of distance learning librarianship. As more time and conferences pass, references may move from the potential core to the core literature or from the core literature to the historical core. These moves will be based upon the revision of the criteria for reference placement that will occur after each conference. The authors will also review and revise the categories assigned to paper presentations in order to continue tracking future developments in distance learning librarianship research. Reviewing the proceedings of each succeeding Off-Campus Library Services Conference will enhance an awareness of the changes in focus in the field of distance learning librarianship.

REFERENCES

Conference Program: The Tenth Off-Campus Library Services Conference, Cincinnati, Ohio, (2002). Mt. Pleasant, MI: Central Michigan University.

Jacob, C. J. (1991). *The Fifth Off-Campus Library Services Conference Proceedings: Albuquerque, New Mexico, October 30-November 1, 1991.* Mt. Pleasant, MI: Central Michigan University Press.

Jacob, C. J. (Ed.). (1993). *The Sixth Off-Campus Library Services Conference Proceedings: Kansas City, Missouri, October 6-8, 1993.* Mt. Pleasant, MI: Central Michigan University Press.

Jacob, C. J. (Ed.). (1995). *The Seventh Off-Campus Library Services Conference Proceedings: San Diego, California, October 25 -27, 1995.* Mt. Pleasant, MI: Central Michigan University Press.

Lessin, B. M. (Ed.). (1983). *The Off-Campus Library Services Conference Proceedings: St. Louis, Missouri, October 14-15, 1982.* Mt. Pleasant, MI: Central Michigan University Press.

Lessin, B. M. (Ed.). (1986). *The Off-Campus Library Services Conference Proceedings: Knoxville, Tennessee, April 18-19, 1985.* Mt. Pleasant, MI: Central Michigan University Press.

Lessin, B. M. (Ed.). (1987). *The Off-Campus Library Services Conference Proceedings: Reno, Nevada, October 23-24, 1986.* Mt. Pleasant, MI: Central Michigan University Press.

Lessin, B. M. (Ed.). (1988). *The Off-Campus Library Services Conference Proceedings: Charleston, South Carolina, October 20-21, 1988.* Mt. Pleasant, MI: Central Michigan University Press.

Mahoney, P. B. (Ed.). (2002). *The Tenth Off-Campus Library Services Conference Proceedings: Cincinnati, Ohio, April 17-19, 2002.* Mt. Pleasant, MI: Central Michigan University Press.

Mahoney, P. B. (Ed.). (2004). *The Eleventh Off-Campus Library Services Conference Proceedings: Scottsdale, Arizona, May 5-7, 2004.* Mt. Pleasant, MI: Central Michigan University Press.

Thomas, P. S. (Ed.). (2000). *The Ninth Off-Campus Library Services Conference Proceedings: Portland, Oregon, April 26-28, 2000.* Mt. Pleasant, MI: Central Michigan University Press.

Thomas, P. S., & Jones, M. (Eds.). (1998). *The Eighth Off-Campus Library Services Conference Proceedings: Providence, Rhode Island, April 22-24, 1998.* Mt. Pleasant, MI: Central Michigan University Press.

doi:10.1300/J111v45n03_06

On the Road Again: Taking Bibliographic Instruction Off-Campus

Debbi Richard

Dallas Baptist University

SUMMARY. Literature in the field of distance learning librarianship tends to focus on the provision of asynchronous, Web-based bibliographic instruction and reference services. Experience has shown this author, however, that off-campus students attending classes at extension or satellite campuses appreciate, and benefit from, personal interaction with a librarian. This paper describes the author's efforts, some more successful than others, to increase her personal contacts with distance learners in order to more fully realize her department's philosophy of "equivalent access/superior service." doi:10.1300/J111v45n03_07

KEYWORDS. Reference service, bibliographic instruction, satellite campuses, extension sites, public relations, outreach services

INTRODUCTION

A librarian sits quietly at a table, staring at a computer screen. A young man approaches and asks, "Are you the librarian?" At her nod of affirmation, he continues: "I have a research project due in three weeks,

[Haworth co-indexing entry note]: "On the Road Again: Taking Bibliographic Instruction Off-Campus." Richard, Debbi. Co-published simultaneously in *Journal of Library Administration* (The Haworth Information Press, an imprint of The Haworth Press, Inc.) Vol. 45, No. 3/4, 2006, pp. 411-425; and: *The Twelfth Off-Campus Library Services Conference Proceedings* (ed: Julie A. Garrison) The Haworth Information Press, an imprint of The Haworth Press, Inc., 2006, pp. 411-425.

Available online at http://jla.haworthpress.com
doi:10.1300/J111v45n03_07

and my professor says we have to have scholarly articles to support our thesis. Can you help me?" The librarian invites him to sit with her so she can show him where to begin his search. A brief interview ensues while the librarian ascertains the particulars of the student's topic and the project perimeters. While engaged in this conversation, the two are interrupted by a third student, who enthusiastically reports that, thanks to the librarian's assistance, she earned an "A" on her recent research project. The librarian responds with delight and encouragement, and, once the student has gone, continues with the reference consultation.

Librarians will recognize this interaction as a typical scene in an academic library. However, in this case, the setting is a break room in a north Dallas office complex, where the host institution, Dallas Baptist University, holds evening classes for adult students who live or work too far from the main campus for convenient access. Although this satellite campus has no designated area for library services or research, scenes like the one described above happen on a regular basis, usually three to four times a month.

The philosophy of the Distance Learning Library Services department at Dallas Baptist University is "equivalent access/superior service." The department was created in August, 2000, to meet the needs of a growing community of distance learners enrolled in DBU's online courses and in classes held away from the campus in locations such as businesses, churches, and office parks. Initial efforts in providing distance library services focused on the usual array of online databases and tutorials, Web pages, book and article delivery services, and cooperative lending agreements. In 2003, the librarians involved with distance learners began to realize that, in order to more nearly approximate the "equivalent access," at least for students in the Dallas-Fort Worth metroplex, they would need to find ways to establish "face time" with those students. The steps taken, and the results of those efforts, form the subjects of this paper.

BACKGROUND

Dallas Baptist University is a private institution of higher education committed to providing a traditional, liberal arts education in a Christian environment. Total enrollment in fall 2005 was 4,988, with approximately 1,000 students living on the campus. DBU offers 56 undergraduate majors and 11 graduate programs, including doctorates in leadership and education. In the mid-1980s, DBU began offering classes in various north Dallas locations for the convenience of adult commuter students. The popularity of these offerings led to the decision to centralize course offerings in the north Dallas area, and to offer "one stop" service for admissions, financial aid, and advising for students living in the prosperous and growing areas of the north Dallas suburbs–Richardson, Plano, Garland, Carrollton, and Frisco. In 2001, DBU-North opened in Carrollton, with three classrooms and two full time staff members. The facilities were expanded in 2003 to encompass eight classrooms, a break room with drink and snack machines, two lounge/study areas, and office space for six full-time staff. The Carrollton campus is approximately 30 miles from the main campus. The overwhelming success of this venture has resulted in two further developments: the opening in August 2005 of a new satellite campus in Colleyville, northwest of Fort Worth, and the relocation of DBU-North to a new, larger facility in Frisco, known as the Frisco Regional Academic Center, in January 2006. Enrollment at DBU-North for fall 2005 was 602; the opening enrollment at DBU-Colleyville was 114.

Students attending both satellite campuses are working adults who have decided to return to school, either to complete an education that was interrupted by life events in the past, or to pursue an undergraduate or graduate degree that may lead to career advancement. Consequently, the degrees offered at these sites are geared toward the needs of business professionals: business administration, management, communication, and psychology. In addition, master's degrees in education and school counseling meet the needs of area teachers seeking professional advancement. In most cases, these adult students are returning to an academic world totally different from the one they left years ago. Although they may possess advanced computing skills, they remain largely unaware of the resources available to them through their academic library. If they were ever required to write research papers in the past, they have since forgotten any basic research skills they may have possessed at one time. Just like their younger counterparts on the main campus, these students tend to view the prospect of a research project with a sometimes debilitating mixture of alarm, panic, and dread (Mellon, 1988). Additional pressure is felt by some adults whose computer skills may be limited (Jiao & Onwuegbuzie, 2004), or by those whose financial situations limit their Internet access to either slow dial-up connections at home, or solely to computer stations at their workplace. Distance learners' sensations of library anxiety are heightened by their perceptions of disconnectedness from the main body of the institution (Veal, 2002).

Mellon found that her students' feelings of library anxiety dropped significantly when they experienced personal contact and interaction with a librarian (1988). Many distance librarians report that service to an extension site or satellite campus is a component of their job descriptions. Yet the literature aimed at distance learning librarians routinely focuses on technological solutions to the problems of delivering adequate distance library service. Several possible reasons exist for the preponderance of articles and presentations dealing with Web-based, asynchronous distance library services:

1. many institutions' online education programs are their only source of distance learners;
2. the delivery of online course content is relatively new and exciting, and exists in an almost constant state of change and adaptation; and,
3. in some cases, the universities' satellite campuses are so far from the main campus that travel expenses are prohibitive, necessitating other arrangements, such as cooperative agreements with library affiliates.

An examination of the proceedings from the last four Off-Campus Library Services Conferences revealed that only 7.8% of the papers presented dealt directly with the topic of providing face-to-face library service to distance learners.

The percentage of university systems facing the challenges of providing services to remote, non-online patrons may indeed be relatively small. If the situation in the Dallas-Fort Worth metropolitan area is any indication of national trends, then the situation at DBU may be fairly unique. A December 2005 investigation of academic institutions in the DFW area resulted in the following data:

- 33 institutions of higher education in the DFW metroplex
- 6 technical or medical schools
- 8 institutions too small for comparison (less that 500 enrollment)
- 8 institutions with no distance education except online
- 8 institutions with branch system (each location has a fully staffed library)
- 3 institutions with extension or satellite campuses

The three institutions remaining for comparison are Southern Methodist University, the University of Texas at Arlington, and the subject of this paper, Dallas Baptist University.

Southern Methodist University (SMU) maintains an extension site for graduate programs in the north Plano area. Known as SMU-in-Legacy, this facility features a resource room which is supplied and maintained under the aegis of the campus library. The room contains six computers and two printers, allowing students a convenient space for accessing the online resources provided by the university's library system. SMU's distance librarian explained in a telephone interview that he usually visits the site once a month for maintenance purposes, but he rarely works with Legacy students in person. He tries to visit classes at the beginning of each semester to hand out brochures and other literature, and encourages students to contact him via phone, e-mail, or Web-based chat service for reference assistance (B. Jenkins, personal communication, December 9, 2005). According to Jenkins, most of these graduate students are already competent researchers and need very little help with their projects. When the center first opened in 1997, Jenkins offered bibliographic instruction sessions on a volunteer basis. However, the sessions were poorly attended (only two students took advantage of the service), and the decision was made to discontinue this service.

The University of Texas at Arlington opened UTA-Fort Worth in 2001, offering graduate degree programs for working adults. This site includes a library space containing three computers and a printer. General reference librarian for UTA's main campus library, S. Beckett, is tasked with the supervision of the UTA-FW library. Beckett explained to the author via phone interview that librarians man the UTA-FW library on a rotating basis for 12 hours per week. This service is divided into four-hour increments, usually two afternoons and one Saturday morning each week. The librarian on duty provides research assistance and guidance in using the online resources provided by the university. Class-based bibliographic instruction is not offered (personal communication, December 12, 2005).

Both of the situations described above differ from Dallas Baptist University in at least two significant areas. First, the satellite campuses mentioned above exist to provide graduate programs only. In both cases, the librarians interviewed emphasized the competence of graduate students to conduct research on their own, without assistance from library professionals. However, it has not been this author's experience at DBU. Many graduate students received their undergraduate degrees several years ago, and are now returning for graduate work after establishing their families and careers. The average age of adult students attending DBU-North and DBU-Colleyville is 32. That statistic implies an absence from academia of ten years or more. The fast pace of technological change, especially in regard to library services, would necessitate at minimum a new orientation to online library technology for these students in order to optimize their current educational experience.

Another point of difference exists in the facilities provided at these extension sites. While SMU-in-Legacy and UTA-FW have dedicated library areas, DBU's satellite campuses lack any space set aside specifically for library service. While the librarians would prefer to have a space to call their own at these campus locations, the decision was made several years ago that lack of facilities would not equal lack of service. Hence the description which opened this paper, of the librarian providing reference services in the break room of the DBU-North campus. While this situation is not optimal, there have been some benefits accruing from these circumstances, including greater visibility for the librarian, as will be explained below.

The following discussion will highlight some of the activities initiated by DBU's distance learning librarian and her staff to establish personal contact and collegial professional relationships with the community of distance students, professors, and administrators involved in off-campus education under the auspices of Dallas Baptist University. The ideas and initiatives presented were the product of collaboration between the Director of Libraries, Peggy Martin, the University Provost, Dr. Gail Linam, the Assistant to the Distance Learning Librarian, Sharon Dehnel, and the author of this paper, Distance Learning Librarian, Debbi Richard. The activities described can be loosely organized into three initiatives: public relations, instructional services, and reference services. The nature of this narrative is anecdotal rather than prescriptive, and the suggestions contained herein are based on personal experience and are meant to spark creative ideas rather than to serve as a model.

PUBLIC RELATIONS

One of the challenges for librarians working with the public is overcoming the stereotype of the boring, restrictive, shushing librarian (Atlas, 2005). The effort to reverse this attitude among off-campus learners at DBU-North began with the previous Distance Learning Librarian,

Peggy Martin (who now serves as Director of Libraries at DBU). Martin would regularly visit the north Dallas campus with a candy basket, hoping to engage students in conversation by tempting them with sugar or chocolate. This effort was mildly successful, but depended upon random variables of time and place and hunger. At about the same time, a new initiative was established at the main campus library to welcome students during the first two days of the semester by serving homemade cookies and bottled water in the lobby of the learning center building that also houses the library. Tables set up in the lobby to accommodate the cookies and water also held library brochures and bookmarks. The goal of this program was to encourage new and returning students to view librarians as hospitable and friendly, rather than as the forbidding wardens of dusty tomes sometimes depicted in popular culture. In 2004 it was decided that this effort should be extended to the students at DBU-North as well. However, the reality of the evening class schedule for adult students meant that many students would only attend class one night per week. Therefore, the schedule for serving cookies was expanded to become Cookie Week–four evenings of hospitality during the first week of classes each semester.

At the beginning of every semester, trays of cookies are arranged on the countertop in the break room at DBU-North. Bottled water is kept in an insulated cooler at the end of the counter. To insure that students realize that the refreshments are provided by the library staff, special labels containing the library logo are printed and affixed to the bottles in the weeks prior to the beginning of the semester. A large poster advertising the cookies and drinks stands on an easel in the reception area, so students and professors will not miss the opportunity to enjoy a free snack before or after their classes. Library brochures and business cards are arranged artistically around the food trays to encourage students to pick them up and examine their contents. The most crucial element of this initiative is the presence of the librarians themselves. Because this effort requires a good amount of set-up and clean-up, the distance learning librarian is accompanied by another librarian. In this way, not only do the students become familiar with the distance learning librarian, they have the opportunity to meet other librarians they might not otherwise see. These men and women become the face of the library to the students they meet.

Evening classes at DBU are offered in two sessions per evening: 5:15 to 7:45 p.m., and 8:00 to 10:30 p.m. To accommodate the students in both sessions, the schedule of cookie service begins with set-up at 4:30 p.m. so librarians are ready and available for meeting and greeting students and professors when they arrive. The distance learning librarian and accompanying on-campus librarian have a good opportunity to network during the lull between classes. The librarians prepare for the second influx of students at 7:15 p.m. and begin clean up at 8:30 p.m.. The work involved in setting and striking the area is made much easier with the cooperation of the staff at DBU-North, who provide storage space for trays and coolers during the week so that fewer supplies have to be carried back and forth.

The opening of the DBU-Colleyville campus added another Cookie Week to the hectic first month of each semester. However, DBU's librarians have cheerfully and competently met this additional challenge. Not only are they required to commit more time to traveling and staffing during the project, but the emphasis on homemade cookies means that the librarians spend more personal time at home, preparing and baking the cookies that are later distributed to the students.

To library professionals, this emphasis on cookies and refreshments may seem, at first glance, to be unprofessional, counter-academic, or gratuitous. But the response from the distance learning community at DBU-North and DBU-Colleyville has been overwhelmingly positive. The visibility generated by this semi-annual event has resulted in a spirit of enthusiastic collegiality between the distance learning librarian and the professors, administrators, and students at our extension sites. It has provided a welcome introductory episode and an opportunity to promote library services without seeming to be self-aggrandizing. Upon subsequent appearances at the distance campuses, occasionally students will associate me with the cookies. I am able to use the opportunity to respond by explaining the reason for my visit, letting the student or professor know that I am on site to extend reference services or to instruct a class in research techniques. On many occasions, exchanges such as these have led to additional opportunities to provide service to off-campus patrons.

Additional opportunities to promote distance library services to professors, specifically, were presented in meetings outside of the off-campus community. The invitation to speak to adjunct professors at their annual orientation meeting has allowed me to declare my willingness to visit their classes, no matter where they may meet. My inclusion in the program at the annual online education banquet, held for professors teaching online, has also presented opportunities to offer bibliographic instruction in person, because many of the professors who teach online also teach at our extension sites. The crossover between on-campus, off-campus, and online instructors allows for occasions to cement professional relationships that can later lead to further opportunities for providing distance library services.

BIBLIOGRAPHIC INSTRUCTION

I have learned that there is no better way to generate opportunities to deliver bibliographic instruction than good word-of-mouth. A professor who decides to allow a librarian to consume a portion of his valuable class time must be convinced that the time devoted to library instruction will be well spent. Librarians should consider each invitation to deliver bibliographic instruction during class time as a special privilege and distinct honor. Instructors must be convinced that the knowledge and skills gained will be worth their lost classroom time. It is therefore imperative that bibliographic instruction be delivered efficiently and intelligently, with thorough preparation and attention given to the logical chronology of topics presented.

At a distance location, it is impossible to perform the usual library orientation tour. It is also unnecessary, as the majority of these students will never visit the campus library. In most cases, it is also impractical or impossible to present a hands-on research workshop. At DBU-North, there is a room designated as the "computer lab," containing laptop computers and a wireless Internet hub. However, this room is also the largest classroom in the current building, and is therefore scheduled for classes in every possible time slot. Asking the professor assigned to that room to switch places so that another class could receive hands-on library training would only result in resentment, inconvenience, and negative impressions of library services. At DBU-Colleyville, a hands-on presentation would be impractical, at least for a normal class of 12 to 20 students, as the small computer lab contains only four computers and one printer, and no space for instructional display. Therefore, off-campus bibliographic instruction takes the form of demonstration and a virtual tour of the library's virtual space, our Web site.

Fortunately, all of DBU's classrooms, on- and off-campus, are configured as "smart classrooms," containing a ceiling-mounted media projector, projection screen, and podium containing a networked computer and DVD/VCR player. Recently the computers were fitted with front-mounted USB ports, allowing interface with small, portable storage devices. When working properly, this configuration allows me to store PowerPoint presentations linked to Web pages that can be carried in my purse or pocket and displayed in any classroom. The PowerPoint slides are used to highlight the various materials and services provided by the library, and to describe the methods distance students can use to obtain the resources they need. This section of the presentation usually takes 10 to 15 minutes. Another 30 to 45 minutes is expended in demonstrating the features of DBU's most useful databases, executing sample searches based on the topics covered in the class. The presentations, although similar in content, are personalized to the topic of the course, i.e., a presentation to a class on organizational behavior will look quite different from a presentation made to an English literature class. All presentations, however, emphasize the fact that the library demonstration is only a beginning step, and that there is much more to learn.

To help students remember the concepts presented, packets for each student are prepared and distributed. These blue pocket folders are custom-labeled with the professor's name, course designation, and date. Inside, students find a hand-out version of the PowerPoint presentation, printed research guides that provide step-by-step directions for using the databases covered in the presentation, pathfinders for the topic of the course, guides to using NetLibrary, library brochures, bookmarks, and other appropriate literature. Brochures explaining the TexShare program, the open-access cooperative agreement among Texas public and academic libraries, are included, as well as application forms so the students can apply for TexShare cards on the spot. The applications are returned to the library, where the consortium cards are prepared and then mailed to the students. One of the most important items in the folder is my business card. I encourage the students to remove the card and place it in their wallets or purses, so they will have my phone number and e-mail address when they need extra assistance. Students are reminded that they will probably forget much of what was explained to them during the demonstration, but they can be assured of personalized help when they need it by keeping my contact information close at hand. I also encourage the students to play around with the databases that were highlighted after class, searching for articles of personal interest. Their "play" experiences will solidify the learning that has taken place, and allow them to experiment with search techniques without the pressure of a paper or project hanging over their heads.

The previous paragraphs outlined the impressive and convenient features of our smart classrooms. However, it must be noted that problems will occasionally arise that prevent the presentation from proceeding smoothly. It is wise, therefore, to have multiple back-up systems in place and on hand against that eventuality. Although I keep all my PowerPoint presentations on a memory stick, I also have copies burned on CD-ROMs in case something goes wrong with the USB port. I have even made color paper copies of the slides and had them laminated and spiral-bound. Although the paper versions are much more difficult for the students to see, they serve to keep my presentation on track and prevent me from forgetting important points when the computer malfunctions or the power goes out. Occasionally there will be problems with Internet connectivity, so I have pre-recorded database search sessions using Camtasia software which are also saved on both the memory stick and CD-ROMs. If the computer cannot access the Internet, I can still show these pre-recorded sessions and narrate what is happening in person, pausing for questions when necessary. If all else fails, the packets of printed information described above act as talking points for "no-tech" presentations. Though these redundant systems may never be needed, they serve two important purposes: first, I feel more confident knowing I can handle just about any setback with aplomb; and second, the instructors know that they can count on me to deliver information regardless of the potential for negative circumstances.

In addition to the library services/virtual tour presentation, recently a newly developed instructional presentation has become popular with several professors. This seminar focuses more specifically on alleviating library and research anxiety by presenting information about the Big 6 research model developed by Eisenberg and Berkowitz (2005). By encouraging students to focus more intentionally on the research process, rather than agonizing over the final product, this presentation seeks to empower students to become more independent researchers, while at the same time persuading them to appreciate and prepare for the amount of time required for a successful research venture. Also informed by Kuhlthau's information-seeking model, the 45-minute seminar prepares students for the common, but unnerving, sense of potential failure that she termed "the dip" (2004). Since so many adult students have either forgotten what they may have learned about research, or perhaps were never required to write a research paper in the past, the goal of this presentation is to de-mystify the research process while at the same time helping students to view research skills as valuable assets to be acquired and developed. Some professors have written both presentations into their syllabi and recurring course calendars. In some instances, I give both presentations back-to-back, with a break in-between, which fits neatly into the two-and-a-half-hour weekly class period. Other professors prefer I deliver the sessions on consecutive weeks. The professors who have utilized these presentations in past semesters have responded with enthusiasm, claiming that their students' final products have improved significantly. Again, I expect this positive word-of-mouth to result in an increase in invitations to address classes, which will result in more personal contact with more students over time.

REFERENCE SERVICES

While bibliographic instruction sessions, such as the ones described above, can serve to introduce students to the tools and techniques that may one day lead to research proficiency and information literacy, they do not fully meet the needs of distance learners. Many students still need the opportunity to engage in one-on-one reference interviews and consultations in order to make the jump from general to specific research technique. Although I had always sought to provide prompt and comprehensive reference services via e-mail and phone, I began to realize that some learners need a more personal, face-to-face approach. However, difficulties in setting up such a service seemed insurmountable at first. There was no dedicated library space, such as that provided at SMU-in-Legacy or UTA-FW, in which to work. There were not even unoccupied classrooms that could be tapped for service, especially as enrollment continued to grow. The approach to setting up a schedule was complex. Should it be reference "on call" one night a week, if so, which night? How would students who did not have class on that night be served? How would students find the reference librarian, and would they even know why a librarian was there? How would the service be promoted to students?

One major question to be answered from the beginning involved naming the service. It was decided that a library term such as "reference session" would not appeal to the distance learners, especially since many students would not know what "reference" services even are. A brain-storming session among several stakeholders resulted in the adoption of the name "research cyber café." We decided to serve coffee and biscotti to entice patrons to sit and chat about their resource needs. Attractive posters, table tents, and flyers were designed with a French café theme to promote the sessions. I developed a schedule designed to provide this reference service on different nights each week, attempting to be fair and equitable to students attending class on various schedules. The administrators at DBU-North worked with me to find empty classroom space for each of the planned visit times. The stage was set. The project failed.

The coffee and biscotti were popular, however, students were disappointed to discover that the "cyber café" was, in reality, a librarian with a laptop sitting in an empty classroom. The flyers and catchy name failed to convey the real nature of the service. The various times and locations were too confusing, and the cleverly-designed schedule generated was too difficult for anyone but me to understand. It was obvious that a major re-tooling of the effort would be necessary before we could expect success.

The following semester, we re-named the sessions "research consultations." This, we hoped, would more accurately reflect the nature of the service. A new set of promotional materials was designed to resemble (but only loosely) the classic image from the Peanuts cartoons of Lucy offering psychiatric help from a ramshackle stand. This design was placed on flyers, table tents, door hangers, and posters, and was included in blanket e-mails sent to all students enrolled in classes at DBU-North. The image was also used in an announcement in the online course delivery software, Blackboard. We discovered that many of our online students actually live in the Dallas area, and some were excited to have an opportunity for face-to-face interaction. By blanketing our marketing efforts with this image, we hoped to "brand" the concept of face-to-face consultation with a librarian in the minds of our patrons. A large version of the image was created on foam-core board to be displayed on an easel in the reception area of the north campus. Instead of using various empty classrooms, I decided to set up operations in the break room. Two wireless laptops were placed on a centrally-located table, along with a selection of library literature and a large, chocolate-filled candy dish. Another image of the "Librarian is IN" logo was displayed on the table so that students who saw the large poster in the lobby area would recognize that I was the person to whom the poster referred.

The changes in approach were successful. Although I still had to field the occasional questions, more students came to understand my purpose in being there. The candy dish gave me an opportunity to strike up conversations with students, some of which led to actual reference interviews. The fact that I was providing service in the break room actually worked in my favor; as I helped one person, other students could hear what was going on and began to realize that I could help them too. After a few weeks of providing once-a-week service, students began to recognize what the poster in the lobby meant. Students would see me in the hall, or even in the restroom, and tell me they were so glad to know I was there because they had questions or needed help. As in regular, on-campus reference duty, some questions could be answered quickly, while others required more lengthy attention. Students would often make sure I would still be available after their class ended. Sometimes students waited in line for their chance to sit down for a reference interview. Although scheduling allows me to visit only once a week, I simplified the schedule to an easier-remembered formula: the first Monday, the second Tuesday, the third Wednesday, and the fourth Thursday of each month.

The opening of the Colleyville campus provided a new challenge: in this case, there is no break room area to use. A small, empty office has become my space for research consultations. Although it affords more privacy, the space does not encourage as much drop-by business as the table set up in the middle of the break room. I place the large poster on the easel just outside the door, visible up and down the main corridor of the campus. To further encourage students to stop by, the candy dish is just inside the door, and coffee is offered as well. The aroma of hot coffee has proven attractive–students say they can smell it the minute they enter the front door from the street. Although the Colleyville location is new, and the enrollment is small, I feel confident that more students will come to understand how I can help them as the ensuing semesters unfold.

CONCLUSION

Three years' experience in delivering personal library service has convinced me that distance learners greatly appreciate and benefit from face-to-face contact with a librarian. Outdated stereotypes of librarians can be overcome with persistence, personality, and a genuine interest in assisting students to maximize their research experiences. Distance learning librarians who are fortunate enough to have a personally accessible patron base are encouraged to reach out to those students by becoming a constant, recognizable presence in the satellite campus community.

REFERENCES

Atlas, M. C. (2005). Library anxiety in the electronic era, or why won't anybody talk to me anymore? *Reference & User Services Quarterly, 44*(4), 314-319. Retrieved December 16, 2005, from Academic Search Premier database.

Eisenberg, M., & Berkowitz, B. (2005, December 14). *The big 6: Information literacy for the information age.* Retrieved December 16, 2005, from http://www.big6.com.

Jiao, Q. G., & Onwuegbuzie, A. J. (2004). The impact of information technology on library anxiety: The role of computer attitudes. *Information Technology & Libraries*, *23*(4), 138-144. Retrieved December 16, 2005, from Academic Search Premier database.

Kuhlthau, C. (2004). *Seeking meaning: A process approach to library and information services* (2nd ed.). Westport, CT: Libraries Unlimited.

Mahoney, P. B. (Ed.). (2002). *The Tenth Off-Campus Library Services Conference Proceedings: Cincinnati, Ohio, April 17-19, 2002*. Mt. Pleasant, MI: Central Michigan University Press.

Mahoney, P. B. (Ed.). (2004). *The Eleventh Off-Campus Library Services Conference Proceedings: Scottsdale, Arizona, May 5-7, 2004*. Mt. Pleasant, MI: Central Michigan University Press.

Mellon, C. A. (1988). Attitudes: The forgotten dimension in library instruction. *Library Journal*, *113*(14), 137-139. Retrieved December16, 2005, from Academic Search Premier database.

Thomas, P. S. (Ed.). (2000). *The Ninth Off-Campus Library Services Conference Proceedings: Portland, Oregon, April 26-28, 2000*. Mt. Pleasant, MI: Central Michigan University Press.

Thomas, P. S., & Jones, M. (Eds.). (1998). *The Eighth Off-Campus Library Services Conference Proceedings: Providence, Rhode Island, April 22-24, 1998*. Mt. Pleasant, MI: Central Michigan University Press.

Veal, R. (2002). The relationship between library anxiety and off-campus adult learners. *Journal of Library Administration*, *7*(3/4), 529-36. Retrieved December 16, 2005, from Academic Search Premier database.

doi:10.1300/J111v45n03_07

WISPR
(Workshop on the Information Search Process for Research) in the Library

Shauna Rutherford
K. Alix Hayden
Paul R. Pival

University of Calgary

SUMMARY. This paper details how stand-alone instructional elements became the foundation for a new inquiry-based blended learning approach to information literacy on our campus. Based on the information search process research of Kuhlthau and designed to be inserted into blended learning classes, an information literacy workshop consisting of both on-line and face-to-face components was developed. Rather than simply train students on specific research tools, the premise for the workshop is to lay a broader foundation for students' inquiry based on discovery. A variety of assessment features (self-tests, quizzes, graded assignments) are employed throughout the syllabus. doi:10.1300/J111v45n03_08

KEYWORDS. Information literacy, online tutorial, information search process, blended learning, inquiry-based learning

[Haworth co-indexing entry note]: "WISPR (Workshop on the Information Search Process for Research) in the Library." Rutherford, Shauna, K. Alix Hayden, and Paul R. Pival. Co-published simultaneously in *Journal of Library Administration* (The Haworth Information Press, an imprint of The Haworth Press, Inc.) Vol. 45, No. 3/4, 2006, pp. 427-443; and: *The Twelfth Off-Campus Library Services Conference Proceedings* (ed: Julie A. Garrison) The Haworth Information Press, an imprint of The Haworth Press, Inc., 2006, pp. 427-443.

Available online at http://jla.haworthpress.com
doi:10.1300/J111v45n03_08

INTRODUCTION

Two significant trends affecting higher education in recent years are the integration of inquiry-based learning into the undergraduate experience and the move towards blended or hybrid learning, wherein technology plays a major role in the acquisition of knowledge. Both of these trends provided the impetus and opportunity for librarians at the University of Calgary to develop a new approach to delivering information literacy instruction.

BACKGROUND

Inquiry and Blended Learning

In the influential *Reinventing Undergraduate Education: A Blueprint for America's Research Universities* (1998), the Boyer Commission recommended that the freshman year be inquiry-based and that future college years be built on this foundation. Based upon a constructivist theory of education, inquiry-based learning puts student curiosity at the center of the educational experience. In order to be successful in an inquiry-based learning environment, students must be able to formulate researchable questions and then investigate widely to form new knowledge, gain deeper understanding of the issues, or create a novel solution to a problem.

Librarians realize that most incoming undergraduate students do not have the necessary information seeking skills to complete such tasks. Although the connection between inquiry-based learning and the necessity for information literacy skills has been widely written about in a K-12 school environment (Donham, Kuhtlhau, Oberg, & Bishop, 2001; Kuhlthau, 2001; Moore, 2002), surprisingly little has been written about the role of academic libraries and information literacy in enabling inquiry-based learning in higher education. Gilchrist (1993) wrote of her experiences providing information literacy instruction to an inquiry-based history course at Pacific Lutheran University, and a handful of other researchers have addressed the issue in nursing education (Cleverly, 2003; Schilling, Ginn, Mickelson, & Roth, 1995). University of Calgary librarians wanted campus administration to understand that acquisition of information literacy skills is essential to student success in an inquiry-based learning environment across all disciplines, and that a core syllabus should be developed to serve this purpose.

The integration of technology into teaching is another significant trend in higher education. Bonk (2004) pointed out four trends converging on institutes of higher education: emerging technologies, enormous learner demand for e-learning, enhanced pedagogy, and diminishing institutional budgets. Bonk maintained this convergence "generates waves of new opportunities on online learning environments" (p. 2). The Pew Charitable Trusts Program in Course Redesign was created in 1999 to explore the "promise of technology to improve the quality of student learning and reduce the costs of instruction" (Twigg, 2003, p. 28). Thirty institutions took part in the study, all of which incorporated six features: whole course redesign, active learning, computer-based learning resources, mastery learning, on-demand help, and alternative staffing. The results of the study were overwhelmingly favorable. Not only were there considerable cost-savings (an average of 40% across the 30 institutions), but the project showed that meaningful incorporation of technology into the learning experience resulted in "increased course completion rates, improved retention, better student attitudes towards the subject matter, and increased student satisfaction with the mode of delivery" (p. 30).

Prompted by the recommendations of the Boyer Report and the findings of the Pew Program in Course Redesign, the University of Calgary administration actively sought to promote the integration of inquiry-based and blended learning into the undergraduate curriculum. In fall 2004, it invited applications for innovation grants to support the development or redesign of courses.

The authors submitted a successful proposal to develop a blended learning syllabus including an online tutorial that would assist students in acquiring the information literacy skills necessary to be successful in an inquiry-based learning environment. The premise of the proposal was that information literacy skills prepare students for an inquiry-based learning environment at the university level as well as for lifelong learning after their degrees. They enable learners "to master content and extend their investigations, become more self-directed, and assume greater control over their own learning" (ACRL, 2000, p. 2). Integration of information literacy instruction into course content has been shown to be the most effective way for students to learn and apply these skills (ANZIL, 2004); therefore, an essential feature of the proposal was that the final product be customizable to suit the requirements of a specific course or discipline of study.

The online tutorial, or workshop, was intended for use in a blended environment with the librarian as an active collaborator with teaching faculty in course delivery. Librarian involvement in course instruction would allow students to see themselves as part of a broader learning community that included information professionals. However, the tutorial was also designed to be used independently so that all students at the university, not just those in courses that integrate the syllabus, could benefit from the project. Librarians and professors may direct students to the online learning tutorials for independent study, or for review after a library instruction session.

Framework for the Proposed Tutorial

Once funding was secured, the authors met with an instructional designer at the University of Calgary Learning Commons to identify learning objectives, desired layout, and appropriate activities for the project. The librarians quickly came to a consensus that the online tutorial must take a holistic approach to the research process. In an inquiry environment, learners need guidance and support in all aspects of information seeking, from selecting a general topic to research, to question formulation, research techniques, and evaluation of results. A review showed that the majority of online tutorials at other library sites focused predominantly on the mechanics of database searching, without providing guidance in topic selection or developing a researchable question. These aspects of research are vital in inquiry-based education. Additionally, while many of the other tutorials provided excellent support for skill development, they did not emphasize that research is a process with recognizable patterns that allow students to develop strategies to assist in their progress. This understanding of research as a process, with identifiable components and accompanying practices, was central to the project. To incorporate this view of research, the team decided to use Kuhlthau's information search process (ISP) as a framework for the entire online tutorial.

Information Search Process

Models of information seeking behaviors that center on a process approach to library skills and information seeking are now prevalent in the literature. Such an approach is not dependent upon particular sources or libraries. Rather, the emphasis is on developing transferable cognitive skills that increase students' effectiveness in using information. Kuhlthau's (1993) model of the information seeking process is such an approach.

Kuhlthau (1993) developed a model of the ISP from common patterns which emerged from her longitudinal investigation of the information seeking behaviors of numerous groups including high school students, undergraduates, lawyers, and other professionals. Her ISP model goes beyond the mechanics of information seeking; it incorporates three realms: the affective (feeling), the cognitive (thoughts), and the physical (actions and strategies). These realms are common to each stage of the search process, as described in Table 1.

The student's knowledge grows as s/he interacts with the information. More importantly, cognitive processes are involved in information seeking. Throughout the process, the student engages in cognitive strat-

TABLE 1. Information Search Process (Kuhlthau, 2004)

Stage	Stage Description	Thoughts	Feelings	Actions
Task Initiation	Recognizes that information is required to complete an assignment.	Review/think about assignment; consider potential topics	Apprehension; uncertainty	Talking with others; brainstorming; discussing
Topic Selection	Identifies and selects a general topic	Consider personal interest, project requirements, info available, time	Confusion; anxiety; anticipation	Preliminary library search; informal mediators; review general sources
Prefocus Exploration	Gathers general information; intent on expanding knowledge base and personal understanding	Explore general topic; identify possible focuses;	Confusion; doubt; threat; uncertainty	Locating relevant info; reading; taking notes; listing descriptors
Focus Formulation	Forms new understanding of topic based on general exploration; clear focus emerges	Identify ideas	Optimism; confidence	Reading notes for themes; consider possible focuses through listing, merging, surveying
Information Collection	Gathers specific information related to defined focus	Seek info to support focus; organizing info; confirm understanding	Increased interest; sometimes overwhelmed with task to be done	Comprehensive searches of relevant resources; requesting assistance from experts (librarians, profs, etc)
Search Closure	Completes the task	Identify gaps in search, understanding, or knowledge; consider time restrictions	Relief; satisfaction; disappointment	Verify sources; confirm info; prepare to write

egies such as brain storming, contemplating, predicting, consulting, reading, choosing, identifying, defining, and confirming. The model highlights how feelings such as apprehension, uncertainty, confusion, anxiety, anticipation, doubt, optimism, and confidence interplay as the search for information proceeds. Another significant contribution of Kuhlthau's model to the theory of information seeking is that the process is iterative. One does not conduct research in a series of predetermined steps; rather, research involves looping back or returning to previous stages in the process as necessary to refocus a topic, search for missing information, or to verify new concepts discovered.

Given the current emphasis on inquiry and blended learning at the University of Calgary, coupled with the knowledge that the information search process is a universal experience; librarians developed a new blended learning tutorial in the summer of 2005. The workshop incorporates the major components of Kuhlthau's model with some minor, but significant, enhancements. The following describes in detail the development of the inquiry-based ISP tutorial.

OVERVIEW

Development of ISP Graphic

A precursor to the Workshop on the Information Search Process for Research (WISPR) was developed during the summer of 2003 when Kuhlthau's ISP was integrated into an online course in academic writing for nursing and rehabilitation students. Although Kuhlthau has stressed that the ISP model is not linear, but rather is recursive. It is commonly depicted in tabular format, sometimes with the addition of a time line showing that the process takes place over time in a specific sequence. Dyckman (2005) also commented on Kuhlthau's ISP, stating "ironically, for the most part the ISP stages are presented–both in her work and in others'–as a consecutive progression" (p. 352). Byron (1999), in her doctoral dissertation focusing on verifying the ISP in a virtual environment, maintained that "while there is a definite sense of motion in the stages of thoughts, feelings, and actions the model identifies, to date there has not been a way to represent the motion without creating a sense of strict linearity" (p. 71). She contended that a better representation of Kuhlthau's ISP is essential if instructors are expected to teach it to students. Further, students must understand the information search process prior to commencing a research project (Barranoik, 2004).

The project team used Kuhlthau's ISP as both a theoretical framework for the tutorial, and as the visual framework. The ISP is the 'roadmap' that allows students to both plan for and track their progress through their research assignment. In light of the limitations of Kuhlthau's linear depiction of the ISP, it was essential to develop a graphical representation of the ISP that was both meaningful and informative. Therefore, a graphic developed for a different purpose by two colleagues (Vivian Steida and Lorraine Toews) was adapted to reflect the ISP. Figure 1 illustrates the adapted information search process used in WISPR.

The *WISPR in the Library* graphic encapsulates the complexity and recursive nature of the ISP. It must be noted, however, that the WISPR graphic is not a direct representation of Kuhlthau's ISP. Incorporating the work of Bateman (1998) and Hayden (2003) coupled with practical experience, the ISP model was adapted to merge Stage 1 (task initiation) with Stage 2 (topic selection). As Bateman pointed out "information seeking stage 1 was not reported as a single stage but reported in combination with other stages" (p. 136). The information collection stage was split into two, where information refinement affords students the opportunity to revisit the information collected in light of the course assignment. Further modification included changing terminology from Kuhlthau's "stage" for each component of the ISP to "phase." The term *stage* again infers a sense of linearity and sequential steps. *Phase*, however, provides a less concrete, more fluid interpretation of the components of the ISP.

FIGURE 1. WISPR Graphic

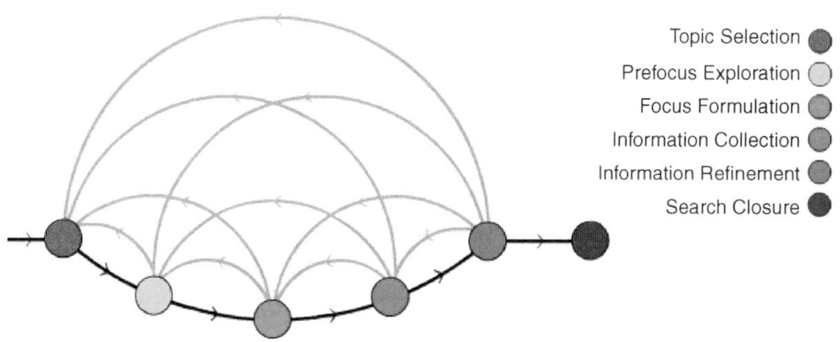

Collaborative Development

Development of WISPR included several key collaborators: librarians, an instructional designer, and technical experts. Throughout the four month development process, the librarians held bi-weekly meetings with the instructional designer and technical experts. The librarians developed all content, and provided the framework for WISPR. The instructional designer had extensive experience working with library tutorials, and provided guidance on developing sound instructional activities throughout WISPR. He also ensured that a variety of learning modalities were considered. As well, he introduced simple technologies to increase interactivity. The technical experts developed the interface and navigation, and created an online journaling mechanism. All work was done in tandem, with short timelines resulting in some technical issues initially, but produced a well-designed, instructionally appropriate workshop in the end.

Components

WISPR follows the components as outlined in Kuhlthau's ISP, with additional instructional aspects and interactivity. Each phase incorporates: overview, actions/strategies; thoughts/feelings; course specific activities; self-assessment; and logbook. Phase components are color-coded to guide the student, and to provide a sense of cohesion to the phase and the entire tutorial. Further, WISPR maintains a friendly, non-academic tone in all phases and the various interactive activities (see Figure 2).

Overview provides an orientation to the phase. *Actions/strategies* guide the student to specific actions that need to be done or considered in the phase. These are based extensively on Kuhlthau's work, as well as expanded based on experience. *Actions/strategies* in topic selection, for example, include: read your assignment carefully; read your lecture notes for ideas; talk to others; start NOW. Each of these guiding actions is further explained with related strategies. The *thoughts/feelings* section validates the common feelings that students experience when searching for information, which are also based on Kuhlthau's work.

One of the guiding principles for WISPR was that it would be meaningful to the students encountering it in their specific courses. An effort was made to ensure that WISPR was not generic. It was designed to be integrated directly into a course, and, therefore, the examples, activities, and information sources presented in WISPR are customizable to

FIGURE 2. WISPR Components

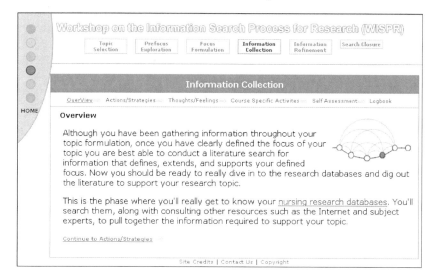

be relevant to the course content. While components of WISPR remain relatively similar across courses (i.e., overview, actions/strategies, thoughts/feelings) other components respond directly to specific course content and requirements. Course specific activities provide the opportunity to include new content, activities, or assignments that respond directly to the course. Instructors may develop the content to be integrated, or the content may be librarian led. In the information collection phase, course content focuses on teaching the various resources, often electronic, that are appropriate for the course. This phase reflects the usual "one-shot" teaching session which represents so much of library instruction. Other course specific activities may have students finding subject encyclopedias, or speaking with experts in a given field. Depending on the course, not every phase will include course specific activities.

As evidenced by the WISPR graphic (see Figure 1), searching for information is an extremely iterative process. However, students often try to either skip a phase, or move forward before they have completed a phase. In order to guide students in their progress, WISPR includes a self-assessment at the end of each phase. The point of the self-assessment *checklist* is to ensure that students have considered all components in the phase, and have something tangible and conceptualized before moving to the next phase.

Finally, WISPR incorporates two modes for tracking the student's search process and knowledge growth on a given topic: a logbook and a KWLF (What I **K**now, What I **W**ant to Know, What I **L**earned, Where I **F**ound it) Chart. The logbook is a diary of students' search progress, where they consider and answer specific questions. The logbook may be considered the deliverable from WISPR. Some logbook entries prompt students to document their actions and strategies related to the corresponding phase. This assists students in recording their progress through the phase and encourages good research skills (e.g., keeping track of references, writing down possible search terms, evaluating sources). Other logbook entries are more reflective in nature, and encourage students to consider what went right and what went wrong, and reasons why they may have been successful or unsuccessful in their information search process. Reflecting on one's ISP might lead to a better understanding of searching and a more critical evaluation of tools, techniques, and sources used in the process. Hopefully, it will assist students in developing more appropriate strategies for research so that future projects are completed more effectively and efficiently.

The KWLF Chart was adapted from the KWL Chart, based on the work of Ogle (1986), which has been used extensively in the K-12 environment as a means of improving student comprehension. The KWLF Chart encourages students to think actively about what they know, what they want to know, and what they are learning. Including an additional element, Found, provides a means for students to be accountable for information retrieved; that is, students might rely less on Google and search out more authoritative resources for academic papers. Table 2 illustrates the KWLF Chart used in WISPR. This sample chart is completed to show how a student might fill in information for each element. The KWLF Chart is inquiry-driven as students are expected to question their own knowledge and learning.

Summary of WISPR Components

Having WISPR delivered online allows students to engage with the material as their schedules and readiness allow. Access to on-demand help, either through face-to-face meetings with librarians or online assistance, is encouraged. The online workshop permits students to revisit phases and their components as they wish, either to ensure mastery of

TABLE 2. KWLF Chart

What I **Know**?	What I **Want** to Know?	What I **Learned**?	Where I **Found** It?
FASD is caused by drinking alcohol during pregnancy	Is there an "okay" amount of alcohol consumption?	Accepted alcohol levels differ from country to country	FASWorld Canada (Web site)
		Canada proclaims zero alcohol amount	CINAHL (nursing database)
		FASD is a non-reversible, but totally preventable, birth defect	MEDLINE

skills or to refer to when particular skills are needed for related course work.

TECHNOLOGY

WISPR was designed to engage the students in as many different ways as possible, not only to address different learning styles, but also to make sure students did not become bored with the same old "read it on a Web site" type of tutorial. A number of technologies were used to construct the various components of WISPR. Some components were built by the librarians involved, while others were built by the campus Learning Commons (see Table 3).

Audio narration was included with all the screencasts and in the KWLF chart to try to engage the students as much as possible. In previous uses of this technology in other online courses, students rated this enhanced content highly, appreciating the opportunity to learn both visually and aurally.

For the reason indicated above, audio was also incorporated into the guided tutorials, which provide an opportunity for students to practice in a hands-on guided session. Librarians felt strongly that it was most important to allow students to practice what they had learned and yet still be in a guided session. Guided instruction appears to be lacking in many online tutorials, and is a feature that most librarians would say is the most important part of their face-to-face sessions with students. The hands-on feature is accomplished through the presentation of a split screen using frames and a little Javascript coding for interactivity provided by the Texas Information Literacy Tutorial (TILT).

TABLE 3. Technology Used for Creating WISPR

Component	Technology	Responsibility
Overall design	XHTML and CSS	Learning Commons
WISPR graphic	*Macromedia Flash*	Learning Commons
Self-Assessment checklists	*Quandry 2.2*	Librarians
KWLF Chart	*Macromedia Breeze*	Librarians
Logbook	*Jakarta Tapestry*	Learning Commons
Screencasts	*Qarbon ViewletBuilder Pro*	Librarians
Guided tutorials	HTML, *Boomer*, Javascript	Librarians

On the left side of the screen students are given instructions on what to do in the live database that appears on the right side of the screen (see Figure 3). Students may search anything they want in the live database, but if they use the guided instructions, there are checks in each tutorial to ensure students are on the right track ("how many results did you get for that search?"). To incorporate audio into the tutorials, a brief audio file was recorded as a WAV file and then quickly converted to *Flash* using a tool called *Boomer* [http://www.segon.com/boomer.html]. The embedded *Flash* [http://www.macromedia.com/software/flash/flashpro/] audio file plays as soon as the left frame loads, allowing the student to both read and listen to the instructions that are to be followed in the live database.

With the exception of the database backend for the logbook, all of the technology used in the original creation of WISPR is easily within the grasp of any librarian with the time and patience to experiment. Full integration into Tapestry [http://jakarta.apache.org/tapestry/] requires more sophisticated skills. WISPR is offered under a Creative Commons NonCommercial ShareAlike license [http://creativecommons.org/licenses/by-nc-sa/2.0/ca/].

IMPLEMENTING WISPR–PILOT COURSES

A key characteristic of inquiry-based learning is allowing students to explore independently with expert help available at critical moments. Ideally, WISPR is introduced by a librarian. This introduction, whether in a face-to-face environment, video streaming, or synchronous chat, promotes relationship-building between the librarians and students,

FIGURE 3. Guided Hands-On Tutorial

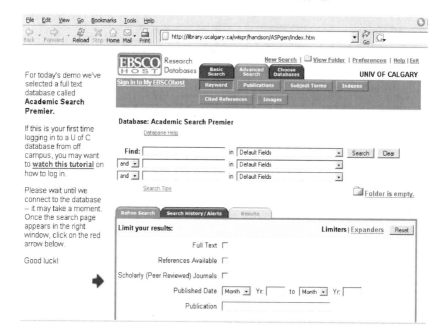

provides a forum for laying the theoretical foundations of information seeking, and provides an opportunity to orient students to WISPR.

A first year nursing undergraduate block course (four week course) was the pilot for full integration of WISPR. The Nursing Liaison Librarian provided an overview of WISPR during the first class. Further, the students were provided with a research day (five hours) where they worked through WISPR in groups, submitted the logbook at the end of the day, with two librarians facilitating the groups in searching for information for course-related assignments. The professor provided 10% of the students' final grade for assignments related to WISPR. Two assignments, developed by the librarian, were handed out as well. The first assignment required students to submit their logbook on a specific date. For this course, the logbook was completed by groups of eight students. This aspect of the assignment was a simple pass/fail. The second assignment required students to provide a two-page reflection on their information seeking process and experience using WISPR. The students were provided with guidance on reflective writing, based on the work of Dr. Jenny Moon, an expert on learning and reflection from the University of Exeter. The assignment was marked by the librarian.

FUTURE DIRECTIONS

WISPR will be piloted in two more courses in January 2006, a first year kinesiology research methodology course and, again, with the nursing undergraduate course. Feedback from students participating in all of the pilot courses will be sought to revise and enhance WISPR in light of actual student experiences and learning. Faculty from across several disciplines at the University of Calgary are showing considerable interest in WISPR.

Although librarians would prefer to have WISPR integrated directly into a course, with WISPR content responding to course curriculum, this may not always be possible. Therefore, a generic version of WISPR is being developed that provides instruction on more multidisciplinary resources, such as Academic Search Premier. The added benefit of a more generic version is that students may direct their own learning, or revisit concepts taught from a more traditional library instruction session.

Further, WISPR will be used at the reference desks throughout the library system, especially in the Information Commons. It has been recognized that Kuhlthau's ISP model has direct implications for reference practice (Isbell & Kammerlocher, 1998; Cottrell & Eisenberg, 2001). Training programs for all reference staff will be developed based on WISPR. Staff will be encouraged to promote the generic version of WISPR, as well as use it as a teaching tool for guiding students in their information search process.

CONCLUSION

The information search process is not easy or linear; however, few library tutorials or instruction sessions acknowledge the complexity of the process. The development of WISPR addresses the shortcomings found in traditional online information literacy tutorials by emphasizing that research is an iterative process comprising identifiable phases, not merely a series of isolated events. Recognition of the process can enable the students to plan ahead, to develop effective strategies to assist their progress, to be prepared for challenges and frustration, and to learn from both their successes and missteps. WISPR also gives far more emphasis to the early phases in the research process–identifying a topic and formulating a researchable question–which are essential elements for student success in an inquiry-based learning environment. Student and faculty feedback have been favorable, and librarians at the University of Calgary are optimistic that the modular nature of the workshop will facilitate its widespread adoption among colleagues both locally and at other institutions.

AUTHOR NOTE

Funding

Building Skills for Inquiry–Inquiry and Blended Learning Course Development and Enhancement Pilot Project, 2004-2005 Grant, University of Calgary.
Nursing Inquiry for Nursing 207–Inquiry and Blended Learning Course Development and Enhancement Pilot Project, 2004-2005 Grant, University of Calgary.

ISP Graphic

Health Knowledge Network, Vivian Steida, and Lorraine Toews for permission to adapt their Search Process graphic.

Instructional Design

Norm Vaughan, PhD. Learning Commons, University of Calgary

Technical Advisors

Patrick Kelly, Learning Commons, University of Calgary
Gord Southam, Learning Commons, University of Calgary
Julian Wood, Learning Commons, University of Calgary

REFERENCES

Association of College & Research Libraries. (ACRL). (2000). *Information literacy standards for higher education.* Retrieved November 5, 2005, from http://www.ala.org/ala/acrl/acrlstandards/standards.pdf.
Australia and New Zealand Institute for Information Literacy (ANZIL). (2004). *Australia and New Zealand information literacy framework: Principals, standards, and practice* (2nd ed.). Retrieved November 5, 2005, from http://www.anziil.org/resources/Info%20lit%202nd%20edition.pdf.
Barranoik, L. K. (2004). *Meaningful research projects: Perspectives from high school students and their teacher.* Unpublished doctoral dissertation, University of Alberta, Edmonton, Alberta.
Bateman, J. W. (1998). *Modeling changes in end user relevance criteria: An information-seeking study.* Unpublished doctoral dissertation, University of North Texas, Denton, TX.

Bonk, C. J. (2004). *The perfect e-storm: Emerging technologies, enormous learner demand, enhanced pedagogy, and erased budgets.* London: The Observatory on Borderless Higher Education. Retrieved November 5, 2005, from http://www.publicationshare.com/.

Boyer Commission on Educating Undergraduates in the Research University. (1998). *Reinventing undergraduate education: A blueprint for America's research universities.* Menlo Park, CA: Carnegie Foundation for the Advancement of Teaching, Retrieved November 5, 2005, from http://naples.cc.sunysb.edu/Pres/boyer.nsf/.

Byron, S. M. (1999). *Information seeking in a virtual learning environment.* Unpublished doctoral dissertation, University of North Texas.

Cleverly, D. (2003). *Implementing inquiry-based learning in nursing.* London: Routledge.

Cottrell, J. R., & Eisenberg, M. B. (2001). Applying an information problem-solving model to academic reference work: Findings and implications. *College and Research Libraries, 62*(4), 334-347.

Donham, J., Kuhtlhau, C. C., Oberg, D., & Bishop, K. (2001). Inquiry-based learning: Lessons from Library Power. Worthington, OH: Linworth.

Dyckman, L. M. (2005). Fear of failure and fear of finishing: A case study on the emotional aspects of dissertation proposal research, with thoughts on library instruction and graduate student retention. *ACRL Twelfth National Conference,* Minneapolis, MN. Retrieved February 27, 2006, from http://www.ala.org/ala/acrl/acrlevents/dyckman05.pdf.

Gilchrist, D. (1993). Collaborative teaching through inquiry based instruction. In L. Shirato (Ed.), *What is good instruction now? Library instruction for the 90s* (pp. 51-56). Ann Arbor, MI: Pierian Press.

Hayden, K. A. (2003). *Lived experience of students searching for information.* Unpublished doctoral dissertation, University of Calgary, Calgary, Alberta.

Isbell, D., & Kammerlocher, L. (1998). Implementing Kuhlthau: A new model for library and reference instruction. *Reference Services Review, 26*(3-4), 33-44.

Kuhlthau, C. C. (1999). Literacy and learning for the information age. In B. K. Stripling (Ed.), *Learning and libraries in an information age: Principles and practice* (pp. 3-21). Englewood, CO: Libraries Unlimited.

Kuhlthau, C. C. (2001). Rethinking libraries for the information age school: Vital roles in inquiry learning. Keynote Address *International Association of School Librarianship Conference & International Research Forum on Research in School Librarianship.* Auckland, New Zealand. Retrieved November 5, 2005, from http://www.scils.rutgers.edu/~kuhlthau/NZtext.htm.

Kuhlthau, C. C. (2004). Seeking meaning: A process approach to library and information services. 2nd Edition. Westport, Connecticut: Libraries Unlimited.

Moon, J. (2005). *Reflective writing–some initial guidance for students.* Retrieved December 12, 2005, from http://www.services.ex.ac.uk/cas/employability/students/reflective.htm.

Moore, P. (2002). *An analysis of information literacy education worldwide.* White Paper prepared for UNESCO, the U.S. National Commission on Libraries and Information Science, and the National Forum on Information Literacy, for use at the Information Literacy Meeting of Experts, Prague, The Czech Republic. Retrieved

November 5, 2005, from http://www.ncils.gov/libinter/infolitconf&meet/papers/moore-fullpaper.pdf.

Ogle, D. M. (1986). K-W-L: A teaching model that develops active reading of expository text. *Reading Teacher, 39*(6), 564-570.

Schilling, K., Ginn, D. S., Mickelson, P., & Roth, L. H. (1995). Integration of information-seeking skills and activities into a problem-based curriculum. *Bulletin of the Medical Library Association, 83*(2), 176-183.

Texas Information Literacy Tutorial (TILT). (n.d.). Retrieved December 8, 2005, from http://tilt.lib.utsystem.edu/.

Twigg, C. (2003). New models for online learning. *Educause Review, 38*(5), 28-38.

Workshop on the Information Search Process for Research (WISPR) in the Library. (2005). Retrieved December 12, 2005, from http://library.ucalgary.ca/wispr.

doi:10.1300/J111v45n03_08

Demand for E-books
in an Academic Library

Ellen Safley

University of Texas at Dallas

SUMMARY. Rather than create a collection solely to support distance learners, libraries should consider the needs of all customers when developing a digital library. The acceptance of digital libraries is dependant upon the conversion of resources to an electronic format that is easy to use and is fully searchable. While electronic journals are widely accepted by most academic library customers, the delivery of online books has had a very different acceptance rate. Rather than support the sequential reading of books, electronic books are commonly used to find information and can be particularly well-suited for reference purposes. This article will provide insight into the history of e-book models and evaluate the usage statistics of a large electronic book collection in an academic library. doi:10.1300/J111v45n03_09

KEYWORDS. Digital libraries, electronic books

INTRODUCTION

With the increased demand for information, libraries are exploring the need for electronic books, the online equivalent of the printed item.

[Haworth co-indexing entry note]: "Demand for E-books in an Academic Library." Safley, Ellen. Co-published simultaneously in *Journal of Library Administration* (The Haworth Information Press, an imprint of The Haworth Press, Inc.) Vol. 45, No. 3/4, 2006, pp. 445-457; and: *The Twelfth Off-Campus Library Services Conference Proceedings* (ed: Julie A. Garrison) The Haworth Information Press, an imprint of The Haworth Press, Inc., 2006, pp. 445-457.

Available online at http://jla.haworthpress.com
doi:10.1300/J111v45n03_09

Many researchers are skeptical that these resources have archival attributes and many librarians believe that the format has a limited audience. While digital libraries are often created by digitizing the contributions created by scholars in their institutions or by scanning the rare materials that make a library collection unique, other libraries are accumulating digital books from commercial e-book publishers/distributors. Most academic libraries have small collections of electronic books and the analysis on the usage of their e-book collections has been limited. This research provides additional information on the usage of a large electronic book collection. Finally, the study urges standardization of the statistics provided by e-book vendors. The usage of electronic books as compared to printed material needs to be explored in the future as libraries change with the introduction of new technologies.

LITERATURE REVIEW

The initial phase of electronic book development was complicated by the rise of different types of hand-held readers and by their limited popularity as a means for reading materials. Coyle (2003) recounted the rise and fall of the Rocket reader, a device weighing and measuring approximately the same as a hardbound book. She noted that "along with the rest of the dot.com bubble" (p. 8), the first phase of e-books never delivered the content in a manner acceptable to devoted readers. O'Leary (2003) outlined that his predictions in 2001 of individual e-books resident in electronic hand-held readers never materialized. He noted that e-book readers may be seen in the "Museum of Forgotten Technologies" (p. 59). Despite the problems with hand-held readers, they were portable. With the rise of Internet delivery, the customer was confined by the equipment and licenses constrained the printing and downloading of the content.

Internet delivery of the book was not initially popular as reading a volume online was not considered acceptable by most users. Bell (2005) stated that reading devices and most computer screens are not conducive to extended reading by library customers. O'Leary (2003) stated "the more time you spend with a book at one sitting, the less attractive it is" (p. 59). On the help page for the Search Inside!™ (connected July 27, 2005), Amazon states that despite the fact that many books are scanned, the images retrieved with this special feature have been "optimized for viewing on a computer monitor; printed pages are usually a much higher resolution and quality."

Brown (2001) suggested that learners using digital text are not reading sequentially but are searching, scanning, selecting, cutting, and pasting in segments. Other researchers have suggested that Internet use and scanning texts online are changing how students conduct research. If segments of text are taken out of context, a student's use of the work can be flawed if not totally inaccurate. While e-books did not cause the changes in reading, Bell (2005) stated that "'search-driven' reading can make for depressingly sloppy scholarship" (p. 31). O'Leary (2003) described this phenomenon as "use, not read" (p. 59).

The literature on electronic books cites success for e-books in delivering resources for use in reference service as many items can be searchable using one interface. Models include the Oxford Reference Online and Gale Virtual Reference Collection. Dorner (2003) stated that Accenture, a consultant firm, predicted that e-books would make up 10% of all book sales in 2005 and that reference works would be amassed in huge online databases. According to Abbott and Kelly (2004) and Coleman (2004), reference works lend themselves to strong acceptance by users because articles are short and can easily be read online, content can be frequently updated, and customers can search across texts. Taken a step further, Miller (2004) cited Sean Devine, the managing director of Safari Books Online, that the e-book market is responding to a subject-focused fully searchable collection. "Users can go to one place to search across thousands of books simultaneously to pinpoint exactly the chapter, section, code fragment or example they need," according to Devine (p. 13). O'Leary (2003) reinforced the concept of aggregated collections to find a specific bit of information. The size of the database increases the ability of locating exactly what is required. Coyle (2003) stated "the ability to turn a collection of books into a searchable whole is ideal for a reference collection" (p. 10). The use of electronic reference collections is not unlike someone searching a phrase on Yahoo or Google. The difference is that locating authoritative works could be much more acceptable academically than the results of an average search.

Librarians must continue to provide electronic content in anticipation of both types of use. Technological developments are likely to change learners' opinions of reading online. Bell (2005) affirmed that "what is needed is a computer that looks and feels exactly like a book" (p. 31). New technological advances such as microencapsulated electrophoretic displays, also called electronic-ink screens, show promise (Lewis, 2004). Electronic ink technology uses millions of white and black capsules floating in liquid. The capsules can be arranged using electric charges that are flipped as the learner needs to turn a page.

What do our learners want with respect to electronic books? There are a few surveys and usage studies that indicate the growing importance of electronic books in academic libraries.

One of the most interesting studies was by Croft and Bedi (2005) of the Royal Roads University in British Columbia, Canada concerning the use of a small collection (under 2,000 works) of NetLibrary titles, a subject specific collection of 2,200 titles (ITKnowledge), and a subscription to 13,000 titles from ebrary. They found that if a student had attended an instructional session and was taught how to connect to and use electronic books, they were more likely to use the resources again for another project. Secondly, the librarians tested the students' preferences for ebrary over NetLibrary because of perceived difficulty with the NetLibrary delivery model (customers must register and create a password for many functions and only one person can use the book at a time). The librarians assumed that users would prefer ebrary over NetLibrary, but the research showed that the users did not prefer one model to another. To test the assumption of preference for print or electronic, the librarians referred students to both versions of certain texts. Students opted for the electronic version over print at a rate of 3 to 1. Similar to other usage studies, students at Royal Roads used e-books for research and reference, but not primarily for reading (Croft & Bedi, 2005).

Littman and Connaway (2004) studied e-book and print book usage at Duke University between February 2001 and August 2002. The e-book collection (7,880 titles) was comprised largely of social science/law, business, and arts/humanities with a small number of medicine and computer science titles. Books on science/mathematics/engineering were not reported, but were less than 2% of the total collection. During the study, the circulation of 7,456 print books for one year prior to the addition of the e-book was compared to the use of the printed book after the addition of the electronic version. The study reported that the circulation of books with e-book equivalents declined 22% while overall circulation of the entire collection increased 5.2%. The authors suggest that the online equivalent is meeting the needs of many users. The subjects of the books circulated and accessed were relatively in proportion with the overall collection. The study concluded that e-books received 11% more use than their print books and that despite their recent introduction to the library, e-books already added value for Duke University users.

Cox (2004) explored the usage of Safari Tech Books among a set of Irish university libraries. A group of librarians from the Conference of Heads of Irish Universities (CHIU) assessed the markets for e-books in 2002 and concluded that they had great potential for certain disciplines including business, law, and computer science. Thus, they purchased a subscription to 54 Safari Tech books using a three seat model, a collection of information technology and business titles. Over a nine month period, there were 1,526 sessions each lasting on average 4 minutes 43 seconds. Halfway through the year, a survey of Safari users was conducted. The majority of students noted that they were using the resource for a project or essay (75%) rather than reading a text; however, faculty use was primarily for resources not held in any other format. In addition, faculty use was highest for preparation of a lecture (65%). Users indicated that they could find information faster, that their work had improved, and that it saved them time, but that it is harder to read online. Overall, they indicated that they would be interested in other electronic book services (87%), although over 90% of respondents still needed print resources for research and reading.

Abbott and Kelly (2004) studied the e-book usage at Bond University, the first private, non-profit university in Australia (established in 1989 and currently enrolls over 2,500 students). In 2003, the library purchased two user seats for 90 titles in Safari Tech Books. When they compared the usage of their print collection to the Safari usage, it was found that the e-books had a great potential for making a set of current resources available to a body of students who were not strong book users. One lecturer had a class subscribe to a set of Safari books rather than purchase a textbook (this option is no longer available) and valued content that was interactive and had multimedia features that appealed to computer science students. Those students had difficulty adjusting to studying with the electronic book as a text, but most said that they would get used to it. A usage survey was conducted and yielded some of the results and opinions expressed previously: the searching and navigating functions were positives, while reading online and lack of mobility with a computer were problems. The adoption of e-books depends on the "experience, information need and expectations of the users" (Abbott & Kelly, 2004, p. 12).

Dillon (2001a, 2001b) wrote a series of articles on the NetLibrary consortial purchases of members of the University of Texas System Libraries initiated in 1999. The system began purchasing electronic books while avoiding proprietary software and personal book devices. Members from 12 institutions selected from monthly lists of offerings, making the approach similar to an approval plan with the notable exception that the purchases were not made at the time the print version was originally published. In addition, the selectors never knew if their purchases would be acquired until bibliographic records were received. Votes were tallied and titles with the most votes were purchased as money was available. The system provided the funds rather than each individual library.

In 2001, Dillon noted that it was too soon to place much validity in usage statistics and he outlined many of the problems intrinsic in comparing print and electronic usage.

> The printed book circulation data is particularly vexing in that, even though we know the patron checked the book out, we don't know how intensively they used each title, or whether they even opened the book at all. With the e-book data we don't know if the usage represents one user intensively reading a title during many different sessions, or if it represents brief examinations by many different people. (2001a, pp. 116-117)

Despite those warnings, the statistics on usage have surpassed expectations and he indicated that usage in business/economics and computer science was fairly high. In addition, the study unveiled that many of the highest used electronic titles were actually lost or missing from the collection and another portion was not owned by UT Austin libraries, calling into question local collection development decisions. Finally, Dillon (2001b) analyzed the consortial approach for e-book purchases as it impacts the type of materials selected. While the selection results followed expectations, there was a larger number of quick reference, non-fiction titles purchased.

METHODOLOGY

The UT System was an early adopter of electronic books through multi-campus librarian selection with NetLibrary (Dillon, 2001a) and the University of Texas at Dallas Library supported the project by selecting titles along with librarians from the other 11 institutions. The library regularly consulted the administrative module to analyze the usage of the collection and quickly realized that the statistics suggested many customers were connecting to the resources. As a result of looking at these statistics, the library actively pursued electronic book acquisition to determine which models of delivery were used and favored by students and faculty.

The library acquired a number of different types of e-book models. Rather than add collections through consortial agreements, the library wanted to subscribe to a model where the items were selected by the vendor. ebrary Academic Collection provided the library a large collection of e-books which were available as a subscription. The collection was used to determine the importance of selectors in choosing electronic books versus a vendor providing a collection. In addition, library administration wanted to determine if the rate of use and subjects being used were similar across e-book collections.

Secondly, because of the strong demand of computer science and business/economics in NetLibrary and because of the print usage of books in the same subjects, the library wanted to subscribe to a product with a narrow subject focus. Safari Tech Books was the product selected. In addition, this model allowed the user to search the words within the volume and allowed precise retrieval to a paragraph in the item.

Librarians wanted to determine how electronic reference items might be selected in preference to printed items. The Oxford Reference Online collection was selected and the Gale Virtual Reference collection was purchased consortially.

The librarians were often faced with explaining some of the problems with the NetLibrary delivery model and wanted to explore a model that allowed the users to manipulate the book in more generous ways. EBL allows an e-book to be downloaded for a day and read offline and 20% of the book to be printed in a session. The initial purchase was small (125 titles) so analysis is somewhat limited.

Finally, the library staff wanted to explore electronic books for historical items because of the limits in the depth of its collections. During 2004 and early 2005, the UT System purchased access to Early English Books Online and the Eighteenth Century collection (Gale). Several Alexander Street Press databases (American Filmscripts Online, North American Women's Letters and Diaries, Early Encounters in North American and North American Immigrant Letters and Diaries) were also selected. These historical materials often allow the users to print the entire book and cut and paste text. Many of the titles and collections were available within the microfilm resources of the library.

In additional to looking at different models, the other goal of the project was to determine how the electronic books were being used. This aspect of the project continues to be a problem because the statistics are supplied by the publisher and each publisher provides different variables to approximate the intensity of the use. Comparing statistics between companies is a problem because of the lack of standards. COUNTER is working to standardize statistical reporting on the usage of electronic books in the same way as standards were set for electronic journals. Some products provide data about time online, the number of sessions, the items retrieved (number and title), items viewed, average time on-line, pages viewed, and pages downloaded to name but a few of the options. Making comparisons between products is as much a problem as comparing online access to print circulation patterns. A customer could connect and use a number of books in each session or connect several times to a book to print a page or read it online. The same library customer could check out a stack of books and return them without opening them.

RESULTS AND FINDINGS

By early 2005, the library had access to over 350,000 electronic books. Nearly all titles were either added to the library's catalog or loading of the records is planned.

The library began to track usage of electronic books each month during 2003 and discovered that many of the publishers had been making the statistics available since 1999. Whenever possible, the statistics on the number of titles used was preferred over other indicators such as sessions, downloads, or pages viewed in an effort to try to compare checkouts of the print collection to the use of online books. The majority of the e-book usage occurs between NetLibrary (49%), Safari Tech (15%), and ebrary (11%). The overall electronic book usage grew from 29,776 in 2004 to 63,079 in the first 11 months of 2005. Part of the usage occurred because of the large increase in titles available. But even within products, the demand for electronic books is increasing at a dramatic rate. During the same period, circulation of print materials declined from 67,465 in 2004 to 50,993 in the first 11 months of 2005. While the university is growing by 1-3% per year and the library is spending over $500,000 on printed monographs, the print circulation is flat or declining.

The statistics indicate a dramatic increase in NetLibrary usage since its initial creation in late 1999. Presently, the library has access to nearly 36,000 titles and they have been used over 20,000 times per year. The growth rate in the use of the collection is slowing as the number of titles

available in other sources increases. In addition, some of the other resources do not require a customer to register for a password. Despite
slight fluctuations of 1-2 % each year, the usage by subject has been
very stable. Computer science and engineering (39%), business, economics, and management (17%), arts and humanities (14%), and natural sciences and mathematics (13%) constitute the majority of the
demand for NetLibrary books. These numbers were anticipated as the
usage of the print collection in computer science and technology is extremely high as compared to other subjects.

The library subscribed to ebrary Academic collection to determine
the importance of selection in the acquisition of e-books. One of the
strongest factors for the usage of ebrary is the delivery model. Unlike
NetLibrary, ebrary does not require passwords and has relaxed the
printing requirements (five pages can be printed at a time rather than
one page for NetLibrary) and the text can be copied and put into another
document. The usage of ebrary is almost identical to the subject use
within the NetLibrary collection so despite the fact that NetLibrary was
selected by librarians across the UT System and ebrary is a package collection, the usage by subject is similar.

Over the past three months, the rate of growth in ebrary increased over
190%. While there is about 25% duplication between the NetLibrary and
ebrary collections, the library is increasing its efficiency in loading and
merging bibliographic records. If the items are duplicates, the library is
attempting to put the print and electronic links to e-books on the same
record. In addition, the librarians prefer ebrary to NetLibrary and whenever possible will refer customers to the delivery method they believe
the users prefer.

Unlike other vendors, ebrary provides slightly different statistics that
give further insight into how the e-books are used. In the 7,600 sessions
conducted in 11 months in 2005, over 163,220 pages were viewed, 2,300
pages were copied, and 18,000 pages were printed. The printing and
copying statistics suggest something beyond casual browsing behavior.
Because of the similarities between the subject usage of NetLibrary and
ebrary, the importance of librarian selection rather than subscription
purchase is questionable and further testing is needed.

Safari Tech provides more statistics on how the titles are being used.
In addition to the titles being accessed, data are available on the number
of successful queries (something retrieved), on the time spent online
during an average session, on the number of turnaways, and the number
of sections retrieved (generally chapters of a book). Safari Tech showed
a 125% increase in sessions between 2004 and 2005. From January-No-

vember of 2005, Safari accounted for over 6,200 sessions despite an 11% decline in students attending classes in the engineering/computer science school. The average session length is increasing. Over the past 12 months, the average session time increased 28% to about 9 1/2 minutes. Clearly, the need for additional resources in computer science and engineering was helped by the subscription to Safari Tech Books and the greater period of time spent online with each item suggests usage or reading rather than other types of browsing/clicking behavior.

What is surprising is the demand for historic materials from databases such as the Eighteenth Century collection, Early English Books, Evans Digital Edition, and many collections from the Alexander Street Press. Only 10% of students major in arts and humanities programs so the audience is smaller than business or computer science. Despite the size of the humanities programs, the usage on these databases constitutes 20% of the e-book usage. These statistics are surprising because many of the collections have not yet been cataloged. The relative number of sessions is small in comparison to the number of titles provided as some of these products are very large. While the loading of the bibliographic records is pending or the library is waiting on the final distribution of the record sets, the databases are being promoted and add depth to a print collection which is limited in older and primary resource materials.

As an example of the type of usage experienced in the historic materials, Early English Books Online (bibliographic records were added to the catalog) was used 470 times in 11 months of 2005. The information collected from the usage is calculated by document/page image views (4,140), pdf downloads (256), and full text (ASCII) views (66). The vendor (ProQuest) provides a statistic on the number of searches returning no hits. In the last 11 months, 42% of the searches resulted in no hits. Because the statistical reports do not provide a list of these searches, it is impossible to tell whether the searches were unsuccessful because the item/subject was not present, because of spelling errors, or because of errors in using the database. The number does seem to be very large and warrants further research.

While the library does yet subscribe to a large number of reference books in electronic format, data are available for the use of the Oxford English Dictionary (OED) and the Oxford Reference Online (ORO) during 2004/2005. For the OED, there have been over 1,500 sessions in 2005. On average, the OED sessions last approximately 6 1/2 minutes and 4.4 pages are viewed per session. The total time spent online was 113 hours (through 11 months of 2005). On average, the ORO sessions lasted 6 1/2 minutes and 10 pages were viewed. There have been 1,363 sessions since July 2004 with a total of over six days spent online.

Usage of ACLS History E-Book Project exhibits above average usage as compared to the average of all subscribers. Since March 2004, UTD learners have conducted 1,061 searches or 18% more than the average site. In addition, users have viewed 4,016 page images or over twice the average for all project sites. Despite the size of the humanities program, demand for quality electronic books in history is impressive.

CONCLUSION

As librarians, we presently are unable to determine how customers are using electronic books as compared to traditional library materials. In comparing circulation transactions, no data are available if the checked-out item was opened, used briefly, or read cover to cover. While we can determine if the book was checked out and how many times it was checked out or renewed, further information about the use is not gathered.

The same problems exist with the statistics available on electronic book usage. If one was to compare session usage to a checkout, the growth in e-book usage is enormous within the library studied. While it is certain that the usage between print and electronic titles could be very different, some of the statistics available indicate that the demand for all things electronic is infiltrating into monographs in the form of e-books. Because of the extensive search systems in many of the models studied, it seems certain that the closer libraries can get to giving customers segments of text, the more useful the item becomes. It is important to note that the ability to find phrases in a large set of texts is new and that tool can be incredibly powerful for locating specific information within a collection.

Despite that many customers frown on trying to read a book much less a chapter online, others are becoming more comfortable with the technology according to two recent user surveys conducted on the customers' knowledge and usage of electronic books at the University of Texas at Dallas. Current reader developments suggest that the devices being developed will become more comfortable for facilitating online reading.

Standards are not currently available to evaluate usage between e-book collections. While the information provided is helpful in determining overall use of the collections, how the statistics are collected is important if librarians are to determine how to invest in electronic book materials and what model is preferable for students and faculty.

The demand for electronic information in academic libraries is pervasive and will continue to increase. Librarians should work to improve these resources as a means to increase the electronic information available to their customers. The ability to search the text of a library's collection can make the difference in finding an answer to a question and releasing the power of the collections amassed by our institutions.

Rather than threaten library traditions, electronic monographs provide traditional and distance learners with a different form of information. In the short term, the printed volume might not be replaced by users wanting to read a long tome cover-to-cover online. This study found that the demand for electronic books as expressed by usage statistics is enormous and growing at an exponential rate. From the overall experiences of an academic library which invests heavily in the format, electronic books are offering library customers a level of interaction with monographs which has never been available. Many users already prefer the online version of a text to a printed resource. Advances in technology can make reading online comfortable. Collecting the e-book format will only make libraries more relevant in the coming decades.

REFERENCES

Abbott, W., & Kelly, K. (2004). Sooner or later!–Have e-books turned the page? *VALA 2004: Breaking boundaries: Integration and interoperability.* 12th Biennial Conference and Exhibition, 3-5 February 2004, Melbourne Convention Centre. Retrieved November 30, 2005, from http://www.vala.org.au/vala2004/2004pdfs/46AbbKel.PDF.

Bell, D. A. (2005). The bookless future, what the Internet is doing to scholarship. *New Republic, 232* (16/17), 27-33.

Brown, G. J. (2001). Beyond print: Reading digitally. *Library Hi Tech, 19*(4), 390-399.

Coleman, G. (2004). E-books and Academics: An ongoing experiment. *Feliciter, 4,* 124-125.

Cox, J. (2004). E-books: Challenges and opportunities. *D-Lib Magazine, 10*(10). Retrieved July 28, 2005, from http://www.dlib.org/dlib/october04/cox/10cox.html.

Coyle, K. (2003). E-books: It's about evolution, not revolution. *Library Journal, 128*(17), 8-12.

Croft, R., & Bedi, S. (2005). E-books for a distributed learning university: The Royal Roads University case. *Journal of Library Administration, 41*(1/2), 113-137.

Dillon, D. (2001a). E-books: The University of Texas experience, part 1. *Library Hi Tech, 19*(2), 113-124.

Dillon, D. (2001b). E-books: The University of Texas experience, part 2. *Library Hi Tech, 19*(4), 350-262.

Dorner, J. (2003). The literature of the book: E-books. *Logos, 14*(3), 144-149.

Grogg, J. E., & Ashmore, B. (2005). Reading the e-book wave. *Against the Grain, 17*(1), 41-49.

Lewis, P. (2004). Prose and cons: Sony's new e-book. *Fortune, 150*(5), pp. 62-63.

Littman, J., & Connaway, L. S. (2004). A circulation analysis of print books and e-books in an academic research library. *Library Resources & Technical Services, 48*(4), 256-262.

Miller, R. (2004). Safari bucks industry e-book trend. *EContent, 27*(4), 12-13.

O'Leary, M. (2003). E-book scenarios updated. *Online, 27*(5), 59-60.

Rogers, M. (2004). Librarians, publishers and vendors revisit e-books. *Library Journal, 12*(7), 23-24.

doi:10.1300/J111v45n03_09

A Study on Using Rubrics and Citation Analysis to Measure the Quality of Doctoral Dissertation Reference Lists from Traditional and Nontraditional Institutions

Johanna Tuñón
Bruce Brydges

Nova Southeastern University

SUMMARY. This study used citation analysis in conjunction with a subjective rubric with five criteria deemed valid by a majority of committee chairs at the writers' institution to assess the quality of 144 dissertation reference lists from a non-traditional program. Criteria included the breadth of resources; the depth of the literature review as shown through the citing of critical historical and theoretical works; depth as demonstrated through the scholarliness of citations chosen; currency; and relevancy. The results were then compared with citations from 59 dissertation reference lists purposively selected from a list of 10 traditional institutions. This social-constructive theory-based approach ascertained that there was no statistically significant difference between traditional or non-traditional scores for any criteria except breadth of resources which measures the number and variety of citation sources. In contrast, the constructivist theoretical approach establishes statistically significant differences in 11 of 17 variables. doi:10.1300/J111v45n03_10

[Haworth co-indexing entry note]: "A Study on Using Rubrics and Citation Analysis to Measure the Quality of Doctoral Dissertation Reference Lists from Traditional and Nontraditional Institutions." Tuñón, Johanna, and Bruce Brydges. Co-published simultaneously in *Journal of Library Administration* (The Haworth Information Press, an imprint of The Haworth Press, Inc.) Vol. 45, No. 3/4, 2006, pp. 459-481; and: *The Twelfth Off-Campus Library Services Conference Proceedings* (ed: Julie A. Garrison) The Haworth Information Press, an imprint of The Haworth Press, Inc., 2006, pp. 459-481.

Available online at http://jla.haworthpress.com
doi:10.1300/J111v45n03_10

KEYWORDS. Online resources, survey, web pages, usage patterns, evaluation, assessment

INTRODUCTION

The increasing importance given to learning outcomes by accrediting agencies has sparked a strong interest on the part of academic libraries in assessment tools in general and ways of quantifying the acquisition of library research skills in particular. Although a number of assessment tools measure the information literacy levels of undergraduates, finding methods that quantify library research skills mastered at the graduate level is still a challenge. For graduate students, simple pretest/posttests are not sufficient to document the efficacy of students' library research skills, particularly skills that are more meta-cognitive in nature. One solution for this problem has been to examine graduate capstone projects for evidence that library research skills have been mastered (Beile, Boote, & Killingsworth, 2003, 2004; Brydges & Tuñón, 2005a, 2005b; Green & Bowser, 2003).

Dissertations have been traditionally seen as the culmination of students' formal academic training (Herubel, 1991). Numerous studies (Budd, 1988; Gooden, 2001; Herubel, 1991; Iya, 1996; Kuyper-Rushing, 1999; Okiy, 2003; Smith, 2003; Thomas, 2000) have used citation analysis to examine dissertation reference lists for a variety of purposes. These studies made the assumption that reference lists provide evidence of the authors' "ability to engage in an extensive scholarly endeavor" (Buttlar, 1999, p. 228) characterized by locating, evaluating, and synthesizing information in specific areas of study. Librarians have often used dissertations and theses to help in collection development decisions (Chambers & Healey, 1973; Gooden, 2001; Haycock, 2004; Herubel, 1991; Kushkowski, Parsons, & Wiese, 2003; Kuyper-Rushing, 1999; Leiding, 2005; Smith, 2003; Thomas, 2000; Walcott, 1991; Waugh & Ruppel, 2004). Although citation analysis has been used to assess the effectiveness of library training at the undergraduate level (Ackerson, Howard, & Young, 1991; Dykeman & King, 1983; Hurst & Leonard, 2005; Kohl & Wilson, 1986; Oppenheim & Smith, 2001; Young & Ackerson, 1995), it has been used less frequently to assess graduate students in particular (Brydges & Tuñón, 2005a, 2005b; Tuñón & Brydges, 2005). Beile et al. (2003) more narrowly focused their study on the use of citation analysis to analyze only the citations used in the literature reviews of 30 Doctorate of Education (Ed.D.) dissertations.

Only two studies have used citation analysis to assess the library research skills of distance students in higher education. Heller-Ross (2002) used 78 reference lists with a total of 441 citations retrieved from research papers by nursing students at Plattsburgh State University in New York to compare classes taught face-to-face with classes taught online. In a research grant at Nova Southeastern University, Tuñón and Brydges (Brydges & Tuñón, 2005a, 2005b; Tuñón & Brydges, 2005) examined 144 dissertation reference lists of students in the Child and Youth Studies Ed.D. program at Nova Southeastern University (NSU) using data collected through citation analysis in conjunction with two assessment tools they developed. They compared dissertation reference lists by 51 students attending classes in the three-county area of south Florida with reference lists of 93 students that attended classes at field-based sites that met at various sites around the United States. The findings of these two research projects that focused on distance and local students were important because neither study found any statistically significant difference between the overall quality of the reference lists cited by the students in traditional and nontraditional methods of delivering educational instruction. It should be noted that traditional institutions as it is used in these previous studies and in this paper refer to institutions of higher education that provided "traditional," face-to-face instruction and support services as distinguished from nontraditional institutions that provide much of the instruction and support services at a distance. The methods of delivery of instruction and support services ranged from face-to-face at field-based sites to asynchronous online classes and the use of various synchronous technologies such as compressed video. The important distinguishing characteristic between the nontraditional institutions and traditional institutions that may offer some distance programs, is that the separation in time or place between the students and the services provided by the nontraditional institution is the norm rather than the exception.

The study by Tuñón and Brydges was also noteworthy because it went one step beyond analyzing the statistical significance of their findings to compare the types of resources used by students at the writers' nontraditional university with two other recent citation analysis studies of more traditional Ed.D. students (Beile et al., 2003; Haycock, 2004). The Haycock study used 43 dissertation reference lists from Ed.D. students at the University of Minnesota. The study by Beile et al. used dissertations from two "top ranked schools of education" (2003, p. 3) as well as a third institution that was described as newer and smaller. Tuñón and Brydges found that the NSU students used journal articles almost 25% more frequently than students in the other two studies while the students in the studies by Haycock and Beile et al. used more traditional print resources, particularly books more frequently (see Table 1). This was noteworthy because the writer's institution has been a pioneer (Riggs, 1997) in meeting the educational needs of working adults at times and places convenient for them since the 1970s and because the institution routinely delivered programs using everything from site-based and online classes to the use of videos and compressed video. Because atypical usage patterns were produced by students from a stereotypical "nontraditional" institution, Tuñón and Brydges' findings raised questions about whether the overall environment of nontraditional institutions such as NSU might impact the types and quality of resources cited by students at these institutions. The authors speculated that factors such as online classes, committee chairs who interact with their advisees at a distance, access to library resources online, and library training that focuses on access to resources online might be characteristics of nontraditional institutions that influence the differences in citation patterns.

CITATION ANALYSIS THEORIES

Theories of citation analysis have traditionally been concerned with using citation counts to assess the flow of information or the quality of contributions (impact) made by individuals (e.g., faculty up for tenure), certain publications or groups of publications (e.g., core library science journals), or even disciplines such as forestry, music, etc. Social constructive and constructivist theories provide two different interpretations about the value of referencing behavior. A social constructive view of the use of reference lists takes into account the social conditions involved in the dissertation writing process. As Moed (2005) noted, a social constructive view factors the social environment that produced a cited work into account or, as the case is in this study, the referencing behavior of students that chose to cite selected documents in dissertation reference lists. The theory takes the position that citation analysis can provide valid and objective indications about the significance of the resources being cited. Although Moed's discussion of this theory focused on using citation analysis to evaluate the quality of scientific re-

TABLE 1. Comparison of Resources Used in Three Citation Analysis Studies of Ed.D. Students

	Tuñón/Brydges (2005)	Beile, Boote, & Killingsworth (2003)	Haycock (2004)
Journals	69%	45%	44%
Books	18%	33%	56%
Other	13%	22%	--

search, the social constructive view can also be applied to the quality of dissertation reference lists. For example, the types of resources in a reference list can be "viewed, evaluated, and analyzed to some extent separately from the text in which they were made" (2005, p. 218) and mark what Moed termed the "socio-cognitive location" (p. 219). For the purpose of this paper, it is assumed that citations can be examined as reflections of a doctoral student's awareness and appropriate use of what should be included in a dissertation reference list. In this approach, the relevance of citation analysis is based on the degree to which it measures the types and quality of resources cited rather than a purely mechanical, quantitative count of dissertation references that is the hallmark of a constructivist approach.

In contrast, the constructivist approach to citation analysis operates on the assumption that citations are a reflection of a wide array of individual motives and special circumstances which cannot be used to make broader generalizations. To put it another way, the constructivist theory does not see citations as having anything in common with each other or as useful for identifying socio-cognitive usage patterns. Instead, a constructivist approach asserts what is important is the number counts. This approach uses the sheer number or quantity of citations being cited to define quality rather than factoring in other cogent considerations.

USE OF RUBRICS IN ASSESSMENT

Rubrics are frequently used as assessment tools to document library research skills. A rubric can be defined as a qualitative tool that uses agreed-upon standards to assess individuals' ability to address expected outcomes. In her article touting the benefits of rubrics for librarians, Stefl-Mabry (2004) noted, "Complex learning cannot be assessed with simplistic measures" (p. 21) that use mere checklists. Rogers and Graham (1998) defined a rubric as any established set of statements (criteria) that clearly, precisely, accurately, and thoroughly describe the varying, distinguishable, quality (or developmental) levels that may exist in something (a product, organization, creation, system, etc.). Currently, the most common uses for rubrics in education are evaluating, scoring, and assessing "student work" in order to accurately determine the work's level of quality. This approach is no different from the way rubrics are used outside of the classroom when one says that a movie gets "two thumbs up," a restaurant is a "five-star" establishment, or the figure skating compulsories' score is a 5.9.

Using rubrics in conjunction with citation analysis is not a new concept for librarians. Dykeman and King (1983) started in that direction with their "scoring guide," but Green and Bowser (2003) actually used the term "rubric" for their criteria for evaluation of the citations used in students' masters-level theses literature reviews. Beile et al. (2003) used citation analysis in conjunction with a more precise subjective rubric to assess education dissertations. The investigators' previous study (Brydges & Tuñón, 2005a, 2005b; Tuñón & Brydges, 2005) went one step further when they validated two different rubrics used in conjunction with citation analysis. They used a social construction approach in a qualitative and subjective rubric. The authors' goal was to provide criteria that were based on the best thinking in the field about what constitutes good performance in order to articulate the essence of what assessors look for when they judge quality (Arter & McTighe, 2001). The second rubric was quantitative in nature and applied a more constructionist use of an objective and mechanical algorithm for counting citations and quantifying quality.

QUESTIONS ABOUT QUALITY IN ED.D. PROGRAMS AND THE RESEARCH CONTEXT

Two studies in 2005 raised questions about the quality of Ed.D. programs. First, a report (Levine, 2005) by the Education Schools Project, which charged that the majority of Ed.D. programs "range[d] from inadequate to appalling, even at some of the country's leading universities" (p. 23), received national coverage (Jacobson, 2005). Later in the same year, Boote and Beile (2005) made a scathing indictment of the quality of literature reviews and students' library research skills. They described what they termed a "dirty secret" (p. 4) known by dissertation committees that dissertation literature reviews (1) are not exhaustive and up-to-date and (2) are poorly conceptualized and written, and they documented these assertions with results from their earlier study (Beile et al., 2003, 2004).

The issues of quality and distance education intersected at the writers' institution. Nova Southeastern University is currently the seventh largest private, not-for-profit academic institution in the United States, and the institution's school of education accounts for 42% of all students enrolled (*NSU Fact Book*, 2004). The fact that more than 50% of the education students attended classes outside of the institution's main campus in Broward County illustrates the prevailing climate of distance education for students in this academic program, and this trend is accelerating as increasing numbers of classes throughout the institution are offered online.

The issue of how to assess the quality of library instruction for NSU's Ed.D. students came to the forefront as the university began preparations for the process of reaffirmation of accreditation in 2007. The library had been concerned with providing all students with equivalent library services (Chakraborty & Tuñón, 2002; Quinlan, Tuñón, & Hutchens, 2002; Ramirez & Tuñón, 2003; Tuñón, 1996, 1997; Tuñón & Pival, 1997), using technology (Pival & Tuñón, 2001, 2002) to provide library training, and preparing for reaccreditation (Tuñón, 2004; Tuñón & Pival, 2001). The quality of the dissertation reference lists of Ed.D. students in the Child and Youth Studies (CYS) program at NSU became a focus of interest initially because Tuñón (1999) had completed a study with this program in 1999, and the Child and Youth Studies program had developed a collaborative team-taught approach to library training for the program's Ed.D. students (Brydges & Tuñón, 2005a, 2005b). Finding effective ways to document that students actually had mastered the library research skills became a more pressing problem as the university prepared for reaccreditation. The library sought to document learning outcomes, and the CYS program wished to quantify the effectiveness of their dissertation process.

RESEARCH QUESTIONS

This study looked at the following questions:

- How do the types of resources cited in a purposive sample of Ed.D. reference lists (N = 59) from 10 traditional Carnegie research insti-

tutions compare with the resources cited by NSU's nontraditional students (N = 144)?
- To what degree are there differences in quality between dissertation reference lists from a purposive sample of traditional Carnegie research institutions (N = 59) and lists produced by NSU's nontraditional Ed.D. students (N = 144) as measured by the Brydges/Tuñón subjective rubric?
- To what degree do the quality and quantity of citations within dissertation reference lists differ as measured by the Brydges/Tuñón subjective rubric and citation analysis data compiled from the 59 traditional and 144 nontraditional dissertation reference lists?

METHODOLOGY

Citations were used in this study as descriptive indicators of document content using a citation analysis method that counted resources used in dissertation reference lists rather than resources cited in the literature review or the number of times that resources were cited. The investigators first compiled the citations from NSU's students as representative of a nontraditional institution of higher education. The data from the original 144 Child and Youth Studies dissertation reference lists consisted of a total of 10,020 citations. Sampling was not a concern for this set of reference lists because all completed dissertations by students during the initial study were included. Acquiring and processing the citations from dissertations produced by students in traditional Ed.D. programs was more complicated and much more time consuming. The investigators adapted Kuyper-Rushing's (1999) selection method of identifying Carnegie dissertations to identify the traditional dissertations used in their study. ProQuest's *Digital Dissertations* database was searched for Ed.D. dissertations that had been completed in 2002 and 2003 and indexed as dissertations in the areas of early childhood, elementary, and secondary education. This pool of top-tier degree-conferring institutions was ranked numerically by number of dissertations retrieved. The top ten institutions that met both the 1994 (Carnegie Foundation, 2000) and 2000 (Carnegie Foundation, 2005) definitions of Carnegie Research institutions were selected. Although some of the institutions of higher education were undertaking some initiatives to offer classes at a distance, the overall structure and focus of these programs were still traditional in nature. A purposeful sample of 59 dissertations from the final list of 213 dissertations was then selected.

Frequency counts were compiled for the various types of resources used based on a review of the types of categories used in several previous studies (Chambers & Healey, 1973; Glenn, 1995; Gooden, 2001; Haycock, 2004; Hovde, 1999; Kuyper-Rushing, 1999; Malone & Videon, 1997; Thomas, 2000). The title page, abstracts, and reference lists were retrieved, the names redacted, and the date of publication and type of record were input into an Excel file. Book publishers, journal titles, and resources retrieved in databases, Web sites, and ERIC documents were also collected. Information about the types of periodicals used was retrieved from *Ulrich's Periodicals Directory* including whether the periodical was identified as academic/scholarly and peer-reviewed. A total of 7,376 of citations from 59 traditional dissertations were normalized and sorted in an Excel software spreadsheet. The citations were then categorized by type (see Table 2). When resources fit into more than one category, the researchers counted function rather than form when possible. Thus, a government report that was retrieved full-text online from the ERIC database was counted as a report rather than a Web page or an ERIC document. Cover sheets with basic data about the numbers and types of citations and their currency were generated using Access.

Once the citations had been processed, the next step was to use the Brydges/Tuñón subjective rubric to score the reference lists in the two groups. (See Appendix A for a copy of the instrument.) This rubric used five criteria validated by committee chairs in the CYS program: the number and variety of types of documents cited, the depth of understanding as demonstrated through the inclusion of theoretical and background documents as well as the scholarliness, currency, and relevancy of the resources. The raters took the title pages and abstracts for the dissertations into consideration when scoring the reference lists. Because of an excellent rate of inter-rater reliability in the previous study (.978) as measured by a Spearman two-way mixed effects model of the intraclass nonparametric correlation coefficient that was significant at the 0.01 level (2 tailed), the investigators divided the work of scoring the traditional lists. Because the traditional dissertations had, on average, significantly more citations, one adjustment was made when scoring the currency section of dissertations with more than 100 citations. When dissertation reference lists had more than 100 citations, the citations published within the last three years fell below 50% but more than 30 citations, the reference list was deemed level 4 for the currency criterion. However, when the reference lists contained more than 100 citations but contained less than 30 citations published within the last three years, the score was raised between half of a level and a level above the

TABLE 2. Citation Categories

	Less than 3 yrs old	Less than 10 yrs
Periodicals (magazines, trade journals)		
Scholarly periodicals*		
Journals		
Academic/scholarly		
Peer-reviewed		
Books/book chapters		
Reports (gov. agencies, foundations, associations, universities, etc.)*		
Conference papers and proceedings*		
Dissertations		
Theses/practicums/action-based research*		
Government laws/legal cases		
ERIC ED documents*		
Newspapers*		
Web sites*		
Miscellaneous*		

*Documents that fit two or more categories were included in category with higher weight.

score it would normally earn for the high ratio of older citations to compensate for the greater breadth entailed in including the greater number of retrospective sources.

Because this study was concerned with the socio-cognitive aspects of the quality of traditional versus nontraditional dissertations, data generated by the citation analysis and subjective rubric were collected. The collected data were input into SPSS, and a two-sample one tailed t-test was conducted to establish mean gains for each of the quantitative and subjective criteria (see Tables 3 and 4).

DATA ANALYSIS

As in Tuñón and Brydges' previous findings, this study found the percentage of journals used by the students at NSU's nontraditional program to be significantly higher (67.53%) than those cited by students from traditional institutions (47.28%). The mean numbers were somewhat closer with 59.91 used by traditional students and 46.99 by nontraditional students. The overall number of citations used by traditional students, however, were more startling: traditional students cited almost double the number used by NSU's nontraditional students while books

TABLE 3. Descriptive Comparison of Traditional and Nontraditional CYS Doctoral Dissertations Using a Social Constructive Theory-Based Approach

Criteria	Nontraditional mean	Nontraditional range	Traditional mean	Traditional range	t test
N =	144	144	59	59	
Breadth	2.49		3.33		**< .0001***
Depth–Understanding	2.74		2.82		0.6279
Depth–Scholarliness	3.11		3.00		0.4855
Currency	2.58		2.61		0.8298
Relevancy	3.78		3.72		0.5112
Subjective Rubric Overall	14.69	9-19	15.55	6.5-20	0.0726

t Test scores marked **bold*** are statistically significant–confidence level 0.95 using a two-sample one tailed t-test for significance.

were used almost 3.5 times more frequently by the traditional students than the nontraditional students.

When the subjective rubric was used to analyze quality, the two groups did vary in the breadth of resources used because traditional students used significantly more resources than NSU's nontraditional students. However, the two groups had very comparable results in the areas for depth of understanding, depth of scholarliness, currency, and relevancy. Thus, it was notable that the overall subjective rubric scores varied less than 1 point (14.69 for nontraditional students and 15.55 for traditional students). As for currency, neither group obtained the majority of their citations in the last three years. Greater breadth of citations utilized in traditional dissertation reference lists may also account for the fact that students in traditional institutions, on average, cited significantly more citations that were older than 10 years than did nontraditional students.

The researchers then used the constructivist theoretical approach to analyze the citation patterns by types of resource and found statistically significant differences between the traditional and nontraditional users in 11 of 17 variables. Traditional students cited more periodical articles as well as more articles from peer-reviewed and/or academic scholarly journal articles. Traditional students, on average, cited more books, dissertations, conference papers, reports, and miscellaneous resources than the nontraditional students.

The numbers of resources reported as retrieved online from databases or the Web were surprisingly low for both groups (see Table 5).

TABLE 4. Descriptive Comparison of Traditional and Nontraditional CYS Doctoral Dissertations Using a Constructivist Theory-Based Approach

Criteria	Nontraditional mean	Nontraditional range	Traditional mean	Traditional range	t test
N =	144	144	59	59	
Total Number of Citations	69.58	23-250	126.71	25-364	< .0001*
Number of Periodical Article Citations	46.99	10-182	59.91	2-212	0.0358*
Number of Citations from Peer-Reviewed Journals	33.16	2-136	42.96	0-138	0.0345*
Number of Academic/Scholarly Journal Citations	23	0-89	30.93	2-59	0.0110*
Number of Books or Book Chap. Citations	12.55	0-104	42.52	4-229	< .0001*
Number of Dissertations	.42	0-9	1.57	0-16	.0057*
Number of Practicum/Theses	.10	0-5	.16	0-3	0.4292
Number of Conference Papers	.81	0-9	2.15	0-9	< .0001*
Number of Reports	3.42	0-24	14.22	0-17	< .0001*
Number of ERIC ED Documents	1.12	0-19	1.49	0-16	0.3940
Number of Laws/Legal Cases	.19	0-5	.16	0-3	0.5488
Newspaper Articles	.62	0-17	.47	0-9	0.5492
Web Sites	1.04	0-11	.47	0-18	0.1169
Miscellaneous	1.45	0-12	3.10	0-16	0.0013*
Citations Published Within 3 Years	16.96	0-56	20.76	0-112	0.2378
Citations Published Within 10 Years	37.67	0-130	49.40	8-171	0.0178*
Citations More Than 10 Years or Not Dated	14.54	0-92	56.52	2-174	< .0001*

t Test scores marked **bold*** are statistically significant–confidence level 0.95 using a two-sample one tailed t-test for significance.

However, the nontraditional students accessed a much higher percentage of resources retrieved online, particularly periodical articles retrieved from databases.

DISCUSSION OF RESULTS

The use of the Brydges/Tuñón subjective rubric and descriptive citation analysis to compare dissertation reference lists produced by students in traditional environments with those produced by students from

TABLE 5. Online Retrieval by Type of Citations

	Nontraditional			Traditional		
	Database	URLs	%	Database	URLs	%
Periodical Articles	360	52	4.1%	98	79	2.4%
Books	1	1	> 0.1%	0	2	> 0.1%
Dissertations/Theses	5	1	> 0.1%	0	0	0.0%
Conference Papers	0	5	> 0.1%	0	13	0.2%
Reports	45	49	0.9%	21	87	1.5%
ERIC ED Documents	5	17	0.2%	0	6	> 0.1%
Laws/Legal Cases	0	4	> 0.1%	0	3	> 0.1%
Newspaper Articles	6	25	> 0.1%	0	6	> 0.1%
Web Sites	0	179	1.8%	0	112	1.5%
Total Percent Retrieved Online	7.5% (755 of 10,020 citations)			5.8% (427 of 7,376)		

nontraditional environments demonstrated that both groups were able to identify quality resources as defined by relevant resources that included landmark and seminal resources, theories, and empirical research. The traditional students, on average, had more breadth both in terms of sheer numbers and in the variety and types of resources used. The citation counts documented that the breadth of the resources used by traditional students included many more print resources in the form of books, but they also used more dissertations, conference papers, and reports. In addition, the more exhaustive nature of the resources cited by traditional students may also account for the fact that they were also, on average, more likely to include a higher number of older resources.

Looking at the data through a constructivist lens proved to be useful. Descriptive data gathered through the citation analysis were useful in taking into account the quality of different types of resources (e.g., consideration whether the majority of journals were classified as academic/scholarly and/or peer-reviewed in Ulrich's, as well as types of resources that did not fall into the categories of periodicals or books). Assessments of the quality of the dissertation must take into account the cognitive aspects of the dissertation under consideration. Or, to put it another way, the sheer numbers produced by quantitative counts is best tempered by qualitative considerations that make more subjective decisions about quality based on the criteria.

Looking at the data through the social constructivist lens raised more questions than the data answered about how the socio-cognitive settings in traditional versus nontraditional institutions may have impacted student outcomes. For example, the fact that traditional students used almost 3.5 times as many books as nontraditional students is a case in point. Did traditional students use more print resources because they had ready access to the traditional brick-and-mortar library? At first glance, previous findings by Tuñón and Brydges (2005) might dispel this interpretation because they found no statistically significant difference between the types of resources used by distance and local students at Nova Southeastern University. However, the fact that NSU is a nontraditional institution has also played a role in the results since both NSU's local and distance students used more journals than did the students from traditional institutions. Thus, the answer may be more complex than just reasonable access to a print collection. The researchers speculated that differences in usage patterns between the two groups may be accounted for by socio-cognitive factors ranging from differing expectations by advisors and academic programs about what is a satisfactory or quality reference list. Other factors may be the difference in the nature of interactions of traditional and nontraditional committee members with their advisees, differences in the method and focus of library training provided to traditional versus nontraditional doctoral students and differences in the types of print and electronic resources provided to the two types of students.

The data in Tables 3 and 4 demonstrate that any use of citation analysis of dissertation reference lists need to assess quality from both a social constructive and a constructivist approach to balance the subjective considerations with the use of mechanical counts. As is the case with citation impact (Moed, 2005), citation analysis that provided absolute citation counts served a straight-forward and important quantitative function while the subjective rubric provided qualitative judgments of quality that take into account the context in which the citations appear (e.g., the focus of the research topic identified in the dissertation title and abstract).

For the purposes of this study, the decision had initially been made to use only the Brydges/Tuñón subjective rubric in conjunction with a citation analysis but not to make use of the Tuñón/Brydges objective rubric (Appendix B) as the planned focus for this study had been on quality defined by qualitative rather than quantitative measures. The researchers had felt that the descriptive data obtained from the citation analysis were sufficient to examine the constructivist approach that measured quality in terms of mechanical counts.

LIMITATIONS

Although citation analysis is quantitative in nature, and the mechanical nature of the activity is inherently objective, the simple quantitative-statistical considerations of citation analysis can still result in errors. Because the data in this study were collected through a mechanical counting of citations, the investigators did not have to worry about the data being contaminated by participant responses and opinions. However, errors in the citations were an issue. Students frequently had errors in their citations. Errors ranged from misspelled words (e.g., *Education Leadership* instead of *Educational Leadership* and *principle* instead of *principal*) to transposed letters and incorrectly formatted citations (e.g., government reports identified as Web sites because they were retrieved online). Data input by students introduced some errors in spelling and incomplete data. Also, the character recognition software used for some of the data used from the previous study of NSU students also introduced some errors. However, the important point was that these types of errors were random in nature. Because of the large data sample, the researchers assumed that any bias introduced by these random errors was likely to cancel itself out.

Errors that were not random in nature were more problematic because they presented the potential for introducing patterns that biased the results. When students made systematic errors that resulted in incomplete citations, the use of citation analysis to look at citation usage patterns in dissertation reference lists could result in a distorted picture of the types of resources used. The lack of retrieval statements is a case in point. The use of retrieval statements for resources retrieved online is important information provided by citations. First of all, the information provides an indication of usage patterns. Secondly, retrieval statements can serve as a "performance measure" (Mercer, 2000, para. 2) of students' knowledge of how to use the library's online resources. Libraries use this type of empirical evidence to quantify learning outcomes (Kelley & Orr, 2003; Tuñón, 2004). When students do not include retrieval statements for resources retrieved online, the errors have important implications for citation analyses because the errors introduced are not random in nature. As a result, any interpretation of the usage patterns would in turn be flawed by factors totally unrelated to the impact of electronic resources on those patterns. The fact that less than ten percent of the citations in both the traditional and nontraditional groups were cited as retrieved full-text is suspect in light of documented student reliance on online resources by students in general (Dunlap &

Stierman, 2001) and distance students in particular (Kelley & Orr, 2003). The suggestion that both groups of students had problems with correctly citing online resources would be in line with the problem with correct formatting of citations in several other studies (Beile et al., 2003; Gooden, 2001; Malone & Videon, 1997).

AREAS FOR FURTHER RESEARCH

Research using citation analysis in conjunction with the Brydges/ Tuñón subjective rubric presents a number of areas for more study:

- The high percentage of journals by nontraditional students may be attributed in part to the focus in library training sessions on online resources that are equally accessible by students on- and off-campus. However, this may be an over-simplistic explanation that does not take into account other possible factors such as dissertation committee members that meet with their advisees by phone or e-mail rather than in more traditional on-campus settings. The impact of bias that skews resources retrieved to favor resources available on the Web must also be taken into account.
- Citation analysis of dissertation reference lists from a broader group of nontraditional programs is needed.
- Studies that include dissertations from a broader spectrum of types of Ed.D. programs than just the Child and Youth Studies area of specialization are needed.
- A longitudinal study of changes in citation patterns that appear in Child and Youth Studies dissertation reference lists is necessary. This study should include CYS dissertations that predate students' access to online databases.
- The Tuñón/Brydges objective rubric was not utilized in this study. However, given findings that point to the impact of quantitative data, analysis of a broader spectrum of dissertation reference lists comparing data from the subjective/qualitative rubric with the objective/quantitative rubric is needed, particularly as it pertains to the constructivist theory.
- Focus thus far has been on dissertations by students in the United States, but citation patterns by students in other countries may have different results that need to be explored.
- The relative merits of assessing education dissertations using Beile et al.'s (2003, 2004) rubric used to assess citations in the lit-

erature review section could be compared to the results found using the Brydges/Tuñón subjective rubric to assess reference lists.
- In addition to using the Brydges/Tuñón subjective rubric (Appendix A) and the data collected from counting the number of citations in various categories, citations from traditional and nontraditional institutions should be examined using the more nuanced weighting system incorporated in the Tuñón/Brydges objective rubric's algorithms (Appendix B). The results should be compared with those obtained using the constructivist approach of using purely mechanical counts utilized in this paper.

CONCLUSIONS

Citation analysis used in conjunction with the Brydges/Tuñón subjective rubric demonstrated that the quality of dissertation reference lists produced by students at traditional and nontraditional institutions has more in common than differences. Both social construction and constructivist theories had insights to offer into the use of citation analysis as an assessment tool for the library research skills of doctoral students. More research is also needed, however. Directions for further research that emerged include a need for studies using a broader selection of traditional and nontraditional dissertation reference lists that include more specialization areas and more institutions, longitudinal studies that examine the impact of electronic resources on student usage patterns, and surveys that examine possible differences in library services provided to Ed.D. students in traditional and nontraditional programs.

REFERENCES

Ackerson, L. G., Howard, J. G., & Young, V. E. (1991). Assessing the relationship between library instruction methods and the quality of undergraduate research. *Research Strategies, 9*, 139-141.

Arter, J., & McTighe, J. (2001). *Scoring rubrics in the classroom: Using performance criteria for assessing and improving student performance.* Thousand Oaks, CA: Corwin.

Beile, P. M., Boote, D. N., & Killingsworth, E. K. (2003, April). *Characteristics of educational doctoral dissertation references: An inter-institutional analysis of review of literature citations.* Paper presented at the Annual Meeting of the American Educational Research Association, Chicago, IL. (ERIC Document Reproduction Service No. ED478598) Retrieved November 20, 2004, from ERIC database.

Beile, P. M., Boote, D. N., & Killingsworth, E. K. (2004). A microscope or a mirror?: A question of study validity regarding the use of dissertation citation analysis for evaluating research collections. *Journal of Academic Librarianship, 30*(5), 347-353.

Boote, D., & Beile, P. (2005). Scholars before researchers: On the centrality of the dissertation literature review in research preparation. *Educational Researcher, 34*(6), 3-15. Retrieved December 4, 2005, from Wilson Education Full Text database.

Brydges, B., & Tuñón, J. (2005a, April). *Assessing and improving the library research skills of distance graduate students through citation mining and analysis using two new dissertation bibliometric assessment tools.* Paper presented at the Canadian Association for Distance Education, in partnership with The Centre for Online and Distance Education, Simon Fraser University Vancouver, BC.

Brydges, B., & Tuñón, J. (2005b, May). *Conducting a comparative assessment of doctoral students' library research skills using citation analysis tools.* Poster session presented at the Annual Meeting of the American Educational Research Association Conference, Montreal, Canada.

Budd, J. (1988). A bibliometric analysis of higher education literature. *Research in Higher Education, 28*, 180-190.

Buttlar, L. (1999). Information sources in library and information science doctoral research. *Library & Information Science Research, 21*(2), 227-245.

Carnegie Foundation for the Advancement of Teaching. (2000). *Category definitions.* Retrieved March 9, 2005, from the Carnegie Foundation Web site: http://www.carnegiefoundation.org/Classification/ CIHE2000/defNotes/Definitions.htm.

Carnegie Foundation for the Advancement of Teaching. (2005). *The 2000 Carnegie classification: Background and description (excerpt).* Retrieved March 9, 2005, from the Carnegie Foundation Web site: http://www.carnegiefoundation.org/Classification/CIHE2000/background.htm.

Chakraborty, M., & Tuñón, J. (2002). Taking the distance out of library services offered international graduate students: Considerations, challenges, and concerns. Patrick B. Mahoney (Ed.), *The Tenth Off-Campus Library Services Proceedings* (pp. 131-139). Mt. Pleasant, MI: Central Michigan University.

Chambers, G. R., & Healey, J. S. (1973). Journal citations in master's theses: One measurement of a journal collection. *Journal of the American Society for Information Science, 24*, 397-401.

Dunlap, I. H., & Stierman, J. K. (2001). Full text frenzy: An analysis of periodical database use at Western Illinois University. *Illinois Libraries, 83*(4), 1-12. Retrieved December 11, 2005, from Wilson Library Literature and Information Full Text database.

Dykeman, A., & King, B. (1983). Term paper analysis: A proposal for evaluating bibliographic instruction. *Research Strategies, 1*(1), 14-21.

Glenn, D. L. (1995). A citation analysis of master's and education specialist theses and research papers by graduates of the Library Science and Information Services Department at Central Missouri State University. *Masters Abstracts International, 34*(3), 928 (Publication No. 1377607).

Gooden, A. M. (2001, Fall). Citation analysis of chemistry doctoral dissertations: An Ohio State University case study [Electronice version]. *Issues in Science and Technology Librarianship, 32.*

Green, R., & Bowser, M. (2003, April). Evolution of the thesis literature review: A faculty-librarian partnership to guide off-campus graduate research and writing. In *Learning to Make a Difference: Proceedings of the Eleventh National Conference of the Association of College and Research Libraries.* Charlotte, NC. Chicago: Association of College and Research Libraries.

Haycock, L. A. (2004). Citation analysis of educational dissertations for collection development. *Library Resources and Technical Services, 48*(2), 102-106.

Heller-Ross, H. (2002). Assessing outcomes with nursing research assignments and citation analysis of student bibliographies. *Distance learning: Information access and services for virtual users.* Binghamton, NY: The Haworth Press, Inc.

Herubel, J. P. V. M. (1991). Philosophy dissertation bibliographies and citations in serials evaluation. *Serials Librarians, 20*(2/3), 65-73.

Hovde, K. (1999). Check the citation: Library instruction and student paper bibliographies. *Research Strategies, 17,* 3-9.

Hurst, S., & Leonard, J. (2005, April). *Putting the "B" into BI: An exploratory study of the effect of library instruction on the number, variety, and sources of citations found in business students' term papers.* A poster session at the 12th National ACRL: Currents and Convergence: Navigating the Rivers of Change, Minneapolis, MN.

Iya, J. A. (1996). A citation study of education dissertations at the University of Maiduguri, Nigeria. *African Journal of Library, Archives, and Information Science, 6*(2), 129-132.

Jacobson, J. (2005, March 25). Reports call for abolition of Ed.D. degree and overhaul of education schools. *Chronicle of Higher Education, 52*(29), p. A24. Retrieved March 29, 2005, from http://chronicle.com/temp/reprint.php?id=u9s4moadqbi8oadqzqmibwiwn343ry.

Kelley, K. B., & Orr, G. J. (2003). Trends in distant student use of electronic resources: A survey. *College & Research Libraries, 64*(3), 176-191. Retrieved December 11, 2005, from Wilson Library Literature and Information Full Text database.

Kohl, D. F., & Wilson, L. A. (1986). Effectiveness of course-integrated bibliographic instruction in improving coursework. *RQ, 26,* 206-211.

Kushkowshi, J. D., Parsons, K. A., & Wiese, W. H. (2003). Master's and doctoral thesis citations: Analysis and trends of a longitudinal study. *Portal: Libraries and the Academy, 3,* 459-479. Retrieved October 25, 2004, from ProQuest Research Library database.

Kuyper-Rushing, L. (1999). Identifying uniform core journal titles for music libraries: A dissertation citation study. *College & Research Libraries, 60*(2), 153-163.

Leiding, R. (2005). Using citation checking of undergraduate honors thesis bibliographies to evaluate library collections. *College & Research Libraries, 66,* 417-429.

Levine, A. (2005). *Educating school leaders.* Report 1 from the Education Schools Project. Retrieved April 17, 2005, from http://www.edschools.org/pdf/Final313.pdf.

Malone, D., & Videon, C. (1997). Assessing undergraduate use of electronic resources: A quantitative analysis of works cited. *Research Strategies, 15*(3), 151-158.

Mercer, L. S. (2000, Winter). Measuring the use and value of electronic journals and books. *Issues in Science and Technology Librarianship.* Retrieved July 10, 2004, from Expanded Academic Index database.

Moed, H. F. (2005). *Citation analysis in research evaluation.* Dordrecht, The Netherlands: Springer.

NSU fact book. (2004). Fort Lauderdale, FL: Nova Southeastern University. Retrieved December 9, 2005, from http://www.nova.edu/rpga/factbook/2005/.

Okiy, R. B. (2003). A citation analysis of education dissertations at the Delta State University, Abraka, Nigeria. *Collection Building, 22*(4), 158-161.

Oppenheim, C., & Smith, R. (2001). Student citation practices in an Information Science Department. *Education for Information, 19,* 299-323.

Pival, P., & Tuñón, J. (2001). Innovative methods for providing instruction to distance students using technology. *Journal of Library Administration, 32*(1/2), 347-360.

Pival, P., & Tuñón, J. (2002, June). *How do you spell "support"? Multiple methods of library support to distributed education programs.* Paper presented at the North American Regional Distance Education Conference, ICDE/Canadian Association of Distance Education, Calgary, Canada.

Quinlan, N., Tuñón, J., & Hutchens, J. (2002, May 2). *Getting the story straight: Publicizing services to remote patrons.* Paper presented at the Changing Face of Libraries SOLINET Conference, Atlanta: GA.

Ramirez, L., & Tuñón, J. (2003). Considerations, challenges, and concerns for providing library services to Nova Southeastern University's distance students in Latin America. In B. E. Massis (Ed.), *Models of cooperation in U.S., Latin American and Caribbean libraries: The first IFLA/SEFLIN International Summit on Library Cooperation in the Americas* (IFLA Publication 1005) (pp. 61-66). Munchen, The Netherlands: K. G. Saur.

Riggs, D. (1997). Library services for distance education: Rethinking current practices and implementing new approaches [Editorial]. *College & Research Libraries, 55,* 208-209.

Rogers, S., & Graham, S. (1998). *The high performance toolbox: Succeeding with performance tasks, projects, and assessments.* Evergreen, CO: Peak Learning Systems.

Smith, E. T. (2003). Assessing collection usefulness: An investigation of library ownership of the resources graduate students use. *College & Research Libraries, 64,* 344-355.

Stefl-Mabry, J. (2004). Building rubrics into powerful learning assessment tools. *Knowledge Quest, 32*(5), 21-25. Retrieved December 10, 2005, from Wilson Library Literature and Information Science Full Text database.

Thomas, J. (2000). Never enough: Graduate student use of journals–citation analysis of social work theses. *Behavioral & Social Sciences Librarian, 19*(1), 1-16.

Tuñón, J. (1996, April 18). *A metamorphosis: Electronic access and delivery and its impact on traditional library services.* Paper presented at the Florida Library Association, Tampa, FL.

Tuñón, J. (1997, January 24). *Support services: Differences to consider and pitfalls to avoid.* Paper presented at Third Annual Distance Learning Workshop.

Tuñón, J. (1999). *Integrating bibliographic instruction for distance education doctoral students into the Child and Youth Studies Program at Nova Southeastern University.* Unpublished doctoral practicum, Nova Southeastern University, Fort Lauderdale, FL (ERIC Document Reproduction Service No. ED440639).

Tuñón, J. (2004). When quality assurance, information literacy, and accreditation issues intersect. In D. Biggs (Ed.), *Library instruction: Restating the need, refocusing the response: Papers and session materials presented at the Thirty-Second National LOEX Library Instruction Conference held in Ypsilanti, Michigan* (pp. 71-75). Ann Arbor, MI: Pierian Press.

Tuñón, J., & Brydges, B. (2005, August). *Improving the quality of university libraries through citation mining and analysis using two new dissertation bibliometric assessment tools.* Paper presented at the 71st IFLA (International Federation of Libraries and Associations) Conference and General Council, Oslo, Norway.

Tuñón, J., & Pival, P. (1997). Library services to distance students: Nova Southeastern University's experience. *Florida Libraries, 40,* 109+.

Tuñón, J., & Pival, P. (2001). Reaccreditation at Nova Southeastern University: How reaccreditation can create opportunities for improving library services to distance students. *Journal of Library Administration, 32*(1/2), 409-424.

Walcott, R. (1991). Characteristics of citations in geoscience doctoral dissertations accepted at United State academic institutions 1981-1985. *Science and Technology Libraries, 12*(2), 5-16.

Waugh, C. K., & Ruppel, M. (2004). Citation analysis of dissertation, thesis, and research paper references in workforce education and development. *Journal of Academic Librarianship, 30,* 276-284.

Young, V. E., & Ackerson, L. G. (1995). Evaluation of student research paper bibliographies: Refining evaluation criteria. *Research Strategies, 13*(2), 80-93.

doi:10.1300/J111v45n03_10

APPENDIX A

Brydges/Tuñón Subjective Rubric for Doctoral Reference List Resources

Cluster ID number_____   Rater_____

Subjective Rubric for Doctoral Reference List Resources

Criteria	Level 1 Inadequate	Level 2 Marginally adequate	Level 3 Adequate	Level 4 Superior
Breadth of resources* - number of citations - variety of resources cited	Student used a limited number and/or variety of resources available on topic/Did not show awareness of specialized sources	Limited number and variety of sources cited	Reasonable number and variety of sources used for topic	Exhaustive search that utilizes a comprehensive number and a full range of types of sources available for topic
Depth: understanding as demonstrated through the citing of historical, theoretical background resources.	Depth of understanding undeveloped by a lack of citations from historical, theoretical background resources.	Depth of understanding emerging as demonstrated through the citation of a limited number of historical, theoretical background resources.	Depth of understanding developed as demonstrated through the citation of a substantial number of historical, theoretical background resources available for the topic.	Depth of understanding exemplary as demonstrated through the exhaustive citation of historical, theoretical background resources available for the topic.
Depth: scholarliness (quality of sources cited*) - primary resources - empirical research - peer-reviewed - seminal/landmark studies	Majority of resources superficial/weak	Limited number of scholarly, peer reviewed, resources/too few empirical reviews- superficial	Majority of resources were scholarly, peer reviewed and reasonable no. of empirical research studies	A rich representation of quality, peer reviewed empirical research resources/ very scholarly
Currency* -- Criteria take into consideration the availability of resources on the specific topic being researched	Not current – Majority of references older than 10 years from date of dissertation completion	A disproportionate number of unnecessarily dated resources (majority over 5 years)	The majority of the resources published 5 years or less from completion of dissertation	Extremely current – majority of references within 3 years of dissertation completion
Relevancy to the topic	Majority of sources do not relate/pertain to topic	A disproportionate number of sources do not relate/pertain to the topic	Sources generally support/pertain to the topic	Sources directly on target and support/pertain to topic

* Criteria take into consideration the availability of resources on the specific topic being researched

OVERALL SCORE_____/20

APPENDIX B

Tuñón/Brydges Objective Rubric's Scoring Scale

	points	≥ 3 yrs old	≥ 10 yrs	Max pts
Dissertations*	2	.3	.2	2.5
(published and unpublished)				
Theses/practicums/action-based research*	1	.3	.2	1.5
Periodicals (magazines, trade journals)*	0	.3	.2	.5
Scholarly periodicals*	1.5	.3	.2	2.0
Journals +.3	+.3			
Academic/scholarly +.2				
Peer-reviewed +1				
Books/book chapters (not scholarly)	0	.3	.2	.5
Books/book chap.–scholarly publishers	1	.3	.2	1.5
Books/book chap.–academic presses	1	.3	.3	1.5
Reports (gov. agencies, foundations, associations, universities, etc.)*	1	.3	.2	1.5
Conference papers and proceedings* (published and unpublished)	1	.3	.2	1.5
Government laws/legal cases	1	0	0	1.0
ERIC ED documents*	.5	0	0	.5
Newspapers*	0	0	0	0
Web sites*	0	0	0	0
Miscellaneous*	0	0	0	0

*Documents that fit two or more categories were included in category with higher weight.

Career Paths of Distance Education Librarians: A Profile of Current Practitioners Subscribed to the OFFCAMP Listserv

Allyson Washburn

Brigham Young University

SUMMARY. A growing number of institutions are offering courses and degrees via distance education; however, distance education librarianship is a relatively new and often less defined field of librarianship. This paper will present the results of a survey to discover career paths leading to distance education librarianship. Based on a survey of subscribers to the OFFCAMP listserv, it asked questions such as: Is there a "typical" career path? Does previous or continuing work in other library units benefit a distance education librarian? What are the most important qualifications for a distance education librarian? Profiles of the education and experience of distance education librarians were analyzed for commonalities. The study concluded that distance education librarians come to their positions from a variety of experience, not always in libraries, but predominantly from library public service departments. A typical career path for distance education librarians is not evident at this time. doi:10.1300/J111v45n03_11

KEYWORDS. Career paths, distance education librarians, library services, library careers

[Haworth co-indexing entry note]: "Career Paths of Distance Education Librarians: A Profile of Current Practitioners Subscribed to the OFFCAMP Listserv." Washburn, Allyson. Co-published simultaneously in *Journal of Library Administration* (The Haworth Information Press, an imprint of The Haworth Press, Inc.) Vol. 45, No. 3/4, 2006, pp. 483-509; and: *The Twelfth Off-Campus Library Services Conference Proceedings* (ed: Julie A. Garrison) The Haworth Information Press, an imprint of The Haworth Press, Inc., 2006, pp. 483-509.

Available online at http://jla.haworthpress.com
doi:10.1300/J111v45n03_11

INTRODUCTION

More institutions are now offering courses and degrees via distance education. "In 2000-01, 56% of all postsecondary institutions offered distance-education courses (up from 34% three years earlier). . . . Course enrollments in distance education have increased as well . . . increasing from 1.7 million to 3.1 million between 1997-98 and 2000-01" (NCES, 2004, p. 85). Many distance learners are located in isolated rural areas or are unable to travel to a traditional campus. They are generally older students with jobs, families, and other obligations, who study on their own time. These learners need library materials and services to successfully complete their coursework. Some distance learners may have access to their local public library; however, due to the nonacademic mission of public libraries, the resources available are often inadequate to meet their needs.

What about the librarians who serve distance learners? How does one become a distance-education librarian? Is there a typical career path that leads to becoming a distance-education librarian? The answers to these questions have been unclear because no research about distance-education librarians and their career paths had previously been done. This paper will report the results of a survey of practicing distance-education librarians regarding their career path. In this paper the term "distance-education librarian" will be used to describe those whose titles may include off-campus, extended, or outreach services librarian.

Librarians have been providing service and materials to distance learners via telephone and postal mail for many years and more recently have used e-mail, chat, fax, electronic delivery, and interlibrary loan. Athabasca University in Canada, created in 1970, has been providing library services to distance learners since its inception as an open university. The Off-Campus Library Services Conference has been addressing issues of providing library services to distance learners since 1982, so one could reasonably assume that distance-education librarians have existed for at least a quarter of a century, and probably longer. However, contrary to what one might think, distance-education librarianship is still an evolving and growing field, as witnessed by the following comments typical of librarians new to the distance-education field: "Despite my more than twenty years of experience in a variety of library settings, I had no previous contact with–or even awareness of–this particular type of user" (Goodson, 2001, p. xi). "When I applied for my current position as Extended Campus Services Librarian . . . I had over a decade's experience in libraries, but little with serving off-campus library users" (Jones, 2002, p. 397). Titles of presentations at the Tenth Off-Campus Library Services Conference in the last few years also provide evidence of the growing field of distance-education librarianship.

- The Answer You Get Depends on Who (and What) You Ask: Involving Stakeholder in Needs Assessment
- Help! I'm the New Distance Librarian–Where Do I Begin?
- Documenting Priorities, Progress, and Potential: Planning Library Services for Distance Education
- Starting Small: Setting Up Off-Campus Library Services with Limited Resources

Many programs in library or information studies offer courses or degrees via distance learning; however, a search of the Web sites listed on the Directory of ALA-Accredited Master's Programs in Library and Information Studies revealed that there is very little in the way of specific course work for aspiring distance-education librarians. Hoerman and Furniss (2001) reported that "only recently have some institutions developed courses or workshops that emphasize distance services" (p. 249). The University of Maryland University College offers a graduate certificate in Library Services to Distance Learners; however, only one of the four required courses deals with providing library services. When the author began working as a distributed learning services librarian, there was not a body of literature describing career paths for distance-education librarians. Nor were there many resources available for learning about the job or about how to become a successful distance-education librarian. Hoping to discover educational or professional development opportunities, the author decided to do a survey of current practicing distance-education librarians to determine how others prepared for or developed professionally in distance-learning positions.

The population for this study included subscribers to the OFFCAMP listserv. This listserv addresses issues in services to distance learners and has been active since about 1991. Lessin, founder of the listserv, recounted that the list was started as a way to maintain communication and foster collaboration during the

> long gaps that occurred between the meetings of the OCLS Conference. The purpose then was to make it as easy as possible for off-campus librarians to talk with one another and to share their

successes, challenges, and questions with their colleagues. (Lessin, personal communication, July 27, 2005)

The survey findings document current practices within this population and provide valuable guidance for those aspiring to enter the field of distance librarianship.

LITERATURE REVIEW AND RESEARCH OBJECTIVES

As has been previously stated, there is not a large body of literature about the career paths of librarians who serve distance learners. A review of the literature reveals a myriad of articles addressing the growth of distance education, along with many articles that address the provision of library services to distance learners. A search of Academic Search Premier, ERIC, and Library and Information Science using the subject term "distance education" or "distance learning" yielded more than thirteen thousand articles. A similar search using the terms "distance education" or "distance learning" and "library services" retrieved more than five hundred articles, some dating back to 1981. However, an exhaustive search of the Library and Information Science Database in Dialog, using various terms for distance education, librarianship, and career paths, yielded very few articles on the topic of career paths of distance-education librarians. Reiten and Fritts tracked "career paths of attendees and presenters at the ten [OCLS] Conferences" (2004, p. 366), focusing on the effect of distance-education librarian experiences on a librarian's career path. Yang (2005) also interviewed practicing distance-education librarians and briefly described the amount of time they devote to providing services. Another area in the literature describes educational preparation for those entering the field of distance education; again, there are few articles on the topic. The author was interested in determining if a standard educational or career path exists for distance-education librarians. With this in mind, a set of research issues of interest was developed that guided the study (see Appendix A: Research Questions).

METHODOLOGY–RESEARCH PROCEDURE

The population studied included subscribers to the OFFCAMP listserv as of March 18, 2005. A survey was constructed consisting of twenty-three questions divided into three sections. An open-source product, phpSurveyor, was used to build the survey in a Web format. All sections contained questions that were either multiple choice or "choose all that apply," and open-ended short-answer questions. The first section consisted of eight questions that asked about rank, job title, how the librarian got his or her current position, the most important qualifications for a distance-education librarian, and if providing services to distance-education students was the sole focus of the position. The second section of the survey, consisting of eleven questions, queried previous library experience, what department the librarian currently reports to, experience as a distance-education student, education for the job, challenges, successes, and advice to new and aspiring distance-education librarians. The third and final section consisted of four questions that collected demographic data about degrees held, length of employment in libraries and in their current position, and gender (see Appendix B: Career Paths of Distance-Education Librarians).

The survey was sent to the 673 subscribers of the OFFCAMP listserv with two follow-up reminders, one sent a week after the initial request and the second sent a week later. One hundred twelve valid surveys were returned. Analysis of the returned surveys by the Harold B. Lee Library's (HBLL) statistical officer yielded the following:

> Normal response rate for Web-based surveys varies between 15 to 30%. The rate for this survey is more towards the low end of that tendency at 16.64%, but [that's] not necessarily bad. Those that did respond provided complete and thoughtful answers based on what was evident in most of the open-ended comment questions. In addition, those that responded were representative of the target population in terms of gender. (Roberts, personal communication, July 27, 2005)

Data were collected in an Excel spreadsheet, and the statistics were tabulated and analyzed using SAS®. For some open-ended questions, responses were grouped into themes for purposes of analysis.

RESULTS

In this section of the article, data will be reported from the survey that answer the research questions developed early in the study (see Appendix C: Summary of Distance Education Survey). Not all respondents answered every question and all percentages have been rounded to the nearest whole percent.

Question 1: What kind of training or education for the position do distance-education librarians have? Did it include being distance students themselves?

Multiple questions in the survey provided data on training or education that respondents had for their position. When asked about their rank or title, an overwhelming majority, 96% (108), responded that they were librarians with an MLS degree. Support staff and "other" accounted for the other 4% (4) of responses. Degrees other than an MLS held by respondents varied (see Table 1).

Respondents held degrees in a wide variety of disciplines. Those holding associate degrees all reported different disciplines. English and history were the most common disciplines listed as respondents' first bachelor's degree. History was the most common discipline of those with a second bachelor's degree. Nearly all survey respondents held a master's degree in library/information science, most as their first master's degree, but some as their second master's degree. The MLS degree was the most common among those holding a second master's degree. When asked about PhDs, half of the respondents listed education as the discipline. Other degrees held covered a wide spectrum, as shown below.

- Computer Information Services
- Nursing
- Sociology
- German
- Psychology
- Religion
- Spanish
- Occupational/Technology Information
- Information Technology
- Instructional Technology

- General Studies
- Music
- Economics
- Political Science
- Greek
- Secondary Education
- Translation
- Distance Education
- Instructional Materials
- Aesthetic Studies

More than half, 54%, of the survey respondents answered yes when asked if sometime during their career or as part of their education they had been or currently were a distance-education student. A further ques-

TABLE 1. Degrees Held by Respondents

Degree	Number	Percentage
Associate of Applied Science	4	4%
Bachelor's	87	78%
2nd Bachelor's	8	7%
Master's	91	81%
2nd Master's	32	29%
PhD	8	7%

Note: Percentages total more than 100 due to some respondents' holding more than one degree.

tion asked if they had any education or training specific to distance education. Most, 73% (82), answered no, with 27% (30) answering yes. Of the 27% (30) who answered yes, types of education or training by percentage are illustrated in Table 2.

Question 2: Did they have any previous experience in other library units? If so, which experience do they consider the most valuable?

Work in other library units was common among respondents (see Table 3). Respondents were asked to mark all units in which they had worked. Of the respondents, 61% (67) had worked in two or more other library units before becoming the distance-education librarian. Most had experience working in public service units, but other areas of the library were represented in the responses. Reference work, with 76 respondents (68%), was the most common response, with instruction or information literacy, chosen by 50 respondents (45%), the second most common response. Subject librarian or bibliographer and access services were third and fourth respectively, with 27 respondents (24%) and 19 respondents (17%). Smaller numbers of respondents indicated that they had worked in other library units, including acquisitions, cataloging, periodicals/serials, government information, library computer systems, and archives/special collections. No respondents had experience in human resources, and 18 respondents (16%) had no experience in other library units.

If respondents indicated that they had worked in other library units, they were then asked which experience had been the most valuable to them. Again, reference work and instruction/information literacy dominated the responses, with 49% (54) indicating that reference was the most useful and 12% (13) choosing instruction/information literacy.

TABLE 2. Training or Education in Distance Education

Type of education/training	Number	Percent having training
Distance-education workshops	8	27%
Online course	6	20%
MLS	6	20%
Past distance-education student	4	13%
PhD	3	10%
Other	3	10%

TABLE 3. Previous Experience in Other Library Units

Library unit	Number	Percentage
Access services	19	17%
Acquisitions	12	11%
Cataloging	13	12%
Reference	76	68%
Subject librarian/bibliographer	27	24%
Library computer systems	6	5%
Archives/Special Collections	5	5%
Periodicals/serials	11	10%
Government information	11	10%
Human resources	0	0%
Instruction/information literacy	50	45%
Not applicable	18	16%

Note: Percentages total more than 100 due to some respondents' working in more than one library unit.

These two categories accounted for 87 of the 112 responses. An interesting finding was that of those who had previous reference experience, 37% (41) held a bachelor's degree in either English or history. For those with previous experience in instruction or information literacy, 31% (35) held bachelor's degrees in English or history. Ten percent (11) said access services was their most useful experience. Library computer systems, public services, subject librarian/bibliographer, and outreach had percentages of 4 or lower, and 20% (22) marked "Not applicable."

Question 3: How did they get into the field of distance education librarianship? Did they start in a new position or fill an existing position?

Responses to this open-ended question varied greatly and were classified into eleven categories. The largest number of respondents (25) indicated that they had taken an open position, and for others distance education librarianship was part of their job description. Some indicated that they got into the field via experience or library duties that evolved into serving distance learners. Others wanted to move on to a new position, and distance-education librarian was the position available or of interest to them. Some saw a need for a librarian to serve distance-education students and either lobbied to have a position created or had the duties added to their current position. A few respondents indicated that this was their first position post-MLS (see Table 4). Of those currently in distance-education librarian positions, 53 respondents filled an existing position and 59 indicated that it was a new position.

Question 4: What is the average length of time in the position for distance-education librarians?

While many respondents have been librarians for a number of years, the majority (67%) have been in their current position for five years or less (see Table 5). However, 45% (51) have been in the field of librarianship between six and fifteen years. More than 25% (30) of respondents have been in librarianship for more than twenty years.

Question 5: Is distance education their sole responsibility, or do they have other responsibilities?

Sixty-two percent (69) of respondents said they spend fewer than thirty hours a week working in distance education. The other 38% (43)

TABLE 4. Entry Point Into Distance-Education Librarianship

Entry point	Number	Percentage
Took open position	25	22%
Via experience	12	11%
Wanted to move on	12	11%
Added to current responsibilities	10	9%
First position after MLS	10	9%
Nature of position	10	9%
By accident	9	8%
Interest in distributed learning	7	6%
Promoted to position	7	6%
Recruited to position	6	5%
By necessity	4	4%

TABLE 5. Number of Years in Librarianship Compared with Number of Years in Current Position

Number of years	Years in librarianship	Years in current position
1-5 years	16%	67%
6-10 years	25%	17%
11-15 years	20%	12%
16-20 years	12%	2%
More than 20 years	27%	2%

indicated that they spend from thirty-one to forty hours a week working in distance education (see Table 6). When asked the number of hours worked in other library departments, the majority said they spend their time working in reference or as a subject librarian/bibliographer. None of the respondents spend more than twenty hours a week in any other library department, with the exception of one who indicated spending twenty-eight hours per week in library computer systems. A majority of those who responded to the survey, 79% (88), report either to a public services department or division or to library administration.

When asked about the number of FTE librarians, staff or student assistants employed in serving distance learners, 63% of respondents (70) indicated that only one full-time librarian had responsibility for distance education students. About the same number of respondents, seventy-nine (71%), reported one full-time support staff member supporting distance education students. Nearly 100% (111) of respondents, whether librarian or support staff, had some student help.

Question 6: What are the most important qualifications for distance-education librarians?

For this question respondents were asked to check all answers that applied. Of the six choices for the most important qualifications for distance-education librarians, technology and outreach skills were the overwhelming choices, both at 75% (84). Public service skills and a commitment to public service were close seconds at 72% (81) each. The responses are broken out by percentage in Table 7.

Question 7: What challenges do distance education librarians face?

The responses to the challenges faced by distance education librarians varied, from technology to time, from fair services to frequent changes,

TABLE 6. Number of Hours Per Week Spent in Distance Education

Hours per week in distance education	Number	Percentage
10 or less	31	28%
11-20	23	21%
21-30	15	13%
31-40	43	38%

TABLE 7. Important Qualifications for Distance Education Librarians

Qualifications	Number	Percentage
Public service skills	81	72
Commitment to public service	81	72
Bibliography skills	26	23
Organizational skills	65	58
Technology skills	84	75
Outreach skills	84	75

Note: Percentages total more than 100 because multiple responses were requested.

and from communication to copyright. The responses for this question were analyzed and categorized according to themes. According to the HBLL statistical officer:

> Technology was the theme of the single most important challenge facing distance-education librarians. Almost as frequently mentioned was communication, lack of institutional awareness, providing services for distance-education students that are comparable to those offered on campus, and staying abreast of the frequent changes in the field of distance education. (Roberts, personal communication, July 27, 2005)

See Table 8 for a complete breakdown of responses.

Question 8: What are/have been their biggest successes in distance education?

Responses to this question fell into four major themes–improving relationships, resource improvements, structure improvements (meaning improvements in the functions and processes of distance education),

TABLE 8. Biggest Challenges Facing Distance Education Librarians

Challenge	Number	Percentage
Technology	19	17%
Communication	14	13%
Lack of institutional awareness	14	13%
Fair services	13	12%
Frequent changes	12	11%
Improving student skills	8	7%
Money	7	6%
Access to materials	5	5%
Definition of distance learners	5	5%
Copyright	4	4%
Knowing students	4	4%
Time	4	4%

Note: Percentages total more than 100 percent because multiple answers were given.

and increased awareness. Eighty-seven percent (97) of the responses fell into these four themes. Improving relationships and resource improvements were both chosen as the biggest success by 25% (51) of the respondents. Twenty-one percent (22) said that structure improvements were their biggest success, and 16% (16) listed increasing awareness as their biggest success. Other successes mentioned included improvements in skills 5% (5) and positive feedback, student increases, and personal rewards which accounted for 13% (13) of the responses.

Question 9: What advice would they give to librarians wanting to get into the field of distance librarianship or those new to distance librarianship?

Respondents gave similar responses to both of these questions (see Table 9). Three items dominated the responses. First, being aware of and up-to-date on the technology needed to be a good distance-education librarian accounted for 30% (30) of the responses. Second, knowing what is expected accounted for approximately 25% (25) of the responses. Third, having good experience or past training accounted for approximately 25% (24) of the responses. Having social skills, knowing resources, and miscellaneous other accounted for the remaining 22% (22) of responses.

When respondents were asked what advice they would give to new distance-education librarians, networking was the top response at 31%

TABLE 9. Advice for Aspiring and New Distance-Education Librarians

Advice for getting into distance education		Advice to new distance education librarians	
Technology skills	30%	Network	31%
Know what is expected	25%	Know what is expected	22%
Good experience/training	24%	Good experience/training	19%
Social skills	10%	People skills	10%
Know resources	8%	Technology skills	9%
Other	4%	Flexible with time	7%
		Be creative	3%

Note: Percentages equal more than 100 because multiple responses were given.

(31). Knowing what is expected and having good experience/training were second and third again, at 22% (22) and 19% (19) respectively. People skills, which could be construed to mean about the same thing as social skills, was fourth at 10% (10), and technology skills had 9% (9). Being flexible with time and being creative accounted for the other 10% of responses (10).

DISCUSSION

The driving question (number 10) for this study was, "Is there a typical career path for distance-education librarians?" The hypothesis was that a standard career path for distance-education librarians is not evident at this time. Distance-education librarians come to their positions from a variety of experience, not always in libraries but predominantly from library public-service departments. The survey data indicate that the respondents overwhelmingly hold MLS degrees, but their educational backgrounds are varied, with English and history dominating as the two most common undergraduate degrees. Prior or continuing work in other library units was common among the respondents. A large majority indicated that they had previous reference experience or were currently working in reference in addition to their distance-education duties. The other areas where significant previous or continuing work occurs are in instruction/information literacy and functioning as a subject librarian/bibliographer. This is consistent with the needs of distance-education students for reference assistance, instruction, and access to a librarian with knowledge of subject-specific resources.

Not surprisingly, less than a third of the respondents indicated that they had any education or training in distance education. However, more than half of those with education or training indicated that they had experience as a distance education student and considered that as a part of their training for the position. Other training consisted of distance education workshops, followed closely by online courses, or training/education received as part of their MLS program. Technology and outreach skills were considered the most necessary qualifications for becoming a distance education librarian, with public service skills and a commitment to public service not far behind. Experience as a distance education student could have honed respondents' technology skills, or at least could have made them aware of the various technologies used to deliver instruction and services to distance education students. A large majority of the respondents indicated that previous work in reference and instruction/information literacy was the most useful experience in their training, perhaps accounting for their belief that public service skills are an important qualification for distance education librarians.

Two-thirds of the respondents have been in their current position for five years or less, but the total time in librarianship varied from one year to more than twenty years. A little more than one quarter of the respondents have been in the profession more than twenty years. Entrance points to the field of distance education librarianship varied, with some respondents indicating that experience of being a distance education student led to interest in working in the field. The percentage of those filling new positions and those filling vacancies was about half and half, with slightly more filling a new position. These findings seem to corroborate the expansion and development of this branch of librarianship.

Distance education librarians, by the very nature of their job, face many challenges. Included in these are learning, using, and troubleshooting technology problems; marketing services to both distance education students and the faculty who teach them; providing instruction in the use of library resources; complying with copyright; experiencing frequent changes; dealing with inadequate budgets; and coping with lack of institutional awareness of the need to provide equitable library services for distance learners. Survey respondents confirmed that technology, communication, and lack of institutional awareness are the top three challenges they face. It comes as no surprise that the need to sharpen technology skills is the principal advice survey respondents provided to those wanting to get into the field of distance education librarianship. They advised distance education librarians who are new in their positions to network with those who can assist them in their work. Other advice given to both those wanting to get into the field and those new in the field was the same for both groups–know what is expected and have or acquire experience and training related to the position.

Along with the challenges, distance education librarians also experience success in their work. The successes reported in the survey correspond closely with identified challenges. An outcome of addressing challenges in communication resulted in successes such as improved relationships; increased awareness both at the institutional, faculty, and student levels; and development of ways to improve student skills. Success in obtaining resource improvements occurred when tackling challenges related to budgets. Evaluating functions and processes used in providing services, including the technologies used to provide those services, resulted in structure improvements.

CONCLUSIONS

This survey verifies that, beyond holding an MLS and a bachelor's degree in English or history and having prior library experience in public services, there is not a typical career path for distance education librarians in the population studied. Distance education librarians hold a variety of degrees in addition to the MLS. While a large percentage of distance education librarians have more than five years' prior library experience, that experience could be in access services, acquisitions, archives/special collections, cataloging, government information, instruction/information literacy, library computer systems, periodicals, reference, or subject librarian/bibliographer positions. Slightly over two-thirds of the respondents have been in their current position as distance education librarian for no more than five years. Most report to a public services division or to library administration. Most are one-person operations, while others have some support staff or serve as coordinators of the service throughout the library, as noted by Backhus and Summey (2003). No standard progression through education or library experience to distance education librarian is evident. However, new positions continue to be created, and through attrition and aging of the librarian population, vacancies will occur in existing positions. At this point, an MLS, a familiarity with technology, and good public service skills can form the basis for a successful career in distance education librarianship.

The continuity of distance librarianship as a specific field is in question with the blurring of distinctions between distance learners versus remote users. If it is determined that distance education librarians perform essential functions that differ from other public service librarians, further research should explore whether a standard career path needs to be established to qualify librarians for practicing distance librarianship and what the steps along that path would be.

Distance education librarians are often charting new courses through unfamiliar waters. Whether they acquire the skills to be successful through formal or informal education or through work experience, or a combination of both, above all, they need to possess the commitment, the vision, and the leadership to develop, deliver, and improve library services for distance learners.

REFERENCES

Backus, S., & Summey, T. (2003). Collaboration: The key to unlocking the dilemma of distance reference services. *Reference Librarian, 40* (83/84), 193-202.

Ghandi, S. (2003). Academic librarians and distance education. *Reference and User Services Quarterly, 43*, 138-154.

Goodson, C. (2001). *Providing library services for distance education students: A how-to-do-it manual.* New York: Neal-Schuman.

Hoerman, H., & Furniss, K. (2001). Education for provision of library services to distance learners: The role of the LIS schools. *Journal of Library Administration, 32*, 247-257.

Jones, M. F. (2002). Help! I'm the new distance librarian–Where do I begin? In P. Mahoney (Ed.), *Distance Learning Library Services: The Tenth Off-Campus Library Services Conference.* New York: The Haworth Information Press.

Mahoney, P. (Ed.) (2002). *Distance learning library services: The Tenth Off-Campus Library Services Conference.* New York: The Haworth Information Press.

Reiten, B., & Fritts, J. (2004). The impact of distance learning library services experience on practitioners' career paths. *Journal of Library Administration, 41*, 365-374.

United States Department of Education, National Center for Education Statistics. (2004). Section 5–Contexts of postsecondary education. In *The condition of education 2004.* Retrieved from http://nces.ed.gov/pubs2004/2004077_5.pdf.

Yang, Z. Y. (2005). Distance education librarians in the U.S.: ARL libraries and library services provided to their distance users. *The Journal of Academic Librarianship, 31*, 92-97.

doi:10.1300/J111v45n03_11

APPENDIX A

Research Issues of Interest

1. What kind of training or education for the position do distance-education librarians have? Did it include being a distance student themselves?

2. Did they have any previous experience in other library units? If so, which experience do they consider the most valuable?

3. How did they get into the field of distance-education librarianship? Did they start in a new position or fill an existing position?

4. What is the average length of time in the position for distance-education librarians?

5. Is distance education their sole responsibility or do they have other responsibilities?

6. What are the most important qualifications for distance-education librarians?

7. What challenges do distance-education librarians face?

8. What are/have been their biggest successes?

9. What advice would they give to librarians wanting to get into the field of distance librarianship or those new to distance librarianship?

10. Is there a "typical" career path for distance-education librarians?

APPENDIX B

Career Paths of Distance Education Librarians

Part I

Career Paths of Distance Education Librarians
This is a survey to discover how librarians get into the field of distance education librarianship.

Q1: Which Category best describes your current rank or title? <u>Please choose **only one** of the following:</u>

- ⊓ Librarian (MLS)
- ⊓ Support Staff
- ⊓ Other |_____|

Q2: What is your job title? <u>Please write your answer here:</u>

|_____|

Q3: Was it a new position or did you fill a vacancy? <u>Please choose only one of the following:</u>

- ⊓ New Position
- ⊓ Vacancy

Q4: How did you get into the field of distance education librarianship? <u>Please write your answer here:</u>

Q5: What are the most important qualifications for a distance education librarian? <u>Please choose all that apply</u>

- ⊓ Public service skills
- ⊓ Commitment to public service
- ⊓ Bibliography skills
- ⊓ Organizational skills
- ⊓ Technology skills
- ⊓ Outreach skills
- ⊓ Other: |_____|

Q6: **Please indicate the number of FTE staff employed at your library serving distance learners.**
Please choose all that apply and provide a comment

- ☐ Librarian(s) (MLS)
- ☐ Support Staff
- ☐ Student Assistants

Q7: **How many hours a week do you work in distance education?** Please choose **only one** of the following:

- ☐ 10 or less
- ☐ 11-20
- ☐ 21-30
- ☐ 31-40

Q8: **If you work less than 40 hr per week in distance education, please indicate the number of hours you work, if any, in other library departments/divisions.** Please choose all that apply and provide a comment

- ☐ Access services
- ☐ Acquisitions
- ☐ Cataloging
- ☐ Reference
- ☐ Subject librarian or bibliographer
- ☐ Library Computer Systems
- ☐ Archives/Special Collections
- ☐ Periodicals/Serials
- ☐ Government Information
- ☐ Human Resources
- ☐ Not applicable

Part II

Q9: **Before becoming the distance education librarian, did you work in other library units?** Please choose **all** that apply

- ☐ Access Services
- ☐ Acquisitions
- ☐ Cataloging
- ☐ Reference
- ☐ Subject librarian or bibliographer
- ☐ Library Computer Systems
- ☐ Archives/Special Collections
- ☐ Periodicals/Serials
- ☐ Government Information
- ☐ Human Resources
- ☐ Instruction/Information Literacy
- ☐ Not applicable
  - Other:

APPENDIX B (continued)

Q10: If you worked in another library unit, which experience has been the most useful in your current position? Please write your answer here:

Q11: Which department/division do you report to in your library? Please write your answer here:

Q12: Based on your response to the previous question, do you think distance education would function more effectively if it were part of a different department/division? Please choose only one of the following:

☐ Yes

☐ No

Q13: If you answered yes, in your opinion, where would distance education be placed most effectively? Please write your answer here:

Q14: During your education/career, have you been or are you currently a distance student? Please choose **only one** of the following:

☐ Yes

☐ No

Q15: Do you have any education relating specifically to distance education librarianship? Please explain. Please write your answer here:

Q16: What are the biggest challenges facing distance education librarians? Please write your answer here:

Q17: What do you consider your biggest success in distance librarianship? Please write your answer here:

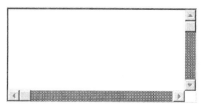

Q18: What advice would you give to librarians wanting to get into distance education librarianship? Please write your answer here:

Q19: What advice would you give to new distance education librarians? Please write your answer here:

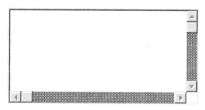

Part III

Q20: Please check the degrees you hold and indicate the discipline. Please choose all that apply and provide a comment

- ☐ Associate Degree
- ☐ Bachelor's Degree
- ☐ 2nd Bachelor's Degree
- ☐ Master's Degree
- ☐ 2nd Master's Degree
- ☐ PhD

APPENDIX B (continued)

Q21: How long have you been employed (as a librarian or as support staff) in libraries? <u>Please choose **only one** of the following:</u>

- ☐ 1-5 years
- ☐ 6-10 years
- ☐ 11-15 years
- ☐ 16-20 years
- ☐ More than 20 years

Q22: How long have you been employed in your current position? <u>Please choose **only one** of the following:</u>

- ☐ 1-5 years
- ☐ 6-10 years
- ☐ 11-15 years
- ☐ 16-20 years
- ☐ More than 20 years

Q23: Please indicate your gender. <u>Please choose **only one** of the following:</u>

- ☐ Female
- ☐ Male

Submit Your Survey
Thank you for completing this survey. Please fax your completed survey to: by 2005-04-08.

APPENDIX C

Summary of Career Paths Survey

(n = 112)

Q01: Description of rank/title:

Librarian (MLS)	108	96.43%
Other	3	2.68%
Support staff	1	0.89%

Q02: Title classification:

Distance education librarian	45	40.18%
Dean or director	15	13.39%
Reference librarian	15	13.39%
Public services librarian	13	11.61%
Coordinator	10	8.39%
Head	7	6.25%
Assistant dean or director	3	2.68%
Instruction librarian	2	1.79%
Other	2	1.79%

Q03: New or vacant position?

New position	59	52.68%
Vacancy	53	47.32%

Q04: How did you get into distance-education librarianship?

Took open position	25	22.32%
Via experience	12	10.71%
Wanted to move on	12	10.71%
Added to current responsibilities	10	8.93%
First position after MLS	10	8.93%
Nature of position	10	8.93%
By accident	9	8.04%
Interest in distributed learning	7	6.25%
Promoted to position	7	6.25%
Recruited to position	6	5.36%
By necessity	4	3.57%

Q05: Respondents that think the following are important qualifications for this position:

Public service skills	81	72.32%
Commitment to public service	81	72.32%
Bibliography skills	26	23.21%
Organizational skills	65	58.04%
Technology skills	84	75.00%
Outreach skills	84	75.00%

Q06a: Number of FTE librarians in distance education:

From 0 to just under 2	70	63.06%
From 2 to just under 4	16	13.42%
From 4 to just under 6	9	8.11%
From 6 to just under 10	8	7.20%
10 or more	8	7.20%

Q06b: Number of FTE support staff in distance education:

From 0 to just under 2	79	71.17%
From 2 to just under 4	15	13.51%
From 4 to just under 6	4	3.60%
From 6 to just under 10	7	6.30%
10 or more	6	5.40%

APPENDIX C (continued)

Q06c: Number of FTE student assistants in distance education:

From 0 to just under 2	92	82.88%
From 2 to just under 4	10	9.01%
From 4 to just under 6	4	3.60%
From 6 to just under 10	1	0.90%
10 or more	4	3.60%

Q07: Hours per week spent in distance education:

10 or less	31	27.68%
11 to 20	23	20.54%
21 to 30	15	13.39%
31 to 40	43	38.39%

Q08a: Number of hours spent in access services:

None	96	85.71%
10 or less	9	8.04%
11 to 20	7	6.24%
21 to 30	0	
31 to 40	0	

Q08b: Number of hours spent in acquisitions:

None	103	91.96%
10 or less	9	8.04%
11 to 20	0	
21 to 30	0	
31 to 40	0	

Q08c: Number of hours spent in cataloging:

None	110	98.21%
10 or less	2	1.79%
11 to 20	0	
21 to 30	0	
31 to 40	0	

Q08d: Number of hours spent in reference:

None	40	35.71%
10 or less	46	41.07%
11 to 20	20	17.86%
21 to 30	4	3.58%
31 to 40	2	1.79%

Q08e: Number of hours spent as a subject librarian/bibliographer:

None	72	64.29%
10 or less	35	31.24%
11 to 20	4	3.58%
21 to 30	0	
31 to 40	1	0.89%

Q08f: Number of hours spent in library computer systems:

None	105	93.75%
10 or less	5	4.45%
11 to 20	1	0.89%
21 to 30	1	0.89%
31 to 40	0	

Q08g: Number of hours spent in archives/special collections:

None	108	96.43%
10 or less	4	3.57%
11 to 20	0	
21 to 30	0	
31 to 40	0	

Q08h: Number of hours spent in periodicals/serials:

None	110	98.21%
10 or less	1	0.89%
11 to 20	1	0.89%
21 to 30	0	
31 to 40	0	

Q08i: Number of hours spent in government information:

None	111	99.11%
10 or less	1	0.89%
11 to 20	0	
21 to 30	0	
31 to 40	0	

Q08j: Number of hours spent in human resources:

None	108	96.43%
10 or less	4	3.57%
11 to 20	0	
21 to 30	0	
31 to 40	0	

Q08k: Number of hours spent in "not applicable":

None	79	70.54%
10 or less	29	25.89%
11 to 20	3	2.68%
21 to 30	0	
31 to 40	1	0.89%

Q09:   Previous work experience:

Access services	19	17.12%
Acquisitions	12	10.81%
Cataloging	13	11.71%
Reference	76	68.47%
Subject librarian/bibliographer	27	24.32%
Library computer systems	6	5.41%
Archives/special collection	6	5.41%
Periodicals/serials	11	9.91%
Government information	11	9.91%
Human resources	0	
Instruction/information literacy	50	45.05%
Not applicable	18	16.22%

Q10:   Which of the above experiences were most useful?

Reference	54	49.09%
N/A	22	20.00%
Instruction/information literacy	13	11.82%
Access services	11	10.00%
Library computer systems	5	4.55%
Public services	2	1.82%
Subject librarian/bibliographer	2	1.82%
Outreach	1	0.91%

Q11:   Which department or division do you report to?

Public services	48	42.86%
Library administration	40	35.71%
Academic service	9	8.04%
Distributed learning office	3	2.68%
None	3	2.68%
Other	9	8.04%

Q12:   Would a distance-education librarian function better in a different department or division?

No	104	92.86%
Yes	8	7.14%

APPENDIX C (continued)

Q13:   If yes, where?

Distance education/learning	3	37.50%
Access services & reference	1	12.50%
Depends on institution	1	12.50%
Continuing education	1	12.50%
Public services	1	12.50%
Instruction	1	12.50%

Q14:   Are you or have you been a distance-learning student?

No	51	45.54%
Yes	61	54.46%

Q15:   Do you have any distance-education-related training or education?

No	82	73.21%
Yes	30	26.79%

Q15other: If yes, what?

Distance-education workshops	8	26.67%
MLS	6	20.00%
Online courses	6	20.00%
Past distance-education student	4	13.33%
Distance education PhD	3	10.00%
Others	3	10.00%

Q16:   What are the biggest challenges facing distance-education librarians?

Technology	19	17.43%
Communication	14	12.84%
Lack of institutional awareness	14	12.84%
Fair services	13	11.93%
Frequent changes	12	11.01%
Improving student skills	8	7.34%
Money	7	6.42%
Access to materials	5	4.59%
Definition of distributed learners	5	4.59%
Copyright	4	3.67%
Knowing students	4	3.67%
Time	4	3.67%

Q17:   What has been your biggest success in distance education?

Improving relationships	26	25.49%
Resource improvements	25	24.51%
Structure improvements	22	21.57%
Increasing awareness	16	15.69%
Skill improvements	5	4.90%
Others	8	7.84%

Q18:   What advice would you give to librarians just getting into distance education?

Technology skills	30	29.70%
Know what is expected	25	24.75%
Good experience/training	24	23.78%
Social skills	10	9.90%
Know resources	8	7.92%
Other	4	3.95%

Q19:   What advice would you give to new distance-education librarians?

Network	31	30.69%
Know what is expected	22	21.78%
Good experience/training	19	18.81%
People skills	10	9.90%
Technology skills	9	8.91%
Flexible with time	7	6.93%
Creative	3	2.97%

Q20a: Associate degrees:

AAS	1	25.00%
Computer info services	1	25.00%
General studies	1	25.00%
Nursing	1	25.00%

Q20b: First bachelor's degree:

English	15	17.24%
History	13	14.94%
Music	7	8.05%
Sociology	7	8.05%
Economics	5	5.75%
Education	4	4.60%
German	3	3.45%
Political science	3	3.45%
Psychology	3	3.45%
Others	27	31.03%

Q20c: Second bachelor's degree:

History	2	25.00%
Education	1	12.50%
Greek	1	12.50%
Religion	1	12.50%
Secondary education	1	12.50%
Spanish	1	12.50%
Translation	1	12.50%

Q20d: First master's degree:

MLS	76	83.52%
English	4	4.40%
History	2	2.20%
Occupational/technological information	2	2.20%
Others	7	7.70%

Q20e: Second master's degree:

MLS	13	40.63%
Distance education	2	6.25%
Information technology	2	6.25%
Instructional materials	2	6.25%
Others	13	40.62%

Q20f: PhD:

Education	4	50.00%
Information technology	1	12.50%
All But Dissertation	1	12.50%
Instructional technology	1	12.50%
Aesthetic studies	1	12.50%

Q21: Years as a librarian:

1-5 years	18	16.07%
6-10 years	28	25.00%
11-15 years	23	20.54%
16-20 years	13	11.60%
More than 20 years	30	26.79%

Q22: Years in current position:

1-5 years	75	66.96%
6-10 years	19	16.96%
11-15 years	13	11.61%
16-20 years	2	1.79%
More than 20 years	3	2.68%

Q22: Gender:

Female	91	81.25%
Male	21	18.75%

Firewalls, Ad-Blockers, Web Accelerators, etc.: Helping Remote Users of Electronic Resources Overcome Barriers to Access

David Bickford

University of Phoenix

SUMMARY

The past ten years have seen remote access to electronic resources emerge as the preferred method of use for many, if not most, library patrons. Unfortunately, the misuse of the Internet has also led to a culture in which many personal computer users feel they must install accessory programs that complicate the normal processes associated with the retrieval of Web-based information. Various programs that users install, often with the best of intentions, can interfere with the authentication processes that many libraries and their vendors use. An exploration of firewalls, ad-blockers, pop-up blockers, Web accelerators, and similar software will examine the complications caused by popular programs in each category when users attempt remote access to library-provided in-

---

[Haworth co-indexing entry note]: "Firewalls, Ad-Blockers, Web Accelerators, etc.: Helping Remote Users of Electronic Resources Overcome Barriers to Access." Bickford, David. Co-published simultaneously in *Journal of Library Administration* (The Haworth Information Press, an imprint of The Haworth Press, Inc.) Vol. 45, No. 3/4, 2006, pp. 511-512; and: *The Twelfth Off-Campus Library Services Conference Proceedings* (ed: Julie A. Garrison) The Haworth Information Press, an imprint of The Haworth Press, Inc., 2006, pp. 511-512.

Available online at http://jla.haworthpress.com
doi:10.1300/J111v45n03_12

formation resources. Additional exploration will focus on similar complications experienced by users behind workplace firewalls. Discussion of each type of software will include minimally invasive remedies to recommend to users and suggestions for managing the technical support burden. Particular attention will focus on the interaction of firewalls and related software with popular remote access solutions such as EZproxy. Finally, analysis of this situation will include consideration of human factors, including suggested messages to convey to skeptical patrons and network administrators.

Copyright
in the Online Course Environment

Hazel M. Davis

Rio Salado College

SUMMARY

Librarians are often regarded, either formally or informally, as the experts on copyright at their institutions. This role can assume added importance in the distance learning environment, where so much copyrighted material is made available in online courses.

Hazel Davis is a faculty librarian and the Library Director at Rio Salado College, a non-traditional community college, which has a current enrollment of 25,000 online students. Part of her responsibilities have included the establishment and supervision of a distance learning copyright permissions department at the college, whereby a systematic and structured copyright procurement process is in place. Course developers submit information about the third party materials they would like to make available to students in their online courses (including such items as book excerpts, journal articles, images and film clips) and these items are then researched and evaluated by Hazel and her staff to gauge whether permission is required to include them in online courses. Considerations include whether the items are in the public domain, covered by the fair use statutes, or are library subscriptions which can be linked within the course via PURL script technology, etc. Once the evaluation has been made, permission is secured by library copyright staff, where

[Haworth co-indexing entry note]: "Copyright in the Online Course Environment." Davis, Hazel M. Co-published simultaneously in *Journal of Library Administration* (The Haworth Information Press, an imprint of The Haworth Press, Inc.) Vol. 45, No. 3/4, 2006, pp. 513-515; and: *The Twelfth Off-Campus Library Services Conference Proceedings* (ed: Julie A. Garrison) The Haworth Information Press, an imprint of The Haworth Press, Inc., 2006, pp. 513-515.

Available online at http://jla.haworthpress.com
doi:10.1300/J111v45n03_13

necessary, via an established permissions process, and the items are mounted in the course.

The college has a centralized course development department, and Hazel is a member of this team, meeting with the course developers and instructional designers in the early stages of course development. She makes them aware of the many resources available through the college online library for use in their courses, and also assists with researching possible resources that might be appropriate, based on their needs for course content to meet course competencies.

Hazel has also presented several workshops on copyright best practices for faculty members at all 10 institutions in her community college district who are teaching in the online or hybrid environment.

The workshop at OCLS will include the following elements:

- an overview of copyright law as it pertains to the online environment
- a description of the systematic copyright process at the presenter's institution
- types of third party materials that can be used in online courses
- avenues for use of third party materials, including the public domain, fair use, the TEACH Act, library subscription databases (including persistent links), free Web links, and requesting permission from the copyright holder
- the permissions process

Assumptions

No prior knowledge of copyright in the online environment is required. However, the most recent developments and best practices will be discussed, for those participants with some prior knowledge. Basic computing skills are required.

Objectives

- Discuss the background to copyright law in the United States
- Describe the copyright issues affecting the online course environment
- Apply copyright principles to online courses, including the public domain, fair use, and the TEACH Act
- Describe a model process for copyright compliance for distance learning faculty, administered through the library at Rio Salado College

- Discuss and provide online library and free Web resources to recommend for instructional use in online courses
- Describe and discuss the copyright permissions process

Instructional Outcomes

Participants will be able to apply the concepts taught in the workshop to assisting online faculty with copyright compliance at their own institutions.

Web Site Usability with Remote Users: Formal Usability Studies and Focus Groups

Beth C. Thomsett-Scott

University of North Texas

SUMMARY. Incorporating usability into any Web site creation or redesign is essential. Capturing the perspective of the user makes the site more efficient and effective for the people who will actually be using it. There are a number of usability techniques and several can be incorporated in a study of remote users. The purpose of this paper is to provide an overview of how the traditional usability techniques of focus groups and formal usability studies can be extended to studies involving off-campus users. doi:10.1300/J111v45n03_14

KEYWORDS. Web site usability, remote users, remote usability techniques

INTRODUCTION

Libraries need to aggressively market their products and actively seek and respond to patron feedback (Balas, 2003). Input from current and future users provides for more effective products (Bruseberg & McDonagh-Philp, 2002). The trend towards "fast and easy" may be replacing the need for quality, especially among teens and young adults, making it even more vital to understand and to know the users' needs and wants (Janes, 2003).

[Haworth co-indexing entry note]: "Web Site Usability with Remote Users: Formal Usability Studies and Focus Groups." Thomsett-Scott, Beth C. Co-published simultaneously in *Journal of Library Administration* (The Haworth Information Press, an imprint of The Haworth Press, Inc.) Vol. 45, No. 3/4, 2006, pp. 517-547; and: *The Twelfth Off-Campus Library Services Conference Proceedings* (ed: Julie A. Garrison) The Haworth Information Press, an imprint of The Haworth Press, Inc., 2006, pp. 517-547.

Available online at http://jla.haworthpress.com
doi:10.1300/J111v45n03_14

As libraries continue to provide more and more information on the Web, the Web site must also undergo user satisfaction studies to ensure that it is meeting the needs of the users. A usable interface is essential to keep the users returning to the site. The usability of a Web site will determine its success or failure (Chak, 2000). In the library world, success means that users find what they need when they need it on the library's site rather than resorting to Google or some other method. Chak stated that users will choose the site that provides them with easy access to the information they need. Given the huge dollar amounts libraries spend to purchase electronic products and to make them available via their Web sites, it is essential that the Web site provides access to the information effectively and efficiently.

Usability has long been an important part of Web design. Initially introduced as user-centered design or usability engineering and primarily used in software manufacturing (Rubin, 1994), usability is now widely employed by anyone trying to attract users to their Web site. Hoover's Online was recently redesigned based on the results from a usability study (Green & Hinder, 2003). Kushniruk, Patel, Patel, and Cimino (2001) discussed a usability study involving an online information site for medical patients. Nielsen and Curtis (1995) reported on a study that employed four home pages of businesses to determine which features users preferred. Johnson (1996) provided a review of government Web pages and offered some design suggestions. Agarwal and Venkatesh (2002) discussed a study which examined multiple business Web sites from airlines, online bookstores, automobile manufacturers, and car rental agencies. They had nearly 1500 participants examine the Web sites using a set of well-defined heuristics (usability criteria).

A number of libraries have been including usability as a part of their Web redesign. See Battleson, Booth, and Weintrop (2001), Chisman, Diller, and Walbridge (1999), and Collins and Aguinaga (2001) as examples.

As distance and online learning continues to increase, it is even more vital that the Web sites of libraries are useable. Cockrell and Jayne (2002) noted that the growth in distance learning and off-campus users necessitates additional concern about the efficiency and effectiveness of a library's Web site. The National Center for Education Statistics reports that during the 2000-2001 academic year, 56% (2,320) of all two-year and four-year Title IV-eligible, degree-granting institutions offered distance education courses. Another twelve percent of all institutions indicated that they planned to start offering distance education courses in the next three years. They added that college-level, credit-granting distance education courses at either the undergraduate or graduate/first-professional level were offered by 55% of all two-year and four-year institutions (NCES, 2003). Thus, it is clear that distance and online learning is increasing and will continue to increase, and that libraries need to be ready with efficient and accessible Web sites.

This paper will provide short introductions to Web site usability and remote usability, and then move into the discussion of remote formal usability studies and focus groups. Formal usability studies and focus groups were selected for this paper as they complement each other and provide significant information on Web site usability issues. As well, both of these techniques can be employed remotely with little impact on the quality and quantity of information. Emphasis will be placed on how remote studies vary from face-to-face studies.

For anyone wanting additional information on usability in general or on the techniques, Rubin (1994) wrote a comprehensive book that focuses primarily on formal usability studies. Any of Jakob Nielsen's works, including information found on his Web site (http://www.useit.com/) provide high quality information as Nielsen was and is today one of the foremost experts in Web site usability. For those particularly interested in usability studies in libraries, Battleson et al. (2001), Campbell (2001a), and Norlin and Winters (2002) provide excellent starting points.

WEB SITE USABILITY

The goals of usability are usefulness, effectiveness or ease of use, ability to learn, and attitude or satisfaction (Rubin, 1994). By involving the users in the design or at least considering the site from users' perspectives, the site will be more effective and efficient for the users and they will be more likely to use the site rather than go to a free search engine or some other source of information. Ebling and John (2000) stated that usability evaluations need more than a yes or no answer, they must provide details about what did not work and why something did not work. Kushniruk et al. (2001) noted that the evaluation must also investigate the thought processes and reasoning behind use of the site.

There are three basic categories of usability techniques: inquiry, inspection, and formal usability studies, also called task-based testing. Inquiry methods include surveys, questionnaires, focus groups, and field observations. Inspection methods consider the site from the user's perspective using a set of heuristics or established usability criteria, and include techniques such as cognitive walkthroughs, heuristic evaluations, and card sorts. Formal usability studies involve having participants complete representative tasks while being observed or recorded in some fashion. Ivory and Hearst (2001) presented a paper that categorizes usability methods by such things as automation level and effort level. This is a comprehensive paper for anyone seeking to learn more about the variety of usability methods available.

Incorporating more than one usability method into a study is recommended. Kushniruk et al. (2001) suggested that a multi-method approach is best to gain an indepth understanding of the usability of the site. Dix, Filay, Abowd, and Beale (1998), Ebling and John (2000), Jeffries and Desurvire (1992), Nielsen (1993), and Rafee, Kassim, and Kochanek (2003) recommended including at least two techniques in a usability study in order to provide the best possible evaluation. As noted above, this paper will discuss formal usability studies and focus groups. Focus groups can be used after formal usability studies as they provide for group discussion and the synergy of ideas (Thomsett-Scott, 2004a, 2004b). Often participants are more relaxed in a group situation than in one-on-one situations (Canning, 1995), and this may be the reason for the additional usefulness of the focus groups. The techniques complement each other and provide valuable information.

REMOTE USABILITY

Remote methods of gathering information from users have been incorporated into usability engineering and human-computer interactions for a number of years, initially for the evaluation of new or redesigned software, and more recently being applied to Web sites. Since software is used by a diverse population with various computer setups and browsers, evaluations by remote techniques are considered to be more effective (Scholtz, 2001). Remote usability in its most basic form involves working with a participant who is not in the same physical location as the tester. Ivory and Hearst (2001) defined remote testing as evaluations with users who are in a different location. Hartson, Castillo, Kelso, Neale, and Kamler (1996) expanded the definition to note that the evaluator is separated in space and/or time from the participant. The earliest remote studies involved using video conferencing, live video feeds, and telephone communication which can end up being time consuming for the observers and expensive (Tullis, Fleischman, McNultry, Cianchette, & Bergel, 2002). Recently, remote usability more generally refers to live-viewing of a remote site (S. M. Thompson, 2003). Preston (1999) noted that the literature she read tended to reserve the term "remote testing" for the type of testing that involves having the test facilitator "live" at one site while watching a participant at a remote site. Hammontree, Weiler, and Nayak (1994) stated that remote testing sites can be anywhere from a room next door to a location on the other side of the world. Although more frequently employed when participants are geographically separated from each other by large distances, remote usability can be used between rooms in a building. This may be helpful when testing faculty who are on campus but who do not want to take the time to come to the library.

Remote usability has become more attractive and feasible in the last few years as improvements in Web technologies have provided for an increase in the number and variety of options available (Hammontree et al., 1994). F. S. H. Krauss (2003) added that for remote usability to work, the facilitator and participant must be able to share information and files over secure, high bandwidth networks, and that the increase in reliable and safe networks provides for a growth in remote usability studies.

Millen (1999) suggested that the rapid increase in new products, such as Web development technology, has challenged design teams to involve users in an effective way. Kushniruk et al. (2001) added that as sites become more technologically advanced, the methods used to evaluate them should also become more high-tech. As new Web technology becomes available and Web sites need more frequent updating to be technologically appealing, designers must engage as many users as possible in usability studies and not leave any group, such as distance learners, out of the usability loop.

Remote Usability Studies

Remote usability can be synchronous or asynchronous. Synchronous usability provides for sending and the receiving data in real time. Examples include videoconferencing and using screen-sharing tools such as WebEx or NetMeeting. Ames (2003) noted that synchronous remote studies most closely simulate local studies. Asynchronous studies do not have a facilitator with the participant and the data are not delivered in real time. Server logs, diaries, surveys, and questionnaires are examples of asynchronous methods. Asynchronous methods normally provide only quantitative data, and basing an analysis on quantitative data alone in usability studies can lead to the misinterpretation of results (Dray & Siegel, 2004).

Hartson et al. (1996) categorized and evaluated seven types of remote evaluation methods: portable (setting up the studies at another location), local (study materials sent to participants who perform the study and send the results back), remote questionnaire/survey, remote control evaluation (participant controls own computer at his/her location and the results are captured by a collaboration software), video conferencing (capture video feed from the participant's site), instrumental remote evolution (involves questionnaires which are used to log various events), and semi-instrumental remote evaluation (participant triggers the logging system when s/he encounters an issue).

This paper will focus on synchronous remote control evaluation which is also referred to as same-time/different-place evaluation (Ivory & Hearst, 2001) as we are particularly interested in formal usability studies and focus groups which are most frequently performed in real time. Examples of asynchronous methods can be found in Ames (2003), Chak (2000), F. S. H. Krauss (2003), and Paternò and Pagenelli (2001). For purposes of this paper, the term local will be used to refer to studies where the participants meet in-person with the test facilitator.

Hammontree et al. (1994) noted that tools developed for cooperative computer-support and group collaboration tools are useful for remote usability. S. M. Thompson (2003) explained that the most basic piece of equipment needed for remote studies is a screen viewer. The preferred capabilities of the software are real-time sharing applications between two or more computers, a whiteboard for annotating screen shots, and providing live video of the participant (Hammontree et al.). Preston (1999) noted that adding screen capture software that will record the actions on the user's screen will enhance the quality of the data. Audio connections may be provided by the software or by using additional phone lines (Scholtz, 2001). Ivory and Hearst (2001) stated that in same-time different-place evaluation and in remote control testing the facilitator observes the participant's screen through a sharing software and may be able to hear what the participant says via a speaker telephone or a microphone affixed to the computer. F. S. H. Krauss (2003) recommended using a screen sharing software, having observers record usability problems, utilizing a data logging tool to record the user's screen or having a video camera recording the test administrator's screen, and setting up a telephone for verbal communication. Software makes it possible for the tester to interact with the participant during the test, which is essential for techniques such as the question-asking or thinking-aloud protocols that require a dialogue.

Disadvantages and Advantages of Remote Usability Studies

One of the major benefits of remote studies is the ability to test a larger number of users since travel time and costs are not a factor (Cheatham & Bartek, 2004; Perkins, 2002; S. M. Thompson, 2003). Test administrators may also find it easier to get people to participate. Cheatham and Bartek reported a lack of local participants when recruiting them to evaluate the IBM portal. Brush, Ames, and Davis (2004) reported that they had many more participants for the remote test than for the local test. Remote usability studies allow participants to take less time away from their normal activities, and thus a greater number of people may be willing to participate (Bartek & Cheatham, 2003a). Remote studies may appeal to users who otherwise might not come forward such as the very shy participant or participants with family or job responsibilities. The number of participants required may be specific to the technique used and the product being evaluated.

Related to the above is the possibility of testing a greater diversity of users. Remote studies can more easily include specialized users (Bartek & Cheatham, 2003a; Cheatham & Bartek, 2004; Perkins, 2002). From a library perspective, these users may include students who use the library remotely with no or infrequent in-person visits, or those who do not use the library's resources at all. Gough and Phillips (2003) added that remote studies can be used to reach small, hard to reach or decentralized groups, or other users that can be difficult to add to a local study. For Web sites that have a global user population, remote assessment and analysis methods are necessary to evaluate usability (Scholtz, 2001). Remote studies also allow for the participation of representative users of the libraries rather than just those who are on campus (Hartson et al., 1996; Winckler, Freitas, & Valdeni, 2000). Scholtz noted that it is becoming more difficult to find representative users due to the increased growth of users and the greater diversity of computer configurations. Ames (2003) concurred that it may be difficult to find representative users, especially if serving wide areas or diverse groups of people. It can cost time and money to include non-local and especially international participants if test administrators need to go to them or bring them to the test location. In libraries, there may be a pool of international students and faculty to select from that can help with the studies. However, an advantage of remote studies is clearly an enlarged pool of users and the possibility of increasing the diversity of the participants.

Several authors stated that working with participants in their own environments is beneficial as they can examine the context of how users actually use the technology and provides a more natural work environment (Brush et al., 2004; Cheatham & Bartek, 2004; Hartson et al., 1996). Kushniruk et al. (2001) added that they prefer to study participants in their own environment due to the advantage of examining the real context of the work. Scholtz (2001) and Winckler et al. (2000) noted that remote studies provide useful data on how the software or Web site works with different computer configurations. Kushniruk et al. added that it is important to consider how the user's system varies from the preferred set-up when assessing usability issues. Web site usability with remote methods has the benefit of being done in the user's real-life workspace to allow the evaluators to gather a full spectrum of usability issues. Formal usability studies normally use specific tasks but the results will still show the user's choice of browser and how this may affect the site's performance, as well as how users actually use the site.

Usability studies carried out in a remote environment may cost less, although this is dependent on how the studies are normally conducted. Most libraries bring users into a room in the library and run the study there. Incentives for participation are usually small. Businesses and software developers frequently have a special usability testing laboratory and will pay the travel costs of the participants so remote studies thus save a great deal of time and money (Cheatham & Bartek, 2004; Gough & Phillips, 2003; Hartson et al., 1996; S. M. Thompson, 2003). The costs of formal usability studies include preparing for the study, performing the study, extracting the raw data, analyzing the raw data, and identifying the usability issues (Ebling & John, 2000). Dray and Siegel (2004) added that facilitators still need time to find participants, schedule the sessions, develop materials, and set up the hardware and software. Gough and Phillips emphasized that the software costs and telephone charges can actually add to their costs over and above what local studies cost them. There will also be extra time to examine and select the remote software. Many authors evaluate several screen-sharing software options and this can add to the time of the study.

While remote studies can be advantageous to show how users employ the technology in their natural environment, there are drawbacks. System performance, network traffic, and the participant's computer set-up can all affect the results (Cheatham & Bartek, 2004; Ivory & Hearst, 2001; Rafee et al., 2003). The size and capacity of the machines, the resolution, the number of colors in the display, and the intricacy of the application or Web site being tested may also affect the results (Preston, 1999). Perkins (2002) added that downloading and connecting to the software can cause technical issues. Additional connectivity and firewall issues may arise, especially if the participants are taking the test from their place of employment. Setting up the software remotely can be painstaking, especially when working with international participants (Dray & Siegel, 2004).

Another challenge is that the user should have a high speed connection. Perkins (2002) emphasized that participants must have a high speed connection. K. T. Thompson, Rozanski, and Haake (2004) noted that one participant was unable to connect to the study software using a dial-up connection. This limits the participant pool to those users who have acceptable connection speeds and to those who may be more technological literate (Gough & Phillips, 2003).

The study may also have unexpected interruptions. The recording software can glitch or crash, either the participant's or the facilitator's computers can crash, or the network can become too slow to allow the test to continue. Cheatham and Bartek (2004) noted that emergency phone calls, e-mail notifications, and other disruptions may occur during the study. Some of these can be mediated by a pilot test as discussed below.

Since the participant is separated from the facilitator, the observation data usually found in formal usability studies are missing. The contextual information and non-verbal cues observed while participants complete the tasks can be highly beneficial (Brush et al., 2004; Cheatham & Bartek, 2004; Gough & Phillips, 2003) but are lacking in remote studies. Audio and/or video can be used in remote studies but facilitators will still miss some information (Rafee et al., 2003). Video quality may be poor as well as difficult to obtain, while Gough and Phillips noted that speakerphones can add extra noise and provide for reduced sound quality. Not being able to observe the participant may add extra challenges since body language cues can assist the facilitator in knowing when a participant is confused about instructions or the tasks, or when s/he are getting frustrated (Dray & Siegel, 2004), and these are missing in remote studies. Facilitators must excel at detecting emotions through verbal cues to ensure a successful remote study.

Cultural differences may also affect study results but be less noticeable if the participants cannot be seen (Olson & Olson, 2000). For example, some cultures are hesitant to ask for assistance or show emotion either visually or verbally. These issues can lead to misinterpretation of the task and/or the results (Dray & Siegel, 2004). Culture can also affect the degree to which technical delays influence participants as some cultures are very patient while others are less so (Olson & Olson). Culture also provides for differences among "business" and "relationship building." In face-to-face meetings, the facilitator can gauge the participant's comfort level and decide when to begin the "test" but the same cues are not available in remote studies.

Cheatham and Bartek (2004) recommended emphasizing the "think aloud" protocol and paying close attention to verbal cues. They added that the facilitator could use question probes to get the necessary information. This is unusual in formal usability studies but may be beneficial in remote studies, especially with quiet participants. While the think aloud protocol is useful for most participants, it may be less useful, especially in replacing observer data, when working with international participants as they may be more reticent to verbalize their thought processes. With remote studies, there is a greater need to be aware of verbal cues as even video may not give the whole story. Trust between the participant and facilitator is essential and needs special attention in remote studies (Olson & Olson, 2000).

Several other advantages exist for remote studies. Remote participants may be easier to schedule (Gough & Phillips, 2003; S. M. Thompson, 2003), although the facilitator may find that a larger number of the sessions will need to occur at times beyond "normal" working hours. Time zones can be a problem for international participants, and may also be a source of confusion with any participant in a different time zone (Dray & Siegel, 2004; Olson & Olson, 2000). Remote studies may be less intrusive to shy participants. Cheatham and Bartek (2004) added that since the remote atmosphere is a more realistic environment, the participants may experience less anxiety. Remote methods also allow for additional observers compared to most local studies. Since more observers can be present, stakeholders may have the opportunity to view the live tests rather than just watching videos or data (Gough & Phillips, 2003), which can be highly beneficial when convincing them that changes to the site are needed.

REMOTE FORMAL USABILITY STUDIES

Formal usability studies involve working with real users of the Web site on a one-on-one basis. It is frequently considered to be the best usability technique. Gough and Phillips (2003) noted that the reality check that comes from watching actual users perform real tasks is invaluable for stakeholders, designers, and developers. The basic elements of formal usability testing involve real users performing real tasks on a Web page or site, usually with a moderator and often an observer (Norlin & Winters, 2002). Observation can be either direct (in the room) or indirect (through one-way glass, screen captures, video recording, etc.) or a combination of both. Nielsen (1993) stated that laboratory testing of users is the most effective source of information for identifying usability data. Prior to technological advances, design teams were restricted to conducting user testing in specially designed labs or rooms (F. S. H. Krauss, 2003), which can be expensive and make it difficult to get representative users. Remote studies, as discussed above, provide options that assist with obtaining participants and make it much easier to work with remote users.

Norlin and Winters (2002) explained that formal usability studies provide both qualitative and quantitative data and thus offer greater scope and breadth to usability studies. This technique can be used to find the more serious difficulties that users have with the site (Jeffries & Desurvire, 1992). Formal usability studies provide useful data to indicate where the terminology or the visual layout may be confusing to users, where information is hidden, and how pages should be arranged for improved utilization. They also show the different strategies users take to answer the tasks. If the atmosphere is conducive and good communication is established, participants may also suggest alternate terminology and design which can be very helpful to design teams.

Equipment Needs

Conducting a formal usability study remotely requires some additional equipment as noted above. A screen-sharing software is a must as this provides the ability to share viewing and control of the Web browser, view the user's mouse movements, and see the pages that are explored. Common screen-sharing software, also called collaboration software, are NetMeeting, Lotus Sametime, and WebEx. A number of authors have used NetMeeting as it comes bundled with Windows XP and 2000 and has downloads available for older editions. NetMeeting also has an audio function that can be used to record the talk aloud comments. Since NetMeeting is free, it is possible to add extra observers which can be useful if stakeholders are interested in viewing the live tests.

Incorporating screen recording software is beneficial. S. M. Thompson (2003) recommended using a screen recording technology as it captures all screen movements and provides automatic timing for questions. The captured data can be converted to movie format and watched at the tester's leisure to fill in gaps from the observation and also be used to provide a visual representation to show stakeholders where the usability problems occurred (Kushniruk et al., 2001; S. M. Thompson, 2003). Reviews of screen-sharing software can be found in Preston (1999), K. T. Thompson et al. (2004), and S. M. Thompson.

An audio connection is fundamental as it is essential to be in voice contact with the participants to reassure them and to encourage the think aloud process (S. M. Thompson, 2003). Hammontree et al. (1994) noted that voice communication provides for a level of personal relationship that is otherwise missing in remote studies. This can assist in building trust between the facilitator and the participant that is valuable for successful studies (Olson & Olson, 2000).

Some form of video communication between the facilitator and the participant is beneficial. Bartek and Cheatham (2003b) videotaped the facilitator's screen which shows the participant's actions and recorded the phone conversation through a speakerphone at the facilitator's desk. Videotape can be helpful to see users' reactions if pointed towards them but may be intrusive for some participants (S. M. Thompson, 2003), and is difficult to arrange in distance usability studies. If video is desired, extra considerations will need to be built into the study.

A shared whiteboard feature is helpful for participant/facilitator discussion. Troublesome pages can be brought up into the whiteboard space and participants can point out problem areas (Hammontree et al., 1994). Both the evaluator and the participant can annotate the pages and suggest modifications for increased usability (Hammontree et al.; Preston, 1999).

Setting Up and Running a Remote Usability Study

Cheatham and Bartek (2004) noted that although local studies need careful planning, a well-defined purpose, and a well-established target audience, these are even more essential with remote studies. Gough and Phillips (2003) added that it is vital to have clear communication with the participants. They need to know when they are supposed to attend the meeting, what they are supposed to do, and how to use the software. Communication with the participants should be personal, either through e-mail or over the phone. Most formal usability studies take one and one-half to two hours. Bartek and Cheatham (2003a) suggested that studies last no longer than three hours.

Gough and Phillips (2003) recommended that the software requirements and the importance of a high speed network be emphasized when recruiting participants. Participants need to be comfortable with using the screen-sharing software and any other software or hardware that is required. Even with fairly simple software, the participants should have a certain degree of technical comfort. Facilitators may also want to select participants based on their potential ability to be coached if something goes wrong during the study. This necessitates talking with the potential participants prior to selecting them which can be unusual for libraries but does have advantages.

Conducting a beta test prior to performing the real study is recommended. Beta testing provides for testing of the tasks or questions and ensuring that the equipment works well. This is again more important for remote studies. All collaboration software should be tested remotely before incorporating it into a usability study. For best results, the software should be tested on a variety of computer configurations and with different browsers to enable easier identification of problems and to allow a fuller knowledge of how to troubleshoot any potential issues. Brush et al. (2004) noted that coping with technical problems remotely can be more difficult as the facilitator will have to guide the participant through the problem rather than simply fixing it his/her self. Remote troubleshooting becomes even more problematic when facilitators or participants are in a hurry (Bartek & Cheatham, 2003a). Dray and Siegel (2004) recommended beta testing in order to avoid problems and making the users figure out the corrections on their own.

H. Krauss and Vigilante (2002) suggested a pilot session as this provides an opportunity to assess the participant's hardware and software against the needs of the testing software and the Web site. Cheatham and Bartek (2004) and K. T. Thompson et al. (2004) also recommended a beta test with the participant prior to the study. The extra session may act to increase the comfort level of the participant with the software, although most respondents did not take advantage of this when it was voluntary (Bartek & Cheatham, 2003b). The pilot test may also reduce the stress to the participant and should provide additional time to establish trust. Bartek and Cheatham (2003a) emphasized that pilot sessions will add increased time for each participant. If a pilot session is not feasible, Brush et al. (2004) recommended having the participants download the software prior to the study.

Since the remote aspect of the test adds some additional steps, such as having the user log into the software, this time will need to be built into the overall test time. Even with encouraging the participants to download the software prior to the study or establishing a beta test prior to the real test, it is still valuable to factor in some extra time. Bartek and Cheatham (2003b) noted that 40% of participants had not set up the equipment ahead of time despite being asked to do this, and therefore strongly recommended an introductory session to ensure that participants are adequately prepared. The average time to set up the screen software was 10 minutes (Bartek & Cheatham, 2003b). Gough and Phillips (2003) recommended allowing for 10-15 minutes at the beginning to set up the software and to demonstrate how it works. Bartek and Cheatham (2003b) recommended sending explicit instructions to the participants which will help to meet the needs of people who prefer to read rather than to hear directions. Observers should log in prior to the participants in order to avoid additional concerns for the participant (Gough & Phillips, 2003). Facilitators may want to add some extra time to allow for general training and glitches (H. Krauss & Vigilante, 2002).

Test materials need to be clearly written, especially with remote studies. The tasks need to be designed for most effective utilization of the session (see Campbell, 2001b and Norlin & Winters, 2002 for excellent overviews on writing tasks). Chisman et al. (1999) and Thomsett-Scott (2004a) recommended providing the tasks in written form to the participants in a face-to-face study as some participants prefer to see the questions rather than to hear them, especially international participants. This should be carried through in a remote study, as relaying tasks over the telephone can be difficult and many people cannot read screen text effectively.

Cheatham and Bartek (2004) recommended that test materials be e-mailed or faxed to the participants prior to the study, while Bartek and Cheatham (2003a) added that putting the materials online may be useful. K. T. Thompson et al. (2004) mailed the tasks and debriefing questionnaire in hardcopy to reduce any inconvenience to the participants and to ensure that they had the task list printed out since it may be easier to read hardcopy than view on the monitor. She also included a self-addressed, stamped envelope for returning the post-test questionnaire. Participants must be strongly encouraged not to open the task list until the session begins. Since participants do not always follow instructions concerning preliminary instructions for the test, facilitators may find it beneficial to send materials in hardcopy even if they hope participants will complete the materials online.

Running the Test

A checklist of steps and their sequence in remote studies was provided by H. Krauss and Vigilante (2002). The first few minutes are taken up with introducing the test and the purpose. As mentioned earlier, remote studies will take a few minutes extra to connect to the software and to ensure that everything is working. Ames (2003) recommended using the same facilitator in order to control for facilitator variations.

The think aloud method involves asking the users to vocalize the reasons for their pathway choices and other thoughts as they work through the tasks. Nielsen (1993) wrote that the think aloud process may be the most important part of the formal usability study process. Walbridge (2000) noted that the think-aloud technique reveals the thought processes of the participants and can indicate why they make particular choices. Usability participants should be encouraged to think aloud as the information obtained is well worth the effort. A good way to encourage participants to "think aloud" is to ask them to read the question aloud (Battleson et al., 2001) and ask them to continue to think aloud while completing the question. Ames (2003) suggested saying "and now" if participants go silent.

Results from Remote Formal Usability Studies

Tullis et al. (2002) and Ames (2003) noted that the task completion rates were similar between remote and local participants, although the differences were larger in the study by Ames with remote results being somewhat lower, but no significant differences were found. Tullis et al. added that the remote and local participants generally had difficulty with most of the same tasks. Cheatham and Bartek (2004) noted that there were similar error rates between both groups. There were more errors in the pathways for the remote group (K. T. Thompson et al., 2004). Remote participants tend to explore the site more which affected the pathway results (Waterson, Landry, & Matthews, 2000). A higher number of remote users think they found the correct answer but really did not (Scholtz, 2001), necessitating an increased level of prompting from the moderator to encourage them to look for other pathways. Ames reported that the remote group had twice the preemptive finish rate of local participants.

Remote participants took longer to complete the tasks, although the times were not significantly different (K. T. Thompson et al., 2004; Tullis et al., 2002). Cheatham and Bartek (2004) noted that both groups took similar times. K. T. Thompson et al. (2004) added that although time is a standard measure for formal usability studies, it is not really a good indicator of usability in remote studies.

The ultimate goal of a usability study is to identify usability issues or problems. Ebling and John (2000) identified something as a usability problem if two or more sources of data suggest it, two or more users report a problem, or if one user provides evidence and the facilitators concur. K. T. Thompson et al. (2004) noted that the remote group reported more usability problems, but that each group found four different types of errors than the other. Hartson et al. (1996) reported that remote participants found two more problems than local participants. Ames (2003) reported similar results. Tullis et al. (2002) performed two studies and noted that in the first study the local participants found more errors, while in the second study the remote participants reported more usability issues. They added that the serious issues were discovered by both groups. Ebling and John reported that remote participants missed some of the more severe issues. Both remote and local studies may need to be performed to allow for identification of all usability issues.

Tullis et al. (2002) made an interesting observation. Several remote users complained that the font size was too small on the test site, but no local participants reported this. Upon further investigation, they discovered that most remote participants used monitor resolutions of 1024 × 768 or 1280 × 1024 while lab monitors were set to 800 × 600. In addition, the local participants noticed some characteristics of the site such as the need to scroll and missing elements that the remote people did not. Perhaps the monitor size affected these issues or the remote group noticed the issues but did not choose to comment on them.

Cheatham and Bartek (2004), Chen, Mitsock, Coronado, and Salvendy (1999), and Hartson et al. (1996) reported no difference in product or site satisfaction between local and remote participants. Tullis et al. (2002) asked participants to provide a subjective rating for their product. Interestingly, in the first study, the local group rated the product higher, while in the second study the remote users gave a higher rating. Although the order changed between the studies, Tullis et al. hypothesized that remote users feel more anonymous which makes it easier for them to provide negative feedback. As well, the lack of social dynamic between the participant and the facilitator may add to an enhanced ability to critique a product.

Remote and local usability participants provide a similar quality and quantity of information from think aloud protocol (Cheatham & Bartek, 2004). Brush et al. (2004) found comparable results. Ebling and John

(2000) noted that the verbal protocol identified 61 of 65 issues and that 40 were only noticed through the think aloud, supporting the importance of ensuring that the participants add verbal comments in both local and remote studies. Tullis et al. (2002) suggested that the level of comments from the remote group overcomes the lack of observer data.

Brush et al. (2004) conducted a questionnaire of a group of participants who performed both remote and local usability tests. The majority of the users felt equally comfortable, found it equally easy to remember to think aloud, reported equal comfort in discussing the questions, and felt they had provided similar contributions to the usefulness of the test with either the remote or the local method. There was a split between the two groups on which type of test they preferred between remote and no preference for either method. Cheatham and Bartek (2004) wrote that the majority of their subjects agree that the remote study was very easy or easy, the study experience was very satisfactory or satisfactory, and the ease of setting up remote software was very easy to easy. All participants replied that the remote method was well suited to the purpose of the study. Ames (2003) also noted that participants had a similar comfort level between the two methods. Bartek and Cheatham (2003b) added that all 26 participants (whether local or remote) wanted to continue participating in usability activities.

There was a slight preference for participants to find it easier to concentrate in a local situation (Brush et al., 2004). Ames (2003) reported that there was no significant difference in distractions between local or remote participants. The possibility of various interruptions in a remote study suggests that participants should be asked to schedule the session when there will be a minimum of interruptions.

Remote participants list the benefits of remote as being convenient and cost-effective (Cheatham & Bartek, 2004). Ames (2003) noted that participants felt it easier to recall the tasks and pathways and thought that test facilitators were more interested in their feedback in the local study.

Local and remote participants had a similar level of tolerance with system failures (Bartek & Cheatham, 2003b). Brush et al. (2004) noted that there were no significant differences in technical difficulties or software problems. Interestingly, some participants who were concerned about unseen observers in a lab setting were not concerned about observers watching them complete the tasks remotely (Bartek & Cheatham, 2003b). Brush et al. (2004) reported that observers felt that either system was easy to observe and that the tone of voice of the participants was useful to sense the frustration of the participants.

Debriefing and Post-Study Questionnaires

After completing the study, participants are usually "debriefed." This normally involves completing a short demographic questionnaire with additional debriefing questions on the test process and asking for general satisfaction of the site. The questionnaire measures opinions, attributes, strengths, weaknesses, and terminology of the site (F. S. H. Krauss, 2003). McGillis and Toms (2001) noted that post-test surveys provide information on the participants' perceptions of using the site and the features. Questionnaires are useful for collecting additional feedback from the study (Campbell, 2001a). Participants are also asked to fill in a demographic questionnaire. The use of a post-test questionnaire and demographic survey allows participants some time to relax and reflect on the study, and may assist in leading them more easily into the debriefing sessions.

In a local study, participants normally complete a paper-based survey and questionnaire. As mentioned above, some authors send the questionnaires and surveys to the participants in advance. F. S. H. Krauss (2003), however, had the participants complete the survey online while recording the results via the screen-sharing software, allowing the facilitators to follow up on questions or to clarify answers. Bartek and Cheatham (2003a) also used online surveys as these reduce printing and provide for increased anonymity. A problem with remote studies can be ensuring that participants return the surveys, even with encouragement and reminders (Bartek & Cheatham, 2003a; Cheatham & Bartek, 2004). If participants are being compensated in some manner, making the return of the completed surveys a part of the requirements prior to payment may help overcome this issue.

The debriefing portion of the study can be the key to fixing the problems indicated by the study results (Rubin, 1994). The informal comments provided are often enlightening and always useful (Battleson et al., 2001). Walbridge (2000) added that the debriefing time offers a chance to provide some information literacy training for the participants. Chisman et al. (1999) stated that debriefing participants and test administrators after each study is essential for a quality result. Debriefing the facilitators and the observers allows for additional discussion on the participants' reactions to the site.

Some authors spend more time on the debriefing than others. Gough and Phillips (2003) asked participants to point at the feature when they discuss problem areas for each task. Green and Hinder (2003) used a modified version of the "formal" technique by asking users to clarify their thoughts and actions after each task as a type of mini-debriefing. This may be more useful in remote studies as it is important to get as many contextual clues as possible since visual observation of the participants may be missing. Ames (2003) asked participants to reflect on the tasks, elaborate on what was difficult, and suggest possible improvements. After the participants have finished discussing their responses, Hammontree et al. (1994) told participants what the predetermined "correct" solutions were and then they discussed the potential usability problems and entertained possible solutions. Ames and Brush et al. (2004) noted that remote participants took several minutes longer to discuss the results. This extra time will need to be built into the session time.

Summary of Remote Formal Usability Studies

Remote formal usability studies work best with screen-sharing capabilities, screen recording software, think aloud, and audio recording. A pretest with each participant is highly recommended. Test materials should be mailed or faxed prior to the study to allow participants to examine the procedure, but mark the tasks as "do not open until session time."

Formal usability studies are currently based on "traditional" measures of success such as less time taken to find answer, greater success rate, and reduced errors. However, remote groups, while possibly doing more poorly on the traditional measures, found more usability issues and that, of course, is the goal of a usability study. Cheatham and Bartek (2004) reported that one participant stated "Tasks like usability testing can be conducted with remote methods as effectively as if it were done in person" (p. 9). Other than some slight modifications to the standard procedures and some extra equipment, remote formal usability studies are a useful means of gathering usability data from remote users and provide similar results to local studies. For a thorough evaluation, both local and remote formal usability studies should be employed in order to discover all of the potential usability issues.

FOCUS GROUPS

Focus groups have been used extensively in a number of disciplines including software engineering. They are an effective way of evaluating the design of software products and Web pages (Crowley, Leffel,

Ramirez, & Armstrong, 2003). Bruseberg and McDonagh-Philp (2002) wrote that the qualitative information garnered from focus groups is particularly useful to product designers at the decision-making stage. Focus groups are beneficial for software and Web designers as they effectively provide information on participants' satisfiers–the tangibles and intangibles that make the product enjoyable and satisfying (Burns & Evans, 2000; Jordan, 2000). Canning (1995) described focus groups as a cost-effective and quick means to elicit relevant information about services and resources. Focus groups are well suited to exploring participants' behaviors, concerns, needs, and desires, and for determining how users will react to new services, products, or ideas (Crowley et al., 2003). Cavill (2002) noted that focus groups are a powerful research tool as they explore participants' feelings about various issues.

Originally used in libraries primarily for user satisfaction, focus groups have more recently been used to evaluate library services. Examples of the use of focus groups for evaluative purposes are Connaway, Johnson and Searing (1997), Massey-Burzio (1998), and Widdows, Hensler and Wyncott (1991).

Incorporating focus groups into a usability study provides additional information that is well worth the extra time. Large, Beheshti and Rahman (2002) noted that focus groups utilize group interactions to solicit a wide range of ideas. By utilizing the synergy of ideas provided by well-functioning focus groups, more information on terminology, design, and layout can be brought quickly to the surface. When incorporated into usability studies, focus groups can be used in several different ways. Groups can look at a site and discuss issues about it. This preliminary information is used to create prototypes for the revised site. Other researchers use focus groups after formal usability studies. Some researchers will perform the formal usability studies in a group setting and then immediately have a focus group (Palmquist, 2001), while others work with the usability participants individually and then bring them together for a focus group (Thomsett-Scott, 2004a).

The past few years have seen the emergence of online focus groups that are carried out in Web-based chat rooms rather than in person (Bird, 1994; Parks, 1997). The participants and the moderator meet in an online chat room simultaneously. They type their comments over the course of the session and a running transcript of these comments is visible to all of the participants. The groups are then conducted similarly to local studies (Gaiser, 1997).

For the reader looking for background information on focus groups, Morgan (1997) provided an excellent comprehensive introduction to the methodology and uses of focus groups. Glitz (1998) offered a highly informative summary on the use of focus groups in libraries.

Advantages and Disadvantages of Remote Focus Groups

Remote focus groups are beneficial for reaching audiences that are geographically diverse, difficult to recruit, or whose interactions with the product or organization have been completely online (Schneider, Kerwin, Frechtling, & Vivari, 2002; Sweet, 1999; Whitlach, 2001). Remote focus groups also offer the potential for working with groups who are difficult to reach via conventional research approaches (Coomber, 1997; Hodkinson & Hodkinson, 1999)

Online focus groups are usually cheaper than in-person groups (Schneider et al., 2002; Whitlach, 2001). Landreth (1998), Maddox (1998), and Miller (1994) noted that online groups do not require special meeting rooms, refreshments, transcription, or videotaping. The transcripts are immediately available for printing and viewing (Marney, 1990; Whitlach, 2001) which saves a substantial amount of time and money.

Remote focus groups are useful for Web site studies (Sweet, 1999). Schneider et al. (2002) added that online focus groups may be particularly advantageous for evaluating Web sites because the participants can easily inspect the Web sites during the discussions. Facilitators may want to send screenshots of specific pages in hard copy with the other test materials to save participants the time needed to switch back and forth between the communication system and the Web site.

Remote focus groups may provide for more open discussions. Since the communications are anonymous, participants may be willing to share personal behaviors and to be more critical of the Web site (Murphy, Durako, Muenz, & Wilson, 2000; Walston & Lissitz, 2000). Hughes and Lang (2004) explained that since all comments are recorded on the transcript and are immediately available to the participants, issues due to poor hearing, participants talking over each other, and missed opportunities to respond to a particular topic or comment are significantly reduced.

Schneider et al. (2002) added that online groups can be unrepresentative as participants must have a computer and Web access, and also be somewhat tech savvy in order to access and use the software. There is also a risk of technical difficulties. Hughes and Lang (2004) presented a very thorough review of the disadvantages and advantages of online focus groups, although not all comments relate to focus groups for Web site usability.

Implementing and Running an Online Focus Group

When employed in usability studies, focus groups are conducted similarly to other disciplines. There are usually eight to twelve participants, a moderator and perhaps an observer, the session may be audio and/or video taped, have eight to ten questions, and last for approximately two hours. Remote focus groups are another relatively inexpensive method of gathering input from users as they can be small, with one or two groups, or large, with several to many groups. Sweet (1999) recommended six to eight participants for online groups, although five members may be the maximum that can be reasonably monitored (Hughes & Lang, 2004). Even with a smaller number of participants, the benefits of having all comments recorded in an error-free transcript can make the online groups more useful.

Some form of chat or collaboration software is needed. Blackboard, WebCT, NetMeeting, and eShare Expressions are all frequently used as are pay-per-use chat software. If libraries already use chat software, this should be investigated as potential software for focus groups. A whiteboard feature may be useful, if available, as the Web pages could be posted and participants be allowed to annotate the pages with their suggestions for improving usability as can be done in formal usability studies.

Participants need clear communication about passwords, usernames, connection instructions, dates, and times (Sweet, 1999). Observers should log in before the participants to avoid any possibility of complications. Participants should sign on in advance of the group session to make sure they can use the software and that their machines are compatible with the software (Gough & Phillips, 2003). This provides them with time to contact either the facilitator or the technical support company for the software if there is a problem. One moderator facilitates the group. Observers can be in private communication with the moderator to ask for follow up on comments (Sweet, 1999). They should be well trained in using the communication software.

After all participants and observers are logged in, the focus group begins. Participants should be quickly introduced. The purpose of the group and the ground rules need to be discussed. When using local focus groups after formal usability studies, an Internet accessible computer should be available or screen shots of the main pages should be provided (Thomsett-Scott, 2004b). Frequently, participants will want to review the pages to remember specific comments they had during completion of the tasks. Remote participants should be reminded of the

URL for the test site and particularly difficult pages may want to be reviewed in advance of the focus group meeting.

Sweet (1999) recommended having the moderator use capital letters so it is easy to see when the moderator has posted a question or a comment. This will also assist with reading the transcripts. Questions should be typed in advance and pasted into the software when needed. Doing this will prevent delays due to slow typing or extra clarifications on unclear questions.

Some additional moderating skills are required for remote focus groups. The moderator must be a fast typist and be able to multitask as s/he may need to be typing a question, answering a technical question, and responding to an observer comment at the same time (Sweet, 1999). Moderators still need to be able to make participants feel comfortable and be able to assure participants that their contributions are worthwhile.

The moderator usually does not respond to comments or offer answers to questions in focus groups. However, Thomsett-Scott (2004a) reported on a study that involved answering or commenting on quick or factual questions during the focus groups and noted the benefits of providing a short response or comment when the majority of the participants have similar concerns. A brief response allows some information literacy training (Walbridge 2000). Allowing participants to free think on the site provides highly useful information (Thomsett-Scott, 2004c). An increased level of interactivity enhances the rapport with the participants and responding to some questions at the point of need increases participant satisfaction.

In-person focus group participants should be provided with comment sheets so participants can record comments they do not want to share with the group (Thomsett-Scott, 2004c). Although online focus groups tend to be more anonymous and participants normally share more, it may be worthwhile to encourage participants to e-mail additional comments to the moderator. Millen (1999) provided an online bulletin board as an opportunity for participants to provide detailed comments on likes and dislikes. An open forum, such as an unrestricted bulletin board used by Millen, could be used to allow all users to expand/agree/disagree with other comments and maintain a level of synergy among the responses.

Results of Remote Focus Groups

Sweet (1999) noted that online and in-person focus groups are generally assumed to have similar results. A review of the literature bears this out.

Ensuring equal participation from all members of a focus group is one of the major challenges. Usually there are some dominant personalities or people to whom the others tend to defer (Schneider et al., 2002). Olmsted and Underhill (2003) found no significant difference in participation level. Other research is mixed with some tendency towards more participation in remote groups (Bordia, 1997; McLeod, 1992; Schneider et al., 2002; Straus, 1997). Olson and Olson (2000) noted that the participants typing or linguistic skills may affect the comment level. As well, different cultural styles, such as the more outgoing Americans and the more reticent Asians and Europeans, may affect the level of participation. Thus, extra care must be taken to make sure everyone has an opportunity to participate.

The remote conversation was more equally shared, possibly because the participants could not see each other and the normal nonverbal cues such as interest, boredom, or surprise that may lead some participants to dominate the conversation and other participants to withdraw are not available (Schneider et al., 2002). Hughes and Lang (2003) noted that while online focus groups lack visual and verbal cues, this lack does tend to allow all participants to contribute equally without the usual dominant and shy personalities. They add that since Web communications have become more widely accessible, a number of substitute cues such as emoticons and standard acronyms have developed. These substitute cues may be useful to add context to the conversations.

Remote groups provide more comments (Schneider et al., 2002). This is most likely due to a freer flow of information since there are no verbal or physical cues to inhibit or encourage participants and comments are not cut of by other participants. The remote group lasted longer, and after analysis Schneider et al. reported that there were a similar number of comments per minute between the remote and local groups. Montoya-Weiss, Massey, and Clapper (1998) concurred that online groups frequently last longer.

Some authors report that remote groups provide more on-topic comments than face-to-face groups (Bordia, 1997; McLeod, 1992; Olaniran, 1994; Parent, Gallupe, Salisbury, & Handelman, 2000). The quality of comments was greater in the remote groups (McLeod), inconclusive (Bordia), and similar to local groups (Barki & Pinsonneault, 2001; Ziegler, Diehl, & Zijlstra, 2000). Olmsted and Underhill (2003) reported that, although there was no significant difference in number of unique comments, the face-to-face group used many more words to describe their ideas. Schneider et al. (2002) reported a tendency towards fewer words per comment in the online group. They also noted that online participants were more uniform in the number of words that they contribute to the discussion. Typing a comment usually takes more effort and time than saying it, resulting in remote participants using fewer words per comment. Remote groups also may not flesh out their ideas as well as local participants, thus, requiring more prompting from the moderator. Hughes and Lang (2003) noted that the lack of a linear environment, as all comments are being recorded as they are typed, affects the normal flow of conversation but can be overcome by having the moderator repost a particularly interesting comment or adding a follow-up question.

Olmsted and Underhill (2003) reported no significant differences in satisfaction level as both remote and local groups were approximately 85% satisfied with the process. McLeod (1992) noted inconclusive results regarding participant satisfaction, while other studies report reduced satisfaction from remote participants (Olaniran, 1996; Parent et al., 2000). More recent studies may show a higher satisfaction as online communications are becoming increasingly commonplace.

Intragroup conflict has been studied less than the other characteristics of online focus groups, and the results are generally inconclusive about which groups have more participant disagreement and conflict (Bordia, 1997). Olmsted and Underhill (2003) reported no significant differences between the Internet-based and face-to-face groups.

Analyzing the Data

Responses to the questions are broken down into specific points which are then collapsed into trends and then grouped into "working areas," such as terminology, design elements, color, etc. The moderator is normally responsible for compiling and analyzing the data. Krueger and Casey (2000) recommended that the analysis be performed by someone who was present at the focus groups to allow for the unspoken comments gained from body language and behaviors of the participants. This may be less important for remote groups, although the moderator may be able to "sense" attitudes within the group and thus be able to add more contexts to the results than someone who was not present during the focus group.

Focus Group Conclusions

Remote focus groups appear to provide similar information as face-to-face groups. Schneider et al. (2002) noted that local groups may be best when looking for indepth information but that remote groups are good for other purposes. Schneider et al. emphasized that remote focus groups frequently provide for a more equal distribution of comments from all participants which in turn provides for a more balanced collection of viewpoints on the Web site or product being evaluated. Thus, remote focus groups are a good usability technique to employ when seeking input from remote users.

LAST WORDS

Scholtz (2001) reported that remote studies are not a substitute for local studies as they provide limited qualitative data but emphasized that they do effectively provide data to identify problem areas of the site, difficult tasks, and user populations that may need extra study. Paternò and Paganelli (2001) added that cheaper and faster ways to evaluate usability of Web applications are needed. Gough and Phillips (2003) noted that there are limitations to the remote studies, such as lack of body language and being limited to users with high speed networks, but emphasized that any feedback is better than no feedback.

Despite some drawbacks and the need to modify "standard operating procedures," both formal usability studies and focus groups held in remote fashion provide valuable feedback for Web site creation and redesign. Libraries will benefit from using these techniques to gather information from remote users concerning the usability of the Web site.

REFERENCES

Agarwal, R., & Venkatesh, V. (2002). Assessing a firm's Web presence: A heuristic evaluation procedure for the measurement of usability. Information Systems Research, 13(2), 168-186.

Ames, M. (2003). Final report. Retrieved December 2, 2005 from http://www.cra.org/Activities/craw/dmp/awards/2003/Ames/report.html.

Balas, J. (2003). How to make your library's Web site your patrons' favorite. Computers in Libraries, 23(1), 55-57.

Barki, H., & Pinsonneault, A. (2001). Small group brainstorming and idea quality: Is electronic brainstorming the most effective approach? Small Group Research, 32, 158-205.

Bartek, V., & Cheatham, D. (2003a). Experience remote usability testing, part 1. Retrieved December 12, 2005, from http://www-128.ibm.com/developerworks/web/library/wa-rmusts1.html.

Bartek, V., & Cheatham, D. (2003b). Experience remote usability testing, part 2. Retrieved December 12, 2005, from http://www-128.ibm.com/developerworks/web/library/wa-rmusts2.html.

Battleson, B., Booth, A., & Weintrop, J. (2001). Usability testing of an academic library Web site: A case study. Journal of Academic Librarianship, 27(3), 188-198.

Bird, L. (1994, February 4). Focus groups meeting in cyberspace. Wall Street Journal, p. B1.

Bordia, P. (1997). Face-to-face versus computer-mediated communication: A synthesis of the experimental literature. Journal of Business Communication, 34, 99-120.

Bruseberg, A., & McDonagh-Philp, D. (2002). Focus groups to support the industrial/product designer: A review based on current literature and designers' feedback. Applied Ergonomics: Human Factors in Technology and Society, 33(1), 27-38.

Brush, A. J. B., Ames, M., & Davis, J. (2004). A comparison of synchronous remote and local usability studies for an expert interface. Conference on Human Factors in Computing Systems. Extended abstracts on Human factors in computing systems (pp. 1179-1182). New York: Association for Computing Machinery.

Burns, A. D., & Evans, S. (2000). Insights into customer delight. In A.R. Scrivener (Ed.), Collaborative design: Proceedings of co-designing 2000 (pp. 195-203). London: Springer-Verlag.

Campbell, N. (2001a). Usability methods. In N. Campbell (Ed.), Usability assessment of library-related Web sites (pp. 1-10). Chicago: Library and Information Technology Association.

Campbell, N. (2001b). Conducting a usability study. In N. Campbell (Ed.), Usability assessment of library-related Web sites (pp. 11-15). Chicago: Library and Information Technology Association.

Canning, C. S. (1995). Using focus groups to evaluate library services in a problem-based learning curriculum. Medical Reference Quarterly, 14(3), 75-81.

Cavill, P. (2002). The power of focus groups. PNLA Quarterly, 66(2), 4-6.

Chak, A. (2000). Usability tools: A useful start. New Architect. Retrieved December 1, 2005, from http://www.webtechniques.com/archives/2000/08/stratrevu/.

Cheatham, D., & Bartek, V. (2004). Experiences in remote usability evaluation. Retrieved December 22, 2005, from http://www-3.ibm.com/ibm/easy/eou_ext.nsf/Publish/50?OpenDocument&../Publish/1116/$File/paper1116.pdf.

Chen, B., Mitsock, M., Coronado, J., & Salvendy, G. (1999). Remote usability testing through the Internet. Proceedings of the HCI International '99: The 8th International Conference on Human-Computer Interaction (pp. 1108-1112). Mahwah, NJ: Lawrence Erlbaum.

Chisman, J., Diller, K., & Walbridge, S. (1999). Usability testing: A case study. College & Research Libraries, 60(6), 552-69.

Cockrell, B., & Jayne, E. (2002). How do I find an article? Insights from a Web usability study. Journal of Academic Librarianship, 28(3), 122-132.

Collins, K., & Aguinaga, J. (2001). Learning as we go: Arizona State University West Library's usability experience. In N. Campbell (Ed.), Usability assessment of library-related Web sites (pp. 16-29). Chicago: Library and Information Technology Association.

Connaway, L. S., Johnson, D. W., & Searing, S. E. (1997). Online catalogs from the users' perspective: The use of focus group interviews. College and Research Libraries, 58, 403-420.

Coomber, R. (1997). Using the Internet for survey research. Sociological Research Online, 2(1). Retrieved January 7, 2006, from http://www.socresonline.org.uk/socresonline/2/2/2.html.

Crowley, G. R., Leffel, D., Ramirez, J. L., & Armstrong, T. S., II (2003). User perceptions of the library's Web pages: A focus group study at Texas A & M University. Journal of Academic Librarianship, 28(4), 205-210.

Dix, A., Filay, J., Abowd, G., & Beale, R. (1998). Human-computer interaction (2nd Ed.). Upper Saddle River, NJ: Prentice Hall.

Dray, S., & Siegel, S. (2004). Business: Remote possibilities?: International usability testing at a distance. Interactions, 11(2), 10-17.

Ebling, M. R., & John, B. E. (2000). On the contributions of different empirical data in usability testing. Proceedings of the conference on designing interactive systems: Processes, practices, methods, and techniques (pp. 289-296). New York: Association for Computing Machinery.

Gaiser, T. J. (1997). Conducting online focus groups: A methodological discussion. Social Science Computer Review, 15, 135-144.

Glitz, B. (1998). Focus groups for libraries and librarians. Chicago: Medical Library Association.

Gough, D., & Phillips, H. (2003). Remote online usability testing: Why, how, and when to use it. Boxes and Arrows. Retrieved December 4, 2005, from http://www.boxesandarrows.com/view/remote_online_usability_testing_why_how_and_when_to_use_it.

Green, K., & Hinder, J. (2003). Should the user be driving?: A comparison of remote testing methods. Paper presented at the Usability Professionals Association Conference, Scottsdale, Arizona.

Hammontree, M., Weiler, P., & Nayak, N. (1994). Remote usability testing. Interactions, 1(3), 21-25.

Hartson, H. R., Castillo, J. C., Kelso, J., Neale, W. C., & Kamler, J. (1996). Remote evaluation: The network as an extension of the usability laboratory. Proceedings of the SIGCHI conference on human factors in computing systems (pp. 228-235). New York: Association for Computing Machinery.

Hodkinson, H., & Hodkinson, P. (1999). Teaching to learn, learning to teach? School based non teaching activity in an initial teacher education and training partnership scheme. Teaching and Teacher Education, 15, 273-285.

Hughes, J., & Lang, K. R. (2004). Issues in online focus groups: Lessons learned from an empirical study of peer-to-peer filesharing system users. Electronic Journal of Business Research Methods, 2(2), 95-110.

Ivory, J. Y., & Hearst, M. A. (2001). The state of the art in automating usability evaluation of user interfaces. ACM Computing Surveys, 33(4), 470-516.

Janes, J. (2003). Wrestling with teens and technology. Voice of Youth Advocates, 26(3), 201-204.

Jeffries, R., & Desurvire, H. (1992). Usability testing versus heuristic evaluation: Was there a contest? SIGCHI Bulletin, 24(4), 39-41.

Johnson, E. (1996). Government Web pages: The lights are on but nobody is home. Electronic Library, 14(2), 149-156.

Jordan, P. W. (2000). Designing of pleasurable products: An introduction to the new human factors. London: Taylor and Francis.

Krauss, F. S. H. (2003). Methodology for remote usability activities: A case study. IBM Systems Journal, 42(4), 582-493.

Krauss, H., & Vigilante, B., Jr. (2002). A reference guide for remote usability activities using NetMeeting and Sametime. Technical Report 29.3493. IBM Research Triangle Park, North Carolina: IBM.

Krueger, R. A., & Casey, M. A. (2000). Focus groups: A practical guide for applied research (3rd ed.) Thousand Oaks, CA: Sage.

Kushniruk, A. W., Patel, C., Patel, V. L., & Cimino, J. J. (2001). Televaluation of clinical information systems: An integrative approach to assessing Web-based systems. International Journal of Medical Informatics, 61, 45-70.

Landreth, D. (1998). Focus groups on the Net: Some pros and cons of doing qualitative research online. Marketing, 103, 16-17.

Large, J. A., Beheshti, J., & Rahman, T. (2002). Design criteria for children's Web portals: The users speak out. Journal of the American Society for Information Science and Technology, 53(2), 79-94.

Maddox, K. (1998). Virtual panels add real insight for marketers: Online focus group use expanding. Advertising Age, 69, 34-40.

Marney, J. (1990). Computerized focus groups faster, cheaper. Marketing, 95, 13.

Massey-Burzio, V. (1998). From the other side of the reference desk: A focus group study. Journal of Academic Librarianship, 24, 208-215.

McGillis, L., & Toms, E. G. (2001). Usability of the academic library Web site: Implications for design. College and Research Libraries, 62(4), 355-368.

McLeod, P. (1992). An assessment of the experimental literature on electronic support of group work: Results of a meta-analysis. Human-Computer Interaction, 7, 257-280.

Millen, D. R. (1999). Remote usability evaluation: User participation in the design of a Web-based e-mail service. SIGGROUP Bulletin, 20(1), 40-45.

Miller, C. (1994). Focus groups where none has been before. Marketing News, 28, 2-14.

Montoya-Weiss, M. M., Massey, A. P., & Clapper, D. L. (1998). Online focus groups: Conceptual issues and a research tool. European Journal of Marketing, 32, 713-723.

Morgan, D. L. (1997). Focus groups as qualitative research (2nd ed.). Thousand Oaks, CA: Sage.

Murphy, D. A., Durako, S. D., Muenz, L., & Wilson, C. M. (2000). Marijuana use among HIV + and high-risk adolescents: A comparison of self-report through audio computer-assisted self-administered interviewing and urinalysis. American Journal of Epidemiology, 152, 805-813.

National Center for Education Statistics. (2003). Distance education at degree-granting postsecondary institutions: 2000-2001. (NCES 2003-017).

Nielsen, J. (1993). Usability engineering. Boston, MA: Academic Press.

Nielsen, J., & Curtis, B. (1995). A home-page overhaul using other Web sites. IEEE Software, 12(2), 75-78.

Norlin, E., & Winters, C. (2002). Usability testing for library Web sites. Chicago: American Library Association.

Olaniran, B. (1994). Group performance in computer-mediated and face-to-face communication media. Management Communication Quarterly, 7, 256-281.

Olaniran, B. (1996). A model of group satisfaction in computer-mediated communication and face-to-face meetings. Behavior and Information Technology, 12, 24-36.

Olmsted, M. G., & Underhill, C. (2003). An experimental comparison of computer-mediated and face-to-face focus groups. Social Science Computer Review, 21(4), 506-512.

Olson, G., & Olson, J. S. (2000). Distance matters. Human-Computer Interaction, 15(2), 139-178.

Palmquist, R. A. (2001). An overview of usability for the study of users' Web-based information retrieval behavior. Journal of Education for Library and Information Science, 42(2), 123-136.

Parent, M., Gallupe, R. B., Salisbury, W. D., & Handelman, J. M. (2000). Knowledge creation in focus groups: Can group technologies help? Information and Management, 38, 47-58.

Parks, A. (1997). Online focus groups reshape market research industry. Marketing News, 31, 28.

Paternò, F., & Paganelli, L. (2001). Short talks: Of mice and measures: Remote automatic evaluation of Web sites based on task models and browser monitoring. Conference on Human Factors in Computing Systems. Extended abstracts on human factors in computing systems (pp. 283-284). New York: Association for Computing Machinery.

Perkins, R. (2002). Remote usability evaluation over the Internet. In R. J. Branaghan (Ed.), Design by people for people: Essays on usability (pp. 153-162). Bloomingdale, IL: Usability Professionals' Association.

Preston, A. (1999). Remote usability testing tools. Usability Interface, 5(3), 5-6.

Rafee, A., Kassim, C., & Kochanek, T. R. (2003). Designing, implementing, and evaluating an educational digital library resources. Online Information Review, 27(3), 160-168.

Rubin, J. (1994). The handbook of usability testing: How to plan, design and conduct effective tests. New York: Wiley.

Schneider, S. J., Kerwin, J., Frechtling, J., & Vivari, B. A. (2002). Characteristics of the discussion in online and face to face focus groups. Social Science Computer Review, 20(1), 31-42.

Scholtz, J. (2001). Adaptation of traditional usability testing methods for remote testing. Proceedings of the 34th Hawaii International Conference on System Sciences (pp. 341-352). Piscataway, NJ: EEE Computer Society Press.

Straus, M. A. (1997). Physical assaults by women partners: A major social problem. In M. R. Walsh (ed.), Women, Men and Gender. Ongoing Debates (pp. 210-221). New Haven: Yale University Press.

Sweet, C. (1999). Designing and conducting virtual focus groups. Quirk's Marketing Research Review. Accessed November 15, 2005, from http://www.sysurvey.com/tips/designing_and_conducting.htm.

Thompson, K. T., Rozanski, E. P., & Haake, A. R. (2004). Learning: Here, there, anywhere: Remote usability testing that works. Proceedings of the 5th conference on information technology education (pp. 132-137). New York: ACM Press.

Thompson, S. M. (2003). Remote observation strategies for usability testing. Information Technology and Libraries, 22(1), 22-31.

Thomsett-Scott, B. (2004a) Turning students on to your Web site using usability testing. In Proceedings of the Victorian Automation and Library Association 12th Biennial Conference and Exhibition. Accessed November 22, 2005, from http://www.vala.org.au/vala2004/2004pdfs/72Thomst.pdf.

Thomsett-Scott, B. (2004b). Yeah, I found it!: Performing Web site usability testing to ensure that off-campus students can find the information they need. In P. Mahoney (Ed.), Proceedings of the Eleventh Off-Campus Library Services Conference (pp. 355-364). Mt Pleasant, MI: Central Michigan University.

Thomsett-Scott, B. (2004c). If you ask, I will tell you: Future users of virtual reference share their thoughts on the design, operation, and marketing of virtual reference. In R. D. Lankes, J. Janes, L. C. Smith, & C. M. Finneran (Eds.), The virtual reference experience: Integrating theory into practice (pp. 63-86). New York: Neal-Schuman.

Tullis, T., Fleischman, S., McNultry, M., Cianchette, C., & Bergel, M. (2002, July). An empirical comparison of lab and remote usability testing of Web sites. Paper presented at the Usability Professionals Association Conference, Orlando, FL.

Walbridge, S. (2000). Usability testing and libraries: The WSU experience. ALKI, 16(3), 23-24.

Walston, J., & Lissitz, R. W. (2000). Computer mediated focus groups. Evaluation Review, 24, 457-483.

Waterson, S., Landay, J. A., & Matthews, T. (2000). Short talks: In the lab and out in the wild: Remote Web usability testing for mobile devices. Conference on Human Factors in Computing Systems. Extended abstracts on Human factors in computing systems (pp. 796-797). New York: Association for Computing Machinery.

Whitlach, J. B. (2001). Evaluating reference services in the digital age. Library Trends, 50(2), 207-217.

Widdows, R., Hensler, T. A., & Wyncott, M. (1991). The focus group interview: A method for assessing users' evaluation of library services. College and Research Libraries, 52, 352-359.

Winckler, M. A. A., Freitas, C. M. D. S., & Valdeni, J. de Lima (2000). Interactive posters: Usability remote evaluation for WWW. Conference on Human Factors in Computing Systems. Extended abstracts on human factors in computing systems (pp. 131-132). New York: Association for Computing Machinery.

Ziegler, R., Diehl, M., & Zijlstra, G. (2000). Idea production in nominal and virtual groups: Does computer-mediated communication improve group brainstorming? Group Processes and Intergroup Relations, 3, 141-158.

doi:10.1300/J111v45n03_14

CONTRIBUTED ELECTRONIC POSTERS

Experiments with Online Tools
to Deliver
Off-Campus Library Instruction

Lisa T. Abbott
Geri Purpur

Appalachian State University

SUMMARY

Delivering library instruction to off-campus students offers numerous challenges. The varying needs of the teaching faculty and user need to be considered. Does the user need general information, specific database searching techniques, or want to know more about ILLiad? What about "point of need"? Can this information be integrated into the off-campus classes? At Appalachian State University Libraries we are using an array of online tools and are exploring others. An interactive guide, Virtual Research @ ASU Libraries: A Guide for Off-campus Students, uses animations to provide information about library services and procedures. With faculty in Instructional Technology, we built a virtual library to deliver research assistance within AppEdTech (a 3-D

[Haworth co-indexing entry note]: "Experiments with Online Tools to Deliver Off-Campus Library Instruction." Abbott, Lisa T., and Geri Purpur. Co-published simultaneously in *Journal of Library Administration* (The Haworth Information Press, an imprint of The Haworth Press, Inc.) Vol. 45, No. 3/4, 2006, pp. 549-550; and: *The Twelfth Off-Campus Library Services Conference Proceedings* (ed: Julie A. Garrison) The Haworth Information Press, an imprint of The Haworth Press, Inc., 2006, pp. 549-550.

Available online at http://jla.haworthpress.com
doi:10.1300/J111v45n03_15

virtual teaching environment). We have provided orientations to the virtual library (led by a librarian avatar) via voice-over-IP. WebCT also provides a number of opportunities to deliver information, including the faculty professional development course, Preparing to Teach Online, which contains a library support and information literacy module. During 2006, we will experiment with screen casting to provide mini tutorials, small group discussions within WebCT and offering Instant Messaging to our distance learning community.

À La Carte Learning

Heather L. Brown

University of Nebraska Medical Center

SUMMARY

Orientation for distance students often does not equal the ideal teachable moment for learning about library resources and services. Seeking ways to provide learning objects for students to use at the point of need, academic health sciences librarians have created printable guides, Flash video demonstrations and simulations, and interactive tutorials. This electronic poster demonstrates how the learning objects were created, modified, and inserted into various delivery platforms, such as the library's web page, course management system, and CD-ROM.

[Haworth co-indexing entry note]: "À La Carte Learning." Brown, Heather L. Co-published simultaneously in *Journal of Library Administration* (The Haworth Information Press, an imprint of The Haworth Press, Inc.) Vol. 45, No. 3/4, 2006, p. 551; and: *The Twelfth Off-Campus Library Services Conference Proceedings* (ed: Julie A. Garrison) The Haworth Information Press, an imprint of The Haworth Press, Inc., 2006, p. 551.

Available online at http://jla.haworthpress.com
doi:10.1300/J111v45n03_16

The Development of RoboDemo Tutorials in an OCLS Blackboard Space

Edward W. Daniels

Southern New Hampshire University

SUMMARY

The geographically, culturally, and academically diverse student population of Southern New Hampshire University encompasses more than 30 time zones and includes students enrolled in bachelors, masters, and doctoral programs. There is a constant challenge to reach out and make them aware that they have at their disposal an academic support resource such as the university's Shapiro Library. Although the Internet is an integral part of how our off-campus students "get to class," its search engines also remain a means for conducting much if not all of their academic research.

RoboDemo (now *Captivate*) tutorials are continuing to be developed to attract and inform our students about the library's capabilities to assist them with their academic work. Housed in a Blackboard OCLS Resource space for SNHU Online faculty, these tutorials are available for downloading and insertion in individual classes. The tutorials are also available directly to students for viewing via the Shapiro Library Web page. This session will walk attendees through the deciding factors behind their development and the accompanying "learning curve" of lessons picked up along the way.

[Haworth co-indexing entry note]: "The Development of RoboDemo Tutorials in an OCLS Blackboard Space." Daniels, Edward W. Co-published simultaneously in *Journal of Library Administration* (The Haworth Information Press, an imprint of The Haworth Press, Inc.) Vol. 45, No. 3/4, 2006, p. 553; and: *The Twelfth Off-Campus Library Services Conference Proceedings* (ed: Julie A. Garrison) The Haworth Information Press, an imprint of The Haworth Press, Inc., 2006, p. 553.

Available online at http://jla.haworthpress.com
doi:10.1300/J111v45n03_17

Online Library Instruction: Building Bite-Size Tutorials for Clinical Nursing Courses

Ulrike Dieterle

University of Wisconsin-Madison

SUMMARY

At the School of Nursing, University of Wisconsin-Madison, librarians and clinical faculty are working collaboratively to produce Web-based learning modules.

The collaboration resulted in four Web-based learning objects, including a virtual tour of the library Web site and three assignment-centered tutorials. Modules are short (15 minutes), focused on specific learning objectives and easily accessible on- and off-campus. They are embedded in an online course environment and free librarians to provide more customized instruction to classes upon request.

This poster presentation will demonstrate sections of the four modules, detail the development process, and explain how modules currently support School of Nursing curriculum and outline implications for future development.

[Haworth co-indexing entry note]: "Online Library Instruction: Building Bite-Size Tutorials for Clinical Nursing Courses." Dieterle, Ulrike. Co-published simultaneously in *Journal of Library Administration* (The Haworth Information Press, an imprint of The Haworth Press, Inc.) Vol. 45, No. 3/4, 2006, p. 555; and: *The Twelfth Off-Campus Library Services Conference Proceedings* (ed: Julie A. Garrison) The Haworth Information Press, an imprint of The Haworth Press, Inc., 2006, p. 555.

Available online at http://jla.haworthpress.com
doi:10.1300/J111v45n03_18

Creating a Logo to Market Distance Learning Services

Mary Edwards
Linda Butson
Ned Davis
Chris Youngblood

Health Science Center Libraries
University of Florida

SUMMARY

With distance education rapidly expanding at many institutions, the successful promotion of services designed for distance learning faculty, staff, and students is essential since most of the students will never visit the library building.

While many libraries have created a logo for their main web page that is also used on publications and handouts, an evaluation of distance learning sites and portals reveals that few libraries use a logo specific for distance learning. Creating a brand identity is a marketing element underutilized in promoting distance learning library services.

In the fall of 2004, it was determined that a distance learning specific logo would help to better promote services. The logo is used on all the library's distance learning sites as well as publications including brochures, bookmarks, and presentations. The goal is to create a unique "brand" to unify all of the library's distance learning materials.

This poster session focuses on the history of the design and selection of the logo. During the creation process, several images were consid-

[Haworth co-indexing entry note]: "Creating a Logo to Market Distance Learning Services." Edwards, Mary et al. Co-published simultaneously in *Journal of Library Administration* (The Haworth Information Press, an imprint of The Haworth Press, Inc.) Vol. 45, No. 3/4, 2006, pp. 557-558; and: *The Twelfth Off-Campus Library Services Conference Proceedings* (ed: Julie A. Garrison) The Haworth Information Press, an imprint of The Haworth Press, Inc., 2006, pp. 557-558.

Available online at http://jla.haworthpress.com
doi:10.1300/J111v45n03_19

ered as logos. The poster describes the reasons for selecting one design over others, and includes tips for the institutional approval process.

This poster demonstrates the uses of the distance learning logo to brand presentations, publications, and Web pages to successfully increase use of distance learning services, and create a name for the services.

From Learning Communities to Learning Objects: Participating in a Faculty Learning Community to Develop Distance Learning Library Instructional Modules

Jill Markgraf

University of Wisconsin-Eau Claire

SUMMARY

A distance learning librarian shares her experience as a member of a faculty learning community devoted to technology innovation in education. Participants in the learning community include faculty from a range of disciplines all working on projects to enhance student learning through instructional technology. The librarian was selected to participate in the community to develop online learning objects using Camtasia. In addition to discussing the practical considerations of developing the learning objects, the poster session will focus on the learning community experience. How did collaboration and dialogue with other faculty affect the project? What did the librarian's participation and unique perspective contribute to the learning community as a whole? Finally, recommendations for establishing similar formal or informal learning communities will be offered.

[Haworth co-indexing entry note]: "From Learning Communities to Learning Objects: Participating in a Faculty Learning Community to Develop Distance Learning Library Instructional Modules." Markgraf, Jill. Co-published simultaneously in *Journal of Library Administration* (The Haworth Information Press, an imprint of The Haworth Press, Inc.) Vol. 45, No. 3/4, 2006, p. 559; and: *The Twelfth Off-Campus Library Services Conference Proceedings* (ed: Julie A. Garrison) The Haworth Information Press, an imprint of The Haworth Press, Inc., 2006, p. 559.

Available online at http://jla.haworthpress.com
doi:10.1300/J111v45n03_20

What Is a "MIVER"
and How Does the Library Prepare for It?

Marcia G. Stockham

Kansas State University

SUMMARY

The Military Installation Voluntary Education Review (MIVER) assesses the quality of selected on-base higher education programs and assists in the improvement of such programs through recommendations to the institutions and the military services. This poster relates the experience of one librarian's participation in such a review of the master's degree program in adult education offered by Kansas State University at Ft. Leavenworth. Topics covered include: the librarian's role in preparing the self-study document; steps taken to gather information; collaboration with responsible administrators/faculty members; pre-visit telephone interview with a site inspector; attending the actual site visit; and recommendations from the site team. Shared highlights and benefits specific to this librarian's experience include: developing a better working relationship with the teaching faculty; implementing a new method of reaching the students; gaining new knowledge of library services needed by this particular group of distance students; exploring opportunities for further activities; and reviewing outcomes and commendations received from the MIVER team.

[Haworth co-indexing entry note]: "What Is a 'MIVER' and How Does the Library Prepare for It?" Stockham, Marcia G. Co-published simultaneously in *Journal of Library Administration* (The Haworth Information Press, an imprint of The Haworth Press, Inc.) Vol. 45, No. 3/4, 2006, p. 561; and: *The Twelfth Off-Campus Library Services Conference Proceedings* (ed: Julie A. Garrison) The Haworth Information Press, an imprint of The Haworth Press, Inc., 2006, p. 561.

Available online at http://jla.haworthpress.com
doi:10.1300/J111v45n03_21

When Faculty Behave Like Students: Teaching Faculty About Online Library Resources

Rachel G. Viggiano

University of Central Florida Libraries

SUMMARY

Each semester, the instructional designers at the University of Central Florida facilitate an innovative course for faculty only. IDL 6543 is an eight-week professional development course that prepares faculty to teach online.

IDL 6543 models how to teach online using a combination of seminars, labs, consultations, and Web-based instruction. A librarian was typically invited to a lab session to present information about the library's online resources. Because there was so much information, this portion of the course was migrated to the online environment in the fall semester of 2004. The in-person presentation was transformed into an online learning module for the faculty to read and participate in at their own pace.

This poster session will address collaborating with instructional designers, creating an online module of library information aimed at teaching faculty, moderating a faculty discussion of library resources, and comparing the in-person training session with an online module.

[Haworth co-indexing entry note]: "When Faculty Behave Like Students: Teaching Faculty About Online Library Resources." Viggiano, Rachel G. Co-published simultaneously in *Journal of Library Administration* (The Haworth Information Press, an imprint of The Haworth Press, Inc.) Vol. 45, No. 3/4, 2006, p. 563; and: *The Twelfth Off-Campus Library Services Conference Proceedings* (ed: Julie A. Garrison) The Haworth Information Press, an imprint of The Haworth Press, Inc., 2006, p. 563.

Available online at http://jla.haworthpress.com
doi:10.1300/J111v45n03_22

Contributor Index

Index

Page numbers followed by f indicate figures; those followed by t indicate tables.

BOOK ORDER FORM!

Order a copy of this book with this form or online at:
http://www.HaworthPress.com/store/product.asp?sku= 5969

The Twelfth Off-Campus Library Services Conference Proceedings

—— in softbound at $90.00 ISBN-13: 978-0-7890-3477-9 / ISBN-10: 0-7890-3477-8.
—— in hardbound at $145.00 ISBN-13: 978-0-7890-3476-2 / ISBN-10: 0-7890-3476-X.

COST OF BOOKS _____

POSTAGE & HANDLING _____
US: $4.00 for first book & $1.50
for each additional book
Outside US: $5.00 for first book
& $2.00 for each additional book.

SUBTOTAL _____

In Canada: add 6% GST. _____

STATE TAX _____
CA, IL, IN, MN, NJ, NY, OH, PA & SD residents
please add appropriate local sales tax.

FINAL TOTAL _____

If paying in Canadian funds, convert
using the current exchange rate,
UNESCO coupons welcome.

❏ BILL ME LATER:
Bill-me option is good on US/Canada/
Mexico orders only; not good to jobbers,
wholesalers, or subscription agencies.

❏ **Signature** _____

❏ **Payment Enclosed: $**_____

❏ **PLEASE CHARGE TO MY CREDIT CARD:**

❏ Visa ❏ MasterCard ❏ AmEx ❏ Discover
❏ Diner's Club ❏ Eurocard ❏ JCB

Account # _____

Exp Date _____

Signature _____
(Prices in US dollars and subject to change without notice.)

PLEASE PRINT ALL INFORMATION OR ATTACH YOUR BUSINESS CARD
Name
Address
City _____ State/Province _____ Zip/Postal Code
Country
Tel _____ Fax
E-Mail

May we use your e-mail address for confirmations and other types of information? ❏Yes ❏No We appreciate receiving
your e-mail address. Haworth would like to e-mail special discount offers to you, as a preferred customer.
We will never share, rent, or exchange your e-mail address. We regard such actions as an invasion of your privacy.

Order from your **local bookstore** or directly from
The Haworth Press, Inc. 10 Alice Street, Binghamton, New York 13904-1580 • USA
Call our toll-free number (1-800-429-6784) / Outside US/Canada: (607) 722-5857
Fax: 1-800-895-0582 / Outside US/Canada: (607) 771-0012
E-mail your order to us: orders@HaworthPress.com

For orders outside US and Canada, you may wish to order through your local
sales representative, distributor, or bookseller.
For information, see http://HaworthPress.com/distributors

(Discounts are available for individual orders in US and Canada only, not booksellers/distributors.)

Please photocopy this form for your personal use.
www.HaworthPress.com

BOF07

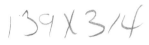

Bibliothèque Université d'Ottawa Échéance	Library University of Ottawa Date Due